Library of Arabic Linguistics

The reasons behind the establishment of this Series on Arabic linguistics are manifold.

First: Arabic linguistics is developing into an increasingly interesting and important subject within the broad field of modern linguistic studies. The subject is now fully recognised in the Universities of the Arabic speaking world and in international linguistic circles, as a subject of great theoretical and descriptive interest and importance.

Second: Arabic linguistics is reaching a mature stage in its development benefiting both from early Arabic linguistic scholarship and modern techniques of general linguistics and related disciplines.

Third: The scope of this discipline is wide and varied, covering diverse areas such as Arabic phonetics, phonology and grammar, Arabic psycholinguistics, Arabic dialectology, Arabic lexicography and lexicology, Arabic sociolinguistics, the teaching and learning of Arabic as a first, second, or foreign language, communications, semiotics, terminology, translation, machine translation, Arabic computational linguistics, history of Arabic linguistics, etc.

Viewed against this background, Arabic linguists may be defined as: the scientific investigation and study of the Arabic language in all its aspects. This embraces the descriptive, comparative and historical aspects of the language. It also concerns itself with the classical form as well as the Modern and contemporary standard forms and their dialects. Moreover, it attempts to study the language in the appropriate regional, social and cultural settings.

It is hoped that the Series will devote itself to all issues of Arabic linguistics in all its manifestations on both the theoretical and applied levels. The results of these studies will also be of use in the field of linguistics in general, as well as related subjects.

Although a number of works have appeared independently or within series, yet there is no platform designed specifically for this subject. This Series is being started to fill this gap in the linguistic field. It will be devoted to Monographs written in either English or Arabic, or both, for the benefit of wider circles of readership.

All these reasons justify the establishment of a new forum which is devoted to all areas of Arabic linguistic studies. It is also hoped that this Series will be of interest not only to students and researchers in Arabic linguistics but also to students and scholars of other disciplines who are looking for information of theoretical, practical or pragmatic interest.

The Series Editors

From code-switching to borrowing: foreign and diglossic mixing in Moroccan Arabic

Library of Arabic Linguistics

Series editors
Muhammad Hasan Bakalla
King Saud University, Riyadh, Kingdom of Saudi Arabia
Bruce Ingham
School of Oriental and African Studies, University of London
Clive Holes
Faculty of Oriental Studies, University of Cambridge

Advisory editorial board
Peter F. Abboud *University of Texas at Austin*
M.H. Abdulaziz *University of Nairobi*
Yousif El-Khalifa Abu Bakr *University of Khartoum*
Salih J. Altoma *Indiana University*
Arne Ambros *University of Vienna*
El Said M. Badawi *American University in Cairo*
Michael G. Carter *University of Sydney*
Ahmad al-Dhubaib *King Saud University (formerly University of Riyadh)*
Martin Forstner *Johannes Gutenberg University at Mainz*
Otto Jastrow *University of Erlangen-Nürnberg*
Raja T. Nasr *University College of Beirut*
C.H.M. Versteegh *Catholic University at Nijmegen*
Bougslaw R. Zagorski *University of Warsaw*

First published in 1989
by Kegan Paul International Limited
P.O. Box 256, London WC1B 3SW

Jeffrey Heath

From code-switching to borrowing: foreign and diglossic mixing in Moroccan Arabic

Monograph No. 9

Routledge
Taylor & Francis Group
LONDON AND NEW YORK

First published in 1989
by Kegan Paul International Limited

This edition published 2013 by Routledge
2 Park Square, Milton Park, Abingdon, Oxfordshire OX14 4RN
711 Third Avenue, New York, NY 10017
First issued in paperback 2014

Routledge is an imprint of the Taylor & Francis Group, an informa business

Unwin Brothers, The Gresham Press, Woking, Surrey

ISBN 978-0-710-30118-5 (hbk)
ISBN 978-1-138-86995-0 (pbk)

Contents

List of tables xiii

Abbreviations xiv

Acknowledgements xv

Map xvi

1 Introduction 1
- Organization 1
- Use of appendices 3
- Significance of this study 4

2 Sociolinguistics of Morocco 5
- 2.1 Traditional variation in MCA 5
- 2.2 Diglossia 8
- 2.3 French 11
- 2.4 Spanish and other European languages 13
- 2.5 Literature on Moroccan sociolinguistics 15

3 Sketch of Basic Features of MCA 17
- 3.1 Consonants 17
- 3.2 Full vowels 18
- 3.3 Short vowels 19
- 3.4 Root structure 19
- 3.5 Noun morphology 21
- 3.6 Verb morphology 21
- 3.7 Verb derivation 22

4 Code-Switching 23
- 4.1 Types of code-switching 23
- 4.2 CA/MCA mixing 25
- 4.3 Examples of CA/MCA code-switching 30

4.4 Fr/MCA mixing: noun phrases 33
4.5 Fr/MCA mixing: verb phrases 37
4.6 Further examples of Fr/MCA code-switching 38
4.7 Code-switching and borrowing 40

5 Adaptation of CA (Classical Arabic) Borrowings 42
5.1 Vowels 42
5.2 Fricatives and affricates 44
5.3 Glottal stop 45
5.4 /r/ vs. pharyngealized /ṛ/ 48
5.5 Pharyngealization spreading 52
5.6 Nominal inflection 52
5.7 Verbal inflection 55
5.8 Verb stems and "conjugations" 55
5.9 Augment /-i-/ with geminate and /CCaC/ stems 61
5.10 Internal (ablaut) passives 62
5.11 Verbal nouns and participles 62
5.12 Prepositions and related elements 65
5.13 Adverbs and short phrases 66
5.14 Syntax: clause introducers 67
5.15 Syntax: conjunctions 70
5.16 Syntax: the genitive 70
5.17 Syntax: number-gender concord 71

6 Adaptation of European Borrowings 74
6.1 Syllabic phonology: pharyngealization 75
6.2 Vocalic conversions: oral vowels 77
6.3 Vocalic conversions: nasal vowels 80
6.4 Truncation, cluster simplification, and desyllabification 83
6.5 Nasals and liquids 85
6.6 Treatment of labial consonants and clusters 90
6.7 Stops /t/, /t^s/ 93
6.8 Affricates [č ǰ] 94
6.9 Other consonants: *k g d ? x h w y s š z ž* 95
6.10 Secondary gemination of consonants 99
6.11 Secondary labialization 100
6.12 Minor and irregular phonological developments 101
6.13 Morphological assimilation of verbs: Sp prototypes 104
6.14 Morphological assimilation of verbs: Fr prototypes 108
6.15 Borrowed triliteral weak and hollow verbs 113
6.16 English verbal borrowings 114
6.17 /CCCeC/ verbal borrowings, including denominatives 114
6.18 Weak denominative verbs 115
6.19 /CuCeC/, /CuCC/ verbs 116

6.20 /CiCC/, /CaCC/ verbs 117
6.21 Verbal nouns 117
6.22 Participles and agentives 119
6.23 Direct borrowing of nouns and adjectives 121
6.24 Definite prefix and treatment of stem-initial vowels 124
6.25 Gender and a type of false borrowing routine 130
6.26 Number (including ablaut plurals) 134
6.27 Diminutives 143
6.28 Back-formation 151
6.29 Fr/Sp crosses and other contaminations 153
6.30 Problematic and unsolved cases 156
6.31 Invariant forms: parallels with pidginization 156
6.32 Native consciousness of foreignness of borrowings 158

7 Semantic Patterns of Borrowings 160
7.1 Nouns vs. verbs: generalities 160
7.2 "Core" vocabulary: verbs 161
7.3 Kin terms 162
7.4 Human category terms 163
7.5 Body parts and other inalienables 164
7.6 Professions and business establishments 165
7.7 Education 166
7.8 The military 167
7.9 Implements and consumer items 168
7.10 Automobile parts 169
7.11 Ecological vocabulary 169
7.12 Adjectives 170
7.13 Sports and card games 171
7.14 Personal characteristics and behavior 172
7.15 Slang and affective language 174

8 Borrowings in Two Special Registers 178
8.1 Radio soccer broadcasts 178
8.2 "Foreigner talk" used by maids 180

9 Borrowing Patterns in Two Neighbouring Arabic Dialects 183
9.1 Northern (Tetouan) MCA: verbs 183
9.2 Northern (Tetouan) MCA: other stems 184
9.3 Algeria: verbs 187
9.4 Algeria: other stems 189

10 Reflections I: Structural Determinism in Borrowing Processes 193
10.1 The problem 193
10.2 Complications 195

11 Reflections II: Pidgins/Creoles vs. "Ordinary" Language Mixing 201
11.1 Identifying parallels 201
11.2 Chronological development 203
11.3 Multiple lexifier languages 204

Appendix A: CA Borrowings in MCA 207

Appendix B: European Borrowings in MCA Verbs 227

Appendix C: European Borrowings in MCA Other Stems 251

Bibliography 326

Glossary of technical terms 329

Arabic section

Acknowledgements

The primary support for the fieldwork behind this study was a grant from the National Science Foundation (BNS 79-04779) and a leave of absence from Harvard University. Fieldwork was carried out in the summer of 1979, and in the summer and autumn of 1980. The primary locations were Fes and Meknes. I have subsequently continued fieldwork in Morocco (and elsewhere with Moroccan dialect speakers), on a different grant, and although the recent fieldwork has concentrated on other topics I have continued to collect and check my data presented below.

My brief data-collecting from Algerian dialects occurred in Berlin in the spring of 1981, and that for the Jewish Casablanca dialect was obtained shortly thereafter in Paris. During that period I was supported by a fellowship from the National Endowment for the Humanities (and, in Berlin, by the Deutscher Akademischer Austauschdienst). The few items from the Jewish Tafilalt dialect were obtained as a by-product of dialect research carried out in Jerusalem in the winter of 1980-81 while still under NSF support.

None of these agencies is responsible for the opinions, analyses, or transcriptions in this work.

I acknowledge assistance from the following overseas universities relevant to my data-gathering: Freie Universität Berlin, Université de Paris, Hebrew University, and the University of Fes.

For general helpfulness over the years in connection with one aspect or another of my Arabic studies I thank Wilson Bishai, Carolyn Killean, Haim Blanc, Otto Jastrow, Moshe Bar-Asher, Norman Stillman, and Ernest Abdel-Massih. To my Moroccan informants, friends, and hosts (who must remain anonymous for their own sakes), I can only say /baṛaka ḷḷah fi-kum/.

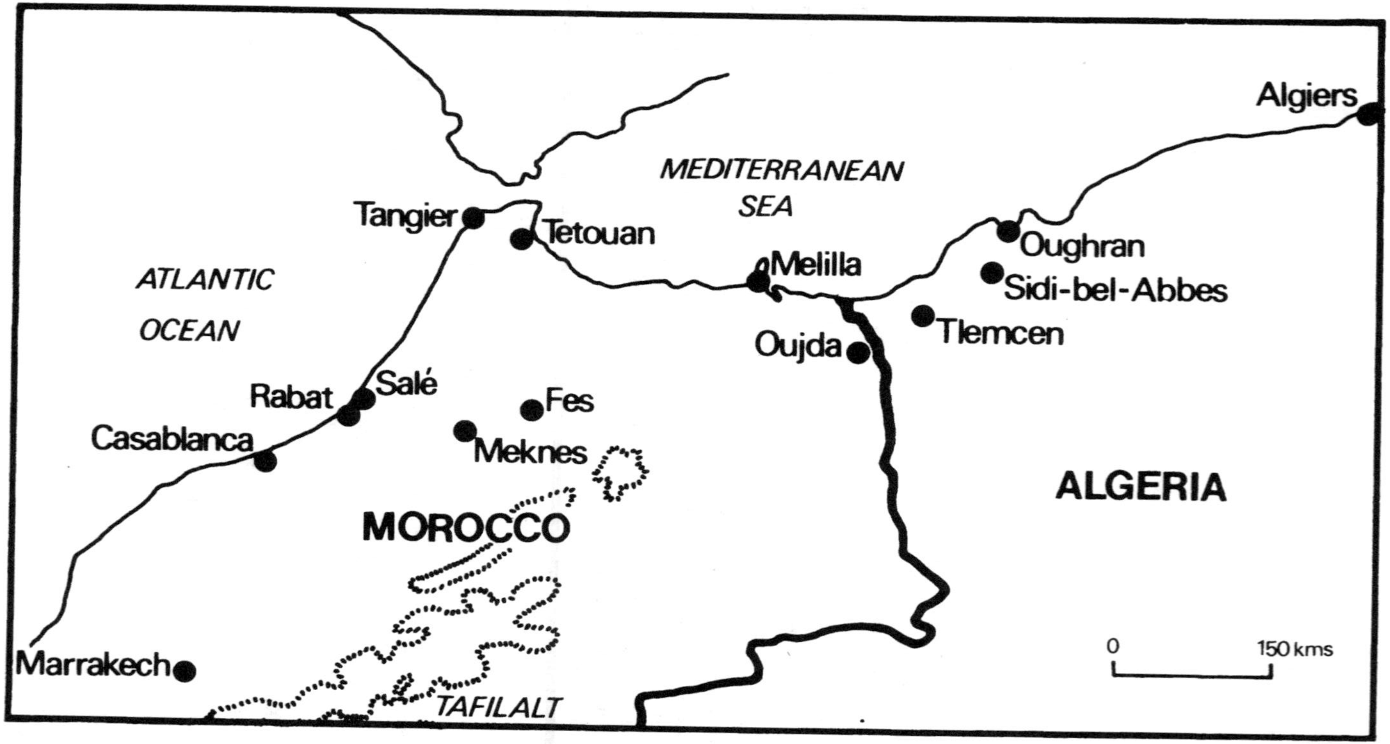

Algiers
MEDITERRANEAN
SEA
Tangier
Tetouan
Melilla
Oughran
Sidi-bel-Abbes
Tlemcen
Oujda
ATLANTIC
OCEAN
Rabat
Salé
Fes
Casablanca
Meknes
MOROCCO
ALGERIA
Marrakech
TAFILALT
0
150 kms

1 Introduction

This is a relatively detailed case study of linguistic changes which have affected and are still affecting Moroccan Colloquial Arabic (MCA) in a rather complex sociolinguistic environment involving several other languages. It has two objectives. First, it is a contribution to the theory of language mixing, and is designed to be intelligible to linguists interested in this field even if they have no specific background in the languages dealt with here. Second, it is a contribution to Arabic dialect studies in general and to studies of Moroccan dialects in particular; for example, data presented here will be cited as evidence in subsequent publications on the theoretical analysis of MCA phonetics/phonology and other grammatical areas.

Organization

Chapter 2 provides a capsule description of the sociolinguistic system in which MCA has been evolving, with primary reference to the colonial ("Protectorate") period (1912-56) and the subsequent post-colonial period. Chapter 3 is a brief, nuts-and-bolts presentation of MCA phonology and morphology, comparing it to the diglossic superordinate language Classical Arabic (CA). These two chapters contain little original material, but will help to make the volume self-contained, so that general readers with no background in Arabic studies will not need to refer constantly to other publications.

In Chapter 4 we discuss code-switching patterns and their relationships to borrowing, which we define informally as involving a greater degree of formal adaptation to the base language (here MCA). It turns out that there are instances of mixing which are difficult to categorize in terms of this binary opposition, either because we seem to have partial adaptation or because there is little difference between code-switched and borrowed forms. There are additional problems involving, for example, items which look formally like unadapted code-switches but which function as borrowings (i.e. are commonly used and have stabilized in form). Although the detailed analysis of code-switching in this society is of great potential interest, our main concern in the present volume is in code-switching as an avenue to borrowing (adaptation), and in partly adapted forms. For example, we identify specific morphological frames in French, such as *le NOUN* and *il VERB-ait*, which coincidentally resemble MCA morphological frames, here /l-NOUN/ and /y-VERB-i/, and which may thus have served as channels to morphological adaptation of borrowed nouns and verbs.

In Chapter 5 we present a detailed analysis of the conversion routines (or diasystemic rules) which have been used and are currently being used to adapt material from CA (the diglossic superordinate) to MCA. Because the phonetics and phonology of MCA and CA are quite different, there are many non-trivial phonological problems which must be resolved to achieve this adaptation. It turns out, moreover, that phonological and morphological factors closely interact, so that it is ultimately very difficult to factor out the purely phonological elements. For example, there are systematic differences between conversion routines for noun and verb stems, the latter showing the most extreme weighting of canonical-shape requirements and paradigmatic consistency. We also analyse verb-class regroupings and selected syntactic topics.

Chapter 6 performs a similar analysis of routines used to convert material from European languages, primarily Fr(ench) and Sp(anish), secondarily It(alian), Eng(lish), and Ger(man). Here we find much greater variation and instability of the conversion routines than we had in Chapter 5 for CA borrowings. We find chronological and regional variations in the forms of the same foreign stem, suggesting that alternative routines are available and have been differentially operationalized in different times and places. We examine the ways in which MCA has adapted foreign materials which grossly violate its most central root-structure and morphological norms — and ways in which MCA has relaxed these norms over time, now accepting noun and verb formations which would formerly have been unthinkable. We pay close attention to the problem of the foot-in-the-door borrowed form (involving, perhaps, identification of a specific MCA morphological frame with a specific source-language frame, cf. our earlier remarks about interlinguistic channels), and then to the further problem of generating (within MCA) affixal and ablaut paradigms for the borrowed stem (ablaut plurals and diminutives, imperfective and perfective verb paradigms, verbal nouns), as well as derivatives (nominalizations, verbalizations). In some instances the foot-in-the-door borrowing is fairly straightforward, while the subsequent internal generation of inflections and derivations is problematic, often requiring MCA speakers to choose among alternative structural analyses of the foot-in-the-door borrowing. Assignment of grammatical gender to borrowings is another highly complex matter.

Chapter 6 in particular is also concerned about crosses and similar complications, where an attested modern MCA form turns out to be (historically) a hybrid involving interaction between two or more source items, often Fr and Sp cognates which entered MCA at different times or in different places and eventually converged. A simple example is MCA /antiris/ "interest (on loan)", whose initial syllable must reflect Fr *intérêt*, but whose final syllable reflects an earlier borrowing from Sp *interés*. Some crosses are more interesting than this one, involving obvious speech play.

Another matter which arises particularly in Chapter 6 is the distinction between fully inflectable borrowings and a pidgin-like stratum (notably adjectives and adverbs) in European loans.

Chapter 7 is a general assessment of the contribution of the European languages to the current vocabulary of MCA, with appropriate comparisons to their competition with alternative borrowings from CA. The central issue is the differential distribution of lexical borrowings over semantic domains, and in slang.

Chapters 8 and 9 present supplementary data on CA and European borrowings, designed to provide sociolinguistic and geographical contextualization for the data in the primary substantive chapters, 5 and 6. In Chapter 8 we discuss special registers of MCA which show significant differences in borrowing patterns from the more usual vernacular styles dealt with in the earlier chapters; the special registers are broadcast MCA (in which European borrowings are avoided while CA borrowings and code-switches are rampant) and a type of "foreigner talk" MCA used by Moroccan domestics with Europeans who know a little MCA. In Chapter 9 we give brief descriptions of the most significant differences in the adaptation of (mainly European) borrowings between our main MCA dialect(s) and two other nearby Arabic dialects. The first is the distinctive regional MCA spoken in northern Morocco around Tetouan, characterized by heavy continuing direct Spanish influence. The second is Algerian Colloquial Arabic. Presently available data on these dialects are limited, but suffice to indicate some important variable structural conversion routines.

Chapters 10 and 11 are theoretical discussions of two basic issues raised by this case study. Chapter 10 is concerned with the question, how much of the linguistic mechanics of borrowing can be predicted in advance by a linguist presented with separate grammatical analyses of the languages in contact? Chapter 11 explores the relationship between "ordinary" language mixing, such as that described in this book, and pidginization/creolization.

The chapters do not have to be read in consecutive order. Some readers may wish to consult the concluding chapters before taking on the primary substantive chapters (5 and 6). Whether the background chapters (2 and 3) are of much value will depend on the reader's own background and on what he or she wants to get out of the volume. The short chapters (8 and 9) on special registers and on neighbouring dialects might be skipped by some readers.

Use of appendices

A great deal of the data base for this study is presented in the appendices. Appendix A contains a representative sample of what is essentially an open-ended stock of attested or easily produced borrowings from CA into MCA; the organization is by the canonical shape and/or morphological class of the CA items. Appendices B and C, for verbs and other words, respectively, present European borrowings; these appendices are organized alphabetically by stem, with each entry usually indicating inflectional and derivational forms, variant forms, etymology, location of attestations, attestations in earlier publications, and competing MCA lexicon.

Throughout the substantive chapters, particularly 5 and 6, many coded cross-references are made to these appendix entries. A particular phonological conversion rule, for example, might be given in the main text with an illustration or two, plus a long list of appendix entries which also display this phenomenon and which can be consulted by any interested reader. This division between descriptive chapters and primary data base will permit readers to get the essentials without drowning in exemplification and documentation, while at the same time providing this documentation to more suspicious or meticulous readers.

Significance of this study

For scholars who share my own interest in MCA or in Arabic linguistics generally, it is unnecessary to discuss the value of a detailed analysis of language mixing involving this dialect. The sheer extent of code-switching and borrowing in MCA is such that almost any linguistic or sociolinguistic study of the dialect will have to come to grips with relevant aspects of language contact. Scholars working on Arabic dialects outside of Morocco should find interesting parallels and differences between the conversion processes reported here and those which they find elsewhere, whether the source languages are the same or different.

For those readers whose interest is in language mixing rather than specifically in things Moroccan, the present study is offered as a case study of sufficient completeness to be useful in the larger theoretical analysis of language mixing and its relationship to both linguistic structures and sociolinguistic contexts. It is obvious that we need a number of case studies of this type, involving various types of language structure and various types of social context (ranging from the transmission of scientific and related vocabulary by academics or language commissions to sugar plantations). In this context, the present case study is characterizable as follows:

a It involves a base language with (originally) very strict canonical shape patterns connected with morphological classes, so that morphological factors interfere with phonological adaptations.
b It involves source (donor) languages of several types, including the diglossic superordinate and several superimposed European (post-)colonial languages, allowing us to examine conversion patterns from several languages (with different sociolinguistic positions) into the same base language at the same time.
c It involves extensive crossing, particularly of Fr and Sp source forms, including some speech play.
d It gives information about chronological and regional developments in borrowing routines.
e It analyses code-switching as (in part) an avenue to borrowing, but as a stage which may now be bypassed because of the availability of (now) productive conversion routines.
f It deals with code-switching and borrowing almost entirely unmediated by literacy (i.e. with few or no spelling pronunciations and with virtually no institutional orchestration).

2 Sociolinguistics of Morocco

The purpose of this chapter is the quite modest one of providing a capsule description of MCA sociolinguistic structure in historical context. Virtually all of the information presented here is available from other sources and much of it is simplified.

In addition to MCA, the indigenous languages of Morocco include a number of Berber dialects generally grouped into three languages: Tarifiyt (in the Rif mountains of northern Morocco and adjacent areas), Tamazight (in the Atlas mountains south of Fes and Meknes), and Tashelhit (in southwestern Morocco inland from Agadir). Nowadays virtually all Berbers speak MCA as well as their native dialect, and interethnic communication is in MCA. Since the Berber dialects have no solid foothold in any of the major cities, they do not appear any longer to be exercising any significant diffusional influence on MCA in the major population centres. We will have no more to say about Berber languages here.

2.1 Traditional variation in MCA

Although we are not going to be able to present a comprehensive dialectological picture of the differential treatment of CA and Fr/Sp borrowings in different parts of Morocco, it is important to explain that there is a considerable range of MCA dialects and that this study is focusing on a few of them only.

The colonial period began in earnest in 1912 with the establishment of the French and Spanish "Protectorates". Precolonial Morocco, except for a few ports, was a highly isolated and inward-looking region (it is difficult to call it a "country" during this period). It was dominated by a number of large, old cities: Fes, Meknes, Rabat (and neighbouring Salé), Tetouan, Tangier, Marrakech, and a few smaller ones. Each city was partly autonomous and geographical mobility was relatively low, favouring the retention of a local dialect in each city. However, each city was internally differentiated; there were, at any given time, both old established families and recent arrivals from the country still speaking rural dialects. Moreover, some self-consciously distinctive tribal groupings retained their own speech forms for many generations.

With some allowance for such subdialects, on the whole one can say that each city (or at least the oldest and best-established families thereof) had its own characteristic urban dialect, differing from the dialects of other major cities and also from rural dialects collectively. Even now, despite significant recent demographic mobility and the gradual emergence of a more uniform national educated MCA, there are some telltale indicators. In Meknes, the merger of /š ž/ with /s z/ is a notorious local trait distinguishing this city's dialect from that of nearby Fes; the latter is characterized by glottal /?/ as reflex of **q* and by an unusual unconstricted articulation of /r/ and /ṛ/. At a more inclusive level, the Fes/Meknes regional dialect is clearly distinguished from the northern dialect of Tangier and Tetouan, the former showing more complete reduction of short vowels in several word classes, the latter showing at least one distinctive phoneme /č/ and some distinctive verb forms, etc.; there are also some important lexical isoglosses such as /drri/ "boy" (Fes, Meknes) vs. /^{c}ayl/ "boy" (Tangier, Tetouan). No single isogloss is completely reliable as a regional or local indicator (some, like /?/ for **q*, crop up discontinuously in several widely separated cities), but a given combination is usually sufficient to permit a well-travelled Moroccan to guess at one's origin. (Younger, better-educated speakers tend to eliminate the most glaring local idiosyncrasies from their speech, but can still usually be identified as to general region of origin.)

Cutting across geographical regional dialect variations was a more pervasive one between urban dialects as a whole and rural dialects. This split goes back to the Arab conquest of North Africa, which took the form of an early wave of settlers who occupied the main cities, and a later wave of Arabian bedouin who displaced some Berber tribes in the agricultural plains around the main cities and in some mountainous territories. Traditionally, the rural MCA dialects have shared a number of common features among themselves, such as preference for /g/ as reflex of **q* and retention of diphthongs (which are monophthongized in several urban dialects).

In present-day Morocco, this urban/rural split has been greatly complicated by demographic developments. The single most important change was the emergence of Casablanca as the largest city and the commercial/industrial capital of Morocco. Before the Protectorate, Casablanca was a minor town, but during the colonial period (and later) it experienced an enormous influx of migrants, many from nearby rural areas such as the Gharb plains and the valleys of southwestern Morocco (including many bilingual Berbers). An adequate sociolinguistic study has yet to be done, but the dominant Casablanca dialect appears to have many "rural" features. The older cities, while still retaining their old dialects to some extent, have also had a considerable influx of persons from rural areas. The urban/rural distinction is thus changing its character, and some "rural" features are now common in the emerging national educated vernacular.

Traditional Moroccan cities were also characterized by an important split between Muslim and Jewish communal dialects. In the last several decades most Moroccan Jews have left the country (the largest number being now in Israel, with respectable numbers in

France and Montreal), but until this exodus there was a substantial Jewish minority in each important city, occupying a special Jewish quarter called /mllaḥ/ ("mellah" is a common informal transliteration). The Jews were mostly artisans and merchants; the wealthier ones owned land which was rented out, or (if agricultural) was leased to Muslim peasants who worked the land in exchange for a percentage of the harvest. Intercommunal marriage was almost unheard of, and social relations with Muslims were primarily limited to workplace and commercial interactions (chiefly involving men). Even in the colonial period there was fairly little interaction, since the Jews had their own schools (often using Fr).

Under these conditions, special Jewish communal dialects developed and stabilized over the centuries. Although many of the Jews were descended from Spanish and Portuguese Jews who fled the purges of the Inquisition in the fifteenth and sixteenth centuries, the attested Jewish Arabic (Judeo-Arabic) dialects of Morocco appear to be basically Moroccan in origin (rather than imported from the Iberian peninsula). However, they are archaic in this context, and tend to reflect older MCA patterns which most Muslim dialects have given up; they also have a number of lexical items of foreign origin (Hebraisms, especially in religious matters, and some Hispanisms going back to the Judeo-Spanish (Ladino) which many of them spoke in Spain). Some characteristics of the major urban Judeo-Arabic dialects are: /ṛa/ "he saw" (vs. /šaf/ in most Muslim dialects), /ḥəbb/ "he liked, wanted" (vs. /bġa/), merger of /š ž/ with /s z/, and some special forms of basic kin terms. However, there were reasonably extensive differences among the Judeo-Arabic dialects, especially if we consider geographically peripheral ones such as that of Oujda in the northeast near the Algerian border, and the occasional rural Judeo-Arabic dialect like that spoken in Tafilalt where most Muslims in the area spoke Berber dialects. I am currently collecting dialectological data on Moroccan Judeo-Arabic but have a long way to go. For Tafilalt see now Heath and Bar-Asher (1982) and for the old Fes dialect see Brunot and Malka (1939). (It should be added that Jews in northern Morocco, i.e. in Tetouan and Tangier, spoke Ladino into this century instead of a special Judeo-Arabic dialect.)

In addition to regional, urban/rural, and Muslim/Jewish variation, we should mention that adult/child, male/female, and elegant/vulgar dimensions appear also to be involved in speech variation. Female speech is characterized by diminutives, other hypocoristics, certain interjections and expressions, and a narrow range of registers. In Meknes, I found that although adults do not have /ʔ/ as a reflex of **q*, children (sometimes up until about the age of twelve) replace not only /q/ but also /k/ and /g/ with /ʔ/, creating a kind of children's dialect quite distinct from the usual acquisition stages (and possibly encouraged by their mothers, who are said to use this pronunciation when talking to young children). Elegant and formal styles were traditionally achieved largely through use of CA admixtures and CA-like pronunciation.

In a complete historical study of CA and Fr/Sp borrowings into MCA, we would have to consider how all of these sociolinguistic dimensions have interacted with the adaptation of borrowings. For the most part, Berber dialects have not been intermediaries in this respect, but Tarifiyt in the north was in an area of extensive Sp influence and may have been a conduit for some Sp borrowings moving into the interior. A few Sp loans may also be very old ones brought in via the Ladino spoken by Jews, though most Sp loans now current in Muslim MCA probably came in from more recent contacts in the northern and coastal areas. During the Protectorate period (and thereafter), Jews were notably Europeanized in dress, language, etc., and seem to have borrowed Fr and Sp lexical items into their speech more than their Muslim contemporaries (though whether the Jews then transmitted these items to the Muslims is questionable). It is likely that urban dialects of MCA adopted Fr and Sp borrowings earlier than most rural dialects, and the former may have been conduits to the latter in many instances. Fr influence in the Protectorate was much stronger in some regions than others — Fr colons were numerous in the area from Casablanca through Rabat to Meknes and Fes, but for lack of manpower the Fr used "indirect rule" in the Marrakech area, relying on local native potentates — and it is likely that the former areas not only now use more Fr loanwords but also that they have served as conduits for many borrowings which have apread to the less Gallicized areas. The effort by men to develop a wide registral range, including an elegant or "fancy" style, may have encouraged them to outpace women in adopting foreign and CA items into their speech.

The present publication does not pretend to begin to work out these sociolinguistic matters even in the limited context of loans from CA and Fr/Sp. However, the present study, focusing as it does on the speech of younger educated persons in the Fes/Meknes area, can (among other things) provide a basis for further comparative work, and one aspect which I hope to check in connection with more general dialectological studies now in early stages is the treatment of selected borrowings in different dialects and varieties. (We do present some limited dialectological data, notably in Appendices B and C in connection with Fr/Sp borrowings, since we do have some relevant data from Algeria, Marrakech, and Tetouan from personal fieldwork, and since variant forms can be cited from published sources for some other locations.)

2.2 Diglossia

Arabic is, of course, one of the "charter members" of the diglossia club (Ferguson 1959). Although the term diglossia has subsequently been diluted by workers in the sociology of language who apply it to bilingual speech communities where there is a significant functional hierarchization (Fishman 1971), the term is here used in Ferguson's original sense, namely, as a designation for sociolinguistic systems in which a "low" vernacular coexists with what speakers regard as a "high" form of the same language, the latter being the normal language of writing and (other) formal contexts.

The grammar and core lexicon of CA was largely fixed in the first few centuries following the death of Muhammad, and has never strayed very far from the language of the Koran. Of course, CA has evolved in many ways, and in some contexts it is appropriate to speak of "Modern Literary Arabic" in contrast to "Classical Arabic", though in the present publication CA represents both unless otherwise specified. The primary changes since the Koran have been the elimination of some archaic morphological constructions, and especially the addition of much new vocabulary based on foreign models (either borrowed outright or internally derived).

On the other hand, MCA has evolved over a millenium as a spoken vernacular and has diverged considerably from CA (which we may take as essentially identical to the proto-dialect, though the historical relationship is not quite this simple). There is a popular belief in Morocco that MCA is very close to CA, closer at least than the other conspicuous living colloquial dialects (Egyptian, Syrian, Iraqi, etc.), but for the most part this is wishful thinking and in some respects MCA is particularly far removed from CA. At any rate, MCA and CA are now quite distinct; Moroccans receive their initial serious exposure to CA in schools (and through Koranic recitation), nowadays also through television (including CA cartoons produced in Iraq), and only a well-educated minority can discourse freely in it.

CA currently functions in Morocco strictly as a language of writing and formal contexts, and effectively no one uses it as a home language. It is, though, the primary language of schools at all levels (though until recently there were some all-French schools). In principle, teachers even in primary schools are supposed to use CA as the classroom language; in practice what they often do is code-switch from CA to MCA, often repeating the same explanations in both languages to ensure clarity. Later on, in secondary and higher education, a relatively pure CA is used where practicable, except where Fr is still used.

In government and other bureaucratic settings, CA is the regular medium for written documents (again, except where Fr is still used) and indeed most Moroccans would have some difficulty writing MCA even if its vocabulary is fit for the task in hand. A Moroccan who finds it necessary to discuss a matter with a postal clerk, police official or business person will normally speak MCA, but any resulting written communication will be in CA (if not Fr). Newspapers and magazines appear in formal CA with few or no Moroccanisms, except for one humour tabloid *ʔAkhbār S-Sūq* ("News of the Market") which does appear in MCA (using Arabic script).

The broadcast media use CA and/or MCA depending on programme type. The news is always in formal CA, and there are many didactic religious programmes and documentaries in CA, many of them originating in other Arabic-speaking countries (Egypt, Saudi Arabia, Iraq). However, local sporting events are broadcast in MCA (with heavy CA borrowing and occasional code-switching), and MCA is also used for soap operas, situation comedies, and similar informal programming. Commentary in Arabic-language music programmes on radio is in MCA. Academic panel discussions, which are common on television and radio, oscillate between CA and a classicized MCA depending on the mood of the participants, and it is quite common for one speaker to use formal CA while another uses classicized MCA on the same programme (there is also a tendency to use CA at the beginning and then shift into MCA as the discussion moves along). Interviews with government ministers, even when subsequently broadcast as part of regular news programmes, are usually in MCA, though the same politicians use CA in public addresses and formal parliamentary sessions. Finally, CA is the predominant language of Islam and is used in most sermons as well as Koranic recitations.

Informal observation of attitudes during my sojourn suggests a widespread positive attitude toward CA even among persons who are unable to speak it fluently. There is little interest even among academics to cultivate an alternative native culture based on MCA (or Berber languages for that matter). Discussions of the value of CA usually emphasize not only its supranational, pan-Arab character and its glorious literature, but also its supposed intrinsic beauty and logic, presumably in contrast to the illogical and unattractive MCA. It is difficult for Moroccans to understand why a foreign linguist would spend his valuable time studying MCA, though they will usually be satisfied with the answer: "So I can talk to the people." Those Moroccans (mostly teachers) who can really speak CA evidently derive considerable pleasure from doing so, in somewhat the same way an American college student who has mastered Fr may enjoy conversing in it for its own sake. I have attended small holiday gatherings involving several guests where, at the end of the festivities, one of the guests arises and (on behalf of the others) gives a short speech in pure CA thanking the host for his hospitality and wishing him well; this is by no means standard but it is a nice touch. Groups of Moroccans may also occasionally switch into more or less pure CA in order to discuss serious topics (politics, philosophy, the economy) if they feel more comfortable in CA with such topics, though roughly the same effect can be achieved by using MCA with substantial use of borrowed CA stems and occasional code-switched segments.

In most modern Arabic-speaking countries there appears to be a developing hybrid involving convergence between CA and the colloquial, generally used as a special register for discussing serious topics or used in interactions between Arabs from different dialect areas (e.g. an Egyptian and an Iraqi). On the basis of my own observations (which are limited to particular groups of people), I do not think that at the present time it is useful to speak of a stabilized hybrid register of this type. It is true, though, that texts do occur with basically MCA grammatical structures but with extensive use of borrowed CA stems and with frequent short code-switched (or at least poorly assimilated) segments so that some parts of a text (especially a section consisting largely of nouns and adjectives) may not have clear MCA/CA switch points. It is also possible, for example in reading a CA newspaper aloud, to make some adjustments such as omitting word-final short vowels (i.e. using "pausal" CA pronunciation even in non-prepausal position) and perhaps pronouncing CA interdental fricatives as stops (as in MCA). It appears that the frequency of intermediate or mixed CA/MCA forms is increasing with more universal education, the expansion of CA at the expense of Fr from some domains, and the increasing importance of the broadcast media, but at the present time I do not think it useful to speak of a stable, well-established hybrid (or mesolectal) form intermediate between vernacular MCA and formal CA. (This conclusion might have to be reconsidered in connection with other groups of Moroccans, and/or in connection with the next couple of generations.)

Some idea of the divergence between MCA and CA, and of the nature of classicized MCA (i.e. MCA base with heavy borrowing and code-switching) can be gotten from chapters 3 and 4 in particular.

2.3 French

The so-called French "Protectorate" was basically a classic colonial structure, thinly disguised, and lasted from 1912 until 1956. There was very little French influence in Morocco prior to 1912, although the French had intensively colonized Algeria much earlier. The Protectorate took the form of an arrangement between the colonial administrators and the Moroccan sultan which gave the latter a modest degree of political power and a substantial ceremonial role, while the French had the major say in matters that they considered important to themselves. There was a substantial French military presence, especially in and around the cities of Casablanca (which the French greatly expanded), Rabat-Salé, Meknes, and Fes. Lacking sufficient military and economic resources to occupy the southwest of the country in the same way, the French relied on a real system of indirect rule in Marrakech, where they made mutually accommodating arrangements with local Muslim leaders. In all cases the French took great pains to obtain the loyalty of some local elements; the colonial administrators attempted to prevent French colons from excessively offending local sentiments, banned Christian missionary activity to a large degree, and made it illegal for Christians even to enter mosques. However, the colonial administrators were not above dumping an uncooperative sultan in favour of a more malleable one when circumstances required this. (A small northern area around Tangier and Tetouan was under a separate Spanish Protectorate.)

French policy was to educate a small, controllable native Moroccan élite rather than to provide mass European education. French military field officers, a vitally important element in the overall colonial system and often men of considerable ability, were encouraged to learn Arabic (or, in mountainous areas, Berber) and to use it with natives rather than teaching the latter Fr, and access of natives to European-type schools was deliberately restricted. The effect of this was that Fr diffused to Moroccans at a limited rate, and the Fr spoken by many Moroccans in contact with the French (as domestics, assistants, liaison people, etc.) was frequently fragmentary. Moreover, some of the colons and colonial administrators in the early Protectorate period were veterans of the Algerian colony, and may have spoken a little Algerian colloquial Arabic along with a somewhat nonstandard North African dialect of Fr (based on southern Fr dialects with some additional peculiarities).

With independence in 1956 (after a relatively peaceful transition, in contrast to the grisly war of independence in Algeria), a programme of mass education (in principle, compulsory at primary level) began. With the increasing number of native Moroccans employed in government bureaucracies, and in clerical and other white-collar jobs, there was a great demand for persons with a knowledge of Fr, which at this time was far better established in such domains than MCA or CA. To satisfy this need it was necessary to greatly expand the teaching of Fr in schools, and for this purpose a large number of French nationals were imported or kept on as teachers not only of the Fr language itself but also of mathematics, science, and other academic subjects. Certain schools, the Missions Françaises, operated more or less entirely in Fr, though the majority of schools included at least some instruction in CA (at the very least, in Islamic subjects).

In this fashion, Fr achieved far greater currency in post-colonial Morocco than it had in the colonial period itself, even though the native French population declined (when most French landowners had their property confiscated). Most Moroccan intellectuals in this period were educated in France; most Moroccan novelists and many poets wrote and published in Fr; the Fr language gradually lost some of its stigma as a language of colonial oppression and becme an avenue for socioeconomic advancement — and, for a new generation of young urbanites, for spiritual liberation.

For some years now there has been an active youth culture (or counterculture) centred on campuses but not confined to them, based at least as much on French and other Western models as it is on any traditional Moroccan or Arab popular culture or life style. As in the West, this revolves around popular music, films, drinking, drugs, sex, and a bit of radical politics. Fr is associated with this youth ambience, and not just with the colonial heritage and with European "high" culture.

Fr has become an important language among the new Moroccan middle class, particularly in Casablanca and Rabat, and throughout Morocco among middle-class Jews (many of whom have regrouped in Casablanca, though most have now left the country). There are even a few families in these segments who use Fr as a home language, though this practice is uncommon in Morocco (in contrast to Algeria) and is declining as it becomes increasingly obvious that Arabic is the dominant language of the present and future in Morocco.

Another significant development is the substantial migration of Moroccan (along with Algerian and Tunisian) "guest workers" to European countries, especially France and Belgium (but also to the Netherlands, for example). These migrants, often single men, work overseas for a few years as factory hands, street sweepers, or other unskilled and semi-skilled labourers. Some then return permanently to Morocco — if they are lucky, with a decent nest egg; but others remain in their European country of adoption, returning to Morocco periodically for vacations. It is difficult to assess the overall effect of these overseas workers in the adoption of Fr borrowings in Morocco itself. Certainly they may bring back with them a heavily Gallicized form of MCA and may sometimes play the role of transmitters of new borrowings. However, many of these people speak macaronic Fr/MCA mixtures which native Moroccans laugh at rather than straining to imitate, and in general they are more likely to code-switch than to adapt Fr items to the structure of MCA. Moreover, extensive direct contact between stay-at-home Moroccans and French nationals (teachers, other professionals, and tourists) along with the extent of Fr films and radio broadcasts seems sufficient to explain the large number of Fr borrowings into MCA in recent decades without having to rely on borrowings mediated by returning guest workers.

At any rate, the significance of Fr in Morocco appears to have peaked in the 1960s and early 1970s and is probably now on the wane. A long-planned educational reform, now in an intermediate stage of implementation, is replacing Fr by CA in Moroccan schools and universities in many subjects (mathematics and the hard sciences being the last to go). Progress is slow due to logistical difficulties (training teachers, developing CA textbooks, standardizing technical vocabulary) but is now in high gear, and it appears that the number of French nationals brought over as teachers (*les coopérants*) is being reduced. Even courses in Fr as a second language are increasingly being taught by Moroccan teachers. Arabization is also proceeding apace in government bureaucracies, despite the resistance of employees whose own education was substantially in Fr and who find it difficult to use CA in their daily routines. International political developments are in concert with these tendencies: European countries caught in deep recessions are not accepting new guest workers and are prodding those already there to depart on the next bus; economic and political regionalization is pulling the European countries and the Arab bloc closer together, but dividing the two groups increasingly from each other (this despite the current local hostility between Morocco and Algeria over the fighting in the Western Sahara). Moroccan workers are now more likely to head for jobs in Libya and Saudi Arabia than for the factories of France and Belgium.

Turning away from gross sociological and demographic facts, my observations are that there is not a profound conflict between a symbolic allegiance to Fr (or other Western languages) and allegiance to CA, whatever may seem to be the case from scrutiny of government language policies. The young, educated, often fun-loving Moroccans in Fes and Meknes that I know are remarkably eclectic. There is no strong feeling of contradiction between Western and Islamic-traditionalist orientations. The same Moroccans who get drunk on bad red wine, smoke hashish joints, and frequent bordellos in nearby mountain resorts nonetheless consider themselves tolerably good Muslims and undergo the rigorous fasting of the holy month of Ramadan (though they may pray in mosques only rarely). They are proud, patriotic Moroccans with a strong sense of national honour and, on another level, of the famous virility of the Moroccan male, while at the same time they adulate the Bee-Gees and John Travolta. We should therefore not exaggerate the "conflict" between Fr and CA, especially at the level of individual attitudes (as opposed to national policy-making). There is very little evidence in vernacular speech of any systematic linguistic purism, say with European-oriented persons making massive use of Fr borrowings while traditionalists take pains to avoid them. (The main exception is that in broadcast MCA, and perhaps MCA in some other public, formal contexts, most Fr/Sp borrowings are avoided.) In everyday speech we find considerable numbers of borrowings from Fr as well as MCA, and even the local slang and other special, affective registers contain large number of both Fr and CA elements.

2.4 Spanish and other European languages

The second colonial language in Morocco is Spanish. The actual Spanish Protectorate was limited to a small part of Morocco including the northern cities of Tangier and Tetouan and some nearby territory along the coast and into the Rif mountains.

Prior to the creation of the French and Spanish Protectorates in

1912, Spanish was the most important European language in Morocco since it was of some importance in the coastal ports. Moreover, Judeo-Spanish (Ladino) was the language brought to Morocco by Jews in the fifteenth and sixteenth centuries; Moroccan Jews in places like Fes have spoken Arabic dialects in recent centuries but retain some old borrowings, and in Tangier and Tetouan Judeo-Spanish remained the home vernacular into this century (when it was gradually replaced by a more standard continental Spanish transmitted through the schools). Spain is still in possession of Ceuta, a small enclave east of Tangier, along with Melilla, a similar coastal enclave in eastern Morocco near Oujda; both Melilla and Ceuta are now centres for duty-free shopping. Until recently Spain was also the colonial power in the former Spanish Sahara, subsequently occupied by Moroccan troops and now the object of fighting between them and Polisario guerillas.

The principal difference between Sp and Fr in Morocco is that the Spanish colonial area (leaving aside the Spanish Sahara, a thinly populated area) was smaller than the French colonial area, that Sp-language educational institutions have never been especially well developed, and that the Spanish presence has declined drastically in the postcolonial period whereas, as noted above, the French postcolonial presence has been substantial. Although Sp is still a useful second language in the north, it is of no communicative use in the remainder of Morocco. Educated Moroccans from Tangier and Tetouan are now finding Fr a more generally useful second language than Sp, since Fr is still used to some extent as a language of instruction in Moroccan universities (most of which are located in the former French zone). Sp also seems to have much lower prestige than Fr, due in part to the failure of former Spanish colonists to push their "high" culture in the fashion of the French (I am thinking here mainly of the postcolonial period), and also to the fact that Fr but not Sp can serve as a useful communicative and political link to a large number of other African countries. Sp is offered as a language of study in many schools throughout Morocco, but is relatively unpopular.

English has no particular historical link to Morocco, though the United States has had a few military bases in the country during much of the post-World War II period. There is no contiguous English-speaking country, with the insignificant exception of the British Crown Colony of Gibraltar. The bulk of foreign tourists in Morocco are French; Americans and British are not only fewer in number but also have less direct contact with the average Moroccan since most of them are well-off tourists who travel in organized groups, while many French (and German) tourists travel in small packs and are more likely to mingle with Moroccans. Furthermore, the French are by far the dominant commercial interest in the country, far ahead of American and British companies.

Despite this, or possibly because of it, English (Eng) is gaining as an international language in Morocco. Though still much less useful within the country than Fr, its prestige is very high. There are some signs that its practical value may be on the verge of a significant increase as French influence declines and as Morocco becomes increasingly dependent on American aid. American multinational corporations are currently avoiding investments in

Morocco, owing mainly to the poor state of the local economy resulting from the expensive war in the Western Sahara, but when the economy begins to improve it may be that American commercial penetration in the area may increase. Moroccan attitudes toward Americans and the United States government seem to be highly positive, particularly since they are not contaminated with the colonial memories which taint attitudes toward France. American popular culture in the form of rock music and Hollywood films, supplemented by their British counterparts, is filling the airwaves and the theatres. The remoteness of English-speaking countries and people, in contrast to the familiarity of France and the French, may contribute to the favourable aura around Eng. My data indicate that Eng words are starting to creep into MCA, chiefly as slang expressions, though it is true that some of these have probably come in via Fr (since colloquial Fr and especially Fr slang contain many Eng words).

The German language (Ger) has not sunk deep roots in Morocco, though before the French Protectorate in 1912 there was some attempt to establish a German foothold in the southwest around Agadir and a few other locations. There is now a reasonable number of German tourists, particularly in some of the southwestern resorts, and Ger is taught as an optional second language in many Moroccan schools. There are some Moroccans working overseas in German-speaking countries or regions (West Germany, Austria, Switzerland), though many fewer than in French-speaking ones. Overall, the prestige of Ger in most of Morocco seems to be intermediate between the high prestige of Eng and the low prestige of Sp (outside the north). A handful of slang expressions of recent German origin occur in my MCA data.

2.5 Literature on Moroccan sociolinguistics

It is worth mentioning, at least briefly, some of the more useful general resources on Moroccan multilingualism for the benefit of those readers who might wish to enter more deeply into these matters or at least to see what various scholars have had to say on them.

We may begin with Lanly (1962), a study of Fr as spoken in North Africa (mainly Algeria) by native speakers. This is a fundamental reference, but in so far as it deals with interference between Fr and local Arabic dialects it is specifically concerned with the adaptation of Arabic materials into Fr, not vice versa. Much of the book is a discussion of relationships between local spoken Fr and other Romance langauges (including Sp) in the Algerian region, and the relationship of this Fr to Sabir (lingua franca), a type of pidgin used in Algiers and elsewhere in the Mediterranean (mainly in earlier centuries). However, this Sabir does not seem to have been a significant factor in Morocco — certainly not during the period of massive European influence on MCA since the beginning of the Protectorate period (1912). Lanly is well aware of the differences between Algeria and Morocco, and states that the relatively recent occupation of Morocco was carried out mainly (though not entirely) by new settlers direct from France (p.111). Thus even Lanly's description of twentieth-century Fr in

Algeria is not necessarily of much relevance to our Moroccan concerns.

Of more immediate interest are three recent unpublished dissertations by Abbassi (1977), Gravel (1979), and Forkel (1980). All three are wide-ranging surveys of social, historical, and some linguistic features of Moroccan multilingualism; they are not focused on any single specific point. In combination, these studies are more detailed and authoritative on the historical and social dimensions than the present volume, but none of them pretends to discuss details of code-switching and (especially) borrowing in the fashion presented here.

Abbassi (1977) contains the following points of interest here: survey of MCA urban and rural dialects; remarks about the incipient supralocal koine (pp.23-5); analysis of local forms of Fr as spoken by Moroccans (pp.29-31); remarks on the one-way bilingualism of Berbers, who use MCA when speaking with Arabs (p.98); an analysis of "Franco-Arabic", presented mainly in terms of code-switching in which MCA tends to be the base language with Fr words and phrases inserted at particular types of switch points; and results of questionnaires on language attitudes and usage (by domains). Abbassi is mainly interested in code-switching for its own sake, whereas I am looking at it here mainly in connection with certain ways in which it functions as an avenue to fuller integration; Abbassi thus has somewhat fuller information on code-switching points than is presented in chapter 4 below.

Gravel (1979) is rather similar in general structure, but with somewhat fewer linguistic details. It includes a more complete sketch of the history of Morocco (especially in the earliest Arab periods) as it relates to language distributions (pp.27-73). A good part of this work is devoted to presentation of another questionnaire on language usage and attitudes (pp.99-189). Gravel's subjects for the questionnaire study were incoming university students in Rabat; Abbassi's were mainly government and business employees and a few students in Casablanca.

Forkel (1980) covers some of the same ground, but is perhaps more concerned with the typology of mixed speech varieties and of stylistic levels. In the case of MCA *vis-à-vis* CA, he distinguishes an unstable mixed form ("Mischsprache") from a more stabilized educated dialect; in the latter he found a great many CA elements but they were integrated into MCA to a greater extent than in the mixed forms. With respect to MCA and Fr, Forkel emphasizes mixtures rather than well adapted borrowings. In the present volume I make informal use of similar typologies of registers, but I do not emphasize them because a single stretch of speech may include clearly code-switched material, clarly well-integrated (borrowed) material, and other material which is not easily classified in these terms. I am therefore somewhat more concerned with classifying and analysing particular stems, words, and phrases than with a global characterization of long stretches of speech (see, however, remarks on special registers, especially in chapter 8).

For Tunisia, we may cite Stevens (1974), another dissertation, which reports language attitudes and usage, based in large part on questionnaires. Verbs of Romance origin are treated in Talmoudi (1986).

3 Sketch of basic features of MCA

For a general description of MCA see Harrell (1962). In this chapter we present elementary data on the Fes/Meknes dialect, covering only "pure" native forms.

3.1 Consonants

In Table 3-1, note that MCA does not have /p v ? θ ð ñ l̃ č ǰ/. Actually, there are certain MCA subdialects which have some of these consonants: affricates occur in some northern dialects, **q* is reflected as glottal stop /?/ in some urban dialects, etc.

Table 3-1 MCA Consonants

	voiceless stop	voiced stop	nasal	voiceless fricative	voiced fricative	voiceless sibilant	voiced sibilant	lateral	rhotic	aspiration	semivowel
labial		b	m	f							
plain alveolar	t	d	n			s	z	l	r		
pharyngealized alveolar	ṭ	ḍ				ṣ	ẓ		ṛ		
palatoalveolar						š	ž				y
velar	k	g									w
uvular	q			x	ġ						
pharyngeal				ḥ	ʕ						
laryngeal										h	

There are also some marginal consonants not shown in the table (in addition to those restricted to borrowings, and which are thus not discussed in this chapter). Pharyngealized /ḅḅ/ and /ṃṃ/ occur in kin terms /ḅḅa/ "father" and /ṃṃ-i/ "my mother", often with labialized release, and /ṃṃ/ occurs in some other nouns as well. It is not clear, though, that these are distinctive phonemes since some other labial clusters like /mw/ are phonetically articulated as [ṃṃ^{w}] in noun morphology under certain conditions. Pharyngealized /ḷḷ/ in /ḷḷa(h)/ and /t-hḷḷa (f-)/ "he took care of" is another rare phoneme, and there are a handful of other cases of /ḅ/ and /ṇ/.

Pharyngealized consonants (distinct from pharyngeal consonants), called "emphatic" in traditional Arabic grammar, involve a secondary approximation of the base of the tongue to the pharyngeal wall, in addition to a primary articulation (usually an alveolar constriction). It is indicated by a dot in /ṭ ṣ ṛ ẓ ḍ ḷ ṃ ḅ p̣ ṇ f̣ ỵ/. However, /ḥ/ is a pharyngeal fricative and is not pharyngealized in this sense.

Pharyngealization is easily heard through allophones of adjacent vowels: phonemes /i/ and /u/ are lowered to allophones [e] and [o], while /a/ has a back articulation here transcribed [ạ]. In unpharyngealized environments we get phonetic [i u æ], except that uvulars and pharyngeals have somewhat the same effect as pharyngealized consonants, and that /a/ has a backed articulation in final, prepausal position.

Consonantal pharyngealization may "spread" from a focal pharyngealized consonant like /ṭ ṣ ḍ/ not only to adjoining vowels but also, under circumstances which differ from dialect to dialect, to noncontiguous consonants and syllables. A detailed study is not presented here. The fullest spreading to affixes is most characteristic of northern and southwestern dialects, not of central (Fes/Meknes) ones.

Because phonetic vowel qualities like [e], [o], and [ạ] are associated in MCA with consonant pharyngealization (and to a lesser extent uvular and pharyngeal consonants), it should be noted immediately that borrowings from Fr and Sp source forms which contained vowels with similar qualities are commonly introduced into MCA by converting appropriate Fr or Sp consonants into MCA pharyngealized consonants, in order to preserve the surface vowel qualities (with many exceptions). For example, a source sequence like **doso* could come into MCA as phonemic /ḍuṣu/, pronounced [ḍoṣo]. However, difficulties would arise with a sequence like **oduso*, since the two *o*-vowels imply MCA /ḍ/ and /ṣ/, but this would entail changing the medial *u* to surface [o] as well; there is no good MCA representation which preserves all source vowels. See §6.1, §6.2.

Another point relevant to borrowings is that MCA /t/ is, in most contexts, phonetically [t^{s}] with distinctive assibilated release (though distinct from /ts/ sequence), while /ṭ/ lacks this. See §6.7. Preservation of Fr and Sp *t* without the release can produce a new MCA phoneme.

In MCA, uvular /q/ is normally pronounced as a glottalized uvular stop [q̓]. It is only slightly farther back than velar /k/, and the glottalization is apparently the primary cue.

Pharyngeal /ḥ/ and /^{c}/ are characteristic Semitic phonemes of great phonological interest, but since they are rarely central to the treatment of borrowings we omit a discussion of them here.

3.2 Full vowels

We make a distinction between full vowels /i u a/, and the rather evanescent "short vowels" discussed in the next section. The full vowels are clearly articulated, and if there are several of them in the same word, the stress pattern tends to be even and staccato. As noted above, /i u a/ are phonetic [e o ạ] before or after a pharyngealized consonant, and phonetic [i ü ae] elsewhere, except that /a/ has backed allophone word-finally, and that uvulars and pharyngeals /q x ġ ḥ ᶜ/ have somewhat the saem effect as pharyngealized consonants. There are occasional cases of morphophonemic alternations /w/~/u/ and /y/~/i/.

3.3 Short vowels

These segments are unstable and have a fairly ambiguous structural status which will have to be clarified in a more specialized publication elsewhere. We will here use three symbols /^/, /ə/, and /ʷ/, though the first of these can perhaps be considered a special case of the second, and the third can (in some analyses) be considered a consonantal feature (as the notation implies).

Basically, /ə/ and /ʷ/ are unrounded and rounded short vowels, respectively. The first of these can be heard as /ă/, /ɛ̆/, or /Ĭ/ depending on consonantal environment, but always quite short. Under syncope (or syllabification of an adjacent sonorant) it disappears. Rounded /ʷ/ occurs as /Ŭ/ (like English *u* in *put*) when syllabic or as the onset to a syllabifying sonorant; when syncope applies it is heard as a labialized release of a consonant or a labialized transition between two consonants: /xʷbz/ is [xŬbz] "bread", but with suffix /xʷbz-i/ is [xʷbz-i]. The /ʷ/ phoneme usually occurs next to a velar or uvular consonant /k g q x ġ/.

It should be noted that the analysis used here makes sparing use of the /ə/ phoneme, recognising it only where clear surface oppositions occur (or are possible). In words with syllabic sonorants, like /kbṛ/ "bigger", I do not usually write the form with /ə/ (/kbəṛ/), though some authors do; to some extent this is due to the fact that /ə/ seems to be distinctive in the particular dialects I know best only in a few positions. The typical positions for /ə/, and to some extent for /ʷ/, are C__CC#, CC__C#, VC__C# — in other words, at the end of a word before the last or penultimate consonant, and even in such positions the possibility of contrasts may be ruled out if one or the other of the last two consonants is a sonorant.

The marginal segment /^/, as in /t^-drib/ "training", indicates that what we would expect to be pronounced as a consonant cluster is in fact pronounced with a clear consonantal release between the segments, here /t/ and /d/. In this case, even if the underlying form is /tə-drib/ we would expect syncope and then assimilation to apply, producing */d-drib/. We take no position here on the phonemic status of this /^/, which does not commonly appear in borrowings.

3.4 Root structure

A prototypical root is of the type $C_1C_2C_3$(triliteral) or $C_1C_2C_3C_4$ (quadriliteral), with one or two noncontiguous consonants here optionally being replaced by root vowels. Actual words are based on such roots but may include intercalated vowels with grammatical (not lexical) value and one or more affixes: /ma-ktəb-t-ha-š/ "I did not write it" from root /ktb/.

The major triliteral root types are these:

CCC	strong
CCV	weak
CVC	hollow
$C_1C_2C_2$	geminate

The vowels (V) in these formulae must be full (not short) vowels.

For verbs, the basic strong pattern is CCəC and the basic geminate pattern is CəCC, with the (non-root) short vowel subject to syncope or absorption depending on the particular word form. There is usually no difference between imperfective and perfective stem shapes.

For the weak and hollow types, the vowel in the root may take different forms, and three distinct contexts must be recognized: (a) imperfective; (b) perfective with subject-marking pronominal suffix beginning in a consonant; (c) other perfective forms (with vowel-initial suffix or zero suffix for 3MSg subject). Weak verb roots have /a/ in context (c), /i/ in context (b), and either /a/, /i/, or /u/ (depending on the root) in context (a). Hollow roots have /a/ in context (c), short /ə/ in context (b) except for two important roots with /^{w}/, and either /a/, /i/, or /u/ in context (a) depending on the root. The basic patterns are therefore these:

	hollow	weak
preconsonantal perfective	CəC-	CCi-
other perfective	CaC	CCa
imperfective	-CVC	-CCV

Examples: /faq/ "he awoke", /fəq-t/ "I awoke", /n-fiq/ "I awaken" (imperf.); /šra/ "he bought", /šri-t/ "I bought", /n-šri/ "I buy".

Geminate roots differ from strong roots not only in that the geminate cluster may not be broken up by a short vowel, but also in taking an augment /-i-/ in context (b): strong /ktəb-t/ "I wrote" but /šmm-i-t/ "I smelled".

Quadriliteral roots and stems do not have a structurally significant distinction between strong and geminate types, so in this context we lump the two together as strong. There are weak quadriliterals with final /a/ in context (c) and final /i/ in contexts (a) and (b). There are also hollow types with either C_2 or C_3 replaced by a vowel, but with one or two exceptions in these cases the root vowel is stable throughout the perfective/imperfective paradigms (unlike the case with hollow triliterals).

There are several statistical or absolute restrictions on allowable consonant sequences within roots. C_1 and C_2 ordinarily may not be identical; exceptions are a few kin terms like /bḅa/ "father" and the verb /dda/ "he carried", along with /ḷḷa(h)/ "God", and the last of these is the only one which appears to occur in all Moroccan dialects. C_1 and C_3 (in triliterals) are very rarely identical, the most common exceptions being /šəmš/ "sun", /žwwəž/ "he married", and /t-qlləq/ "he got worried or angry". Certain sequences of two consonants differing only in one feature, like /rl/ or /lr/, are rare or nonexistent within roots.

3.5 Noun morphology

The definite prefix is /l-/, which assimilates completely to a following stem-initial coronal consonant: /l-fžr/ "the dawn", /š-šəmš/ "the sun", /l-gmṛ-a/ "the moon". The two most common indefinite formations are with /ši/ "some" and /waḥəd/ "one, a", as in /ši ṛažl/ "some/any man" and /waḥəd ṛ-ṛažl/ "a man"; note that the type with /waḥəd/ contains what is morphologically a definite noun (contrast /ṛažl waḥəd/ "one man").

There are various prepositions, mostly written here as prefixes, such as /f-/ "in, at", /l-/ "to", /mn-/ "from", hence /mn-ṛ-ṛažl/ "from the man".

There is a set of pronominal suffixes: /ṛažl-i/ "my husband" ("my man"), /ṛažl-ha/ "her husband", /ṣaḥb-i/ "my friend". The definite prefix is not used in this context.

Stem-ablaut is commonly used to convert Sg into Pl, and is always used to form diminutives (Dimin). Thus /bit/ "room (of house)", Pl /byut/, Dimin /bwiyt/; /wəld/ "boy", Pl /wlad/, Dimin /wliyd/. The Dimin Pl is formed by adding Pl suffix /-at/ to the Dimin Sg and is not based directly on the ordinary Pl. The Dimin form is generally predictable from the ordinary Sg, involving insertion of /i/ and /iy/ after C_2 (when C_1 and C_2 in the ordinary form are not separated by a full vowel), or of /wi/ after C_1 (replacing a full vowel between C_1 and C_2). There are some minor irregularities which need not detain us. The stem-ablaut Pl, on the other hand, is more difficult to predict since there are many Sg/Pl paradigm types; sometimes a fixed Sg form has two or more possible Pl forms. A Pl suffix /-at/ is used instead of an ablaut pattern for some nouns (especially those with FSg /-a/, see below, or those with unusual Sg forms) and for almost all participles. For Pl/Dimin ablaut in borrowings see §6.26, §6.27.

Fsg (feminine singular) suffix /-a/, becoming /-t-/ before a pronominal suffix, is found with most nouns which take feminine concord, though there are a handful of nouns like /šəmš/ "sun" which take feminine concord even without this suffix. There is no Msg suffix. Whether a given Pl noun is formed by adding /-at/ or by ablaut is not significant for concord, since in general gender is neutralized in the Pl. For gender in European borrowings see §6.25.

3.6 Verb morphology

Each verb has imperfective and perfective paradigms; the perfective is basically a punctual or perfective past tense form, while the imperfective is the normal present and future form and may be used in the past (usually with a preceding past tense form of /kan/ "he was") to indicate continuity, repetition, etc. For some stems the active participle is in common use as a stative perfect or (present) progressive form, so there is a three-part system: perfective /fṭṛ/ "he ate breakfast", imperfective /ta-y-fṭṛ/ "he (usually) eats breakfast" (present) and /ġadi y-fṭṛ/ "he will eat breakfast" (future), and participle /faṭṛ/ (usually with a preceding independent pronoun) "(he) has already eaten breakfast". The participle agrees only in gender and number with the subject (FSg /-a/, Pl /-in/), but the perfective and imperfective have complete series of pronominal affixes cross-referencing the subject (see Table 4-2 in chapter 4).

Most verbs have a corresponding verbal noun. For simple triliterals the verbal noun is often of the form /CCVC/ or /CCC-an/ and can take regular nominal affixes.

3.7 Verbal derivation

Some quadriliteral verb stems are simply derived from triliterals by doubling C_2, hence from /dx^wl/ "he entered" we get /dxxl/ "he put (something) in". Other quadriliterals are underived and have four distinct consonants. The type /dxxl/ is historically derived from the "conjugation II" of CA, and has factitive-causative sense.

From this is formed a (medio-)passive form by adding prefix /t-/ as in /d-dxxl/ (with /dd/ from /td/) "he was put in"; this is the "conjugation V" of CA. Other (underived) quadriliterals also have this form with /t-/.

The morphological MCA reciprocal verb has /t-/ prefix and inserted /a/ vowel when formed from triliteral stem: /qtl/ "he killed", reciprocal /t-qatl-u/ "they killed each other" (with 3Pl perfective suffix /-u/). This is historically the CA "conjugation VI". It is usually not formed from non-triliteral stems and is not fully productive. (There is also an alternative periphrastic reciprocal: /ši qtl ši/ "they killed each other".)

The usual (medio-)passive of triliteral verbs has no CA counterpart and has prefix /tt-/, as in /tt-qtl/ "he got killed".

There is a handful of residual MCA forms based on other CA conjugations (VII, X), but most have been shortened or reshaped and these are no longer identifiable stem-types. A type /CCaC/ with adjectival roots, like /ġlaḍ/ "he got fat" (cf. /ġliḍ/ "fat"), is related to the semantically corresponding CA types ("conjugation IX" or "XI").

4 Code-switching

We begin by again remarking that the principal concern of this book is the gradual integration of borrowed lexical materials. We are concerned with code-switching primarily in so far as it functions as an avenue for more complete integration. We are therefore particularly interested in code-switching at the phrasal and lexical levels of linguistic structure rather than in switching at clausal and supraclausal levels.

4.1 Types of code-switching

It is convenient to begin with an idealized binary distinction between code-switching and borrowing, though we will soon see that this requires extensive elaboration. By "code-switching" is meant a pattern of textual production in which a speaker alternates between continuous utterance segments in one language L_x and another language L_y with abrupt and clear-cut switching points, often at phrasal or clausal boundaries. By "borrowing" is meant the adaptation of a lexical item P_y from L_y into L_x, becoming P_x (that is, a regular lexical item in L_x satisfying phonological, canonical-shape and morphological rules for this language).

This binary distinction is conceptually useful, and these terms will be used from time to time in this publication. However, it is important to understand that it is not completely satisfactory.

First, there are occasions where it is difficult to decide whether certain particular items in texts are instances of code-switching or borrowing in these senses. Code-switching at clausal boundaries is usually easy to distinguish from borrowing, but there is no reason in principle why code-switching cannot occur at the level of individual words (and, some would argue, morphemes within words). Suppose, for example, we hear the utterance: "We need a little more *Gemütlichkeit* around here." A decision as to whether *Gemütlichkeit* is a case of code-switching or borrowing will have to be based on considerations of pronunciation, and perhaps frequency of usage, but such parameters are problematic; we often find pronunciations intermediate between those of L_y (here, German) and L_x, while frequency of usage is difficult to determine, individually variable, and gradient rather than binary. Moreover, classifications based on two or more parameters may be messy since evidence from the various parameters diverges. For example, L_y items retaining most features of L_y pronunciation (thus violating some L_x phonological norms) may none the less become current lexical items in L_x, so that we might speak of code-switching on formal grounds but borrowing on functional ones. In addition, phonological considerations may be unhelpful if the lexical item happens to be one which is already acceptable in terms of L_x norms; morphological considerations are equally unhelpful with stems which require no affix in either language (e.g. adverbs in many instances), or when the particular affixes in an L_y word happen to resemble functionally similar affixes in L_x.

Moreover, even when an L_y stem shows up in an L_x context with unmistakably L_x affixation, we must be careful about automatically considering this to be a borrowing. The reason for this is that in cases of prolonged language contact, speakers of L_x may develop productive routines for spontaneously inserting L_y stems into L_x frames. In the case of verbs, for example, speakers of L_y may add a thematization marker to L_y verbs so that regular L_x inflectional affixes may be added; alternatively, there may be a convention that borrowed verb stems belong to a particular morphological verb class in L_x so that borrowed stems can be directly inserted into inflectional frames without thematizers. We will see some extreme examples of this type of minimal morphological adaptation, as in /ma-ta-y-t-?ütiliza-w-š/ "they are not utilized", a spontaneous adaptation of Fr *utiliser* retaining the Fr vowels and Fr canonical shape of the stem but with an entirely MCA affixal frame. Again, some forms of this type may actually become current in the borrowing language (this particular instance is not).

Another complication is that L_y word forms (including L_y affixes) for some stems may become current in L_x, so that a full or partial L_y paradigm (Sg/Pl, for example) may reappear within L_x. We see this in English Sg/Pl pairs of Latin or Greek origin (*formula/formulae*, *datum/data*). Eventually such paradigms may acquire the status of minor inflectional classes within L_x. However, the transition from sporadic word-level code-switching (with affixes) to establishment of a minor inflectional class is gradual, and involves a settling down of usage rather than significant formal changes.

In the Moroccan case, all of these factors are further complicated by the wide range of bilingualism present in the community. Bilingual Fr/MCA speakers, for example, may continue to use code-switched forms for lexical items which have already found their way into common usage in borrowed (fully assimilated) form. One manifestation of this is the appearance of several variants for many long-established borrowings, some of these variants being recently reborrowed forms which closely approximate the L_y source form.

For these reasons, in some contexts it may be useful to elaborate the distinction between code-switching and borrowing. However, a profusion of terminology is not entirely desirable, since it suggests a greater classificatory rigour than is in fact warranted by the complex and often ambiguous or unstable reality we are trying to describe. We will normally apply the term code-switching to L_y forms (at word level or higher level) used in otherwise L_x

contexts when the forms show little or no formal adaptation to L_x. We use the term borrowing for word-level items with overtly L_x affixes and/or phonology; we extend the term to cases like /ma-ta-y-t-?ūtiliza-w-š/ but usually point out in connection with such items that they are uncommon and/or restricted to the speech of educated bilinguals; we also extend the term cautiously to cases like/(ḷa-)gaṛ/ "(the) train station" where the definite prefix is based on Fr *la* (rather than being regular MCA /l-/), since here the definite prefix allomorph is well established with the lexical items in question (cf. definite Pl /ḷa-gaṛ-at/ with MCA Pl suffix). The most difficult cases are those like /kliṛ/ "clear, obvious" (Fr *clair*), where the form used in MCA typically has no affixes (MCA or Fr); for those items of this type which seem to be commonly used in MCA we include them in our appendices (lists of borrowings) but take pains to point out that the form is invariable. In general, although we do not apply an elaborate taxonomy of types of code-switching and borrowing, the lexical entries in our appendices have sufficient information on morphology and usage to permit readers to appreciate their status.

For a general discussion of code-switching and borrowing, indicating the range of terminologies employed and the difficulty of applying any systematic taxonomy, see Pfaff (1979).

4.2 CA/MCA mixing

Because of the many phonological, grammatical, and lexical differences between MCA and CA it is in principle moderately easy to identify switching from MCA to CA utterance segments. On the other hand, in educated MCA we may find a considerable admixture of CA stems and short phrases; this is particularly common when the speakers are in an informal context (hence use MCA as primary language) when discussing topics of an academic, political, commercial, or Islamic nature (that is, topics which are commonly discussed elsewhere in CA). It may be difficult to classify some CA admixtures as code-switched or borrowed. In addition, traditional MCA vocabulary does retain a considerable number of lexical items which have CA cognates; in this event, deciding whether a given textual occurrence is from CA at all is possible only when there is some kind of formal difference between the native MCA form and the borrowed or code-switched form. There is also the possibility that the native MCA form may have a different primary meaning from its CA cognate, so that one possible interference process is purely semantic (the native MCA form acquiring the CA meaning, at least as a secondary meaning). We may speak of "reclassicizations" in those cases where an existing native MCA form has been adjusted in form and/or meaning by analogy to a CA cognate.

To give some idea of the formal significance of MCA/CA switching, we now describe some of the most significant features which distinguish the two systems and which thus serve as diagnostic indices.

First, CA has some phonemes not found in MCA: *ǰ*, *θ* (voiceless interdental fricative), *ð* (voiced interdental fricative), and *ḍ̣* (pharyngealized cousin of the preceding); glottal stop *?* is also common in CA but only marginal in MCA. CA distinguishes long and short vowels, giving words like *al-mu-ta-fāhim-ū-na* "the ones who understand each other" an undulating syllabic (and intonation) contour not found in MCA (where the cognate form is /l-m-t-fahm-in/.

Largely due to reductions of the vocalic system in MCA, canonical shapes in MCA and CA usually differ for basic stem types. For example, the most common nonparticipial adjective shape is *CaCīC-* in CA (*kabīr-* "big") but /CCiC/ in MCA (/kbir/ "big"). For verbs the difference is even more striking, since (leaving aside hollow and weak roots) we get such forms as /CCəC/ and (quadriliteral) /CCCəC/ in MCA with just a weak short vowel (highly vulnerable to deletion by syncope or by absorption into a syllabifying sonorant), whereas CA has *CaCaC-* and other *CVCVC-* patterns (*-CCVC-* in the imperfective) for triliterals and *CaCCaC-* and so forth for quadriliterals.

Retention of CA-type vowel patterns is in many cases sufficient to indicate CA admixture into MCA utterances. However, whether this admixture is code-switching or borrowing depends on the particular case involved. Many CA nouns, for example, have been borrowed into MCA with only a slight adjustment of vocalism and these forms have stabilized within MCA. On the other hand, borrowed verbs are immediately converted into MCA-type canonical shapes with no full vowels (except for hollow, weak, and some derived stems). Therefore retention of CA-like vocalism is a reliable index for code-switching in the case of verbs, but is not so reliable for nouns (where this index may fail to distinguish code-switching from borrowing).

In addition to these fairly simple phonological and canonical-shape factors, there are a large number of grammatical differences between MCA and CA which often signal that code-switching is at hand. In CA, both nouns and verbs have suffixes (mostly consisting of just a short vowel) which do not occur in MCA. For nouns these are case markers, the most common set being Nominative *-u*, Accusative *-a*, and Genitive *-i*. For verbs they are modals (used with imperfective stem), the ordinary set being Indicative *-u*, Subjunctive *-a*, and Jussive *-Ø* (zero). In spoken CA these are not usually pronounced in "pausal" (i.e. prepausal) position but they are pronounced medially within clauses: *sa-ya-xruǰ-u r-raǰul-u min dār-i-hi* "the man will go out from his house" (*-u* Indicative, *-u* Nominative, *-i-* Genitive), with the final word reducing to *dār-i-h* prepausally. Utterance segments including such short-vowel endings can be safely regarded as code-switched CA segments with the exception of a fixed set of individual borrowed forms which have now become fairly well established in MCA (mostly forms with MCA /-an/ or /-n/ borrowed from CA nouns with *-a-n* consisting of Accusative *-a-* and Indefinite *-n* where this suffix combination functions adverbially, Appendix A-3-42 ff.).

For the nouns, another significant CA/MCA difference is the Dual, which in CA is regularly expressed by suffix *-āni* (Nominative) or *-ayni* (Accusative/Genitive). In MCA, on the other hand, this morphological Dual form survives only for a handful of commonly counted nouns, in the form /-ayn/ regardless of case, as in /šhṛ-ayn/ "two months" (CA *šahr-āni, šahr-ayni*). MCA also has a few "pseudo-duals" in suffix /-in/ which are etymologically Dual (*-*ayni*) but have become the regular Pl form for certain nouns (such as paired body parts), as in /ᶜin-in/ "eyes" (semantically dual or plural) from CA Dual *ʿayn-ayni*. In code-switched segments it is, of course, possible to use the CA Dual endings with any noun and to use the full range of CA forms (*-āni*, *-ayni*, and prepausal counterparts *-ān*, *-ayn*) according to CA rules.

For the suffixal (non-ablaut) plurals, which are most characteristic of adjectives (rather than nouns), including participles, there are again some important differences. For CA the basic masculine Pl forms are Nominative *-ūna* and Accusative/Genitive *-īna*, prepausally *-ūn* and *-īn*. In MCA there is a single form /-in/. Therefore the use of Nominative *-ūn(a)* in particular is a conspicuous classicism and is almost always an indication of code-switching (for one apparent example of /-un/ in a borrowed form see A-1-105).

The corresponding feminine suffixal Pl forms in CA are Nominative *-ātu* and Accusative/Genitive *-āti*, which merge as prepausal *-āt*. This is not easily distinguished from MCA /-at/.

In general, nominal prefixation shows fewer CA/MCA distinctions than suffixation. The definite prefix is /l-/ in MCA, while in CA it has a maximal form *ʔal-* after a pause but medially is heard as *al-* or *l-*. In both MCA and CA the lateral assimilates to a following coronal consonant (there are some differences in this respect between the two languages in details, but the differences affect a fairly small set of nouns). The prepositions of MCA are basically identical to those of CA with some of the vowels reduced, hence CA *fi l-madīn-a* (prepausal, written *fī l-madīn-at-i*) "in the city" and MCA cognate /f-l-mdin-a/ "in the (Arab) city". The forms of the prepositions and of the definite prefix are therefore of possible value in identifying code-switching, but not so useful as suffixes.

For the verbs, morphology (as well as stem canonical shape, noted above) is usually reliable in distinguishing code-switching from borrowing. Leaving aside temporarily the pronominal affixes and focusing on other components of the morphological frame, let us compare the basic MCA and CA structures for the major categories. We exemplify here with 3MSg forms of the root √dxl "to enter".

Table 4-1 MCA/CA verb frames

MCA	CA	gloss
ġadi y-dx^{w}l	sa-ya-dxul(-u)	he will enter
ta-y-dx^{w}l	ya-dxul(-u)	he enters
dx^{w}l	?udxul	enter!
dx^{w}l or dxl	daxal(-a)	he entered
ma-dx^{w}l-š	lam ya-dxul	he did not enter

The simplified data in Table 4-1 indicate the major differences. MCA dialects have a future tense with preverb /ġadi/ "going" or /maši/ "going" plus imperfective, while CA uses future prefix *sa-* or preverb *sawfa*. In the present tense, and the continuative imperfective in any tense, MCA commonly has prefix /ta-/ or /ka-/, while CA has the simple imperfective form. The imperative forms shown are perhaps not significantly distinct since the initial *ʔu* in *ʔudxul* is inserted by phonological rules, and the perfective forms translated "he entered" likewise have no major difference in affixes, especially in pausal forms where 3MSg suffix *-a* is dropped in CA. Negative forms, of which only the perfective (past) ones are shown, differ systematically between CA and MCA; CA has preverbs *mā*, *lā*, *lam* (past), and *lan* (future) plus a given modal form (Jussive for *lam*), while MCA has /ma-___-š/, /ma-___-ši/, or /ma-___-šay/ across the boards (with /la-/ optionally replacing /ma-/ in imperatives). (In the table, (*-u*) in CA is the Indicative marker, omitted in pausal forms.)

Ablaut passives like *kutib-* "was written" from *katab-* "wrote" are common in CA, but do not occur in MCA, which instead uses prefixes /tt-/ and /t-/: /tt-ktəb/ "it was written". (See also §5.10.)

Table 4-2, below, compares MCA and CA pronominal affixes in the imperfective and perfective paradigms. CA and MCA share this basic stem opposition, and several of the pronominal affixes are exactly cognate. However, aside from historical loss of vowels, MCA diverges due to a number of categorial mergers and analogical restructurings.

Table 4-2 MCA/CA Perfective/Imperfective paradigms

	Perfective		**Imperfective**	
	MCA	CA	MCA	CA
1Sg	-t	-tu	n-	?V-
2MSg	-ti	-ta	t-	tV-
2FSg	-ti	-ti	t-__-i	tV-__-īna
3MSg	-∅	-a	y-	yV-
3FSg	-ət	-at	t-	tV-
1Pl	-na	-nā	n-__-u	nV-
2MPl	-tu	-tum	t-__-u	tV-__-ūna
2FPl	-tu	-tunna	t-__-u	tV-__-na
3MPl	-u	-ū	y-__-u	yV-__-ūna
3FPl	-u	-na	y-__-u	yV-__-na

As usual, CA pausal forms are produced by omitting a word-final short vowel. The endings *-īna* and *-ūna* lose the *na* syllable in some modal forms. These fine points can be taken as reducing the distinctness of the MCA and CA paradigms, but there are still some important differences. The special feminine Pl endings *-tunna*, *-na* of CA do not exist in MCA, which has merged gender in the Pl. MCA has also replaced the CA 1Sg imperfective prefix *?V-* with /n-/, which etymologically matches CA 1Pl *nV-*, whereupon MCA has developed /n-__-u/ as the 1Pl form by adding Pl /-u/ (formerly not used in the 1Pl). The use of /-ti/ for 2MSg (as well as 2FSg) in MCA, while *-ti* is specifically 2FSg in CA, and the shortening of CA 2MPl *-tum* to MCA 2Pl /-tu/, further differentiate the two languages (though there are some Moroccan dialects with 2MSg /-t/ instead of /-ti/). On top of this, the CA imperfective prefixes are of the form *CV-* (*Ca-*, *Cu-*) while the MCA counterparts lack this vowel, so MCA prefixes like /n-/ and /t-/ usually form consonant clusters with the following stem-initial consonant (at least in the dialects I know best). Not shown in the table are special Dual forms which occur in CA but not in MCA.

In addition to such morphological differences, there are a

number of very deep-seated lexical differences involving high-frequency stems. On the whole, lexicon is not the most reliable indicator of the distinction between MCA and CA, particularly in view of the large number of borrowings from CA now in use in MCA. However, some of the lexical oppositions appear to have the status of fundamental dialect indicators, as in other Arabic colloquials. Among the verbs, for example, we may mention MCA /mša/ "he went" (CA *ðahab-*), /šaf/ "he saw" (CA *raʔā*), and /naḍ/ "he got up" (CA *qām-*). (These differences will have to be amended in connection with some Moroccan dialects; thus /ṛa/ "he saw" occurs in most Jewish dialects, and some dialects do have a cognate of CA *qām-*.)

Many MCA personal and demonstrative pronouns closely resemble the CA counterparts. However, note the difference between MCA /ḥna/ and CA *naḥnu* "we", and MCA /d-i-k/ and CA *tilka* "that (FSg)", for example.

We probably should add that MCA has a large number of important particles, conjunctions, etc., which are distinctive dialect forms: /baš/ "so that" (also quotative), /awlla/ "or", /ᶜla-ḥqq-aš/ "because", and so forth. However, CA counterparts are now creeping into the MCA of educated persons, and these particular items are thus no longer rigorous indicators of code-switching. While /baš/, for example, occurs only in MCA (not in CA), similar CA forms such as quotative /biʔnna/ do occur frequently in some of my basically MCA texts.

We may give a better idea of the differences between MCA and CA by giving a few sentential examples illustrating some of the preceding remarks along with some additional CA/MCA differences.

a) CA: sa-ʔa-ðhab-u ġad-a-n li-d-dār-i li-ʔa-rā ʔab-ī
MCA: ġadi n-mši ġdda l-ḍ-ḍaṛ baš n-šuf ḅḅa
I will go tomorrow to (my) home to see my father

Here CA *ġad-a-n* resembles MCA /ġdda/ "tomorrow", *li-d-dār-i* is quite similar to /l-ḍ-ḍaṛ/ "to home", and *ʔab-ī* is vaguely similar to /ḅḅa/ "father", but overall the forms are clearly distinct. Perhaps with the exception of "to home", any replacement of an MCA word or phrase by its CA counterpart, even with slight adaptation of segmental phonemes, would be immediately perceived as a classical intrusion, and since none of the CA words in the example is an established borrowing I would not hesitate to classify them as instances of code-switching if they were to occur in a text.

b) CA: māðā ta-fᶜal-u hunā-ka?
MCA: aš ta-d-dir tmma?
What are you (MSg) doing there?

Here we have several very basic lexical differences: *māðā* vs. /aš/ "what", *-fᶜal-* vs. /-dir/ (perfective *faᶜal-* and /dar/) "to do", and *hunā-ka* vs. /tmma/ "there". (Some other MCA dialects do have /hnak/ "there"; for "to do" some MCA dialects have /ᶜml/.) In the verb there are further differences due to morphological frames; 2Sg *ta-* in CA corresponds to /-d-/ (underlying /-t-/ in /ta-d-dir/, but the latter also has the characteristic MCA continuative prefix /ta-/ (or /ka-/). Again, any intrusion of CA words into the MCA sentence would be obvious and I would consider them cases of code-switching.

4.3 Examples of CA/MCA code-switching

In the preceding section we have given a general (though far from complete) contrastive analysis of the two languages, along with resultant criteria for identifying CA utterance segments. We now give a few textual examples to illustrate these principles, and perhaps the difficulty in applying them.

First, consider this text (basically in MCA), with asterisks placed before the more interesting items.

Text 1

*ḥasab *l-žuw, *qaḍiy-t l-ʿṛbiy-a
according to the atmosphere matter of Arabic
w-l-fṛanṣawiy-a, had-a maši *muškil ġi dyal waḥəd,
and French this not problem only of one
*li?anna ta-t-ᶜṛf *bi?anna l-mġrib kan-t *stᶜmṛ-at-u
because you know that Morocco it was colonized it
fṛanṣa, w-mnin stᶜmṛ-at-u fṛanṣa bqa-t
France and when it colonized it France it remained
l-luġ-a lli kan-u ta-y-hḍṛ-u bi-ha
the language which they were they spoke by it
l-fṛanṣawiy-in bqa-t hna, *fa-li-had-a kayn-in
the French (people) it remained here and therefore there are
ḥtta *f-ḍ-ḍiṛaṣ-a dyal-na f-l-qṛay-a, ta-n-qṛa-w
even in the studying of us in the studying we study
bəᶜḍ *ḍ-ḍuṛuṣ b-l-fṛanṣawiy-a, ...
some studies by French

This text was the beginning of an answer to my question translated "When you are with your friends, do you speak French or Arabic?". The answer translates: "Depends on the situation, (this) business of Arabic and French. This is not just a problem of one (individual), since you know that Morocco was colonized by France, and when France colonized it the language which the French people spoke with remained here (afterward); therefore even in our education, we study some subjects in French ..."

The forms marked by asterisk are CA intrusions (and there are perhaps others not so marked). In general, I consider these to be borrowings rather than code-switched items. The only form with CA affixal trappings is /fa-li-had-a/ in the third-last line, but this particular expression is now fairly common in educated speech; the CA version is *fa-li-hāðā* (note that the usual conversion of ð to /d/ does apply). In the other cases the affixes, if present, are basically MCA rather than CA. Actually, /li?anna/ and /bi?anna/ in line 3 can be decomposed into a preposition plus CA *-?anna*, but again the combinations occur in educated MCA as fixed expressions. In the case of /l-žuw/ in the first line, the definite form /l-/, not /ž-/, is characteristic of CA borrowings with initial /ž/ (from CA ǰ), but many of these words are in common use in educated MCA with /l-/ definite allomorph, and they cannot properly be called code-switched. The verb in /stᶜmṛ-at-u/ in line 3 (repeated in line 4), from CA *(?)ista-ᶜmar-at-hu*, shows extensive adaptation to MCA both in stem canonical shape and suffixation.

This textual fragment is characteristic of educated MCA, having an unmistakably dominant MCA foundation but with frequent individual borrowed lexical items (with MCA affixes) and the occasional more complex word or phrase (usually an adverb or conjunction functionally).

More extreme cases of CA/MCA mixing do occur, however. Persons of mediocre educational level sometimes produce macaronic texts when attempting to approximate CA in Koranic disquisitions, but more systematic (and easily accessible) types are to be found in sports broadcasts (if originating in Morocco and not, for example, Egypt), formal panel discussions, and similar situations. In news broadcasts the usual language is a very formal CA, but interviews with politicians (which may be presented in part within the newscasts) are generally in a highly classicized MCA. An excerpt from a 1979 ministerial interview:

Text 2

*f^{c}l-an ġadi, *bi-ḥawl lla, *n-twžžəh
in fact will by the power of God I head for

had *l-yom, lə-žənɛv, *l-ḥuḍuṛ d-dawr-a
this the day to Geneva to attendance of the session

*xams-a *w-sitt-in, dyal *munəẓẓam-at *l-^{c}amal *d-dawl-iy-a,
five and sixty of organization (of) labour international

*w-kama huwa *ma-^{c}ṛuf *?inna *l-wəfd
and like it known (quotative) the delegation

*l-maġrib-i, *mu-ṛakkab mn tlata dyal *l-^{c}anaṣiṛ,
Moroccan composed from three of the elements

*mu-mttil-in ^{c}ənd *l-ḥukum-a, mu-mttil-in ^{c}ənd
representatives of the government

*l-mu-šaġġil-in , w-mu-mttil-in ^{c}ənd *l-^{c}ummal, w-had-a
the employers and- the workers and this

huwa *mbda? *t-t-mtil *f-munẓẓam-at l-^{c}amal
it beginning (of) representation on organization (of) labour

d-dawl-iy-a, mn n-nuqaṭ lli hiya ġadi t-tt-bḥət
international from the points which it(FSg) will will be studied

fi-ha, ...
in it

Since we have no samples of this minister's more casual MCA speech, we will analyse it assuming that he has the same type of style range as other educated Moroccans whom I do know. I should begin by cautioning that transcription, notably of vowels, is not always easy in texts of this type because of background noise and the impossibility of eliciting repeats.

In this text there is still a basic MCA core, some characteristic MCA elements being /ġadi/ (future tense, twice), /dyal/ "of" (twice), relative /lli/ (penultimate line), etc. However, the number of individual CA intrusions (borrowings or otherwise) is so high that in some passages we can no longer be sure the text is basically in MCA. A general translation: "Indeed I will, by the grace of God, be heading today to Geneva, to attend the session number sixty-five of the International Labor Organization, and as is known the Moroccan delegation is composed of three elements: representatives of the government, representatives of the employers and representatives of the workers. And this is the beginning of (our?) representation in the International Labor Organization; among the viewpoints (matters) which will be studied in it ..."

In the case of /n-t-wžžəh/ (line 1), the form is modelled on CA stem *ta-waǰǰah*-"to head tor", but the form has been MCA-ized both in canonical shape (vocalism) of the stem and in the prefix, 1Sg /n-/. However, /bi-ḥawl lla/ "by the power of God" in the same line, a stock expression with Koranic flavour, is only slightly modified from CA *bi-ḥawl-i llāh*(pausal form) and does not shorten preposition *bi*- to normal MCA /b-/. In line 2, /had l-yom/ seems to be based on CA *hāðā l-yawm(-a)* "this day (adverbial form)". MCA has /l-yum/ "today" from the same source, but note the /u/ here, and this MCA expression does not usually co-occur with the demonstrative pronoun; the normal MCA word for "day" is now /nhaṛ/, so "this day" would be /had n-nhaṛ/. It looks as though /had l-yom/ is a sort of semi-code-switched phrase with partial adaptation to MCA, e.g. with /o/ as a partial adaptation of CA diphthong *aw*. (It is possible that /had l-yom/ is a fixed phrase in this speaker's educated style, but I do not recall hearing it from other speakers.)

In the string "to attend the session number sixty-five of the International Labor Organization", the string of nominal forms (even "attend" is in verbal noun form) and the relative absence of diagnostic morphological frames make identification of language difficult (lines 2 to 3). Preposition /l-/ in the first word in this string has its MCA form, vs. CA *li*-, and /dyal/ "of" later on is clearly MCA. The expression "sixty-five", /xams-a w-sitt-in/, is not pronounced in the usual MCA fashion as /xms-a w-stt-in/, and seems to be modelled on the CA form *xams-a wa-sitt-īn(a)*, though *wa*- "and" is reduced to the MCA form /w-/. If my transcription of "organization" as /munəð̣ð̣am-at/, and later (line 8) as /munð̣ð̣am-at/, is correct, preservation of the interdental fricative points toward the CA pronunciation *mu-nað̣ð̣am-at*- with only slight MCA adaptation (weakening or elision of the first *a*). Moving on, the expression /w-kama huwa ma-ᶜṛuf/ "and as (it) is known" is basically code-switched, cf. CA *wa-kamā huwa ma-ᶜrūf* with *-kamā* "like, as" (compare normal MCA /ḅ-ḥal/ in this sense). Similarly, the ensuing "the Moroccan delegation (is) composed of three elements" is essentially CA (up to the final numeral phrase) minus the expected CA short-vowel case endings (i.e. with each word in pausal form); in CA this segment would be *ʔinna l-wafd-a l-maġrib-iyy-a mu-rakkab-u-n min* ...

One can describe this text in general terms as follows. For the most part the basic language is MCA, as shown particularly by the MCA shape and inflection of verbs, the generally MCA form of prepositions, and the systematic use of MCA elements like /dyal/ "of" and future /ġadi/. However, the style is heavily nominal, and there is a tendency for some phrases to be pronounced in CA or compromise CA/MCA style even when a distinct MCA form is readily available (as with "sixty-five"). Some short phrases appear to be clear code-switches, and because of the strings of educated nouns there are stretches where the distinction between MCA (with individual CA borrowings) and code-switched CA is difficult to make. However, the speaker does not go all the way to pure CA style by putting in the word-final short-vowel suffixes (case for nouns, modals for verbs).

For analysis of additional materials of the same general type, see chapter 8.

Aside from spontaneous code-switched segments in educated speech and a few which have become stable in this style, we should mention that a number of frozen expressions such as greetings occur in everyday speech. For example, /šukṛ-an/ "thank you" and the standard response /la šukṛ-a ᶜla wažib/ (lit. "no thanking for duty", i.e. "don't mention it") are from CA *šukr-an* and *lā šukr-a ᶜalā wājib* with only minimal adaptation (note the preservation of the short-vowel case suffix of *šukr-a* in the second phrase). There are also some Koranic lines that virtually everyone knows and can be spoken or chanted in appropriate contexts. Since these are isolated, frozen expressions or scriptural passages, they are not a significant factor in the larger-scale system of code-switching and borrowing from CA into MCA which is going on chiefly among younger educated persons.

4.4 Fr/MCA mixing: noun phrases

Code-switching from MCA to Fr is relatively common among persons who have been educated in schools where Fr was used as an important medium of instruction; this applies to most university-educated persons (except, perhaps, those trained mainly in Islamic subjects) and to many others with secondary-school training or with experience in élite private French-language primary schools (Missions Françaises). I have heard (but not yet recorded) rather extreme macaronic Fr-MCA code-switching among certain Moroccans who have returned after working for several years in France or Belgium, and among bank officers. In the latter case, the tendency to use MCA as background language (when the bank officers are Moroccans, as they usually are) conflicts with the fact that bank-related matters are commonly discussed by the same persons (with different addressees) in Fr, the fact that until recently official written communications (memoranda, operating instructions, and reports) have been mainly in Fr, and the fact that some of the technical language of banking in CA is not yet fully standardized and current.

In any event, we are here mainly concerned with switching at word and phrase levels, since this is the type of code-switching that is most closely related to borrowings.

In our sections on CA/MCA switching, above, we took pains to point out various types of differences between the two languages in order to emphasize to readers who do not know much about Arabic dialects that MCA is in fact quite distinct from CA in basic grammatical structure. Nevertheless, MCA is obviously a good deal more similar to CA than either is to Fr. The grammatical categories of CA and MCA are mostly similar or identical, and many of the differences are merely in the phonological form of affixes, presence or absence of vowels among root consonants, etc. In the case of Fr and MCA, on the other hand, our initial working assumption must be that the two grammatical structures (as well as phonological systems) are so radically different that code-switching ought to be very transparent and borrowing (with structural adaptation) ought to be quite problematic. There is considerable truth to this, but it turns out on finer analysis that, as chance would have it, there are some similarities in morphological framing which appear to have served as avenues for diffusion.

Turning now to specific instances of code-switching, we first observe that the typical pattern in Morocco is for MCA to be the basic language with Fr phrases inserted from time to time. One very common pattern is the insertion of a NP (noun phrase) including a Fr article (usually definite, sometimes indefinite).

a) kayn 1-ᶜid 1-kbir ka-n-dbḥ-u fi-h *les moutons*
there is holiday great we slaughter in it the sheep
"There is (also) the Great Feast, in which we slaughter sheep."

b) ka-d-dir l-ḥaž-at lli ġad d-dir bi-hum *les tagines*
it does the things which will it does by them the tagines
"It (FSg) makes the things which it will make the tagines (a native dish) with."

In both of these examples the speaker could perfectly well have used standard MCA forms /l-ḥwala/ "the sheep", /ṭ-ṭwažn/ "the tagines". Only a bilingual speaker would code-switch in this way.

When a code-switched NP containing a Fr article occurs in an MCA context where a prepositional phrase is syntactically appropriate, the normal output is a combination of an MCA preposition with the Fr NP. Similarly, MCA conjunctions like /w-/ "and" commonly precede Fr NPs.

c) xdəm-t f-waḥəd *la société d'assurances*
I worked in a the insurance company
"I worked in (i.e. for) an insurance company."

d) *un* [sic] *pile* ka-d-dir ᶜənd-na ḥna b- *un dirham*
a battery it does of us we by one dirham
"A battery costs us one dirham."

e) kayn-in lli sakn-in f- *les villas*
there are which living (Pl) in the villas
"There are some (people) living in villas (nice homes)."

f) b-ḥal *un professeur marocain* ka-y-dir *cent cinquante deux cent*
like a teacher Moroccan he does 150 200
"For example a Moroccan teacher gets (paid) 150 (or) 200."

g) kayn hna ḥda-na sakn-in bzzaf d- *les romanis*
there is here among us living many of the Europeans
"There are many Europeans living among us."

While the form of the NP in these examples is Fr, not only the preposition or prenominal element, but also the syntax, is that of MCA. Note, for example, in the first example in this block that the Fr NP is in definite form; this is because the MCA indefinite NP with /waḥəd/ "one" functioning as indefinite article "a(n)" requires what is formally a definite noun following, as in /waḥəd l-bənt/ "a girl" with /l-bənt/ "the girl" (contrast /bənt wḥd-a/ "one girl" without definite prefixes and with postposed numeral agreeing in gender). The alternative is to omit /waḥəd/ and use a Fr indefinite form; this is seen in *un professeur marocain* (fourth example), but is not very common. Note also the use of the Fr definite form in the final example, following the normal use of Pl definite nouns with /bzzaf d-/ "many (of)", as in /bzzaf d-r-ržal/ "many men".

Of course, there are types of code-switching in which the Fr chunks are much larger in size (clauses or larger segments), but those of the types just seen are particularly interesting. Since Fr indefinite articles (*un, une*) are not very common (partly because of the alternative MCA construction with /waḥəd/ "one" plus definite noun), and since Fr FSg *-e* and Pl *-s* are commonly "silent" even in standard Fr, the conspicuous morphemic accompaniment of Fr noun stems is limited to the Fr definite articles (*le, la, les*, and contracted *l'*). It is highly significant that the MCA functional counterpart, definite prefix (l-/, is also phonologically similar.

The full set of Fr forms in phonetic transcription is as follows:

	before vowel	masculine before consonant	feminine before consonant
Sg	l-	lə- or l-	la-
Pl	lez-	le-	le-

The MCA prefix has the form /l-/ except that it assimilates to a following coronal consonant, and is independent of plurality (which is marked by stem-internal ablaut and/or by suffixation). There is a significant overlap between the MCA and Fr allomorphs in the crucial Sg forms, and there is consequently a set of forms where *we cannot distinguish between code-switching and borrowing* (with full morphological adaptation). For example, any Fr noun beginning in a vowel and in Sg form will begin with /l-/ whether it is a stabilized borrowing or an on-the-spot code-switch like those just illustrated, and we can only attempt to restore the distinction on other grounds (precise phonological form of the noun stem, paraidgmatic behaviour observed by eliciting the corresponding Pl, or stability of usage). In many specific instances no principled decision can be made, as with /waḥəd l-aṇaṇaṣ/ "a pineapple" (Fr *ananas*, Sp *ananás*). The same is true for a large number of masculine nouns not beginning with coronal consonants.

It would appear that this fortuitous similarity between the definite markers of MCA and Fr has functioned as a facilitator of borrowings. Given that an initially code-switched form like *l'ananas* "the pineapple" (Fr) looks exactly like an MCA word with no further adjustment, we can easily understand how such words may, if semantically appropriate, develop additional morphological forms (Pl, Diminutive) within MCA and thus come to be treated as relatively well-integrated borrowings. In going from such a structurally different language as Fr to MCA, it is likely that getting the foot in the door is the major problem; once a particular borrowed form can occur in what looks like a fairly good MCA shape, generation of further MCA inflectional or derivational forms is relatively unproblematic. Moreover, once a reasonable set of "vanguard" borrowings have entered MCA, bilingual speakers can develop standardized routines for bringing in new borrowings.

What, then, of those Fr allomorphs like [la-], [le-], and [lez-] which do not fit into traditional MCA definite allomorphs? Since these Fr prefixes are quite common in code-switched NPs (see examples above) involving Fr feminine or plural nouns, there is a substantial likelihood a priori that MCA will accept these as stabilized definite-prefix allomorphs for the relevant borrowed nouns. That is, while many borrowed nouns will fit perfectly into the MCA system, others will bring along with them their original definite allomorph in the Sg and/or Pl. It is also possible that a new MCA form based on Fr *la* will retain its feminine gender value and thus require feminine concord in MCA.

In the event, this does not normally happen in Morocco, though my initial material from Algeria suggests that it does there. In Morocco, the usual treatment of Fr and Sp borrowings is to use the regular MCA definite prefix /l-/, with assimilation to coronal stem-initial consonant if present: /l-bḷaṣ-a/ "the place" (Fr *la place*, perhaps Sp *la plaza* also involved historically). Definite Pl [le] or [lez] is characteristic of spontaneous code-switching but not of stable borrowings, and such forms are virtually never used by nonbilingual speakers in my experience (the Pl of borrowed nouns has the regular definite /l-/, with plurality marked by MCA-type stem-ablaut or suffixation). For Fr feminine nouns, the usual definite prefix is /l-/ and its normal allomorphs; in other words, the definite prefix is based on the analogy of other MCA nouns and not directly on the Fr definite form with *la*. However, some Fr feminine nouns which appear to be in the process of stabilizing as loanwords show fluctuation between definite /l-/ and a syllabic form /la-/ or /ḷa-/ based on the Fr definite form, and a few important and highly stabilized earlier borrowings show /la-/ or /ḷa-/ as the normal definite prefix: /ḷa-gaṛ/ "the train station", /la-pisin/ "the swimming pool". For these stabilized borrowings, /la-/ or /ḷa-/ is merely a definite allomorph, and concord is masculine (unless they happen to end in FSg suffix /-a/, which these particular examples do not).

In classifying individual textual occurrences as code-switching or borrowing, for the Moroccan varieties that I know best the following criteria are used. Pl [le] or [lez] is regularly interpreted as an indication of code-switching (except for a handful of loans where the segments indicated are now an inseparable part of the stem, as in the case of /liḅ-a/ "stocking", definite /l-liḅ-a/, from Fr *les bas* treated as a fused stem). Definite [la] pronounced as in Fr *la* is usually taken as an indication of code-switching, but is accepted as an MCA allomorph in the case of stems which have clearly stabilized with this prefix or which appear to be in the process of stabilizing (obviously there is a transitional area here). See also §6.24.

My limited material on Algerian colloquial Arabic indicates that most recent Fr borrowings retain essentially their Fr definite form with little phonological adjustment, and that most take Pl definite forms based on Fr *les*. Moreover, nouns with /la-/ or /ḷa-/ definite prefix based on Fr *la* are treated as FSg for concord purposes even though most lack the Arabic FSg suffix /-a/. I would speculate that the much greater extent of Fr-Arabic bilingualism in Algeria (and indeed the appreciable number of Algerians who know Fr much better than Arabic, classical or colloquial) is a significant factor behind this wholesale importation of Fr definite articles with functions preserved.

4.5 Fr/MCA mixing: verb phrases

For present purposes we can consider such Fr forms as *il faisait*, *il m'a donné*, and *je te vois* as verb phrases (without worrying about independent NPs functioning as complements). In general, a Fr verb phrase consists minimally of a finite (inflected) verb form and an unstressed subject pronoun, with or without direct or indirect object pronoun (all of these pronouns are proclitic). For MCA a minimal verb phrase is a complete verbal word, with or without a preverbal element like future /ġadi/; see Table 4-1 above, and chapter 3.

There is little danger of analysing, e.g. *il m'a donné* "he gave me" as anything other than a code-switching, since such Fr verb phrases are characteristically multiply marked with unambiguously Fr morphemes (quite aside from the fact that most Fr verb stems have canonical-shape patterns which violate traditional MCA norms). However, there are once again certain specific morphological frames which are approximately congruent between the two languages.

Let us look at the difference between Fr verb phrases with verb *changer* "to change" and two different potentially possible borrowed MCA forms /šạ̃ž/ and /šạ̃ža/ (the citation form, as usual, is 3MSg perfective). Of these two, the second is actually attested (though not very common). Let us assume further than the nasalized vowel /ạ̃/ is stable and thus does not undergo perfective/imperfective ablaut change.

In the case of /šạ̃ž/, the following would be the most precise formal/functional parallels:

2Sg imperative	Fr *change!*	(familiar)	MCA /šạ̃ž/
3MSg present	Fr *il change*		MCA /y-šạ̃ž/

Since in colloquial spoken Fr the *l* of 3MSg *il* is commonly not pronounced before a consonant, and since MCA /y-/ is syllabic and approaches /i-/ pronunciation before a nonsyllabic, *il change* and /y-šạ̃ž/ would be difficult to distinguish phonetically. (It should be noted, though, that many MCA dialects add prefix /ta-/ or /ka-/ to imperfective forms like /y-šạ̃ž/ in a high proportion of present-tense cases.) From the historical development point of view, the significance of these cross-linguistic pairs is that a code-switched item like *change!* or *il change* can be taken, with no overt phonological changes, as being forms within the MCA system, whereupon additional paradigmatic forms can be generated: /n-šạ̃ž/ "I change" with 1Sg /n-/, etc. To my knowledge, this particular form /šạ̃ž/ does not occur (as a stable borrowing) in MCA, but there are some approximately similar forms (from other Fr verbs) attested as early borrowings and still used in some dialects (see 6.14).

If the borrowing is of the type /šạ̃ža/ in the 3MSg perfective (as citation form), that is, if it comes in with final vowel (weak conjugation), the cross-linguistic pairs of greatest interest are these:

2Sg imperative	Fr *changez!* (polite)	MCA /šạ̃ži/
3MSg imperfective	Fr *il changeait*	MCA /y-šạ̃ži/

There are phonetic differences here, notably in the pronunciation of the final vowel, but these differences are probably slight to a

Moroccan ear since [e] and [ɛ] are within the allophonic range of /i/. For this particular verb /i/ would have allophone [i] because of the preceding /ž/, but we can counteract this by using a different verb (Fr *poster* "to mail", MCA /puṣṭa/ pronounced [poṣṭa]) where the last consonant is pharyngealized: 2Sg imperative /puṣṭi/ pronounced [poṣṭe]. It should be noted that final /i/ in MCA verbs is characteristic of a large number of "weak" roots in the imperfective forms (of which the imperative is a subtype). Taking forms like /š̃ạži/ and /y-š̃ạži/ as the foot-in-the-door borrowed inflected forms, others like /š̃ạža/ "he changed" (perfective) can be generated by internal MCA analogies with no necessary reference to specific Fr inflected forms (/š̃ạža/, of course, has nothing to do with Fr "simple past" *changea*, a purely literary form to which few Moroccans would be exposed in speech).

On the basis of my modern texts and other observations, I would say that code-switching with a Fr verb phrase inserted into an otherwise MCA utterance frame is uncommon. That is, sentences like /*il m'a donné* dak s-sarut dyal-u/ "he gave me that key of his" are not often heard and are looked upon dimly by informants when I try them out. Given that Fr/MCA code-switching is commonly an MCA base with occasional Fr phrases interspersed, it seems that Fr NPs are much more likely than complete Fr verb phrases to occur. Much the same effect can be created by spontaneously providing a Fr verb with MCA affixes, following borrowing routines which have come to be quite productive. An elementary verb like *donner* "to give" would scarcely be likely to be borrowed or code-switched (at phrasal level) at all, but a verb like *utiliser* "to utilize" can be easily borrowed on the spot, as in the form /ma-ta-y-t-?ütiliza-w-š/ "they are not utilized". This type of spontaneous borrowing is typical when the Fr item to be mixed into an MCA utterance is just a verb form. Of course, in contexts where code-switching is more extensive (as in the macaronic style of some atypical speakers), or when the switching involves entire clauses or larger segments, complete Fr verb phrases can occur.

4.6 Further examples of Fr/MCA code-switching

Among the more common types of short code-switched Fr words and phrases we may mention the following: place names, locative adverbs (especially prepositional phrases), other adverbs of various kinds, numerals, and other quantified expressions. A few examples are given to illustrate the type of switching one can find in conversation among educated bilinguals:

a) huma f- *l'Algérie* ka-d-dir *mille francs* ᶜənd-hum
they in Algeria it does 1000 centimes of them
"The Algerians, it costs them 1000 centimes."

b) bqa-w ši *six personnes* wlla *sept familles, je crois,* wlla *cinq*
they remain some six persons or seven families I think or five
"There are about six persons left — or seven families, I think, or (maybe) five."

c) lli ^{c}nd-u ḍaṛ ma-y-qdr-š y-šri *la deuxième, seulement*
who of him house he cannot he buys the second only
une, ila kan-t ^{c}nd-ək žuž ḍyuṛ ma-y-xlli-w-ək-š d-dir
one if it was of you two houses they won't let you you do
žuž, *seulement une,* ma-t-qdr-š d-dir *deux fois, deux*
two only one you cannot you do two times two
maisons, t-xlləs ġi wḥd-a
houses you (will) pay only one (FSg)
"He who has a house may not buy a second one, just one. If you have two houses – they will not let you get two, just one. You can't do it twice, (buy) two houses. You (can) pay for just one." (talking about Algeria)

d) *chaque semaine* ka-y-ddi-w s-sl^{c}-a k^{w}ll-ha mn wžda
every week they take the merchandise all of it from Oujda
"Every week they take all of the merchandise from Oujda (city)."

e) w-ka-y-mši-w, *des fois* ka-y-ži-w
and they go sometimes they go
"and they go; sometimes they go"

f) sakn-in *en centre ville* m^{c}a-na
living (Pl) downtown with us
"They are living downtown with us."

g) š-šluḥ? *pas beaucoup* ^{c}ənd-na *seulement* lli m-qabl-in
not many of us only which taking care of
l'épicerie
grocery
"Schleuch (Berbers)? We don't have many (in Oujda), just those who run the groceries."

Turning to longer switches, the following examples show typical switch points, including the point immediately following a clause-introducer such as "because" or following a topicalized constituent.

h) li?inna *c'est une ville économique*
because it's a city economic
"because it's a commercial city"

i) li?nna ḍ-ḍar l-biḍ-a *c'est une ville économique*
"because Casablanca is a commercial city"

Sometimes relativizer /lli/ can function as a switch point, as in this somewhat unusual example:

j) *les gens* lli *habitent* f-n-nawaḥi
the people who live in the area
"the people who live in the general vicinity"

Even within a verb form I have occasionally heard switches. In a typical imperfective MCA form like /ta-y-ži-w/ (variant /ka-y-ži-w/) "they are coming", the initial syllable consisting of prefix /ta-/ or /ka-/ and the pronominal element, here 3MSg /-y-/, may be pronounced separately from the remainder of the verb form; this is common in hesitation forms where the speaker is trying to think of which verb stem to use. The Fr/MCA switches which I am thinking of occur at this same point, as in /-ka-y- *habitent*/ "they live", pronounced [ka-y-abit]. The absence of Pl imperfective suffix /-u/ indicates that this is not a borrowing. Such forms are not very common and are usually rejected by informants when I try them out on them, but they do occur now and then in actual speech.

Among brief Fr items which are commonly found in styles with substantial code-switching are a few elements which seem to be used systematically by some speakers in the absence of exactly similar MCA forms: *donc* "so" (competes with /idan/, from CA), *y-compris* "including" (with following noun), and *à part* "aside from" (with following noun). MCA has several expressions meaning "instead of", but nonetheless I have heard Fr *au lieu de* fairly often, and it can precede a clause as well as a noun: /*au lieu d'* y-gul-u/ "instead of (them) saying".

Switching with a Fr preposition or similar element followed by an MCA noun phrase or the like is rare (the opposite pattern being much more typical). I do not have any examples of Fr *dans*, *en*, *pour* or other high-frequency monosyllabic prepositions in such constructions. I do have one example with *jusqu'à* "until", and a number of examples of complete all-Fr prepositional phrases.

k) ka-ta-k^{w}l-u *jusqu'à* l-m^{w}ġṛb
you (Pl) eat until the nightfall
"You eat right up till nightfall."

l) m-žwwž-a *avec un algérien*
married (FSg) with an Algerian
"She is married to an Algerian."

4.7 Code-switching and borrowing

The relationship between code-switching and borrowing is always a problematic one, and since the presently observable borrowings and code-switches are the product of decades of language contact (involving a complete range between fluent bilinguals and completely monolingual peasants and herders) the Moroccan situation is especially complex. Our remarks on the historical relationship of the two types of mixing are therefore conjectural.

It does appear that despite the seemingly wide gulf between the morphological systems of Fr and MCA, there are some crucial correspondences (by pure coincidence) in morphemic frames which may have permitted originally code-switched NPs and verb forms from Fr to be reinterpreted (with little or no surface change) as semantically similar MCA forms. These foot-in-the-door borrowed inflected forms could then have suggested, by analogy to already productive paradigmatic structures, additional MCA inflected forms not directly modelled on Fr.

In the case of CA and MCA, we have taken pains to emphasize that the two are distinct languages with many differences in segmental phonology, canonical-shape norms, and morpheme structure. However, even where the actual CA and MCA affixes are different, the basic structure of nouns, NPs, and verbs is similar in the two languages.

While there are many lexical divergences, there are also many cognate noun and verb stems, and Moroccans with a reasonable knowledge of CA are aware of many of them.

On the basis of these cognates, it is easy for Moroccans to develop generalizations about diasystemic relationships between CA and MCA, which are then put into practice in the form of borrowing routines (conversion rules) applied to other CA forms. We will see that this is particularly important for CA verbs, which must undergo significant canonical-shape restructuring to fit into the MCA system (while noun borrowings are usually based more directly on the current CA form). Similarly, in the case of Fr and Sp borrowings, once a certain number have come into MCA, bilingual speakers can develop generalizations about Fr/MCA and Sp/MCA correspondences on the basis of these cognate pairs (even though some such generalizations are in fact false, since Fr/MCA bilinguals not knowing Sp often produce spurious Fr-MCA diasystemic rules based on what are in fact historically Sp borrowings). These generalizations likewise lead to dynamic borrowing routines applied to new words, sometimes on a spur-of-the-moment basis.

These conversion routines, which are discussed in detail in the following chapters, mean that ongoing borrowings need not be mediated by code-switching. A bilingual speaker who knows, for example, many hundreds of Fr verbs, along with the basic conversion rule which can convert these into MCA inflected verbs, can spontaneously borrow a particular item (like *utiliser* "to utilize"). It is not necessary for him first to make frequent use of code-switched short verb phrases like *j'ai utilisé* "I utilized" or *nous l'avons utilisé* "we utilized it" before finally producing a form with MCA affixation; indeed, as we have seen, use of Fr verb phrases in otherwise MCA clauses is relatively rare (in my data). It is, presumably, necessary that the Fr verb in question be sufficiently common or important (to addressee and speaker) to justify the borrowing functionally, but this frequency or importance may relate to all-Fr domains (such as most university classrooms).

For these reasons, we must be cautious about assuming that what we are calling borrowing is, in each instance, the final product of a uniform pattern of sequencing beginning with word-level or phrasal code-switching, mediated by the particular cross-linguistically ambiguous morphemic frames discussed above (due to the fortuitous similarity between Fr definite *le* and MCA /l-/, or that between Fr imperative and 3MSg indicative forms and corresponding MCA types). Instead, it seems that diasystemic borrowing routines are now of crucial significance, and permit newer borrowings to bypass a good part of the trail blazed by earlier, pioneering borrowings.

5 Adaptation of Classical Arabic borrowings

CA borrowings into MCA are subject to comparatively predictable conversion rules, but these involve not only phoneme replacements but also canonical-shape restrictions (notably for verbs) and the use of MCA rather than CA affixes. We proceed from phonology to morphology and syntax, but factors from all three are commonly at work together.

Appendix A is a companion to this chapter and constitutes its primary data base. However, the appendix lists only a representative set of CA borrowings, consisting primarily of items from a specific recorded corpus with some supplementary elicitation to fill in word-class gaps. Occasionally in this chapter we refer to a borrowing not listed in the appendix. Formulae like A-1-23 mean appendix A, section 1, item 23.

5.1 Vowels

As noted in chapter 3, MCA has full vowels /i a u/ and three short vowels /^ ə ^{W}/. The segment /^/ is merely an indication that the flanking consonants are not bonded into a tightly knit consonant cluster or that normal consonantal assimilations do not apply. Segments /ə/ and /^{W}/ are "real" phonological segments but have limited syllabic distribution, are highly vulnerable to loss by syncope or by absorption into a syllabifying sonorant, and are in the process of being reanalysed as epenthetic or as consonant features. CA, on the other hand, has long *ī ā ū* and short *i a u*, the latter being almost as long phonetically as the full vowels of MCA. Although the short vowels of MCA regularly correspond to CA short vowels in inherited forms which have been subject to historical sound changes, in more recent borrowings we should not necessarily predict that CA short vowels will become MCA short vowels.

Indeed, the regular pattern (i.e. seen in forms not subject to tight canonical shape restrictions) in borrowings is for CA long and short vowels to merge in MCA as full vowels. Thus such CA canonical shapes as *CVCVC-*, *CV̄CVC-*, *CVCV̄C-*, and *CV̄CV̄C-* are collapsed into undifferentiated MCA patterns (in this case /CVCVC/). This results in occasional new homophones like CA *^{c}alam-* "flag" and *ᶜālam-* "world" merging as /ᶜalam/. Similarly, MCA has /?aṭar/ "monument(s)" both for CA *?aθar-* "monument" and its plural *?āθār-* (see discussion of A-1-174 for lexical ramifications of this). The first several pages of appendix A give many examples of these CA canonical shapes and their forms as MCA borrowings.

However, the merger of CA long and short vowels in borrowings does not always take place. When a CA short vowel occurs before a consonant cluster, the MCA borrowing may either follow the rule above and give an MCA full vowel, or the borrowing may show a short vowel (which may then disappear if a following sonorant syllabifies).

It is difficult to determine, in such pre-cluster environments, whether MCA full or short vowels are the "regular" borrowing outputs from CA short vowels. In any given item, one could argue that the particular output attested has been influenced by some analogical pattern or another and is thus not a regular (i.e. purely phonetic or phonological) output.

This is patently true of verb forms, but is possibly true to some extent of other word classes. For example, consider the type /muxriž/ "producer" (A-1-290, cf. also A-1-291 to 296) from CA *mu-xriǰ-*. Here the MCA form has full vowel /u/ before a cluster. One could, however, plausibly argue that the choice of full vowel has been influenced by the analogy of /mu/ at the beginning of other participles borrowed from CA like /muṛaqib/ "supervisor" A-1-286 and /mumttil/ "actor" A-1-278 (CA *mu-rāqib-*, *mu-maθθil-*), where the full vowel is required because it is followed in CA by just a single consonant. On the other hand, seeing occasional occurrences of /m/ instead of /mu/ in such participial borrowings (for a few /m/ vs. /mu/ alternations see A-1-278, 285, 287, 297 and 299), we can explain this as due to the analogy of regular (inherited) MCA participles in /m-/, and indeed the forms with /m/ for /mu/ appear to be regular in internally derived forms based on verbs (which may or may not themselves have been borrowed from CA).

It may therefore be best to look at simple *CVCC-* and *CVCC-a* noun forms in CA and consider their borrowed MCA forms, on the assumption that these are less subject to analogical contamination than participles, infinitives and other well-defined derivational categories. Appendix A lists many *CVCC-* items beginning with A-1-196, and *CVCC-a* (feminine) items beginning with A-1-215. Unfortunately, no very clear overall patterns emerge; both the full-vowel and short-vowel MCA forms are frequently attested. Some of the items appear to have two distinct pronunciations (one with full, the other with short, vowel), and more intensive elicitation with additional speakers would certainly produce many more examples of this variation.

One subset of CA *CVCC-* items, namely when C_3 is a sonorant and syllabifies (C_2 must be an obstruent or a nongeminate sonorant other than *r* or *ṛ*), tends to show the full-vowel borrowed form rather consistently, as in /qism/ "class", /ṭifl/ "small boy", /ṣifṛ/ "zero", /šuġl/ "work" etc. (A-1-205, 206, 207, 212). (Some of these are reclassicizations of coexisting inherited MCA forms like /ṭfl/; some educated speakers avoid full-vowel pronunciation of borrowed forms so the appendix entries include variant pronunciations for some items.) In this environment, a short vowel between /C_1/ and /C_2/ is subject to syncope, so the vowel must either be full or be zeroed (except in cultivated speech).

Even with this subset differentiated, we still have what appears to be considerable unpredictability in the remaining *CVCC-* and *CVCC-a* borrowings. It is possible that a clearer pattern would begin to emerge after intensive analysis of these forms using a much greater data base with minute analysis of each item (dialect variants, historical development, particular related forms providing analogical pressures), but we will not push the matter further here.

We can observe, however, that when the word-initial segment is glottal stop /?/, whether (in CA terms) a root consonant, a prefix consonant, or an epenthetic element inserted before phrase-initial vowel, an immediately following short vowel is usually retained as an MCA full vowel even when itself followed by a consonant cluster. We find several examples in the group A-1-230ff., comparatives A-1-187ff., plurals A-1-249ff. and 169ff., and verbal nouns A-1-342ff. As we will note below, /?/ in MCA is typical only in CA borrowings (most of them still felt to be cultivated CA items), and it may be that forms (other than inflected verbs) with /?/ tend to be pronounced in a way which approximates the CA form (with MCA full vowels for CA short vowels).

Ordinarily, when CA short *i a u* are reduced to the (very) short vowels of MCA, *i* and *a* merge as /ə/ while /u/ becomes the rounded /^{w}/. The MCA /ə/ segment, when not syncopated or absorbed, has allophones ranging from approximately [Ĭ] (English *bit*) to approximately [ă] (both very short), the choice of allophone depending on environment, with [ă] expected only adjacent to pharyngealized C (and to a lesser extent uvular or pharyngeal consonants). In a few cases, a borrowing based on CA short *a* retains its low back articulation in an MCA borrowing even though the consonantal environment would point to the [Ĭ] or some similar allophone of /ə/. It is therefore, in principle, necessary to recognise a marginal phoneme /ă/ occurring in some CA borrowings involving roots not containing any pharyngealized C. The forms in question are not well established in MCA and are used by educated speakers only, to my knowledge, but I have heard them often enough to consider them worth mentioning. The examples are /l-?ăhl/ "the family", /l-?ăb/ or /l-?ăbb/ "the father", and /dăwq/ (alongside /dəwq/) "taste" (A-1-235, 246, 229). The latter is presumably a cultivated variant. The two examples involving kin terms are sporadic forms reflecting reclassicization of established MC stems /hl/ and /ḅḅa/, and the forms shown above occur only with definite prefix /l-/ (which is uncommon for these stems since they are normally in possessed forms without this prefix). In the case of /l-?ăb(b)/ "the father" it is possible that pharyngealization of the usual form /ḅḅa/ has affected the vowel allophone, but in the definite form I do not hear the labial stop(s) as pharyngealized.

5.2 Fricatives and affricates

There are a small number of automatic consonantal conversions which apply to all CA borrowings in MCA. These involve CA consonants which do not occur as such in MCA, and which Moroccans (aside from highly educated ones) usually have difficulty pronouncing even when speaking or reciting CA texts.

The CA consonants which do not occur in MCA are glottal stop *ʔ*, interdental fricatives *θ ð ð̣*, and affricate *ǰ*. The glottal stop is often retained in MCA and is discussed below. For the other consonants, the following conversions apply:

θ → /t/ *ð* → /d/ *ð̣* → /ḍ/ *ǰ* → /ž/

The last of these conversions is entirely predictable (given that the *ǰ* is not retained without change in the borrowings), since of the existing MCA consonants /ž/ is unquestionably that most similar to *ǰ*.

In the other cases (those involving fricatives), it is notable that the result is always the corresponding stop and never the corresponding sibilant /s z ẓ/. It is well known that many English-L_2 speakers (e.g. French) pronounce English interdental fricatives as sibilants (Zey sink zat zey would razzer baze in zee basstub), while other (e.g. Germans) sometimes pronounce them as stops (Dey tink dat dey would radder bade in dee batt-tub), but these stereotypes of foreign accents conceal a more complex reality in which many English-L_2 speakers fluctuate from sibilants to stops.

In the present case, the consistent conversion to stops suggests that the CA/MCA correspondences of the type *θ* to /t/, attested in a great many inherited MCA words which Moroccans are able to identify with their CA prototypes, have created a clear-cut diaphonic pattern which is then applied to new borrowings as well.

Some examples of the basic conversions: /taqaf-a/ "culture" from CA *θaqāf-a*, /ʔasatid-a/ "teachers" from *ʔasātið-a*, /ḍuṛuf/ "conditions" from *ð̣urūf-*, and /žaʔiz-a/ "prize" from *ǰāʔiz-a*. Numerous other examples occur here and there in appendix A.

5.3 Glottal stop

As mentioned in an earlier chapter, in some Moroccan dialects (mostly Judeo-Arabic, along with archaic Muslim dialects of a few cities like Fes and Tetouan) we find /ʔ/ reflecting old *q (sometimes this /ʔ/ splits into a pharyngealized and plain type). However, most existing Muslim dialects retain *q or shift it to /g/ and therefore have no cases of internally generated secondary /ʔ/. As for *ʔ, it has disappeared in inherited forms in all Moroccan dialects, though it has sometimes left behind indirect traces due to a restructuring after the loss designed to restore something like the usual MCA root shapes (we omit details here).

Essentially, glottal stops in present-day MCA are therefore found only in borrowings, and chiefly in CA borrowings (or partially reclassicized forms of old MCA items reshaped under CA influence). (We will see later that stem-initial glottal stops are found in some Fr borrowings as well.)

When we find /ʔ/ as a root consonant we are in all cases dealing with CA borrowings. Moreover, there appears to be little resistance to permitting retention of CA *ʔ*, and most relevant items show consistent /ʔ/ among those speakers who use the word. In general, the words in question are cultivated vocabulary (or elegant, reclassicized pronunciations of existing words) and are used rarely or never by uneducated elderly or rural persons. Some examples involving root /ʔ/ in verbs are A-2-1, 7, 8, 10, 82. The only clear examples of deletion of *ʔ* in verb stems borrowed from CA are

A-2-71 and 73, involving CA "conjugation X" derivatives with shape *(?)ista-CCaC-a*. In these two cases C_1 (first root consonant) is *?* in CA but is deleted in MCA, e.g. *(?)ista-?naf-a* "he prolonged" becoming /stanəf/. However, we will see below that one factor here is analogies to other similar verbal patterns; compare the shape of /stanəf/ to that of /stažəb/ "he heeded", CA *(?)ista-ǯāb-a*, suggesting a regrouping within MCA of distinct CA stem stypes.

Stable glottal stop in CA borrowings is also commonly found among nouns, whether it is a root consonant or part of a morphological frame. A miscellany of nominal examples is given in A-1-230ff., and further examples involving specific morphological frames (plurals etc.) can be found scattered throughout part A-1 of the appendix and in denser concentrations in A-1-169ff., 187ff. and 249ff.

In the cases of some nouns, a form with stem-initial /?/ represents a reclassicization of an inherited form in which the original *? was lost. One interesting case is that of the kin terms A-1-245-248, where even among educated speakers the /?/ is absent in the most common forms (namely, those with possessive pronominal endings). Thus "brother" normally shows up as /xu-/ (dialect variant or contextual allomorph /xa-/) in possessed forms like /xu-ya/ "my brother" and /xu-h/ "his brother". A simple definite form "the brother" is uncommon, but when it is used I have usually heard /l-?əx/, showing the influence of CA *al-?ax-* "the brother". Similarly, for "father" the usual possessed form is /ḅḅa-/, "mother" has /ṃṃ-/, and "sister" has /x^{w}t-/, but the uncommonly used definite forms are now often heard as /l-?ăb(b)/, /l-?^{w}mm/, and /l-?^{w}xt/. It appears that these are partial reclassicizations of older (and still attested) forms /l-^{w}bb/ "the father", /l-^{w}mm/ "the mother", and /l-^{w}xt/ "the sister", the latter two reflecting CA *al-?umm-* "the mother" and *al-?uxt-* "the sister" with historical loss of **?* (the MCA form /l-^{w}bb/ is from *al-?ab-* but has been reshaped by analogy to /l-^{w}mm/).

It would seem that the following factors are involved in the restoration of CA *?* in the definite but not possessed forms of these kin terms: (a) the definite forms are of comparatively low text frequency for kin terms; (b) inherited definite forms like /l-^{w}xt/ and /l-^{w}mm/ are structurally anomalous in appearing to show /^{w}/ as a stem-initial segment, violating ordinary MCA restrictions on this segment; (c) the logical solution to the preceding problem, namely reshaping inherited definite forms by analogy to inherited possessed forms, is unsuitable since it would produce forms like */l-ḅḅa/ "the father" with awkward stem-initial geminate cluster and */l-ṃṃ/ "the mother" with no vowels and with otherwise at best marginally acceptable final pharyngealized cluster. The (re-)introduction under CA influence of stem-initial /?/ in definite forms seems therefore to be motivated by therapeutic considerations.

Further complications arise in connection with verbal nouns which show variable (deletable) glottal stop in CA. This involves a few simple nouns but is most conspicuous in verbal nouns of "conjugations" numbered VII to X in CA, examples of which are shown in A-1-353-363. The CA forms are of the type *?iqtiṣād-* with *?i* present in postpausal position (e.g. sentence-initially), and *(i)qtiṣād-* "economy" after a prefix or another word within a punctuation group. It is possible to take *qtiṣād-* as the underlying form, with the *?* and *i* inserted by rules. This type contrasts with verbal nouns of "conjugation IV" like *?išhār-* "publicity" where the *?i* sequence, even though prefixal rather than root elements, is stable, hence *al-?išhār-* (vs. *al-iqtiṣād-*) with definite prefix. However, in some "modern" pronunciations of CA this difference is becoming blurred, and under analogical influence from the *?išhār-* type the *?i* is stabilized across contexts (especially after the definite prefix) in the *?iqtiṣād-* type as well.

Since the CA input itself is in this case variable, with traditional *al-iqtiṣād-* and innovative *al-?iqtiṣād-* "the economy" both present, it is difficult to trace what further changes have occurred in the process of assimilating these elements into MCA. The items in A-1-353-363, involving CA prototypes of the *(?)iqtiṣād-* type, sometimes show initial /?i/ in the borrowed form and sometimes eliminate these segments, hence /?iqtiṣad/ or /qtiṣad/ "economy". In one case (A-1-358) a variant is recorded with the /?/ but not the following /i/, hence /?xtilaf/ "difference" (along with at least one other variant).

The appendix does not indicate morphophonemic behaviour, and the transcriptions with initial /?/ must be qualified here. Specifically, with definite prefix /l-/ the stem-initial /?/ is often omitted, so that from variant /?iqtiṣad/ we can get definite /l-iqtiṣad/ alongside /l-?iqtiṣad/. The social distribution of these variants appears to be complex, since on the one hand /l-iqtiṣad/ is closer to the traditional form *al-iqtiṣād* and might therefore be favoured by highly cultivated speakers who stigmatize CA *al-?iqtiṣād-* as incorrect and avoid it even in MCA contexts, while on the other hand uneducated older and rural speakers make little use of /?/ (a phoneme characteristic of cultivated, classicized items) at all and thus prefer ?-less forms like /l-iqtiṣad/. We might therefore have ?-less variants favoured on different ends of the social scale and for different reasons.

Without pretending that my observations are sufficient to describe treatment of /?/ across the social continuum (or across Morocco), I have the following remarks based mostly on monitoring speech from my regular informants and acquaintances (mostly men around 20, educated in some cases but not snobbish and members of lively peer groups). I found /?iqtiṣad/-type forms regularly in unprefixed forms, /l-iqtiṣad/ about as common as /l-?iqtiṣad/ with definite prefix (we here disregard the alternate forms like /qtiṣad/ which are not subject to morphophonemic alternations). Similarly, this pattern was extended to MCA borrowings based on CA stems with stable initial *?*. This includes the "conjugation IV" verbal nouns like /?išhaṛ/ "publicity" (See A-1-342-350), hence definite /l-išhaṛ/ alongside /l-?išhaṛ/; it also applies to some (but apparently not all) simple nouns with initial /?/ followed by full MCA vowel, hence /?insan/ "human being" (A-1-237), definite /l-insan/ or /l-?insan/; /?ustad/ "teacher (A-1-235), definite /l-ustad/ or /l-?ustad/. There is a possible ongoing reanalysis of all these forms whereby the base form is being taken as ?-less, hence /iqtisad/, /išhaṛ/, /insan/, and /ustad/, with /?/ being inserted as an epenthetic element in word-initial position before a vowel to protect against vowel-initial words. However, for the speakers observed this reanalysis is by no means fully implemented, and the /?/ is often heard after definite /l-/. It would appear that considerable variation among speakers occurs and that this reflects the conflict between continuing pressures to retain or restore CA pronunciations on the one hand, and internal developmental tendencies of MCA (including its borrowings from CA) on the other. (For further evidence suggesting a developmental trend toward inserting /?/ as epenthetic element before otherwise stem-initial vowels, recall our discussion of kin terms above, and compare the addition of /?/ to Fr vowel-initial borrowings, especially verbs like /?ütiliza/ "he utilized", discussed in §6.9.)

5.4 /r/ vs. /ṛ/

The normal MCA consonantal inventory (see Table 3-1) contains two phonemes not found (as phonemes) in CA, /ṛ/ and /ẓ/. Essentially what has happened here has been that CA *r* has split into plain /r/ and pharyngealized (emphatic) /ṛ/ in MCA; CA *z* has likewise split into /z/ and /ẓ/. The exact historical processes involved are complex, and some items with /ẓ/ are borrowings from non-CA sources. However, we can disregard the history of the inherited MCA items showing these oppositions, and take as our point of departure the fact that /r ṛ z ẓ/ are distinct phonemes in MCA.

So far as new borrowings are concerned, CA *z* becomes MCA /z/, except that when the stem contains another pharyngealized consonant we get /ẓ/, presumably by spreading. For a general discussion of pharyngealization-spreading in borrowings, see §5.5.

On the other hand, CA *r* in new borrowings can appear either as /r/ or as /ṛ/ when pharyngealization-spreading does not require that /ṛ/ be chosen. Before proceeding to discuss the principles behind the choice of /r/ and /ṛ/ in stems lacking other pharyngealized consonants, it is necessary to describe the broad nature of the distribution of /r/ and /ṛ/ in inherited lexical material.

The general pattern in MCA, as in CA, is for pharyngealization to function as an inherent feature of root consonants, rather than as a feature introduced by phonological rules (aside from the spreading rule). That is, a given consonant normally does not acquire pharyngealization due to vocalic environment or the like. There are no major exceptions to this generalization in CA. Howeven, in MCA, /r/ and /ṛ/ constitute a major exception to the rule.

For example, consider /kbir/ "big", its plural /kbaṛ/ or /k^wbaṛ/, its comparative form /kbṛ/ "bigger", and its verbal counterpart /kbr/ "to grow up, to get big". Since */kbiṛ/ and */kbar/, for example, are perfectly pronounceable and otherwise acceptable sequences in MCA, and since /kbṛ/ and /kbr/ differ only in pharyngealization of the rhotic consonant, we must conclude that the alternation of /r/ and /ṛ/ is not a matter of low-level allophonic variation and must therefore be phonemic in some sense. On the other hand, since we are dealing with different forms of the same root, we cannot account for the data merely by putting /r/ or /ṛ/ in our representation of the root and allowing it to appear on the surface in all forms thereof.

Further analysis shows that in such cases the /r/ variant is favoured by position next to /i/, /ṛ/ being favoured when next to /a u/. Thus an environment like /i__i/ is maximally favourable to unpharyngealized /r/, while /a__a/ maximally favours /ṛ/. In the case of forms like /kbṛ/ and /k̄b̄r̄/ with no vowels (or with at most a possible underlying short vowel subject to loss by syncope or absorption), no such rule is applicable synchronically (though short vowels formerly present in such stems may have determined the choice between /r/ and /ṛ/). Even in words containing full vowels, no purely phonological generalization is workable except as a statistical observation, since for many roots what may once have been alternations between *r and *ṛ in different morphological environments have been levelled out one way or the other. Nevertheless, there is still a reasonably visible correlation between /i/ and /r/ on the one hand, and between back vowels /a u/ and /ṛ/ on the other.

In analysing the behaviour of recent CA loans, partly assimilated phrases, etc., it is advisable to bear in mind two factors which may be operative: (a) phonological environment, particularly vowels, favouring /r/ or /ṛ/ as the borrowed output; and (b) analogical levelling pressures involving not only relationships among several forms of a single CA root (e.g. verb, verbal noun, agentive participle) borrowed more or less simultaneously and independently, but also (in the case of reclassicizations) the influence of an inherited cognate stem which has /r/ or /ṛ/ for historical reasons. Furthermore, /ṛ/ is overall more frequent than /r/ in MCA and can thus tentatively be taken as the less marked form (even though it is more marked in phonetic terms).

Of the forms listed in the appendix, and leaving aside stems where /ṛ/ is clearly or arguably a case of secondary pharyngealization (i.e. another pharyngealized consonant occurs and the latter is the historical source of pharyngealization in /ṛ/), I count 69 items with /ṛ/, 31 with /r/, and 5 attested with both pronunciations (in these instances, I believe that /ṛ/ is more common among educated speakers). The figures for appendix subsection A-1 (nouns, adjectives) are 54, 23, and 4; and those for A-2 (verbs) are 12, 5, and 0. (The few remaining items are in appendix subsection A-3, containing particles and some adverb-like phrases, and there are not enough forms for statistical comparisons to be useful.)

The fluctuating examples are A-1-20, 163, 209, 315 and A-3-42. Some examples of /ṛ/ are A-1-8, 16, 19, 21 and A-2-5, 9, 10, 25. Some examples of /r/ are A-1-32, 46, 100 and A-2-14, 23, 35.

Although I cannot account for every detail, there are some very clear overall patterns which emerge from analysis of the full set of examples. Looking first at appendix subsection A-1 (nouns etc.), of the 23 forms with /r/, 6 involve the environment /i__#/, 1 involves /#i__/, 10 have /a__i/, 1 has /aC__i/, 1 has /uC̄__i/, 1 /ay__a#/, 1 /i__a/, 1 /īC̄__a/, and 1 /āC̄__a/. The role of /i/ and /y/ is conspicuous here, and as a general rule we can say that CA r becomes MCA /r/ in borrowings whenever it is followed by /i/ or when as stem-final consonant it is preceded by /i/. The less clear-cut environments are the last four in the list above, all of which involve following /a/ and the last of which involves preceding and following /a/. The examples are /buḥayr-a/ "lake" (A-1-168), /stiraḥ-a/ "recreation" (A-1-363), /?ižra?/ "measure" (A-1-344), and /?afraḋ/ "individuals" (A-1-178).

Of the 54 items with /ṛ/ in the same appendix subsection A-1, we find the following environments: 14 with /a__a/, 4 with /aC__a/, 4 with /a__Ca/, 7 with /a__#/, 2 with /aC__#/, 3 with /u__u/, 2 with /u__#/, 1 with /u__Cu/, 1 with uC__a/, 3 with /u__a/, and 1 with /u__Ca/, totalling 42 out of 54. Since only one of the examples of unpharyngealized /r/ is in any of these environments, it is obvious that /a/ and /u/ favour /ṛ/ in borrowings from CA in much the same way that /i/ favours /r/. Moreover, of the 12 remaining cases of /ṛ/ all but one involves /a/ or /u/, including one case where CA *a* has been lost by absorption. We now discuss these 12 remaining cases.

One, /ʔasṛaṛ/ "secrets" (A-1-183) was omitted from the lists above only because it has two rhotics and thus straddles two of the environments listed; it is clearly consistent with the general pattern. Four examples of /ṛ/ involve /i__a/ (A-1-8, 72, 75, 87). There being just one example of /r/ in this position (/stiraḥ-a/ A-1-363 "recreation"), it appears that /ṛ/ is regular in this environment (in other words, the following /a/ rather than the preceding /i/ is decisive). It is likely that /stiraḥ-a/ shows /r/ by analogy to the related verb /starəḥ/ A-2-64 "he rested".

In /qṛn/ A-1-197 "century", we are dealing with a CA form which already has an inherited MCA counterpart, dialectally /qṛn/ or /gṛn/, in a second sense "horn", the CA form being *qarn-*. Choice of /ṛ/ in the new borrowing is favoured by several factors: a-vowel in prototype, uvular *q*, and analogy of the existing MCA form. In /muṛšid/ A-1-294 "guide" we get /ṛ/ despite the following /i/, but the intervening /š/ keeps the rhotic in a distinct syllable where it is subject to the influence of the tautosyllabic /u/, favouring /ṛ/ instead of /r/.

Three forms, A-1-280 /muqṛṛiṛ/ "clerk" (CA *mu-qarrir-*), A-1-282 /muqṛṛaṛ/ "program" (*mu-qarrar-*), and A-1-324 /t-qṛiṛ/ "report" (*ta-qrīr-*), are all based on the same CA root (and indeed on its factitive form with C_2 geminated). In /muqṛṛaṛ/ the pharyngealized /ṛ/ is quite expectable, because of the phonological environment with two back vowels (three in the CA prototype) and with uvular /q/ to boot. However, the presence of /i/ in /muqṛṛiṛ/ and /t-qṛiṛ/ makes the choice of /ṛ/ problematic. It would appear that two factors are at work here: (a) influence of the important related verb /qṛṛəṛ/ "he decided, he reported" (CA *qarrar-a*), and (b) presence of the uvular /q/.

The remaining unexplained case of /ṛ/ is in A-1-123 /taṛix/ "history", where uvular /x/ is presumably a crucial factor. However, in addition to /taṛix/ (which occurs in the data corpus used for appendix A), I have also heard /tarix/ for this item from some speakers.

The basic conclusion for nouns is that /a u/ favour /ṛ/ while /i/ favours /r/, with the relevant vowel normally being an immediately adjacent, tautosyllabic vowel (V_2 in V_1__V_2, but V_1 in V_1__CV_2 and in V_1__#). There are few exceptions, and for some of them my most recent data (generally not included in appendix A) indicate alternative variants consistent with our generalization. Thus alongside /ʔižraʔ/ A-1-344 I recorded /ʔižṛaʔ/ in several cities in the latest trip and now consider this regular. I likewise recorded /ʔafṛad/ instead of /ʔafrad/ A-1-178, and /buḥayṛ-a/

instead of /buḥayr-a/ A-1-168. I did confirm /stiraḥ-a/ in Tetouan. I also confirmed /taṛix/ as the usual form for A-1-123 despite the remarks just made above about variant /tarix/, and /t-qṛiṛ/ A-1-324 was confirmed in Fes and Meknes though /t-qrir/ was recorded in Tetouan.

Analysis of /r/ vs. /ṛ/ in borrowed verbs from CA is messier because MCA has reduced or eliminated the CA vowels between stem consonants. If we assume that the quality of the CA vowels is what determines the /r/ vs. /ṛ/ in the borrowing, we still have to decide which CA inflected forms are basic in this respect; note alternations like perfective *ᶜabbar-* and imperfective *-ᶜabbir-* for "to express", with suffixes providing further complications. Theoretically, we could get MCA aspect alternations like perfective /ᶜbbṛ-/ vs. imperfective /-ᶜbbr-/, but this would be quite unusual (use of consonantal features to distinguish aspects being otherwise nonexistent) and this does not occur. We assume that paradigm levelling occurs, but the historical details are very difficult to unravel in given cases.

Of the verbs recognized in appendix A as CA borrowings (and recall that it is often difficult to identify them as recent borrowings), the following show /ṛ/: A-2-5, 9, 10, 25, 30, 31, 44, 52, 59, 66, 77, 78. The following have /r/: A-2-14, 23, 35, 36, 64. We may bracket A-2-35 in the latter list since it is an existing MCA stem which has been semantically reclassicized.

In view of the small number of verbal forms in these lists, and the absence of clear-cut phonological patterns, I cannot resolve the issue definitely. The data appear to me to hint at the following trends: (a) C_1 position seems somewhat more favourable to /r/ than do C_2 or C_3 positions; (b) some consonants including /ᶜ x q/ (and presumably /ġ/) seem to favour /ṛ/, while others such as /k s š/ appear to favour /r/; (c) there are some indications that position in MCA between two obstruents so that the rhotic syllabifies may favour /ṛ/. However, in individual instances there may be additional special factors at work, such as analogical influences from a semantically related noun based on the same root, or even influences from a synchronically derived form such as an agentive participle (through back-formation).

On the other hand, in general the role of paradigmatic analogy in the treatment of rhotics in borrowings from CA is very limited. IN particular, the majority of verbal nouns and /mu-/ participles are based directly on corresponding CA forms, with /r/ or /ṛ/ chosen on the basis of vocalism in the particular form, rather than generalized throughout the paradigm. Thus compare /mudir/ "director" A-1-32 with verbal noun /?idaṛ-a/ "administration" A-1-350 from the same root and (causative) pattern; moreover, /?idaṛ-a/ has an adjectival form /?idar-i/ "administrative" A-1-351 with change of /ṛ/ to /r/. Another example is verb /?ttṛ/ A-2-10 "he influenced" and its own verbal noun /t-?tir/ A-1-327 "influence". Alternations of Sg and (ablaut) Pl show the same pattern in many cases: /mḍṛaṣ-a/ A-1-266 "school" (*ma-dras-a*), Pl /madaris/ A-1-151 (*ma-dāris-*). Levelling of /r/ vs. /ṛ/ alternations, except in inflected verbal forms, is unusual in CA borrowings, though noticeable in European borrowings (§6.5).

5.5 Pharyngealization spreading

With reference to CA borrowings, pharyngealization-spreading refers to the process by which a plain consonant in the CA form becomes pharyngealized in MCA by assimilation to a nearby pharyngealized C.

To a considerable extent, MCA merely carries over the CA pattern of pharyngealization, since CA itself has restrictions on the co-occurrence of nearby pharyngealized and plain consonants. However, the restrictions in CA are a little looser than those in MCA, due perhaps to the fact that MCA has reduced or eliminated many CA short vowels and thus brought consonants closer together. Thus CA *s* or *d* may be pharyngealized to /ṣ ḍ/ in MCA borrowings next to another pharyngealized consonant (or sometimes a uvular consonant). Also, MCA /ṛ/ (a new phoneme) may cause pharyngealization of nearby /s d z/.

Elicitation is hampered by the slight phonetic distinction between plain and pharyngealized /s d z/ in some words, and by the influence of CA literacy on phonemic judgements by informants. Maximally careful pronunciation tends to lead to exact reproduction of CA consonantism. With some allowance for this, we may observe that there is a fundamental tendency in MCA to spread pharyngealization to /s d z/ from another pharyngealized consonant, and sometimes uvulars (especially /q/), within a stem, especially if no full vowel intervenes. Phoneme /ṭ/ resists this assimilation, presumably because its affricated offglide [t^s] differentiates it from /t/ by release as well as pharyngealization. The opposing tendency to retain CA consonantism due to literacy factors is seen even in old, well-established MCA items which are sometimes reshaped to restore a long-lost CA consonantal pattern, as with /ṣafṛ/ "he travelled", an old MCA item now sometimes reshaped to /safṛ/ because of CA *sāfar-*. Of course, informants who insist that the sibilant is /s/ rather than /ṣ/, and pronounce it /s/ in careful speech in the elicitation context, may well "lapse" into pronunciations of the type /ṣafṛ/ in less guarded speech styles. Even /safṛ/ shows partial pharyngealization of the initial segments in phonetic terms.

The CA items listed in appendix A include a few items with pharyngealization-spreading: A-1-6, 19, 55, 69, 75, 183, 266 and A-2-6. Note, however, absence of spreading in A-1-144 and 263. I should add that transcription is very difficult since pharyngealization is the kind of secondary articulation which naturally has gradual on- and offsets; for some of the items the appendix lists two alternative pronunciations and the two are very hard to differentiate in some cases.

5.6 Nominal inflection

For the most part, simple nouns borrowed from CA do not show adaptation to traditional MCA stem shapes. That is, the CA stem is taken as the basis for the borrowing and the stem itself is then converted into an MCA form on the basis of the phonological rules described above. The result is that the borrowings often have two or more full vowels, forming stem-shapes like /CVCVC/ which are unusual in inherited MCA nouns.

However, the borrowed forms behave like native MCA items in their inflection. The definite prefix is therefore regularly /l-/ instead of CA *(ʔ)al-* (the CA form reduces to *l-* when not initial in the phrase and preceded by a vowel, but MCA has /l-/ in all positions). As in CA, the /l-/ becomes, by a specialized morphophonemic rule, /C_1-/ when the stem-initial segment is a coronal (alveolar, interdental, palatoalveolar) consonant, hence CA *ad-duwal* "the countries", MCA /d-duwal/. Since the same assimilation applies in inherited MCA items, in general this assimilation works the same for inherited and recently borrowed items.

There is one exception to this. While there is some variation among MCA dialects, in the dominant ones the assimilation of /l-/ applies when the stem-initial consonant is /ž/ just as with other consonants like /š s ṣ t/. This is distinct from the CA pattern, where the corresponding segment is affricate ǯ, which does not induce the assimilation. Compare CA *al-ǯamal-* "the camel" with inherited (not borrowed) MCA /ž-žml/. (That assimilation of /l-/ before /ž/ is well established in MCA is also suggested by the consistent use of /ž-/ as surface definite allomorph with Fr loans beginning in /ž/.)

Nominal loans from CA, on the other hand, retain /l-/ as the definite prefix, hence /l-žumhur/ or l-žumhuṛ/ "the crowd" (A-1-163), and so on for the other CA borrowings in the appendix beginning with /ž/. While there is undoubtedly some variation in usage among MCA speakers, for my informants there was basically one set of items which consistently take /ž-/ and another set of (recently borrowed, or perhaps in some cases secondarily reclassicized) items which consistently take /l-/. From a purely formal point of view, we might therefore set up a distinction between underlying stem-initial /$ž_1$/ and /$ž_2$/, only the former triggering assimilation of preceding /l-/. However, the distinction is not simply arbitrary as this analysis would suggest, since /z_2/ is predictable in lexical items which are still felt to be cultivated (classical) in nature. (I did not record any hypercorrect forms, which I would not expect to be common with my principal informants, but they are almost certain to occur among younger students, for example.)

Borrowed CA nouns like inherited MCA nouns may be preceded by "prepositions", which I generally prefer to represent as prefixes, and these take MCA (not CA) form except in the case of phrasal code-switching or poorly assimilated CA phrases. Thus /f-l-žumhur/ "in the crowd", /ᶜl-l-žumhur/ "against (or for) the crowd" with the regular MCA forms of these prefixes, cf. CA *fi l-ǯumhūr-i* (orthographically *fī l-ǯumhūr-i* with long vowel in preposition) and *ᶜala l-ǯumhūr-i* (orthographic *ᶜalā l-ǯumhūr-i*). In a number of the short phrases based on CA found in appendix subsection A-3 we do find CA-like variants such as /fi-/ and /ᶜala-/ in poorly assimilated pronunciations, with MCA full vowels representing CA long or short preposition vowels. For example, note /bi-/ (vs. usual MCA /b-/, cf. CA *bi-*) in A-3-10, 13, 16, 27 (but some of these have /b-/ variants, and contrast A-3-11, 31); also /li-/ (MCA /l-/, CA *li-*) in A-3-8, 17, 70, 71 (but not A-3-36). (One factor favouring /li-/ is that it cannot be confused with definite /l-/.) These are fixed phrases, and in spontaneous usage the simple MCA forms like /f-/, /ᶜla/ (/ᶜl-/ before definite /-l-/), and /b-/ abound.

Turning to suffixes, we begin by noting that MCA borrowings from CA feminines show MCA FSg /-a/, identical to the inherited MCA FSg ending. Thus /wžb-a/ A-1-215 "meal" (borrowing) has the same shape as /bgṛ-a/ "cow" (inherited). In CA this FSg suffix has pausal form *-a*, along with a fuller form *-at-* when followed by a case-marking vowel (and, perhaps, a following indefinite suffix *-n*), as in *wajb-at-u-n* "a meal (Nominative)", *al-wajb-at-a* "the meal (Accusative)", and *al-baqar-at-i* "of the cow (Genitive)". The normal MCA form is thus based on the CA pausal form, generalized to other syntactic contexts. In the case of CA *ḥayāt-* "life" (from underlying **ḥayay-at-* under one possible analysis), the FSg suffix is less easily detachable in CA and the *t* is pronounced in pausal forms, hence MCA /ḥayat/.

In MCA, FSg /-a/ becomes /-t-/ when immediately followed by a possessive pronominal suffix, hence /klb-a/ "female dog", /klb-t-i/ "my female dog". However, in MCA only a small set of nouns (mostly inalienables and other commonly possessed nouns) permit this suffix construction, and most FSg borrowings from CA do not permit it. If we wanted to say, for example, "my meal", we could only get /l-wžb-a dyal-i/ "the meal of me", rather than */wžb-t-i/ "my meal".

The usual plural of FSg *-a(t-)* in CA is *-āt-* (when an ablaut Pl is not used), and this suffix occurs in borrowings as /-at/, matching inherited Pl suffix /-at/ from the same historical source: /wžb-at/ "meals" (borrowing), /klb-at/ "female dogs" (inherited). As in CA, /-at/ is used to pluralize some masculine nouns as well.

For participles, CA has plural suffixes *-ūn-* (Nominative) and *-īn-* (Accusative and Genitive). In inherited paradigms, MCA has merged these as /-in/, and this suffix is extended to virtually all newer CA borrowings of these types. Usage of Nominative /-un/ would strongly suggest an approximation to code-switching. Thus from /mumttil/ "actor" A-1-278 (CA *mu-maθθil-*) we get MCA Pl /mumttil-in/ "actors" (for all-female Pl we get /mumttil-at/ "actresses", cf. FSg /mumttil-a/ "actress"). A form */mumttil-un/ is bad because it shows basically the CA nominative Pl suffix while at the same time showing phonological changes within the stem (including syncope of a vowel) characteristic of well-integrated loans. However, in one isolated instance /-un/ has become common in a plural form (A-1-105).

The dual suffixes of CA have been lost in inherited paradigms in MCA except for a few duals and pseudo-duals (Blanc 1970), the latter old dual forms now used as plurals (e.g. with paired body-part terms like "eye"). True dual forms of recent CA borrowings are not used in MCA, though of course they occur in code-switching.

In their full (nonpausal) forms all CA nouns end in case suffixes, which take the forms *-u-* (nominative), *-a-* (accusative), and *-i-* (genitive) for singular nouns and internal (broken) plurals; the case suffix may be followed by indefinite *-n*, as in *suʔāl-u-n* "a question" (definite form *as-suʔāl-u*). However, even in CA the case suffix (and *-n*) is (are) omitted in the pausal form (before a pause, as at the end of a clause), and it is clearly this pausal form which is the basis for borrowings, hence MCA /suʔal/ A-1-231. Since case distinctions are also lost in MCA suffixed plurals (cf. above), borrowings (like old stems) lack suffixal case marking.

5.7 Verbal inflection

We defer discussion of the shape of borrowed verb stems themselves and here concentrate on their inflectional affixes.

Very simply, borrowed verbs from CA have identical affixal frames to ordinary inherited verbs. This is not simply because phonological adaptation of inflected CA forms converges with the affixal patterns of old MCA verbs. For example, in the imperfective the 1Sg and 1Pl prefixes in CA are *?a-* (*?a-s?al-u* "I ask) and *na-* (*na-s?al-u* "we ask"), respectively. By contrast to this, in inherited forms MCA has generalized /n-/ (reflecting *na-) to both of these forms, and has added /-u/ (taken over from second and third person paradigms) to set off the plural (hence /n-ktəb/ "I write", /n-ktb-u/ "we write"). In borrowing "to ask" (see CA forms above), MCA therefore must choose between merely applying minimal phonological and canonical-shape rules to the two CA forms, giving /?-s?l/ "I ask" and /n-s?l/ "we write", or using the normal MCA frames, hence /n-s?l/ and /n-s?l-u/. As we might expect, the latter system is in fact used, and the result is that √s?l is indistinguishable in its morphology from inherited roots like √ktb (we can tell it is a borrowing since it contains /?/, which does not occur in inherited MCA items). Use of non-MCA affixes like CA 1Sg *?a-* is limited to code-switched material and is uncommon.

In addition to the imperfective prefixes, all other inflectional prefixes and suffixes are used with borrowed verbs in the same way as with inherited verb roots. This applies, for example, to negative /ma-...-š/, perfective subject suffixes, and direct or indirect object suffixes.

5.8 Verb stems and "conjugations"

We are here concerned with the form of verb stems (i.e. of verbal words minus affixes), including derived stems reflecting what are usually called "conjugations" or "measures" in CA grammar.

In the case of simple triliteral roots of the type √$C_1C_2C_3$ with consonants as root phonemes, the regular CA forms are of the type *CaCVC-* plus suffix in the perfective and *-CCVC-* plus prefix and suffix in the imperfective. (The *V* may be *a*, *i*, or *u* depending on root and may be a different vowel in the imperfective and perfective.) According to the phonological conversion rules seen in borrowed nouns (e.g. A-1-1ff.), we should expect the verb forms to occur in MCA as /CaCVC-/, /-CCVC-/, or both, with full vowels /a/ and /V/. However, this does not occur. As the examples A-2-1 and 3 show, the MCA borrowings are based on the pattern /CCəC/ as in A-2-3 /zhəd/, which may become indistinguishable from /CCC/ when /C / syllabifies as in A-2-1 /s?l/ (the glosses are "he was devout" and "he asked" respectively). When /C_2/ and /C_3/ are identical, we get /CəCC/ (/dəll/ "he pointed" A-2-2).

These surface patterns are not directly derived from the CA prototypes by ordinary phonological adjustments in borrowing. Instead, they show adjustment of the borrowings to the very tight MCA norms for verbs, in which /CCəC/ is the regular pattern except that /CəCC/ is regular for geminate roots with /C_2/ and /C_3/ identical. This convergence has undoubtedly been favoured by the existence of many CA/MCA cognates, like CA *katab-/-ktub-* "to write" and MCA /ktəb/ "to write". From such patterns it is possible to derive diasystemic conversion rules which can then be applied to new borrowings. It should be noted that a form like *sa?al-/-s?al-* could conceivably have come into MCA as */sa?l/ or */s?al/, since canonical shapes of this sort (though not very common, and in the case of /CCaC/ semantically restricted) do occur: /ṣafṛ/ "he travelled", /ġlaḍ/ "he became fat". The existence of pre-established diasystemic rules could have helped to insure /s?l/ (i.e. /s?əl/ with syllabification of /l/) as the output for "to ask".

Hollow roots (with vowels instead of /C_2/) likewise show assimilation to MCA patterns described in §3.4. Thus /qam/ "to undertake" (with following /b-/ preposition) A-2-4 produces such inflected forms as 1Sg perfective /qm-t/ (/qəm-t/ with syllabification of /m/) and 1Sg imperfective /n-qum/. These MCA forms are similar to those of CA anyway so no significant restructuring occurs here. I do not happen to have any clear examples of weak verb roots (with vowel instead of /C_3/) which have recently been borrowed from CA (in the relevant textual corpus), but it is clear that any such borrowings would be assimilated to the MCA weak-root patterns (§3.4) since these are very similar to those of CA anyway.

In the case of hollow (and presumably weak) triliteral roots, we can see that both the CA perfective and imperfective forms are borrowed; in the examples with "to undertake" just given, note /qam/ "he undertook" resembling CA *qām-a*, and /y-qum/ "he is undertaking" resembling CA *ya-qūm-u*. Since /CaC/ is the only allowable basic perfective form for hollow roots, while /-CaC/, /-CiC/, and /-CuC/ are all possible (depending on lexical item) in the imperfective, it is actually conceivable that the imperfective form is the basic borrowed stem and that the perfective forms are then produced by predictable internal constraints. In the case of strong roots (with all root phonemes as consonants), it is impossible to decide whether the CA perfective or imperfective is the model, since in either case restructuring (loss and reduction of vowels) occurs.

Quadriliteral CA roots, like the triliterals, are adapted to prevailing MCA stem shapes and thus undergo loss or reduction of CA short vowels. Quadriliterals include a few unanalysable root quadriliterals A-2-5,6, and a number of "conjugation II" verbs, derived from a triliteral verbal or other root by geminating C_2 (see A-2-7ff.). The CA patterns are perfective *CaCCaC-* and imperfective *-CaCCiC-*, but in MCA we get just /CCCəC/, with the remaining vowel subject to absorption if the final /C/ is a sonorant, and in any case being subject to syncope if there is a suffix with a vowel, as in /ṭbbəq/ "he practised" A-2-13 (vowel retained) and /sžžl/ "he registered" A-2-17 (with absorption), 3Pl perfective /ṭbbq-u/ and /sžžl-u/.

Since triliteral and quadriliteral roots borrowed from CA thus look exactly like old MCA verb forms (unlike nominal borrowings which often show several full vowels in patterns found almost exclusively in borrowings), it is in fact rather difficult to determine whether particular roots now used in MCA are recent borrowings or inherited forms. The forms listed as borrowings in appendix A-2 are in some cases only tentatively considered borrowings. In a few cases we can be sure (e.g. when /?/ is a root consonant), but in most cases a decision to include an item has been based on informant opinions, context of usage (e.g. academic/ cultivated), precise semantic identity to CA prototype, etc. It is possible that some of the items have actually been in usage for a long period and are thus really old borrowings which continue to be thought of as cultivated or classical vocabulary.

What, then, of the other derived "conjugations"? It turns out that we can find examples of borrowed derived stems representing all of the really productive CA types, but that some regrouping has occurred in the borrowing process so that the CA types do not precisely correspond to the types of borrowed forms in MCA.

Conjugation III of CA is of type *CāCaC-* (perfective), *-CāCiC-* (imperfective) with long ā as its characteristic marker. It is usually transitive in form but indicates that the subject is engaging in an activity involving another party. Some individual CA form III verbs have been inherited by MCA, like /ṣafṛ/ "he travelled" (CA *sāfar-* without pharyngealization), but they do not pattern as derivatives and simply constitute a set of semantically simple verbs which happen to have the form /CaCəC/ or /CaCC/. A fair number of new borrowed verb stems of this type have come in, see A-2-19-26, and they have full vowel /a/ for CA ā but lose the short vowel following C_2 in the CA form, e.g. /naqḍ/ "he contradicted" A-2-20 from *nāqaḍ-/-nāqiḍ-*. Note that these borrowings thus have the same shape as /ṣafṛ/. The new borrowings, like the inherited form III stems, are for the most part best treated in MCA as underived basic stems since they are not productively derived from simple (triliteral roots). In the case of /nada/, imperfective /-nadi/ "to call (for)" A-2-19 we have a weak stem of this type and, as usual in both CA and MCA, the final vowel shows grammatically determined alternation of /a/ and /i/ (the latter in all imperfective forms and in the perfective when following by consonant-initial subject suffix).

The CA causative form IV is of the type *?aCCaC-/-CCiC-*. It has not survived in inherited forms, except for a handful of cases where it has been restructured (or perhaps altered by regular phonological rules) to merge with the usual simple triliteral verb type. There are two apparent cases of recent CA borrowings, A-2-27 and 28, and if so these likewise show restructuring. The form /mkn/ "to make (it) possible" corresponds semantically to CA *?amkan-/-mkin-*, but in MCA it is now formally identical to its own underlying simplex form /mkn/ "to be possible" (perhaps originally a passive of form IV), the two differing in sense and syntactic frame ("to make possible" requiring an object). Similarly, /ᶜln/ "he called (for)" from CA *?aᶜlan-/-ᶜlin-* A-2-28 looks like a simple triliteral strong root in MCA. It is possible that this merger is phonologically natural (i.e. if imperfective stem *-ᶜlin-* is taken as the basis of the borrowing, since underived triliterals are also of the form *-CCVC-*, including *-CCiC-*, in the imperfective); whether due to morphological or phonological factors (or some combination), the CA form IV does not constitute a separate formal class in MCA in either borrowed or inherited stems.

Form V of CA with prefix *-ta-* (following pronominal prefixes in the imperfective) has the shape *(-)ta-CaCCaC-* in both aspect forms.

The corresponding form in MCA is /t-CCCəC/. In both languages this derivative functions as the (medio-)passive of quadriliterals, including derived quadriliterals of form II. We recognise as direct form V borrowings a modest number of examples A-2-29ff. whose MCA form does not appear to be an internal derivative; these are generally cases where the CA form V stem has a specialized meaning or does not have a related form II or quadriliteral base. The treatment of stem vowels is as in quadriliterals.

Form VI in CA is *(-)ta-CāCaC-* and in MCA is /t-CaC(ə)C/. It is essentially reciprocal in sense. In CA it can be thought of as regularly derived from form III (see above), but since form III is not a well-established derivative in CMA this approach does not work for the dialect. Rather, /t-CaCəC/ is the standard reciprocal form for triliteral verb roots and does not require an intermediate derivational level. We recognize as direct form VI borrowings a number of stems A-2-36-40 which do not seem to be internally generated in this way and which seem to be directly taken from CA form VI stems. (It should be noted, though, that transitive triliteral borrowed roots like √s?l "to ask" can have internally generated reciprocals, here /t-sa?l/ "to ask each other".)

Form VII is the derived passive in CA (distinct from an ablaut or internal passive, see below) and is of the type *(?)in-CaCaC-* (perfective), *-n-CaCiC-* (imperfective). In the dominant MCA dialects this form has been eliminated and replaced by a new (medio-) passive form with prefix /tt-/ (for triliterals). As a result, it now can only appear in recent borrowings based directly on CA form VII stems, and only a few of the most common CA forms of this type are attested (A-2-41, 42). They can be considered synchronically as frozen, unanalysable stems.

The regrouping of derived stems begins to occur in form VIII, having CA forms with infixed *ta* following C_1, hence *(?)iCtaCaC-* and *-CtaCiC-*. In the MCA borrowings, we get /ta/ with full vowel when the root is not a geminated one. Among the examples A-2-43-59 note that when /C_2/ and /C_3/ are not identical the MCA stem is of the form /CtaC(ə)C/, as in /ktas(ə)b/ "he possessed" A-2-56. With weak roots the same basic structure occurs, except that C_3 is replaced by a vowel, as in /ntaha/ "it ended" A-2-43 (see also A-2-53). As our data in appendix A show, form VIII borrowings are rather common, and it would seem that they are beginning to constitude an identifiably distinct stem-type. However, form VIII is not a productive internal derivation in MCA, and almost all attested examples involve cultivated items of recent CA origin.

When C_2 and C_3 are identical (i.e. when the root is geminate), we get a pattern /CtəCC/ with only a short vowel (which may be absorbed if followed by a syllabifying sonorant), hence /htəmm/ "he was interested" A-2-48 (others are A-2-47, 49). In CA these are of the type *(?)iCtaCC-*, imperfective *-CtaCC-*, differing from the strong type *(?)iCtaCaC-*, imperfective *-CtaCiC-* only by syncope of the vowel between C_2 and C_3 (a device permitting a surface geminate cluster). In MCA, on the other hand, /CtəCC/ is not so obviously related to /CtaC(ə)C/, since there is no regular phonological rule relating /ə/ to /a/ (though a parallel applies in hollow triliterals: /daz/ "he passed", /dəz-t/ "I passed"). For further remarks on geminates see §5.9 below.

A more significant morphological recombination appears to be going on in borrowings of form X stems from CA of the type *(?)ista-CCaC-*, imperfective *-sta-CCiC-*. Since there is here a sequence *ta* in position similar to that of *ta* in form VIII, there is the possibility of some convergence of borrowings from the two stem types.

When the root is triliteral with three root consonants, the MCA borrowing from CA form X is of the type /st^CCəC/, with the /^/ vacuous in some cases and the /ə/ often syncoped or absorbed. Note that here the CA vowel in *ta* is reduced to a very weak "short vowel" whose only effect is to prevent bonding of the /t/ with a following alveolar consonant. Indeed, in our list of items in the appendix, the /^/ actually affects the surface form in a few examples only.

Examples of /st^CCəC/ are A-2-60,61,66,67,68,72,77,78. Effects of /^/ are seen in /st^dṛk/ A-2-77 "he reached", also A-2-78 and the weak type /st^tna/ A-2-75 "he excluded".

It is probable that these form X borrowings of type /st^CCəC/ (and weak /st^CCa/) are, if associated with any other MCA type, most strongly associated with geminate form VIII borrowings of type /CtəCC/ on the basis of general canonical shape. Note that /^/ and /ə/ are often deleted or vacuous, and are arguably identical anyway.

On the other hand, the CA form X stem with a hollow root has *(?)ista-CāC-*, imperfective *-sta-CīC-*. The perfective shortens *-CāC-* to *-CaC-* before consonant-initial perfective pronominal suffix: *(?)ista-ṭāᶜ-a* "he was able", *(?)ista-ṭaᶜ-tu* "I was able", imperfective *ya-sta-ṭīᶜ-u* "he is able". In MCA, the usual form is /staC(ə)C/, though /staCaC/ is an occasional variant (notably with zero suffix). Both variants are attested for A-2-62 and 64, while only /staC(ə)C/ is attested for A-2-65,74,80,81. Thus /statᶜ/ "he was able".

Since the most common and analogically basic CA forms here have long vowels, we must explain why the usual MCA pattern is /staC(ə)C/ with a short vowel often lost by syncope or absorption and optional elsewhere. Perhaps several factors are at work. First, the preconsonantal perfective type *(?)ista-ṭaᶜ-tu* "I was able" with short vowel is consistent with the MCA pattern, in that CA short vowels in verbs are usually lost or reduced. However, the relevant forms (1Sg, 2Sg, 1Pl, 2Pl) are not usually analogically more basic than the imperfective (which includes present, future, imperative, and imperfective past). A more subtle but perhaps more real factor is that reducing the CA long vowel to an MCA (very) short vowel eliminates internal ablaut distinctions between perfective and imperfective. Aside from triliterals like /šaf/ "he saw", /y-šuf/ "he sees", non-stem-final vowels in other MCA verb patterns do not show ablaut variation: /ġlaḍ/ "he got fat", /y-ġlaḍ/ "he gets fat" (a marginal exception is /ṣafṭ/ "he sent", /y-ṣifṭ/ "he sends", but many speakers level this out and generalize /ṣifṭ/ as stem form). A third factor favouring reduction of the CA forms to /staC(ə)C/ is the analogical influence of the /CtaC(ə)C/ MCA form for some CA form VIII verbs (see above).

On this last analogical influence, if indeed it has been a dynamic historical factor, it is probable that the influence is purely formal (i.e. involving canonical shape). In CA, forms VIII and X are distinct (though partly.similar) in form, and have only marginal semantic similarities. However, neither has a consistent, unitary derivational meaning in CA, and even less identifiable meaning in MCA, so there is no objection against a secondary formal merger on these grounds. Thus, /staC(ə)C/ can now be taken as /CtaC(ə)C/ for the special case where C_1 is /s/.

The MCA shape /staC(ə)C/ is found not only from CA form X with hollow root, as in the examples cited above; it also occurs in some cases of CA form X with C_1 the glottal stop *?*, if this segment is deleted in the borrowing. Thus /stahl/ A-2-71 "he deserved" from CA *(?)ista-?hal-*. A similar example is A-2-73. However, in a third form, A-2-72, the *?* is preserved, so we get /st^?CəC/ (eventual surface form /st?CC/ with final consonant syllabifying); this type with preservation of CA *?* is probably characteristic of the most recent stratum of borrowings. The two forms which lose the *?* retain /a/ as a full vowel in the MCA borrowing, while the form which retains *?* reduces this to /ə/, in this instance vacuous. The patterns /staC(ə)C/ and /st^?CəC/ are not very similar, and it would be difficult to associate them closely on the basis of MCA data alone. It is likely that the /staC(ə)C/ type has been influenced in its final form by /staC(ə)C/ from hollow roots in form X, and by /CtaC(ə)C/ from form VIII, constituting a new MCA grouping.

Form X from geminate root is also, in part, a component of this grouping. From CA *(?)ista-CaCC-*, imperfective *-sta-CiCC-*, we get either /staCCC/ or /st^CəCC/, the first of these resembling /staC(ə)C/, etc. For example, note /sta^{c}dd/, /st^{c}ədd/ "he prepared (self)" A-2-63. The type /staCCC/ seems more common and is the only form I recorded for /staḥqq/ A-2-70 "he deserved" and /stadll/ A-2-79 "he based (decision) on". It is therefore reasonable to group these geminate form X borrowings with types like /staC(ə)C/ and /CtaC(ə)C/ already discussed above.

Table 5-1 Borrowings of forms VIII and X

	MCA borrowing
CA form VIII	
strong root	/CtaC(ə)C/
geminate root	/CtəCC/
hollow root	/CtaC/
CA form X	
strong root	/st^CCəC/
strong root with initial ?	/staC(ə)C/
geminate root	/staCCC/
hollow root	/staC(ə)C/

Note: dotted lines indicate suggested regroupings; only the predominant MCA output types are shown; for further details see discussion above.

The forms of borrowings of CA forms VIII and X are summarized in Table 5-1. The table omits stems from weak (vowel-final) roots, but these are identical to the forms shown for strong roots except that the final C is replaced by the weak vowel. Again, we emphasize that the regroupings suggested in the table are formal rather than semantic, since the majority of form VIII or X borrowings are not obviously derived from simpler roots (synchronically), nor are there many oppositions in MCA of old CA form VIII and X stems from the same root.

5.9 Augment /-i-/ with geminate and /CCaC/ stems

MCA shares with CA the pattern of stem-final vowel alternations for perfective/imperfective of the weak roots in all forms ("conjugations"), hence (to use a form VIII borrowing) CA *(?)intamā* "he belonged", imperfective *-ntamī*, preconsonantal perfective type *(?)intamay-tu* "I belonged", becoming MCA /ntama/, /-ntami/, /ntami-t/ (MCA /i/ regularly represents CA *ay* as well as *i* in inherited forms, and to some extent in borrowings). However, MCA has innovated in its inflections of geminate roots, giving them an extension /-i-/ in the preconsonantal perfective (i.e. in perfective forms with consonant-initial subject suffix). This extension has parallels in many Arabic dialects and seems to involve analogical interaction with weak forms. Thus CA *šamm-a* "he smelled", *ya-šumm-u* "he smells", *šamam-tu* "I smelled" in MCA becomes /šəmm/, /y-šəmm/, and /šmm-i-t/, where the first two MCA forms are directly inherited but the third has been reshaped. The most direct analogy is with weak factitive-causative (form II) derivatives like /smma/ "he named", /y-smmi/ "he names", /smmi-t/ "I named", where the last form resembles /šmm-i-t/ "I smelled" in vocalic structure. (The analogy here is rather awkward, but makes sense when we realize that the change to /šmm-i-t/ was a therapeutic device which satisfied the developmental tendency favouring keeping the two identical root consonants in a surface cluster unless broken up by a full vowel.)

The /-i-/ augment in the preconsonantal perfective applies to borrowings as well as inherited stems; moreover, in addition to simple triliteral stems it applies also to derived forms which end in a geminate cluster. Thus /ḥtəžž/ "he protested" A-2-49 and /ḥtžž-i-t/ "I protested"; /staḥqq/ "he deserved" A-2-70 and /staḥqq-i-t/ "I deserved". The CA forms are *(?)iḥtajj-a*, *(?)iḥtajaj-tu*, *(?)ista-ḥaqq-a*, and *(?)ista-ḥqaq-tu* with surface geminate cluster in the 3Sg but not 1Sg.

The augment /-i-/ cannot be used with form II derivatives (nor, therefore, with form V, which is form II plus a prefix), even with /C_2/ identical to /C_3/. For example, in /ḥqqəq/ "he confirmed", /C_2/ itself is doubled and forms a medial geminate cluster, leaving the final consonant unclustered; the 1Sg form is /ḥqqəq-t/ without /-i-/.

In addition to stems with final geminate cluster, MCA has one other stem-type which takes /-i-/ in the preconsonantal perfective: stems of the shape /CCaC/, most of which are inchoative adjectival verbs like /ġlaḍ/ "he got fat". While many MCA dialects do not use /-i-/ with these stems, in the Fes/Meknes area the augment is usual: /ġlaḍ-i-t/ "I got fat".

I am not aware of any borrowings from CA of this adjectival type. However, /xtar/ "he chose" (possibly a recent borrowing) has 1Sg form /xtar-i-t/ "I chose", and /ḥtaž/ "he needed" gives /ḥtaž-i-t/ "I needed" (see A-2-51). These are, in CA, hollow form VIII derivatives with *-ta-* infix. If the MCA forms just listed are borrowings, they have been assimilated to the /ġlaḍ/ type, suggesting yet another realignment of the system of forms (conjugations).

5.10 Internal (ablaut) passives

Among its passive forms, CA has an internal (ablaut) passive formed from any transitive stem (and some intransitives) by vowel changes: *katab-a* "he wrote" but *kutib-a* "it was written", *ya-ktub-u* "he writes" but *yu-ktab-u* "it is (being) written". This can be formed from simple or derived stems.

In MCA the internal passive has been lost (along with passive form VII, see above). Form V, of the type /t-CCCəC/, is used as (medio-)passive of form II and other quadriliterals. A new type /tt-CCəC/ has been developed as the regular passive of simple triliteral verbs.

New borrowings fit these MCA patterns. A simple triliteral will form passive /tt-CCəC/ while a quadriliteral will form /t-CCCəC/. Moreover, transitive borrowings of more elaborate CA types like form X can form MCA passives; curiously, the prefix is /tt-/ rather than /t-/, hence /ta-y-tt-^{c}tabṛ/ "it is considered" from /^{c}tabṛ/ "he considered" A-2-44. This suggests that the allomorph rule for /tt-/ vs. /t-/ has to do with syllabic structure: /tt-/ used in forms where the following /C_1/ and /C_2/ form a cluster which is followed by a vowel, /t-/ used with three following consonants with /C_2/ and /C_3/ (out of four consonants) the most tightly bound together and with a weak epenthetic vowel often heard (but not written) after /C_1/.

5.11 Verbal nouns and participles

In MCA, the great majority of verbs (simple or derived) have a corresponding verbal noun (infinitive). There is also an active participle and for transitives a passive participle (for some verbs the active participle is very common and is commonly used as predicate, e.g. for present perfective; for other verbs the active participle is not often used and may be unelicitable).

For simple triliterals, the usual forms are the verbal noun /CCVC/ with /V/ depending on the root (usually /i/ or /a/, rarely /u/); active participle /CaC(ə)C/ and the passive participle /m-CCuC/. For the other, derived forms the active and passive participles are no longer distinct, both having prefix /m-/; there are various verbal noun patterns depending on the particular derivational verb type.

When dealing with borrowed lexical items, there are two options: (a) just borrow the verb stem from CA, then generate the verbal noun and participle(s) by productive internal MCA mechanisms, or (b) borrow the verbal noun and participle(s) directly from CA. Usually the formal difference is in the vocalism: internally generated forms ordinarily show the same deletion or reduction of CA vowels seen in the verb forms themselves, while directly borrowed participles and verbal nouns usually keep CA vowels (short or long) as MCA full vowels (in other words, the regular conversions applied to CA nominal borrowings are applicable here). This is slightly oversimplified but basically correct. Frequently we find, in MCA, both an internally generated and directly borrowed verbal noun or (more often) participle; in this event, the internally generated form is semantically very closely based on the meaning of the verb stem, while the directly borrowed form is often semantically specialized.

For example, for simple triliterals the active participle is /CaC(ə)C/ if internally generated, /CaCiC/ if borrowed; the CA prototype is *cāCiC-*. Examples of direct borrowings are A-1-100,101,102,103,104 (note occupational glosses like "goalkeeper" and "delegate"); there are some others in the same list (A-1-98,99,105,106,107,108) which have even less clear verbal significance. Not all of these have internally generated alternates, but compare /xariž/ "exterior" A-1-107 (borrowed) with /xarž/ "(he has) already gone out" (based on inherited /x^wrž/ "he went out").

Similarly, from form III the active participle is /muCaCiC/ if directly borrowed, but if internally derived from a verb of the shape /CaCC/ we get /m-CaCC/. See A-1-286-289 for borrowed examples (for two of these an internally derived counterpart is mentioned in the listing). Other active participle types are form IV /muCCiC/ (borrowed, no internal counterpart since IV is not a distinct MCA form); form VI /mutaCaCiC/ (borrowed, see A-1-299) or /m-t-CaCC/ (internal); and form VIII /muCtaCiC/ (borrowed, see A-1-300,301) or /m-CtaCC/ (internal).

However, partial reduction of vocalism does occur in some types of directly borrowed active participles. In particular, those of the important form II (factitive-causative) are *mu-CaCCiC-* in CA and become not */muCaCCiC/ but /muCCCiC/ in MCA: /mumttil/ "actor", /mufttiš/ "inspector", etc. (see A-1-276-281). This pattern is now well established and any more recent borrowings of this type will adopt it. A similar example is /mutwṣṣiṭ/ "Mediterranean" A-1-297, formally an active participle of form V (which is form II plus a (medio-)passive prefix /-t-/). Note that in this form we end up with four consonants squashed together in the middle, flanked by /mu/ at the beginning and /iC/ at the end. This general pattern is also found in active participles of form X, as in /musthlik/ "consumer" (A-1-314, CA *mu-sta-hlik-*), cf. also A-1-315 (the example in A-1-313 is different but involves a hollow root). In all of these types the prefix /mu/ with /u/ retained, and the /i/ before the final root consonant, show that we are dealing with direct borrowings from CA and not internally generated participles.

Moreover, whereas the internal participles with /m-/ do not distinguish active from passive participles (except in simple triliterals, where /m-/ is passive only), in borrowings the two are distinguished by having /i/ vs. /a/ in the final syllable. The preceding paragraph has examples of active forms with /i/; a passive example is /mušddad/ "doubled (letter), fortified" A-1-285 (the active form does not occur in my data but would be /mušddid/ "fortifier"); see also A-1-282-285, 296, 305-312, 316. Again, many of these are cultivated forms similar to Latinate adjectives in English, and may coexist with internally derived passive participles more closely related in meaning to the verb (see A-1-282-285).

The only other remark I have to make about participles is that in the simple triliteral passive type, *ma-CCūC-* in CA, the borrowed forms seem to all take the MCA form /mCCuC/ rather than */maCCuC/ (see A-1-271-275). This applies also to semantically specialized examples like /mžhud/ "effort", which are clearly based directly on CA participial forms. The inherited MCA participial form is likewise /m-CCuC/ for these triliterals, and this analogical pattern plus the closed first syllable and perhaps the stress pattern of the CA models have encouraged reduction of the vowel in *ma-*.

There are a few verbal nouns in the data from simple triliteral roots which appear to be based directly on CA verbal nouns and not internally generated. These include /ṣiyam/ "fasting" A-1-29, /muyul/ "inclination" A-1-47, and /ḥuḍuṛ/ "attendance" A-1-48, all from CA *CVCV̄C-*. The usual inherited MCA verbal nouns from such roots are of the form /CCVC/, historically from *CVCV̄C-. Some examples of a shorter type *CVCC-* are /fə^{c}l/ "act" A-1-198, /ḥəfḍ/ "memorization" A-1-200, and others in the same group in the appendix.

Each of the derived stem types has a characteristic verbal noun formation in CA, and examples of borrowings based on them are given in the section from A-1-318-365. In the form II type *ta-CCīC-* we get /t-CCiC/, with the same reduction of the first CA vowel seen in the passive participle *ma-CCūC-* (see above); examples are A-1-318ff. The usual MCA verbal noun for this pattern is /t-CCaC/ rather than /t-CCiC/.

For form III the regular verbal noun is /muCaCaC-a/, ending with the feminine suffix; examples are A-1-328ff. The inherited MCA form, though not common, is /mCaCC-a/ with some vowels lost, so here we can distinguish the recent borrowings. An example of the less common CA type *CiCāC-*, usually more specialized semantically than the other, is /niḍam/ "organization" A-1-30.

From form V and form VI we find, respectively, CA *ta-CaCCuC-* and *ta-CāCuC-*. In MCA borrowings, form V becomes /taCCCuC/ or less often retains its medial vowel as /taCaCCuC/, see A-1-333ff. The reduction of medial vowels here is related to that in participles of the same form. The form VI verbal noun in borrowings is /taCaCuC/ as we would expect; see A-1-336ff. The forms A-1-339-341, e.g. /tasawi/ "equality", are from weak roots and show a vowel change at the end which is also present in the CA counterparts. There is no productive inherited MCA counterpart to these form V and VI verbal nouns (form V is essentially the passive of form II and does not have a distinct verbal noun; form VI functions as the reciprocal of simple verbs and likewise does not normally have its own verbal noun).

With the form IV type, CA *?iCCāC-*, we move to types with an initial glottal stop, in this instance obligatory in CA in all positions. Examples of MCA /?iCCaC/ are A-1-342-344. There are also several examples of /?iCCaC-a/ (A-1-350) or /?iCaC-a/ (A-1-345-349) with feminine ending; the second of these two subtypes is the usual form IV verbal noun for hollow roots. In the form VIII (A-1-353ff.) and form X (A-1-360ff.) types, the initial ? in CA is omitted in some positions; the MCA borrowings sometimes omit the *?* and the following vowel as in /stqbal/ "reception" A-1-361, but sometimes keep them as in /?imtiyaz/ "benefit" A-1-356 (see also variants with initial /i/ without glottal in A-1-361,362). In the form VIII type the medial /i/ is preserved in all of our examples, hence /mtiḥan/ "exam" (not */mtḥan/ or the like); in form X, on the other hand, the medial /i/ is sometimes dropped:

/stqbal/ or /istiqbal/ "reception" (A-1-354,361, respectively). Since forms IV, VIII, and X are effectively absent from traditional MCA there is no clear contrast between inherited and borrowed verbal nouns of these types.

5.12 Prepositions and related elements

Part 3 of Appendix A contains a number of attested borrowings in MCA from CA prepositions (simple or complex) A-3-20-41. Most of these are typical of cultivated speech styles, but they may be quite common now in such styles.

It should be noted that most of the simple inherited MCA prepositions (including several which I prefer to transcribe as prefixes) are already closely related to CA prototypes: *bi-* and /b-/ "by", *li-* and /l-/ "to". *fi* and /f-/ "in", *ᶜinda* and /ᶜənd/ "with, at" (Fr *chez*), *ᶜalā* and /ᶜla/ or (before definite noun) /ᶜl-/ "against, for", *min* and /mn/ "from", *maᶜa* and /mᶜa/ or /mᶜ-/ "with". Similarly, several locational prepositions are shared (through inheritance) by CA and MCA; *fawqa* and /fuq/ "above", *taḥta* and /təḥt/ "under", etc.

For this large set of CA/MCA cognate prepositions, the only possible new CA influence would take the form of restoration of vowels and/or rearranging some details of usage of the various prepositions where MCA has diverged somewhat (for example, MCA /ᶜla/ has expanded into dative and benefactive functions as /l-/ has retreated from them). In general, restoration of vowels does not occur except in code-switched material and some poorly integrated CA phrases (A-3-8, 15-17, 41, 70, 71). Restoration of details of CA distribution of the prepositions also seems to be limited (except of course in so far as newly borrowed phrases reflect CA prepositional uses).

While the set of attested borrowings in the list A-3-20 to 41 may seem impressive on first glance, it should not be thought that recent borrowings are particularly extensive in this area. In particular, some very important MCA prepositions which do not have an obvious resemblance to specific CA prepositions generally have resisted replacement. Thus the usual genitive preposition in MCA is /dyal/ or /ntaᶜ/, depending on the dialect; despite the fact that there is no phonologically similar element in CA (which normally uses a "construct" or quasi-compound construction or else uses *li-* "to" to express genitive), these MCA prepositions remain in full usage even in relatively cultivated styles. Similarly, the preposition for "like, resembling" in CA is *ka-* or *kamā* but in MCA it is /bḥal/ (perhaps /b-ḥal/; there is a dialect variant /f-ḥal/), and outside of a handful of poorly assimilated phrases (A-3-12,68) we do not find extensive new intrusions of the CA forms. One intrusive CA preposition which is attested, /dun/ "without" A-3-26 (cf. also /bi-dun/ "without" A-3-27), is nevertheless still much less common than inherited /bla/ reflecting a second CA form *bi-lā*. On balance, then, new borrowings of prepositions are insignificant and tend to involve cultivated items with glosses like "on the basis of", "with respect to", and "for the sake of", often compound. CA *ʔilā* "to" as well as CA *li-* "to" become MCA /l-/.

Our final remark on prepositions concerns the question of whether final vowels in the CA forms are retained in new borrowings. Most of the CA prototypes in the relevant cases, like *dūn-a* "without" and *ḥasab-a* "according to", end in a short vowel, often accusative indefinite *-a*. By their very nature, prepositions occur with nouns immediately following and therefore do not occur in "pausal" position (which would regularly produce deletion of the final vowel even in CA pronunciation). Still, most new MCA borrowings fail to retain the final vowel: /dun/ "without", /ḥasab/ "according to" (A-3-26, 20). Optional retention has been found with /ḥəwl/ or /ḥəwla/ "concerning" (*ḥawl-a*) and with /ḍəḍḍ/ or /ḍəḍḍa/ "against, in opposition to" (*ḍidd-a*) (see A-3-25, 30). It should be stressed that feminine singular *-a* (the CA pausal form of *-at-*) is kept in MCA borrowings and that the treatment of this suffix is an entirely different matter.

The preference for forms like /dun/ instead of expected */duna/ appears to require an explanation which is not purely phonological. I would suggest that Moroccans who know CA (and thus function as initiators of borrowings) recognise that the final vowels of *dūn-a*, *ḥasab-a*, and the like are really case endings and not stem elements. Since there is a very well-established diasystemic pattern where MCA nouns lack the case endings found in CA cognates, it is reasonable to expect that when Moroccans analyse the CA prepositions as being really special adverbial accusative forms of nouns, they drop the case ending in the borrowing. As to what the reason is why /dun/ and /ḥasab/ lack the final CA *-a* while /ḥəwl(a)/ and /ḍəḍḍ(a)/ may retain it, the limited number of forms in question makes analysis difficult (and a more detailed study might turn up /duna/ or the like with some speakers); however, we might speculate that the nominal status in CA of *dūn-* and *ḥasab-* might be more transparent than it is for *ḥawl-* and *ḍidd-* (e.g. because the former are more commonly preceded by other prepositions than the latter).

5.13 Adverbs and short phrases

Appendix subsection A-3 also has a representative set of adverbs and short adverbial phrases.

In the section beginning A-3-42 we present a large number of examples of adverbs involving CA suffix *-an*, which is actually a special adverbial usage of indefinite accusative *-a-n*. Some of the borrowed forms reduce this to /-n/, others keep /-an/, others have either form. A number of the borrowings are now quite common and not necessarily limited to elite speakers: /tqrib-n, tqṛib-n/ "approximately" A-3-42, /tamam-n/ "completely" A-3-67, /da?im-an/ and variants "always" A-3-49, /matal-an/ "for example" A-3-43, and of course /šukṛ-an/ "thank you" A-3-65. It is unlikely, however, that any of the examples listed is a direct inheritance from its CA prototype, since CA *-an* does not seem to have survived in authentic old dialect forms. (There is some evidence that MCA /-a/ occasionally represents *-an* in inherited forms, hence /dima/ "always", now often reclassicized to /da?im-an/ and variants A-3-49.) Although /-(a)n/ as adverbial suffix is restricted to CA borrowings, there are so many of these that we can consider this to be a recognizable type in modern MCA. Note in this connection that some of the (noun) stems in these forms also occur in other forms without the /-(a)n/, e.g. /xuṣuṣ-an/ "especially A-3-45 vs. /b-l-xuṣuṣ/ "especially" A-3-10.

A few adverbial phrases not involving /-(a)n/ are given in A-3-8ff. Some of these involve a noun stem with affixes including a preposition. In this event the preposition sometimes takes its CA form, sometimes its MCA form (the latter usually by reducing or dropping a vowel). The forms listed in this section are basically cultivated expressions and are only marginally assimilated to MCA patterns. The adverbial phrases involving demonstrative stems A-3-68-71 should also be mentioned here.

A CA syntactic arrangement *lā NOUN-a* "(there is) no NOUN" occurs in two expressions which are now in fairly common use. First, /la ba?s-a bi-hum/ "they are doing fine" (economically, medically, etc.), a reclassicization of /la bas/ "fine", /la bas ᶜli-hum/ "they are fine", is sometimes heard. The more common example is /la šukṛ-a ᶜla wažib/ "you're welcome", the standard reply to /šukṛ-an/ "thank you" (see A-3-13, 66, respectively). The forms with /la NOUN-a/ in MCA do not constitute a clear syntactic configuration and it is probable that many Moroccans have learned them as fixed phrases with no clear internal structure.

5.14 Syntax: clause introducers

Probably the most significant non-lexical influence of CA on MCA in recent times has been the restructuring of the forms of certain types of subordinate clauses.

Some of the most important traditional clause-introducers in MCA are these:

billa	that (quotative complement, etc.)
b-aš	(so) that; that (quotative)
f-aš	(at the time/place) when/where
mnin	when
ᶜla ḥqq-aš	because

(We omit regional variants, which are plentiful for the first, fourth and fifth of these in particular.)

All of these clause-introducers are invariable in form and are followed by complete finite clauses. None of them is clearly identifiable as having a precise CA counterpart.

These forms are still, for the most part, in common use. However, some CA forms have become common in the speech of students and other educated persons and may eventually become quite general. Moreover, some of the borrowed clause-introducers require a somewhat different syntax.

Consider "because" to begin with. One form, /ḥet/ A-3-3, if correctly identified as a CA borrowing, causes no syntactic changes since it merely replaces the older MCA clause-introducer. However, the other new form /li?inna/ and variants A-3-1 is from CA *li-?anna* "because", which requires an immediately following NP or pronominal suffix, usually the clause subject: *li-?anna-nī xaraǰ-tu* "because I (*-nī*) went out", *li-?anna l-wazīr-a xaraǰ-a* "because the vizier went out". The bound NP or pronominal suffix takes accusative case (regardless of its case role within the clause) and must precede the predicate (whereas unmarked CA word order is VSO). The old MCA counterparts would be /^{c}la ḥqq-aš (ana) x^{w}rž-t/ (the 1Sg pronoun /ana/ being usually omitted) "because I went out" and /^{c}la ḥqq-aš l-wazir x^{w}rž/ "because the vizier went out" with the further possibility of putting the subject noun or pronoun after the verb, as in /^{c}la ḥqq-aš x^{w}rž-t ana/ and /^{c}la ḥqq-aš x^{w}rž l-wazir/.

When /li?inna/ and its phonological variants is used in MCA, we find a partial but not complete accommodation to inherited MCA syntactic patterns. That is, /li?inna/ sometimes occurs as an invariable form which has no pronominal ending and need not be followed by a NP, but sometimes it does bring in its CA syntax and shows a pronominal suffix. A survey of a small body of texts with an educated speaker using fairly cultivated style showed a basically even frequency of the two types.

An example of /li?inna/ as an invariable and formally independent particle:

a) li?inna ḥtta ḥna-ya ka-y-^{c}žəb-na n-šuf-u l-byut
because too we it pleases us we see goals
"because we too like to see goals"

In CA, an example of this type would have to begin with *li-?anna-nā* "because we" or *li-?anna-hu* "because it", depending on which NP is taken as theme. (In some contexts there is no convenient NP to be theme, and in this event a dummy 3Sg masculine pronominal element is used.)

An example of /li?inna/ with pronominal suffix:

b) ^{c}žəb-ni li?inna-hu ḥsn ml - l-msid
it pleased me because it better than the msid
"I liked it because it was better than the msid (Koranic school)"

This is not merely a calque, since the form of the 3Sg masculine pronominal suffix, /-hu/, is directly based on CA *-hu* instead of the usual MCA forms, /-h/ after vowel and /-u/ after consonant. This is true of the other pronominal suffixes as well, to the extent we can distinguish CA from MCA forms. (Rarely, I have recorded forms like /li?inna-h/ "because he" with MCA suffix allomorph; it is far more common among my informants to use the CA suffix form or else to omit pronominal suffixes.)

The other important case of this type is CA *bi-?anna* "that" (mostly a quotative complement with certain verbs, also used with complements of verbs like "know", "see", and "find"). The MCA form is /bi?inna/ and phonological variants. We find the same optional importation of CA pronominal suffixes already seen with "because" (above).

An example of the invariable use of /bi?inna/ is this:

c) w-ġadi y-žbṛ bi?inna kayn tmma ši ^{c}šr-in
and will he find that there is there about twenty
"and he'll find that there are about twenty there"

In CA we would expect something like *bi-?anna-hu* (with dummy 3Sg suffix).

An example of pronominal suffix with /bi?inna/ is:

d) l-bhž-a bi?anna-hu qḍa š-šhṛ dyal ṛamaḍan
the joy that he he finished the month of Ramadan
"(he expresses) his joy that he has finished the month of Ramadan (month of fasting for Muslims)"

Again the pronominal suffix is directly based on CA *-hu*.

The same speaker still uses the older form /billa/ in essentially the same syntactic contexts:

e) qṛi-t f-ž-žuṛnal billa kayn waḥəd l-mᶜhəd
I read in the paper that there is one centre
"I read in the paper that there is a centre...

As the segmentation suggests, CA *li-?anna* "because" and *bi-?anna* "that" both involve a clause-introducer *?anna* (preceded by prepositions). In CA, the simple form *?anna* is quite common, and there is another clause-introducer *?inna* used with "to say" (but not other quotative verbs) and used by itself (with no higher clause) as a topicalizer. Moreover, *?anna* can be preceded by various prepositions other than *li-* and *bi-*, although these two are by far the most common.

In educated MCA, some of the forms crop up here and there. The forms *?anna* and *?inna* are uncommon without prepositions, and there is some tendency to use /bi?inna/ where CA uses simple *?anna*. However, an occasional example of *?anna* shows up as /?anna/ or /anna/:

f) kan dak d-diplum, ta-yᶜtabṛ-u anna-(h)u diplum ᶜali
it was that degree they consider that it degree high
"that degree, they considered it an advanced degree"

(I did not hear the /h/ on the tape but regard this as a low-level casual-speech deletion, the suffix being from CA 3Sg masculine *-hu*.)

An example with *?inna* is:

g) walakin lli bġi-t n-gul huwa ?inna-ni stafd-t bzzaf
but what I wanted I say it that I I gained much
"but what I wanted (meant) to day was that I gained (profited) a lot (from the experience)"

Scattered examples occur in my texts of *?anna* used in borrowed forms with a preceding preposition; this is usually in cases where the matrix verb is associated with a following preposition-plus-NP sequence and where clausal complements take the same preposition plus *?anna* and a clause. The matrix verbs themselves are usually CA borrowings:

h) bṛhn-t ᶜla ?anna ma-kayn-š t-tasawi bayn d-duwal
I proved that is no equality among nations
"I proved that there is no equality among nations"

Here we have a borrowing from CA *barhan-* "to prove", which takes *ᶜalā* as its characteristic preposition.

An example not involving a higher clause in the usual sense:

i) ḥtta ?inna-hum ma-ta-y-lqa-w-šay l-bḷayṣ
until that they they do not find places
"(they crowd into the mosques) to the point where they can't get places (to sit)"

The extent to which these CA clause-introducers are used in MCA will vary greatly with generation, degree of education, context of discourse, and so forth. However, among educated speakers these forms, especially /li?inna/ and /bi?inna/ and their variants, are already quite common and are introducing a new syntactic construction involving what are (from the viewpoint of MCA) special allomorphs of pronominal suffixes.

5.15 Syntax: conjunctions

In addition to the syntactic clause-introducers used in subordinated clauses (preceding section), MCA has a number of simple logical conjunctions, notably /w-/ "and" (prefixed to first word of conjoined clause or phrase), /awlla/ "or", and several forms meaning "but" such as /walakin/, /walaynni/, and /b-l-ḥəqq/.

These conjunctions remain in use even among educated speakers. There are, however, occasional intrusions of CA forms. While /w-/ "and" is not often expanded to /wa-/ on the model of CA *wa-*, MCA /awlla/ "or" and its phonological variants is sometimes replaced by /?aw/ from CA *?aw*. The CA form for "but" is *lākin* or, with pronominal suffix or bound accusative NP, *lākinna*, and can be preceded by *wa-* "and". The MCA variant /walakin/ "but" is therefore evidently similar to the CA form, and one form of CA influence is favouring this variant over the others like /walaynni/ and /b-l-ḥəqq/, which are not used by younger educated speakers as often as they are by older and uneducated speakers in my experience. A more extreme CA interference, namely, use in MCA of /(wa)lakinna/ plus bound NP or pronominal suffix, is attested but uncommon.

In general, while there is a limited amount of replacement of old MCA conjunctions with new borrowings from CA, this replacement in most cases has no syntactic consequences (the borrowing fitting into the same syntactic frame as the old conjunction it replaces). If a form like /(wa)lakinna/ becomes established in configurations with a pronominal suffix (parallel to patterns seen in the preceding section), this generalization will require modification.

5.16 Syntax: the genitive

In MCA there are basically two patterns for attributive (non-predicative) genitive of the type "the X of Y" or "Y's X". The first is an analytic construction /l-$NOUN_X$ dyal l-$NOUN_Y$/ with genitive /dyal/ before the possessor noun, here $NOUN_Y$. Both nouns can take definite /l-/. The pronominal equivalent is of the type /l-$NOUN_X$ dyal-i/ "my $NOUN_X$" with pronominal suffix added to /dyal-/. The second, synthetic construction is of the type /$NOUN_X$ l-$NOUN_Y$/, where only the possessor noun can take the definite prefix; the pronominal form is /$NOUN_X$-i/ "my $NOUN_X$". The synthetic type is often called the "construct" (i.e. nexus) form in Arabic grammar and the two elements are said to be "in construct".

In CA we have formal analogues to both the analytic and construct genitives. However, the analytic type with preposition *li-* (or *la-* with pronominal suffix) is the less common of the two forms in CA and is considerably less common and more restricted than the construct form. The opposite is true in MCA: the type with /dyal/ (or dialectal variant /ntaᶜ/) is almost always possible and very common while the construct forms are subject to various restrictions (mostly of a subtle semantic nature) and are generally uncommon for many stems.
(The stem acting as possessed noun, $NOUN_X$, is generally decisive in determining whether the construct form is possible.) The possessed nouns most often occurring in construct forms in MCA are commonly possessed (quasi-inalienable) stems such as kin terms. We omit a detailed discussion here.

It would be reasonable to expect that some MCA speakers who are under strong CA influence might tend to shift away from the /dyal/ genitive to the construct type. Whether this is correct, and if so to what extent, cannot be established at this time since we would need extensive before-and-after textual corpora and would have to factor out the many interfering factors (such as semantic type of $NOUN_X$) before a suitable statistical study could be undertaken. I will therefore make the general remark that my data are consistent with the suspicion that young educated speakers are making somewhat greater use than others of the construct type.

There are certain specific types of this construction which do not occur to my knowledge in ordinary MCA and which are therefore probable CA borrowings. One type is seen in /?axir muqabal-a/ "the last match (of the season, etc.)", with adjective /?axir/ "last, final" as $NOUN_X$. A similar type is seen in /mn ?ahmm l-ᶜyad/ "one of the most important (religious) holidays", with /mn/ "from" (i.e. "one of") and /?ahmm/ "more/most important". The CA prototypes would be *?axīr-u mu-qābal-a* (pausal form) and *min ?ahamm-i l-?aᶜyād*. These constructions in CA are typical of comparative adjective forms like *?ahamm-* and of the adjectives meaning "first" and "last".

Similarly, we have MCA construct forms involving /ġiṛ/ "other than, different from, except" which may be modelled on CA configurations with *ġayr-*. An example:

a) kayn ᶜuṭal li-munasab-at ?aᶜyad
there is vacations on the occasion of holidays
waṭan-iy-a ?aw din-iy-a ?aw ġiṛ-ha
national or religious or other than them
"there are vacations during national, religious, and other holidays"

The whole passage shows numerous CA borrowings and it appears that /ġiṛ-ha/ may be based on CA *ġayr-V-hā* (in this instance the CA form would be genitive *ġayr-i-hā*).

5.17 Syntax: number/gender concord

In both CA and MCA, number/gender concord is significant since adjectives agree with nouns, inflected verbs have pronominal affixes agreeing with subject (and sometimes object), and relative clauses often have "resumptive" pronouns coreferential to the head noun.

The possibility of ongoing syntactic interference between CA and MCA is due to the fact that the two differ in some details of how concord works. Specifically, CA has the following restrictions. First, when an inflected verb is followed (but not preceded) by the subject NP, the verb agrees (anticipatorily) in gender but not number: *xaraǰ-a r-raǰul-u* "the man went out", plural *xaraǰ-a r-riǰāl-u* "the men went out", both with 3Sg masculine verb *xaraǰ-a*, contrast *xaraǰ-ū* "they went out" (used without following subject NP or with subject NP preceding). Second, inanimate plural NPs are treated as feminine singular in agreement in all positions: *xaraǰ-at il-malik-at-u* "the queen went out", *xaraǰ-at il-?aflām-u* "the films came out (appeared)", with 3Sg feminine verb.

In MCA, the first of these restrictions is not applied, hence /x^{w}rž ṛ-ṛažl/ "the man went out" but /x^{w}rž-u r-ržal/ "the men went out", with 3Pl verb in the second example. (It is worth noting in this connection that the order of verb and subject NP is more variable in MCA than in CA.) Examination of my texts suggests that no significant CA interference in this matter is visible, even in texts with large numbers of CA borrowings and phrases and with a generally cultivated style. I have noticed a few apparent examples of 3Sg agreement for plural nouns which follow the verb, but they involve an existential verb and thus appear to represent a minor internal MCA restriction rather than CA interference. An example: /kan ^{c}ənd-na mu^{c}llim-in ?ažanib/ "we had (lit., was to us) some foreign teachers", with /kan/ "he was", not /kan-u/ "they were". (In this type with /kan/, gender agreement is regular and plural agreement is possible but not required.)

On the other hand, quite a bit of interference from CA appears to be in operation regarding the concord patterns of inanimate plurals. The situation is somewhat complex, since MCA retains a few idiomatic patterns in which a Pl noun shows FSg agreement; Harrell (1962:158) has /daz-t ši yyam-at/ "a few days passed" (my transcription), for example. Harrell states, however, that the great majority of inanimate plural NPs have regular plural concord; he specifically includes numerals (apparently with inanimate as well as human/animate reference), and says that the few surviving true duals (/šhṛ-ayn/ "two hours", etc.) generally take plural concord in modifying adjectives though they usually take FSg concord in verbs (1962:157-8).

We may compare Harrell's description with data from a number of my texts involving a fairly cultivated MCA with a significant number of CA borrowings. In the texts surveyed I found 10 examples of plural agreement for nonhuman plural NPs, vs. 34 examples of feminine singular agreement. Some examples of the FSg type: /l-luġ-at l-ḥayy-a/ "living languages"; /d-i-k š-šhṛ-ayn/ "those two months"; /wq^{c}-ət waḥəd l-mašakil/ "problems developed"; /l-ši ?amakin lli fi-ha ġaṛ ṛ-ṛbi^{c}/ "to some places in which (lit. which in it) is nothing but grass"; /^{c}ənd-na ts^{c} šhuṛ k^{w}ll-ha ka-n-duwz-u-ha f-l-mḍṛaṣ-a/ "we have nine months all of which we spend (them) in the school". The feminine forms here are adjectival suffix /-a/ in l-ḥayy-a/ "living", distant demonstrative /d-i-k/ "that", /-ət/ perfective subject suffix in /wq^{c}-ət/ "it/she fell" (literal gloss), and /-ha/ oblique suffix (direct object, genitive, object of preposition) in the remaining examples. The examples involve true duals with suffix /-ayn/ and other numeral expressions. FSg agreement is also attested with code-switched Fr plural NPs, as in /d-i-k *les billes*/ "those marbles".

Usage of Pl, versus FSg, concord for inanimate plurals appears to be highly unstable, with younger educated speakers showing the greatest preference for the FSg. Moreover, while for a given speaker some NPs may take either pattern, there is a tendency visible even in the small textual corpus examined for Pl concord to apply to old MCA vocabulary not associated with cultivated style, while FSg agreement is most common with CA borrowings. There is also a suggestion that true duals and other numeral phrases are often treated as FSg (except regarding immediately following adjectives), as indicated by Harrell. Leaving the numeral phrases aside, we may mention that such common MCA nouns as /ḥwayž/ "things, clothes" and /l^c b-at/ "games" ordinarily have Pl agreement even among young educated speakers, while such borrowed forms as /?aflam/ "films" occur repeatedly with FSg agreement. The fact that 34 out of 44 instances in the texts surveyed showed FSg agreement reflects to a large extent the type of vocabulary present in those texts, and this percentage would not be likely to hold up in recordings of mundane domestic conversations in which fewer cultivated NPs occurred.

There are a few other details in which CA and MCA concord differs in detail (e.g. MCA generally merges masculine and feminine plural into a general plural category in concord for human referents). We omit discussion here, but remark that CA interference is less substantial in these areas than in the inanimate plural cases just discussed.

6 Adaptation of European borrowings

The mechanics of assimilating borrowings from Fr, Sp, and other European languages is more complex than it is for CA borrowings. Some European borrowings are more completely assimilated than others; some attested borrowings are much older than others and were produced by different diasystemic conversion processes than those now in productive usage; there are difficulties in determining which particular form (of an inflected paradigm) in the source language is to be the model; once a foot-in-the-door borrowed form has come into MCA it is still necessary to generate inflectional and derivational forms, and this is often problematic with borrowings since the canonical shapes of the initial borrowings are atypical by MCA standards; similar borrowings of Fr and Sp origin (and a few from other Romance languages) may combine over time, forming hybrids of composite origin; for all of these reasons there are often two or more variant forms for the same borrowed item.

In this chapter we attempt to clarify the basic principles at work in the assimilation of such foreign borrowings, and indicate where appropriate how these principles conflict with each other. We begin with relatively "simple" phonological regularities (though we will quickly see that they are complex and far from automatic), moving gradually into morphological structure.

Most of the raw material for this chapter is in Appendices B (verbs) and C (other word classes). Many of the generalizations made below will be illustrated by one or two examples spelled out, with an additional list of appendix entries with supportive data; thus B-100,121, C-65,455 would indicate that the appendix entries B-100, B-121, C-65 and C-455 contain additional examples of the point at issue. When an actual form is given, like /srba/ B-145 "he served", often only a single form is presented here while others (variants, inflected and/or derivational forms) may be given in the appendix entry. Those appendix entries listed by number with an asterisk * are cases where one or more (but not all) variants listed in the appendix entry are instances of the generalization; thus B-100,*121, C-65,*455 would indicate that B-100 and C-65 are clear cases of the generalization, while B-121 and C-455 contain some variants which satisfy it along with variants which do not. By using this system of cross-reference to appendices, we can keep this chapter reasonably brief and avoid cumbersome documentation of all points, while at the same time providing the serious analyst with a significant quantity of primary data.

6.1 Syllabic phonology: pharyngealization

Before presenting data on conversions involving single segments (vowels, consonants), it is advisable to begin with some remarks about pharyngealization ("emphasis"), which in MCA tends to be a syllabic phenomenon, at least in its phonetic realization.

As we have seen (§3.1), MCA has a set of pharyngealized coronal consonants of which /ṭ ḍ ṣ ẓ ṛ/ are the primary phonemic ones. Pharyngealization infects immediately preceding and following vowels, lowering /u i/ to surface [o e], and giving backed [ạ] as surface allophone of /a/ (which is otherwise phonetic [æ] in most nonfinal positions). The obvious problem for borrowing Fr/Sp forms is that the European languages lack a pharyngealization feature for coronal consonants but have vowel oppositions resembling the allophonic contrasts of MCA vowels; thus Sp has *e o a* resembling the three pharyngealized MCA allophones, and *i u* resembling plain (unpharyngealized) MCA /i u/ (word-final MCA /a/ is like Sp *a*). A specific problem is that MCA will allow phonetic [oṣo] and [usu], for example, but not *[osu] or *[uso] and so forth. In MCA, either the sibilant is or is not pharyngealized; if it is, both flanking vowels must be in pharyngealized allophones, and if it is not, neither flanking vowel can have such an allophone (we omit further complications involving longer stems with many syllables).

It is difficult to make any clear generalization as to how MCA borrowings treat such complex inputs as *osu* and *uso*. Indeed, even in the simpler cases where the Fr/Sp vocalism does match the vocalic allophones of a possible MCA word form, the predicted MCA form does not always result. As expected, in the most recent and least phonologically altered Fr borrowings used by bilinguals, there is maximal retention of Fr vowel qualities, so that some previously unacceptable MCA strings result — in which case it is necessary to recognize some instances of [ạ e o] and other vowels as new phonemes /ạ e o/, instead of merely as surface pharyngealized allophones. However, even excluding such examples, and focusing on stabilized borrowings adapted to MCA sequential norms, the diasystemic rules are partly unpredictable.

Let us look first at a few examples where the MCA surface vowels in assimilated borrowings do approximately match the source vocalism. From Sp *moda*, Fr *mode* we get /muḍ-a/ C-518 "fashions, mode", which is pronounced [moḍ-a]. This pronunciation is basically identical to that of Sp and is similar (except for the FSg suffix) to the Fr form. Similarly, /muṛṣu/ C-522 "piece" from Fr *morceau* is pronounced [moṛṣo] in MCA, coming fairly close to the source form (though the latter has a more open vowel in the initial syllable). In /ṃukiṭ/ C-519 "rug" from Fr *moquette*, the MCA pronunciation [ṃokeṭ] is again similar to that of Fr, though the MCA vowel allophones are again a little higher than those of Fr.

As far as our phonemic transcription is concerned, note that we specifically mark /ṃ/ with the pharyngealized diacritic where this is necessary to produce the attested pronunciation, as in /ṃukiṭ/, where /k/ cannot be pharyngealized for articulatory reasons; without a pharyngealized consonant in the first /CVC/ sequence we might get *[mukeṭ]. However, in /muḍ-a/ and /muṛṣu/ there is already a pharyngealized C in the initial /CVC/ sequence, and this is one of the primary pharyngealized consonants /ṭ ḍ ṣ ẓ ṛ/, so we simply mark the latter pharyngealized. There is no direct corroborating evidence that /m/ in /ṃukiṭ/ is phonemically pharyngealized while /m/ in /muḍ-a/ and /muṛṣu/ is not, since prefix allomorphs do not make this distinction clearly for nouns. (There is some indirect evidence, from play speech, that this is a complex matter involving native as well as borrowed stems and is best discussed in another publication; see now Heath (1987), chapter 8.)

In a considerable number of examples, a borrowed form alters the source vocalism, adopting unmarked (unpharyngealized) MCA pronunciation. In the case of /nibru/ C-530 "wrapping paper for cigarettes" from Sp *libro* "book", we might have gotten */nibṛu/, pronounced *[nibṛo], or /libṛu/ [libṛo] (attested in the north), with acceptable MCA sequences reproducing the source vocalism. However, the usual MCA form is just /nibru/, phonetic [nibru]. In the case of /munik-a/ C-521 "doll" from Sp *muñeca*, an MCA pronunciation *[munek-a] or the like matching source vocalism would have violated MCA norms; the [e] allophone of /i/ requires an adjoining pharyngealized consonant, but /k/ has no pharyngealized counterpart, and if the /n/ were pharyngealized it would have to lower the preceding /u/ to [o] allophone. It would seem that MCA had to choose between [munik-a] (plain) and [moṇek-a] (pharyngealized), neither closely matching the Sp prototype, and that the choice of [munik-a] was either arbitrary, or favoured by marginal markedness considerations.

There are a great many examples of a similar nature where a mid vowel in Fr or Sp has been replaced in the borrowed MCA form by high vowel [u] or [i] (that is, by /u/ or /i/ phoneme, with no neighbouring pharyngealized consonant). A few examples of *o* or *ɔ* becoming MCA [u] are B-19, 27, *46, 69, 90, and C-10, 87, 128, 129, 132, 137, 138, 141, 142, *144. Some examples of *e* or *ɛ* becoming [i] are B-33, 99, 105, *112, *113, 127, 128, 170, and C-1, *77, 78, 81, 84, *90, 94, 100, *109, 137, 138, 142, 148, 166.

On the other hand, there are also a great many cases where the Fr/Sp mid vowel shows up in MCA as a pharyngealized mid allophone of /i/ or /u/; we have exemplified this above with /muḍ-a/ and so forth, and it is not necessary to give a list of the many examples in appendices. However, there are also a number of cases of what is apparently an unmotivated pharyngealization in an MCA borrowing so that Fr/Sp *i* or *u* (phonetic [u] in the latter case, not Fr orthographic "u") shows up in MCA as surface [e] or [o] with a neighbouring pharyngealized consonant. Let us look at these now.

For *i* becoming [e] in MCA, we start with /aṛbiṭ/ C-18, phonetic [aṛbeṭ] from Sp *árbitro*, Fr *arbitre*. A form */aṛbit/, pronounced *[aṛbit], would more closely have matched source vocalism. Perhaps pharyngealization of *t* to /ṭ/ was favoured by the presence of pharyngealized /ṛ/ in the same word (though this is by no means a regular phonological rule), and/or by the fact that MCA /ṭ/ lacks the conspicuous assibilated release of MCA /t/ [t^s], and is thus sometimes the direct segmental reflex of Fr/Sp *t* (which has no corresponding release). In /bṣṭil-a/ C-122 "pastilla (baked dish)" from Fr *pastilla* (Sp *pastilla*), perhaps the /ṣ/ was the first consonant pharyngealized, inducing the adjacent *t* to become pharyngealized as well. In /ṣigaṛ/ variant of /sigaṛ/ C-637 "cigar" (Fr *cigare*), pharyngealized /ṛ/ in the second syllable may have favoured the variant with /ṣ/, though the existence of the other variant shows that this is far from automatic. In the uncommon variant /ṣṭilu/ of /stilu/ C-660 "ballpoint pen" (Fr *stilo*), there is no obvious external source for pharyngealization; once again we may have had Fr *t* directly becoming MCA /ṭ/ to avoid the assibilated release of MCA /t/. (Fr/Sp *t* can also become unreleased [t], a new MCA phoneme; see §6.7.)

The number of cases of Fr/Sp phonetic [u] becoming pharyngealized [o] in MCA is considerably greater: C-133, *145, 146, *149, *150, 190, 246, 392, 415, 423, 612, 620, 704, 705. It appears that there are two distinct principled explanations for this. First, in some cases an apparent borrowing from Fr [u] may really involve a hybrid formation in which a Sp or It cognate with *o* plays a role. Thus /buṛṣ/ [boṛṣ] variant of /burs/ C-145 "scholarship stipend", ostensibly from Fr *bourse*, could perhaps be reanalysed as a recently partly Gallicized form based on an earlier borrowing from Sp *bolsa*. I have hinted at similar explanations for a few of the other cases just listed by appendix number.

However, I believe that in many of these cases what we really have is a tendency for Fr/Sp *r* to become MCA /ṛ/ next to tautosyllabic /u/ (or /a/), with the subsequent automatic lowering of the /u/ to [o]. This effect of /u/ on /ṛ/ is very clear in CA borrowings (§5.4). It is not so clear in European borrowings, but does seem to be in operation as a sporadic tendency, and it is noteworthy that an /ṛ/ is present in a large percentage of the fourteen items just listed. For example, /ṛubyu/ C-612 "blond" (Sp *rubio*) and /ṛutin/ C-620 "routine" (Fr *routine*) seem to have no other explanation for pharyngealization of /ṛ/, and hence of [o] allophone for /u/.

To sum up, MCA has implicational relationships among segments in surface strings (representable analytically as a plain/pharyngealized consonantal opposition, with allophonic consequences for adjacent vowels). They are factors in the treatment of borrowings, but do not work in a particularly simple or automatic fashion.

6.2 Vocalic conversions: oral vowels

Some aspects of borrowing conversions for vowels have been dealt with in the preceding section. Here we give a more complete description of how the various Fr and Sp vowels are treated.

The regular treatment of Fr/Sp back rounded vowels, phonetic [u o ɔ], is MCA /u/ (phonetic [u] or [o] depending on context). A number of examples involving Fr/Sp [u] were given above and many others could be cited were this necessary. Some examples of Fr/Sp [o] or [ɔ] becoming MCA /u/ are /brikula/ B-19 "he improvised" (Fr *bricoler* with [ɔ]), also B-27, *46, 69, 90 and C-10, 87, 105, 128, 129, 132, 137, 138, 141, 142, *144 and many others. In a few cases, however, we get an MCA form (not fully assimilated) with phonemic (not merely phonetic) /o/ or /ɔ/, at least in variants recorded from my informants. For /o/ see /koki/ C-364 "shellfish" (Fr *coquille*), also C-365, 366, 456, *495, *723. For /ɔ/ see /šwiŋgɔm/ variant of C-718 "chewing gum" (Eng via Fr *chewing-gum* [šwiŋgɔm]), also C-227, *284, *513.

The regular treatment of Fr/Sp [i e ɛ] is, of course, MCA /i/ (allophones [i] and [e] depending on context). This treatment of Fr/Sp [i] is unremarkable and the examples given in transcription in the preceding paragraph reveal this. Some instances of Fr/Sp [e ɛ] becoming MCA /i/, sometimes but not always with neighbouring pharyngealized C to guarantee [e] allophone in MCA, are /dimirda/ B-33 "he acted by himself" (Fr *démerder*), also B-99, 105, *112, *113, 127, 128, 170 and C-1, *77, 78, 81, 84, *90, 94, 100, *109, 137, 138, 142, 148, 166 and many others. However, Fr [ɛ] (orthographic è, or *e* before consonant cluster) does become MCA /a/ (in unpharyngealized form [æ]) in a few words. Those known to me are: /byas-a/ C-162 "spare part" (Fr *pièce*), /ban/ C-45 "dump-truck" (Fr *benne*), /syas/ or /syast/ C-665 "siesta" (Fr *sieste*, more likely than Sp *siesta*), and /siran/ C-647 "siren" (Fr *sirène* more likely than Sp *sirena*); these seem to me to be basically recent Fr loans, except that /byas-a/ may be fairly old and may possibly have a more complex history. There are some other apparent examples of MCA /a/ from Fr/Sp [e ɛ], but they are dubious because they involve analogy with a pre-existing stem-shape (like agentive /CCCaC/), possible contamination with a semantically similar form, or an uncertain etymology: C-163 (/CCCaC/), C-368 (contamination), C-462 (trisyllable with possible irregular "harmony" affecting first syllable), C-472 (probably based on Eng, not Fr/Sp), C-490 (false example if Sp is correct source).

Clearly, then, /i/ is the usual reflection of Fr/Sp [i e ɛ], with /a/ allowed as an occasional reflex of Fr [ɛ], after interfering factors are removed from consideration. However, as we would expect, in some of the half-assimilated borrowings used mostly by bilinguals, [e ɛ] are retained and must be set up as phonemes since they are not predictable as allophones of regular MCA vowel phonemes: /e/ occurs in C-*168, *307, 381, 456, while /ɛ/ is found in C-221, *428. There are a couple of examples of MCA diphthong /ay/ representing either long monosyllabic [e:] in the source (C-529, from German) or [ey] (variant for C-605). An irregular form /ilyan/ "it's there!" (exclamation after goal is scored) shows /a/ with extra nasal, perhaps as a device to differentiate this from /ilyi/ C-294 "wing (player in soccer)" (Fr *ailier*), and/or due to phonetic distortion of the input form due to exclamatory nature.

Fr/Sp [a] is normally realized in borrowings as /a/. The most common pronunciation of the Fr/Sp phonemes is close to the MCA pharyngealized allophone [ạ], and in many borrowings a neighbouring consonant is pharyngealized to retain this as the MCA allophone. (This is less of a factor when the /a/ is the word-final segment in the borrowing, since here unpharyngealized /a/ is also somewhat backed, and it is less distinct from the pharyngealized allophone than in medial position.) There are also many borrowings in which Fr/Sp [a] appears as MCA /a/ with no pharyngealization, hence (except finally) in the allophone [æ]. A few examples of this allophone are /gažạ/ B-63 "he enlisted" (Fr *s'engager*), /ankul/ or /alkul/ C-10 "alcohol" (Sp *alcohol*, Fr *alcool*), also C-*20, 21, *28, 33, 37, 42, 46, 61, *66, *77, 81, *95, *98, 107, 108, 112, 137, 159, 197, and many others. In some borrowings the pharyngealized articulation [ạ] appears, though no neighbouring phoneme can be considered pharyngealized, so phoneme /ạ/ must be recognized: /uṛgạniza/ B-2 "he organized", also B-130, 166 and C-*3, *20, *25, *95, *115, *208, 337, 338, *339, *342, *344, 345, 372, 433, 464, 481, *811, and many others. Note that several of these numbers occur with asterisks and are in both lists, indicating considerable fluctuation between [æ] and [ạ] in borrowings. There is no well-established [æ] phoneme (that is, in an environment where the regular /a/ phoneme would have a backed allophone), but perhaps a marginal example occurs in [læm-æ] "hand-ball" C-436 (soccer infraction), where the second [æ] is unusual in that it occurs in word-final position. However, this is not a well-integrated borrowing.

Front rounded vowels [ü ö] are a problem in borrowings, since the MCA dialects studied do not have similar phonetic entities. In the case of Fr [ö] (orthographic *eu*), the common output is MCA /u/ (usually with no pharyngealized consonant nearby), though /ö/ is retained as a new phoneme for recent Fr borrowings, in certain words, in the speech mainly of bilinguals. Fluctuation between /u/ and /ö/ occurs in C-101, 117, 218, 361, 413, 433, 614; we have /ö/ in C-175, 610, 819; and we have /u/ in B-13, C-80, 129, 147, 277, 563, 652, 662, 735 (if from Fr), 795, 826. There is one possible case of /i/, namely /firuž/ variant of C-218 "stoplight" (Fr *feu rouge*), but it is hard to know what to make of this and it may be an irregular case of vowel dissimilation. There is also one case of Fr [öy] becoming MCA /i/, namely /f̣uti/ variant of C-251 "armchair" (Fr *fauteuil*).

The regular treatment of [ö] is therefore /u/ in the better-assimilated stems. It is conceivable that this was favoured by secondary association of Fr words like *inspecteur* with older carry-over borrowings based on Sp words like *inspector*, where o would have become MCA /u/ regularly. However, /u/ is a reasonable conversion of [ö] anyway, and the forms cited based on Fr ending *-eur* (feminine *-euse*) do not show clear Sp traits (like pharyngealization of /ṛ/ in the MCA form of this suffix because of the o-vowel in Sp *-or*).

The treatment of Fr [ü] (orthographic *u*) is more irregular. In the less well-assimilated cases we can get /ü/, which of course represents a new phoneme restricted to such borrowings: B-3, 102, *172, and C-96, 523, 573, 674, *730. However, the most common borrowed form is with /i/, as in /biru/ C-87 "office" (Fr *bureau*, not Sp *buró*), also B-*172, C-78, *85, 91, 143 (unless metathesized), 533, 552, 649, *730, 733, *737, 771, *778. On the other hand, there are some examples with MCA /u/, and while it may be possible to analyse some of these as really based on Sp [u] rather than cognate Fr [ü], this is not possible for all of the forms: /sura/ B-150 "he insured" (Fr *assurer*, contrast B-149 /sugr/ from Sp), also C-23 (Fr), 24 (Fr), 143 (only if metathesized), 197 (Fr or Sp possible), 209 (Sp likely), 419 (Fr), 628 (possible Fr/Sp cross), 662 (possible contamination of two distinct Fr words), *737 (also variant with /i/), 822,3 (Fr, though Algerian variant has /i/). There is one case of semivowel /w/, namely /wzin/ C-801 "factory" (Fr *usine*), where stem-initial position favours (partial) desyllabification. It is difficult to identify a clear pattern in the treatment of Fr [ü] from this set of data, and it is possible that some of the variation reflects Fr dialectal differences (i.e. some of the older loans might have /u/ while more recent ones, based on the clearly high front rounded Parisian [ü], might tend to become /i/).

Fr [ə] (orthographic *e*) is most often borrowed as /u/, though we should immediately point out that Fr FSg ending *-e*, which is normally "silent" in modern spoken Fr, is not involved here. Examples are /rutira/ B-136 "he took out" (*retirer*), /dublsumil/ C-176 "walking (basketball infraction)" (*double semelle*), /galuri/ C-255 "spectator gallery" (*galerie*), /kruvi/ C-377 "flat tire" (*crevé*), /ṛupp-a/C-617 "meal (in hotel)" (*repas*), /ṛuppu/C-618 "rest time" (*repos*), /ṛuṣul/ or /ṛusul/ C-619 "spring (metal)" (*ressort*), /ṛuṭaṛ/ C-621 "late (for work)" (*en retard*). From *tournevis*, where the *e* is weakly pronounced, we get /tuṛnuvis/ C-746 "screwdriver" as one variant. The fact that /u/ is the common MCA borrowed form suggests that [ə] is not clearly distinguished by Moroccans from Fr [ö], except that the former is more likely to be dropped. (We discuss omission of Fr/Sp vowels in 6.4, below.)

A possible example of /i/ from Fr [ə] occurs in verb /t-liva/ B-95 "it (ball) hooked" and related noun /livi/ C-449 "hooking shot", if these are from *(se) lever* and (participle) *levé* ("to get up" and "lifted", respectively), but this etymology is doubtful for semantic as well as phonological reasons. In C-640, the F variant /siman-a/ in particular is now associated with Fr *semaine* "week", but as the other forms show Sp *semana* is historically the primary source with perhaps some later reshaping under Fr influence, so there is no simple historical equation of Fr [ə] with MCA /i/ here.

6.3 Vocalic conversions: nasal vowels

Traditional MCA has no phonemic nasalized vowels, and no common surface-phonetic nasalized vowel allophones. There are therefore several options in dealing with Fr nasalized vowels [æ̃] (written *in*, *im*, etc.), [ã] (*an*, *am*, *en*, *em*), and [õ] (*on*, *om*). (We disregard Fr *un*, which does not occur in any known source for an MCA borrowing.) Basically, the options are these: (a) retain the Fr pronunciation, thus introducing yet another set of new phonemes restricted to borrowings; (b) convert the Fr nasal vowel to an MCA oral vowel; and (c) expand the nasal vowel as a sequence of MCA vowel plus nasal consonant. All three types are found.

There is, however, an important asymmetry between the three Fr nasal vowels, reflecting a natural tendency for vocalic nasalization to be most common with low back vowels. Fr [ã] is commonly retained in MCA borrowings, where it will be written /ạ̃/, indicating that it is phonetically a nasalized low back (not low front) vowel; that is, it does not have a fronted (low front) allophone in unpharyngealized environments, rather it is always low back.

Fr [ã] can have other realizations, as oral vowel /a/ or as sequence /an/, /aṇ/, /am/, or the like (with /m/ before labial). However, /ạ̃/ is the most common realization (in terms of number of lexical items, not text frequency) in my data. With Fr [õ], there are a fair number of realizations as /õ/ (or /ɔ̃/ or /ạ̃/), but the number of such lexical items is less than that for either of the other major outputs, /u/ and /un/ (or similar sequence). Moreover, for Fr [æ̃], the output /an/ (or /am/, etc.) in unpharyngealized environment (hence phonetic [æn] etc.) is overwhelmingly the favoured output, with the other types very marginal.

We begin by exemplifying Fr [ã]. We get MCA /ạ̃/ in /bṛạ̃ša/ B-16 "he branched off" (contrast /bṛašm-a/ C-106 "intersection", an earlier loan without nasalization in MCA; the sources are Fr *brancher* and *branchement*), /ḍạ̃tifris/ C-181 "toothpaste" (*dentifrice*), also B-38, 44, *98, 111, 117, 126, 163, 179, 180, and C-*13, 26, 31, 32, *195, *260, 296, *318, *333, *382, *405, *411, 501, *588, 631, *667, 668, *677, 678, 695, 696, *702, 765, 767, 768, 769. (note that many of these are asterisked, indicating that there is considerable variation in the acceptability of the nasalized vowel.)

Fr [ã] becomes oral /a/ in /bṛašm-a/ C-106 "intersection", just cited, and in B-*85, C-207 (root syllable), *588, 810. There are also a number of cases, mostly involving Fr ending *-ment*, where the MCA borrowing is reanalysed as ending in FSg /-a/, which usually (but not always) results in denasalization of the vowel by analogy to the regular non-nasal forms of this suffix: /kṛwaẓm-a/ C-380 "intersection" (*croisement*), also C-379, *382, *405, 443, 639.

An example of the output /an/ word-finally, without pharyngealization, is /kliyan/ C-360 "client" (Fr *client*); the other similar example that I know of is /saṛžan/ C-630 "sergeant" (*sergent*). Here absence of pharyngealization may be characteristic of word-final position or may have been influenced by the nature of the preceding consonants /y/ and /ž/. In general, though, the output /aN/ with some nasal consonant for Fr [ã] occurs before another consonant (to which /N/ is homorganic) and the syllable is pharyngealized. Thus /kuṃanḍa/ B-84 "he bossed around" (Fr *commander*), /tṛaŋkil/ variant of C-765 "alone, unbothered" (*tranquille*), /šạmbwan/ variant of C-702 "shampoo" (Fr *shampooing*); see also B-*85, *98, 160; C-8, 23, 183, *195, *260, 398, *411, *667, *677, possibly *766.

Occasionally I have recorded /õ/ or /ɔ̃/ for Fr [ã], perhaps reflecting some difficulty on the part of Moroccans in discriminating Fr [ã] and [õ]. The examples of /õ/ are C-*318, 537; the examples of /ɔ̃/ are B-77, C-*318, *333.

There is no simple phonological rule for determining what the MCA output from Fr [ã] is. It would seem that oral /a/ is not typical of newer borrowings which have not been reshaped later. For the main bulk of Fr source forms, it is likely that a complete dialectological study would show that most such items have variant pronunciations with bilinguals tending to prefer /ã/ and monolinguals to prefer /aN/, but with considerable lexical variation.

Fr [õ] is recorded as MCA nasalized /õ/ in /t-bṛõza/ B-22 "he got a suntan", see also B-54, 114, 118, C-363, *399, *404, *407,

*410, 547, *724. Note that many of these have other variants recorded. Variant /ɔ̃/ was recorded in C-227, 609. There is a possible variant /aN/ in B-185 if the etymology given there is correct (further evidence for confusion among the various Fr nasal vowels); a possible case of /o/ is C-203 but again there is an etymological problem; a better case for this latter output is C-43 /baḷko/ "balcony", but it is possible that this is a crossing of Sp *balcón* with Fr *balcon*.

Another output from [õ] which is at least as common as any of the preceding is just /u/: /gufl/ B-68 "he inflated" (*gonfler*), /bidu/ C-75 "canister" (*bidon*), also C-194, 268, *313, 347, 349, 359, 389, 390, (perhaps) 427, 485, 649, *675, *688, 756. Several of these are early, well-established borrowings.

An equally common borrowed form of Fr [õ] is /uN/ with some nasal consonant (/n/ word-finally, otherwise homorganic to following consonant): /bṛmsyun/ C-111 "military leave" (*permission*), also C-136, 152, 153, 157 (unless from Sp), 158 (same remark), 270, *383 (if from Fr), 331 (if from Fr), 355, 399, *404, 405, *407, 408, 409, *410, 411, 412, 413, *675, *688, *724, 729. It is possible, though present evidence is not very strong, that Sp/Fr cognates with Sp [on] and Fr [õ] (orthographic *on* in both cases, cf. Sp *permisión* "permission, leave") may be involved in establishing /un/ as the word-final MCA output from Fr [õ]. I am hesitant about this idea here, since /u/ instead of /uN/ occurs in some of the earliest Fr borrowings involving Fr [õ], and since Fr/Sp mixing should have peaked during this early period.

It should also be noted that some confusion may be occurring due to the occurrence of doublets with final /u/ vs. /un/ (like /ṣaḷu/ and /ṣaḷun/ C-675 "guest salon"), and that some borrowings which ought to end simply in /u/ are now analogically developing variants with /un/, thus /ṛaḍyun/ as a variant of /ṛadyu/ C-589 "radio" (Fr and Sp *radio*). Other stems ending in /u/ have Pl allomorphs in /-nat/ for expected /-wat/ or /-yat/ (with basically epenthetic /w/, /y/).

Turning now to Fr low front nasal vowel [æ̃] (written *in*, *im*), we have (unpharyngealized) /an/ or /am/ (before labial) as the regular outputs: /fanta/ B-48 "he dodged, faked" and noun /fant/ or /fant-a/ C-201 "(a) fake" (Fr *feinte* "(a) fake"), /kwansa/ B-94 "he collided with" (*coincer*), /tambr/ variant of C-734 "postage stamp" (*timbre*), also B-121, 142, 155, C-11, *13, 14, 15, 16, *25, 49, 50, 100, 127, 228, 663, *702, 715, 728, *736, 743. Note that most of these are quite stable.

There are some other attested outputs, none common. One variant of the poorly assimilated form in C-25 has /æ̃/ as in Fr; in C-436 I hear the final vowel as /æ/, which would have to be set up as a marginal phoneme; in C-702 we can get final /æ̃/ or /aṇ/, where pharyngealization in the latter variant is probably induced by the preceding labial cluster; in C-827 and 828 we find final /a/ vs. /an/ from the same Fr source in two different meanings; /a/ is also found in the old loan C-441 and, as FSg suffix /-a/, in C-461 /magaz-a/ "store" (Fr *magasin*).

To summarize, retention of a French-like nasal vowel (instead of a denasalized oral vowel or a vowel-nasal sequence) is most common with Fr [ã] and least common with Fr [æ̃], with [o] intermediate.

There is an interesting piece of evidence bearing on the synchronic structural status of nasalized vowels. Although examples are hard to come by, I have recorded a handful of diminutive (Dimin) forms involving the change of a stem vowel to /i/. Thus from /ṭulạ̃ṭi/ C-779 "clever, smart aleck" we get /ṭwiliṇṭi/. The important point is that /ạ/ in the normal form becomes /iṇ/. Thus suggests, though it does not prove, that nasal vowels like /ạ̃/ can be analysed conceptually by MCA speakers as equivalent in some fashion to vowel-nasal sequences, or at least that they can be "resolved" into such sequences in environments where a nasal vowel cannot occur.

6.4 Truncation, cluster simplification, and desyllabification

In this section we discuss a number of distinct ways in which Fr/Sp borrowings are reduced through the loss of segments or reduction in the syllabicity of segments. It should immediately be indicated that most such reductions are, at least in part, motivated by MCA canonical-shape norms rather than by simple phonological diasystemic conversion rules.

To begin with, we observe a significant tendency to drop Fr/Sp vowels in the first and sometimes also second syllable, resulting in an MCA pattern with several initial consonants followed by one full vowel (usually itself followed by a final consonant). This is perhaps particularly common when the Fr/Sp source form has a consonant cluster between the first and second vowels, but can occur even when there is just one consonant here. This type of reduction is characteristic of word classes other than verbs, hence mainly nouns. The reduction is very common in the earlier borrowings, including some quite old, precolonial borrowings from Sp. Appendix C has many examples of which the following will suffice here: /bḷḷuṭ/ C-103 "acorns" (Sp *bellota* or similar Romance form), /blyun/ C-105 "an old coin" (Sp *vellón*), /brgad-i/ C-107 "brigadier" (contrast /brigad/ C-108 "brigade", more recent loan), /brmil/ C-110 "barrel" (Sp *bermil*), /bṛmsyun/ C-111 "military leave" (Fr *permission*), /bṛṭal/ C-113 "small bird" (Sp *pardal*), /bṛwiṭ-a/ C-118 "wheelbarrow" (Fr *brouette*), /ḍbḷun/ C-182 "doubloon" (Sp *doblón*), /fṇaṛ/ C-225 "flashlight, torch" (Sp *fanal*), /qbṭan/ C-583 "(military) captain" (Fr *capitaine*), /srdin/ C-658 "sardine(s)" (Sp *sardina* or similar source), /ṣblyun/ C-683 "Spaniards" (Sp *español*, Fr *espagnol*), /ṭnbuṛ/ C-763 "drum" (Sp *tambor*, Fr *tambour*), /šḷaḍ-a/ C-712 alongside variant /šaḷaḍ-a/ "salad" (Sp *ensalada*). Some examples appear to involve relatively modern Fr borrowings, showing that this type of initial-syllable reduction is still operative, though more weakly than before: /srtifik-a/ C-659 "certificate" (Fr *certificat*). In those cases where the vowel lost is Fr [ə], it is not clear whether these are parallel to the examples above (involving clearly articulated Fr/Sp vowels), or whether [ə] is simply perceived as a weak vowel particularly highly vulnerable to deletion: /rmiz/ C-607 "rebate, discount" (Fr *remise*), see also C-571, 608, 715, *746, 785, etc.

Similar loss of Fr/Sp vowel near the end of a borrowed word is rare. We may perhaps cite /nikl/ C-532 "money; cash" (Fr *nickel*, Sp *níquel*), where perhaps the Sp penultimate stress is a factor. With verb stems, on the other hand, /CVCəC/ or /CVCC/ is a popular shape in MCA and several borrowings adopt this form, sometimes through vowel reduction, as in /t-fubṛ/ B-57 "he gave tip", denominative from /faḅuṛ/ C-193 (Sp *favor*). These verb forms clearly involve morphological restructuring, as is shown by their co-occurrence with earlier nominal borrowings like /faḅuṛ/.

Another very important type of loss of segments from the source form is truncation, by which I mean (here) the lopping off of syllables. The usual context for this is that the Fr/Sp source form begins with a vowel which is lopped off in the borrowing (sometimes with a following tautosyllabic consonant). In the case of recent borrowings, especially among bilinguals, this truncation is usually not applied, and there are some doublet forms where the longer type is most often used by bilinguals.

In the case of verbal borrowings based directly on a Fr verb, either the initial syllable is dropped, or the initial vowel of the Fr/Sp stem is "protected" by the addition of glottal stop /?/ in the borrowing. Thus /ṣṭala/ or ?anṣṭala/ (pronounced [?ænṣṭạla]) "he installed" B-155 (Fr *installer*), see also B-4, 126, 176. In two poorly assimilated verbs used sporadically by bilinguals, B-2 and B-3, only the form with initial /?/ is attested.

For non-verb words, retention of the Fr/Sp initial vowel is a little more common on the whole, and /?/ is not usually added (except sometimes as a low-level insertion in absolute word-initial position). However, some cases of initial truncation do occur: /trisinti/ C-742 "electricity" (Fr *électricité*), /trisyan/ C-743 "electrician" (Fr *électricien*), /frmli/ C-241 "male nurse" (Fr *infirmier*), /bṛṭm-a/ C-114 "apartment" (Fr *appartement*).

There are also a few cases of syllable truncation with stems whose Fr/Sp form begins with a consonant, so the truncation is motivated not by a problem in handling stem-initial vowels (a local phonological problem), rather by the more general, word-level tendency to avoid long, multisyllabic stems which do not fit into traditional MCA patterns. Hence /t-frma/ B-56 "it became worn out" (old loan from Fr *réformer* in military context), /muṇaḍ-a/ C-520 (Sp *limonada*, cf. /limuṇaḍ/ C-445 from Fr *limonade*, a more recent loan).

In one or two cases, what appears on the surface to be a simple case of syllable truncation may, historically, have involved vowel deletion with subsequent consonant cluster reduction. Thus /ẓin-a/ C-806 "dozen" (Sp *docena*, Fr *douzaine*) has variants like /ṭ^ẓẓin-a/ and /t^{w}ẓẓin-a/, suggesting that the *ṭ (or *t) may have fused with the /ẓẓ/ into a consonant cluster in which the stop was difficult to hear and was finally dropped to produce /ẓin-a/.

In general, consonant clusters are retained in borrowings, but some reductions occur, principally in stem-final positions. Thus /aṛaf/ C-17 "police van" (Fr *(la) rafle* "police round-up"), /turis/ or /turist/ C-744 "tourist" (Fr *touriste*), /aṛbiṭ/ C-18 "referee" (Fr *arbitre*), /kiluṃiṭ/ or /kiluṃiṭṛ/ C-353 "kilometre" (Fr *kilomètre*), /kuṇṭak/ or /kuṇṭakt/ C-409 "(car) ignition)" (Fr *contact*, with *t* not always pronounced), see also C-631, 665, 721. In general, these simplifications involve loss of consonants which (in this position) are difficult to perceive and are probably not always pronounced clearly by native Fr speakers.

Some examples showing retention of a variety of types of

consonant cluster in various positions: /aṃaṛš/ C-7 "in motion", /anṭṛinm-a/ C-16 "training", /dyaṃanḍ/ C-178 "diamond", /biškliṭ/ C-90 "bicycle", /skwil-a/ C-654 "school", /buṛṭfuy/ C-147 "wallet".

The final point for this section is the occasional desyllabification of a Fr/Sp vowel. The two examples I have are /wzin/ C-801 "factory" (Fr *usine*) and /yṭṛu/ variant of C-298 "litre" (Sp *litro*, resegmented). In both cases, the semivowel is in a structural position where it must be pronounced as a "half-syllabic" surface allophone; they sound a little bit like full vowels /u/ or /i/ but are not fully syllabic, are clearly less stressed than a full vowel would be, and (in the case of /yṭṛu/) do not show allophonic variations in vowel quality (here vowel height) characteristic of full vowels (a representation */iṭṛu/ would be pronounced with /i/ becoming [e], due to a pharyngealized environment, but in fact /yṭṛu/ does not show this).

6.5 Nasals and liquids

We now consider the treatment of consonants in Fr/Sp borrowings, beginning with nasals and liquids. As it happens, these consonants are highly unpredictable, with a significant number of unpredictable and apparently random interchanges among /l/, /r/, and /n/ (and their pharyngealized counterparts).

Since MCA has /l r ṛ n m/ as basic native phonemes, all with considerable freedom of distributional occurrence, we would expect that Fr/Sp *l r n m* would regularly be borrowed as MCA /l r n m/, with /ḷ ṛ ṇ ṃ/ as possible variants when the Fr/Sp prototype contains vowels such as [e o], like the pharyngealized allophones of MCA full vowels. Not surprisingly, this prediction is borne out statistically. We will give a few examples of the regular outputs before turning to exceptions.

Some examples of MCA /l/ or /ḷ/ for Fr/Sp *l* are /blisa/ B-12 "he wounded", /bḷuka/ B-14 "he blocked (shot)", /ḅal-a/ or /baḷ-a/ C-40 "shovel" from Fr *blesser*, *bloquer*, and Sp *pala* (Fr *pelle*). Examples of MCA /r/ or /ṛ/ from Fr/Sp *r* are /briya/ B-20 "it shone" (Fr *briller*), /baṛa/ B-5 "he blocked off" (Fr *barrer*), and /adris-a/ C-1 "address" (Fr *adresse*).

Examples of /n/ or /ṇ/ from Fr/Sp *n* are /t-nirva/ B-105 "he was worried" (Fr *nerveux* and/or *énervé*), /t-ṇuma/ B-106 "he was appointed" (Fr *nommer*), /nuṭa/ B-108 "he took notes". Examples of /m/ or /ṃ/ from Fr/Sp *m* are /maṛka/ B-97 "he scored (goal)" (Fr *marquer*, Sp *marcar*), /kuṃanḍa/ B-84 "he bossed around" (Fr *commander*), /aṃaṛš/ C-7 "in motion" (Fr *en marche*). All of these correspondences have dozens of additional examples scattered through appendices B and C.

Except for /m/, however, there are a significant number of cases of interchange between /n l r/ (or pharyngealized counterparts). There are a small number of cases where we simply have a metathesis involving two of these segments changing places within the same stem; we disregard such cases here but present them in 6.12. The remaining cases appear to involve simple segmental replacements. The largest number of these irregular replacements involve Fr/Sp *l*, but there are also a few involving Fr/Sp *n* and *r*.

The following are the attested examples of Fr/Sp *l* becoming /n/

or /ṇ/: /ankul/ C-10 (more common than variant /alkul/) "alcohol" (Fr *alcool*, Sp *alcohol*), /fsyan/ C-245 "military officer" (if from Sp *oficial*), /fuṇaṛ-a/ variant of /fuḷaṛ-a/ C-246 "kerchief" (Fr *foulard*), /kabṛan/ C-305 "corporal" (Fr and Sp *caporal*), /kaṣṛun-a/ or /kaṣṛuṇ-a/ C-336 "cooking pot" (Fr *casserole*), /kʷṇiniṛ/ and variants C-362 "colonel" (Fr *colonel*, Sp *coronel*), possibly /niṛ-a/ variant of /liṛ-a/ C-447 "type of flute" (related to It *lira*, etc.), /minitir/ variant of /militir/ C-502 "soldier" (Fr *militaire*), /mnyaṛ/ variant of /mlyaṛ/ C-509 "billion", /nibru/ C-530 "cigarette wrapping paper" (Sp *libro* "book"), /šan/ alongside /šal/ C-700 "shawl" (Fr *châle*, Sp *chal* but possibly involving contamination), /ṭiṇifizyu/ variant of C-724 "television" (Fr *télévision*), /žuṛnan/ variant of /žuṛṇal/ C-824 "newspaper" (Fr *journal*). One can try out various local "explanations" for individual cases, but none works for all of them. The most promising explanation is that *l* often becomes /n/ or /ṇ/ in words also containing /r/ or /ṛ/. (It is not the case that native MCA roots may not have /l ḷ/ and /r ṛ/ together: /ṛml-a/ "sand", /lxxr/ or /lxxṛ/ "last", /lṛḍ/ "earth". It is true, though, that this is a less favoured combination.)

Examples of MCA /r/ or /ṛ/ for Fr/Sp *l* are these: /bakaṛuṛiya-a/ variant of /ḅakaḷuṛiya/ C-36 "baccalaureat diploma" (Fr *baccalauréat*), cf. metathesized variant /ḅakaṛuḷiy-a/, /biḍaṛ-a/ C-77 "pedal" (Fr *pédale*, Sp *pedal*) along with other variants, /fnaṛ/ C-225 "flashlight, torch" (Sp *fanal*), /kriru/ along with /kliru/ C-359 "in a single gulp" (Fr *clairon*), /manifir/ C-467 "crank" (Fr *manivelle*), /ṣbiṭaṛ/ C-682 "hospital" (It *spedale*, etc.), /ṭiṛifun/ variant of C-723 "téléphone" (Fr *téléphone*), /ṭiṛigṛam/ variant of C-760 "telegram" (Fr *télégramme*), /ṭṛibiṇaṛ/ C-771 "tribunal" (Fr *tribunal*), /nutir/ and /nuṭiṛ/ variants of /util/ C-784 "hotel" (Fr *hôtel*). It is difficult to find a clear pattern to these forms; the presence of a distinct /n/ or /ṇ/ might be a factor (at least in the choice of /r/ or /ṛ/ instead of /n/ or /ṇ/), but in the preceding paragraph we have examples inconsistent with this.

We now consider irregular reflexes of Fr/Sp *n*. We find /l/ as a variant in two cases: /kaṛabil/ alongside /kaṛabin/ C-321 "small rifle" (Fr *carabine*), /silim-a/ and /sulim-a/ as uncommon variants of /sinim-a/ C-643 "cinema" (Fr *cinéma*). On the other hand, we find /ṛ/ in /anṭiṛ/ C-13 "antenna" (Fr *antenne*) and /kuṃanḍaṛ/ C-398 "(army) major" (Fr *commandant*); both of these involve word-final Fr/Sp *n* in a word with another nasal. There is one case of irregular addition of /n/, namely /trisinti/ C-742 "electricity" (Fr *électricité*).

Borrowings based on Fr/Sp [ŋk] and [ŋg] clusters, with nasal phoneme /n/ assimilated to following velar, differ as to whether the homorganic articulation is retained. We find borrowed /ŋg ŋk/ in /žaŋgla/ B-185 "he zigzagged' (apparently Fr *jongler*), /ḅaŋk/ and /ḅaŋk-a/ variants of C-48 "bank", variant /iŋgliz/ of C-295 "English (people)" (Sp *inglés*, perhaps Fr *anglais*, FSg *anglaise*), /fṛəŋk/ C-242 "franc (centime)", /šwiŋgɔm/ variant of C-718 "chewing gum" (Fr *chewing-gum*), /ṭəŋg/ C-764 "(military) tank" (Fr *tank*), and /ṭṛaŋkil/ variant of C-765 "alone, unbothered". However, we find /ng nk/ in variants for C-48, 295, 718 (cf. the preceding list), and in /ḟangaḷ-a/ C-200 "penis" (vulgar slang, etymology problematic) and related verb /ḟngḷ/ B-52 "he copulated with", and

/zəng/ C-808 "zinc" (Fr *zinc*). Moreover, /ṭəŋg/ "tank" (see above), though showing homorganic velar cluster, has Pl /ṭnug-a/, with /n/ when separated from the velar stop by a vowel.

In a somewhat similar way, there is evidence that /mb/ clusters in borrowings are interpreted as underlying /nb/ with low-level homorganic assimilation. Thus from /kambu/ C-311 "country hick" (Sp *campo* "field", countryside") we get Pl /kwanəb/, and the related verb is /t-kunəb/ B-87, where even a weak vowel between nasal and stop is sufficient to induce the change from /m/ to /n/. Whereas in the case of /ŋg ŋk/ analysed as /n/ plus /g k/, the re-analysis is obviously related to the absence of velar nasal /ŋ/ as an MCA phoneme, the analysis of /mb/ as really /nb/ is more difficult to explain, since /m/ as well as /n/ is a full-fledged phoneme. Apparently we are here dealing with a minor canonical-shape norm of MCA which prevents the sequence /m/ plus /b/ as contiguous root consonants (though /m-/ participial prefix or nominalizer can immediately precede /b/ as initial root consonant). There is no precise MCA analogy for an alternation of the type /mb/ vs. /nəb/ within a single paradigm, but the absence of sequences of /m/ and /b/ as contiguous root consonants appears to have been strong enough to affect these borrowings.

For Fr/Sp *r*, we have noted that the regular borrowed reflexes are /r/ and /ṛ/ in MCA. There are several minor irregular reflexes, however. To begin with, in a tiny number of cases, Fr *r* or Ger *r* is found as /ġ/ (voiced uvular fricative): /hiġipuġ/ C-292 "airport" (rare borrowing) from Fr *aéroport*, /dihuġ-a/ C-167 "prostitute" from Ger *(die) Hure*. This is, of course, related to the uvular pronunciation of *r* in these source languages in their current standard pronunciations. We get /l/ for *r* in a small number of cases: /faḷgaṭ-a/ variant of /fṛgaṭ-a/ C-231 "large rowboat" (Sp *fragata*, Fr *frégate*), /kuliyi/ variant of /kuryi/ C-425 "mail, letters" (Fr *courier*, but variant with /l/ possibly influenced by /kuliy-a/ C-395 "package, parcel" from Fr *colis*), /ṛuṣul/ alongside /ṛuṣuṛ/ C-619 "metal spṛing" (Fr *ressort*). We get /n/ for *r* in these examples: /antrit/ C-12 "retirement pension" (Fr *la retraite* with resegmentation), /grisun/ C-277 "bus driver's assistant" (Fr *graisseur*), and /maṛšaṛyan/ alongside /maṛšaṛyar/ C-477 "reverse gear" (*marche arrière*). The other reflexes recorded are zero in /msyu/ C-516 "Frenchman" (*Monsieur*, often pronounced without *r* in Fr) and /ẓ/ in /ẓiẓwaṛ/ C-606 "razor" (alongside /ṛiẓwaṛ/, Fr *rasoir*).

There are three remaining points to be dealt with in this section: (a) the morphophonemic status of /r/ and /ṛ/; (b) treatment of Fr/Sp palatoalveolar sonorants; and (c) syllabic status of sonorants in borrowings.

The question of the status of /r/ and /ṛ/ is just a special case of the more general problem which these consonants present for MCA phonology. In the case of the primary opposed plain vs. pharyngealized consonants like /ṭ ḍ ṣ/ vs. /t d s/ (and normally /ẓ/ vs. /z/), each root is consistent in either having the plain or pharyngealized form of the consonant in all inflected forms and derivatives. With /ṛ/ vs. /r/ this is normally true within verbal paradigms, but there are a number of morphophonemic alternations of /r/ and /ṛ/ in Sg/Pl pairs in nouns and adjectives. Examples with old MCA forms are: /kbir/ "big", Pl /kbaṛ/ (or /k^{w}baṛ/), comparative /kbṛ/ "bigger", related verb /kbr/ "he became big, grew up"; /tažr/ "rich man, merchant", Pl /tžžaṛ/, often reduced to /džaṛ/. Historically, the /ṛ/ vs. /r/ opposition is a dialect innovation, with CA *r splitting into two phonemes, initially on the basis of neighbouring vocalism (*i favouring /r/, other vowels favouring /ṛ/) but with subsequent partial loss of this conditioning environment.

What is interesting about Fr/Sp borrowings is that morphophonemic /ṛ/ vs. /r/ alternations are not developed, even when the borrowings fit precisely into morphological patterns which favour the alternation. Consider the inherited, traditional MCA type of noun with Sg /CVṛ/ (usually /Caṛ/) and Pl /Cir-an/, not /Ciṛ-an/, which includes such important and high-frequency items as /žaṛ/ "neighbour" (Pl /žir-an/), /faṛ/ "mouse" (Pl /fir-an/), and /tuṛ/ "bull" (Pl /tir-an/), along with the literary term /naṛ/ "flame", Pl /nir-an/. There is only one stem with this Sg/Pl pattern where pharyngealized /r/ occurs in both Sg and Pl forms: /ġaṛ/ "cavern", Pl /ġiṛ-an/. Here retention of /ṛ/ in the Pl was apparently favoured by the uvular /ġ/. The stem /ġaṛ/ is relatively uncommon in MCA, cf. the more common term /k̇af/ "cave" (not a loanword), Pl /kif-an/. There is no reason to think that /ġaṛ/ would counteract the analogical influence on new borrowings of the much more common stems /žaṛ/, /faṛ/, and /tuṛ/.

However, there are two well-attested Fr/Sp borrowings whose MCA Sg form is /Caṛ/ by regular conversions, but which consistently have pharyngealization in /Ciṛ-an/. These are: /kaṛ/ C-320 "intercity bus" (Fr *car*), Pl /kiṛ-an/ (these forms recorded from several dialects in Morocco and Algeria and confirmed by other authors); also /baṛ/ C-52 "bar", Pl /biṛ-an/ (alongside irrelevant Pl variant /baṛ-at/) from Fr and Sp *bar*. Obviously the /Ciṛ-an/ pattern is analogically modelled on that of /žaṛ/ and the others, but in the borrowings the /r/ vs. /ṛ/ alternation is levelled in favour of /ṛ/. Since the initially borrowed form is the Sg, with /ṛ/, this amounts to saying that the internally derived Pl form shows the analogically expected canonical shape, but avoids the traditional split of /r/ vs. /ṛ/.

Since the uncommon noun /ġaṛ/, Pl /ġiṛ-an/ by itself is insufficient to motivate this as an analogical development, my explanation is this. If we expand our perspective from the /r/ vs. /ṛ/ problem to the larger one of pharyngealization as a distinctive feature of MCA, we see (as noted above) that the dominant tendency in the language is for consonant pharyngealization to be an invariant feature of particular root consonants; this pattern is regular with other plain/pharyngealized oppositions, and operates to some extent (notably in verbal paradigms) even for /r/ and /ṛ/. This suggests that there is a fundamental underlying tendency (imperfectly realized) for consonant pharyngealization to be an invariant feature of root consonants. The development of Pl /kiṛ-an/ and /biṛ-an/, retaining the /ṛ/ of Sg /kaṛ/ and /baṛ/, appears to be a case where this very general and abstract principle of word structure has overridden what would normally be expected to be a simple, local analogical pluralization with */kiṛ-an/ and */biṛ-an/ modelled on the specific, local morphological pattern seen in /žaṛ/ Pl /žir-an/ and so forth.

Now for the treatment of Fr/Sp palatoalveolars. Both source languages have [ñ] (Sp *ñ*, Fr *gn*); Sp also has [λ] (written *ll*), but the corresponding phoneme in Fr is now usually pronounced like [y] (e.g., *ll* in *briller*).

For [ñ] we get either /ny/ cluster or just /n/: /sinya/ variant of /sna/ or /sina/ B-140 "he signed (name)" (Fr *signer*), /ḅanyu/ C-51 "bathtub" (Sp *baño*), /buny-a/ C-140 "fist" (Sp *puña*, Fr *poignée*), /sinyal/ C-645 "blinker" (Sp *señal*, Fr *signal*), and /sinyuṛ/ "señor" (Sp, but also "senior" league from Fr *sénior*) C-646. Examples of /n/ output are the variants of B-140 just given and /munika-a/ C-521 "doll" (Sp *muñeca*). Fr [ny] (orthographic *ni* or *nni*) does not seem to be clearly distinguished from [ñ] (orthographic *gn*) and shows similar outputs: /ny/ in /panyi/ C-541 "basket" (in basketball) from Fr *panier*(cf. also /sinyuṛ/ C-646, just mentioned, when it is from Fr *sénior*), but /n/ in /kuṛḍuni/ alongside /ny/ in variant /kuṛḍunyi/ C-417 "shoemaker" (Fr *cordonnier*).

Sp [λ] is usually found in MCA as /y/, hence /ḅumbiy-a/ C-135 in Tetouan dialect form "light bulb" (Sp *bombilla*), /p̣ay-a/ C-548 "paella" (Sp *paella*), and /sbniy-a/ C-634 "shawl" (early loan, Sp *sabanilla*). There is, however, one important borrowing with /ly/, /šly-a/ C-714 "chair", perhaps a still earlier borrowing (Sp *silla*) found, for example, as an archaism in several Judeo-Arabic dialects.

There is one apparent case where MCA has /ny/ from Fr/Sp *n* by an irregular conversion: /ạ̃ṭṛinyur/ C-26 "coach" (Fr *entraîneur*, Sp *entrenador*).

The final problem for this section has to do with syllabicity of sonorants. The normal MCA pattern is to allow what occur in transcriptions as long sequences of consonants, but which in reality are often syllabically complex, with such sonorants as /n m l r/ and pharyngealized counterparts achieving syllabicity in favourable environments (between two obstruents, between obstruent and word boundary, etc.). Fr/Sp borrowings, however, do not always respect this pattern.

Consider first /l/. In the cases of /mlyaṛ/ C-509 "billion" (Fr *milliard*) the /l/ is syllabic, which is appropriate since /ml/ here corresponds to a syllable in the Fr form; the same happens with /mlyun/ C-510 "million" (Fr *million*, Sp *millón*). However, Fr *client* "client, customer" occurs as /kliyan/ or /klyan/ C-360. The variant /klyan/, which may be influenced by the /CCCaC/ agentive noun pattern of MCA, is pronounced as one syllable, with nonsyllabic /l/.

With /r/ and /ṛ/ we also have to specify syllabicity in some types of borrowing, but several examples show fluctuation between two forms. Thus in /kṛwaṣ-a/ C-379 "croissant (pastry)" (Fr *croissant*) the /ṛ/ is syllabic for some informants but not others; the same was noted (but with different results for individual informants) for /kṛw-a/ C-378 "cross" (Fr *croix*, also meaning "belts in motor" from Fr *courroie*). I have recorded syllabic /ṛ/ in /kṛwel-a/, variant of /kaṛwel-a/ C-381 "cart, jalopy" (Fr *carriole*, etc.), and in /bṛwiṭ-a/ C-118 "wheelbarrow" (Fr *brouette*); but /ṛ/ is nonsyllabic in /kṛwaẓa/ B-82 "he crossed" (Fr *croiser*) and related noun /kṛwaẓm-a/ C-380 "intersection", and in /ṣạ̃fṛwa/ C-668 "fearless" (*sang-froid*). Generally though not always exactly, the cases of syllabic /ṛ/ represent Fr/Sp source syllables, while those of nonsyllabic /ṛ/ represent nonsyllabic Fr/Sp *r*. It should be added that the distinction between syllabic and nonsyllabic /l/ and /ṛ/ in these MCA borrowings appears to be somewhat unstable, and a more thorough investigation would probably reveal some more or less free variation.

Occasional occurrences of /rr/, /ll/, and so forth as geminated MCA reflexes of simple or geminated Fr/Sp consonants are dealt with in 6.10 along with other cases of secondary gemination.

6.6 Treatment of labial consonants and clusters

We begin by recalling that traditional MCA has /b/ but not /p/ as an inherited, full-fledged phoneme. We should also note that MCA does have two important cases of initial geminate labials in kin terms, /ḅḅa/ "father" and /ṃṃ-/ "mother" (/ṃṃ-i/ "my mother"). These geminate labials are normally pronounced with pharyngealization and often with a brief labialized release, except that these features are absent before /u/ vowel (/mm-u/ "his mother" being the relevant case). There is a more general process of gemination, pharyngealization, and labialization in the language, seen particularly in ablaut Pl and Dimin forms of nouns with underlying /w/ inserted after C_1 of the root. With C_1 other than a labial, we have /swart/ (Pl) and /swirit/ (Dimin) from /sarut/ "key". However, when C_1 is a labial /bmf/ (or, in borrowings, /v p/), the combination /C_1w/ is regularly realized as /C̣C̣/ with a labialized release: /ṃṃal-in/ "owners of" for underlying /mwal-in/ (Sg /mul/), /f̣f̣iyṛ/ Dimin of /faṛ/ "mouse", etc. The pharyngealization is also found in Sg stems with initial clusters historically involving a labial consonant plus **w* before a vowel, as in /f̣f̣ad/ "entrails" (**fwad*). Moreover, the rule applies to other labial-labial clusters, as in /f̣ṃam/ "mouths" (Pl of /f^{w}mm/). However, the rule does not apply in these cases: (a) verbs; (b) combinations of participial /m-/ prefix plus root-initial /w/ or other labial consonant. Moreover, the rule applies only sporadically (i.e. in selected forms only) to non-initial labial clusters within the stem: for many speakers we get /f^{w}ṃṃ-i/ "my mouth" and /ṛḅḅ-i/ "(my) God", but /dmm-i/ "my blood". In all of these transcriptions /ṃṃ/ /ḅḅ/ /f̣ṃ/ and other labial clusters with the pharyngealization diacritic are to be interpreted as permitting a labialized release although the latter is not specifically indicated. (All of these data are from the Fes/Meknes Muslim dialect group and are not necessarily correct for all Moroccan dialects.)

Turning to Fr/Sp borrowings, we have the following questions: (a) how are Fr/Sp *p* and Fr *v* borrowed, and (b) do the pharyngealization and labialized release of MCA labial clusters apply to borrowings? It turns out, in addition, that borrowed reflexes of Fr/Sp *f* and *b* are not always the expected MCA /f/ and /b/.

For Fr/Sp *p* we get a large number of different borrowed forms. The most common are /p/, /b/, /pp/, and /bb/, along with pharyngealized counterparts. Pharyngealized forms /p̣ ḅ p̣p̣ ḅḅ/ are usually motivated by the retention of vowel allophones approximating those of the source form, on the basis of general principles applying to all consonantal positions of articulation (6.1), but there are also many cases of Pl and/or Dimin ablaut forms with, e.g., underlying /bw/ becoming /ḅḅ/ along the lines just indicated.

The cases of *p* becoming /pp/ or /p̣p̣/ (not including /p̣p̣/ due to coalescence of underlying /pw/ cluster) are primarily in intervocalic position: /ṛupp-a/ C-617 "meal" (Fr *repas*), /ḍṛap̣p̣u/ C-186 "flag" (Fr *drapeau*), also B-51, 72, *90, 91, 96, 132, 156 and C-224, 254, 280, 291, 314, *404, *414, 553, 564, *565, *577, 608, 618, 655, 701, *782, 815, 823. There are also a few cases after full vowel in stem-final position with nouns, where (however) the geminate pronunciation is heard consistently only with Pl suffix /-at/, hence /grupp/ C-280 "group", also C-224, 414, 655, 815 (sometimes alternating with simple /p/). Other examples of /pp/ are C-404 (from *p* preceded by *m* or by nasalized vowel), C-564 (stem-initial *p*), and B-90 (/kuppya/ variant with only preconsonantal instance, possibly via earlier */kuppiya/).

There are somewhat fewer examples of /bb/ from *p* in my data, though it is probable that /bb/ is commoner in some rural dialects. There are five examples of intervocalic position including /ṣubb-a/ C-690 "soup" (Sp *sopa*, Fr *soupe*); some variants with /bb/ alongside /p/ as stem-initial, as in /bbisin/ as rural variation of/pisin/ C-556 "swimming pool" (Fr *piscine*); one stem-finally after full vowel (C-351); and two variants with /bb/ in consonant clusters (C-172 before lateral, C-545 after sibilant). The other intervocalic and stem-initial cases are C-*349, 350, 387, *551, *557, *577, and perhaps *782.

Reflex /p/ or /p̣/ for Fr/Sp *p*, though probably not well established until recent decades, is now regular in many borrowings except among elderly or rural speakers. Examples can easily be found of stem-initial /p/ or /p̣/ in the appendices, which are alphabetical. There are also numerous cases of /p/ or /p̣/ in other positions: /dipaṛ/ C-171 "departure" (Fr *départ*), /dipḷum/ C-172 "diploma" (Fr *diplôme*). A complete list will not be given here.

Reflex /b/ or /ḅ/ is also common for *p*, though most of the recent loans have /p/ or /p̣/. It would appear that formerly /b/ or /ḅ/ was the regular borrowed form of *p* in stem-initial position, and between a consonant and a following vowel. There are about forty examples in the appendices of stem-initial /b/ or /ḅ/ from *p*, including about twelve beginning with /bC/ with some other consonant (the consonant is in some cases a syllabic sonorant, and in some other cases there may formerly have been a short vowel between the /b/ and the consonant). A few examples are: /bakiy-a/ C-37 "packet" (Fr *paquet*, with Sp *paquete* perhaps also involved), /bḷaṣ-a/ C-102 "place" (Fr *place*), /sbiktur/ C-632 "inspector" (Sp *inspector*, Fr *inspecteur*). There are no examples known to me of /b/ or /ḅ/ from *p* in intervocalic or word-final position (B-87 is superficially an instance of word-final /b/ from *p*, but is an internal MCA formation based on previously borrowed noun with intervocalic /mb/ from *mp*).

On the treatment of underlying /pw/ and /bw/ in ablaut forms with inserted /w/, see the end of this section.

We now consider the treatment of Fr/Sp *b* (orthographic *b* and, for Sp, also *v*). It is appreciated that Sp *b* and *v* are often pronounced [β], but in most examples the Sp consonant has the same reflexes in MCA as Fr *b*.

The usual treatment of Fr/Sp *b* is, as expected, MCA /b/, with some cases of /ḅ/ where appropriate to retain vowel allophones approximating the Fr/Sp vowel articulation. There are many examples in the appendices including many which begin with /b/ or /ḅ/ (B-4ff., C-30ff.). Note, for example, /baḅuṛ/ C-30, representing Sp *vapor*, Fr *vapeur* "steamboat" but also Fr *bâbord* "port (side of ship)" in different meanings.

There are, however, a few examples of a reflex other than /b/ or /ḅ/ for Fr/Sp *b*. First, from my Marrakech (Mr) informant I recorded a small number of variants with /v/ or /ṿ/: /vaṭim-a/ for /baṭim-a/ C-68 "apartment building" (Fr *bâtiment*), /kuṇṭṛaṿan/ C-411 "contraband" (Fr *contrebande*, Sp *contrabando*). Without a more detailed study of the phonology of this dialect we cannot tell what is going on here, but it is conceivable that this dialect (or this speaker) has established /v/ or /ṿ/ as a characteristic segment of European borrowings, with sporadic "hypercorrection". The other irregular reflexes of Fr/Sp *b* are instances of geminated /bb/, /ḅḅ/, or /pp/. In /ṣbbn/ B-153 "he washed" and /ṣbbəṭ/ variant of B-151 "he attacked (verbally)" we do not really have a simple shift of *b* to /bb/, rather (in all likelihood) a restructuring modelled on the factitive /$C_1C_2C_2$əC_3/ pattern of traditional MCA. However, /klupp/ was recorded in Marrakech as a variant of C-316 (Fr *club*), /ppikini/ occurs alongside /bikini/ "bikini" (C-565, Fr *bikini*), and we have /ṛuḅḅ-a/ C-611 "robe, gown" (Fr *robe*) unless this is really a recent semantic shift from an older loan from Sp *ropa* "clothing".

We now consider reflexes of Fr *v*. We include Fr orthographic *v* and *w* under this rubric. Since /v/ is not a traditional MCA consonant, it is not surprising that Fr *v* is often borrowed as /f/ or /f̣/. However, most of the recent borrowings now coming in have /v/ or /ṿ/, and there are many doublet forms with /f/ or /f̣/ preferred by older and rural speakers and /v/ or /ṿ/ by younger and urban speakers, especially those who know Fr reasonably well. There are a few examples of /b/ or /ḅ/.

Some examples of /f/ alternating with /v/ are /fil-a/ and /vill-a/ (among other variants) C-211 "villa" (Fr *villa*), also C-221, 367, 746. Examples of /f/ are /t-ṣufəž/ B-157 "he acted wild" (verbal derivative from Fr *sauvage*), also C-194 (Fr *w*, Sp *v*), 195, 219, 227, 389, 418, 467, 588, 785ff. We get /f̣/ or /ṿ/ in f̣ayạž/ or /ṿayạž/ C-208 "load, haul" (Fr *voyage*). Voiced /v/ occurs in /t-nirva/ "he was worried" B-105 (verb from Fr *nerveux* and/or *énervé*), see also B-95, 131, 182ff. and C-2, 20, 92, 117, 408, 449, 450. Pharyngealized /ṿ/ occurs in /aṿuka/ C-27 "lawyer" (Fr *avocat*) and /ṣuṿaž/ C-694 "wild" (Fr *sauvage*, contrast /f/ in the related verb already cited); we get /ṿ/ or /b/ in C-28 (possibly due to Fr and Sp confluence) and /ṿ/ or /ḅ/ in C-193 (same remark). In addition to some variants already mentioned, /b/ occurs alongside /v/ in B-145 (Fr and Sp confluence), but the most likely clear cases of /b/ from Fr *v* are /baliz-a/ C-42 "suitcase" (Fr *valise*) and /kab/ C-301 "cellar" (Fr *cave*).

Naturally, Fr/Sp *f* is normally realized as MCA /f/ with a few cases of /f̣/ when pharyngealization guarantees vowel allophones approximating those of the source form. There are many examples in the appendices including those beginning with /f/ and /f̣/

(easily found in the alphabetical listings in appendices B and C). There appear to be a handful of exceptions with /v/ or /v/: B-93 (probably involving contamination with another form listed in the same entry), B-*134, C-*220, 326 (from German), *367.

We conclude this section with comments about the treatment of such sequences as /bw/, /pw/, /vw/, /fw/, which in native MCA words usually are pronounced /ḅḅ/ (with labialized release) and so forth in the positions mentioned at the beginning of this section (i.e. most often at the beginning of a noun or adjective stem). We first consider cases where these combinations occur as the result of plural or diminutive ablaut. While the data on this point are not exhaustive, it does appear that this secondary pharyngealization (and labialized release) applies to the relevant Pl and Dimin forms from borrowed Sg stems among my informants (my data on Pl and Dimin forms, however, are mostly from the Fes area). Some examples are /muṇaḍ-a/ C-520 "soft drink", Pl /mwaṇ(ə)ḍ/ [ṃṃ^{w}aṇ(ə)ḍ]; /mašin-a/ C-487 "train", Pl /mwašn/ [ṃṃ^{w}ašn], Dimin /mwišin-a/ [ṃṃ^{w}išin-a]; /vill-a/ and variants C-211 "villa", Dimin /vwill-a/ [ṿṿ^{w}ill-a]. (The transcriptions in the appendix entries do not specifically mark this pronunciation of /mw/, /vw/, etc., but if pharyngealization is not present we indicate this fact.) In a somewhat different morphological construction also involving infixed /w/, we get /mwagn-i/ [ṃṃ^{w}agn-i] C-528 "watch seller", derived from /magan-a/ C-460 "watch, clock".

In underived, directly borrowed stem forms we have some examples of pharyngealization of labial cluster, but counterexamples as well. First, /bwan/ C-159 "broke, without money" (Fr *en panne*) is often unpharyngealized. In the noun /bwaṭ-a/ (collective /bwaṭ/) "canned, in cans", I do not hear any special phonetic effects, but the stem is pharyngealized anyway (due to the /ṭ/), so the special treatment of the labial cluster would be partly vacuous even if present (the only special effect would be an increase in the duration of the /b/, which I did not hear — at least consistently). However, I did hear verb /pwanta/ B-121 "he punched in" (Fr *pointer*) as [p̣p̣^{w}anta], even though native MCA verbs do not show special treatment of labial clusters. Further data are /bwandi/ (often but not always pharyngealized), variant /ḅandi/ C-160 "bandit" (Fr *bandit*); cf. also the humorously constructed slang kin terms C-527 and 581 (where pharyngealized onset in MCA synonyms /ḅḅa/ "father" and /ṃṃ-/ "mother" is a factor). Pharyngealization of Fr [pw] occurs at least as a variant in borrowings C-609 (from Fr *rond point*) and 702 (Fr *shampooing*).

6.7 Stops /t t^s/

An additional difficulty has to do with the fact that what we normally write as MCA /t/ is pronounced [t^s] with an affricate-like release, while MCA /ṭ/ lacks this. Actually, MCA /t/ has this type of release mainly in certain positions, such as word-finally, before vowels, before /r/ or /ṛ/, and before noncoronal consonants, while the release is absent or inconspicuous before most other coronal consonants. In any event, most cases of /t/ in MCA have the release, and since Fr and Sp *t* has no similar release the question arises whether borrowings preserve unaffricated [t] as a new MCA

/t/ phoneme distinct from old MCA [t^s] (which we would then have to write as a phoneme /t^s/), or whether the borrowings adopt the MCA affricated /t/ [t^s] so that no new phoneme is present.

My data on this matter are not complete, and to avoid confusion the appendix entries do not specify precise pronunciation of what is there transcribed /t/. I have two basic points, however. First the existence of a new, unaffricated phoneme /t/ distinct from /t^s/, but limited to European borrowings, is present in the northern MCA dialect of Tetouan, in a number of Judeo-Arabic dialects, and (to some extent) in the central area around Fes and Meknes. My data on Marrakech are presently inadequate for a judgement concerning that dialect.

Second, certain patterns emerge from a more detailed analysis of the speech of my primary Fes-area informant. In this dialect, unaffricated /t/ vs. /t^s/ is retained in some but by no means all borrowings. We get /t/ regularly before /r/ or /ṛ/, as in /tran/ C-736 "train" (also C-735, 737, 738, 740-743, 766). We get /t^s/ almost always before /i/, as in /antiris/ C-11 "interest" (also C-120, 154, 175, 181, 309, 316, 390, 405, 486, 502, 546, 572); before /y/ we have /t^s/ in C-327 but /t/ in C-251. We seem to get /t^s/ before /a/ (C-139, 219, 719) but C-319 has /t/. Before /u/ we get /t^s/ in C-49, 50, 197, 383, 735, and /t/ in C-746, 747, 325, 745. Stem-finally we get /t^s/ in C-91, 201, 250, 336, but /t/ in C-3, 12, 53, 131, 557, 744. There is one case of /t^s/ before /e/ (C-168), and of course only /t/ occurs before /s/ (C-430). Variant /t/ and /t^s/ forms were recorded for C-12 (first /t/), 221, 234, 196, 506, 731, 734, 744, 748. Recent, half-assimilated Fr borrowings tend to take /t/ more than older borrowings; thus C-196 has /fakt^sur/ or /faktör/, and C-221 has /fit^sεs/ or /vitεs/, where /t/ co-occurs with unassimilated non-MCA phonemes. These data are from nouns; similar data emerge from verbs (appendix B).

6.8 Affricates [č ǰ]

In native vocabulary, the major MCA dialects do not have affricate phonemes (though they do occur, often as marginal phonemes, in the northern dialect of Tetouan and in Algeria). MCA does have /tš/ and /dž/ as consonant clusters, as in /džaž-a/ "chicken". How, then, are Fr/Sp affricates borrowed — as new affricate phonemes, clusters /tš/ and /dž/, or simplified sibilants /š ž/?

From phonetic [č] (Sp *ch*, Fr *tch*) we usually get an MCA form which is compatible with a representation /tš/, hence /kawatšu/ C-343 "rubber" (Sp *caucho*, Fr *caoutchouc*), also C-430, 489, 677. With /ganšu/ or /gantšu/ C-258 "pitchfork" the nasal makes it difficult to hear the difference between /tš/ and /š/. An earlier borrowing from the same source (Sp *gancho*) is /ġanžu/ C-288. In cases like /šk ḷaṭ/ C-711 "chocolate", we could have /š/ from [č] if the source is Sp *chocolate*, but this may in fact be a hybrid involving Fr *chocolat* with initial [š].

There are a few cases of [ǰ] in a Fr/Sp borrowing, since this affricate is not well established in modern Fr or Sp. However, there are some cases involving Eng [ǰ] in a source form, probably in many cases with Fr as intermediary, and here we seem to get /dž/ regularly: /bidžiz/ C-76 "Bee-Gees" (name of rock band), also C-179,

*821 (/dž/ or /ž/). In the case of /džikit-a/, variant recorded in Marrakech of /žạkiṭ-a/ and other variants C-811 "jacket", it is not entirely clear from which language the /dž/ variant came.

It is difficult to determine whether /tš/ and /dž/ in such forms are clusters or unit phonemes. Absence of /č/ and /ǰ/ phonemes in native MCA, and data from play language (not presented here), generally point to a cluster analysis. However, informant hesitation in producing Dimin forms of /ltšin-a/ C-452 "orange", and Dimin variant /lčičin-a/, point to a possible analysis /lččin-a/ even for central dialects. Ambiguity in phonemic interpretation seems present.

In light of the occurrence of /dž/ for recent borrowings from [ǰ], it is worth recalling that borrowings from CA consistently have MCA /ž/ for CA *ǰ* (5.2). In the standard pronunciation of CA *ǰ*, it sounds like [ǰ] in other languages. It would appear that educated Moroccans who can spontaneously borrow new CA forms into MCA with *ǰ* deaffricating to /ž/, and who at the same time are capable of introducing new European borrowings with /dž/ for [ǰ], are applying *different diasystemic conversion rules to the same segment* depending on which language it comes from. The decision to deaffricate the CA phoneme, but not the European one, rather than vice versa, is perhaps motivated structurally by the fact that CA borrowings are normally fit into native-like MCA patterns, and bringing in CA *ǰ* as /dž/ could complicate the root structure (e.g. converting a triliteral root into a quadriliteral, which would have further consequences including redistribution of vowels between the root consonants); European borrowings, on the other hand, are only sporadically converted into native MCA word shapes nowadays.

MCA /žạṇṭ-a/ C-812 "wheel axle" is apparently an old loan from Sp *junto* or a form of the verb *juntar*. If very old it could go back to the time when Sp orthographic *j* was still an affricate; otherwise it might really be from some other Romance language or dialect.

6.9 Other consonants: *k g d ʔ x h w y s š z ž*

The voiceless velar stop *k* (usually orthographic *c* or *qu*) in Fr/Sp source words is now borrowed regularly as MCA /k/, hence /buks/ C-128 "boxing" (Fr *boxe* [bɔks]) and many other examples in the appendices. In the precolonial period *k* was frequently borrowed as MCA /q/, and there are a few forms of this type still found in my modern data: /qarṭuš/ as variant of /karṭuš/ C-325 "shells, bullets" (Fr *cartouche*), also C-582-586 (contrast /qbṭan/ C-583 with more recent loan /kapitan/ C-319, both from Fr *capitaine* or Romance cognate). In the currently dominant pronunciation of MCA, /q/ is distinguished from /k/ by its glottalization as much as by its more uvular point of articulation, and this glottalized /q/ does not sound much like Fr/Sp *k*. In /qṣṣa/ B-122 we do not have a direct borrowing of *k* as /q/, rather semantic extension of an inherited lexical item under the influence of a phonologically similar Fr verb. Possible examples of MCA /g/ as a minor alternative to /k/ for Fr/Sp *k* are /g^wṭaṛ/ variant of /kṭaṛ/ C-385 "hectare" (Fr *hectare*), and /magan-a/ C-460 "clock" if this is from Sp *máquina* or similar form. A possible example of /xx/ for *k* is the Marrakech (Mr) variant /mxxiy-at/ for /mikiy-at/ C-498 "cartoons" (ultimately Eng *Mickey (Mouse)*), but the development of this form is unclear.

Similarly, MCA /g/ is a well-established native phoneme, and is now the regular borrowed form of Fr/Sp *g* (orthographic *g* or *gu*). For some of the many examples in the appendices see B-62ff. and C-255ff. However, in the precolonial period Sp *g*, which is frequently pronounced as a fricative [ġ] ([ɣ] in the IPA transcriptional system), was borrowed as MCA /ġ/ in a number of words, some of which are still in use and appear in my lists: /ġanžu/ C-288 "country hick" (Sp *gancho* "pitchfork", cf. more recent borrowing /ganšu/ or /gantšu/ C-258 "pitchfork" from same source), /ġiwan/ C-289 "great" (apparently a former Pl form based on /ġan-a/ from Sp *gana* "wish, whim", which appears in my list as /gan-a/ C-257 with /g/ instead of /ġ/, perhaps a more recent borrowing). A minor example with /k/ for *g* is the variant /bikbuṣ/ for /bigbuṣ/ C-79 "giant" (Eng *big boss*), but here we cannot rule out the possibility that the source form (as pronounced by Fr speakers) available to Moroccans may have had a variant already with [k].

For Fr/Sp *d* the regular borrowed form is MCA /d/, with /ḍ/ as a common alternative to preserve vocalic allophones approximating the source vocalism. Thus /dimirda/ C-33 "he acted by himself" (Fr *démerder*), /ḍubl/ or /dubl/ B-46 "he doubled" (Fr *doubler*, Sp *doblar* along with Fr *double*, Sp *doble*), /ḍikuṛa/ C-41 "he decorated" (Fr *décorer*, Sp *decorar*), and many other examples.

Glottal stop [?] does not occur as a Fr/Sp phoneme, but is added in some cases to borrowings with stem-initial vowel (if the vowel is not dropped by truncation or desyllabified to a semivowel, see 6.4). This treatment is regular with borrowed verb stems, including spontaneous new ones like /?uṛg̣aniza/ B-2 "he organized" (see also B-1 and B-3, also variants of B-4, 126, 155, 176). With borrowed noun stems, there is an optional, low-level insertion of /?/ in absolute word-initial position, hence /adris-a/ C-1 "address" has definite form /l-adris-a/, word-initial indefinite form /adris-a/ or sometimes /?adris-a/. This inserted /?/ does not seem to be treated as an inherent stem phoneme and is not indicated in the lexical lists; we do indicate the verb-stem-initial /?/ since with verbs the /?/ occurs even after prefixes: /ġadi n-?uṛg̣anizi/ "I will organize".

The segment [x] occurs in input forms from Sp with orthographic *j* or *g* (the latter before front vowels *e i*). This sound is very close to MCA uvular fricative /x/ and this is the normal borrowed counterpart: /xiṇṭi/ C-802 "people (slang)" (Sp *gente*), perhaps /xuṛuṭu/ C-803 "fellow (slang)" (source unidentified, possibly somehow also related to Sp *gente* via slang deformation). However, in the older strata of precolonial Sp borrowings we can get /ž/, reflecting the pronunciation of orthographic *j* and *g* in old Sp (see C-812).

The consonant *h* does not occur as a sound in modern Fr or Sp, where orthographic initial *h* is "silent". However, there are a few borrowings from older Sp or Eng (some possibly transmitted via Fr slang or the like) with initial *h* which is kept in MCA as /h/: /himri/ C-290 "hungry", /hippi/ C-291 "hippie" (and related verb

B-72). In one poorly assimilated form obtained only from the Marrakech informant, we get a secondary /h/, hence /hiġipuġ/ C-292 "airport" (Fr *aéroport*); it is possible that the /h/ was inserted to permit retention of the hiatus between *a* and *e*, hence *l'aéroport* "the airport" might have been heard as [lạheġopoġ] or the like, then resegmented as [lạ-heġopoġ] and reproduced with some irregularity as /hiġipuġ/. Another possible instance from another region of this hiatus-retaining function of secondary MCA /h/ in a borrowing is /p̣ahiy-a/, the pronunciation recorded from a Tetouan (Tt) informant of Sp *paella* (a Spanish dish), recorded as /p̣ay-a/ C-548 elsewhere. These sporadic examples do not suffice to establish this as a regular conversion rule for loanwords.

The regular borrowed reflex of Fr [w] (chiefly in orthographic *oi* [wa]) is, as expected, MCA /w/, hence /kṛwaẓa/ B-82 "he crossed" (Fr *croiser*), also B-94, 121, C-174, 433. In /wiski/ C-800 "whiskey" we have orthographic *w* in Fr *whisky*, Sp *wiski*. We find /w/ also in /tawzn/ C-721 "money (slang)" from Eng *thousand* or Ger *Tausend*; and from Fr/Sp diphthongs like Sp *ue* ([we]) in C-624 (Sp *rueda*) and 625 (Sp *ruína*, Fr *ruine*, cf. denominative verb B-137), also Sp *ua* in forms like /kwaṭṛu/ C-435 "four (card)" (Sp *cuatro*). In /kṛwel-a/ or /kaṛwel-a/ C-381 "cart" we may have something similar going on, but it is not clear exactly which Romance form is the source. In /bṛwiṭ-a/ C-118 "wheelbarrow" (Fr *brouette*) there has been a shift of syllabicity to the /ṛ/, with Fr *ou* (syllabic in Fr) reduced to /w/. In such stems as /guḷ/ C-283 "goal" and /bun/ C-136 "coupon" (Sp *gol*, Fr *bon*) we get full vowel /u/ in the initially borrowed Sg form, but following the usual analogical pattern of /CuC/ singulars we get Pl forms like /gwal/ and /bwan/; by some analyses of MCA root structure (which I do not fully endorse) we should take /w/ as the underlying C_2 of the root. There are also dozens of examples of infixed /w/ in Pl and Dimin ablaut forms for all kinds of nouns (see morphology sections, below). We should also mention that Fr front rounded semivowel [ẅ] (orthographic *u* in diphthongs) is treated like back rounded semivowel [w] in MCA borrowings: /dilwi/ "tell him!" (Fr *dis-lui!*) C-169 and /kwizinyi/ variant of /kuzin-i/ C-432 "cook, chef" (Fr *cuisinier*). On the question of pharyngealization and gemination of borrowed labial-plus-w sequences like /pw/, see the end of 6.6 above. On the short vowel /^{w}/ see 6.11 and 6.12 below.

The other semivowel, *y*, is normally borrowed as MCA /y/. The source forms in question have these orthographic representations: for Sp *y* along with *i* as nonsyllabic element in diphthongs; for Fr these same representations plus *ll* (*lle*, *ille*, etc.) where this represents old palatalized [λ] now pronounced [y] in modern Fr. Some examples are /byas-a/ C-162 "spare part" (Fr *pièce*), /pḷay-a/ or /bḷay-a/ C-560 "beach" (Sp *playa*), /ḍiṭay/ C-185 "retail" (Fr *détail*), /biyi/ C-94 "ticket" (Fr *billet*). Sp diphthong *ea* becomes /ya/ in /ryal/ C-626 "riyal (money)" (Sp *real*), suggesting that *ea* is not easily distinguished from *ia*. In cases like /gid/ C-269 "guide" Pl /g̣yad/, we can, under certain analyses, take /y/ as underlying C_2 though the only directly borrowed form is /gid/; cf. /guḷ/ and /bun/, preceding paragraph. We get /y/ as a kind of epenthetic consonant between /i/ and following /a/ in several borrowings involving FSg suffix /-a/, whether the latter represents a segment of the source form or is added gratuitously in MCA: /ḅumbiy-a/ C-135 "firemen" (Fr *pompiers*), /paṛtiy-a/ and variants C-542 "part, piece" (Fr *partie*, Sp *parte*, with FSg /-a/ added in MCA). In the form /g̣rayd-i/ C-276 "graded, ranked" (Fr *gradé*), the addition of /y/ is based on the requirements of the particular morphological type which this is analysed as an instance of; for a similar development in a native form see /skayr-i/ "drunk, intoxicated", cf. verb /skr/ "he got drunk" showing the triconsonantal root without /y/. For cases with geminate /yy/ as C_2 in factitive-causative denominative verbs from initially borrowed nouns with /i/, see /myyək/ B-104 and /t-šyyək/ B-167. We have noted above (toward the end of 6.5) that /y/ in borrowings can also be from Sp palatized [λ], and that /ny/ is a common output for Fr/Sp [ñ].

Fr and Sp orthographic *s* differ phonetically in that the latter language has a retroflexed pronunciation (especially in Castilian and related continental dialects). MCA lacks a retroflexed sibilant, but in many of the older Sp loans we find palatoalveolar /š/ instead of /s/ or pharyngealized /ṣ/. Thus in C-62 and 63, the references to forms cited by early authors from the colonial or immediate precolonial periods show /š/ which is replaced in forms I recorded by /s/; in C-63 the /š/ appears to be from Sp *s*, while in C-62 it is not entirely clear which Romance form is responsible (perhaps /š/ was older */ž/ from Sp orthographic *j*). My data show /š/ as a variant in /frišk/ alongside /frisk/ C-233 "fresh" (Sp *fresco* or similar form), /fišṭ-a/ or /fižṭ-a/ C-220 "celebration" (Sp *fiesta* or possibly It *festa* from Algeria); and /š/ is the only pronunciation attested in such forms as /maṭiš-a/ C-491 "tomatoes" (but this may be a semantic shift of a native term), /šḷaḍ-a/ or /šaḷaḍ-a/ C-712 "salad" (Sp *ensalada*), and /šly-a/ C-714 "chair" (Sp *silla*). The form /kššin-a/ C-384 "kitchen" may be another example, with secondary gemination, if this is from Sp *cocina* (in Andalusian Sp pronunciation with *c* pronounced like *s*) rather than It *cucina*. Two apparent cases of MCA /š/ from Fr unretroflexed *s* probably involve secondary assimilation to another /š/ in the same word: /šakuš/ C-698 (Fr *sacoche*) "bag" and /šišwaṛ/ variant of C-709 "hair-dryer" (Fr *séchoir*). (For native MCA parallels cf. /šəmš/ "sun" from CA *šams-*, /žwwəž/ "he married" from CA *zawwaǰ-*, etc.)

In any event, the most common reflex of Sp *s* as well as Fr *s* is MCA /s/ or pharyngealized /ṣ/ to retain vocalic allophones approximating the source vowels. The appendices have many examples of forms beginning in /s/ or /ṣ/ from these Fr/Sp sources: B-138ff. and C-627ff. The MCA /s/ reflex is found even in some relatively early Sp loans like /skwil-a/ C-654 "school" and /sbniy-a/ C-634 "shawl" (Sp *escuela*, *sabanilla*). There are also a few cases where voiced /z/ or /ẓ/ occurs: /bizagr-a/ C-95 "hinge or jamb of door" (Sp *bisagra*), /ẓṭaṭ/ variant of /ṣṭaṭ/ or /ṣṭaḍ/ C-686 "stadium" (Fr *stade*). This might be going on also in /ẓin-a/ C-806 "dozen" if direct from Sp *docena* (Andalusian pronunciation), but here the voiced [z] in Fr *douzaine* is a possible contaminating factor. In the preceding paragraph we note /fižṭ-a/ as a variant of /fišṭ-a/ C-220 "celebration" (Sp *fiesta*, It *festa*). Cf. C-789.

The question of the treatment of Sp [θ] (voiceless interdental fricative, orthographic *z*, or *c* before *e i*) does not arise in MCA borrowings, since in my data this Sp sound is not differentiated from Sp *s* (retroflexed voiceless sibilant). This is undoubtedly because the Sp dialect relevant to Morocco is principally Andalusian, which differs from the better known, more northerly continental Sp dialects in merging *z* with *s* (as in Latin American Sp). Hence /siŋku/ "five card" (not in appendices) from Sp *cinco*, Andalusian pronunciation [siŋko] vs. Castilian [θiŋko].

Fr [š] (orthographic *ch*) is realized, as expected, as MCA /š/, hence /bṛašm-a/ C-106 "intersection" (Fr *branchement*) and many other examples (see also B-160ff. and C-695ff.)

Fr phonetic [z], orthographic *z* or (intervocalic) *s*, is realized regularly as MCA /z/, with the usual variant /ẓ/ in some words to retain vowel allophones resembling the source vowels. In addition to the borrowings beginning with /z/ or /ẓ/ in C-805ff., we may mention /šwaẓa/ B-166 "he chose" (Fr *choisir*), and /bḷasuz/ C-101 "female usher" (Fr *placeuse*), among many others. Devoicing occurs in /faṣm-a/ C-207 "bandage", an old, well-established colonial loan (Fr *pansement*).

Fr [ž], orthographically *j* or *g* (the latter before front vowels or "silent" *e*), regularly appears as MCA /ž/. Hence /pḷaž/ C-561 "beach" (Fr *plage*), and many others including B-44, 63, 98, 114, 185ff. and C-810ff. We have previously noted that /dž/ occurs in one variant of C-811, but this might involve Sp *ch* instead of Fr [ž].

6.10 Secondary gemination of consonants

We have already pointed out (6.6) that Fr/Sp *p*, which does not correspond to a traditional MCA phoneme, has frequently been borrowed as /bb/ or /pp/. This is a specific, local, segmental conversion which does not concern us in the present section. Here, we are concerned with cases of segmentally unmotivated gemination of a consonant in a borrowing.

First, there is carryover of consonants which are already geminated in the source form. The clearest cases involve Sp or It double *rr*, which frequently appears in MCA as /rr/ or /ṛṛ/, hence /birr-a/ C-86 "beer" (It *birra*), /brrak-a/ C-112 "shack" (if from Sp *barraca*, not Fr *baraque*), /gaṛṛu/ C-263 "cigarette" (Sp *cigarro*), /girr-a/ C-271 "war" (Sp *guerra*), /kṛṛuṣ-a/ C-374 "cart" (if from Sp or It), /tirr-a/ C-731 "open square" (if from Sp *tierra* or similar cognate), /ṭaṛṛu/ C-758 "metal pail" (Sp *tarro*).

Second, there are some cases where the vowel of the initial syllable of the source form has been dropped or reduced to a very weak transitional short vowel (which in this position may lose its syllabicity entirely). It appears that C_2 can be geminated secondarily in this case to preserve an approximation to the source syllabic pattern. Thus from Sp *peseta* (the currency unit) we get /bṣṣiṭ-a/ C-121, where the doubled /ṣṣ/ makes the word sound more like the original than */bṣiṭ-a/ would. Similar examples are /kššin-a/ C-368 "kitchen" (Sp *cocina* or similar cognate), /ṭ^ẓẓin-a/ variant of C-806 "dozen" (Sp *docena* or cognate), /žṇṇiniṛ/ C-817 "general" (along with other variants), /mṛṛuk/ C-515 "Morocco, Moroccan" (if from Fr *Maroc*, but Sp *Marruecos*, *marroquí* may have contaminated the form here), possibly /bḷḷuṭ/ C-103 "acorns; card game" (Sp *bellota* in first sense, perhaps a very old loan; Fr *belote*). We do not find such secondary gemination in cases like /mṛmiṭ-a/ C-514 "pot" (Fr *marmite*, Sp *marmita*), where we already have three (not two) consonants before the full vowel (here the /ṛ/ is syllabic).

However, in addition to cases like /kššin-a/ where the gemination is interpretable as compensatory lengthening to retain an approximation to the source syllable structure, we have other cases of apparently unmotivated consonant doubling in borrowings where a full vowel precedes and follows. The following are the candidates, some dubious, for this: /vill-a/ or /vil-a/ (along with variants with /f/) C-211 "villa" (if from Fr *villa*[vila], not It *villa*), /gaṭṭu/ C-266 along with /gaṭu/ "cake" (Fr *gâteau*), /buṛṛu/ or /bwaṛṛu/ C-144 "leek" (Fr *poireau*), /maṣṣ-a/ C-484 "sledgehammer, mass" (Fr *masse*, Sp *masa*, unless It *massa* is involved), /maṣṣu/ C-485 "mason, bricklayer" (Fr *maçon*), /miss-a/ C-505 "cards and money on table in card game" (Sp *mesa* influenced semantically by Fr *mise* "ante"), /trikku/ C-739 "knitted shirt" (Fr *tricot*), /qamižž-a/ and /qmžž-a/ variants of C-582 (Sp *camisa*). Most of these appear to be fairly early loans, some precolonial, and it is difficult at this point to analyse the individual cases without more extensive dialectological data. In several cases the consonant which is geminated in the MCA form is preceded in the (Sp or It) source by a stressed vowel, and the gemination might therefore be motivated historically by prosodic factors; it should be stressed that this is not a regular process. With /krballu/ C-368 "sieve" (Sp *cribello* or similar cognate) we cannot be very confident of the precise reason for the MCA doubling; in /bulasarrut/ C-131 "highway police" the entire form is rather irregular (Fr *police de route*) and the doubled /rr/ might be a kind of fusion of Fr *d* and *r*; with /šaff/ variant of /šaf/ C-697 there may be an interfering factor, namely the influence of other labial consonants, where /CVbb/ and the like are common noun forms due to factors dealt with in 6.6.

6.11 Secondary labialization

We have noted (3.3) that MCA has a native phoneme, written /^{w}/ in this publication, which is realized either as a brief short rounded vowel or, when nonsyllabic, as a brief labialized release linking one consonant to another (or simultaneous with a syllabified sonorant). A few cases where /^{w}/ occurs in borrowings, corresponding to a Fr/Sp vowel, are presented in 6.12.

In addition, however, there are a small number of instances of /^{w}/ being introduced, as a nonsyllabic release, in borrowings where there is no obvious corresponding segment or feature in the source form(s). The examples involve stem-initial /k/ or /g/ in a noun stem, followed by another consonant then a full vowel: /g^{w}ṛam/ variant of /gṛam/ C-275 "gram" (Fr and Sp *gram*), /k^{w}ṭaṛ/ and /g^{w}ṭaṛ/ variants of /kṭaṛ/ "hectare" (Fr *hectare*), and /k^{w}rik/ variant of /krik/ C-370 "jack" (Fr *cric*). In each of these cases the form with /^{w}/ coexists with a corresponding form without /^{w}/, and there are many other stems with similar /kCV/ or /gCV/ onsets which do not have an attested variant with /^{w}/. All we can say here is that /k__CV/ and /g__CV/ are perfect positions, in MCA terms, for the phonemically distinct presence vs. absence of /^{w}/, and that (because of the weak articulation of /^{w}/) there is considerable dialectal and idiolectal fluctuation in particular forms which may have led to the occasional introduction of /^{w}/ into borrowings of similar shape. However, we have no good explanation for why these particular stems were chosen.

6.12 Minor and irregular phonological developments

In this section we discuss a number of irregular segmental correspondences for Fr/Sp segments whose normal correspondences have already been described, along with discussion of special cases of metathesis and other larger-scale reshapings. It should be noted that truncation, consonant-cluster simplification, and desyllabification of vowels to glides (semivowels) have been discussed in 6.4 above.

Most of the irregularities involve vowel correspondences. For Fr/Sp *a* we get /i/ in /aṃḅṛiyaž/ C-8 "transmission" (Fr *embrayage*), /kriyu/ C-373 "pencil" (Fr *crayon*), /qimṛun/ C-584 "shrimp, squid" (Sp *camarrón*), and /ṛiẓwaṛ/ C-606 "razor" (Fr *rasoir*, contrast Algerian /ṛaẓwaṛ/). In the first two the following /y/ might be a factor (but contrast /pḷay-a/ C-560 "beach", Sp *playa*, and similar cases). We get /ṭṛumbiy-a/ with /u/ in C-774 "top; bus" (Sp *tranvía* in the second sense), but here there are ample possibilities of contamination with other forms related to the first sense (see also C-772), and there is also a labial cluster in the stem.

Fr/Sp [u o ɔ], which ordinarily become MCA /u/, irregularly show up as MCA /i/ in these cases: /šifluṛ/ variant of C-704 "cauliflower" (Fr *chou-fleur*), where the palatoalveolar /š/ may have had an effect or where Sp *coliflor* may have had a contaminating effect; /šifuṛ/ variant of C-705 "driver" (Fr *chauffeur*, Sp *chófer*), again with initial /š/, and also with the possibility of vowel metathesis based on the Sp form (some interference between these two items, "cauliflower" and "driver", is also possible); /ṭṛinbu/ or /ṭṛimbu/ C-772 "top" (Sp *trompo* or similar cognate); /ṭṛiṭwaṛ/ variant of /ṭṛuṭwaṛ/ "sidewalk" (Fr *trottoir*) C-777. The same Fr/Sp vowels irregularly become /a/ in /faṛguṇiṭ/ C-204 "police van" (Fr *fourgonette*); /ṭamubil/ variant of /ṭuṃubil/ C-780 "car" (Fr *automobile* , Sp *automóvil*); and /mikṛafuṇ/ variant of /mikṛufuṇ/ C-499 "microphone" (Fr *microphone*). Fr [ü], which ordinarily becomes /i/ or /u/ in fully assimilated loans, shows up as /a/ in /ẓaḷamiṭ/ C-805 "match" (Fr *les allumettes*), perhaps a case of progressive assimilation.

Fr/Sp [i e ɛ], which normally become MCA /i/ (with /a/ occasionally found for Fr [ɛ]), show up as /u/ in these items: /burmid-a/ C-143 "Bermuda shorts" (Fr *Bermuda*), unless this is a case of vowel metathesis; doubtfully in /buftik/ C-124 "steak" (Fr *bifteck*, Sp *biftec*), since the /u/ may really reflect a Fr variant *boeufteck* or else direct analogical influence of Fr *boeuf*, which should become MCA /buf/; /kuḷumiṭ/ variant of /kiluṃiṭ/ C-353 "kilometre" (Fr *kilomètre*), where regressive vowel assimilation is likely; and /sulim-a/ variant of /sinim-a/ C-643 "movie theatre" (Fr *cinéma*). These vowels become MCA /a/ only in /srtafik-a/ and metathesized /srfatik-a/ variants of /srtifik-a/ C-659 "certificate"

(Fr *certificat*); and /ḅagaḍu/ variant of /ḅugaḍu/ C-125 "lawyer" (Sp *abogado*).

Fr [ə] or Sp *e* becomes /a/ in /kafatir-a/ C-309 "coffee-brewer" (Fr *cafetière*, Sp *cafetera*), with progressive assimilation likely. Fr stem-final [ɛy] becomes /a/ in /kuṛḅ-a/ C-416 "crate" (Fr *corbeille* [korbɛy]), but this involves reanalysis of the ending as FSg suffix /-a/.

Loss of vowels, particularly in stem-initial closed syllables, is not uncommon, particularly in early borrowings (6.4; cf. discussion of occasional compensatory lengthening of consonants in 6.10). There are a few other examples where instead of an expected vowel-nasal sequence we get a syllabic nasal (written /N/ or /əN/ in our transcription, with /N/ some nasal consonant /m n ŋ/): /fṛəŋk/ C-242 "centime" (Fr *franc*); /tnbr/ alongside /tanbr/, /tambr/ C-734 "postage stamp" (Fr *timbre*); northern /trən/ vs. southern /tran/ "train" C-736 (the former from Sp *tren*, the latter probably from Fr *train*); /zəng/ C-808 "zinc" (Fr *zinc*); and /ṭəŋg/ C-764 "(military) tank" (Fr *tank*).

We get MCA /^{w}/, realized as a brief rounded vowel when syllabic and as a labialized release between consonants otherwise, in a few items corresponding to vowels (usually [u o ɔ] or nasalized [õ]) in the Fr/Sp (or It) source: /f^{w}ṛšiṭ-a/ variant of /fṛšiṭ-a/ C-243 "fork" (Fr *fourchette*); /k^{w}bbaniy-a/ alongside /kubbaniy-a/ C-349 "business enterprise" (Sp *compañía*, Fr *compagnie*); /k^{w}ššin-a/ variant of /kššin-a/ C-384 "kitchen" (Sp *cocina* , It *cucina*); /k^{w}ṃanḍaṛ/ alongside /kuṃanḍaṛ/ C-398 "(army) major" (Fr *commandant*); /k^{w}ṛniṭ-a/ alongside /kuṛniṭ-a/ C-421 "bugle" (Sp *corneta*, Fr *cornet*). The forms with /^{w}/ are parallel to cases where an unrounded vowel is simply deleted in this position; with rounded vowels we have the possibility of leaving behind /^{w}/. Since Fr [ə] often becomes MCA /u/ (see end of 6.2), it is not surprising that an example of [ə] showing up as /^{w}/ in this syllabic position turns up: /r^{w}ppiṛa/ B-132 "he noticed (landmark)" (Fr *repérer*).

There are some cases of apparent contraction of Romance diphthongs to single vowels. For example, we have /fišṭ-a/ and /fižṭ-a/ C-220 "celebration" (cf. Sp *fiesta*). It is rather difficult to analyse such examples with Sp *ie*, since there is a regular correspondence of Sp *ie* to [ɛ] in Italian and also to the other Romance languages of the Iberian peninsula, Catalan and Portuguese. Relatively early loans like /fišṭ-a/ might thus be most directly related to a prototype like [fɛ́sta] from a language other than Sp, or be hybrid forms showing multiple influences. In the more recent borrowings known to me there is no similar monophthongization of source diphthongs.

There are some alternations of the type /CyV/ and /CiyV/ which may be briefly mentioned: /kamyu/ or /kamiyu/ C-313 "truck" (Fr *camion*, Sp *camión*); /klyan/ or /kliyan/ C-360 "customer" (Fr *client*), with native MCA agentive pattern /CCCaC/ a possible influence; and /maryu/ or /mariyu/ C-482 "wardrobe" (Sp *armario*, resegmented). The phonetic distinction here is slight.

Some minor cases of consonantal metathesis: /diks/ variant of /disk/ C-173 "record" (Fr *disc*); /sirfakit-a/ C-659, variant of /srtafik-a/ or /srtifik-a/ "certificate" (Fr *certificat*); /ṣblyun/ C-683 "Spanish (people)" alongside /ṣpnyul/ (Sp *español*, Fr

Table 6-1 Regular segmental correspondences in European borrowings

Fr/Sp/It/Eng/Ger	MCA
u o	u
i e	i
ɛ	i or sometimes a
a	a
ü	u, i, now often ü
ö	u, now often ö
ə	u
æ̃	aN (N is n, or homorganic to next consonant)
ã	ạ̃ or aN "
õ	u, uN, or õ "
b	b/ḅ, rarely v/ṿ
p	p/p̣, b/ḅ, pp/p̣p̣, bb/ḅḅ
v	v/ṿ, f/f̣
f	f/f̣
t	t ([t^s] or [t]) or ṭ
d	d/ḍ
č	tš
ǰ	dž
k	k, formerly q
g	g, formerly ġ (from Sp)
s	s/ṣ, rarely z/ẓ, formerly š (from Sp)
š	š, rarely ž
z	z/ẓ
ž	ž
x	x (recent Sp borrowings)
h	h (Eng)
w	w
ẅ	w (Fr)
y	y
m	m/ṃ (in mb, mp may be taken as allophone of n)
n	n/ṇ, rarely l, ṛ
ñ	n or ny
ŋ	ŋ or n/ṇ (even ŋ may be taken as allophone of n)
l	l/ḷ, with several examples of n/ṇ or r/ṛ
λ	y, rarely ly
r	r/ṛ, occasionally l/ḷ or n/ṇ, rarely ġ (from Fr)

Notes: Pharyngealized forms like ṣ and ṇ are normally possible when Fr/Sp vowels resemble appropriate variants of MCA full vowels. Such matters as truncation, cluster simplification, desyllabification, and prosodically based secondary gemination are not considered here but are dealt with in 6.4 and 6.10. Further details and lists of exceptions for segmental correspondences are considered in earlier sections.

espagnol); /tiniful/ variant of /tilifun/ C-723 "telephone" (Fr *téléphone* and cognates). If we take /n ṇ/ as manifestations of *l* (see examples in 6.5) we have two other possible examples in /šifṛuṇ/ variant of /šifḷuṛ/ C-704 "cauliflower" (Fr *chou-fleur*) and /žṇinaṛ/ variant of C-817 "general" (Fr *général*).

Some problematic cases, most of which show more than the usual minor irregularities, are C-131, 143, 218, 343, 362, 429, 460. See appendix entries for details.

See Table 6-1 above for a summary of regular segmental correspondences.

6.13 Morphological assimilation of verbs: Sp prototypes

In this and the next few sections we discuss the mechanics of borrowing verbs from Fr, Sp, and (rarely) other European languages. In the present section we consider direct, verb-to-verb borrowings from Sp, and in the next section we do the same for those from Fr. We defer discussion of internally generated denominatives (based on an earlier nominal or adjectival borrowing) until 6.17. However, we do count as verb-to-verb borrowings those where the initial borrowing may have been in participial form.

The first order of business is to determine which of the many Sp verb forms (infinitive, participle, inflected forms) was the direct basis for verb-to-verb borrowings. However, we should immediately emphasize that no verb-to-verb borrowings are currently going on from Sp in the Fes/Meknes area, where my fieldwork was concentrated (though the old Jewish dialects of the area retain a few very old Sp loans). Indeed, very few Sp verb-to-verb loans which enter Morocco in the area of Spanish influence (the north and northwest) reach the Fes/Meknes area even indirectly, by intra-MCA diffusion. Therefore most of the points to be made here apply only to the Spanish-influenced area — primarily the former Spanish Protectorate (Tangier, Tetouan and vicinity) but also to some extent down the coast to Casablanca.

If we think of the Sp verbal paradigms, it would seem reasonable a priori to expect one or the other of the following forms to be the most likely to serve as direct prototype: (a) infinitive *-ar*/*-er*/*-ir*; (b) participle *-ado*/*-ido*; (c) past imperfective *-aba*/*-ía*; or (d) 3Sg present and 2Sg familiar imperative *-a*/*-e*. (The first form in each pair or triad is that of the *-ar* conjugation, followed by that of the *-er* or *-ir* conjugations, which are merged in most cases.)

Further analysis suggests that (b) and (c) are less likely than (a) or (d). Neither (b) nor (c) resembles any particular MCA suffix, and both have an extra syllable. Moreover, (b) and (c) are fairly highly marked forms in Sp, the participle since Sp does not have a "compound past" like that of Fr or German functioning as high-frequency preterit, the imperfective since *-aba*/*-ía* is confined to past tense and competes with the very common preterit type with endings like 3Sg *-ó*/*-ió*. The infinitive *-ar*/*-er*/*-ir* has the disadvantage that there is no MCA parallel to *-Vr* as a stem-final element. However, the infinitive does have the advantage of being unusually conspicuous in Sp, since it is found not only in the infinitive itself but also (with additional pronominal endings) in the future, the conditional, and (at least superficially) in the 3Pl preterit. Thus from *cantar* "to sing" we get *cantará* "he will sing", *cantaría* "he would sing", and *cantaron* "they sang".

The advantage of the simple *-a*/*-e* ending is that it can be directly associated with the native MCA weak endings, which (except for some triliteral /CCV/ roots) have stem-final /i/ in all imperfective (including imperative) forms and in perfective forms preceding original suffix-initial consonants, but stem-final /a/ in other perfective forms (hence 3MSg, 3FSg, and 3Pl). To be sure, there is the problem that some Sp verbs have *-a* while others have *-e* (interpretable as MCA /i/) in the presumably most conspicuous Sp input forms (3Sg present, also used as polite 2Sg present, and familiar 2Sg imperative), so there is clearly no precise match of *-a* vs. *-e* in Sp with the MCA weak /a/ vs. /i/ alternation. The Sp subjunctive, with *-e* replacing *-a* and *-a* replacing *-e*, adds a further complication, but this does not improve the match with MCA (which has no subjunctive form), and in any event the subjunctive is not the most conspicuous Sp form.

What in fact happens in borrowings is that Sp infinitive *-ar*/*-er*/*-ir* is the regular prototype, becoming MCA /-aṛ/, /-iṛ/, or /-ir/, with /-ar/ the most frequent type. There are, however, a small number of documented borrowings ending in weak /a/ vs. /i/; most of these appear to be based directly on the Sp familiar Sg imperative and involve verbs commonly used in commands (the examples are mostly nautical in nature).

One old Sp borrowing, now treated in MCA as a noun, is /kumir/ C-401 "long thin bread loaf" (French bread) from Sp *comer* "to eat". This occurs widely in Morocco. However, borrowings functioning synchronically as verbs occur in my recent data from Tetouan and are well documented in earlier publications on northern and northwestern dialects.

One of many similar examples from Tetouan (Tt) is /fṛinaṛ/ "he braked (car)", which in this (citation) form is both 3MSg perfective and 2Sg imperative in MCA, but directly reflects Sp infinitive *frenar* "to brake". Other MCA forms are predictable: /maš n-fṛinaṛ/ "I will brake", /fṛinaṛ-t/ "I braked", /m-fṛinaṛ/ (participle), etc. There is no real morphological difficulty in assimilating such borrowings; however, the stem-forms are unlike the usual MCA ones in that they usually have two or more stem-medial vowels.

The pattern of using the Sp infinitive as the basis for most borrowings of the verb-to-verb type appears to apply to precolonial and early colonial loans as well, and (to the extent that present data permit conclusions) is true of old loans in Jewish dialects going back to Judeo-Spanish. We now give some examples from earlier publications (for abbreviations see p.xiii). From NLVM, which deals with maritime vocabulary, we can cite: /buṛdyaṛ/ "(ship) passed close by" < Sp *bordear* (NLVM 7); "đûšer" (perhaps /dušr/) "he tied up" < Sp *aducir* (NLVM 44); /žunṭaṛ/ "he attached" < Sp *juntar* (NLVM 27 suggests /ž/ rather than /x/ here on the analogy of earlier Sp borrowings with /ž/); /ṛašpaṛ/ "he scraped" < Sp *raspar* (NLVM 47); /ṛmukar/ (perhaps /ṛmukaṛ/) "he towed, tugged" < Sp *remolcar* (NLVM 51, but cf. Fr *remorquer*); /zngaṛ/ "he steered with rudder or oar" < Sp *singlar* (NLVM 55); /skanṣaṛ/ "(wind) calmed down", where NLVM 62 gives Sp *cansar (de)* as the source but where we should amend this to Sp *descansar*; /ġanžaṛ/, verb related to /ġanžu/ C-288 "harpoon, pitchfork" (Sp *gancho*), the verb perhaps from Sp *enganchar* (NLVM 97-8); /wanṭaṛ/ "(wind) kept blowing for long period", where Sp *ventear* is given by NLVM 150 as the source but where I suspect Sp *aguantar* "to wait". For Tangier, our early source is TAT, which has /panṣaṛ/ "he pierced bread (before baking)" apparently < Sp *pinchar* (TAT 242); perhaps /čunčaṛ/ "small cleared space on the side of oven pit" (TAT 258) is another case of a Sp infinitive now functioning as a noun, but here the etymology is mysterious. For the old Judeo-Arabic dialect of Fes, far from the Sp colonial zone, GJA 18 has "ṭpẹsyâr" (perhaps /t-piṣyar/ or /t-piṣyaṛ/) "he took a stroll"; the source given here is Sp *pisar*, but I would prefer Sp *pasear(se)* on both phonological and semantic grounds.

As noted above, not a single form based directly on Sp *-ar/-er/-ir* is in use, as a synchronic verb, in the major (Muslim) dialects of the interior (Fes, Meknes, etc.). However, one old borrowing given as /bnṭṛ/ or /pnṭṛ/ "he coated (boat) with tar" in NLVM 13, apparently reflecting Sp *pintar* "to paint", is now widespread in much of Morocco; see /bntr/ B-15 for my own data. It is not clear if these forms are really a simple verb-to-verb borrowing, since they could also be internal MCA denominatives from nominal borrowings like /bantur-a/ C-49 "paint". In any event, the fact that this form has become widespread, while the forms ending in /-aṛ/ and so forth are largely confined to the Spanish zone of influence, suggests that the latter type may sound awkward (because of the unusual overall stem-shape) to most Moroccans.

Still, within the Spanish-influenced area the type with /-aṛ/ (or /-iṛ/, /-ir/) has managed to become well established for Sp verb-to-verb borrowings. My brief data from Casaj (i.e. Jewish dialect of Casablanca) include a form /sinyaṛ/ "he signed (name, contract, etc.)", which appears to be a pseudo-Sp borrowing based actually on Fr *signer* (cf. noncognate Sp *firmar* "to sign") with /-aṛ/ added by analogy.

We noted above that the alternative to taking *-ar/-er/-ir* as the prototype for borrowings was to take the most unmarked finite forms, *-a* for the *-ar* conjugation and *-e* for *-er/-ir*. Most of the examples involve *-a*, and in most cases it is clearly the 2Sg familiar imperative which is most directly involved. From NLVM we can cite these: /larga/ (or /laṛga/?) "cast off!" < Sp *larga!* (NLVM 128, also MAG 50); /kaṣa/ "hoist!" < Sp *caza!* (NLVM 120; or should we suspect a deformation or crossing involving Sp *alza!*?); /hiṣa/ "hoist!" < Sp *iza!* (NLVM 147); /kaṛga/ "put up!" < Sp *carga!* (NLVM 122); and /manda/ in /manda ᶜl l-fluk/ "put out the jib for the boat!" < Sp *manda!* (NLVM 122). (Some of my gloss translations are only approximate, but we need not discuss this matter here.) A form /traka/ is given in MAG 50 in the sense "bring in (other boat)!" < Sp *traiga!* (polite, not familiar, 2Sg imperative), but this is probably an error; other sources (NLVM 21, ZLMA 26) have /tṛaka/ "attack (other boat)!" < Sp *atraca*.

These forms pose something of a problem for MCA, since the *-a* of the Sp imperative has been retained in the MCA form, also used mainly as imperative. However, in MCA the imperative is a formal subtype of the imperfective, and weak (vowel-final) stems with final /a/ or /i/ should have /i/, not /a/, in all imperfective forms, unless they have mediopassive /t-/ prefix. In the case of /ṭraka/ (see above), I suppose the form (though not the meaning) is consistent with this "mediopassive" analysis, but this is not true for the others. Therefore, to the extent that these borrowings function as true verb forms (not merely as frozen commands with just one form), they represent a slightly anomalous type. (They are not totally anomalous, since they seem to resemble the preexisting type consisting of weak root with mediopassive /t-/ prefix.) NLVM 128 states explicitly that /laṛga/ "cast off!" does have a full set of inflections, giving 3MSg imperfective /y-laṛga/ ("ilárga") as an example. (It is not clear whether the final /a/ becomes /i/ before consonant-initial perfective suffixes; I would certainly guess that it does, since this is what happens with weak roots prefixed with /t-/.) It may well be because of these anomalous features that Sp *-a*/*-e* (in practice mostly *-a*) has not become the standard prototype for verb-to-verb borrowings, leaving infinitive *-ar*/*-er*/*-ir* as the regular prototype. This amounts to the (untestable) hypothesis that had the majority of Sp verbs likely to be borrowed had a form in *-e* or *-i* (both of which would become MCA /i/) as the usual familiar 2Sg imperative (and 3Sg present tense form), this would have been the most common foot-in-the-door borrowing, with a regular weak paradigm subsequently developed by analogy to existing weak stems (with /i/ in imperatives and other imperfectives, /a/ or /i/ in the perfective depending on following suffix).

Two special individual cases remain to be mentioned. First, a verb /ḍala/ B-37 "he was obsessed with" is now widespread in Morocco (including Fes/Meknes), and according to EDA 351 this is from Sp *dale* "give him!" (*dá* "give!" plus 3Sg dative *-le*). This has a regular weak paradigm, hence /y-ḍali/ (3MSg imperative), etc. It appears that this is a case where an idiomatic verb form with suffix was taken as a single unit, with the Sp imperative form directly connected with the MCA imperative as /ḍali/ and with a regular weak paradigm constructed therefrom.

The second special case is /brda/ B-17 "it came off" and /piṛda/ B-113 "he wasted", along with /srba/ B-145 "he served". The first two are from Sp *perder* and/or Fr *perdre* (or forms thereof), the third from Sp *servir* and/or Fr *servir* (or forms thereof). These are regular weak paradigms.

For /piṛda/, we can mention the participle /m-piṛdi/ "(ship) in distress", which NLVM derives from Sp *perdido* "lost" (participle of *perder* "to lose"). I have some doubts about this, since we have possible Fr (and It) sources, in addition to the problem of deciding which particular inflected form is involved (Fr *perdu* could quite regularly become MCA /-piṛdi/, with participial prefix /m-/ added to this). However, it is possible that the particular form cited by NLVM is based on Sp, possibly on a composite of forms like *pierde*, *perder*, *perdí*, and *perdido*. If so, this would be a case where a regular weak paradigm results from a Sp verb-to-verb borrowing because this particular stem belongs to a Sp conjugation with frequent *e* or *i* vowel corresponding structurally to the MCA imperfective stem-final /i/. Similarly, /srba/ "he served" (imperfective /-srbi/, participle /m-srbi/) could possibly be based on

Sp *servir* (*sirve, serví, servido*) with the same kind of cross-linguistic morphological identification. (If /srba/ came in from Algeria the prototype might really be It *servire*, but the borrowing process within Algeria would have been along the same lines.)

A fuller study of the development of Sp verb-to-verb borrowings would be interesting, but would require much more fieldwork in and around the old Spanish colonial zone than I have done to date. Some further information about current usage of such borrowings in Tetouan is given in chapter 9.

6.14 Morphological assimilation of verbs: Fr prototypes

For Fr verb-to-verb borrowings we have to repeat the intellectual exercise of the preceding section on Sp borrowings. We begin by observing that the dominant Fr conjugation is that with infinitive *-er* (while *-re* and *-ir* conjugations tend to involve smaller numbers of stems which are also often high-frequency stems unlikely to be borrowed.)

If we set out the most basic inflected forms of the *-er* conjugation, we make a striking discovery. Of the several forms which would seem, a priori (e.e. on grounds of formal and semantic markedness), to be possible candidates for prototype form, after applying regular Fr-to-MCA diasystemic segmental conversions we get just two possible forms. First, there is a series of forms which would have stem-final /i/; second, there is another series with the same stem except for absence of this /i/.

If we take the verb *déclarer* as an example, we get MCA /ḍiklaṛi/ from any of the following forms: *déclarer* (infinitive), *déclaré* (participle), *déclarez* (2Pl or polite 2Sg present or imperative), and *déclarais/t* or *déclaraient* (Sg and 3Pl imperfective past). Perhaps we can throw in future and conditional forms like *déclarerai* and *déclarerais*, which would be very hard for the average Moroccan with a little Fr to distinguish from the preceding set. Now if /ḍiklaṛi/ is associated with the MCA imperfective (including all imperative, present, and future as well as past imperfective), we can easily derive a regular weak paradigm with 3MSg perfective /ḍiklaṛa/ and so forth by internal analogies. If the participle (in adjectival use, not as part of the "compound past" type *j'ai déclaré* "I declared") is the initial borrowing, we could add participial /m-/ prefix, hence /m-ḍiklaṛi/ "declared", and we can still derive a regular weak inflected paradigm from this by internal MCA analogies (e.g. with mediopassive /t-/, /ḍ-ḍiklaṛa/ "to be declared"). But we do not even need such morphological additions to produce fully assimilated MCA forms. Fr *déclarez* in the polite 2Sg imperative can simply be taken as /ḍiklaṛi/, the regular MCA 2Sg imperative (there being no polite/familiar opposition in MCA. In addition, a past imperfective form like *il déclarait* "he was declaring", where the *il* is often pronounced just as [i], can be directly equated with MCA /y-ḍiklaṛi/ (3MSg imperfective), which can be past imperfective (as well as present or future). This fortuitous cross-linguistic conversion frame was discussed in 4.5 where we mentioned the difficulty in sharply distinguishing borrowing from code-switching in such verb forms.

The other real possibility for Fr verb-to-verb borrowings is to take Fr verbs with (phonetic) zero suffix as the prototype. This would be Sg and 3Pl present or subjunctive forms like *déclare(s)* and *déclarent*, 2Sg imperative *déclare*, or a composite of these. In this event, the MCA borrowing would be /ḍiklaṛ/ with invariant stem: /ḍiklaṛ-t/ "I declared", /ḍiklaṛ-u/ "they declared" or 2Pl imperative "declare!", etc.

Of these two possibilities, /ḍiklaṛa/ with weak paradigm or /ḍiklaṛ/ with invariant stem, the regular choice is in fact /ḍiklaṛa/. Bilinguals who now spontaneously introduce new borrowings (i.e. productively use Fr verbs with MCA morphological frames) regularly use this weak type; for /ḍiklaṛa/ see B-40, and appendix B has a large number of other cases of weak borrowings from Fr *-er* conjugation verbs.

We deal with exceptions to this below, but right now we want to ask a further question. Whereas the *-er* conjugation in Fr shows extensive syncretism among surface forms, so that most of the important forms would become either /ḍiklaṛi/ or /ḍiklaṛ/ after regular segmental conversions, other Fr verbs show greater surface differentiation of the relevant forms, so examination of borrowings based on them may reveal more precisely which of the /i/-final forms is the real prototype. Is it the infinitive *-er*/*-re*/*-ir* (as in Sp), the participle *-é*/*-u*/*-i*, the polite 2Sg (and 2Pl) present *-ez*/*-issez* (usually we can treat past imperfective Sg *-ais/t* and *-issais/t* the same way), or the familiar Sg imperative *-∅*/*-is* (usually not differentiated clearly from the Sg present forms)?

Unfortunately, relatively few relevant stems have been borrowed, and it is difficult to persuade informants to reveal how they would borrow a given Fr stem if their lives depended on being able to borrow it. We do, however, have some relevant data, and the participial form seems to be the best predictor (though we will qualify this below).

For example, three recent borrowings (none very well established but all recorded in the Fes/Meknes area) have citation forms /ṛiyạža/ B-130 "he reacted" (Fr *réagir*), /šwạza/ B-166 "he chose" (Fr *choisir*), and /kura/ B-92 "he ran" (Fr *courir*). The first two of these Fr stems take *-iss-* augment in the past imperative and 2Pl or polite 2Sg present forms (*réagissais/t*, *réagissez*) and the related forms. Possible prototype forms are thus those lacking the *-iss-* augment, which is absent from the borrowed form: participle *réagi*, Sg present forms like *réagis/t*, and familiar Sg imperative *réagis*(and similar forms for *choisir*). The infinitive forms in *-ir* are unsuitable since the *r*, which is pronounced in Fr *-ir* (though not Fr *-er*), is not present in the MCA form. In the case of *courir*, the fact that the MCA form has weak endings eliminates familiar Sg imperative *cours* along with Sg present forms like *cours/t*. Remaining possibilities are the participle *couru*, past imperfective Sg and 3Pl forms like *courais*, and 2Pl or polite 2Sg present or imperative *courez*, all of which would produce /-kuri/ in MCA and thus lead to a regular weak paradigm (with /kura/ as citation form). By combining the data from *réagir* and *choisir* with those from *courir*, only the participle (*réagi*, *choisi*, *couru*)is consistent with all forms. This could lead us to suspect that even in the *-er* conjugation, participial *-é* is the "real" prototype form, and we could try to explain this by emphasizing the use of the Fr participle not only as an adjective but also in "compound past" forms (*j'ai réagi* "I reacted", etc.).

There is, however, another explanation. First, we take the *-er* conjugation as historically and analogically primary and recognize that within this conjugation the combination of several forms with final mid or central front vowel (*déclarer, déclaré, déclarais/t, déclarez*) is sufficient to make the usual MCA borrowing the weak type /ḍiklaṛa/ (imperfective /-ḍiklaṛi/). Then, the occasional new borrowing from a verb of a different class will take an MCA form which most closely resembles this predominant borrowed type. In the case of *courir*, the combination of participial *couru*, polite 2Sg and 2Pl *courez*, and so forth produces /-kuri/, hence the weak type /kura/; in the case of *réagir* and *choisir*, either /-ṛiyạži/ (from *réagi, réagis/t*) or */-ṛiyạžisi/ (from *réagissez*, etc.) would permit construction of a suitable weak paradigm, and the former is chosen (hence citation form /ṛiyạža/) because it is shorter. In this explanation, we have no grounds for singling out a particular Fr verb form as the prototype; the initial pattern is established by a group of forms from the *-er* conjugation which are phonologically indistinguishable from each other (after conversions), then analogical patterns apply to new borrowings.

One piece of evidence for this is the fact that, when arm-twisted, my Fes informant indicated that if Fr *boire* "to drink" were borrowed, it would take the form /büva/, imperfective /-büvi/. This would be incompatible with the irregular Fr participle *bu* [bü], but would be compatible with polite 2Sg and 2Pl form *buvez*, and with past imperfective Sg *buvais/t* and 3Pl *buvaient*. Note that these inflected forms cannot be the direct prototypes for the MCA forms of *choisir* and *réagir*. What does seem to unify these cases is that the resulting MCA canonical shape is always a weak form (with final /a/-/i/ alternation) with at least one stem-vowel but without unnecessary suffix increments.

We now consider evidence that weak MCA stem forms are not the only possibility. While recent Fr verb-to-verb borrowings are normally assimilated in weak forms, it is possible to hear consonant-final forms in everyday speech among bilinguals, although this seems to be possible only when the MCA verb form itself has no suffixes. Thus in 4.6 we have mentioned the odd case like /ka-y- *habitent*/ "they live", where we have a kind of code-switching with the switch point in the middle of the verb form, so that MCA 3Pl ending /-u/ is not used. This type is not very common, and it should be noted that this particular switch point also coincides with a frequent hesitation point (i.e. when speakers begin with prefixes, then pause to find a verbal lexical item). A similar form, /ta-y-šuṃ/ "he is unemployed" (Fr *il chôme*) is mentioned in B-165 along with the better-assimilated weak form /šuṃa/.

In addition to sporadic examples of this type, which usually do not become well established, there is some evidence that strong (non-weak) forms of Fr verb-to-verb borrowings were formerly fairly common in some MCA dialects.

First, preliminary inspection of data on some Judeo-Arabic dialects (e.g. Rabat) spoken by Jews who left Morocco two or three decades ago (and whose dialect thus reflects local Judeo-Arabic of that period) produces examples of the type /ḍiṛā̃ž/ "he distributed", in contrast to weak /ḍiṛā̃ža/ B-44. Moreover, even in my more modern Moroccan data we may find strong variants of borrowings also attested in weak form. Thus /buksa/ or /buks/ B-27 "he boxed" (Fr *boxer*), /t-frma/ or /tt-frm/ B-56 "it became worn out" (Fr *réformer*), /t-müskla/ or /t-müskl/ B-102 "he showed off muscles" (Fr *musclé*), /ṭṛafika/ or /ṭṛafik/ B-177 "he swindled" (Fr *trafiquer*), /ẓṛṭa/ or /ẓṛṭ/ B-183 "he deserted" (Fr *déserter*). Some of these are difficult to analyse; some may involve denominative derivation (e.g. /buks/ C-128 "boxing" may be involved in the first of these), and /t-müskl/ variant of B-102 cannot be based directly on a Fr verb with zero suffix since such a form (**il muscle*) does not exist (though noun *muscle* "muscle" exists alongside *musclé*, a pseudo-participle like its Eng gloss "muscled"). However, at least some of these forms do appear to be genuinely based on short Fr verb forms with zero suffix. Since we have seen, in the preceding section, some clear cases of Sp imperatives being the basis of a verb-to-verb borrowing, there is no reason why this should not happen occasionally in a Fr borrowing. Moreover, there are a couple of cases (at least) where a Fr verb-to-verb borrowing (with complete paradigm, including Sg imperative with stem-final /i/) coexists with a special alternative imperative without the stem-final vowel: /rul/ "let her roll!" (to bus driver, see /rula/ B-135), and /ṣṭup̣/ "stop!" (see /ṣṭup̣p̣a/ B-156). The first of these is presumably Fr *roule!*, while the second could be either Eng *stop!* or Fr *stoppe!* in the short imperative form.

We will discuss in a later section the denominative verbs which are derived internally after a noun or adjective has been borrowed. However, we should mention now that some of those cases are problematic, since the MCA form (though compatible in form with denominative origin) seems to have at least a partial direct relationship to a Fr verb (perhaps as well as a relationship to the corresponding Fr noun or adjective). Thus /gyyəd/ B-71 "he guided (tourists)" might be denominative from noun /gid/ C-269 "tourist guide", Pl /gyad/, but we might also consider it to be directly based on Fr *guider*. If we disregard the noun /gid/ entirely, we would have to say that Fr forms like *guide!* (imperative), *guides*, *guident*, etc., with phonetic zero suffix, give aninitial prototype [gid] which is fashioned into /gyyəd/ in MCA. This reshaping might perhaps be motivated in that /-gid/, taken as imperfective, would require analogical perfective /gad/ "he guided", and there might be resistance to this type of form since the perfective stem would be quite different from the Fr prototype [gid] and since triliteral hollow verbs in MCA are a relatively closed class which rarely admits a Fr borrowing. Some other examples of borrowed verbs which can be taken either as internal denominatives or direct verb-to-verb borrowings put into /CCCəC/ stem-shape are B-15, 30, 32, 36, 112, 146. Two examples where a very good case can be made for direct verb-to-verb origin, but where the Algerian dialect is the locus of the change, are /mṇṇək/ B-101 "he did not show up (for work)" (Fr *manquer*), also used now in Morocco, and /ṛmməṣ/ B-124 (Alg only) "He collected (things)" vs. MCA /ṛamaṣa/ (Fr *ramasser*). We should also mention /gufl/ B-68 "he inflated" (Fr *gonfler*) and perhaps /ḍubl/ or /dubl/ B-68 "he doubled (Fr *doubler* or denominative from C-187). There is a good chance that Fr verb forms (with zero suffix) have been at least a contributing influence in several of these borrowings. But we also have canonical-shape pressures from within MCA at work simultaneously. Note, for example, that /faḷṭ/ B-47 "he made a mistake" can only be taken as a denominative from noun /faḷṭ-a/ C-198 (Sp *falta*); it has been shaped by analogy to existing /CaCC/ (or /CaCəC/) stems already in MCA.

This essentially exhausts what I know about the question of choice of Fr prototype form. However, I should add that in a number of cases, for essentially semantic reasons, the primary borrowed form in MCA is a participle with /m-/ prefix. Sometimes (B-1, 29, 39, 129) the participle is the only form recorded (in my present data), more often we have recorded both the participle and the semantically associated mediopassive form with prefix /t-/ (B-22, 45, 51, 56, 59, 60, 76, 105, 120, 143). There are also several where the participle, though coexisting with a complete verbal paradigm, does seem particularly common and prominent (B-10, 12, 17, 41, 65, 72, 80, 82, 106, 115, 116, 127, 137, 146, 147, 159, though this list is somewhat arbitrary). It is likely, then, that a number of verb-to-verb borrowings have initially come in as participles and then (in most cases) developed complete paradigms, though we do not suggest here that all verb-to-verb borrowings have followed this route; indeed, some borrowed verbs occur rarely or not at all in participial form. The type with participle as foot-in-the-door borrowing probably involves this scenario: a Fr participle used commonly as adjective, like *énervé* or *blindé*, is introduced as a code-switched form like */nirvi/ or */blandi/; this is then elaborated as an MCA participle /m-nirvi/, /m-blandi/ by adding participial /m-/, with no further change since the stem is already in the correct form for a weak participle; by analogy we can internally generate mediopassive /t-nirva/ "he was agitated" and then transitive /nirva/ "he agitated (someone else)". Of course, the existence of Fr verbs *énerver, blinder* could act as a reinforcing factor in the latter stages. (Of these two Fr borrowings, the actually attested borrowings for *énerver*, with the further influence of Fr *nerveux*, are participle /m-nirvi/ and mediopassive /t-nirva/, though */nirva/ would be understood and may be found in later fieldwork; for *blinder* we do have all relevant stages attested, though /blandi/ C-100 is listed separately from the participle and verb forms of B-10.)

In general, other Fr derivatives of verbs, notably agentive nouns in *-eur* and verbal nouns in *-age*, do not directly produce verb-to-verb borrowings. However, /bntr/ B-15 and variants "he painted" could possibly be an internal denominative based on /bantur-a/ C-49 "paint", and as variants of /sira/ B-141 "he shined (shoe)" (Fr *cirer*) we have /siřž/, apparently internally derived from MCA verbal noun /siraž/ (Fr *cirage*), and even /siřža/, which is based on /siřž/ with an added vowel to produce a weak stem. For some other problematic cases see the discussion of denominatives below. See also /sdr/ B-139 and /t-šumr/ p.117, below.

6.15 Borrowed triliteral weak and hollow verbs

The basic point here is that there are very few established borrowings of the types /CCa/ and /CaC/ (citation forms based on 3MSg perfective, with /a/ changing to a lexically determined vowel /a/, /i/ or /u/ in the imperfective). In other words, these seem to be basically closed classes which tend to avoid admitting new members. Let us look at the possible examples we do have.

There appear to be three weak triliterals of shape /CCa/ (3MSg perfective), at least two of which are defective. First, from Fr *briller* "to shine" we get, alongside /briya/ B-20 "it shone" (with full weak paradigm), a stem /-bri/ used only in the imperfective (B-18), hence /ka-t-bri/ "it (e.g. sun) is shining", clearly based on Fr 3Sg present (*il/elle*) *brille* [briy]. The corresponding weak form would be /ka-t-briyi/, which might be disfavoured because of the final /iyi/ sequence (for a case of haplology involving a similar sequence see the Pl form of C-667).

The second case is /sna/, a variant of /sinya/ and /sina/ B-140 "he signed (name, contract, etc.)". The short form can produce regular finite forms like /sni-t/ "I signed" and /ka-y-sni/ "he signs", but not participial */m-sni/, since only fuller forms like /m-sini/ and /m-sinyi/ are acceptable. The source is Fr *signer*. The existence of a short form /sna/ seems to be an idiosyncrasy of this lexical item, since others of similar canonical shape never shorten to /CCa/.

The last case is /tka/, imperfective /-tki/ B-169 "he knocked out (other boxer)". Unfortunately, it is difficult to determine the precise source of the borrowing, though Fr *K.O.* (from Eng *knock-out* or *K.O.*) is involved somehow (cf. C-342, also C-429).

We now consider cases of triliteral hollow stems of the type /CaC/. The only one which seems to be really established (in the Fes/Meknes dialect at any rate) is /šat/, imperfective /-šut/ B-162 "he shot (e.g. in soccer)", which may well have come in from outside Morocco through the language of soccer broadcasts (presumably from Egypt, where this verb is commonly used), though Fr *shooter* may have been a supportive influence.

Aside from this, we can perhaps cite /fuk/ B-58 "must" (Fr *il faut*) as in /fuk t-mši/ "you must go". This seems now to be a frozen, unanalysable form, but it would seem that in some MCA or Algerian dialects, where it takes forms like /y-fuk/ with 3MSg imperfective prefix, it is interpreted as the imperfective form of a verb whose 3MSg perfective would be */fak/ if it existed. In this case we could take /-fuk/ as a defective hollow triliteral.

The isolated imperfective form /rul/ "let her roll!" (shout to bus driver) could be taken as an MCA triliteral hollow imperative, with analogical processes producing 3MSg perfective */ral/. However, only the imperative is attested; other forms of the Fr stem (*rouler*) are attested in the usual weak form /rula/ B-135.

Similarly, alongside weak /šuṃa/ "he was unemployed" (Fr *chômer*), we have recorded /ta-y-šuṃ/ "he is unemployed" (See B-165), which can be taken as a regular triliteral weak form (cf. native /ta-y-nuḍ/ "he gets up"). However, we do not get analogical 3MSg perfective */šaṃ/, and /ta-y-šuṃ/ itself is only a sporadically attested type (vs. regular /ta-y-šuṃi/ with weak stem) and can be considered a special type of code-switching (see 4.5, 4.6) involving Fr 3Sg present *chôme*. See also /t-šumr/ below, p.117.

6.16 English verbal borrowings

Aside from a small number of internally derived denominative verbs not considered here (see 6.17, 6.18), Eng verb-to-verb borrowings are vanishingly rare among the general Moroccan population. We can, however, mention a couple of examples used chiefly in humorous or other marked styles by Moroccans who know a little Eng. These examples suggest that Eng verb-to-verb borrowings are treated by analogy to Fr borrowings.

First, we have /spika/ B-144 "he spoke", as in /ta-y-spiki myzan/ "he speaks well" (Eng *speak*); this is used mainly in the context of learning to speak Eng, and might be used among students taking an Eng course. Note that the weak stem-final vowel /a/, alternating regularly with /i/, is added, making this look like most Fr verbal borrowings, even though there is no corresponding syllable in any common Eng form (other than *speaking*, which is hardly the most conspicuous form for this verb).

Second, I have recorded borrowings based on Eng *screw* in the slang sense "to copulate with". The Eng pronunciation can be directly converted into /-skriw/, which is analysed as imperfective (weak) stem /-skri-/ plus imperfective Pl suffix, hence /n-skri-w-ha/ "let's screw her!", from which 3MSg perfective /skra/ can be derived by analogy. However, I have also recorded /skruwa/ for this Eng verb, with a regular weak paradigm.

It is probable that more examples could be obtained by studying the slang developed among university students studying Eng, or perhaps tourist guides specializing in Eng-speaking suckers. My informants and friends were not in these categories; however, some last-minute items from Eng are given at the end of section 7.15.

6.17 /CCCəC/ verbal borrowings, including denominatives

A respectable number of MCA verbs of European origin show up as /CCCəC/, which is represented as /CCCC/ when C_4 is a syllabic sonorant; we also include here cases of /t-CCCəC/ with mediopassive prefix. Many of these quadriliteral stems, which join an established native MCA stem type, are internally derived denominatives which presuppose the earlier borrowing of a Fr/Sp (or Eng) noun or adjective, but some seem to be direct borrowings.

We first consider cases where all four consonants are distinct (or at least where C_2 and C_3 are). First, we have a series of apparently recent borrowings of the type /t-CCCəC/ meaning "he acted like (a certain type of person, often pejorative)", all clearly modelled on previously borrowed nouns. These are: /t-fnṭəẓ/ B-53 "he acted like a big shot, put on airs" (cf. C-226), this being perhaps the oldest of the set; /t-bgbəṣ/ B-6 "he acted like a big shot" (cf. C-79); /t-bṛžəz/ B-24 "he acted like a (rich) bourgeois" (cf. C-149, 150); /t-bznəs/ B-31 (Fes form) "he was a drug dealer" (cf. C-163); /t-frkəs/ B-55 "he acted like a dandy" (cf. C-232); and /t-gṛṣn/ B-67 "he did servile labour" (cf. C-264). These are a special case of a more general, highly productive derivational type with similar meaning with /t-/ and quadriliteral (or longer) root, these examples being those where the root has four consonants and thus patterns like a usual MCA strong quadriliteral.

Other /CCCəC/ borrowings (with C_2 and C_3 distinct) lacking /t-/ prefix are these: /m-?ntək/ B-1 "elegant" (now participial only); /brnəz/ B-21 "he varnished" (cf. C-789); /bẓwəṭ/ B-32 "he hazed (new student)" (cf. C-96, C-164); /ḟngḷ/ B-52 "he copulated with" (slang, cf. C-200); /ḅyḍṛ/ variant of B-112 "he pedalled" (cf. C-77); /srkl/ B-146 "he surrounded" (cf. C-650); /škləṭ/ B-164 "he masturbated" (cf. C-711); and /bntr/ B-15 "he painted" (cf. C-49, 50). Most of these are of probable denominative origin.

Parallel to the above we have a number of cases of /t-CCCəC/ and /CCCəC/ which reflect a triconsonantal root with C_2 doubled, as in the native factitive-causative stem. The type /t-CCəC/ occurs in /t-šyyək/ B-167 "he acted suave" (cf. C-707). The type /CCCəC/ occurs in /bwwəṭ/ B-30 "he beat up" (cf. C-161); /dwwəš/ B-36 "he took a shower" (cf. C-177); /gyyəd/ B-71 "he guided" (cf. C-269; there is also an alternative verb /gida/ B-64); /rwwn/ B-137 "he mixed together" (cf. C-625); /ṣbbəṭ/ variant of B-151 "he attacked; he kicked"; /ṣbbn/ B-153 "he washed (with soap)" (cf. C-666). These examples appear to be denominative in origin, though some may also have been directly influenced by Fr verb forms. Some other slightly more problematic cases: /gwwəd/ B-70 "he guided" is really an inherited form; /k^{w}rrəz/ B-79 "he embraced" is recorded only for Marrakech and is of doubtful origin; /mṇṇək/ B-101 "he failed to show up" is a verb-to-verb borrowing from Fr *manquer* but may have come in from Algeria; /myyək/ B-104 "he avoided (person)" is now considered denominative from /mik-a/ C-496 "plastic" but, as indicated in the discussion of B-104, appears to derive historically from a verb form still used in Algeria, unrelated to /mik-a/; /ṛmməṣ/, Algerian variant of /ṛamaṣa/ B-124 "he gathered in (cards)" is another direct verbal borrowing from Fr *ramasser* but is not attested for Morocco.

6.18 Weak denominative verbs

In this section we consider cases where MCA has a borrowed verb ending in the stem-final /a/ or /i/ characteristic of weak verbs, usually with one or two other full vowels in the stem. We are interested in verbs of this type which appear to be internal MCA derivatives based on earlier borrowed nouns or adjectives, but which do not take the /CCCəC/ factitive-causative or /t-CCCəC/ mediopassive form described in the preceding section.

Many possible cases of weak denominatives are etymologically problematic since the Fr (or Sp) prototype might be either a verb or a paired noun of similar shape. However, consider /žwana/ B-187, meaning either "he put (it) into envelope" or "he gave (him) a joint of hashish". This appears to be denominative, in the first sense from /žwa/ C-827 "envelope" and in the second sense from /žwan/ C-828 "joint (of hashish)", both from Fr *joint*. It does not appear possible to consider /žwana/ a direct verb-to-verb borrowing, since no Fr verbs with these meanings appear to be current. Similarly, /fanta/ B-48 "he dodged, faked (in soccer)" seems to be from noun /fant-a/ C-201 (also /fant/) "(a) fake, (a) dodge", which is

Fr *feinte*. It is doubtful that Fr verb *feindre* is the direct source of /fanta/ B-48. Likewise, /bḷana/ B-9 "he schemed, made plans" seems to be a denominative from noun /bḷan/ C-99 "plan" (Fr and Sp *plan*).

It seems likely that this particular denominative formation is analogical, based on the model established by paired noun-verb borrowings where both the noun and verb exist in Fr or Sp. For example, noun /gum-a/ C-285 "eraser" (Sp *goma*, Fr *gomme*) and verb /guma/ B-69 "he erased" (Fr *gommer*) can both be plausibly derived from specific Sp or Fr prototypes, as can noun /glaṣ/ C-273 "ice cream" and verb /glaṣa/ B-65 "he froze" (Fr *glace*, *glacer*). There are a large number of similar paired noun-verb borrowings, where the verb shows stem-final /a/ in the citation form matching either zero or FSg /-a/ in the noun. From this well-represented set it is possible to establish the generalization that borrowed nouns ending in zero or /-a/ correspond to semantically related verbs with /a/ in the 3MSg perfective (i.e. weak verb stems). It would appear to be this pattern which is responsible for cases like those in the preceding paragraph, where the MCA verb is of analogical origin. (For other possible examples see B-11, 34, 74, but these are not clearcut cases.)

An example involving an Eng loan is /t-spida/ B-143 "he used 'speed' (harmful narcotic)", presumably reflecting denominative formation from /spid/"speed". However, it is conceivable that Fr slang has been a mediating agent here and if so some Fr verb forms may be involved.

In the case of /t-hippa/ B-72 "he acted like a hippie" from noun /hippi/ C-291 "hippie", the formation is a little different; the /t-/ mediopassive prefix here requires that the final vowel of the stem be /a/ except in the perfective before a consonant-initial subject suffix. See also B-51 and 102.

6.19 /CuCəC/, /CuCC/ verbs

There are a fair number of obvious denominatives with mediopassive /t-/ of the form /t-CuCəC/ varying with /t-CuCC/ (the latter normal if the last C is a nongeminated sonorant). The Tetouan variants are of the form /t-CawCaC/ or the like. Some examples go back to the early colonial period: /t-fuḅṛ/ B-57 "he gave a small gift to" (from /faḅuṛ/ C-193), /t-ṛufəẓ/ B-134 "he was insolent" (ultimately Fr *refuser* "to refuse"). Both of these involve some restructuring beyond the minimal segmental conversions, to assimilate them to a minor but pre-existing type /t-CuC(ə)C/ in MCA. Note that both /faḅuṛ/ and a direct segmental conversion of Fr *re* (as /ru/) contain /u/. In the case of B-134 a denominative basis is possible but uncertain.

The more recent cases also involve an initially borrowed noun containing /u/, usually before but sometimes following C_2. The examples involve the sense "he acted like a ...", already exemplified with slightly different stem-shapes in the two preceding sections. Examples are /t-buḍr/ B-25 "he acted like strong man, flexed muscles" from /budr-a/ C-123 "pillar"; /t-ḅugəṣ/ B-26 "he acted like a dandy" from /ḅuguṣ/ C-26; t-kumək/ B-86 "he clowned around" from /kumik/ C-400; /t-kunəb/ B-87 "he acted like a hick" from /kambu/ C-311 (with /mb/ in noun reanalysed as /n/ plus /b/; /t-ṣufəž/ B-157 "he acted wild" from /ṣuyaž/ C-694 or regional variant; /d-zufr/ B-184 "he acted like a playboy" from /zufri/ C-809; and /t-šumr/ (not in appendix) "he was idle, unemployed" (participle /m-šumr/ "idle", Fr *chômeur*).

Some /CuC(ə)C/ stems lacking /t-/: /šukəš/ (not in appendix) "he packed clothing" from /šakuš/ C-698 "bag"; /gufl/ B-68 "he inflated" (early colonial loan from Fr verb *gonfler*); denominatives from borrowed noun with /u/ like /buks/ B-27 "he boxed" (cf. C-128); /dubl/ or /ḍubl/ B-46 "he doubled" (cf. C-187); /kufṛ/ B-83 "he preserved in alcohol" (see entry for discussion of etymology); the variant /musəq/ of B-103 "he played music for"; /numr/ B-107 "he numbered" (cf. nouns /nmr-a/ C-534 and /nimiru/ C-533, perhaps unattested MCA */numiru/ at an earlier time from Sp *número*); /sugr/ B-149 "he matched" (earliest attested meaning "he insured" from Sp noun *seguros*, verb *asegurar*).

It would appear from these data that /CuCəC/ or /CuCC/ functions much as an extension of the strong quadriliteral type /CCCəC/, with C_2 in the latter formula replaced by /u/. However, the type with /u/ is clearly more prominent and more productive than alternative types with /a/ or /i/, though the latter do occur (see below). The fact that the noun /kambu/ C-311 "country hick" forms a verb /t-kunəb/ rather than */t-kanəb/, for example, suggests that /t-CuCəC/ is a favoured type and that a /u/-vowel in the model form, even if it follows C_2, is enough to suggest the /t-CuCəC/ stem shape.

6.20 /CiCC/, /CaCC/ verbs

For /CiCC/ we can cite a few examples from our data on borrowed verbs. First, among a number of variants for "he pedalled" B-112 we have /biḍṛ/, probably denominative from /biḍaṛ-a/ C-77, though /ḅyḍṛ/ is another attested variant for B-112. Second, /sirž/ occurs along with /sira/ and /sirža/ B-141 for "he shined (shoe)", where /sira/ is direct from Fr verb *cirer*, while /sirž/ is a secondary formation based on verbal noun /siraž/ (Fr *cirage*), and /sirža/ is a tertiary formation based on the preceding. Others are /rigl/ B-127 "he repaired" (Fr *régler* with some influence of *rigoler*), and /mitr/ "he took long strides" (not in appendix) related to noun /mitr/ C-506 "metre (unit of distance)".

For /CaCC/ we can cite only /faḷṭ/ B-47 "he made a mistake". This may be a relatively early formation, and seems to be an irregular denominative from noun /faḷṭ-a/ C-198.

It is striking how few verbs of the type /CaCC/ exist since there are native MCA forms of this shape: /ᶜawn/ "he helped", /ᶜayn/ "he waited", /ḥawl/ "he tried", etc. The type /CiCC/ also seems to admit new borrowings very sparingly.

6.21 Verbal nouns

In native MCA paradigms, the form of the verbal noun is predictable or nearly so from the form of the inflected stem: usually /CCaC/ or /CCiC/ for strong triliterals, /t-CCaC/ or /t-CCiC/ for factitive-causative derivatives, /t-CCCiC/ for other strong quadriliterals, /m-CaCC-a/ for most /CaCC/ stems, and so forth.

Attempts were made to elicit verbal nouns for the borrowed verbs. Some verbal nouns were easily elicited; some were elicitable but of uncommon usage or else semantically specialized; others could not be elicited.

The principal mechanical difficulty in producing verbal nouns is that many of the borrowed verbs have stem-shapes which do not fit into traditional MCA canonical patterns; it is therefore not clear how speakers can construct MCA-type verbal nouns from them. Frequently, what happens is that a Fr or Sp noun closely related to the borrowed Fr or Sp verb is also borrowed into MCA and functions more or less like a verbal noun (though often having a more concrete meaning). Thus, along with verb /brikula/ B-19 "he improvised" (Fr *bricoler*) we have verbal noun /brikul/ (Fr *bricole*). In this particular pattern the borrowed verbal noun lacks the stem-final vowel of the borrowed verb. (This pattern is the analogical source for a few weak denominative verbs, see 6.18.)

The Fr derivative in *-age* is also fairly common in borrowed nouns which function approximately (in many cases) like verbal nouns. The suffix is pronounced [ạž] or [æž] in borrowings, depending on the particular form. To account for this surface opposition, in the case of [ạž] we take the preceding consonant as pharyngealized. Frequently, the relevant consonant is clearly pharyngealized in the corresponding verb as well, hence /ḍimaṛa/ B-42 "he moved forward" and verbal noun /ḍimaṛaž/; see also B-110 and 178, and compare /baṛa/ B-5 "he blocked off" with /baṛaž/ C-56 "police checkpoint". However, in some other cases the [ạž] pronunciation in the verbal noun is simply carried over from Fr *-age*, despite the fact that the relevant preceding consonant is not pharyngealized in the finite verb forms. Thus /ḍipana/ B-43 "he repaired" with unpharyngealized /n/, but /ḍipaṇaž/ as the verbal noun; see also B-22, 172, 174. There are also a number of examples where the stem-final consonant is unpharyngealized in both finite forms and verbal noun so that the latter has phonetic form [æž], as with /dribla/ B-35 "he dribbled" and /driblaž/; see also B-66, 90, 141. Incidentally, these verbal nouns are normally presented in appendix B under the entries headed by the borrowed verb form; a few cases of borrowings from *-age* which do not function (in MCA) as verbal nouns are listed with the nouns in appendix C (e.g. C-278, 464).

In addition to such cases where the MCA verbal noun is directly borrowed from a Fr or Sp noun, there are many cases where a native MCA verbal noun pattern is derived on the basis of the initially borrowed finite verb.

For stems of the factitive-causative type (quadriliteral, but with $C_2 = C_3$), the productive verbal noun is /t-CCaC/. The /t-/ prefix is released separately when C_1 is an alveolar. Thus we get /t^-dwaš/ as verbal noun from /dwwəš/ B-136 "he took a shower". Others of /t-CCaC/ type are seen in the entries B-71, 101, 151, 153. These data show that /t-CCaC/ is the productive factitive-causative verbal noun type for the Fes/Meknes dialects in question, and suggest that the alternative type /t-CCiC/ is primarily characteristic of CA borrowings (see A-1-318ff.). This is one example of how data on borrowings can help us get at questions of synchronic productivity.

For nongeminate strong quadriliterals and for stems with /u/ or /i/ in the position of C_2 (/CuCəC/, /CiCəC/), the regular verbal noun in this dialect is /t-CCCiC/, /t-CuCiC/, or /t-CiCiC/, respectively; FSg suffix /-a/ is occasionally added (not always with individuating force). Thus from /t-bgbɔṣ/ B-6 "he acted like a big shot", /numr/ B-107 "he singled out", and /bidr/ variant of B-112 "he pedalled", the verbal nouns are /t-bgbiṣ/, /t-numir/, and /t-biḍiṛ/. The /t-/ prefix is used for verbal nouns whether based semantically on simple strong quadriliteral verbs, or on derivatives with mediopassive prefix /t-/, and it is best to regard these as distinct /t-/ prefixes. Other examples of strong quadriliteral verbal nouns with four consonants are in the entries for B-15, 23, 31, 32, 53, 67; examples with a vowel in the position of C_2 are B-26, 86, 134, and two of these with added FSg /-a/ are B-57, 149.

A number of weak stems with at least four root segments (including the final "weak" vowel) take either or both of these verbal noun patterns: (a) one modelled on native /m-CaCy-a/ from /CaCa/, but in the case of borrowings extended occasionally to longer stems; (b) a verbal noun type modelled on /t-CCCy-a/ from verb /CCCa/ (weak quadriliteral). Type (a) is natural enough in the case of /gaža/ B-63 "he enlisted", vbl.n. /m-gažy-a/, since the stem shares the /CaCa/ shape of native forms like /qaḍa/ "he finished", vbl.n. /m-qaḍy-a/. However, type (a) also extends to borrowed verbs with slightly different shapes, hence /m-glaṣy-a/ from /blaṣa/ B-65 "he froze", /m-sury-a/ from /sura/ B-150 "he insured", /m-ṭṛaṣy-a/ from /ṭṛaṣa/ B-178 "he drew". On the other hand, the type (b) pattern with prefix /t-/ instead of /m-/ is found in /t-bṛõzy-a/ from /t-bṛõza/ B-22 "he got a suntan" and /t-maṛky-a/ from /maṛka/ B-97 "he scored". Both type (a) and (b) forms are attested without sharp difference in meaning in /m-grisy-a/ and /t-grisy-a/ from /brisa/ B-66 "he greased; he attacked"; see also B-72, 145.

Because of low text frequency, some such verbal nouns were elicited only with some difficulty, and not confirmed by observation in natural speech. It is likely that individuals will differ fairly substantially in their choice of type (a) and (b) forms, and indeed in their willingness to produce such verbal nouns at all.

6.22 Participles and agentives

True participles are entirely predictable in form. As with MCA participles in general, the uncertainties mainly have to do with whether a given stem will have a participle in normal usage, and (if transitive) whether the participle is active or passive.

It is difficult to find any examples of MCA participles based on borrowed triliteral stems, since such stems are rare and usually are variants coexisting with longer stem forms; see B-139, 183. In the case of /sna/ variant of B-140 "he signed", even speakers who use the form /sna/ in inflected verb forms like /sni-t/ "I signed" use the variant /sina/ as the basis for the participle /m-sini/ "signed". Therefore we cannot produce clear examples of triliteral participles in borrowed paradigms.

For the quadriliteral and longer stems it is much easier to find participles. Here, as in native forms, the participial prefix is /m-/, while the stem is the same as in the verb forms except that for weak stems the final stem segment in the participle is /i/

word-finally and /y/ before FSg /-a/ and Pl /-in/.

The sense of the /m-/ participle in MCA can be active or passive. With the borrowings both senses are attested, with much idiosyncratic lexical variation; there is no need for a long discussion here. Examples of the active sense are /m-bṛẓəṭ/ "pestering (someone)" from /bṛẓəṭ/ B-21 "he pestered", /m-kaṣi/ "taking sharp corner (in motorcycle race)" from /kaṣa/ B-73 "he cut corner", perhaps also those in B-82 and 121. In /m-rigl/ "sarcastic (person), teaser" the sense is active, but the simple verb form is of the type /t-rigl ᶜli-ya/ "he teased me" with the teaser formally in mediopassive form (and with the person teased in a prepositional phrase).

The majority of attested /m-/ participles with borrowed stems are semantically passive: B-2, 10, 12, 17, 19, 22, 30, 39, 59, 65, 80, 106, 115, 137, 140. Some which do not really have a passive sense but which indicate personality or the like are /m-hippi/ "hippie, acting like a hippie" from B-72, cf. B-45, 60, 72, 105, 146, 147, and 159.

For some borrowed verbs, it is worth again pointing out that the participle may have been the initial and most salient borrowed form (for other borrowings this was clearly not the case). For example, /m-nirvi/ "worried" may well have been a direct borrowing from Fr *énervé* (and *nerveux*), with /m-/ added because the meaning suggested that of a participle or because speakers could recognise the diasystemic equivalence of participles in the two languages; the inflected verbal form /t-nirva/ B-105 "he became worried" could then have been created on the basis of many similar participle-verb paradigms by analogy. Note that /blandi/ C-100 and /m-blandi/ in the entry B-10, both meaning "armoured" (Fr *blindé*) seem to represent early and late stages of adaptation along the same lines.

Synchronically, some borrowings where the participle seems to be the only form now in common use for my informants are B-1, 29, 129 (though for B-1, as the entry indicates, finite verb forms are attested in an earlier source). Some other cases where the participle seems to be quite common or has meanings not shared by the finite forms are B-2, 17, 30, 39, 41, 45, 51, 59, 60, 65, 80, 82, 105, 106, 127, 146, 147, 154, 159; some of these are also candidates for verbs whose initial borrowed form may have been participial.

There are also some agentive nouns related formally and semantically to borrowed verbs. Unlike true participles, their forms are not always totally predictable from the inflected verb form. Some, in fact, are direct borrowings from Fr agentives in *-eur* (or feminine *-euse*). The borrowed forms sometimes retain (approximately) the front rounded Fr vowel, hence /ör/ and /öz/, but more assimilated variants /ur/ and /uz/ are also common and are preferred by the less well-educated speakers. Some examples are /brikulur/ "improviser, handy-man" (see B-19), /sirur/ "shoe-shiner" (see B-141), and /bḷasuz/ and variants "(female) usher in theatre" C-101 (Fr *bricoleur, cireur, placeuse*). These borrowed *-eur*/*-euse* agentives come in independently of the associated verbs, and there are many cases where the agentive borrowing (used as a label for an occupation or characteristic) does not correspond in MCA to a related verb, as with /kʷafur/ C-433 "barber" (*coiffeur*).

Aside from such direct nominal borrowings, there are some examples of the MCA agentive pattern /CCCaC/ from borrowings, with FSg

/-a/ and MPl /-a/, the usual suffixes for this MCA pattern. Examples are /bṛẓaṭ/ "parasite, pest (person)" C-119 (cf. B-23) and /ṣbban-a/ C-680 "washerwoman" (see B-153). The form /bznas/ C-163 "(drug) dealer" is of this morphological type, but may be a direct borrowing (slightly reshaped) from Fr *business*(see also B-31; note that C-163 includes other variants). It is likely that /fsyan/ variant of "officer" C-245, and /qbṭan/ C-583 "captain" are at least vaguely associated with this /CCCaC/ formation, but they have /-at/ instead of /-a/ as Pl suffix, and they are not connected with any MCA verbs.

A difficult form /bẓwiṭ/ C-164 "new student subjected to hazing", related to verb /bẓwəṭ/ B-32 "he hazed" (cf. /bizu/ C-96, the relevant Fr forms being *bizut*, verb *bizuter*, verbal noun *bizutage*), is probably of complex origin. A native noun pattern /CCCiC/ does exist, cf. /bttix/ "melon", /gṛṭiṭ/ "country hick", but it is not exceptionally common and does not usually have a clear relationship to a verb. It is not clear to what extent /bẓwiṭ/ is an internal MCA derivative and to what extent it might be directly based on the Fr forms.

Another important agentive pattern in MCA is /CCaCC-i/, MPl or FSg /CCaCC-iy-a/. There are a few examples of this involving borrowings. First we mention internal MCA derivatives based on an earlier borrowing: /ṣbabṭ-i/ C-679 "shoemaker" from /ṣbbaṭ/ C-681 "shoes" (if the latter is a borrowing); /mwagn-i/ C-528 "watch-seller" from /magan-a/ C-460 "watch, clock" (again, if this is a borrowing). The primary forms in these cases are nouns, but the derivatives have agent-like meaning.

In addition to these possible cases of internal generation of /CCaCC-i/, there are a few cases where a Fr borrowing which happened to have approximately similar shape has been borrowed directly as /CCaCC-i/. Hence /gṛayd-i/ C-276 "graded, ranked (officer)" (Fr *gradé*), /bwand-i/ C-160 "bandit" (Fr *bandit*), perhaps /ṭṛanži/ C-766 "foreigner" (obsolescent, Fr *étranger*). Another borrowing, /blandi/ C-100 "armoured (unit)" (Fr *blindé*) looks formally as though it belongs in this type but does not fit semantically and does not appear to take Pl */blandi-ya/. Cf. C-527, 581, and 804.

The bizarre form /mu-bṛẓiṭ/ "pest (person)" (see B-23) involves the verb /bṛẓəṭ/ B-23 "he pestered", denominative from /baṛaẓiṭ/ C-55 "parasite, pest" (/bṛẓaṭ/ C-119, discussed above, is an internal agentive derivative). The form /mu-bṛẓiṭ/ has the form of borrowed CA participles (used as agentives) of the type /mufttiš/ "inspector", /mumttil/ "actor",etc. (see A-1-276ff.) with CA prefix *mu-*. Thus /mu-bṛẓiṭ/ "pest", co-occurring with true participle /m-bṛẓəṭ/ "pestering (someone)", is an analogical, pseudo-CA formation which would presuppose a CA verb **barzaṭ-* "to pester".

To complete this section we point out that the productive MCA formation for abstract nouns of profession (cf. Eng. *carpentry*, *dentistry*, etc.), with /ta-/ prefix and /-t/ suffix sandwiching a stem denoting the relevant agent, occasionally occurs with a stem being one of the borrowed agentive forms just described, usually /CCCaC/. In the case of /ta-gyyad-t/ "profession of being (tourist) guide", the form /gyyad/ actually does not often occur except in this derivative, since elsewhere /gid/ C-269 is usual for "guide" (the form */ta-gid-t/ is, however, impossible).

6.23 Direct borrowing of nouns and adjectives

In this and the next few sections we deal with nouns and adjectives, two word classes which are not sharply distinct formally (though some subtypes of each are distinctive).

The usual pattern is for a Fr (or other European) stem to enter MCA as a Sg stem permitting various MCA affixes, with other stems (Pl, Dimin, sometimes a denominative verb) then being generated internally by existing MCA patterns of ablaut and/or affixation. There are, however, some exceptions which will be mentioned.

The inherited MCA FSg (feminine singular) suffix is /-a/, which contrasts for many stems with MSg -Ø (zero), the latter not usually being indicated in the transcription. The grammatical gender of a borrowed noun is determined, with very few exceptions, by the form of the borrowing; if /-a/ is present the borrowing is FSg, otherwise the borrowing is MSg in its simple form. Frequently the borrowing ends in /-a/ simply because the Fr input form happens to end in a similar vowel; however, in 6.25 below we discuss a number of cases where MCA has added /-a/ in a borrowed noun whose original form (in Fr or some other language) has no corresponding vocalic segment.

Consider, for example, /duš/ C-177 "shower" from Fr *douche*. Here the Fr form ends (phonetically) in a consonant (the *e* is "silent"), and the MCA form is produced by a regular segment-by-segment transposition. Since /duš/ does not end in /-a/ in MCA, it is grammatically masculine for purposes of gender concord, as in /d-duš l-mzyan/ "the good shower", not */d-duš l-mzyan-a/. On the other hand, consider /anṭiṛṇ-a/ C-15 "campus" from Fr *internat* (with "silent" *t*). Again, the MCA borrowing is produced by simple segmental conversions, but since the borrowing happens to end in /a/, the latter is interpreted as the FSg suffix /-a/ and the borrowing is feminine: /l-anṭiṛṇ-a l-mzyan-a/ "the good campus". Additional forms of /duš/ and of /anṭiṛṇ-a/ are derived internally in MCA; hence Pl /duš-at/ or /dwaš/, denominative /dwwəš/ "he took a shower" B-36, and Pl /anṭiṛṇ-at/, to all of which (except the denominative verb) we can add definite prefix /l-/ (becoming /d-/ before /d/) and/or a "preposition".

However, things are not always so simple. We will see below that vowel-initial borrowings like /anṭiṛṇ-a/, which are rare in inherited MCA stems, pose problems regarding the segmentability of the definite prefix /l-/ (6.24). In the present section we will consider the more general question of how simple segmental conversions interact with standardized MCA canonical-shape patterns.

First, recall (6.4) that a large number (though perhaps less than a majority) of multisyllabic noun borrowings show loss of one or more vowels in the first syllable or two of the source form, sometimes with compensatory lengthening of a consonant: /bṛmsyun/ C-111 "(military) leave" (Fr *permission*), /šḷaḍ-a/ C-712 "salad" alongside /šaḷaḍ-a/ (Sp *ensalada*, Fr *salade*), etc. This could possibly be taken as a simple phonological process involving reduction of pretonic syllable (in the source form), but it is equally reasonable to take this as a restructuring to conform with MCA stem-shape norms for nouns, which are not as rigid as they are for verbs but do none the less favour shapes like /CCVC/ and /CCCVC/ (with or without following /-a/ suffix for FSg). In any event, this type of restructuring is not typical of recent borrowings, and occurs chiefly in precolonial or very early colonial loans.

Second, we have noted in the previous section that some borrowings come into MCA in forms like /CCCaC/ and /CCaCC-i/ which correspond exactly to existing MCA patterns for agentive and other derivatives. In some such cases, it would appear that the borrowing has been slightly bent to fit it into the pattern in question; that is, regular segmental conversions would have resulted in a slightly distinct borrowed output (though one sufficiently similar to the existing MCA pattern that a conversion into this pattern would require only minor tampering). Naturally, such twisting occurs primarily when the borrowing fits naturally into the existing MCA type on semantic grounds as well. Thus /bwandi/ C-160 "bandit" (Fr *bandit*) and /g̣rayd-i/ C-276 "ranked (officer)" (Fr *gradé*) seem to have been slightly reshaped to fit the /CCaCC-i/ agentive pattern; we might have expected /bandi/ (attested from Marrakech informant) and */g̣ṛaḍi/ if only regular segmental conversions had been at work.

Third, since compounding is not productive in MCA, and since "conjunct" possessive nexus is lexically restricted, several Fr or other compounds or noun-adjective sequences come into MCA as unit stems. Hence /firuž/ C-218 "stoplight" (Fr *feu rouge*), /bulasarrut/ C-131 "highway police" (Fr *police de route*), /buṛṭfuy/ C-147 "wallet" (Fr *portefeuille*), /dublsumil/ C-176 "walking, steps" (infraction in basketball) (Fr *double semelle*), /kaṛṭbuṣṭ-a/ variant of C-330 "postcard" (Fr *carte postale*, perhaps contaminated with /buṣṭ-a/ C-151 "post office", Fr *poste*), and several others. Usually there is no clear evidence (e.g. from intonation) that these are anything other than unsegmentable unit stems.

As time has gone on, and as the number of borrowings (particularly from Fr) has increased, canonical-shape restrictions formerly applied to borrowings have been relaxed (just as foreign phonemes are now often retained, as noted earlier). New borrowings, especially among bilinguals, now tend to come in with few changes in pronunciation from the Fr (or other) original, and it is difficult in these cases to draw a line between spontaneous code-switchings and integrated borrowings (except in Pl and other forms where the speaker must choose between MCA and Fr morphology).

This general phenomenon can be seen in the number of variant forms recorded for some of the borrowings, where (leaving regional variations aside) we notice some MCA forms quite different from that of the Fr prototype and others closely approximating it. Usually in such cases we are dealing with one or more early borrowings showing substantial formal restructuring to fit MCA patterns (perhaps with a Fr syllable lopped off or desyllabified, foreign segments replaced by MCA segments, perhaps FSg suffix /-a/ added, etc.). In addition to the old borrowed forms, which may still be in active use in rural areas and among older, monolingual, or uneducated persons, there may be one or several more recent re-borrowings based on the same Fr prototype. The newer borrowings are, in some cases, entirely independent of the earlier borrowings, in which case the newer ones can be described merely by reference to the Fr form and the currently productive adaptation processes. In other cases we have a triangular relationship, whereby the newer reborrowings are based partly on the Fr form and partly on the pre-existing (older) borrowing; the old borrowing is taken as starting point and is partially reshaped so that it is somewhat closer than previously to the Fr prototype.

An example of separate, independent borrowings is /qbṭan/ C-583 "(military) captain" and the more recent /kapitan/ C-319 "(team) captain (in sports)", both from Fr *capitaine* (some other Romance cognates possibly involved as well in the earlier borrowing). I am not aware of any intermediate forms between /qbṭan/ and /kapitan/ which would suggest interaction between them. On the other hand, a good candidate for a partial reshaping of an old borrowing is /žṇinaṛ/ variant of C-817 "(military) general", which seems to be a partly modernized form of /žṇṇiniṛ/ (Fr *général*); another variant, /žiṇiṛal/, is an independent recent reborrowing based directly on the Fr form. A similar type of partial (but incomplete) remodelling is also seen in a number of cases of Fr/Sp crossing (6.29 below).

The detailed analysis of reshaping and reborrowing is probably best postponed to a future moment when more extensive material on dialect variants is available. Fieldwork for the present publication did make some provision for dialect variation, but does not suffice for thorough studies of chronological relationships among variant forms, which are necessary for adequate historical analysis. The general theoretical points can be made using the data on Fr/Sp crossings just referenced.

6.24 Definite prefix and treatment of stem-initial vowels

As noted earlier, most noun and adjective borrowings come in as MCA singular stems. Among other affixes, they normally may take definite prefix /l-/, which regularly assimilates to a following coronal (alveolar or postalveolar) consonant in C_1 position, as in /d-duš/ "the shower". Note that the MCA definite form is not directly based on Fr *la douche*.

There are, however, some subsidiary patterns requiring attention. In this section we treat the following topics in order: (a) treatment of Fr *la* and *les*; (b) choice of /l-/ or /ž-/ as definite allomorph for borrowed stems with C_1 = /ž/; (c) reinterpretation of /l/, and /z/ from Fr prevocalic *les*, as stem-initial segment; (d) cases where no distinction is made between definite and indefinite forms; (e) reanalysis of Fr/Sp stem-initial *l* as MCA definite prefix /l-/.

There is little difficulty in assimilating Fr nouns whose definite prefix in Fr is *le* before noncoronal consonant, or *l'* (masculine or feminine) before vowel. In such cases the Fr definite noun form can be more or less directly converted into the MCA definite form, taking advantage of the fortuitous similarity between these Fr elements and MCA definite /l-/. Thus MCA /l-gaṛṣun/ "the waiter" could be a direct borrowing from Fr *le garçon*, while /gaṛṣun/ without /l-/ could be related to the simple Fr stem *garçon*. Or, we could hypothesize that either /l-gaṛṣun/ or /gaṛṣun/ entered MCA, with the other then generated internally by analogy to the hundreds of native nouns with /l-/ definite prefix and zero prefix for the indefinite.

It should be noted in this connection, though, that the syntactic usage of definite and indefinite forms is rather distinct in the two languages. The Fr definite form usually implies the MCA definite in translations. However, in Fr there are two other forms: those with indefinite article (*un*, *une*, *des*), and a form without article used in some adverbial phrases and with preceding numeral: *deux garçons* "two boys" (or "two waiters"). In MCA there are only two forms, definite /l-gaṛṣun/ and indefinite /gaṛṣun/. Moreover, the most common semantically indefinite NP type in MCA involves /waḥəd/ "a, one" followed by what is morphologically the definite noun, as in /waḥəd l-gaṛṣun/ "a waiter". The morphological indefinite form without prefix /l-/ is used in another construction with /ši/ "some" (the construction with /ši/ generally indicates that the referent is truly unknown or indefinite, while the form with /waḥəd/ may be used, for example, to introduce a new referent at a given discourse point), as in /ši gaṛṣun/ "some/any waiter". The morphological indefinite is also used with certain numerals, as in /^{c}šrin gaṛṣun/ "twenty waiters"; but definite forms are used with certain other numerals.

In the case of /(l-)gaṛṣun/ "(the) waiter" we cannot really tell whether the definite (prefixed) or indefinite (simple) MCA form is the primary borrowing (or the chronologically earliest). In some other types of nouns we can make such a determination on formal grounds, but some cases point to the definite form as primary while others point to the indefinite as primary.

Evidence for taking the definite form as primary comes from examples showing Fr or Sp stem-initial *l* reanalysed as /l-/ prefix in MCA, with back-formation of the MCA indefinite lacking this segment. However, this phenomenon (see end of the present section) is observed only in a few items. This marginal evidence is outweighed by the very large number of borrowings whose initial segment is a coronal consonant, and which take assimilated forms of definite /l-/, as in /d-difili/ C-166 "the parade" (Fr *le défilé*), /s-sigaṛ/ C-637 "the cigar" (Fr *le cigare*), and /t-tir/ C-727 "the shot" (Fr *le tir*). Since the assimilation of the definite article in MCA is a morphophonemic idiosyncrasy rather than a general, productive phonological rule (it does not apply to preposition /l-/ "to/for"), the occurrence of assimilated definite allomorphs in the forms just listed shows that they are not based on direct segmental conversions from the Fr definite forms, rather they are internally generated by applying the usual morphophonemic rules to MCA definite /l-/. This is consistent with the position that what is really borrowed is just the simple stem, here /difili/ and so forth, with MCA (not Fr) supplying affix frames.

Let us pursue this matter by considering what happens to Fr feminine nouns with definite *la* (excluding contracted *l'* before vowel-initial feminine nouns). There would seem to be three possible treatments, a priori: (a) borrow both the simple Fr stem as the MCA indefinite, and the definite Fr form as the MCA definite, so that /la-/ or /ḷa-/ must be recognised now as a new allomorph of the MCA definite prefix; (b) borrow only the definite form with Fr *la*, resegment this as having prefix /l-/ (or /ḷ-/), and back-form the indefinite so that it begins with /a/; (c) borrow just the simple form from Fr as the MCA indefinite and generate the definite by the regular MCA patterns.

In fact, the most common treatment of Fr borrowings is (c). Hence Fr *(la) douche* "the shower" becomes /(d-)duš/ C-177; Fr *(la) gomme* or perhaps Sp *(la) goma* "the rubber eraser" becomes /(l-)gum-a/ C-285, etc., with definite forms shown in parentheses. Unless otherwise indicated, borrowed nouns and adjectives in appendix C can be assumed to have this treatment.

However, in a sizeable minority of instances treatment (a) is attested; in other words, a given borrowing has a definite prefix /la-/ or /ḷa-/ which is (more or less) stabilized in MCA (examples below). On the other hand, treatment (b) is quite uncommon; we can cite only /(l-)aṛaf/ C-17 "(the) police van" from Fr *(la) rafle*, and /(l-)antrit/ C-12 "(the) retirement pension" from Fr *(la) retraite*; in the latter example, moreover, the indefinite form /antrit/ is uncommon and for speakers who do not use it the segmentation is ambiguous.

In the numerous examples of treatment (a), there is a second formal problem requiring comment, involving the distinction between /la-/ and /ḷa-/. There are three cases: those with phonetic [læ-], always represented as /la-/; those with phonetic [lạ-], where the pharyngealization cannot be ascribed to the following stem-initial segments and so we must recognise /ḷa-/ as the transcription of the prefix; and those with phonetic [lạ-] but where the pharyngealization may be attributed to the stem-initial segments. The last type is one where no surface distinction between underlying /la-/ and /ḷa-/ is possible, so we arbitrarily represent the prefix as /la-/ in keeping with our conservative policy on recognizing pharyngealization in phonemic transcriptions.

The type with distinctively unpharyngealized /la-/ is seen in /(la-)ban/ "(the) dump-truck" C-45 (Fr *la benne*, see entry for details); others are C-66 (sense 2), 108, 301, 303, 422, 556, 557, 569, 647, 648, 748, and one variant in C-250. The type with distinctively pharyngealized /ḷa-/ is seen in /(ḷa-)fut/ C-250 (Marrakech variant), where the /f/ is not pharyngealized (since the /u/ is not lowered); others are C-259, 328, 371, 376, 446, 561, 568, 665, 695, and variants of C-272 and 273. The type with surface pharyngealization attributable to the stem-initial segments is seen in /(la-)ḅal/ C-39 "(the) ball"; others are C-47, 73, 116, 488, 507, 591, 688 (Marrakech variant), 692, and 761.

Leaving aside this third, indeterminate set (where only one surface pronunciation is possible), the choice between /la-/ and /ḷa-/ cannot be determined rigorously from the form of the following noun in this dialect. However, /ḷa-/ does tend to be used in stems which do have a pharyngealized segment somewhere, perhaps at the end of the stem, while /la-/ is characteristic of stems lacking pharyngealized consonants. This (Fes/Meknes) material is distinct, however, from data from other Moroccan locations (notably Tetouan), where /ḷa-/ is the dominant form regardless of stem. Even for Fes/Meknes, it may be that /ḷa-/ is on its way to becoming regular for the most recent batch of borrowings, since /ḷa-/ is closer than /la-/ to Fr *la*; hence /(ḷa-)lin/ C-446 "(the) line" from Fr *(la) ligne*, with /ḷa-/ despite the absence of pharyngealization in the stem.

In addition to the question of choosing between /la-/ and /ḷa-/, there is also the question of why certain nouns retain a syllabic definite prefix based on Fr *la* while others simply adopt the usual MCA definite prefix /l-/ or assimilated /C_1-/ replacing Fr *la*. It is possible that short stems of the shape /CVC/ tend to keep the syllabic definite prefix more than longer stems — note /(ḷa-)gaṛ/ C-259 "(the) train station" (Fr *la gare*) in addition to examples in the two preceding paragraphs — but /(d-)duš/ C-177 "(the) shower" from *(la) douche* is one of several counterexamples. No clear patterns depending on choice of stem-initial consonant are discernible; several stems, moreover, show fluctuation between syllabic /la-/ or /ḷa-/ and the regular MCA form /l-/ or /C_1-/.

There are no cases where Sp definite article *la* has resulted in /la-/ or /ḷa-/ coming in as a definite allomorph with a borrowing. Such Sp borrowings come into northern MCA dialects with regular MCA definite prefixes, and so of course they remain regular as they trickle down into more southerly dialects.

Retention of syllabic /la-/ or /ḷa-/ from Fr *la* does not serve as a marker of feminine gender in MCA; instead, gender is marked by presence or absence of FSg suffix /-a/. Thus /(la-)pisin/ C-556 "(the) swimming pool" (Fr feminine *la piscine*) is grammatically masculine in MCA, hence /la-pisin mzyan/ (not */mzyan-a/) "the swimming pool is good". Actually, in the case of a code-switched NP or a half-assimilated borrowing, an educated bilingual Moroccan may transfer the Fr grammatical gender to MCA (e.g. in concord), but in the case of the relatively well assimilated and stabilized borrowings the presence of definite /la-/ or /ḷa-/ is disregarded in determining grammatical gender. (In Algeria, on the other hand, /la-/ and /ḷa-/ does appear to be a regular marker of feminine gender in borrowings from Fr.)

Fr definite plural *les* has not become established in MCA as a plural form of definite /l-/; this is another difference between MCA and Algerian Arabic. One hears *les X* frequently (with some noun X) in Fr code-switched phrases in MCA, but as a borrowing becomes established it is usual to develop a regular MCA plural by ablaut or suffixation, with the regular definite prefix /l-/ or /C_1-/ as in the corresponding singular.

In two cases involving very short Fr nouns, *les* has been reanalysed as the initial syllable of the stem. Thus /liḅ-a/ C-442 "stocking" is actually from Fr *les bas*, but the MCA form is now singular, cf. Pl /liḅ-at/. Similarly, we have /lig-a/ "glove" C-443 from Fr *les gants*, with Pl /lig-at/ and Dimin /lwig-a/. Definite /l-/ can be added to any of these forms, hence /l-liḅ-a/ "the stocking". It is clear that although *les* has been incorporated into these forms, it has lost its plural (and definite) meaning and is just part of the stem; moreover, this reshaping is almost certainly a functional device to prevent these forms from having an anomalously brief canonical shape. Later on in this section we discuss a couple of cases where Fr *les* [lez] before a vowel has left behind a trace in the form of stem-initial /z/ or /ẓ/ in the borrowing. (In Algeria, /li-/ or /ḷi-/ from Fr *les* occurs in numerous paradigms of borrowed Fr nouns as a definite plural marker.)

We now consider choice of /l-/ or /ž-/ as allomorph of definite /l-/ in borrowings with stem-initial /ž/. This question arises because traditional MCA has /ž-/ in this case (with exceptions in some dialects), while recent borrowings from CA show /l-/; thus old MCA /ž-žu^{c}/ "the hunger", but recent CA borrowing /l-žumhuṛ/ A-1-163 "the crowd" from *al-ǰumhūr-* (see p.53).

The borrowings from Fr all take /ž-/, not /l-/, hence /ž-žuṛṇal/ C-824 "the newspaper" from Fr *le journal*. This applies to all European borrowings beginning with /ž/, provided they can take definite prefixes at all. (Of course, a form like *le journal* can occur as a code-switching.) This treatment of Fr borrowings indicates that the morphophonemic rule for assimilating definite /l-/ to coronal C_1 of the stem is still productive, even though it does not apply to recent CA borrowings (5.6).

We now discuss cases where a Fr or Sp definite noun form has undergone reinterpretation and resegmentation. First, there are cases where *l* in the definite article of the source form is now treated as a stem consonant. We have already mentioned the type /liḅ-a/ C-442 "stocking" from Fr *les bas*, where definite Pl *les* has been taken as part of the MCA stem. A possible case of Fr feminine *la* in a similar resegmentation is /lam-a/ C-436 "hands, hand ball (infraction in soccer)" from Fr *la main*, but this is usually an interjection and is difficult to analyse morphologically in MCA.

Other examples involving *l* are /ltšin/ C-452 "oranges" (Sp *la China* "China"), /ḷažnyuṛ/ C-441 "engineer" (Fr *l'ingénieur*), /laṣ/ C-440 "ace (card)" (Sp *el as*, Fr *l'as*), and /luṭuṣṭup/ C-455 "hitch-hiking" (Fr *l'autostop*). In these cases the *l* of the original is retained even in MCA indefinite forms, and definite forms are of the type /l-laṣ/ "the ace" and /l-ltšin/ "the orange" (however, /ḷažnyuṛ/ for some speakers is either definite or indefinite without further prefix, and /luṭuṣṭup/ usually does not take a further definite prefix except in the truncated variant /ṭuṣṭup/). Note also Pl /liṣ-an/ "aces" (cf. /fir-an/ "mice"), presupposing /laṣ/ (not /aṣ/) as Sg counterpart.

The fact that /ḷažnyuṛ/ and /luṭuṣṭup/ do not readily admit a further definite /l-/ (or variant /ḷ-/) prefix for many speakers suggests that there is some ambiguity in speakers' minds as to whether the initial lateral in the simple form is really a stem segment or already the definite prefix. Thus, if /ḷažnyuṛ/ is used both as the definite form and the indefinite, it seems to be intermediate between an analysis of the stem as /ḷažnyuṛ/ (which gets the indefinite form right but predicts definite */l-ḷažnyuṛ/, which this set of speakers does not use), and an analysis of it as /ažnyuṛ/ or perhaps /ạžnyuṛ/, which would result in correct /ḷ-ažnyuṛ/ (equivalent to /l-ạžnyuṛ/) for the definite but incorrect */ažnyuṛ/ (or */ạžnyuṛ/) for the indefinite (I know of no speakers who show this pattern, though perhaps there are some somewhere in Morocco).

Similarly, some items listed in appendix C with initial /a/ (see first few pages in that appendix) tend to be used, especially by older and rural speakers, with definite /l-/ in all contexts (indefinite as well as definite), and here again we may have ambiguity as to whether the lateral is synchronically a stem-initial or prefixal segment. For these items, my primary Fes/Meknes informants (mostly fairly well educated) did have indefinite forms without the /l-/ at least as a possible surface form; in this case, a glottal stop may be introduced before word-initial /a/. Thus the form given in the appendix as /aṇaṇaṣ/ C-9 "pineapples", when combined with /ši/ "some" (which regularly takes the indefinite form of a following noun), can give /ši aṇaṇaṣ/, /ši ?aṇaṇaṣ/, or /ši l-aṇaṇaṣ/ "some (quantity of) pineapple(s)". In my experience, the same speaker may use more than one of these forms, and some speakers appear uncomfortable in producing this type of example in elicitation. There are only a few MCA nouns (old, or recent borrowings) beginning in /i/ or /u/, but those that do occur show somewhat similar patterns. Thus, from Fr *hotel* we get MCA /uṭil/ C-784 "hotel", where most of my informants could produce /ši uṭil/ "some hotel" (optionally /ši ?uṭil/). However, the northern form is /?uṭil/ with consistent stem-initial glottal, as in definite /l-?uṭil/ "the hotel" (cf. /l-uṭil/ in Fes and Meknes), and a rural variant /nutir/ or /nuṭiṛ/ is also well attested (the /n/ could be a case of sporadic nasalization of former /l/ from Sp *el hotel*, Fr *l'hôtel*, or could result from resegmentation of indefinite Sp *un hotel*, Fr *un hôtel*). In either case, the initial stem consonant (/?/ or /n/) in the MCA form can be seen as an increment designed to avoid a stem-initial vowel, which is very rare (and morphophonemically problematic) in native MCA words.

Ordinarily, borrowings in which the stem-initial segment is /l/, matching stem-initial *l* in the prototype, are morphophonemically regular; that is, they take /l-/ in definite forms: /ḷamb-a/ C-437 "lamp", def. /ḷ-ḷamb-a/. However, in the case of /lastik/ C-439 "rubber band" (Fr *élastique*), for many speakers the definite form is also /lastik/, suggesting that these speakers are not sure whether the /l/ is really a stem segment or the Fr definite morpheme *l'*.

There are at least two borrowings from the early colonial period in which Fr definite Pl *les* [lez] before initial vowel has been resegmented, so that the MCA form now begins with /z/ (or /ẓ/). These are /zufri/ C-809, Pl /zufriy-a/ "playboy(s)", where the original borrowing was the Pl form, from Fr *les ouvriers* "the workers" (perhaps analysed by Moroccans as **les zouvriers*); and /ẓaḷamiṭ/ C-805 "match" ultimately from Fr *les allumettes*. The definite forms are now /z-zufri/ and /ẓ-ẓaḷamiṭ/. The generalization in MCA of the form with initial sibilant is again motivated in part by avoidance of stem-initial vowels, a tendency we have observed earlier in connection with resegmentation of Fr *l'*. In these two lexical items it would seem that the Fr plural form was prominent, and thus served (instead of the Sg) as the basis for the resegmentation.

In the preceding paragraphs we have argued that for some lexical items the identical form of definite and indefinite nouns, as with /luṭuṣṭup/ C-455 "hitch-hiking", is due to ambivalence in segmentation of the initial /l/, which in turn reflects the uncomfortable status of nouns with initial vowel. However, it should be mentioned here that there are some other nouns of foreign origin in MCA which avoid definite prefix /l-/ for no obvious phonological reason, and that at some chronological stages there was a tendency to treat "synchronically foreign words" in this fashion. Although the various Moroccan dialects vary on specifics, a number of nouns like /atay/ "tea", /xizzu/ "carrots", /bllarž/ "storks", and abstract nouns of profession of the type /ta-X-t/ (e.g. /ta-nžžaṛ-t/ "carpentry") regularly omit /l-/ even in clearly definite syntactic contexts (see 6.31 for further discussion of pidgin-like features of borrowings).

To conclude this section on definite morphology, we note a handful of instances where initial *l* in the prototype has been reinterpreted as the definite prefix /l-/, whereupon an indefinite form without /l-/ is back-formed. The best example is /iṭṛu/ or /yṭṛu/ C-298 "liter" from Sp *litro*, which was borrowed as definite /l-iṭṛu/ or /l-yṭṛu/ (the variant with /y/ is apparently another adjustment to avoid stem-initial vowel). Another example is the variant /iṭṛ-a/ of /liṭṛ-a/ and /ṭṛiṭ-a/ C-773 "monthly payment"; here /liṭṛ-a/ is from Sp *letra* and /iṭṛ-a/ represents reanalysis of this as /l-iṭṛ-a/ with definite prefix, while /ṭṛiṭ-a/ has a more complex history involving contamination with a Fr word and can be disregarded here. A somewhat similar example is /filil/ C-213 "safety pin", probably from Sp *alfilel*, where Sp *al* may have been confused with Sp definite *el* and in any event was treated as MCA definite /l-/ (*alfilel* itself is ultimately of Arabic origin, but /filil/ must be from the Sp form for phonological reasons). In the Tetouan (northern) dialect of MCA, we get /kul/ and definite /l-kul/ "alcohol" from Fr *alcool*, Sp *alcohol* (again, ultimately of Arabic origin) with a similar history, though in most of Morocco we get /ankul/ or /alkul/, definite /l-ankul/ or /l-alkul/ C-10.

To summarize this section: ordinarily, borrowed nouns from European sources enter MCA through regular segmental conversions in the simple prototype form not including definite markers, and definite MCA forms are generated internally with the regular prefix /l-/, which assimilates to following coronal C_1; there are a fair number of cases, however, where Fr *la* has been retained in MCA as a definite allomorph /la-/ or /ḷa-/; rarely (two examples) the Fr form with *la* acts as the primary borrowing but undergoes resegmentation with /a/ now the stem-initial segment; when /la-/ or /ḷa-/ is the MCA definite allomorph this does not affect MCA grammatical gender, which in many of the relevant examples is masculine (despite being feminine in Fr); Fr *les* has been incorporated into borrowed stems (losing its definite and plural meaning) only with two otherwise very short stems, and in general Fr *les* has not become established as a new morpheme or allomorph, being confined to essentially code-switched rather than integrated material; European stems beginning in /ž/ take /ž-/, not /l-/, as definite allomorph; in a number of borrowings involving vowel-initial prototype stems, definite /l-/ may occur in syntactically indefinite as well as definite contexts and there may be some ambiguity as to segmentation; in two early colonial loans from vowel-initial prototypes we get an extra stem-initial /z/ or /ẓ/ deriving from resegmentation of Fr definite Pl *les* [lez]; these problems involving vowel-initial prototypes reflect the MCA avoidance of stem-initial vowels and thus have a therapeutic function.

6.25 Gender and a type of false borrowing routine

In native MCA nouns, grammatical gender (as seen in concord) is very largely dependent on whether or not the noun ends in FSg /-a/.

There are a few grammatically feminine nouns which lack /-a/, mostly high-frequency items like /šəmš/ "sun" and /ḥanut/ "shop"; the Dimin form usually does have /-a/, as in /šmiš-a/ "sun (Dimin)".

In European borrowings, gender is likewise very largely determined by whether the MCA form ends in FSg /-a/; those which have /-a/ are feminine (except for a handful of nouns denoting male human beings), and those which lack /-a/ are masculine. In very short stems of the shape /CCa/ there is the option of taking /a/ as a stem segment, so gender is not predictable in advance; see /žwa/ C-827 "envelope".

In the majority of nominal borrowings from Fr and Sp, the MCA form is produced by regular segmental conversions, and if this happens to produce a stem with final /a/ the latter is taken as the FSg marker. As a result, many masculine Fr nouns show up as feminine in MCA. In some cases a stem-final vowel which should (by regular conversions) be a slightly different vowel is bent into /a/, apparently under the influence of the many other nouns with FSg /-a/.

Cases where a Fr masculine ending in [a] becomes a FSg noun in MCA include /anṭiṛn-a/ C-16 "campus" from *internat*; see also C-143, 211, 312, 378, 389, 399, 402, 410, 558, 617, 643, 659, 711 (one variant), 749, 796. Fr stem-final [ã] (*ant*, *ent*) is frequently denasalized and becomes /-a/ as well, as in /kṛwaṣ-a/ C-379 "croissant"; cf. C-382, 392, 415 (sense 3), 507, 639, 798; to this list we may add several cases involving Fr suffix *-ment* like /anṭṛinm-a/ C-16 "training" from *entraînement*, also C-68, 106, 114, 207, 380. The regular segmental output for Fr [e] is MCA /i/, but at the end of a noun stem we sometimes get FSg /-a/ instead; the two attestations are /kabin-a/ C-304 "bathroom" from Fr *cabinet* and /ṭabliy-a/ C-751 "apron" from Fr *tablier*; contrast, for example, /ṣãdriyi/ "ashtray" C-667 from Fr *cendrier*, showing the regular treatment. Likewise, the usual segmental treatment of Fr [æ̃] (written *in*) is MCA /an/, but we get FSg /-a/ in two cases: /magaz-a/ C-461 "(large) store" from Fr *magasin*, /žṛd-a/ C-820 "garden" from Fr *jardin*. In three other cases a Fr *VC* sequence is irregularly reduced to FSg /-a/, hence /kanz-a/ C-317 "fortnight" from Fr *quinzaine*, /gaṛṣuniy-a/ C-265 "studio apartment" from Fr *garçonnière*, and /kuṛḅ-a/ C-416 "crate" from Fr *corbeille*. In these three instances, the fact that the Fr word is feminine may have influenced the reshaping; note that in the earlier examples in this paragraph the Fr prototype was feminine.

In all of these examples the Fr prototype has final segments which at least vaguely resemble FSg /-a/, even when the conversion shows signs of having been morphologically motivated rather than phonologically automatic. However, there are a substantial number of borrowings where FSg /-a/ has been added (actually or apparently) to a Fr noun which has no comparable final segment.

The historical analysis of these forms is rather tricky; it is necessary to distinguish two basic historical types, though for some individual items it may not be determinable to which type they belong. First, there is a set of items which were originally not from Fr at all, rather from Sp and/or It. In these two languages the regular FSg ending is *-a*, whereas in Fr this has been reduced to phonetic zero. In cases where the Sp/It form with *-a* has a close Fr cognate with -∅, if MCA at an early time borrowed the Sp/It form it may now appear (to Moroccans bilingual in MCA and Fr, and to an incautious linguist) that the MCA item is a borrowing from Fr with /-a/ added. However, possibly by analogy to these spurious Fr/MCA identifications by Moroccans, there is also a set of genuine cases where MCA has borrowed a Fr item and added FSg /-a/ to it. (We are here anticipating somewhat our discussion of contaminations involving Fr and Sp/It inputs in 6.29.)

The following is a list of likely or certain cases where the original borrowing was a Sp/It noun with FSg *-a* but where Fr-and-MCA-speaking Moroccans might consider the borrowing to be related to a Fr cognate: /ḅal-a/ C-40 "shovel" (Sp *pala*, Fr *pelle*), /birr-a/ C-86 (It *birra*, Fr *bière*, cf. Sp *cerveza* in this meaning), /blak-a/ or /bḷak-a/ C-98 "sign, badge" (Sp *placa*, Fr *plaque*); others are C-32, 48, 69, 112, 134, 139, 140, 146, 154, 156, 197, 205, 209, 220, 256, 271, 272, 285, 309, 316, 329, 367, 374, 381, 384, 394, 476, 505, 514, 520, 521, 553, 582, 591, 599, 625, 635, 640, 654, 657, 690, 712, 731, 750, 793, 797, 806. One of the more interesting examples is /bluz-a/ C-104 "blouse" from Fr *blouse* [bluz], which probably began as /blus-a/ from Sp *blusa* (still attested in northern Morocco) but partially reshaped to approximate the Fr consonantism (while retaining the old FSg /-a/).

The apparent examples in which /-a/ has been added to a strictly Fr borrowing, on the analogy of the spurious Fr/MCA pairs just listed, are these: /adris-a/ C-1 "address" from Fr *adresse*, /baliz-a/ C-42 "suitcase" (*valise*), /baṛmiṭ-a/ alongside /baṛmiṭ/ C-60 "barmaid" (Eng, probably via Fr), /basin-a/ C-61 "basin" (*bassine*), /biḍaṛ-a/ variant of C-77 "pedal" (*pédale*), /buṣṭ-a/ C-151 "post office" (*poste*), /bušun-a/ C-153 alongside /bušun/ C-152 "bottle-cap" (gloss of C-153, *bouchon*), /buṭun-a/ C-158 vs. /buṭun/ C-157 "button" (*bouton*), /byas-a/ C-162 "spare part" (*pièce*), /firm-a/ C-217 "(large) farm" (*ferme*); /kaṣṛun-a/ C-336 "cooking pot" (*casserole*); /kḷaṣ-a/ C-356 (alongside /kḷaṣ/) "class" (*classe*), /kuliy-a/ C-395 "parcel" (*colis*, but possibly contaminated with northern MCA /kuliy-a/ "cigarette butt" from Sp *colilla*), /puppiy-a/ C-577 "doll" (*poupée*), /šãbṛ-a/ alongside /šãbṛ/ "hotel room" (*chambre*), /tikiy-a/ variant of C-722 "label; ticket" (*étiquette* and *ticket*), /trimis-a/ C-740 "quarter of year" (*trimestre*), /ṭumubil-a/ or /ṭumubil/ C-780 "automobile" (*automobile*), /žaḳiṭ-a/ and variants C-811 "light coat" (if from Fr *jaquette*), /župp-a/ C-823 "skirt" (*jupe*). For some of these items the precise history is not clear (without fuller dialectological information than is presently available). However, in several of these cases there is no Sp/It word which could have served as prototype; in a few others there may be a Sp cognate (e.g. *pedal* "pedal") but it lacks final *-a* anyway; in a few there may be an It item with *-a* but, in view of the very limited (and always indirect) contribution of It to MCA lexicon it is unlikely that an It prototype is involved for a given item. Even if we eventually transfer a few of the items in the list above to another historical category, the examples just given are sufficient to establish the existence of Fr borrowings with secondary MCA /-a/ added, presumably influenced by the spurious Fr/MCA equivalences in the earlier list.

There are two further comments to be made about these data. First, in the list just given of addition of /-a/ to a Fr borrowing with no obvious direct Sp/It influence, a clear majority involve items which are grammatically feminine in Fr (though there is no phonological marker for gender in the Fr forms). This suggests that bilingual speakers can make the connection between the genders in Fr and the corresponding MCA ones, and that Fr grammatical gender can occasionally influence the gender of the borrowing, with FSg /-a/ being added to feminine nouns to index gender overtly. At the same time, recall from our discussion above that MCA gender is frequently determined by purely phonological factors, with stem-final *a* or similar vowel in Fr masculine nouns leading to feminine gender in MCA. There are also many Fr feminine nouns which become masculine in MCA because they lack a final segment resembling FSg /-a/, as with /duš/ C-177 "shower" (Fr *douche*).

In some borrowings we find alternations between a collective (grammatically masculine) in /-Ø/ and an individuative Sg in /-a/ (grammatically feminine). This follows a preexisting MCA pattern chiefly affecting terms for fruits, vegetables, and certain small objects for which a collective sense is useful but which can also be individuated (e.g. counted). A number of borrowings show this alternation. Thus for plants and foods we can cite /ạṇạṇaṣ/ C-9 "pineapples" (Fr *ananas*, Sp *ananás*) and individuative /ạṇạṇaṣ-a/, also C-34, 46, 92, 236, 444, 451, 452, 658, 704, 711; for small manufactured products and the like we have C-161 (cans), 325 and 586 (bullets), 331 (cardboard), 552 (thumbtacks), 576 (sponges), 653 (tape), 666 (soap), 726 (tennis balls), and for some speakers 805 (matches). After stem-final /u/, we find FSg allomorph /-ya/ instead of /-a/, as is regular in the Fes/Meknes dialect: /gaṭṭu/ and individuative /gaṭṭu-ya/ C-266 "cake" (Fr *gâteau*). Other examples of individuative /-a/ are C-178 (diamonds), and possibly C-714 (chairs) if Pl /šli/ is interpreted as Sg /šly-a/ minus the /-a/ suffix. In most of these cases it appears that the unsuffixed collective in MCA is the form which matches the Fr (or Sp) prototype. However, occasionally it is the suffixed form with /-a/ in MCA which matches the prototype, so that the MCA unsuffixed collective is a back-formation; hence /ltšin/ and /ltšin-a/ C-452 "orange(s)" from Sp *la China* "China". In any event, forms of this type with collective /-Ø/ and individuative FSg /-a/ should, in principle, be distinguished historically from the cases discussed earlier where FSg /-a/ has been secondarily added to a Fr borrowing.

In verbal nouns, individuative /-a/ can be added (as with native MCA items) to indicate a single event as opposed to the abstract action, though /-a/ may become general with some such verbal nouns and lack a precise aspectual sense. In the case of /fant-a/ and /fant/ C-201 "dodge, dodging" (Fr *feinte*), and in that of /paṣ-a/ C-544 "(a) pass" (Fr *passe*) the /-a/ may have this individual-action sense.

In MCA, FSg /-a/ regularly becomes /-t-/ before a possessive pronominal suffix and in "construct" possessive phrases with following possessor noun: /klb-a/ "female dog", /klb-t-i/ "my female dog". There are few examples of this involving borrowed nouns, since relatively few MCA nouns occur freely as possessed noun in these constructions (the type /l-klb-a dyal-i/ "the-female-dog of-me" being the more productive construction) and since borrowings are not usually included in this privileged set. However, we can cite a few such forms including /famil-a/ C-199 "family" and possessed /famil-t-i/ "my family" to show that when this construction does occur, borrowings show the usual morphophonemic rule.

6.26 Number (including ablaut plurals)

Ordinarily, the actual form of a nominal borrowing is singular (in both MCA and the European source language). Instead of also borrowing a plural form (say, with Fr *les*) along with the singular, the Pl is produced internally in most cases by regular MCA morphological patterns. (In northern Morocco, Sp borrowings with FSg /-a/ take regular FPl /-at/, but many masculine borrowings from Sp bring in their Sp plural form with suffix /-s/ or /iṣ/.)

Both suffixal and ablaut plural forms occur in MCA and both types are widely attested with borrowed nouns and adjectives. (For cases where the basic borrowed form is Pl, with a Sg generated by back-formation, see 6.28.)

We have indicated in the preceding section that FSg /-a/ occurs with some borrowings as an individuative singular marker, contrasting with a /-∅/ collective. Such stems have an individuative plural (used, e.g., with numerals) in FPl /-at/, like their counterparts in inherited MCA lexicon: /ạṇạṣ-at/ "(individual) pineapples".

The ending /-at/ in MCA is not only FPl (i.e. the Pl corresponding to FSg /-a/), a function seen most clearly in adjectives; it is also a moderately common general Pl marker with nouns (but not adjectives), and is especially common with long or otherwise unusual nouns that do not fit into an ablaut pattern. (For non ablaut adjectives, especially participles, we regularly get MPl /-in/ and FPl /-at/, but /-in/ is not productive with any nominal category.) Since many borrowings do not fit the usual Sg canonical shapes and thus have no obvious ablaut Pl, /-at/ is very common as a Pl suffix with them. Even when a borrowed noun from Fr or Sp happens to have the canonical shape of an existing ablaut pattern, /-at/ may be preferred to the ablaut Pl; many borrowings are attested both with suffixal and ablaut plurals. To some extent the frequency of particular ablaut Pl types can be used as an index of productivity for the various ablaut plural patterns.

The /-at/ plural ending occurs with so many borrowed stems that no list is necessary here; virtually any page of appendix C will have several examples.

A second, much less common Pl suffix is /-a/, which occurs in MCA as the plural of agentive /CCCaC/ and /CCaCC-i/, as in /fllaḥ/ "farmer, peasant" and Pl /fllaḥ-a/. For such stems the MPl is thus identical to the FSg, also with /-a/ (the marked FPl is with /-at/). For borrowings, this PL /-a/ occurs only with stems that fit the two agentive patterns just mentioned (see 6.22), and a few other stems with /-i/ suffix. For /CCCaC-a/ see /gyyad-a/ "guides" C-287, /srbay-a/ "waiters" C-656, and /bznas-a/ "drug dealers" C-163; for types with /-i/ see /aṣuṛṭi/ C-24 "security policeman" and its Pl /aṣuṛṭiy-a/, also C-50 (Mk variant), 107, 132, 135 (old form cited in DMA-AE), 160, 276, 528, 679, 766 (Algerian form),

809, 810. FPl /-at/ is found with /ṣbban-a/ C-680 "washerwoman" and its Pl /ṣbban-at/.

Some borrowings, particularly involving nationalities, have Sg /-i/ and FSg /-iy-a/ contrasting with a zero Pl or collective /-Ø/, as in /ṣblyun/ C-683 "Spanish people" and /ṣblyun-i/ "(a) Spaniard"; the Sg can also be the basis for a marked Pl form for some of these stems (see also C-6, 132, 295, 472, 515, 683, 708, some of which also show ablaut plurals). Since several of these nationality terms go back to the immediate precolonial period and are mostly of Sp origin, we can speculate as to whether /ṣblyun/ cmae in directly from Sp *español* with /ṣblyun-i/ then derived internally by adding /-i/ (a preexisting Gentilic Sg suffix), or whether /ṣblyun-i/ was also related to a resegmented form of Sp plural *españoles*.

Another Pl suffix, /-in/, is fairly uncommon with borrowed nouns but only because it is morphologically restricted in ordinary MCA. It is used with selected types of adjective, especially participles. It is the normal Pl form for participles derived from borrowed verbs (appendix B). In other nouns and adjectives (appendix C), it occurs chiefly with adjectives of nationality or the like with suffix /-i/ (Pl /-iy-in/), as in /buržwaz-iy-in/ "bourgeois" (See C-150), though many of these also have unsuffixed collective forms, here /buržwa/ C-149 "bourgeois (class)" (Fr *bourgeois*); see also C-229, 291, 472. With regard to morphologically simple adjectives of European origin, we can cite /frisk/ C-233 "fresh" with Pl /frisk-in/ in one dialect (Casablanca Jewish), elsewhere invariable; and /stitu/ C-661 "small" (distinctive to far northern dialects except in Dimin form, but known elsewhere) with Pl /stitw-in/ (old loan, apparently from Sp *chico* and/or *chiquito*).

A Pl suffix /-wat/ or /-yat/ is really just an allomorph of Pl /-at/, already described. When a stem ends in /u/ and a suffixal Pl is indicated, the regular form is with /-wat/ or /-yat/, with /-yat/ common around Fes and Meknes and /-wat/ farther west (but both forms occur in the former region). The morphophonemic rule at work here is also seen in FSg /-ya/ instead of /-a/ after such stems. Moreover, /-wat/ or /-yat/ is used instead of /-at/ with short /CCV/ nouns taking a suffixal Pl; in my data (mostly Fes area) we seem to get /-wat/ in this case except when C_2 is /w/, hence /bṛa-wat/ "letters" but /dwa-yat/ "medicines" (not loanwords). The best example of a loanword is /žwa/ C-827 "envelope", Pl /žwa-wat/ or /žwa-yat/.

With the longer stems, in addition to the fluctuation between /-wat/ and /-yat/ we can get an additional form /-nat/. The latter form is initially puzzling, since it does not occur as a variant of /-at/ in any native MCA nominal paradigm. Instead, /-nat/ originates in a number of borrowed paradigms due to alternative treatments of stem-final nasalized vowels, with /n/ occurring in the borrowed form only in Pl (i.e. suffixed) case; subsequently, /-nat/ starts to generalize by analogy and becomes a variant of the Pl morpheme often co-occurring with /-yat/ and /-wat/.

For example, consider /fagu/ C-194 "car (of train)", which is most likely from Fr *wagon*, though Sp *vagón* may also be involved. In the Sg, Fr nasalized vowel [õ] is denasalized. However, the Pl can be /fagu-wat/, /fagu-yat/, or /fagu-nat/, where the first two forms are produced regularly by adding /-wat/ or /-yat/ following stem-final /u/. The form /fagu-nat/ suggests that bilingual Moroccans were conscious of the nasalization feature even though they dropped it in Sg /fagu/, and that they retained this feature in the form of a nasal segment when a suffix was added (a linking consonant was necessary in any event, and instead of /w/ or /y/ it might as well be a consonant suggested by the original Fr pronunciation). We might also consider the possibility of some Fr/Sp crossings, with /fagu/ based on Fr *wagon* while /fagu-nat/ is a survival of an older */fagun/ (cf. Tetouan dialect /vagun/) from Sp *vagón*; however, this analysis seems contrived in the absence of a specific reason why the Fr/Sp crossing should take this particular paradigmatic pattern.

Other cases where /-nat/ is attested as a Pl suffix, regularly alongside /-wat/ and /-yat/, are C-43, 313, 482, 485, 499, 540, 589, 675, 688, 752, 756, 772. In some of these cases the form with /-nat/ is not justified by any nasal consonant or nasalized vowel in the prototype, so that /-nat/ must be analogical to the type /fagu/, Pl /fagu-nat/ just analysed: thus /ṛadyu/ C-589 "radio", Pl variant /ṛadyu-nat/. There is also a back-formed Sg variant /ṛadyun/, suggesting that /ṛadyu-nat/ has an alternative segmentation /ṛadyun-at/ for some speakers; similar cases with Pl /-nat/ not justified by the foreign prototype are C-482, 499, 752, 772. On the other hand, there are a number of borrowings ending in /u/ for which /-nat/ is not attested as a Pl variant: C-44, 51, 58, 71, 75, 125, 170, 184, 186, and about fifteen others.

We now consider "broken" or ablaut plurals expressed by any of several types of stem-internal change, occasionally also involving a suffix. The least predictable aspect of this problem is whether or not a given borrowing will have an ablaut plural at all, since the suffixal type with /-at/ or a morphophonemic variant thereof is almost always available as an alternative. Once we know that a given borrowing has an ablaut Pl, it is usually possible to guess or at least narrow down what the Pl will be, on the basis of fairly regular implicational relationships between Sg and Pl patterns.

Table 6-2 summarizes most (but not all) of the details concerning ablaut Pl patterns attested with the European borrowings in appendix C. Some qualifications will be made in the following commentary.

The great majority of borrowed nouns of the type /CCCVC/, with or without following FSg /-a/ (which is disregarded in some, but not all, Sg-Pl ablaut relationships), have /CCaCəC/ as their ablaut Pl if they have an ablaut Pl at all (the schwa vowel is absorbed if the last consonant is a sonorant which syllabifies, and some speakers omit the schwa even if this does not happen). Appendix C has twenty-one relevant examples, including /blyun/ C-105 "a coin" (Sp *vellón*), Pl /blayn/, also C-85, 110, 112, 113, 118, 121, 164, 243, 350, 374, 384, 509, 510, 515, 654, 657, 681, 711, 763.

The same ablaut Pl is used with /CVCCVC/, a less common Sg type, again with or without FSg /-a/, hence /bigbuṣ/ C-79 "huge man" (Eng *big boss*), Pl /bgabṣ/, also C-85, 264, 515, 676 (C-85 and 515 appear in both lists since they have alternate Sg forms). Similarly, in the only example of an ablaut Pl from /CCCC/ noun, /tnabr/

Table 6-2 Ablaut plural patterns

Singular	Plural
CCCVC(-a)	CCaCəC
CCCC(-a)	CCaCəC (one ex.)
CVCCVC(-a)	CCaCəC, rarely CwaCCC
CV$_1$CVC(-a)	CwaCəC if V_1 is /u/ or /a/, a few exx. of CyaCəC if V_1 is /i/
CV$_1$CC(-a)	same as preceding type
CV$_1$CCV	same as preceding type, or (especially with Gentilic nouns) CwaCCa
CCVC(-a)	CCayC
CVCVCV	CwaCəC (one ex.)
CCCiy-a	CCaCi (one ex.)
CaCiy-a	CwaCi (one ex.)
CCVCC-a	CCaCCi (one ex., now obsolete)
CCCVC-i (Gentilic)	CCaCCa
CCCC-i (human)	CCaCC-iy-a (one ex.)
CVCC-i (human)	CwaCC-iy-a (one ex.) or treated like CV$_1$CCV
CVCCVC (occupation)	CaCaCiCa (one ex., but probably via CA)
CaC	CiC-an
CuC	usually CwaC, rarely CwəC
CiC	ablaut not usual but CyaC occasional; CyuC in two exx. involving probable MCA homonym influence
CCəC	CCuCa (one ex. in northern dialect)
CCC-a	CCaCi (three exx.)
CuC-a	CwaCi (one ex.)
CuCi	CwaCa (two exx.)

Note: schwa vowel /ə/ in formulae like CCaCəC is often omitted, or absorbed by a syllabified sonorant.

from /tnbr/ C-734 "postage stamp" (Fr *timbre*), the same ablaut pattern is observed.

These examples indicate that /CCaCəC/ is the productive ablaut Pl for quadriconsonantal noun stems. There are relatively few such stems which take different ablaut patterns, and most of these exceptions belong to specific human noun formations (occupational or Gentilic) which take their own characteristic ablaut patterns (see C-188, 241, 295, and a variant Pl of C-515, all to be mentioned below). One serious exception not involving a human noun, Pl /ṣwanḍl/ from /ṣanḍal-a/ C-767 "sandal", is modelled on other ablaut patterns (to be presented below but shown in the table) beginning with /Cwa.../; the form /ṣwanḍl/ was recorded in Marrakech, while the more regular /ṣnaḍl/ was recorded in my primary field area.

A number of other ablaut patterns like /CyaCəC/, /CwaCəC/, and /CCayC/ have obvious resemblances to /CCaCəC/, and essentially involve adding a semivowel to fill a consonant slot when the Sg stem does not have four distinct consonants.

The types /CyaCəC/ and /CwaCəC/ are regular for Sg /CV$_1$CVC(-a)/, /CV$_1$CC(-a)/, and /CV$_1$CCV/, with /y/ used when V_1 is /i/ and /w/

used when V_1 is /u/ or /a/. However, there is an imbalance in productivity between the type with /y/ and that with /u/, in spite of the apparent formal symmetry. Thus /CyaCəC/ appears to be low in productivity among borrowings in the dialects studied, while /CwaCəC/ remains productive. I have found /CyaCəC/ occurring only with /disk/ C-173 "record", and /šifuṛ/ C-705 "driver" (Fr *disc, chauffeur*). The entries C-75, 197, and 213 indicate /CyaCəC/ plurals recorded by earlier sources, but notably not confirmed by my recent data. Since there are plenty of borrowings with the appropriate Sg shapes, the shortage of /CyaCəC/ plurals seems to be a significant fact about the treatment of borrowings; just to take initial /p/, we can cite /piḍal/ (see C-77) "pedal", /piluṭ/ C-551 "pilot", /piniz/ C-552 "thumbtack(s)", /pipp-a/ C-553 "pipe", /pisin/ C-556 "swimming pool", /pist/ C-557 "highway", and /pižam-a/ C-558, none recorded with /CyaCəC/ plural.

On the other hand, /CwaCəC/ plurals are abundant. From Sg /CV_1CVC(-a)/ where V_1 is a back vowel we can cite /baḅuṛ/ C-30 "ferry", Pl /bwaḅṛ/ (Sp *vapor*, Fr *vapeur*), also C-42, 302, 306, 520, 521, 524, 582, 666, 698, 811 (in earlier sources also C-132, 778). From Sg /CV_1CC(-a)/ or /CV_1CCV/ we get this Pl pattern in /bunt-a/ C-139 "cigarette butt", Pl /bwant/ (Sp *punta*), also C-217, 311, 466, 691, 750, 809, 812, and a variant of C-288.

Perhaps further showing that /CwaCəC/ is more productive than /CyaCəC/ is the Pl /nwamr/ from /nimiru/ C-533 "number" (Fr *numéro*), where it looks as though /CwaCəC/ is encroaching on the territory of /CyaCəC/ (i.e. with a stem whose V_1 is /i/). However, /nwamr/ might have another historical explanation; for example, /nimiru/ might be a recently Gallicized form overlain on an earlier borrowing based on Sp *número* such as */numiru/, where V_1 was */u/ rather /i/; or there may have been some contamination and paradigm juggling involving /nmr-a/ C-534 "number" (Fr *nombre*?) or an earlier form thereof.

We have noted above the aberrant Marrakech Pl form /ṣwanḍl/ from Sg /ṣanḍal-a/ C-767 "sandal". This Pl type /CwaCCC/ is clearly just an extension of the type /CwaCəC/, allowing the final consonant string to expand further. Perhaps this extension can be found with other items in the Marrakech dialect, which is presently understudied; it suggests further that the /CwaCəC/ type is currently productive.

The remaining high-frequency ablaut Pl for Sg stems with at least three true consonants is /CCayC/. This is regular for singulars of the shape /CCVC(-a)/. We can cite /blak-a/ C-98 "sign, badge", Pl /blayk/ (Sp *placa*, Fr *plaque*), also C-102, 104, 225, 356, 357, 382, 569, 585, 712 (and, in earlier sources, C-596, 624, 582, though in the latter there may have been some analogical contamination involving C-585 despite some difference in canonical shape). Other examples are /slipp/ C-655 "underpants", Pl /slayp/, where the Pl pattern reflects a tendency to treat stem-final /pp/ as a unit consonant; and /filil/ C-213 "safety pin", Pl /flayl/, where the aberrant Pl is apparently a device to avoid the declining pattern /CyaCəC/ whose lack of productivity was commented on above (the form /fyaləl/ is indeed recorded in earlier sources but has been replaced for my informants with /flayl/).

Some of the other Pl patterns are essentially variations on

those just given. From /gaṛṛu/ C-263 "cigarette" we can get /gwaṛṛu/ where the rules above would suggest */gwaṛṛ/ with the second /ṛ/ syllabified independently (equivalent to */gwaṛəṛ/), as in /kwanəb/ from /kambu/ C-311 "country hick"; perhaps the oddity of such a sequence of nonsyllabic and syllabic /ṛ/ is what discourages the regular form from /gaṛṛu/. Another variant, /gṛaṛu/, is reported by TAT for Tangier at an earlier period. Similarly, a number of Pl patterns (or subpatterns) which are found with one attestation each in my European borrowing material seem to be offshoots of the regular types listed above. From /baṭaṭ-a/ C-67 "potatoes" (collective or Sg) a Pl /bwaṭaṭ/ is recorded, where */bwaṭəṭ/ might be more regular. A Pl type /CCaCi/, presumably a manifestation of /CCaCəC/ with C_4 replaced by /i/, is seen in Sg /sbniy-a/ C-634 "shawl" (Sp *sabanilla*, old loan), Pl /sbani/; also /bakiy-a/ C-37 "pack, packet" (Fr *paquet*), Pl /bwaki/. The Sg/Pl alternations in C-634 and 37 have exact parallels in inherited MCA paradigms. From /ṭṛumb-a/ C-772 "top (spinning implement or toy)", a Pl form /ṭṛambi/ is reported in an early source for Tangier in the north, and perhaps this should be associated with the Pl types /sbani/ and /bwaki/ just given.

There are also some ablaut Pl patterns in MCA involving addition of /-a/ (superficially resembling the FSg suffix /-a/), or replacement of a high vowel by final /a/. The patterns in question are /CCaCCa/, /CwaCCa/, /CCaCCiy-a/, and /CwaCCiy-a/; the segmentability of final /-a/ in the first two of these is not clear and so is not indicated. These Pl patterns generally refer to humans (occupational terms, Gentilics, etc.), though there are a couple of marginal nonhuman instances of /CwaCCa/.

Attestations of /CCaCCa/ in borrowings are /hippi/ C-291 (arguably /hipp-i/ with Gentilic suffix) "hippie", Marrakech variant Pl /hpappa/, in other dialects /hwappa/; /maṛṛuk-i/ or /mṛṛuk-i/ C-515 "Moroccan (person)", Pl /mṛaṛka/ (along with /mṛaṛk/); and /ngliz-i/ C-295 "Englishman", Pl /ngalza/. The inherited model for this Sg/Pl alternation is seen in /mġrib-i/ "Moroccan (person)", Pl /mġarba/, with Gentilic /-i/.

The type /CwaCCa/ is evidently the same as /CCaCCa/ with /w/ added to fill one consonantal slot when the root has just three true consonants. The examples are /ġanžu/ C-288 "country hick", Pl /ġwanža/ (along with /ġwanž/); /hwappa/ Pl variant from /hippi/ C-291 (cf. preceding paragraph); /kutši/ C-430 "cart", Pl /kwatša/ reported by one earlier publication; and /ṣulḍi/ C-691 "an old coin", Pl /ṣwalḍa/ or /ṣwalḍ/. Cf. inherited forms like /fas-i/ "(resident) of Fes", Pl /fwasa/; /wžd-i/ "(resident) of Oujda", Pl /wžada/, with Gentilic /-i/. The Gentilic suffix is not present in /ġanžu/, and is semantically incompatible with "cart" and "an old coin", but the Gentilic Sg/Pl pattern seems to have spread to these borrowings due in large part to phonological resemblances (involving stem-final high vowel in Sg).

We have one example each in borrowings of /CCaCCiy-a/ and /CwaCCiy-a/: /pumbi/ C-135 "fireman", Pl /pwambiy-a/ (Marrakech variants); /frmli/ C-241 "male nurse", Pl /framliy-a/. These Pl patterns occur in inherited paradigms chiefly in the type where Pl /-a/ is added directly to a Sg agentive form /CCaCC-i/ or /CwaCC-i/ (hence Pl /CCaCC-iy-a/, /CwaCC-iy-a/). However, /CCaCC-iy-a/ or a variant is attested once in a while as an ablaut Pl of a native noun, as in /ṭbib/ "doctor", dialectal Pl /ṭbaybiy-a/ (Marrakech, cf. /ṭ^{w}bba/ elsewhere). Note that there is a semantic similarity between "doctor" and "male nurse", and (to some extent) between these and "fireman".

The one example of /CaCaCiCa/ in Table 6-2 is /dạkạtiṛ-a/ "doctors" from Sg /duktuṛ/ C-188 and its variants. This is modelled on the type /?ustad/ "teacher", Pl /?asatid-a/, a well-established CA borrowing (A-1-141, 234). It is very possible that /duktuṛ/ and /dạkạtiṛ-a/ were initially shaped in modern CA, then entered MCA from CA- in this case /dạkạtiṛ-a/ should not be considered an internal development in MCA.

Using the loanword material, it is fairly difficult to study the plural forms based on very short Sg stems, since few borrowed nouns take this shape. However, we can make a few generalizations. We begin by considering plurals based on singulars of the shape /CaC/, /CuC/, and /CiC/.

For /CaC/ we can identify /CiC-an/ as the regular ablaut Pl, and for /CuC/ we can thus identify /CwaC/. The treatment of Sg /CiC/ is a little more problematic. Examples of Sg /CaC/and Pl /CiC-an/ are /laṣ/ C-440 "ace (card)", Pl /liṣ-an/; also C-52, 320, 669, 697, and (in older sources) 700. Examples of Sg /CuC/ and Pl /CwaC/ are /bun/ C-136 "coupon", Pl /bwan/; also C-177, 283, 781, and (in one variant) 155.

A less productive Pl for Sg /CuC/ is /CwəC/. We can cite /buṭ/ C-155 "boots", Pl /bwəṭ/ (alongside /bwaṭ/). For Algeria we can also mention /ṛuḍ-a/ "wheel", Pl /ṛwəḍ/, but the Moroccan forms differ (see C-624). In the case of /gwri/ C-286 "foreigner", Pl /gwr/ (Pl equivalent to /gwər/, with syllabified /r/), it would seem that we have an opposition of Gentilic /-i/ vs. plural without suffix, rather than an ablaut Pl.

As for Sg /CiC/, there is in MCA an inherited type with Pl /CyaC/, nicely paralleling the type Sg /CuC/, Pl /CwaC/ just exemplified. An inherited example is /bir/ "well (water)", Pl /byar/. There is also a type with Sg /CiC/ and Pl /CyuC/, hence /bit/ "room", pl /byut/.

Looking at borrowed singular nouns of the shape /CiC/, we find Pl /CyaC/ clearly in the paradigm Sg /gid/ C-269 "(tourist) guide", Pl /gyad/. One other possible example is /ṛiy/ C-605 (Sp *rey*) "king (playing card), Pl /ṛyay/ (Tetouan has Sg /ṛay/, Pl /ṛyuy/); however, here there may have been contamination involving /ṛiy/, Pl /ṛyay/ "opinion(s)" from CA. For the Tetouan paradigm the analogical source may be the type /ṛaṣ/ "head", Pl /ṛyuṣ/ (native MCA). As for the type Sg /CiC/, Pl /CyuC/ , my data include only /bit/ C-91 (sense 2) "goal (in soccer)" (Fr *but*) and its Pl /byut/, but this is almost certainly due to contamination with the homonym /bit/ "room", Pl /byut/.

In addition to these cases, there are a number of /CiC/ borrowed (Sg) nouns for which no ablaut plural is attested despite attempts at elicitation (C-210, 446, 549, 727). This suggests that Pl /CyaC/ and /CyuC/ from Sg /CiC/ are less than fully productive with borrowings. Recall, in this connection, our earlier observations indicating that Pl /CyaCəC/ from Sg /CiCC(-a)/ and variants was significantly less productive than the parallel Pl /CwaCəC/ from Sg

/CuCC(-a)/ and associated Sg shapes. Since /CyaC/ and /CyaCəC/, both based on Sg forms beginning with /Ci.../, can be considered variants of the same basic ablaut pattern (the difference being in the number of stem consonants), our separate remarks on the low productivity of /CyaC/ and of /CyaCəC/ can now be combined into a more general comment. Scanning the various ablaut Pl types in Table 6-2, we can see a kind of maximal schema /$C_1C_2a(C_3)C_4(V)$/ emerging as an abstraction. We can now see that C_2 is a favoured position for /w/, and C_3 a favoured position for /y/. In those paradigms where the structural logic points to /y/ in C_2 position, commonly the ablaut Pl is avoided (and suffix /-at/ is used instead), while cases with /w/ in this position are quite common. We may point out that these remarks about synchronic productivity are much more convincingly made on the basis of loanword evidence than on other bases since a number of the older, inherited nouns beginning in /Ci.../ do retain old Pl forms in /Cya.../. For further evidence concerning favoured positions for /w/ and /y/ pointing to similar conclusions, see the following section on diminutives.

Another Pl pattern in MCA is /CCəC/, of which /CwəC/ (see above) is perhaps a special variant. In the Fes/Meknes area, /CCəC/ in general seems to be of low productivity; a number of nouns listed in earlier dictionaries as having such plurals do not seem to have them now in this region, at least in active use among younger speakers. This lack of productivity is borne out in connection with borrowings, where /CCəC/ does not occur in my data (except for one example of /CwəC/ already mentioned; this coexists with another Pl /CwaC/, see C-155). For the northern dialect of Tetouan we can additionally cite /miss-a/ "table", Pl /msəs/, but here the /CCəC/ plural may have been suggested directly by Sp plural *mesas* "tables" (Sg *mesa*) by reanalysis.

Other productive ablaut plurals in MCA include /CCuC/, /CCuCa/, and /CCaC/, usually based on singulars like /CCəC/, /CəCC/, or /CCC-a/. Since these Sg patterns are very rare in European borrowings, our loanword material does not tell us much about the productivity or lack thereof of these Pl types in new vocabulary items. For Tetouan in the north we can cite /trən/ C-736 "train", Pl /truna/, but elsewhere we get /tran/, Pl /tran-at/ or a distinct lexical item (C-487). The best example of /CCuCa/ is /ṭəŋg/ C-764 "(military) tank", Pl /ṭnuga/. A possible example of /CCaC/ plural is C-97, but it is not certain that the lexical item in question is a European borrowing.

Another high-frequency Sg/Pl pattern in MCA is Sg /CCC-a/ with feminine ending, Pl /CCaCi/. Since /CCC-a/ is uncommon as a borrowed Sg noun form, we do not have many data but those we have seem to confirm productivity: /ṭbl-a/ C-750 "table", Pl /ṭbali/; /žṛd-a/ C-820 "garden", Pl /žṛadi/. A similar type is /ḅul-a/ C-130 "light bulb", Pl /bwali/. Perhaps we may add /liṭṛ-a/ C-773 "monthly payment", Pl /liṭaṛi/, where there seems to be an alternative reanalysis taking /l/ as definite /l-/, with the /i/ (perhaps treated as /y/ in this reanalysis) occupying C_1 position in the stem.

Another kind of alternation is seen in /kuri/ C-419 "stable", Pl /kwara/, and /ḍusi/ "dossier" (From Fr), Pl /ḍwasa/. Observe that we find inherited paradigms with similar oppositions (though with a consonant instead of /u/ in C_2 position), hence /ḥwli/ "sheep", Pl /ḥwala/. The alternation of stem-final /i/ in Sg with /a/ in Pl is seen in other paradigms (see Gentilic and human paradigm types in Table 6-2), as is the opposite alternation.

In ordinary MCA, there are some specifically adjectival Sg/Pl ablaut alternations. These patterns appear to be consistently inapplicable to borrowings from European languages. In part, this may be due to the coincidental lack of borrowed adjectives which happen to match the relevant Sg canonical shapes, which are quite rigid: /CCiC/ for ordinary adjectives (especially of physical shape and the like), and /CCəC/ for colour adjectives and adjectives of physical infirmity. The pattern /CCəC/ is rare since few borrowings occur without a full vowel; /CCiC/ also happens to be rare. However, /kliṛ/ C-358 "clear, certain" (Fr *clair*) does, by chance, match the /CCiC/ type formally and (more or less) semantically, and the fact that an ablaut plural (which would be */klaṛ/ or */k^{w}laṛ/) is unattested and vehemently rejected by informants seems to suggest that this Sg/Pl pattern cannot apply to borrowings. We will see below (6.31) that borrowed adjectives tend to be morphologically inert and pidgin-like in MCA, often even avoiding FSg /-a/.

Having surveyed the attested ablaut plurals, we conclude this section with remarks on the phonology of such forms. We discuss, in turn, the r/ṛ alternation, homorganic nasal-stop clusters, and some matters involving the status of /ə/ (schwa).

First, in most cases inherited MCA stems with Sg /Caṛ/ take ablaut Pl /Cir-an/ rather than /Ciṛ-an/; the only case of the latter is the uncommon noun /ġaṛ/ "cave", Pl /ġiṛ-an/, where the uvular fricative was probably responsible for inducing pharyngealization historically. In European borrowings, on the other hand, /Caṛ/ Sg produces /Ciṛ-an/ ablaut Pl. It appears that a principle is at work favouring consistency in choice of /r/ or /ṛ/ within a paradigm, and that this principle outweighs (among European borrowings) a distinct principle favouring /r/ next to /i/ and /ṛ/ next to /u/ or /a/. This latter tendency is seen not only in the type /Caṛ/, Pl /Cir-an/ but also in the vast majority of recent CA borrowings. This matter, which seems to me to be of capital theoretical interest, has been discussed in 6.5 above; for CA see also 5.4.

Second, there is the question whether surface homorganic nasal-stop clusters like /mb/ and /ŋg/ are structurally what they appear to be, or really underlying alveolar /n/ plus a labial or velar stop with low-level point-of-articulation assimilation. Evidence from some ablaut plurals suggests that the latter analysis is applicable, even when there is no evidence of this type in the European source language. Thus /kambu/ C-311 "country hick" (Sp *campo*) has ablaut Pl /kwanəb/, cf. also verb /t-kunəb/ B-87, while /ṭəŋg/ C-764 "(military) tank" produces /ṭnuga/. It is likely that these alternations reflect a complex set of considerations, including the following: velar nasal /ŋ/ does not occur phonetically in the language except in such nasal-stop clsuters, so when the ablaut pattern breaks up the cluster alveolar /n/ (as the unmarked nasal) is the appropriate output; analysis of /mb/ into /n/ plus /b/ could be, in part, by analogy to the treatment of /ŋg/, even though /m/ (unlike /ŋ/) is separately pronounceable; there appear to be subtle restrictions on sequences of nonidentical homorganic consonants within stems, favouring historical dissimilations in point of articulation (especially in ablaut forms with the two relevant consonants separated by a vowel). For further remarks on this matter see middle of 6.5 above.

Finally, we return to the issue of whether a weak vowel /ə/ is structurally present in ablaut Pl patterns like /CCaCəC/. As we have noted, in the Fes/Meknes area the /ə/ is often not pronounced in such items. However, there is a reasonable body of evidence favouring recognition of this vowel even in this dialect. First, in list intonation (with stress and rising pitch on final syllable of nonterminal items in list), we get /CCaCə́C/ with the final vowel stressed and drawn out. Second, when the two final stem consonants are identical, they are separately released (not pronounced as a geminate cluster); thus /filil/ C-213 "safety pin", Pl /fyaləl/ not */fyall/ (i.e. clearly having a final syllabic /l/ after a nonsyllabic /l/). Third, our discussion in the preceding paragraph of the type /kambu/ C-311 "country hick", Pl /kwanəb/ involves recognition of some element separating the nasal from the /b/; even though /kwanb/ with no overt short vowel is an alternative pronunciation, the fact that we get /nb/ rather than homorganic /mb/ as seen in the Sg would seem to indicate that an underlying short vowel is structurally present.

There is, however, one complication to this problem. On one occasion, an informant made an explicit distinction between /mwaṇəḍ/ as Pl of /muṇạḍ-a/ C-520 "soft drink", and /mwaṇḍ/ as Pl of /maṇḍ-a/ C-466 "paycheck" (respectively, Sp *limonada* and Fr *mandat*). This comment, though not rigorously borne out by actual speech practise, suggests an additional minor principle to the effect that consonants clearly separated by a vowel in the Sg may be kept apart (at least by a weak short vowel) in the Pl even when, in the same kind of Pl ablaut pattern, consonants already bound together in the Sg are kept apart. There is some additional evidence for the reality of a principle along these lines, though it usually conflicts with other principles and with canonical-shape specifications so its operation is not very obvious.

6.27 Diminutives

In MCA, most native nouns denoting beings or objects, and even some more abstract terms, can form an ablaut Dimin. Some nouns have no readily elicitable Dimin, either because of semantic incongruity (as with "teacher") or because the regular Sg form has an unusual stem shape which makes Dimin formation difficult. The Pl Dimin is regularly the Sg Dimin plus /-at/ suffix, so the Pl Dimin is ordinarily not based on the non-Dimin Pl form.

Attempts were made to elicit Dimin forms for a large number of borrowed nouns (and some adjectives) from European sources. The results are summarized in Table 6-3.

In general, the Dimin forms resemble those applied to native MCA stems of similar input phonological shape. Inspection of Table 6-3 indicates that the various Dimin patterns have a common core, notably involving an initial sequence /CCi(C)C.../, where one or both of the consonants flanking the /i/ vowel may be a semivowel

Table 6-3 Diminutive Ablaut Types

ordinary Sg	Dimin Sg
CVC	CwiyəC
CVC-a	CwiyC-a, CwiC-a
CCVC	CCiyəC
CəCC	CCiyəC
CCC-a	CCiC-a
CCVC-a	CCiyC-a
CVCC	CwiCC
CCCC	CCiCC, CCiCiC (one example)
CCV	CCiyu, CCiw, CCiwa
$C_1C_2VC_3$*V...	$C_1C_2iC_3$*i...
$C_1C_2C_3$*V...	$C_1C_2iC_3$*i...
C_1VC_2*V...	C_1wiC_2*i...
where C* may be a single consonant or a cluster; in the last three formulae the shift of the V to /i/ in the second Dimin syllable is blocked if the V is FSg /-a/, a stem-final vowel, or /u/ after a consonant cluster.	
verb	add /i/ between C_1 and C_2 (quadriliteral only)

inserted in the ablaut process. Note that /w/ typically precedes the /i/, while /y/ commonly follows it, when these semivowels are added by rule.

From Sg /CVC/ the Dimin is /CwiyəC/, with the usual syllabification of the last consonant if a sonorant or /ᶜ/. Examples are /bar̩/ C-52 "bar", Dimin /bwiyr̩/; also C-91, 136, 155, 177, 269, 320, 669, 697, 821. We also get it in /ryal/ C-626 "riyal" (currency unit), Dimin /rwiyl/, where theoretically we should get */ryiyl/ (or possibly */ryiwl/ with semivowel dissimilation). Preference for the slightly irregular /rwiyl/ is presumably due to the fact that */ryiyl/ would have two /y/ segments flanking a homorganic vowel, and to the tendency to avoid having surface /y/ in C_2 position in the Dimin (recall that /y/ is also disfavoured in C_2 position in the structurally similar ablaut Pl patterns described in the preceding section).

For /CCVC/ the regular Dimin is /CCiyəC/. Thus /džin/ C-179 "(pair of) jeans", Dimin /džiyn/; note, parenthetically, that this Dimin proves that /dž/ here is a consonant cluster in MCA rather than a unit affricate phoneme. Other examples of /CCiyəC/ are C-222, 228, 385, 434, 585, 686, 689, 736, 828. The same Dimin pattern applies to triconsonantal nouns lacking a full vowel, as in /ţəŋg/ C-764 "(military) tank", Dimin /ţniyəg/; another example is C-97, but this may not be a true loanword. In the case of /uţil/ C-784 "hotel", Dimin /uţiyl/, the same type of Dimin form is found, suggesting that /u/ here patterns structurally as though it were /w/ (although it is definitely not pronounced as /w/ would be).

Typically, feminine nouns with suffix /-a/ are treated in Dimin formation just like the corresponding unsuffixed stems, with the /-a/ retained in Dimin form. However, slight differences in the stem form may occur. In my Fes/Meknes data, corresponding to masculine /CCiyəC/, we can get either /CCiC-a/ or /CCiyC-a/ for the FSg, where only /CCiyC-a/ might be expected. For some FSg nouns, both Dimin patterns are attested, though the tendency is to favour /CCiC-a/ when the Sg input form has no (full?) vowel between C_2 and C_3. Thus we get /nmr-a/ C-534 "number", Dimin /nmir-a/ (another Dimin form, /nwimr-a/, may involve contamination with the Dimin of synonym /nimiru/ C-533); cf. also /ṭbl-a/ C-750 "table", Dimin /ṭbil-a/ (the other Dimin form is /ṭwibl-a/, but this appears to be based on the variant form /ṭabl-a/). The type /CCiyC-a/ is found in /blak-a/ C-98 "sign, badge", Dimin /bliyk-a/, and also in C-102, 104, 161, 356, 357, 382, 712.

Along the same lines, from simplex /CVC-a/ either /CwiC-a/ or /CwiyC-a/ can be used. I heard both /gwim-a/ and /gwiym-a/ as Dimin forms of /gum-a/ C-285 "(rubber) eraser"; for /CwiC-a/ see also C-130 and 394, and for /CwiyC-a/ see C-136.

For /CVCC/ input with full vowel, the usual Dimin is /CwiCC/. Thus /disk/ C-173 "record", Dimin /dwisk/; cf. C-214, 717. The conceivable alternative would be */CwiCiC/ with an additional /i/ in the second Dimin syllable, but I have no examples of this; it may well be that the principle here is that a consonant cluster in the Sg should be retained as such in the Dimin (unless this conflicts with the pattern of inserting /i/ after surface C_2 in the Dimin). There is one example of a borrowed noun of shape /CCCC/, namely /tnbr/ C-734 "postage stamp", and here both /tnibr/ and /tnibir/ are found; note that /tnbr/, because of its two sonorants, is bisyllabic, unlike the /CVCC/ examples just given, and this may account for the existence of the variant /tnibir/.

In the case of /CCV/ nouns, Dimin forms from native nouns tend to be unstable and variable; perhaps this is because /CCa/ is often ambiguous as to whether the vowel is FSg /-a/, and because /CCi/ and /CCu/ are uncommon. The most common outputs for native /CCV/ stems are Dimin /CCiwa/ (MSg or FSg, in the latter case analysable as /CCiw-a/), /CCiyu/ (perhaps really /CCiyw/), and /CCiwi/. It is difficult to pursue this matter in connection with European borrowings, since few of these are of /CCV/ shape. However, from /žwa/ C-827 "envelope", my informants (when pressed) produced /žwiyu/ or /žwiw/ (these two being rather close phonetically). On the other hand, the slang word /ptiwa/ C-571 "short person", while not obviously functioning synchronically as a Dimin, is apparently a historical Dimin based on /pti/ C-571 "small" (Fr *petit*). From /pnu/ C-563 "tyre" (Fr *pneu*) one informant, rather reluctantly, produced /pniyu/, agreeing with the type /žwiyu/.

In northern Morocco there is a very common adjective /stitu/ C-661 "small", apparently an old bo-rowing from Sp *chico* "small" and/or its own Dimin *chiquito*. It is likely that the Dimin-like shape of /stitu/ (cf. /žwiyu/ and /pniyu/, just given; also /ḥlilu/, Dimin of /ḥlu/ "sweet", a native MCA item) favoured the propagation of this form, because of the lexical sense "small", and there may have been some reshaping influenced by these Dimin patterns in the actual process of forming /stitu/ from those Sp prototypes. In any event, /stitu/ is apparently not (or no longer) treated synchronically as a Dimin, hence a new Dimin /stiwt/ (or perhaps /stiwət/) is recorded in the north; it is also heard in central Morocco even though /stitu/ itself is not. The form /stiwt/ differs from others we have seen in having /w/ after the characteristic /i/-vowel of the Dimin. There could be a confluence of two factors at work here:

(a) the common Morocco-wide synonym for "small" is /ṣġiṛ/, which has an irregular Dimin /ṣġiwṛ/ rather than */ṣġiyṛ/ in most subdialects, and /stiwt/ might well reflect analogy from this semantically similar form; (b) /stiwt/ shares with /stitu/ essentially the same segments (except for /w/ *vis-à-vis* /u/), and could possibly be thought of as showing a kind of metathesis (though this is not a regular MCA process).

Our material on Diminutives from borrowed nouns is particularly rich in connection with stems with large numbers of segments. It appears that the preferred Dimin pattern is of the form /CCiC*i.../ where C* is a single consonant or a cluster. That is, not only do we get /i/ in the first Dimin syllable, we also (often) get /i/ in the second Dimin syllable, whether this is done by changing an input vowel to /i/ or by adding /i/ between adjacent input consonants. The second C in /CCiC*i.../ is a stem consonant if the input begins with two consonants, and is usually an inserted /w/ if the input begins with /CV.../.

Some examples are /kṛṛuṣ-a/ C-374 "cart", Dimin /kṛiṛiṣ-a/; /fṛṃaž/ C-240 "cheese", Dimin /fṛiṃiž/; /bušun/ C-152 "cork", Dimin /bwišin/; and /baṭaṭ-a/ C-67 "potato", Dimin /bwiṭiṭ-a/. However, as noted in Table 6-3, word- or stem-final /u/ or /a/ is not shifted to /i/ in the second Dimin syllable: /bidu/ C-75 "tank", Pl /bwidu/ not */bwidi/; cf. /ṭbil-a/, mentioned earlier, Dimin of /ṭbl-a/ C-750 "table". Other examples of Dimin /CCiC*i.../ are C-118, 379, 421, 542, 635, 654, all from input /CCC*V.../, and /gṛafaṭ-a/ C-367 "necktie", Dimin /gṛifiṭ-a/ from /CCVC*V.../. Other examples of /CwiC*i.../ from simplex /CVC*V.../ include C-37, 42, 46, 67, 84, 86, but a complete list based on the appendix would run over a hundred since this is a very common type with borrowings.

In addition to /bidu/, /bwidu/ just mentioned, further examples of failure of final /u/ to shift to /i/ are C-87, 184, 268, 308, 482, 530, 603, 612, 733, 752, 807; likewise, unshifted /u/ but this time in the third (not second) syllable is seen in C-533 and 671. In the case of /gaṭṭu/ C-266 "cake", individuative Sg /gaṭṭu-ya/ (with FSg allomorph /-ya/ after /u/), the Dimin /gwiṭṭu-ya/ is based on the individuative Sg; since the /u/ is not shifted to /i/ it looks as though stem-final (not only word-final) /u/ in the second Dimin syllable is resistant to the shift.

The exceptions noticed to the rule that /u/ is retained if stem-final but shifted if non-stem-final in the second Dimin syllable are a handful of instances where /u/ fails to undergo the shift. In two of these instances, there is almost surely interference from a variant with stem-final /u/. Thus /ṛadyun/ C-589 gives Dimin /ṛwidyun/, not */ṛwidyin/, but aside from the awkwardness of having /i/ after /y/ we can certainly suspect the influence of stem-variant /ṛadyu/, Dimin /ṛwidyu/, where retention of stem-final /u/ is perfectly regular; the other such example is /ṣaḷun/ C-675, Dimin /ṣwiḷun/ "(guest) salon", cf. variants /ṣaḷu/ and regular Dimin /ṣwiḷu/. In the other counterexamples, it is possible that consonant clusters between the first and second syllables are a factor in the failure of shift to /i/ to take place: /kaṣkṛuṭ/ C-335 "sandwich" (Fr *casse-croûte*), Dimin /kriṣkṛuṭ/ not */kwiṣkṛiṭ/; /ṭiṛmus/ C-762 "thermos bottle", Dimin /ṭwiṛmus/ not */ṭwiṛmis/.

The cases where second-syllable /u/ shifts to /i/, listed by appendix citation above, all involve a single consonant (not a cluster) between first and second syllables. However, /a/ does shift to /i/ after a cluster in /kabṛan/ C-305 "corporal", Dimin /kwibṛin/, and also in C-824, so there may be a slight difference in the conditions under which /a/ and /u/ shift to /i/ in these second Dimin syllables.

Having described the regular patterns for Dimin nouns (see below for additional remarks on irregularities and phonological twists), we briefly digress to consider Dimin verbs. In regular MCA, this construction is uncommon but does occur with some quadriliteral stems; typically it has a jocular or teasing nuance, and is characteristic of verbs denoting behavioural idiosyncrasies and the like, especially in slang. It is formed simply by adding /i/ between C_1 and C_2, hence /(t-)CCCəC/ becomes /(t-)CiCCəC/, where mediopassive /t-/ may or may not be present. Since many of the verbs in this semantic category happen to be borrowings (usually, internal verbalizations based on an earlier noun or adjective borrowing), Dimin verbs are common in our loanword data. Thus /t-bgbəṣ/ B-6 "he acted like a big shot" has Dimin /t-bigbəṣ/, literally "he acted like a little big shot", cf. /bigbuṣ/ C-79 "giant" (Eng *big boss*). In this particular instance, the fact that the noun begins in /big.../ may have favoured the development of the Dimin form of the verb; indeed, /t-bigbəṣ/ may have been the earliest verbalization, subsequently reanalysed as Dimin with /t-bgbəṣ/ arrived at by back-formation. In another similar example (B-24), the noun does not have an /i/ so the Dimin verb must be historically (as well as synchronically) dependent on the regular (non-Dimin) verbalization. Another Dimin verb (see B-180) presents interesting phonological alternations involving nasalized vowels and is discussed below. In B-1 we have a possible case of a Dimin verb, but the only form now attested is the participial, and it is not clear whether this is the participle of a Dimin verb or a Dimin form based on the regular participle without reference to any Dimin verb.

In the remainder of this section we discuss some phonological problems and other minor points involving Dimin forms from borrowings. In order, we consider (a) Dimin forms lacking an expected vowel in the second syllable; (b) mysterious addition of FSg /-a/ to the Dimin form; (c) cases where the non-Dimin simplex happens to already have the shape of a Dimin stem; (d) Dimin forms from stems beginning in a vowel; (e) treatment of nasalized vowel; (f) problems involving pharyngealization.

An example of an unexpectedly short Dimin is /mliyn/, not */mliyin/, from /mlyun/ C-510 "million". It is likely that having /y/ as C_3 in this stem is the key to the unusual Dimin form; recall that /CCiyəC/ with /y/ inserted by rule is an important Dimin type. In the case of Dimin /mwitr/ alongside regular /mwitir/ from /mutur/ C-524 "motorcycle", it may be that Dimin */mwitr/ (not recorded by me, but possibly in use) from /mitr/ C-506 "meter" has been involved by contamination. However, no similar ad hoc explanations suggest themselves for the short Dimin variants /šwif̣ṛ/ and /škiḷṭ/ (alongside regular /šwif̣iṛ/ and /škiḷiṭ/) from /šif̣uṛ/ C-705 "driver" and /škḷaṭ/ C-711 "chocolate". It may just be that short /CCiCC/

can crop up sporadically for expected /CCiCiC/ even without a specific analogical stimulus. Another somewhat puzzling set of data is /tnbr/ C-734 "postage stamp", Dimin /tnibir/ (along with more expectable /tnibr/), and /ṭnbuṛ/ C-763 "drum", Dimin /ṭnibṛ/ (expected variant */ṭnibiṛ/ not recorded, though possibly in use somewhere). Note that the /CCCC/ noun has a Dimin variant /CCiCiC/, while the /CCCuC/ noun has Dimin /CCiCC/, instead of the reverse; since the two Sg stems (non-Dimin) are phonologically similar, there may have been some kind of mutual contamination resulting in irregular types.

There are two examples where FSg /-a/ seems to be added in the Dimin though not present in the simple Sg: /burs/ C-145 "scholarship (stipend)", Dimin /bwirs-a/, and /pist/ C-557 "highway", Dimin /pwist-a/. It is possible that these Dimin forms reflect the bilingual's consciousness of these items as having feminine gender in Fr, although /burs/ and /pist/ in non-Dimin forms can now take masculine agreement in MCA. It is also possible that we may have historical paradigm mixing involving variants */pist-a/ (from Fr *piste* with /-a/ added to preserve gender, or straight from Sp *pista*) and */burs-a/ (this is attested as /burs-a/ C-146, though not used by the Fes informant who produced the forms shown above). It should be noted that native MCA vocabulary includes a number of stems lacking FSg /-a/ which none the less require feminine concord (e.g. /šəmš/ "sun"), and these regularly take overt /-a/ in Dimin forms (/šmiš-a/); the two borrowings just discussed are not precisely the same in patterning but perhaps have some affinities.

Diminutives based on input singular forms which are already "diminutive" in form (i.e. begin with /CCi.../) do not seem to be in use in the borrowings. In principle, one could conceivably generate oppositions of simplex vs. Dimin either by creative usage of a less regular Dimin pattern (in normal MCA we get /CCiwəC/ or /$C_1C_2iC_2əC_3$/ as special patterns for some types of adjectives), or by taking the borrowing as Dimin and creating a new simplex by back-formation (6.28). However, despite its frequent occurrence the Dimin is not a crucially important category, and it seems that if no obvious Dimin pattern is available that would differentiate simplex from Dimin, we just do not get a Dimin form. This is the case with /swirti/ C-664 "game of chance" (Sp *suerte* "luck"), which already has Dimin-like shape and for which no Dimin could be elicited. In a case like that of /wiski/ C-800 "whiskey", the regular Dimin would be /wwiski/, with an initial doubled /ww/ which does not otherwise occur and which sounds awkward; such a form was actually elicited from one speaker, but it was given reluctantly and is almost certainly not in actual use.

Another problematic type is stems beginning with a vowel, a pattern largely limited to European borrowings. Despite elicitation attempts, informants were usually quite unwilling to produce Dimin forms based on nouns beginning in MCA with /a/, and were unsure what the Dimin would be even if one had to be produced. In the case of /uṭil/ C-784 "hotel", a Dimin /uṭiyl/ was obtained from some informants, though it is not very common; what seems to be happening here is that the initial /u/ is treated for purposes of Dimin formation as though it were /w/, the phonetic difference between /u/ and /w/ in this position being slight (though present).

Of course, no similar fictitious semivowel-like status is available for /a/. Nevertheless, attempts to elicit Dimin forms from stems beginning in /i/ were unsuccessful as well.

There is one especially significant phonological alternation between simplex and Dimin in a borrowed noun which may shed light on the phonological status of nasalized vowels, which occur only in borrowings (6.3). This is /ṭulạ̃ṭi/ C-779 "clever", Dimin /ṭwiliṇṭi/. We can see that /iṇ/ is the output when /ạ̃/ undergoes the regular Dimin conversion to /i/, suggesting that /ạ̃/ can be analysed into two components, a low vowel and a nasalization feature (whether simultaneous or linearly sequential); recall that Fr nasalized vowels are sometimes reflected in MCA borrowings as vowel-nasal sequences. The forms just seen are compatible with the observation that /ạ̃/ is now a fairly well established phoneme in borrowings, distinct from /an/ or /aṇ/ sequences, while neither MCA nor Fr has high nasalized vowels like /ĩ/. The one unclear aspect of /ṭulạ̃ṭi/, /ṭwiliṇṭi/ is whether the pharyngealization of the /ṇ/ (i.e. of the /iṇ/ sequence) is due to spreading of this feature from surrounding segments or is regular as the output from /ạ̃/ in any environment.

This remark leads to a more general analysis of pharyngealization in borrowings. Ordinarily, we can disregard the question since the stem consonants retain their usual value for this feature in the Dimin, with the vowels automatically coloured by the consonants. As a result, vowel allophones [ạ o e], the pharyngealized forms of phonemes /a u i/, in the simplex usually correspond to [e] in the Dimin assuming the usual conversion ot /i/ phoneme. There are, however, a couple of cases where a given informant (usually my main Fes informant) gave simplex and Dimin forms with slightly distinct pharyngealization patterns.

For example, the borrowed noun pronounced [ḷokaḷ] (equivalent to [ḷokạl]) is analysed as /ḷukạl/ C-453 "premises" with phonemic back /ạ/ but with the final /l/ nonpharyngealized, because in Pl [ḷokạl-æ̇t] the suffix vowel is not pharyngealized, as it should be if the preceding consonant were distinctively pharyngealized. However, the same informant gave the Dimin as [ḷwekeḷ], Pl [ḷwekeḷ-ạt], where Pl suffix allomorph [-ạt] with back vowel requires analysing the stem-final /ḷ/ as pharyngealized. Another way of looking at this is in terms of a tendency toward vowel harmony within words, with surface [ạ o e] and [æ u i] forming the two harmonic sets. Vowel harmony is not a clearly established independent principle in MCA phonology, but there is some evidence for it as an underlying tendency, and it may be that in Dimin forms (which already have a kind of partial phonemic vowel harmony through the regular occurrence of /i/ in first and second Dimin syllables) this tendency is a little more visible. Similarly, for a few speakers we can get [ṃotur] C-524 "motorcycle", phonemic /ṃutur/, but Dimin /ṃwiṭiṛ/ pronounced [ṃweṭeṛ] at least as a variant for regular /ṃwitir/, showing that pharyngealization-spreading (or vowel harmony) tends to be a little more extensive in Dimin than ordinary forms. Another example is /qamižž-a/ or /qamiž-a/ C-582 "shirt", where /q/ has effects on vocalic allophones similar to the effects of pharyngealized consonants; the regular Dimin is /qwimiž(ž)-a/, pronounced [qwemiž(ž)-a], with distinct vowel qualities in the first two syllables; however, a variant [qwemež(ž)-a] is also recorded, requiring a representation /qwiṃiž(ž)-a/ with pharyngealized /ṃ/, and I interpret this as another instance of the same phenomenon.

In some simplex words, as we have observed earlier, we have a vowel [ạ], [o], or [e] which would normally presuppose an adjoining pharyngealized (or uvular) consonant, but where no such consonant occurs; this is characteristic only of European borrowings. Aside from cases like /ḷokaḷ/ just mentioned above, where there is a consonant (here the final /l/) which acts as though it were phonemically pharyngealized in some forms (here Dimin) but not others (here non-Dimin Pl), we also have some instances where the surrounding consonants are palatoalveolar or velar and therefore cannot be considered to be pharyngealized. In such cases, the Dimin form preserves the "vowel harmony" pattern as though there were a pharyngealized consonant around, giving [e] as the pronunciation for /i/ in the first (and second) Dimin syllable. Since [e] cannot easily be considered a regular surface allophone of /i/ in this case, we write the phonemic transcription of the Dimin with /e/. Thus /kokuṭ/ C-365 "stewpan", pronounced [kokoṭ] with the second [o] due to following /ṭ/ but with the first [o] phonemic (since /u/ here would regularly be pronounced [u]), has Dimin [kweketֽ], transcribed phonemically as /kwekiṭ/. See also C-811.

We may briefly mention a few other instances in which analysis of Dimin forms provides data for the phonological interpretation of the form of borrowings. The noun /ltšin-a/ C-452 "orange", collective /ltšin/, seems not to have a very clear phonemic representation to speakers, to judge by their reluctance to produce Dimin forms and by the variety of such forms which do occur under elicitation. A variant Dimin /lčičin-a/ suggests a representation /lččin-a/ for the simplex, but other forms like /ltitin-a/ are attested, pointing to an ambivalent representation (there is no ablaut Pl to help us). Some rural dialects near Fes solve the problem by changing the simplex to /links-a/, from which Dimin /lšišin-a/ is readily formed. These data are of interest in considering the structural interpretation, as unit /č/ or sequence /tš/, of MCA reflexes of [č] in borrowing; basically, /č/ is reasonably well established as a unit phoneme in northern dialects (Tetouan), but only marginally in the centre of Morocco (e.g. Fes).

We may also mention that homorganic nasal-stop clusters /mb/ and /ŋg/ or /ŋk/ can occur in borrowings in positions where the Dimin requires breaking up the cluster. In view of suggestions that these clusters may be structurally reanalysed as alveolar /n/ plus a labial or velar stop (see middle of 6.5, also discussion of relevant ablaut Pl forms near the end of 6.26), evidence from Dimin forms may be of phonological interest here. In the case of homorganic velar clusters, the Dimin forms do suggest that the nasal is dental. Thus /ṭəŋg/ C-764 "(military) tank" has Dimin /ṭniyəg/, where the Dimin /i/ vowel breaks up the cluster. Similarly, in the case of /fṛəŋk/ C-242 "franc, centime", Dimin /fṛinək/ and variants suggest an underlying alveolar nasal, though here the homorganic cluster is broken up not by the /i/ but rather by the schwa vowel /ə/ in the pattern /CCiCəC/. On the other hand, for /ḅaŋk/ C-48 "bank" and variants, the Dimin evidence is mixed. No clear examples involving labial nasal-stop clusters were recorded.

In borrowings like /šḷaḍ-a/ C-712 "salad", Dimin /šḷiyḍ-a/ [šḷeyḍ-a] could possibly be taken as indicating that /ḷ/ is independently pharyngealized and is not merely affected by low-level spreading of pharyngealization from the /ḍ/. From */šlaḍ-a/ with just /ḍ/ pharyngealized we might expect a Dimin pronounced *[šliyḍ-a]. Using this criterion, we can show that a number of other similar borrowings like /kḷaṭ-a/ C-357 "rifle" and /bḷaṣ-a/ C-102 "place" also have two phonemic pharyngealized consonants, one of them being /ḷ/. In the case of /fnaṛ/ or /fṇaṛ/ C-255 "flashlight", with alveolar nasal rather than lateral, the evidence is mixed: Dimin [fniyṛ] and [fneyṛ] are recorded.

For /šly-a/ C-714 "chair", informants in the Fes/Meknes area were reluctant to produce Dimin forms, but suggested either /šliwy-a/ or /šliy-a/. The variant /šliwy-a/ is technically irregular since the strictly regular form would be /šliyy-a/, and perhaps /šliy-a/ is a slightly reduced form of the latter. However, /šliwy-a/ is fairly reasonable in view of the fact that C_3 is already /y/, and the fact that /w/ does occasionally occur instead of /y/ in a similar position in certain minor inherited Dimin patterns like /ṣġiṛ/ "small", Dimin /ṣġiwṛ/. (Note also /lḥy-a/ "beard", Dimin /lḥiw-a/ for many speakers, with /w/ substituted for /y/ as C_3 to give a surface pattern like that of /mṛa/ "woman", Dimin /mṛiw-a/.) In any event, /šly-a/ is not a common lexical item in MCA except in the north and in Jewish dialects, neither of which is our main concern here.

It is apparent by comparing the Dimin data in this section with the ablaut Pl data in the preceding section (summarized, respectively, in Tables 6-3 and 6-2, above), that the two patterns have much in common. Ablaut Pl is usually based on some variant of a pattern /CCaC.../, Dimin on some variant of /CCiC.../, and in both cases C_2 position is often occupied by an inserted /w/ while C_3 position is often occupied by inserted /y/. The two are not exactly parallel; for example, diminutive forms often show /i/ in the second syllable under the same conditions (though, in some human noun types, stem-final /a/ is switched to /i/ or vice versa).

6.28 Back-formation

Back-formation is a historical process by which a particular form (perhaps an initial borrowing) is analysed as a derived or otherwise morphologically complex formation, with a simpler or unmarked stem-form subsequently created by analogical processes. Once the back-formation has occurred as a historical event, the original form comes to function as a synchronic derivative or marked form, though it was historically primary. We are here concerned with identifying back-formations involving borrowings interpreted as FSg, Pl, or Dimin. It turns out that this is a relatively marginal historical process.

We begin by mentioning instances where the MCS Sg form is based on a Pl form in the original language, where it is reasonable to assume that the initial borrowing was Pl. One such case is /zufriy-a/ "playboys" from Fr *les ouvriers* "the workers", from which Sg /zufri/ C-809 was created by back-formation (the MCA /z/

reflects [z], orthographic *s*, in the Fr definite article). Cf. also /ẓaḷamiṭ/ C-805 "match", ultimately from Fr Pl *les allumettes* with the same resegmentation. Examples in which Fr definite Pl *les* has been completely incorporated into the MCA stem are /liḅ-a/ C-442 "stocking" (Fr Pl *les bas*) and /lig-a/ C-443 "glove" (Fr *les gants*). It should be noted that all of these cases involve stems which would otherwise be phonologically non-optimal in MCA, either because they would begin in vowels or because they would consist of just /Ca/ (an excessively short noun-stem type seen in native MCA only in /ma/ "water"). In other words, the reanalyses which have produced these MCA forms have a strong external motivation. They appear to all have been relatively early, colonial-period borrowings from Fr and would thus have entered MCA at a time when these canonical-shape generalizations concerning stem forms were still enforced fairly rigidly. (Newer loans do not undergo these processes.)

In two cases, a borrowing has been reanalysed as Pl (by some speakers or dialects) because it looked like an existing MCA ablaut Pl pattern. In the case of /fsyan/ C-245 "officer" (Sp *oficial*, old loan), my Marrakech informant used this as a plural "officers" by analogy to other /CCC-an/ (including /CCy-an/) ablaut plurals. Similarly, my main Fes informant considered /ṛḍum-a/ C-596 "bottle" (Sp *redoma*, common in MCA only in the north) a plural by analogy to other /CCuCa/ ablaut plurals such as /ktuba/ "books". However, neither of these reanalyses resulted in a back-formed Sg; either a distinct variant, or a distinct lexical item, was used with singular meaning.

There are numerous cases in borrowings of a collective with zero suffix being opposed to an individuative Sg with FSg suffix /-a/. In such cases, the initial borrowing was in most cases probably the unsuffixed collective, but in some cases may have been the form with /-a/ with the collective then back-formed in MCA. In some cases it is difficult to determine what happened, since there is often a Romance cognate set with the Sp and/or It forms showing final *a* versus phonetic zero (orthographic *e*) in Fr, and we may not know which Romance form was the immediate prototype (and in view of the many Fr crossings with and contaminations of earlier Sp and It borrowings, discussed in the following section, it is quite possible that the MCA form has a multiple Romance source). In the case of /srdin/ "sardines", individuative /srdin-a/ C-658, I would guess that the form is from Sp *sardina* or a similar Mediterranean Romance form, since it seems to be a very old lexical item; if this is correct, /srdin/ is back-formed. (If this were from Fr, we would most likely get */sardin/ with the vowels better preserved, but /srdin/ would be possible in the early colonial period.) The best example of back-formation is /madriy-a/ C-458 "beam" (Fr *madrier*), from which collective /madri/ "beams" is attested, but the latter form is absent from most idiolects examined.

Diminutive back-formation seems nonexistent. From nouns like /swirti/ C-664 "game of chance" (Sp *suerte*), /ṛwiḍ-a/ C-624 "wheel" (Sp *rueda*), and /rwin-a/ C-625 "mixture, disturbance" (Sp *ruína*), which have the proper form for MCA diminutives, back-formed simplexes */sVrti/, */ṛVḍ-a/, and */rVn-a/ might be expected, but none is recorded in Morocco. Algerian /ṛuḍ-a/ "wheel" is a possible back-formation, but could just as easily be a separate borrowing from an Italian dialect. Similarly, corresponding to MCA /skwil-a/ C-654 "school" an Algerian form /škul-a/ is attested, but again this could be from an Italian dialect (or a Sp/It cross). We leave the Algerian forms aside pending more information.

Other apparent MCA Dimin back-formations are /kuzin-a/ C-431 "kitchen" (cf. Fr *cuisine*) and /kuzin-i/ variant of C-432 "cook, chef" (Fr *cuisinier*), which can also be /kwizinyi/. However, these are probably not Dimin back-formations. The form /kuzin-a/ is probably a cross of Sp *cocina* and Fr *cuisine* with It *cucina* possibly also involved, and the variant /kuzin-i/, while not directly from Sp or It, has probably been analogically influenced by /kuzin-a/ since /kuzin-i/ can be taken as a derivative with Gentilic suffix /-i/. There are thus no clear cases of Dimin back-formation.

The question of the roles of European definite vs. indefinite noun forms has been raised in 6.24 above. We have mentioned, toward the end of that section, two or three examples such as /iṭṛu/ C-298 "litre" (Sp *litro*) where stem-initial *l* has been reinterpreted as the definite prefix /l-/ in MCA with subsequent development of an indefinite form lacking this segment. However, this is a low-frequency development, and it is more common for Fr *le* or *l'* to be resegmented as part of an MCA stem, especially in the case of *l'* before Fr vowel.

There is also one marginal example of back-formation involving another nominal prefix /d-/, which is used in certain types of genitive constructions, as in /xms-a d-l-biḍ-at/ "five eggs" (/l-biḍ-at/ "the eggs") and /xms-a d-maṭiš-at/ "five tomatoes". In earlier literature there are reports of forms like /yaṃanḍ/ instead of /dyaṃanḍ/ C-178 "diamond" in some northern dialects, and it would seem that this involves resegmentation of /dyaṃanḍ/ as /d-yaṃanḍ/ with subsequent generalization of /yaṃanḍ/. This reanalysis would require taking /yaṃanḍ/ as one of the nouns which, like /maṭiš-a/ "tomato", fails to take definite prefix /l-/. My own data for northern as well as other MCA dialects show /dyaṃanḍ/ or a similar variant with initial stop.

In summary, back-formation has been a marginal historical process in the adaptation of European borrowings. The only exception would be in verbs, if we consider cases where a participle was the first form borrowed to be cases of back-formation (6.22, also end of 6.14); if so, this is apparently a recurrent process.

6.29 Fr/Sp crosses and other contaminations

By a "cross" we mean an MCA borrowing which is, historically, a hybrid involving more than one protoform, usually a Fr stem in addition to a Sp (or It) one. It could be that there were initially two independent borrowings, one from Sp in northern dialects and one from Fr in other MCA dialects, with subsequent confusion of the two. However, in view of the chronology of colonial penetration, we should also expect cases where a Sp (or It) borrowing became established at an early time, with a similar Fr stem subsequently entering the picture, producing a full or partial reshaping and/or semantic shift of the earlier borrowing to make it more closely resemble the Fr form. Although there are undoubtedly many cases where an existing borrowing apparently directly from Fr was really the result of complete Gallicization of an older Sp/It borrowing now lost, there are also cases where the Gallicization is only partial. It is precisely this latter case, where the attested MCA form is indisputably of hybrid origin, that is of greatest theoretical interest to us.

While many such forms display lexical idiosyncrasies, there is at least one very general pattern involving several borrowings. This is the case where a Sp/It feminine noun with *-a* comes into MCA, but where a Fr cognate with (phonetic) zero suffix (usually written *-e*) subsequently comes into play, so that Fr-MCA bilinguals believe the form to be from Fr with /-a/ (FSg) added in the borrowing process. We have discussed this matter above (6.25); recall examples such as /bal̩-a/ C-40 "shovel", now associated by Fr-MCA bilinguals with Fr *pelle* but actually most likely originally from Sp *pala*. As noted above, there are quite a few cases of this sort, enough to generate a diasystemic conversion routine by which MCA FSg suffix /-a/ is sometimes added gratuitously to new borrowings from Fr with no relevant Sp origin. (We have also observed that addition of this /-a/ is most common with feminine Fr nouns, so that one function of the suffixation is gender preservation, but that /-a/ is added only to a minority of borrowings from Fr feminines and that it is added to some borrowings from Fr masculines.)

We now turn to other cases of possible or probable crossing of Fr with Sp/It borrowings, bearing in mind that we do not always have the complete information on dialectal variants which we would need for authoritative word histories. In /antiris/ C-11 "interest (on loan)", we almost certainly have an early borrowing /intiris/ (attested in early sources) from Sp *interés*, with the initial syllable then reshaped on the basis of Fr *intérêt*, since MCA /an/ is a regular output from Fr [æ̃]. In /bantur-a/ C-49 "paint" we may have a cross between Sp *pintura* and Fr *peinture*; /baṣaḍuṛ/ C-62 "ambassador" appears to involve Sp *embajador* and Fr *ambassadeur*; /baṣažiṛ/ C-63 "passenger(s)" may involve Sp *pasajero* and Fr *passager*; /bluz-a/ C-104 "blouse" involves Fr *blouse* and Sp *blusa*; /buṛṣ-a/ C-146 "stock exchange" may be based on Fr *bourse* and Sp *bolsa*; /ḍubl/ C-187 "double", phonetic [ḍobl], is a compromise between Sp *doble* and Fr *double*; /fayuṛ/ C-193 "small gift" involves Fr *faveur* and Sp *favor* (Sp *v* should give MCA /b/); /gṛabaṭ-a/ "necktie" (see C-367) is based on Sp *corbata* and Fr *cravate*; /paṣpuṛṭ/ C-545 "passport" seems to involve Sp *pasaporte* and Fr *passeport* (the latter with "silent" *t*); /santur/ C-628 "belt" involves Fr *ceinture* and perhaps also Sp *cintura*; /ṭṛiṭ-a/ C-773 "monthly payment" is a mixture of Sp *letra* and Fr *traitement*; /ṭulãṭi/ C-779 "clever" is problematic but may involve several Romance forms such as Sp *teniente* and Fr *intelligent*; /kuṇṭṛaỵan/ C-411 "contraband" is from Fr *contrebande* and Sp *contrabando*; /kuṇṭṛ-a/ C-410 and variants "contract" involve Fr *contrat*, Sp *contrato*, and perhaps the phonologically similar Sp *contra* "against"; /ṭṛãkil/ C-765 "unbothered" may involve Fr *tranquille* [trãki(y)] and Sp *tranquilo*. Many of the MCA forms just cited have other variants shown in the relevant appendix entries, and these other variants may be "pure" Sp or "pure" Fr borrowings not showing such contaminations.

Another kind of historical development is the phonological convergence of two distinct borrowings, perhaps one from Fr and another from Sp or It, resulting in a case of homophony in MCA. Thus /baḅuṛ/ C-30 has meanings including "steamer, ferry" (Sp *vapor*, Fr *vapeur*) and "port (side of ship)" (Fr *bâbord*); likewise, /gaṛṣun/ C-264 means both "waiter" (Fr *garçon*) and "underpants" (Sp *calzón*). In this second example, the regular MCA output from Sp *calzón* should be */kaḷṣun/ or the like, and it is probable that the Sp and Fr borrowings were originally slightly distinct in MCA but that they became associated due to the phonological similarity and eventually merged formally. In some other cases, it would seem that an attested borrowing retains the form of an old Sp/It loan, but has more recently acquired the meaning of a similar Fr word. Thus /ḅul-a/ C-130 "light bulb" may be from Sp *bola* but has the meaning of Fr *ampoule*; /kuḷ-a/ C-394 "glue, paste" would seem to be from Sp *cola* (reinforced by Fr *colle*), but in a second meaning "drunkard" has apparently been influenced by /ankul/ or northern dialectal /kul/ "alcohol" C-10 (Fr *alcool*, Sp *alcohol*). C-505 may be another example.

There are also occasional crossings or contaminations involving a European prototype along with an MCA (or CA) stem. Thus /diwan-a/ C-174 "customs bureau" appears to involve CA *dīwān-* along with Sp *aduana* (and Fr *douane*). (The fact that here the Romance forms are themselves ultimately CA borrowings is immaterial; this is also the case, incidentally, with the "alcohol" example just given.) Similarly, /bit/ C-91 is both an inherited noun meaning "room" (cf. CA *bayt-* "house") and a borrowing meaning "goal" from Fr *but*, both senses sharing Pl /byut/ inherited from CA *buyūt-* (Pl of *bayt-*). However, /faṛ/ C-202 "bright headlights" (Fr *phare*), though homophonous with inherited /faṛ/ "mouse", does not adopt the latter's Pl form /fir-an/, and instead has its own non-ablaut Pl /faṛ-at/. Another somewhat vulgar Fr/MCA crossing is discussed in B-104.

A few instances of contamination affecting Pl and/or Dimin formations have been mentioned in earlier sections of this chapter. For example, we have pointed out that /nmr-a/ C-534 "number" has an unexpected Dimin variant /nwimr-a/ (alongside /nmir-a/); this may involve the influence of a synonymous borrowing /nimiru/ C-533, Dimin /nwimiru/.

Some of the most interesting crossings are slang expressions which can only have arisen when some unknown genius concocted a humorous hybrid form; see 7.15 for a general discussion of slang borrowings. Two types involving Sp, but recorded in Fes among persons who do not know this language and thus cannot have been the originators, are so remarkable that I cannot resist repeating them. First, /aṣṭa ḷa muxiṛṛ-a/ (see C-526) "some other time (not now)", is based on Sp *hasta la* "until the" (as in *hasta la vista* "until the sight", i.e. "see you later"), Sp *mujer* "woman", and MCA /mṛṛ-a x^{w}ṛ-a/ "other time"; /muxiṛṛ-a/ has roughly the same segments as /mṛṛ-a x^{w}ṛ-a/, along with its meaning, but the order of the segments has been scrambled to resemble Sp *mujer*. Similarly, associating Sp *madre* "mother" with MCA /ṃṃ-/ "mother" and Sp *padre* "father" with MCA /ḅḅa/ "father" has resulted in the concoctions /mwaḍṛi/ "mother" C-527 and /pwaḍṛi/ C-581 "father" (/mw/ and /pw/

are virtually identical to /mm/ and /bb/ in this position); taking this one step farther, the perpetrators of these forms have created /xwadri/ C-804 "brother", modelled on /mwaḍṛi/ and /pwaḍṛi/ but with /x/ taken from MCA /xu-/ (or /xa-/) "brother".

At the present time, a few similar cases involving English are starting to crop up in slang. For example, Eng *-man* (perhaps on the basis of compounds like *fireman*, *policeman*, etc., cf. C-59) is the basis for a slang suffix /-man/ in MCA which can be added to various human nouns. This has also resulted in at least one humorous crossing, /žumžu-maṇ/ "bright fellow, intelligent fellow, whiz", based on the (apparently inherited) MCA noun /žumžum-a/ "top of head; intelligent fellow".

6.30 Problematic and unsolved cases

There are quite a few borrowings listed in Appendices B and C for which there is some historical problem or other which could perhaps be resolved if more information on dialectal variants is obtained. However, in the present section I will merely mention a smallish number of cases where I have a more serious problem at the present time; namely, where I do not know what the European source is or where I do not know whether the MCA form is of European origin at all. I would greatly appreciate information on any of these items from other scholars.

Verbs (Appendix B) are /blaka/ B-8 "he slammed on brakes", /k^{w}rrəz/ B-79 "he embraced", /kufṛ/ B-83 "he stuffed, preserved (animal)", /liva/ B-95 "he made (ball) curve", /sbira/ B-135 "he exploited (him)", /stika/ B-147 "he made (it) pretty", /tka/ B-169 "he knocked (him) out". Nouns and adjectives (Appendix C) are /biṇiṭ/ C-82 "national guard", /b^{w}kk/ C-97 "pretty, handsome", /f̣angaḷ-a/ C-200 "penis (vulgar, used in slang)", /fil/ C-210 "commission", /friy-a/ C-235 "no good (slang)", /ġiwan/ C-289 "great!", /kabus/ C-306 "pistol", /k^{w}bb-a/ C-348 in sense "wine", /sarut/ C-629 "key", /šlux/ C-713 "homosexual (slang)", /taff-a/ C-719 "stack of wheat grains". See the entries for more information. See also the discussion of folk etymologies below, 6.32.

6.31 Invariant forms; parallels with pidginization

One notable feature of European borrowings in MCA is the number of stems functioning syntactically as adjectives or adverbs which have a single, invariant form. This pattern is atypical of inherited MCA stems, since adjectives in this language normally have inflectional paradigms and derivatives (FSg with /-a/, Pl usually by ablaut, often a Dimin by ablaut, a related verb, and/or an abstract noun), and since its "adverbs" are mostly prepositional phrases (except for a few adverbial particles like /hna/ "here" and /daba/ "now"). Moreover, the European prototype for the borrowings often has an inflectional paradigm and derivatives. We therefore have a segment of the borrowed vocabulary which constitutes what might be called a pidgin-like stratum within MCA. Furthermore, as in pidgins, some of these items appear to be of ambiguous or inconsistent word-class status.

The aspect of this problem which has attracted attention in earlier descriptions of MCA is the fact that some nouns, mostly borrowings (from Berber or Romance languages), do not take definite prefix /l-/ though they occur in the same syntactic frames which require this prefix in ordinary nouns. For example, Harrell (1962: 190) lists eleven nouns which idiosyncratically fail to take /l-/, and adds that proper nouns (names for persons and places) are usually of this type, and that a productive derivative for abstract noun of profession /ta-X-t/ (with -X- an agentive noun) also takes no definite prefix. The idiosyncratic common nouns which avoid /l-/ vary slightly from dialect to dialect, but some nouns such as /atay/ "tea", /maṭiš-a/ "tomatoes", and /xizzu/ "carrots" belong to the list in most dialects. On the other hand, these nouns in some cases do permit Pl suffix /-at/, and some have attested Dimin ablaut forms, so they are not necessarily immune to all regular morphological processes.

The well-known items of this sort, such as those just mentioned, are old, usually precolonial borrowings from Berber or other languages. However, Brunot (in EDA) remarks in his discussion of Fr borrowings then entering MCA in the early and middle colonial period that several of the borrowed nouns failed to take definite /l-/. In other words, there is evidence that at some chronological stages in the recent development of MCA, there has been a general tendency to avoid adding definite /l-/ to borrowed nouns from these languages, and that some of these items have stabilized with this morphological idiosyncrasy.

However, even in Brunot's description quite a few of the newer Fr borrowings did take definite /l-/, and my more recent data suggest that this prefix is ordinarily found under the usual conditions with Fr and other European nominal borrowings; those items specifically labelled by Brunot as not taking /l-/ now do take it in the speech of my (mostly youngish) informants, although such archaic items as /atay/ "tea" and the others listed above continue to avoid the prefix. The only exceptional case is that of some borrowings mentioned in 6.24 where there is some ambivalence as to whether an initial /l/ (or /ḷ/) is the definite prefix or the stem-initial consonant, but this involves segmentation ambiguities rather than anything like a pidginized stratum.

On the other hand, such a stratum is recognizable in a number of borrowings, usually functioning as adjectives or adverbs but sometimes noun-like and sometimes of indeterminate word class, which appear to avoid Pl and FSg markers (in the case of adjectives) or avoid semantically expectable prepositions (in that of adverbs). For expository purposes we divide the relevant items (from Appendix C) into nouns, adjectives, and adverbs, though in some cases this categorization is dubious.

Nouns which avoid FSg and Pl marking, and for which Dimin forms are difficult or impossible to elicit, include /f̣akạ̃ṣ/ C-195 "overseas Moroccan guest worker (while back in Morocco on vacation)", /buržwa/ C-149 "bourgeois, middle class", /baṣažiṛ/ C-63 "passenger(s)", and /primiṛ/ C-567 "primary school". These stems usually take definite /l-/ where appropriate, though /f̣akạ̃ṣ/ sometimes does not.

Adjective-like forms with similar avoidance of FSg and Pl are /flipp/ C-224 "flipped out", /f̣ranṣiṣ/ C-230 "French", /friks/ C-232 "chic, modish", /frišk/ C-233 "fresh", /himri/ C-290 "hungry",

/kaḷm/ C-310 "calm", /kliṛ/ C-358 "clear, certain", /mɔš/ C-510 "ugly", /pṛi/ C-566 "ready", /pti/ C-571 "small" (used with following personal name), /ṣāfṛwa/ C-668 "fearless", /ṣpuṛtif/ C-685 "athletic", /ṭimid/ C-725 "timid", /ṭṛākil/ C-765 "alone, unbothered", /žõn/ C-819 "young", and /ṣuyaž/ C-694 "wild". These forms in most cases also sometimes occur without definite /l-/ where this prefix is called for, but the resistance to FSg and Pl marking is stronger than the resistance to definite marking.

Adverbs based on Fr adverbial phrases are sometimes reproduced in MCS as parallel phrases involving the substitution of MCA preposition and definite prefix for the corresponding elements in Fr. Thus /b-l-kridi/ C-369 "(buy) on credit" (Fr *à credit*), /d-l-kõfuṛ/ C-363 "de luxe, luxurious(ly)", /b-ḍ-ḍiṭay/ C-185 "(buy) retail", /b-l-gṛu/ C-279 "(buy) wholesale". However, in a considerable number of cases the adverb-like MCA borrowing occurs in a stripped-down, unsegmentable stem form not displaying prepositions or the definite prefix. Some examples are /aṃaṛš/ C-7 "in motion" (Fr *en marche*), /bwan/ C-159 "broke, destitute" (Fr *en panne*), /ḍifanḍi/ C-183 "prohibited", /ḍubl/ or /dubl/ C-187 "double", /faḅuṛ/ C-193 (adverbial sense) "free, as a gift", /fɔlɔ̃ṭi/ C-227 "willingly", /kạš/ C-337 "(in) cash", /kạw/ C-342 "(by) knockout", /kazyu/ C-347 "second-hand (purchase)", /kriru/ C-359 "(drink) in one draught, by chugging", /luks/ C-454 "de luxe" (also prepositional phrase /d-l-luks/), /nikl/ C-532 (adverbial sense) "(in) cash", /õp̣an/ C-537 "having had an accident", /pil/ C-549 in the sense "(hour) on the dot", /pḷizir/ C-562 "as (someone) wants", /ṛup̣p̣u/ C-618 "off work, on vacation or break", /ṛuṭaṛ/ and /ṭṛuṭaṛ/ (C-621 and 776) "late for work", and /anṭiṛdi/ C-14 "prohibited".

In some of these adverbial cases, as with /pil/, the Fr prototype is used in the same context without prepositions (*cinq heures pile* "five o'clock on the dot"), so there is no actual pidginization process in the borrowing. However, several of the examples just given are based on Fr adverbial phrases including prepositions, where the MCA borrowing either drops the preposition or reinterprets it as part of a now unsegmentable stem. The effect is to create a distinctive set of unanalysable adverb-like elements (some also used like adjectives and/or nouns), which (along with the examples listed earlier) constitute a pidgin-like stratum.

Some of the most recent Eng borrowings (often confined to slang) are put in this syntactic category. We may mention in this connection /kipkul/ C-354 "undaunted, cool" (*keep cool*), and /dörti/ C-175 "dirty". These occasionally take definite /l-/ but do not permit (in my data) FSg or Pl markers, for example.

6.32 Native consciousness of foreignness of borrowings

In general, my main informants (young male adults, fairly well educated, reasonably literate in Fr and CA but not other literary languages) were very good at identifying MCA items of foreign origin. Of course, many of the Fr borrowings are quite transparent to Fr-speaking bilingual Moroccans. However, these people were also reasonably good at spotting Sp borrowings, although many of these borrowings are precolonial imports which are well assimilated and have canonical shapes like inherited MCA stems, and although these speakers live in areas where Sp has never been a colonial language (i.e. in the Fes/Meknes area). One clue that a given MCA word may be of European origin is its absence from CA, since much of the inherited MCA lexicon is directly based on that of CA. However, it seems that there is also a word-of-mouth tradition as well, whereby Moroccans hear someone mention that a given word is from Sp and file this away in their memories. (In addition, strange-sounding words which are frequently heard in the speech of Moroccans from the northern, Sp-influenced area around Tangier and Tetouan can be presumed to be of probable Sp origin.)

On the other hand, these speakers are by no means always correct in their suppositions. As we have observed before, in many cases an old Sp or It borrowing has subsequently become associated with a Fr word, often with full or partial reshaping of the borrowing and/or a semantic shift, and there have even been some analogical extensions of false diasystemic conversion routines based on spurious Fr-MCA "cognate" equivalences (6.25, 6.29). Thus MCA /ḅal-a/ C-40 "shovel" from Sp *pala*, secondarily associated with Fr *pelle*, and so forth. Moreover, some of the earlier colonial-period loans from Fr are not obvious to all Moroccans, because of semantic and/or formal changes. Thus /zufri/ C-809 "playboy, swinger" is difficult to associate nowadays with Fr *ouvrier* "worker" (Pl *les ouvriers* being the actual form borrowed). In other cases, my informants claimed that an MCA word was a borrowing from a particular Fr stem, but I find this claim dubious because of major phonological and/or semantic problems. Thus /ṣlguṭ/ C-684 "rascal" was connected with Fr *sale gosse* "dirty lad", but I have a hard time accepting this for a number of reasons. I am likewise suspicious of informants' correlation of /iššir/ C-297 "little boy" with Fr *(le) cher* "(the) darling", especially since /iššir/ seems to be reasonably old in MCA. For the same reason it does not seem possible to agree with some younger speakers' connection of /gud/ "straight (adverb)" and Eng *good*, since /gud/ is well established and probably much too old in MCA to be of Eng origin.

Obviously, there are many individual variations in knowledge of and beliefs about word origins, since colloquial Arabic is not taught as an academic subject in the schools and since foreign lexicon is largely absent from the formal CA which is taught. Naturally, multilingual speakers know much more about foreign word origins than do uneducated monolinguals.

7 Semantic patterns of borrowings

In this chapter we are no longer concerned with the actual mechanics of borrowing and adaptation, rather with the extent of lexical borrowing in various significant lexical domains. For reasons which by now have become clear, it is relatively difficult to address this question with respect to CA borrowings. Much MCA vocabulary in all basic domains is already cognate to CA items, so that many new CA borrowings would be identical to already existing forms, making quantitative studies of borrowing patterns unfeasible. For many attested MCA lexical items I simply do not know whether they were directly inherited or recently borrowed. Moreover, in some cases an MCA paradigm contains one or more forms which appear to be inherited and one or more others which have been borrowed more recently (the plural for nouns, the verbal noun for verbs). Accordingly, in this chapter we will concentrate on diffusion from Fr, Sp, and other European languages into MCA, while making occasional remarks on CA borrowings.

7.1 Nouns vs. verbs: generalities

The majority of borrowings from European languages are nouns and adjectives; an extended list is given as Appendix C and some of these examples are mentioned in the following sections. In general, there is little structural difficulty in borrowing noun stems (and adjectives are very similar to nouns morphologically). Productive inflectional and derivational processes are available to produce plurals and diminutives where appropriate.

The extent of borrowing of verbs directly from Fr varies sharply according to the educational level and degree of bilingualism of speakers and their addressees (hence, indirectly, according to generation, urban vs. rural experience, etc.). Among university students who have received an extensive French-language education, or among Moroccans who have worked extensively in France or Belgium or who interact regularly with tourists, Fr verbs can now be borrowed with relative freedom and spontaneity. Such verb stems as /?uṛgạniza/ "he organized" and /?ütiliza/ "he utilized" can be heard in such contexts on a sporadic basis, though these particular examples are not common: /ġadi n-t-?uṛganiza-w/ "we will get organized". While in some instances a borrowed verb of this type has no good MCA equivalent, in these particular examples and most others there is a perfectly good MCA counterpart (possibly borrowed from CA) which can also be used in these sociolinguistic contexts and would be regularly used when addressing persons who know little Fr (/nḍḍm/ "he organized", /stᶜml/ "he used").

It should also be recalled that there are many borrowed verbs listed in Appendix B which are, historically, internal MCA denominative derivatives from previously borrowed nouns, like noun /ḅuguṣ/ C-126 and verb /t-ḅugəṣ/ B-26, meaning "dandy" and "he acted like a dandy", respectively.

In short, while a very large number of Fr and Sp nouns and adjectives are now well-assimilated MCA borrowings, the number of Fr and Sp verbs which are directly borrowed as MCA verbs is quite limited in the population as a whole, though it becomes extensive among certain bilingual subgroups.

Some examples of relatively well-integrated verbal borrowings: /gaža/ B-63 "he enlisted", /ḍubl/ or /dubl/ B-46 "he doubled, repeated", /gufl/ B-68 "he inflated, beat up", /srba/ B-145 "he served", /sira/ B-141 "he shined (shoes)", /šaṛža/ B-161 "he loaded (truck)", /trina/ B-170 "he trained", and /rigl/ B-127 "he fixed".

Borrowings from CA appear to be more evenly spread across the major word classes; verbs as well as nouns are structurally incorportated into MCA with relative ease. For example, the usual word in MCA for "he opened (it)" is /ḥəll/, but if we wanted to borrow CA *fataḥ-* (imperfective *-ftaḥ-*) there would be no formal problem in doing so and we can immediately produce such forms as /ftəḥ/ "he opened", /ġadi n-ftəḥ/ "I will open", etc. Even the more complex derived stems of CA, like conjugation VIII in *(?)iᶜtabar-* "he considered" and *(?)istaᶜmal-* "he used", can be readily borrowed although MCA has no productive derivations of these types: /ᶜtabr/, /stᶜml/.

7.2 "Core" vocabulary: verbs

As a general rule, the most basic and frequent nouns and verbs in MCA are native items, mostly directly inherited from CA. In several cases we now find a well-entrenched MCA item co-existing with one or more semantically similar borrowed items used in some dialects or perhaps in some registers of MCA.

Some very basic and mundane verbal senses (the sort which usually show up on lexicostatistical lists) include "eat", "drink", "sleep", "go", "come", "sit", "stand", "hit", "kill", "throw", "pick up", "carry", "see", "hear", "smell", "touch", "urinate", "defecate", "copulate", "open", and "shut".

The regular MCA forms, cited in the 3MSg perfective, are /kla/ "he ate", /šṛb/ "he drank", /nᶜəs/ or /rgʷd/ "he slept", /mša/ "he went", /ža/ "he came", /gləs/ or /gᶜʷd/ "he sat", /wqəf/ "he stood", /ḍṛb/ "he hit", /qtl/ "he killed", /ṛma/ or /laḥ/ "he threw", /xda/ "he picked up", /dda/ "he carried", /šaf/ "he saw", /smᶜ/ "he heard", /šəmm/ "he smelled", /qas/ "he touched", /bal/ "he urinated", /xṛa/ "he defecated", /ḥwwa/ "he copulated with", /ḥəll/ "he opened", and /sədd/ or /šədd/ "he shut". These forms are from the Fes/Meknes area (Muslim speech).

There is little evidence that any of these is a borrowing from CA, though a few are formally compatible with such an analysis. Most of them show the results of historical linguistic changes (segmental replacements, analogical reshaping, formal renewal) which make a recent CA borrowing analysis impossible: /kla/ "he ate" from *ʔakal-*, /ža/ "he came" from *ǰāʔ-*, /dda/ "he carried" from *ʔaddā*, /gləs/ "he sat" from *ǰalas-*. Were these to be (re-) borrowed we would expect */ʔkl/, */žaʔ/, */ʔdda/, and */žləs/, respectively. Some of the other items are characteristic colloquial items not commonly used in CA at all: /mša/ "he went", /šaf/ "he saw". Some like /ḥəll/ "he opened" occur in CA but with different primary meaning, and others like /n^{c}əs/ "he slept" occur in CA but are much less common than another high-frequency CA item which is not commonly used in MCA, here *nām-* "he slept". Our overall conclusion is that none of these items can plausibly be regarded as CA borrowings.

Obviously none of these items is from Fr or Sp either, so the question now is whether some of them co-exist with synonymous borrowed forms from Fr or Sp. For most of these items I have recorded no such borrowing even among speakers who have high rates of usage of such European borrowings. For "he ate" I did once hear /mạ̃ža/ (Fr *manger*) from a teenage boy who knew a little Fr and who tended to use an exaggerated number of borrowings in some social contexts. My main informants, who were more thoroughly bilingual and had well-developed norms for appropriate forms of borrowing and code-switching, indicated that /mạ̃ža/ is not regularly used by them except perhaps in fun, and that speakers who make extensive use of borrowed forms of such basic Fr verbs are considered boorish show-offs. For "he touched" I did hear forms of MCA /tuša/ (Fr *toucher*) (B-175), but it is apparently used most often in special extended senses like "he earned (a certain amount of money" (Fr *il touche cinq mille francs*, etc.). I did not hear any Fr verbs meaning "he defecated" (though I intensively elicited vulgar and slang expressions in this and similar domains), but loanwords related to Fr *merde* "excrement" do show up as verbs in other meanings: /mirda/ "he pestered" B-99 (Fr *emmerder*), /dimirda/ "he acted by himself" B-34 (Fr *démerder*). Overall, we can say that there is no significant extent of Fr/Sp borrowing of such high-frequency, core verbs.

These remarks are based on observation of ordinary speech among Moroccans. When speaking MCA to a foreigner who knows Fr and just a little MCA, a Moroccan may develop a special register with MCA as the grammatical base but with many Fr borrowings including some high-frequency verbs. At early stages of my fieldwork I occasionally was the addressee in such cases; thus /kura/ B-92 "he ran", in the form /y-kuri/ "he runs", was recorded as a kind of gloss for a form of MCA /žra/ (the normal verb) intended for the linguist's benefit; it is not in regular use elsewhere.

7.3 Kin terms

This is one of the nominal domains which intuitively is most basic. A limited amount of borrowing has occurred in this domain, however.

Ordinarily, MCA kin terms occur in possessive constructions with immediately following pronominal (possessive) suffix or immediately following possessor noun. In the Fes/Meknes area we get /ṃṃ-i/ "my mother", /mm-u/ "his mother", and /ṃṃayn ṣaḥb-i/ "the mother of my friend"; there are many regional MCA variations (especially in the "construct" form, here /ṃṃayn/). The CA form is *?umm-*, as in *?umm-ī* "my mother", and several other MCA/CA cognate pairs show presence of initial *?* in the CA form and its absence in the MCA form. The pair MCA /ḅḅa/ "father" and CA *?ab-* shows further differences, as does the pair MCA /xu-/ (regional variant /xa-/) "brother" and CA *?ax-*. The ongoing CA interference in the MCA forms primarily affects the relatively uncommon unpossessed definite forms of the kin terms, as in /l-?^{w}mm/ "the mother" based on CA *al-?umm-*, apparently replacing an older MCA form /l-^{w}mm/. The particular type of borrowing going on here is essentially a matter of eliminating canonically awkward preexisting forms in MCA, rather than a simple matter of lexical intrusions, and readers are referred to the discussion in 5.3 for details.

Fr intrusions (some possibly also involving Sp) are sporadic but do occur frequently in some forms used by European-oriented bourgeois and Jews. The principal forms are /baba/ C-29 "father" and /ṃaṃa/ C-465 "mother", often used among these social groups as address forms ("dad!", "mom!"). Fr *Madame* occurs in elegant style as /madam/ or /maḍam/ C-457 "wife" with possessive construction: /madam dyal-i/ "my wife". None of these forms are especially current among the common people in my experience, though /madam/ seems to be gaining currency in some areas. Aside from this there is a set of cleverly manufactured slang terms /mwaḍṛi/ C-527 "mother", /pwaḍṛi/ C-581, and /xwadri/ C-804 "brother" based directly or indirectly on Sp (*madre, padre*), but these are used only by a small segment of the population.

The general term for "family" is now usually /family-a/ or /famil-a/ C-199 (Fr *famille*, Sp *familia*) or /^{c}a?il-a/ (CA *ᶜā?il-a*). Both of these are now well established and very common, though /ḥbab/ "relatives, loved ones" can still be used in roughly the same sense. Such old forms as /hl-u/ "his family" seem to be uncommon now in the areas I worked in, though still known; a newer CA borrowing of the same root, /?ăhl/ "family", is found in the definite form /l-?ăhl/ (see A-1-235), showing the same type of reclassicization of definite forms observed above for some simple kin terms, but neither /hl-/ nor /?ăhl/ occurs very often in my data.

7.4 Human category terms

A basic list of the most important terms in this area should include: /ṛažl/ "man", /mṛa/ "woman" (Pl /nsa/ in some dialects), /wəld/ "boy" (also "son"), /drri/ "boy, child, youth", /bənt/ "girl" (also "daughter"), /šiban-i/ "old man", /šarf/ "old man", and /^{c}guz/ "old man" (the last three having FSg counterparts with suffix /-a/). Adjectives /ṣġiṛ/ "small" and /kbir/ "big" are also used to mean "young" and "adult", respectively.

These basic, high-frequency stems are traditional MCA forms which show no sign of recent borrowing or reclassicization from CA, though most have CA cognates.

From Fr, the stems /msyu/ "man" (Fr *Monsieur*) C-516 and /madam/ or /maḍam/ "woman" (Fr *Madame*) C-457 are heard from time to time, but mainly when speaking about foreigners, or in special registers like the foreigner talk MCA used by some maids (8.2). For their use as kin terms ("husband", "wife") see the preceding section. MCA /gaṛṣun/ C-264 from Fr *garçon* is common, but in the sense "waiter" rather than "boy". Fr *fille* does not seem to be in use in a borrowed form.

Respectful expressions used chiefly in polite direct address are /sid-i/ "sir" and /lalla/ "madam, ma'am", both of which are traditional MCA forms.

In general, then, this domain has been largely unaffected by recent CA or Fr/Sp borrowing. Note, however, /žȫn/ C-819 "young", which fills a partial lexical gap.

7.5 Body parts and other inalienables

This is another conservative lexical field with a strong predominance of old MCA forms not attributable to recent CA or Fr/Sp interference.

The following is a basic list of representative body-part terms which do not appear to be recent borrowings: /ksd-a/ "body", /ṛaṣ/ "head", /^{c}əyn/ or /^{c}in/ "eye", /nif/ "nose", /wdn/ "ear", /f^{w}mm/ "mouth", /š^{c}ṛ/ "hair", /lḥy-a/ "beard", /m^{w}xx/ "brain", /šnaf-a/ or /šnnaf-a/ "lip", /snn-a/ "tooth", /lsan/ "tongue", /^{c}ənq/ "neck", /ḥəlq/ "throat", /ṣḍṛ/ "chest", /bzzul-a/ or /nhd-a/ "(female) breast", /ḍhṛ/ "back", /krš/ "belly", /ṣṛṛ-a/ or /ṣ^{w}ṛṛ-a/ "navel", /ktəf/ "shoulder", /baṭ/ "underarm", /yədd/ "hand", /mṛfəq/ "elbow", /fxəḍ/ "thigh", /qlw-a/ "testicle", /ṭbbun/ "vagina", /ṭiẓ/ "anus", /ržl/ "foot, leg", /ṛk^{w}b-a/ "knee", and /gdm/ "heel". Some items for internal organs and bodily substances: /qəlb/ "heart", /kbd-a/ "liver", /riy-a/ "lung", /klw-a/ "kidney", /bul/ "urine", /^{c}ṛq/ "sweat", /xṛa/ "excrement", /^{c}ḍm/ "bone", /šhm-a/ "fat", /lḥṃ/ "meat, flesh", /dəmm/ "blood".

There are, however, a few such concepts where external intrusions have occurred. The usual word for "penis" is /zəbb/, but /dkṛ/ (CA *ðakar-*) is a less common and more polite form (still felt to be a classicism). The word for "chin" is /dqn/ or /dəqn/, the second variant being a recent reclassicization of the first, from CA *ðiqan-* (variant *ðaqan-*). The MCA dialects I worked on do not seem to have an established traditional term for "jaw", and for this sense both /fəkk/ from CA *fakk-* and /ṃašwaṛ/ C-488 (Fr *mâchoire*) are in use.

Though not really a body-part term, /smiy-a/ "name" is a similar inalienable term. This form is an old MCA one, but borrowings from CA *?ism-* occur occasionally in the form /?əsm/ A-1-238. (Some dialects have /l-ism/ as a definite form.)

Clearly there is little overall CA or Fr/Sp influence in this domain. Pl forms also use overwhelmingly old MCA patterns with no recent reclassicization under CA influence: /nyuf/ "noses", /snan/ "teeth", /kruš/ "bellies", /ṛ^{w}kabi/ "knees", /qlawi/ "testicles", /^{c}ḍum-a/ "bones", /fmam/ or /fwam/ "mouths", etc.

7.6 Professions and business establishments

The traditional MCA stem-formation for a member of a given trade or profession is (MSg) /CCCaC/ or /CCaCC-i/. Examples are /nžžaṛ/ "carpenter", /ḥddad/ "smith", and /nqayṛ-i/ "silver jeweller". The abstract term for the trade or profession itself is /ta-STEM-ət/ where the -STEM- is usually a form like /CCCaC/. In the stem /CCCaC/ the four consonants may be the root consonants of a quadriliteral root, or (if formed from a triliteral root) we may get C_2 doubled: /nḥḥal/ "beekeeper" (/nḥl/ "bees"), /ṣmṣaṛ/ "real-estate agent" (verb /ṣmṣṛ/ "to deal in real estate"). The nouns of profession are /ta-nḥḥal-t/ "beekeeping" and /ta-ṣmṣaṛ-t/ "real estate profession". Ordinarily there is no native MCA term referring to the corresponding business establishment; it is usual to say "I am going to the beekeeper" (not "I am going to the beekeepery" or the like), or in the case of a special market for the commodity with many shops, "I am going to the beekeepers".

A considerable number of European loans, chiefly Fr, are now in common use in this lexical area. It is not surprising to find foreign elements in such modern or modernized professions as these: /bantur-i/ "painter (of walls)" C-50, /kumik/ "comedian" C-400, /mikanisyan/ "mechanic" C-497, /frmasyan/ "pharmacist" C-239, /frmli/ "nurse" C-241, /ḍukturṛ/ "doctor" C-188, /aṛbiṭ/ "referee" C-18, /bulis/ "police" C-132, /ḅumbiy-a/ "firemen" C-135. A few Eng words also crop up, mainly via Fr, as in /baṛmiṭ/ "female bartender" (*barmaid*) C-60, /baṛṃan/ "male bartender" (*barman*) C-59. Sp has contributed /ḅugaḍu/ "lawyer" C-125.

What is less expectable is that many long-established MCA terms for professions are facing competition from newer Fr loans which cannot be said to represent new concepts. Thus alongside /ṣbabṭ-i/ "shoemaker, cobbler" we have /kuṛḍuni/ (Fr *cordonnier*); alongside /ṭbbax/ "cook, chef" we find /kuzin-i/ (Fr *cuisinier*); and alongside /ḥžžam/ "barber" and synonyms we find /kwạfur/ (Fr *coiffeur*); see C-417, 432, 433. In these cases the native term is not threatened with extinction, but the borrowing is at least moderately common. It should be noted in this connection that trades or professions of these types are exercised sometimes in all-native environments, at other times in "European" contexts. For example, /kuzin-i/ "cook" is likely to be the term used to refer to a chef in a hotel or restaurant in the European part of a major city, while /ṭbbax/ can be used in other contexts. For store-front trades like "cobbler" and "barber" it should be mentioned that, especially in the modern (European) part of each city, commercial signs are commonly in Fr (or in both CA and Fr with the latter more conspicuous).

CA is also contributing some new borrowings in this lexical area, particularly for positions in the educational system, government bureaucracies, and commercial organizations. Thus alongside /aṛbiṭ/ "referee" C-18 we have /ḥakm/ from CA *ḥakam-*, used (for example) in broadcasts, and instead of /ḅugaḍu/ "lawyer" C-125 we can now get /muḥami/, also from CA. Some other common CA terms can be found in the lists of borrowed participles in Appendix A (e.g. A-1-100-103, A-1-276ff., A-1-286ff., A-1-315). Terms for political and Islamic dignitaries commonly mentioned in (CA) news broadcasts are also often borrowed: /l-wazir l-?awwal/ "the Prime Minister", /?imam/ "imam (religious leader)", /malik/ "king".

7.7 Education

This is a domain in which borrowing is heavy, but where Fr/Sp borrowings compete head-on with CA items. Of course, this vocabulary is known and used primarily by the educated segment of Moroccan society, most of which is multilingual (MCA, CA, and Fr nowadays). Therefore many foreign (especially Fr) items take the form of code-switched phrases or borrowings which are only slightly assimilated to MCA patterns. At the present time, the relative importance of Fr (*vis-à-vis* CA) as language of instruction increases as we go from primary through secondary to tertiary levels, and it is reasonable to assume that this has some effect on the distribution of borrowings and code-switching among students at various levels.

Some Fr or other European loans which can be said to be reasonably well assimilated are these: /lisi/ C-448 "secondary school (especially its second cycle)", /skwil-a/ C-654 "primary school" (Sp *escuela*), /ḅakaḷuṛiy-a/ C-36 or /ḅak/ C-35 "baccalaureat diploma" (on graduation from secondary to tertiary level), /burs/ or /buṛṣ/ C-145 "scholarship stipend", /dipḷum/ C-172 "diploma", /kḷaṣ/ or /kḷaṣ-a/ C-356 "class", and /anṭiṛṇ-a/ "campus (primary or secondary school)" C-15. Some verbs usually related to the educational domain are /paṣa/ B-110 "he advanced (e.g. from secondary to tertiary level)", /kuppya/ or /kupa/ B-90 "he copied (homework)", /bẓwəṭ/ B-32 "he hazed (new student)". Some other verbs which have more general meanings, but are often used in this domain: /pṛipaṛa/ B-115 "he prepared (e.g. lesson)", /mṇṇək/ B-101 "he didn't show up (for class)", /ṛaṭa/ B-125 "he missed (exam)". (See appendix entries for Fr/Sp sources.)

School levels can be classified in Fr as *primaire* (see C-567), *secondaire*, or *université*; synonymous borrowings from CA are /btida?-iy-a/ "primary (school)" (see A-1-359), /tanaw-iy-a/ "secondary (school)" (see A-1-118), and /žami^{c}-a/ A-1-112 "university". The two divisions of secondary school are *premier cycle* and *deuxième cycle* in Fr, or /s-silk l-?awwl/ "first cycle" and /s-silk t-tani/ "second cycle" (from CA, slightly assimilated). CA borrowing /šahad-a/ is usual for the degree permitting advancement from primary to secondary (perhaps a calque on Fr *attestation*), but Fr *brevet* or a slightly assimilated borrowing from it (C-117) is the term I have heard most often for the degree permitting advancement from first to second cycle within secondary school. We have already seen Fr borrowings (from *baccalauréat* or short form *bac*) for secondary school diploma.

Students are called /tlmid/ "pupil" from CA in primary and secondary school (Fr *élève* is not in common use in MCA), but /ṭalib/ (also from CA) at university (tertiary) level (Fr *étudiant* is not especially common, though it can be used as a code-switching).

Scholarly subjects include arithmetic and mathematics, called *les maths* (Fr) or /ṛ-ṛiyaḍ-iy-at/ (from CA); literature, called *la littérature* or /l-?adab/ (CA); and geology, called *la géologie* or /l-žiyulužiy-a/ (from CA, though of course the CA form is itself based on European forms).

Pupils may live on a primary or secondary school campus (/anṭiṛn-a/ C-15 from Fr, /d-daxil-iy-a/ from CA), while tertiary students live on the university campus (*la cité universitaire* or /l-ḥəyy l-žamiᶜ-i/ from CA), may do experiments in a lab (*laboratoire* or /muxtabaṛ/), and later on have a few hours of recreation (*récréation*, /stiraḥ-a/). As we can see from such examples, there is a duplicate vocabulary in this domain involving Fr items (often code-switched rather than borrowed) competing with slightly assimilated CA forms (only occasionally, as with "geology", cognate with the Fr items).

7.8 The military

Although no detailed study was done of the technical language of members of the armed forces, a certain amount of vocabulary in this domain is known to everybody, and it is clear that this is a lexical area showing extensive European influence. During the early part of the French Protectorate (1912-), much contact between the French and the Moroccans involved French military officers (many of whom had served extensively before that in Algeria). Despite the policy of encouraging these officers to use local dialects (not Fr) in such contexts, inevitably the establishment of a French-run army using unfamiliar weaponry and organizational structures led to the adoption of mnay borrowings (Sp may have had a similar effect in the north, but probably to a lesser extent). Continued Fr influence in this domain is due not only to persistence of these early colonial-period borrowings, but also to the introduction of up-to-date equipment items, some continuing French-Moroccan military cooperation, and above all the exposure of much of the population to war films (including Hollywood movies presented in Morocco with Fr dubbing).

Some relevant verbs are /gaža/ B-63 "he enlisted", /t-ṛufəẓ/ B-134 "he was disobedient", and /t-frma/ B-56 (now meaning "it became worn out", formerly meaning "he was discharged from the army for injury or illness"); all of these are old loans and some may have come in ready-made from Algeria. Some other verbs which are not restricted to military contexts but which may have acquired their currency there are /dimirda/ B-33 "he saved his own skin, looked out for himself" and /ẓṛṭa/ or /ẓṛṭ/ B-183 "he escaped, deserted". All of these loans are from Fr (see appendix entries for exact sources).

Some terms for garments commonly associated with the military are /biriy-a/ "beret" (worn by cadets) C-84, /bṛuḍkạn/ "military boots" C-115, also from Fr.

Terms for military ranks are mostly European borrowings, but it is difficult to sort out their exact history in many cases (most CA terms are also adaptations of European forms and some of these CA variants have influenced some of the MCA forms). Typically we now find several quite different pronunciations in use: see the entries for "corporal" C-305, "captain" C-583 (but also C-319 in sporting sense), "colonel" C-362, "major" C-398, "sergeant" C-630, and "general" C-817.

Some other military terms are /baṭṛwi/ C-70 "patrol", /kuf-a/ C-389 "convoy", /ṭṛa̰ši/ C-759 "trench", /min-a/ C-503 "mine, bomb",

/ṭəŋg/ C-764 "tank", /kaṛabin/ C-321 "carbine", and /kaṛtuš/ C-325 "shell". These terms are from Fr (or occasionally Sp) and there is usually no alternative synonym (say, from CA) which is widely used among the general population.

7.9 Implements and consumer items

This is an area where many European (mostly Fr) borrowings have become established as the regularly used terms for most of the more modern items. In many cases a CA equivalent exists, at least in some official dictionary somewhere, but the CA term is not commonly used and may be unknown to most Moroccans. With time, it is likely that some of these Fr borrowings will be gradually replaced by competing CA terms.

There is no point in presenting a huge list of Fr/Sp borrowings here since our Appendix C is full of them. A few whose MCA form starts with the letter /a/ or /b/ are: /album/ C-5 "(record, photo) album", /aspirin/ C-21 "aspirin", /bakiy-a/ C-37 "pack, packet", /ḅal-a/ C-40 "shovel", /baliz-a/ C-42 "suitcase", /ḅanyu/ C-51 "bathtub" (Sp), /bidu/ C-75 "canister", /bluz-a/ or /blus-a/ C-104 "blouse" (Fr and Sp), /briki/ C-109 "flashlight", /bṛwiṭ-a/ C-118 "wheelbarrow", /biškliṭ/ C-90 "bicycle", /bukan-at/ C-127 "comics", /ḅul-a/ C-130 "light bulb" (Fr or Sp), /buḷun/ C-133 "bolt", /burmid-a/ C-143 "Bermuda shorts", /bušun/ C-152 "cork, stopper", and /buṭ/ C-155 "pair of boots".

In such domains as clothing there is a fairly sharp difference between a traditional set of MCA terms for old types of garment like /žllab-a/ and /ḍṛṛa^{c}-a/ (two types of Moroccan robe), and a set of mostly Fr borrowings (along with a few from Sp) for more modern European-type garments (in the north of Morocco these terms are mostly from Sp). In addition to some Fr/Sp loans in the list just given, we may mention /župp-a/ C-823 "skirt", /sutyan/ C-663 "bra", and /pižam-a/ C-558 "pajamas" as examples (among many). In some individual cases, though, an old MCA form has resisted intrusions from Fr: /tqašr/ "socks", /srwal/ "pair of pants" (Fr *chaussettes* and *pantalon* have not caught on, though the latter is recorded as a borrowing, C-540).

Basic tools in carpentry and gardening show a mixture of sources, and each tool must be discussed separately. Some Fr borrowings are /turnvis/ C-746 "screwdriver", /ṛaḅu/ C-587 "lathe, plane" (cf. B-123), /šalimu/ C-699 "blow torch", and another example not in the appendices is /klaṃuniṭ/ "wrench" (Fr *clef à molette*). Some other tools are usually called by native MCA terms, some of which may be (well-assimilated) CA borrowings: /m-ṭṛq-a/ "hammer" (more common in my data than /maṛṭu/ C-480 from Fr), /m-xṛṭ-a/ "drill" (Fr *perceuse* is occasionally used), /kawy-a/ "soldering iron". Most gardening and farming tools are native: /ṣabb-a/ or /^{c}tl-a/ "large hoe", /gadum-a/ "small hoe", but /ganšu/ C-258 "pitchfork" is an old loan from Sp (see also /ġanžu/ C-288 from the same source but with later semantic shift).

Kitchen utensils are likewise of mixed origins. Some important European loans are /gamil-a/ C-256 "cooking pot", /kafatir-a/ C-309 "coffee-brewer", /kokuṭ/ C-365 "stewpan". Native MCA terms tend to be retained where they exist, often even when there is an exact Fr synonym: /ṭbṣil/ "plate", /m-ᶜlq-a/ "spoon", /mus/ "knife" (but /fṛšiṭ-a/ C-243 "fork", apparently a new item).

7.10 Automobile parts

Young Moroccan men frequently have a good working knowledge of the internal construction of radios, appliances, motorcycles, and automobiles, since their economic level is usually such that they try to repair defective ones rather than discarding them and buying new ones. Even men who are unable to afford their own cars usually know something about how engines work and therefore know much of the relevant vocabulary.

Most automobile-part terms are from Fr and are only slightly assimilated formally; typically, Moroccans do not know MCA or CA synonyms. (This is true, for example, of one person I knew who was employed as a teacher of automobile mechanics.)

Some terms of Fr origin which have been at least partly assimilated are: /byas-a/ C-162 "spare part", /ksiratur/ C-383 "accelerator", /kḷaksun/ C-355 "horn, honker", /aṃḅriyaž/ C-8 "transmission", /fitɛs/ Č-221 "gear(s)", /ṛwiḍ-a/ C-624 "wheel", and /kuṇṭak/ C-409 "ignition".

Many verbs derived from Fr are used in connection with automobile driving and repair: /t-kruva/ B-80 "it (tyre) went flat", /ḍimaṛa/ B-42 "it (motor) started up", /ḍiḅana/ B-43 "he repaired (car)", /gufl/ B-68 "he inflated (tyre)", /kwansa/ B-94 "he collided with (other car)".

7.11 Ecological vocabulary

Under this rubric we consider terms for topographic zones, physical features, and flora/fauna. In general, there are few surprises — most of the terms in use are old MCA forms, but a small number of new CA forms are observed, and European borrowings occur in connection with recently introduced species (mostly vegetables and fruits).

Examples of MCA terms showing no external influence: /ṣḥṛ-a/ "desert", /žbl/ "mountain", /badiy-a/ "rural areas, country", /ᶜəyn/ "spring (of water)" (also "eye"), /wad/ "river", /ṛml-a/ "sand", /ṭin/ "clay", /ḥžṛ/ "stone(s)", /ṛbiᶜ/ "grass", /šžṛ/ "tree(s)", /qṣəb/ "cane", /ṭir/ "bird", /bhim-a/ "domestic animal", /kəlb/ "dog", /ḥənš/ "snake", /ᶜəwd/ "horse", /bgṛ-a/ "cow", /ġnm/ "sheep", /ḥmaṛ/ "donkey". Many of these have CA cognates but the forms appear to be old rather than recently borrowed, and in general the Pl forms also appear to be old MCA forms.

Some examples of probable CA borrowings: /(l-)žazir-a/ "island", Pl /(l-)žuzur/ (where the /l-/ definite prefix allomorph and the vocalism of both Sg and Pl show CA influence); and several generic terms like /ḥayawan/ "animal", /fakih-a/ "fruit" (Pl /fawakih/), and /xuḍaṛ/ "vegetables". The MCA term for "ground, earth", /lṛḍ/, may be reclassicized as /(l-)?ṛḍ/, like so many other cases of common nouns whose CA form begins with glottal ? which has been lost in the inherited MCA form. For "city", /mdin-a/ is now common and may be a case of semantic extension under CA influence (its more basic meaning is "Muslim part of city" in opposition to /mllaḥ/ "Jewish quarter", and in some archaic dialects /blad/ is the usual word for "city"); although the Sg form /mdin-a/ has not been formally reshaped (if it were, it would be */madin-a/ from CA *madīn-a*), the usual Pl form is now /mudun/, which is clearly based on CA *mudun-*.

Fr influence is very limited in this domain. I have heard *(la) cascade* "(the) waterfall" and *(le) village*"(the) village" a few times in MCA speech, but I take them as code-switchings (or weakly assimilated borrowings at best). Items relating to the sea are more likely to be of Fr/Sp origin, but most of my work was in the interior and I can only cite a few relevant items like /maṛi/ C-471 and /mariy-a/ C-474 "tide" (Fr *marée*, Sp *marea*, respectively). European loans are more common in connection with introduced agricultural commodities such as /aṇaṇaṣ/ C-9 "pineapple(s)" and /baṛb-a/ C-57 or /biṭṛav/ C-92 "beets" (It and Fr).

For a much more detailed discussion of Fr/Sp borrowings in the nautical domain, see Brunot (1920), abbreviated NLVM in this book.

7.12 Adjectives

We consider, in order, participles, adjectives of colour and defect, and adjectives of size, shape, quality, etc. These divisions correspond to formal categories within MCA.

Since participles are formed productively from verbs, it follows that MCA verbs which have been borrowed from CA or Fr/Sp will normally have one or more regular participles, and since the form is predictable there is nothing special to say here. However, we should recall that in the cases of certain verbal borrowings, the participle was the first and most basic borrowed form, from which the regular inflected verb forms appear to have been derived analogically. We should also mention the fact that many CA participles have come directly into MCA where they usually have specialized meaning (e.g. as agentives), and these direct borrowings may be distinct from internally generated MCA participles derived from the (borrowed or original) verb stem.

Adjectives of colour and defect have MSg pattern /CCəC/, FSg /CCC-a/, Pl /CuCC/ except that /CiwC occurs when C_2 is /w/. Examples are /ḅyəḍ/ "white", /kḥl/ "black", and /ṭṛš/ "deaf" (MSg forms).

This class of adjectives is productive, but the stems I know of are old MCA ones rather than borrowings so far as I can tell. If some of them are in fact CA borrowings they are completely assimilated morphologically, with no telltale traces of CA origin. European borrowings in this domain are also uncommon; we can mention /limun-i/ "yellow", derived from /limun/ "lemon" or "orange (fruit)" but as noted in the entry for this item (C-444) it is not even certain that this noun is a Romance borrowing. In any event, /limun-i/ obviously does not belong in terms of canonical shape with the /CCəC/ MCA type.

The basic residual (nonparticipial, non-colour/defect) adjectival pattern in MCA is Sg /CCiC/ and Pl /CCaC/ or /C^wCaC/. Examples are /kbir/ "big", /ṣġiṛ/ "small", /ġliḍ/ "fat", /ṛqiq/ "thin", /ḍᶜif/ "weak", /ṣḥiḥ/ "strong, healthy", /ṛxiṣ/ "cheap", /ṭwil/ "long", /qṣiṛ/ "short", /qdim/ "old", and /ždiḍ/ "new". The corresponding CA pattern is Sg *CaCīC-*, Pl *CiCāC-*, which should give MCA /CaCiC/

and /CiCaC/ in new borrowings. In fact we do find occasional reclassicization of Sg MCA forms to /CaCiC/ from /CCiC/, as in /kabir/ as a variant of /kbir/ "big", but this reclassicization is uncommon for most of these stems and is typical of affected registers. However, a few adjectives do habitually occur in the /CaCiC/ form: /baṣiṭ/ "simple". This also happens with a few nouns which happen to have the same canonical shape as these adjectives in CA, as with /ṣadiq/ "friend" A-1-45 (CA *ṣadīq*-).

Fr/Sp intrusions into the set of high-frequency adjectives of size, shape, and similar qualities are relatively uncommon. I have heard *fatigué* from time to time but it seems to be basically code-switched and is much less common than /ᶜyy-an/ "tired" (but this also means "sick", which may explain the need for an occasional Fr code-switching in the case of "tired"; CA /tᶜb-an/ can also be used to mean "tired" more strictly, but this is not common). Such adjectives as /ž̈ön/ C-819 "young" and /kliṛ/ C-358 "clear, certain" are used occasionally, mostly by bilinguals; the first of these is another case of a partial semantic gap. Note that /kliṛ/, by coincidence, satisfies the /CCiC/ Sg canonical shape; as indicated in the appendix entry I have once recorded FSg /kliṛ-a/, but Pl */klaṛ/ or */kʷkaṛ/ is out of the question for my informants and even the FSg with /-a/ is not normally used (/ž̈ön/ seems never to take overt FSg or Pl forms).

In northern Morocco (Tetouan, Tangier), /stitu/ C-661 "small" seems to be as common as the usual Moroccan form /ṣġiṛ/ (which is the only common form in the rest of the country); /stitu/ is apparently an old loan based on Sp *chiquito*.

Other Fr/Sp adjectival borrowings tend to be much more specialized semantically, so we can say in general that Fr/Sp penetration into the set of basic adjectives of colour, shape, and so on is small. One particular area of high levels of borrowing is personal characterisitcs and behaviour (see below, 7.14), which has a close connection with slang (7.15).

7.13 Sports and card games

In this general domain we find extensive Fr and Sp borrowing with Sp influence heavy in card games (which are usually played with Spanish cards) and Fr influence heavy in soccer (football) and other sports. Some of the Fr borrowings are really Eng words ultimately but transmitted to MCA via Fr. It should be noted that radio and television broadcasts of local sporting events generally avoid using Fr/Sp borrowings, so broadcast MCA uses a substantially different vocabulary (including many CA borrowings and code-switches) than ordinary spoken MCA (Chapter 8). (However, international soccer broadcasts emanating from Egypt use an Egyptian colloquial with numerous Eng borrowings.)

Some verbs in ordinary MCA related to soccer are: /maṛka/ B-97 "he scored", /tira/ B-168 "he shot", /bḷuka/ B-14 "he blocked (shot)", /fanta/ B-48 "he faked", /gaṛḍa/ B-62 "he guarded (opposing player)", and perhaps /t-liva/ B-95 "it (ball) curved or swerved". Another verb for "he shot" is /šat/ B-162, which may have come in through Egyptian and other dialects (in which case it is from Eng *shoot*, rather than Fr *shooter* or the like).

Some nouns: /bit/ C-91 "goal, score" (homonym with old MCA /bit/ "room in house" related to CA *bayt-*), /aṛbiṭ/ C-18 "referee", /kufṛ-a/ C-392 "free kick (after foul)", /bilanti/ C-81 "penalty shot", /fuṛfi/ C-248 "forfeit", and /ṃiṭ-a/ C-507 "halftime".

Some of these terms are used in other team sports, of which basketball is the most popular in Morocco. This sport also has some of its own special vocabulary, often half-assimilated Fr borrowings: /dribla/ B-35 "he dribbled", /p̣anyi/ C-541 "basket", /dublsumil/ C-176 "walking (infraction called by officials)".

I have not elicited much vocabulary related to such sports as tennis, golf, and polo since these are elite sports which are played mostly by a small leisure class and are not even commonly seen in broadcasts, so most Moroccans do not know much of their vocabulary.

Card games like poker involve largely Fr vocabulary, much of it code-switched. Some general terms relating to card games in general are /blufa/ B-13 "he bluffed", /miza/ B-100 "he anted", /ṛamaṣa/ B-124 "he gathered in, raked in (cards and money)", and /srba/ B-145 "he dealt out (cards)". These are primarily Fr in origin. However, "he shuffled" is MCA /ḍməṣ/, not a borrowing.

There are some card games of Spanish origin, played with a special Spanish (and Italian) card deck, roughly resembling the familiar international deck. The cards themselves are called by Sp borrowings, including the ones referred to only by number. Hence /ḍuṣ/ C-191 "two card", /tris/ or /ṭṛiṣ/ C-741 "three card", /kwaṭṛu/ C-435 "four card" and so forth, with the higher-valued cards showing human figures called by names like /ṣuṭ-a/ C-693, /kaḅal/ C-302, and /ṛiy/ or /ṛay/ C-605, all from Sp (or in a few cases possibly another Iberian dialect or It). Some games played with this deck are /ṛunḍ-a/ C-616, /škamb-a/ C-710, and /tuti/. The four suits of cards have names like /ṣpaḍ-a/ "spades" (Sp *espada* "sword"). A reasonable number of such terms are given in Appendix A, but we have not tried to elicit a complete lexicon in this area. The general term for "playing card(s)" is /kaṛṭ-a/ C-329, and games of chance in general are called /swirti/ C-664.

7.14 Personal characteristics and behaviour

The evaluation of individuals is a particularly rich area for European loans into MCA, especially when the evaluation is pejorative and/or humorous, or when the evaluation is in terms of westernization or social class symbolism. A large number of loans in this area have been recorded and are in more or less common use at least among students. This vocabulary often verges on or clearly is slang, which we discuss in the following section.

For many of the evaluative terms there is both a simple nominal or adjectival form, and a derived verb form translated roughly "to act like ...", with a mediopassive /t-/ prefix (here in a specialized sense) and following quadriliteral stem. If the input root has four distinct consonants, stem-formation in the derived verb is unproblematic. If the root has only three consonants, but with /u/ vowel after C_1, we often get /t-CuC(ə)C/, a preexisting MCA formation. We also have at least one example of doubling of root C_2 to produce the desired quadriliteral stem in the derivative. Some of these derived verbs permit a further diminutive (Dimin) derivation, with inserted vowel /i/ after root C_1, hence /t-CCCəC/ vs. Dimin /t-CiCCəC/, the diminutive form having a strongly affective flavour (cf. Eng *little* in *he's acting like a little jerk*).

Some of the most important derived verbs in this /t-/ derivation are: /t-fnṭəẓ/ B-53 "he acted like a big shot", /t-ḅugəṣ/ B-26 "he acted like a dandy", /t-frkəs/ B-55 "he acted like a dandy", /t-šyyək/ B-167 "he acted suave", /t-bṛžəz/ B-24 "he acted bourgeois", /t-kumək/ B-86 "he acted like a comedian, acted funny", /d-zufr/ B-184 "he acted like a swinger or debauchee", /t-gṛṣn/ B-67 "he did servile work, acted like a servant or waiter". In the case of /t-hippa/ B-72 "he acted like a hippie" from /hippi/ C-291 "hippie", the verb seems to have the form of a diminutive but */t-hppa/ does not occur (obviously the /i/ in the noun form has influenced the verb); similarly, /t-bgbəṣ/ B-6 "he acted like a big boss" is less common than its own diminutive /t-bigbəṣ/, where again the influence of /i/ in the noun /bigbuṣ/ C-79 is felt.

An unusual case is that of adjective /ṭulạ̃ṭi/ C-779 "clever, wise guy" and related verb /ṭulạ̃ṭa/ B-180 "he acted smart", where imperfective forms like /ta-y-ṭulạ̃ṭa/ "he is acting smart" (not */ta-y-ṭulạ̃ṭi/ with the usual /a/-to-/i/ shift of stem-final vowel in weak verb) suggest that this is treated grammatically like /t-ṭulạ̃ṭa/ (with the /t-/ prefix seen in the forms in the preceding paragraph).

Further examples of this morphological type occur in connection with mental conditions such as insanity (real or figurative) and intoxication. Hence /tt-flippa/ B-51 "he was flipped out", /tt^-ḍṛuga/ B-45 "he was drugged, on drugs", /t-ṣuṭa B-159 "he was nuts, crazy", /t-srkl/ B-146 "he was nuts", /t-ḅwwəṭ/ B-30 "he was plastered (drunk or on drugs)".

These verbs with /t-/ often have related nominal forms which are mentioned in the lexical entries in Appendix B (the nominal forms can be found in Appendix C). It should be noted that some of the /t-/ verbs listed above are particularly common in participial forms, which (by regular rules) involve prefix (m-/ replacing prefix /t-/ (and for weak stems stem-final /a/ becoming /i/): /m-srkl/ "nuts, crazy", /m-ḅwwəṭ/ "plastered". In some cases the participle was probably the initial borrowed form, but in many individual cases we are unable to determine the chronology exactly.

Turning to verbs for illegal or otherwise offensive acts, we find a few additional /t-/ stems like those cited above: /t-bznəs/ B-31 "he engaged in dealing (e.g. in drugs)", cf. /bznas/ C-163 "dealer"; /t-ṛufəẓ/ B-134 "he was disobedient or insolent". However, most such borrowings in this subdomain do not involve /t-/, hence /bṛẓəṭ/ B-23 "he pestered (him)", /sbira/ B-138 "he took advantage of (person)", /ḍiṛạ̃ža/ B-44 "he bothered (him)", /grisa/ B-66 "he attacked, mugged", /šaṇṭa/ B-160 "he blackmailed", /ṭṛafika/ B-177 "he swindled".

The vast majority of the borrowings listed in this section have been of Fr origin (including a couple of Eng stems transmitted via Fr); for etymological details see the appendix entries.

7.15 Slang and affective speech

By "slang" I mean a range of speech forms characteristic of speech within peer groups (but not necessarily secret), revolving around interpersonal relationships, sex, bodily functions, etc. Vulgarities are included, but phonological speech disguise is not considered here.

Most slang words and expressions are old MCA forms or are of origin unknown to me. Some items appear to have been very durable but others appear and disappear. The majority of terms elicited with such meanings as "penis", "testicles", "vagina", "to urinate", "to defecate", "excrement", and "to copulate" (for most of which I have recorded numerous terms) are to all appearances native MCA forms or old forms of Berber origin; in any case most of them are clearly not of CA or Fr/Sp origin. There are, however, certain specific areas in slang where external intrusions have occurred.

The most striking case of CA influence is not in connection with vulgarities, rather in a series of words and expressions meaning "great!, wonderful!" and the like, being considerably more emphatic than the mundane MCA /mzyan/ "good" and its regional variants. Two very common exclamations are /l-^{c}aḍam-a/ "great!" (formally a noun, from CA *al-^{c}að̣ām-a* "magnificence" and/or *al-^{c}að̣am-a* "majesty"), and /haniyatun/, often with protracted vowel as /ha:::niyatun/ "great!". This latter is from CA *hāniʔ-at-u-n*, of which *hāniy-at-u-n* is an acceptable alternative pronunciation; it means "(very) happy (FSg)", and is very unusual in that the MCA pronunciation contains the full suffix complex (Nominative *-u-* and Indefinite *-n* following FSg *-at-*) rather than being based on the CA pausal pronunciation *hāniy-a* (as in virtually all other borrowings from CA nouns and adjectives). The fuller CA phrase of which *hāniy-at-u-n* is an abbreviation, *ad-dunyā hāniy-at-u-n* "the world is happy", is also sometimes transferred into (slightly assimilated) MCA as a whole: /d-dny-a ha:::niyatun/; I have also recorded /d-dnya ha:::niya/ where the second element is in fact based on the CA pausal pronunciation.

Other CA terms are also found as terms of strong praise for a person or thing. Two of them are ostensibly negative in meaning but are in fact used as expressions of admiration. These are CA *al-halāk-* "(the) destructive or harmful thing" and *al-xawar-* "(the) incoherent speech, raving", which occur in MCA as /l-halak/ and /l-xawaṛ/. They can be used as strong expressions of praise for a popular teacher, a good hashish joint, a delicious meal, etc. They are generally used as isolated expressions or as (nonverbal) predicates and do not show gender/number concord; this is also true of /l-^{c}aḍam-a/ and /ha:::niyatun/ (see above). Note that there are some parallels for such inverted meanings (pejorative epithet used as term of praise); Eng *bastard*, *hell*, and *motherfucker* are often used in such contexts ("He's a ... of a player", etc.).

Speaking of *motherfucker* and its abbreviation *mother* in Eng, there is a calque of this in MCA itself, where /mm-u/ "his mother" C-511 is another expression of admiration (it is possible that this was directly calqued on a Fr expression itself calqued on the Eng forms). Another new slang word, /nug^{c}-a/ "great, wonderful" is of unclear origin (it does not seem to be from CA, which lacks /g/, nor from Romance languages, which lack /ᶜ/, but it seems to be a recently popularized word). It forms an antonymic pair with /friy-a/ "terrible" C-235, of possible Romance origin. Another similar form is /ġiwan/ C-289 "great", also of unclear origin. These forms permit definite /l-/ but do not show gender/number concord with different referents.

Words which mean "very bad", "terrible", etc. (and are not used with reversed meaning as terms of praise), do not usually show CA influence. From Fr we get /kuf̣ṛ-a/ C-392, literally "free kick (after foul in soccer)" but also used in slang as derogatory epithet (e.g. for an ugly girl); however, general terms for "great" or "terrible" are usually not Fr/Sp borrowings. (For example, the conspicuous Fr term *formidable* "great" is notably infrequent in MCA.)

We have already noted extensive Fr influence in vocabulary dealing with personality characteristics, insanity, and drug- or crime-related activities (7.14). In the subdomains of sexual behaviour, body parts, drunkenness, and bodily functions, Fr influence is present but sporadic; in some cases we have a simple Fr borrowing with a different meaning which acquires a secondary (e.g. metaphorical) meaning in one of these areas as an internal MCA development after the borrowing.

A very common slang term for "drunkard" is /kuḷ-a/ C-394, a secondary meaning of the borrowing meaning "glue, paste" (Fr *colle*, Sp *cola*). The sense "drunkard" may have been influenced by the phonologically overlapping /ankul/ C-10 "alcohol". In the sense "drunkard" the form is normally Dimin /kwiḷ-a/. It seems clear that "drunkard" is a secondary semantic shift within MCA and unrelated to the initial borrowing process.

Some other drunkenness-related vocabulary can be briefly mentioned. One common slang expression is /ḍṛb ṭ-ṭaṣ-a/ "he got drunk" (lit. "he hit the cup"); this may or may not be a calque from a Fr slang expression (cf. Eng *he hit the bottle*), see also the discussion of the etymology of /ṭaṣ-a/ or /ṭas-a/ C-759. There is a local slang expression /šṛb-ha kliru/ "he chugged it (drank it in one draught)" with /šṛb-ha/ "he drank it (e.g. beer)" plus a sort of adverb from a Fr noun (C-359). However, there are a number of other slang terms produced internally within MCA, including some metaphorical ones: /m-klbn/ "drunk as a skunk, hopelessly alcoholic" (lit. "acting like a dog"), /m-šṛwəṭ/ "alcoholic" (lit. "in tatters, wearing rags").

The term /baliz-a/ C-42 is a routine borrowing in the sense "suitcase" (Fr *valise*), but is also used in slang as a humorous word for "rear end, butt (buttocks)". One of several slang words I have recorded for hashish is /šit/, which may possibly be from Eng *shit* (which is occasionally used in this sense), perhaps again mediated by Fr slang. The most common slang term for "money" (like Eng *bread*, *dough*, etc.) is /mik-a/ C-496, whose literal meaning is "plastic". There are also several other, less common slang words for "money" including several words whose literal meaning is a particular coin or currency unit (for "dollar" see C-189); others of foreign origin are given in the entries C-532, C-721, C-740.

The two slang words for "he masturbated" that I know of are /kffət/ and /škḷəṭ/ B-164. These are both denominative; /kffət/ is from native MCA /kft-a/ "ground meat, hamburger meat", while /škḷəṭ/

is from the borrowed noun /šk!aṭ/ C-711 "chocolate". To my knowledge there are no Fr or Sp slang words for this sense involving "chocolate", so again it appears that the stem meaning "he masturbated" is an internal MCA development which postdates the initial borrowing.

Words for genitalia are, of course, abundant in slang, but the ones I have recorded appear to be almost all of native (or Berber) origin. For "penis" we can mention one uncommon slang term /ḟangaḷ-a/ C-200, which looks like a Romance form (I have not yet found such a Romance word, however); denominative verb /ḟngḷ/ "he copulated with (her)" is also an uncommon slang word. There are ten or so other terms for "to copulate", but the only one of Fr/Sp origin is the euphemistic /kunṭakṭa/ B-88 (lit. "he contacted (her)"). We may also mention the recent metaphorical slang expression /mša-w b-l-fuṭukoppi/ "they shacked up (lived in sin)", lit. "they went by photocopy" (C-254).

Other referents of large numbers of slang expressions are prostitutes, beautiful women, homosexuals, policemen, thieves, and informers (stool pigeons). Terms for "prostitute" are native MCA forms (or possibly in a few cases from CA); prostitution in Morocco is not a specifically colonial or postcolonial phenomenon. To be sure, MCA has been enriched by the term /burdil/ C-142, originally referring to colonial bordellos (Fr *bordel*), but it now refers generally to any noisy or disorderly place or to an unpleasant commotion. Terms for police, however, do sometimes have foreign origin; see /bidžiz/ C-76 and /biṇiṭ/ C-82 for slang words, and /bulis/ C-132, /bulasarrut/ C-131, and perhaps /š^{w}ṛṭ-a/ C-716 for more standard terms (for "gendarme" see /žaḍaṛmi/ C-810). There are several words for "thief" but they are of local origin, except for /bwandi/ C-160 "bandit", used mainly for organized groups of thieves (e.g. in the country) and now often applied to the "bad guys" in films. Informers are usually referred to by pejorative native terms, but Fr *sans fil* "wireless" is sometimes used as an epithet. Terms for "beautiful woman" (cf. Eng *chick*, *broad*) and "homosexual" (cf. Eng *gay*, *queer*) are normally native MCA forms; my F informant believes that /šlux/ C-713 "homosexual" is of German origin, but this is doubtful (I have found no Ger term of this type).

Of course, individual Moroccans who happen to know a large number of Fr (or Sp) vulgarities or other slang terms may use them in certain in-group contexts. However, many Moroccans who can speak Fr reasonably well have limited knowledge of esoteric Fr slang, since their Fr has mostly been learned in academic settings. While in some circles we may find a greater number of Fr/Sp borrowings in this domain, I can say with considerable confidence that Fr/Sp words of this type have only occasionally become current in MCA slang. In cases where usage of Fr/Sp slang words and vulgarities is more common, I would expect that this usually takes the form of code-switching, with little or no structural adaptation.

There are occasional slang words which crop up in unexpected lexical fields. For "potato" we have /baṭaṭ-a/ or /bṭaṭ-a/ C-67 from Sp, which is fair enough in view of the history of the introduction of this plant; but we perhaps do not quite expect a special recent slang term /kaṛtuvn/ C-326 (German *Kartoffeln*)!

There are also some remarkable cases where borrowed material has been put to unusually good use by some anonymous genius. One of the most unusual is /aṣṭa ḷa muxiṛṛ-a/ "some other time" (i.e. not now). This is pronounced roughly like Sp **hasta la mujerra* would be, and readers might like to try their hand at guessing why Sp *mujer* "woman" has been extended suffixally in this fashion and why the semantic shift has occurred; for the solution see C-526, which also gives additional forms with /muxiṛṛ-a/. Similarly, from Sp *padre* "father" and *madre* "mother" someone has coined MCA /pwaḍṛi/ and /mwaḍṛi/ C-581 and 527), and with even greater ingenuity a new form /xwadri/ C-804; again, readers are challenged to explain these forms (answers given in the appendix entries cited). All forms in the present paragraph are slang forms only, but are in use in Fes (far from the region of direct Sp influence) and have obviously spread across cities through the usual slang networks.

The slang words we have discussed belong to fairly ordinary slang accessible to members of what might be called an extended or secondary "peer group" encompassing street-wise, fun-loving students, urban youth, and others involved in similar networks. There is also, of course, a large number of small, primary peer groups who may develop their own private slang, used perhaps in some contexts as a secret language with outsiders within listening distance. Jews apparently used to have an in-group language of this type to prevent Muslim eavesdroppers from listening in, but Moroccan society is such that very intense same-sex (especially male) peer groups can develop and last well into adulthood, and even a group as small as a pair of friends may develop their own private speech, consisting of phonological perturbations and/or special lexical items (including special metaphorical extensions). Our remarks in this section are obviously not intended to cover all types of slang which may develop in such varied contexts.

[We may here add a few items obtained too late to be included in the appendices, suggesting increasing usage of English-based slang vocabulary particularly in the context of narcotics: /ḥaš/ "hashish" from Eng *hash*; /ḥaša/ "he got high on hashish", derived from preceding; /tt-ṣṭuna/ "he got stoned", participle /m-ṣṭuni/ "stoned", Eng *stoned*; /tt-fḷaya/ "he got high, stoned", Eng *fly*; /t-ḥayya/ "he got high (on drugs)", Eng *high*; participle /m-trippi/ "tripping (using drugs)", Eng *trip* or *tripping*; hollow /fak/, imperfective /-fuk/ "he fucked", alternatively weak stem /f̣aka/ with same gloss, Eng *fuck*; there is also a fixed expression of unclear morphological structure /f̣ak f̣aki/ with this sense but showing no paradigmatic variation; /fḷaša ʿla-/"he pestered (someone)", participle /m-fḷaši/ also meaning "crazy, stoned, out of it", Eng *flash*.]

8 Borrowings in two special registers

In this chapter we deal briefly with ways in which the extent and type of borrowings (from CA and/or European sources) can vary depending on register. We select two comparatively specialized varieties of speech: a heavily classicized MCA used in a radio soccer broadcast, and a type of "foreigner talk" used by a hotel maid. These are, of course, only two of many types of registers on which we happen to have some information, but they will suffice for present purposes to indicate something of the range of variation.

8.1 Radio soccer broadcasts

The data source is a transcription of about a half-hour of a radio broadcast of an international match between Morocco and Togo played in Morocco on 17 June 1979 as an elimination match in a larger competition to determine African entries to the World Cup tournament. Morocco won this match easily and eventually was selected for the World Cup.

The base language for the broadcast is MCA. However, the language is heavily classicized and contains some code-switched CA phrases and some unusual hybrid CA-MCA formations. On the other hand, the broadcasters strictly avoid European borrowings, even though in ordinary vernacular MCA a large percentage of the technical vocabulary of soccer is in the form of obvious Fr borrowings (many replaced by corresponding Sp borrowings in northern dialects); see 7.13.

A few examples of CA-based items in the technical soccer vocabulary are these: /l-žanaḥ l-?aymn/ "the right winger", /l-mudafiᶜ/ "the defenceman", /ḥaris l-maṛma/ "the goalie (goalkeeper)", /ḍ-ḍahir/ "the back", /l-faṛiq/ "the team", /l-?iṣab-a/ or /l-hadaf/ "the goal, the score", /l-xaṭa?/ "the foul", /hužum muḍaḍḍ/ "counterattack", /liyaq-a badan-iy-a/ "physical condition", and /ᶜamal-iy-a/ "(a) play". Ordinarily, such items show partial assimilation to MCA phonological patterns including shortening of CA long vowels and the shift of CA interdental fricatives to MCA stops; these items are therefore similar to the CA borrowings into MCA described in Chapter 5. However, in ordinary street MCA many of these items are usually or always replaced by alternative forms of European origin, or by distinct MCA forms of ultimate CA origin, (via sound shifts, etc.), as with /bit/ C-91 "goal" (Fr *but*) and /fṛq-a/ "team" (occasionally /kibb/ "team" C-351).

In addition to such technical vocabulary, the broadcast includes a considerable number of other classicized phrases or lexical items with only minimal adaptation to MCA. A few examples are /makan-u/ "his place" (usually /bḷaṣ-t-u/, see C-102), /žadid/ "new" for usual MCA /ždid/, /ṛaqm/ "number" for usual /nimiru/ C-533 or /nmr-a/ C-534, /l-xamis-a/ "the fifth (FSg)" for usual /l-xams-a/, /l-?iṣab-a l-?ula/ "the first goal" with special CA FSg form of this adjective (usually /l-lwwl-a/), /?aḥad l-mudafiᶜ-in/ "one of the defencemen" with the CA numeral form (usually /waḥəd ml l-mudaf̣iᶜ-in/), /li-ṣaliḥ l-faṛiq/ "(score) in favour of the team" with CA prepositional expression, /muqabil la šay?/ "(a given score) to nil", and so forth. Some adverbs and particles from CA are also used, including /l-?an/ "now" (for /daba/), /kama/ "as (with following clause)", /?itra/ "after" (for usual /mn bəᶜd/), /li-ḥadd l-?an/ "up until now" (for /ḥtta l-daba/), /ḥaytu/ "since, seeing that" (for /ḥet/ A-3-3 or synonyms), /tumma/ "then" (for /mn bəᶜd/), /bal/ "however" (for /walakin/ and synonyms), /hunak/ "there is" (for /kayn tmma/ or the like), and /naḥwa/ "toward (a certain minute mark)" (perhaps for /ḥda/).

While the examples above involve nouns and other non-verb stems, we also observe the same trends when we look at verbs. For example, /qdəf/ is standard for "to shoot (ball)", whereas ordinary MCA generally uses a loanword like /šat/ B-162 or /tira/ B-168. Similarly, the broadcasters repeatedly use /ṛawġ/ for "he dodged, faked"; compare the very common MCA term /fanta/ B-48. The heavy classical lexicon carries over into nontechnical vocabulary: /y-ᶜud/ "he goes back" (for /ka-y-wlli/ or /ka-y-ṛžəᶜ/), /ḥdət/ "it occurred, took place" (for /wqəᶜ/ or synonym), /?adda ?ila t-t-šzil/ "it led to scoring" (all three words classical in form), /y-wḍəᶜ/ "he puts (ball down)" (for /ka-y-dir/ or the like), and /ltaṭm-at b-/ "it (ball) collided with (something)".

To a considerable extent, the above patterns suggest that this register resembles ordinary educated MCA in formal contexts (with European borrowings eliminated), differing only in the extent of the classical material. However, in some respects this broadcast register goes farther, and becomes qualitatively distinctive. In particular, we find CA vowels retained in many of these forms where we do not ordinarily get them in reasonably well-assimilated borrowings from CA. In nouns and other non-verbs, CA vowels are commonly retained in borrowings (with CA long vowels shortened), but in this broadcast register we often find even verbs retaining CA vowels which are dropped in the borrowing process in normal MCA (see 5.8). Thus, note in the preceding paragraph the form /?adda/ "it led" instead of */?dda/. Similarly, the form given above as /ṛawġ/ "he dodged" is also often pronounced /ṛawaġ/ (CA *rāwaġ-*). The most striking divergences from normal MCA are occurrences of /CV-/ rather than /C-/ imperfective pronominal prefixes: /ta-sir/ "it (game) continues" (CA *ta-sīr-u*), /yu-ṛawiġ/ "he dodges" (CA *yu-rāwiġ-u*), /yu-ᶜlin ᶜla-/ "he calls (foul)" (CA *yu-ᶜlin-u ᶜalā*), etc. In such forms the only adaptation to MCA is shortening of CA long vowels (loss of /-u/ indicative suffix is really a matter of choosing the CA "pausal" form as the basis for the borrowing).

The transition between this heavily classicized MCA to code-switched CA is not easy to identify in every instance. However, some more or less pure CA segments occur here and there, chiefly in the most solemn and formal portions of the commentary — just after a goal has been scored, or at the very end of the broadcast just before signing off. Here we find such phrases as *ʔayyu-hā l-mustamiᶜ-ūn l-ʔaᶜizzāʔ* "dear listeners (vocative)" with no morphological and very little phonological adaptation.

Although there is thus some internal variation in this broadcast language, one aspect of it is quite consistent: the avoidance of obvious European borrowings. At no time during the recorded boradcast did any of the (three) announcers let his guard down and permit an obvious Gallicism to slip out.

8.2 "Foreigner talk" used by maids

The term "foreigner talk" is suggested by Ferguson (1971 and elsewhere) as a term for a simplified register of a language used by a native speaker when speaking to a non-native with a limited knowledge of the language.

During the period when I was in Meknes, living mainly in cheap hotels, a few recordings were made of interviews with the hotel maids. Ordinarily, the language used by the maids was conventional MCA with perhaps some slowing down and other minor adjustments to my own knowledge of the language, which at that time (summer 1979) was limited. However, one of the maids, who had previous experience as a domestic for foreign residents in the area, used a distinctive register including certain systematic morphological and lexical features. My Moroccan research assistant at the time, a young man then working in the tourist office and who had considerable experience with foreigners living in Meknes, diagnosed this as a "foreigner talk" register used primarily by domestics working in the homes of foreigners.

The opportunity to verify this formally by obtaining samples of the same woman's speech in other environments was lost. Moreover, since this woman had Berber roots, there is some possibility that the recorded sample shows some similarities to her regular MCA and that some of the simplifications are due to imperfect learning rather than to a secondary reversion to "foreigner talk". Nevertheless, I believe that this is indeed foreigner talk rather than imperfect MCA, since my research assistant argued strongly in favour of this analysis, since a number of the lexical features of the register involve Fr borrowings, and since Berbers are normally bilingual from an early age with few obvious defects in their MCA.

The characteristics of this material can be observed in this sample:

Text 3

n-zid	f-l-bṛbaṛ	w-n-ži
I am born	in the Berber (country)	and I come

n-kbr mnna f-mknas, n-skn-u f-l-b^{w}ṛž, f-l-b^{w}ṛž,
I grow up here in Meknes we live in the Bourj

w-t-mut ṃaṃa mskin-a, w-n-gl s ᶜawd ana-ya,
and she dies Mother poor(FSg) and I sit also I

w-wl d-t tlat-a dyal *les enfantṣ*, w-n-d-žww ž,
and I bore 3 of children and I get married

waḥ d msyu, w-y-mut y-xlli-l-i tlat-a
a man and he dies he leaves for me 3

dyal *les enfants*.
of children

"I was born in Berber country. I came and grew up here in Meknes. We were living out in the Bourj [name of a slum on the outskirts of Meknes]. My mother died, poor thing. I stayed (and lived here). I have had three children. I got married to a man, but he died and left me with three children."

In the lexical area, the salient substitutions are /mnna/ for /hna/ "here" (specifically designated as a feature of "foreigner talk" by the research assistant), and Fr terms for basic kin and human age/sex categories ("mother", "children", etc.). Although the speaker knows very little Fr, she does use code-switched plurals with *les*.

Morphologically, the one major feature of this register is the use of the imperfective verb form (without the progressive prefix /ka-/ or /ta-/) as an all-purpose verb form. The preceding textual fragment does show one instance of the perfective ("and I bore"), but the remainder is strictly in the imperfective even when reporting punctual past tense events ("I was born", "he died", etc.). This is absolutely ungrammatical in normal MCA in all regional dialects which I know. Moreover, even given the use of the imperfective, we would expect the progressive prefix now and then for explicitly durative contexts (here probably in "we were living"); however, this prefix is uncommon in our material in this register. (There are some MCA dialects where the progressive prefix is used sparingly or is restricted in some way, but in the Fes/Meknes area it is very common.)

Aside from this simplification of verb forms, the morphology is fairly standard. The imperfective forms do show correct pronominal prefixes and suffixes, adjectives show gender concord, and so forth. Moreover, the pronunciation shows no significant distortions (for example, there are no added vocalic segments to make consonant sequences more easily audible), though of course the speed is slowed down somewhat.

There is some evidence that such a register was once moderately widespread, near the end of the Protectorate and in the first decades of the post-Protectorate period when there were still many well-to-do French landowners who employed domestics on a long-term basis. Although there is no detailed documentation of characteristic inter-ethnic communication patterns during this period, all indications are that it was usual for the French lady of the house to learn a simplified form of MCA and use it with domestics, who in turn developed a "foreigner talk" involving morphological simplification and usage of French vocabulary of certain types set in an MCA framework. This particular maid specifically stated that her own former employers had spoken a rudimentary form of MCA to her.

9 Borrowing patterns in two neighbouring Arabic dialects

Like the preceding chapter, this one will be kept brief. In it, we discuss variations in the way European borrowings are adapted to MCA from one region to another. Whereas the bulk of this publication deals with borrowings attested in the Fes/Meknes area (with data from other areas added in the appendices to shed historical light), here we are focally concerned with two other nearby dialects. First, we discuss European borrowings in the distinctive northern MCA dialect of Tetouan (in the zone of Spanish rather than French colonial influence), then we consider Algerian dialects. Our material in both cases is rather limited, but does permit us to identify certain significant variations.

9.1 Northern (Tetouan) MCA: verbs

For some historical background on the assimilation of Sp verbs into northern and coastal MCA dialects, see 6.13. It was noted in that section that, early in this century (and mainly in maritime contexts), forms borrowed from Sp verbs generally entered MCA in the Sp infinitive form (*-ar*, *-er*, *-ir*) or else as Sp imperative Sg forms (mainly in *-a*).

My recent data from this area (from Tetouan, hence not involving specialized nautical vocabulary) show a large number of borrowed verbs from Sp infinitives: /p̣ḷanč̣aṛ/ "he ironed (clothing)" (Sp *planchar*), /čokaṛ mᶜa-/ or /čakaṛ mᶜa-/ "he collided with" (Sp *chocar con*), /dučč̣aṛ/ "he took a shower" (Sp *duchar*), /fṛinaṛ/ "he braked (Sp *frenar*), /ṛiglaṛ/ "he fixed" (Sp *arreglar*), /nčufaṛ/ "he plugged in" (Sp *enchufar*), and /ṭakaṛ ᶜla-/ "he attacked" (Sp *atacar*, with added MCA preposition). Two variants are recorded in the case of /paṛaṛ/ or /paṛa/ "he stopped" (Sp *parar*, 3Sg present or 2Sg imperative *para*), where /paṛa/ is a regular weak stem (/paṛi-t/ "I stopped", /ta-y-paṛi/ "he stops") and may have been influenced by the large number of weak borrowed verbs (of Fr origin) which are in use in Tetouan. In the case of /piḍaḷ/ "he pedalled", we probably have a denominative formed internally within MCA on the basis of the nominal borrowing /piḍaḷ/ "pedal" (Sp *pedal*, cf. Fr *pédale*).

There is some variation within Tetouan MCA in the paradigms of borrowed verbs of these types. The background problem relevant here is that in this dialect, old CA short vowels are retained to a much greater extent than in more southerly MCA dialects, and indeed in many cases old short vowels now seem to be merging with old full vowels. Thus verb stems of the type /CCaC/, /CCiC/, and quadriliteral /CaCCaC/ (shown in unsuffixed form) occur in Tetouan MCA where other dialects have just /CCəC/ or /CCCəC/. However, old short vowels in this position are subject to syncope when a suffix beginning in a vowel is added, so that /CCaC/ becomes /C(V)CC-.../ and /CaCCaC/ becomes /CaCCC-.../. If we add a suffix beginning in a vowel to a borrowed verb like /pḷančaṛ/, we find some inconsistency in this matter of syncope: /pḷančaṛ-u/ or /pḷančṛ-u/ "they ironed". However, the syncoped form is rather common with many of the stems. A more detailed exposition of factors involved is not possible at this time.

Occasionally, borrowed verbs ending in consonant (usually /ṛ/ or /r/) add the /-i-/ augment (see 5.9 for background) before pronominal perfective suffixes beginning with a consonant. Thus /fṛinaṛ-i-t/ "I braked" and /piḍaḷ-i-t/ "I pedalled", for example. However, simpler forms like /fṛinaṛ-t/ and /piḍaḷ-t/ also occur and seem more common.

Two borrowed hollow triliteral verbs deserve mention. First, the local variant of MCA /šat/ "he shot" (B-162) in this area is /čaṭ/. Since this dialect shows variable vowel (depending on the root) in preconsonantal perfective forms of hollow verbs, we get such forms as /čuṭ-t/ "I shot" and /čuṭ-na/ "we shot". However, a variant type with /-i-/ augment is also recorded: /čaṭ-i-na/ "we shot". The other hollow verb is /ǰok/ "he joked", as in /ǰok ᶜli-na/ "he joked at us, made fun of us". The imperfective is /(ka-)y-ǰuk/ "he jokes"; the only attested preconsonantal perfective is /ǰok-i-t/ "I joked", which has the same structure as /čaṭ-i-na/ (just given). Both /čaṭ/ and /ǰok/ are from English, though there may have been intermediate carrier languages involved.

There are many verbs of Fr origin in the Tetouan dialect which are not discussed here since their structure is basically the same as that of the Fr borrowings discussed in Chapter 6 for the main MCA dialects. Indeed, these Fr borrowings originate for the most part in the more central and southerly parts of Morocco and filter up into the Tetouan area indirectly, so it is natural that the forms be largely uniform across the entire area.

9.2 Northern (Tetouan) MCA: other stems

As is to be expected, there is an extensive nominal vocabulary of Sp origin in this dialect, even though the period of primary Spanish influence has passed (Fr and to some extent Eng are the major languages taught in schools, after CA). Roughly, the vocabulary of Sp origin in this area corresponds functionally to the Fr-based vocabulary of the rest of Morocco (see Chapter 7).

In this section we give some samples of this vocabulary, but make no pretence of completeness; our goal is to illustrate the vocabulary and make pertinent observations about structural features of adaptation.

Probably the most significant observation about nominal morphology concerns plurals. Whereas in the rest of Morocco, Fr plurals have not taken root and borrowings from Fr normally end up with regular MCA plurals (by ablaut or by suffixation of MCA Pl suffix /-at/), in the north things are not quite so simple. It is necessary to distinguish feminine from masculine nouns. In both Sp and MCA the basic FSg suffix is /-a/, and it is clear that Sp borrowings of this type are interpreted as ending in MCA /-a/. As a result, the MCA plural form is usually generated by replacing /-a/ with Pl /-at/, and occasionally by an ablaut change patterned on existing native paradigms of feminine nouns. On the other hand, Sp masculines in *-o* or with zero suffix (ending in consonant or *e*) do not fit any particular inherited MCA pattern in most cases. Very frequently, with masculine nouns from Sp MCA borrows the regular Sp plural form as well as the singular. Thus Sp *bocadillo* "sandwich", Pl *bocadillos* becomes MCA /bukadiyu/, Pl /bukadiyu-s/. In MCA, the suffix should be represented as /-s/ after unpharyngealized vocalic allophone, /-ṣ/ after pharyngealized allophone; there are also cases of Sp *-es* after consonant coming into MCA as /-iṣ/, as in Sp *gol, goles* becoming MCA /guṇ/ "goal (in soccer)", Pl /guṇ-iṣ/.

The primary pattern is thus for feminines in /-a/ to take strictly native Pl formations (mostly suffixal, occasionally by ablaut), and for masculines to take borrowed Sp plural forms. I am aware of no exceptions to the generalization about feminines. However, some Sp masculines are attested as MCA borrowings with a native Pl form, sometimes by suffix /-at/ and sometimes by ablaut. In my limited data, the Sp masculines which do not bring in their own plurals tend to be long stems with several syllables, along with some (probably quite old) terms for military ranks, such as /kuṛuṇiḷ/ "colonel" (Pl /kuṛuṇiḷ-at/).

There is at least one case of a "false" Sp plural form involving a Fr borrowing apparently associated with Sp masculine borrowings because it happens to end (in MCA) with /u/, which is also a common MCA borrowed form of Sp *-o* suffix. This is /stilu/ C-660 "ballpoint pen" (Fr *stilo*, the continental Sp equivalent being *bolígrafo*). Whereas in the rest of Morocco the Pl is /stilu-wat/ or /stilu-yat/, in Tetouan I have recorded /stilu-s/. (There could conceivably have been some contamination involving Sp *estilo*, Pl *estilos* "style[s]").

We now give a modest sample of some of the recorded borrowed nouns of Sp origin in use in Tetouan:

/ḅaḷinsyaṇ-a/ "intercity bus" (obsolescent), Sp *valenciana*.
/ḅanyo/ (cf. C-51) "bathtub", Pl /banyo-ṣ/, Sp *baño*; note that some borrowings preserve the quality of the Sp *-o* suffix even without a tautosyllabic pharyngealized consonant.
/baṛko/ "boat", Pl /baṛko-ṣ/, Sp *barco*.
/buṛṛačo/ or /bṛṛaču/ "drunk", Pl /buṛṛačo-ṣ/ or /bṛṛaču-s/, Sp *borracho*; the FSg can be either /buṛṛač-a/ (direct from Sp *borracha*) or internally generated /bṛṛaču-wa/.
/čaṃpwan/ [čaṃpwæn] "shampoo", apparently a hybrid involving contamination between the widespread Fr borrowing seen in C-702, and Sp *champú*.

/čawfir/ or /čawfiṛ/ "driver", Pl usually /-at/, Sp *chófer* but probably affected by the set in C-705.
/čik/ (or /ček/) (see C-706) "(bank) cheque", Pl /čik-at/ or ablauted /čyuk/, Sp *cheque* but probably influenced by the Fr-based set in C-706.
/čiklin/ "chewing gum", Sp *chicle* with irregular change, or perhaps directly from a Sp brand name.
/faḷd-a/ "dress", Pl /faḷḍ-at/ or /fḷadi/, Sp *falda*.
/glisy-a/ "church", Sp *iglesia*, with unpharyngealized /i/ possibly reflecting influence of Fr *église*.
/guṇ/ "goal (score)", Pl /guṇ-iṣ/ or /guḷ/, /guḷ-iṣ/ from Sp *gol* (Pl *goles*); see C-283 but note that the usual meaning elsewhere is "goalie (goalkeeper)".
/kaṃ-a/ "bed", Pl /kaṃ-at/, Sp *cama*.
/kaṃp̣u/ "(playing) field", Pl /kaṃp̣u-ṣ/, Sp *campo* (see C-311 for a southerly form which is ultimately cognate but showing drastic semantic shift).
/kaṛṣusiyu/ "(pair of) underpants", Pl /kaṛṣusiyu-s/, Sp *calzoncillo* (cf. C-264, sense 2).
/kuči/ "cart", Pl /-yat/ or /kuči-s/, Sp *coche* (cf. C-430).
/kučiy-a/ "razor", Sp *cuchilla*.
/kuṛč-a/ "bedspread", Pl /-ạt/, Sp *colcha*.
/kwaṭṛu/ "four (card)", Pl /kwaṭṛu-s/, Sp *cuatro*.
/ḷabrigo/, definite /ḷ-ḷabrigo/ "(the) overcoat", Pl /ḷabrigo-ṣ/, Sp *(el) abrigo*, with resegmentation involving the Sp indefinite article.
/ḷaḍu/, def. /ḷ-ḷaḍu/ "(the) ice cream", Pl /ḷaḍu-ṣ/, Sp *helado*.
/lappis/, Pl /lpapəs/ "pencil(s)", also /lapiz/, Pl /lwapəz/, Sp *lápiz*.
/maḷiṭ-a/ "suitcase", Pl [-ạt], Sp *maleta*.
/maḷṭ-a/ "blanket", Pl [-ạt] or ablauted /mḷaṭi/, Sp *manta*.
/map̣p̣-a/ "map", Pl [-ạt], Sp *mapa* (takes masculine concord in Sp but treated as feminine in MCA).
/miss-a/ "table", Pl [-æt] or /msəs/, Sp *mesa*; here the ablaut Pl /msəs/ may have been directly suggested by Sp plural *mesas*; different meaning in C-505.
/muṛṭ-a/ "fine (payment)", Sp *multa*.
/piḍaḷ/ "pedal", Pl /piḍaḷ-iṣ/, Sp *pedal*; cf. C-77.
/pḷanč-a/ "iron (for ironing clothing)", Sp *plancha*.
/pṛupin-a/ "tip", Sp *propina*.
/publiku/ "audience, crowd (at soccer match etc.)", Sp *público*; cf. C-573.
/ṛiṭiṛu/ "retirement (with pension)", Sp *retiro*.
/says/ "six (card)", Pl /says-as/ or /says-at/, Sp *seis* (Pl *seises*).
/siyu/ "postage stamp", Pl /siyu-s/, Sp *sello*.
/srbis-a/ "beer", Pl /srabəs/, Sp *cerveza* (also recorded as /srbis-a/).
/ṣabaṇ-a/ "bedsheet", Pl /-at/, Sp *sabana*.
/tris/ "three (card)", Pl /tursan/ (ablaut pattern), Sp *tres*; cf. C-741.
/waṇṭiṣ/ "gloves", individuative Sg /waṇṭiṣ-a/ "(a) glove", Sp plural *guantes*; for parallel cf. C-443.

While we do not have enough data (or enough evidence concerning relative chronology) for a more thorough analysis of the phonological and morphological assimilation of these items, on the whole the changes and adaptations seem within a reasonable range of expectations based on our earlier analysis in Chapter 6. As usual, there are a few unusual and problematic features, such as the precise conditions under which a Sp consonant shows up in doubled form in MCA, but we cannot now address this issue.

Mention should also be made of one curious nominal borrowing from English: /žips/ "Jeep", Pl /žbusa/, where Eng plural *Jeeps* seems to be the form actually borrowed with the sibilant reinterpreted as part of the root.

Regarding particles, prepositions, and the like, since our present data are mostly from direct elicitation we prefer to defer a decent analysis until after we have more real textual material from this area showing actual speech patterns. On the whole, Sp borrowings of this type do not seem common in current Tetouan speech, perhaps since nowadays rather few natives know Sp well enough to engage in extensive code-switching. We can cite /kuṇṭṛa/ "against", a preposition (from Sp *contra*) often used in discussing soccer matches (e.g. "Tetouan is playing against Fes"). Moreover, whereas Fr *ni..., ni...* ("neither..., nor...") has not become established in the rest of Morocco, the corresponding Sp sequence *ni..., ni...* does seem to be common in Tetouan MCA.

One final remark is in order. The Tetouan dialect is particularly sensitive to sociolinguistic pressures. Locally, there is variation between the old urban dialect, and the speech of the many rural persons who have migrated into the city from the Rif area in recent decades. More seriously, inhabitants of Tetouan who move into central Morocco (e.g. to attend a university, there being few major educational institutions in the north) find that they must make drastic changes in their MCA to avoid ridicule or even to ensure minimal communication. Thus, well-travelled Tetouanis are likely to have an extensive dialect repertoire sensitive to context. Over time, the better-educated Tetouanis are gradually shifting to a higher-status, less local dialect variety and are using this even among friends within the confines of the city. Because the vocabulary of Sp origin is in most cases used only in the north (in Tetouan and Tangier and their surroundings), this vocabulary is particularly sensitive sociolinguistically.

Some additional items from the Tetouan dialect are to be found here and there in Appendices B and C insofar as the entries give information about dialect distributions and dialect variants of items initially documented from the Fes/Meknes area.

9.3 Algeria: verbs

Our direct information about Algerian Colloquial Arabic (ACA) is based on two elicitation sessions with an Algerian couple whom I met in West Berlin. Some caution should be exercised in connection with this material, particularly since my knowledge of the dialects in this region is insufficient even to be certain of phonemic transcriptions. However, since our objective is the limited one of adducing significant parallels and contrasts with our primary Moroccan corpus, we will proceed.

The sociolinguistic situation in Algeria is rather different from that of Morocco. Referring to the older period, we should note that Sabir (a late version of Lingua Franca) was an important contact language in Algiers and some other ports, and served as a medium for introducing foreign items particularly from Italian but also other Mediterranean dialects into local ACA varieties. Sabir was not a significant factor in Morocco, since it was largely out of use by the time of the major French intrusion into that country in 1912.

In the twentieth century, Morocco had both Spanish and French as colonial and postcolonial languages in its two respective zones. In Algeria, Sp was not an administrative language, though at street level Sp was reasonably visible in the form of numerous Sp-speaking sailors and settlers. On the other hand, French became significant in Algeria many decades before it gained its first foothold in Morocco. Even following the grisly war of independence, postcolonial Algeria has kept Fr as the major administrative and (higher) educational language, and Arabization has had a fairly difficult time gaining momentum. French influence in Algeria has been so strong for such a long time that many native Algerians are considerably more fluent in Fr than in ACA (let alone CA), and at the very least a large percentage of the urban population (especially in Algiers) is bilingual. In Morocco, on the other hand, rather few persons (aside from the odd returning overseas working family) speak Fr better than MCA.

With respect to verbs, my data suggest that the basic principles for adapting Fr items are the same in ACA as in MCA. In particular, the most productive adaptation process involves creating weak stems, and many of those recorded for ACA are identical (perhaps with some minor phonological variation) to those recorded in MCA: /dribla/ "he dribbled" (B-35), /fanta/ "he dodged" (B-48), /kḷakṣuna/ "he honked horn" (B-74), and /pṛipaṛa/ "he prepared" (B-115) are examples (Fr *dribbler*, *feinte* [noun] and *feindre*, *klaxonner*, *preparer*); for a case of phonemic variation see ACA /fṛina/ and MCA /frana/ "he braked (car)" (Fr *freiner*, perhaps with the ACA form influenced by other Romance cognates).

Although there are many ACA-MCA matches involving such vocabulary, in many of these cases it is likely that the dialects have independently accomplished the borrowings; it is not likely that large numbers of these items originated in Algeria and were diffused into Morocco (and the reverse is even less likely). However, for the earliest stratum of Fr borrowings in colonial Morocco, some direct or indirect Algerian influence is probable, particularly in the military sphere (some Algerian Arabs came into Morocco with the French army, and a number of French military and civilian officers had served earlier in Algeria and had acquired some knowledge of ACA). Some items such as /srba/ "he served" (B-145) and /ẓṛṭa/ "he deserted" (B-183) common to MCA and ACA may reflect this early influence, but such words often show several variant forms here and there in Morocco, so that whatever diffusional element there may be in the word histories is overlain and complicated by local reshaping and borrowing.

In a considerable number of examples, moreover, the ACA forms recorded differ in phonology or stem shape in a fashion pointing rather clearly to independent ACA and MCA developments. Some relevant ACA forms (with the MCA counterparts to be found in the appendix entry cited) are /dipaṇa/ "he fixed, he helped out" (*dépanner*), /kröva/ "it burst" (*crever*), /kwæ̃sa/ "it bumped, rammed into" (*coincer*), /maṇka/ or /mãka/ "he was absent" (*manquer* or perhaps It *mancare*), /niṛva/ "he got (someone) angry" (*énerver* reinforced by adjective *nerveux*), /šaṛža/ "he loaded (e.g. truck)" (*charger*), and /šuta/ "he shot (ball)" (*shooter* from Eng *shoot*); see MCA entries B-43, 80, 94, 101, 105, 161, 162. The ACA and MCA forms differ in various ways including retention or modification of foreign Fr vowels, extent of indirect retention of Fr vocalic qualities by having pharyngealized consonants in the borrowed form, and by some more far-reaching structural features. However, much of this variation is at the level of lexical idiosyncrasies. The only more general remark that can be made is that ACA is more likely than MCA to retain Fr nasalized vowels and front rounded /ö/ (which is also used in ACA for Fr unstressed orthographic *e*, i.e. schwa, as in /kröva/ above).

9.4 Algeria: other stems

Whereas ACA and MCA agree in basic principles for adapting Fr verbs, they do not agree with regard to nouns. True, to a considerable extent the two Arabic languages agree in which types of Fr noun are borrowed. The major difference, however, is in such areas as rules for determining gender concord of borrowed nouns, the retention of FSg and Pl definite articles from Fr, and the grammatical value assigned to these articles.

To begin with, we have noted that in MCA a borrowed noun is normally treated as feminine for concord purposes if and only if it ends in /-a/, with some allowances for a few specifically human nouns whose semantic gender overrides morphology. In ACA, on the other hand, many borrowed nouns based on Fr feminines are treated for concord purposes as feminine even though the borrowed noun itself may lack any overt marker of gender. Some examples: /ṭunubil/ "automobile" (Fr *automobile*), /kumḅinizo/ "(clothing) combination" (*combinaison*), /(la-)pisin/ "swimming pool" (*la piscine*), /(l-)uṭu/ "automobile" (said to be used chiefly in Oran) (*l'auto*), /(l-)asiṛą̃ṣ/ "insurance" (*l'assurance*), /paṛti/ "(sports) match" (*partie*), /(ḷa-)pil/ "(flashlight) battery" (*la pile*), /tilivizyõ/ "television" (*télévision*), /(la-)batri/ "(car)battery" (*la batterie*), /bisklat/ "bicycle" (*bicyclette*), /(ḷa-)burs/ "scholarship stipend" (*la bourse*), /(ž-)žip/ "skirt" (*jupe*; variant /žipp-a/ recorded), /(l-)antrit/ "retirement (with pension)" (*la retraite*), /(ḷa-)glaṣ/ "ice cream" (*la glace*), /(ḷa-)gaṛ "train station" (Algiers dialect), /(ḷa-)kol "glue" (*la colle*). In my data, these items require feminine forms of adjectives or verbs which cross-reference them: /žip kbir-a/ "big skirt". A number of these items are identical or nearly so to MCA counterparts, with the crucial difference that in MCA these items are commonly treated as masculine for concord purposes.

Nevertheless, even in ACA there are some cases where the original Fr gender is not retained. For example, /magaz-a/ "large store" (Fr *magasin*, masculine) is treated as a FSg noun with suffix /-a/

in ACA as in MCA; another example of this type is /(l-)ạksid-a/ "accident (collision)" (Fr *accident*, also masculine). My data show fluctuation in the case of /(l-)biṭṛav/ "beets" (Fr *betterave*, veminine), for which both masculine and feminine concord was recorded; a larger data corpus would presumably show more cases of this kind. Some cases of stem-final /a/ which are interpreted in MCA as the FSg suffix are not thus interpreted in ACA, which retains Fr masculine gender in concord: /sima/ "cement" (Fr *ciment*), /kuṛa/ in sense "(electric) current" (Fr *courant*, contrast native /kuṛ-a/ "ball" with feminine concord); MCA has FSg /sim-a/ and /kuṛ-a/ in these borrowings. In general, then, ACA retains Fr grammatical gender much better than MCA, though even in ACA there is some reassignment.

A number of the ACA nouns listed above are shown with parenthesized /la-/ or /ḷa-/ before them. These are cases where the Fr FSg definite article *la* is brought in with the borrowed noun, creating a new definite prefix allomorph in ACA. We have seen a few cases of this even in MCA (6.24), and with some of the same lexical items. However, in most such cases the MCA borrowed noun is treated as grammatically masculine, so the /la-/ or /ḷa-/ definite allomorph does not signal feminine gender. In ACA, on the other hand, all examples I have of these definite prefixes involve nouns whose grammatical gender is feminine. Thus these special definite allomorphs do seem to indicate gender in ACA. (However, there are some grammatically feminine borrowings which now take ordinary ACA definite prefix allomorphs, like /žip/ "skirt", def. /ž-žip/ from Fr *jupe*, just as there are some native ACA and MCA nouns which take grammatical feminine gender despite the absence of FSg suffix /-a/; nouns like /antrit/ beginning in vowels can only take definite prefix allomorph /l-/ or perhaps /ḷ-/ for phonological reasons, so no opposition of /l-/ vs. feminine /la-/ or /ḷa-/ is possible with them.)

It is possible that some of the nouns listed above with /la-/ or /ḷa-/ definite prefix, or with /l-/ or /ḷ-/ before a stem-initial vowel, may be cases where the definite prefix is tightly fused with the noun so that unprefixed stem forms are uncommon or not possible. Some cases of full or partial fusion in MCA counterparts have been noted earlier (6.24).

In MCA, we noted (6.26) that Fr borrowings normally take MCA plural forms *suffixation of /-at/ or a similar suffix, or internal ablaut) rather than borrowing Fr *les* (Pl definite article), though forms with *les* are common in code-switching. In ACA, on the other hand, quite a few Fr borrowings do use a borrowed form based on *les* as a Pl prefix marker. Other Fr borrowings take suffixed or ablaut plurals using native patterns.

Some examples of /li-/ as Pl prefix in ACA are /ṣak/ "sack, bag" (Fr *sac*), Pl /li-ṣak/; /tambr/ "postage stamp" (*timbre*), Pl /li-tambr/; /šaf/ "boss" (*chef*), Pl /li-šaf/; /bis/ "(local) bus" (*bus*), Pl /li-bis/; /pnö/ "(automobile) tyre" (*pneu*), Pl /li-pnö/. It appears that /li-/ in these forms functions as either definite or indefinite without further affixes.

It may be recalled that in MCA /lig-a/ "glove" and /liḅ-a/ "stocking" are synchronically FSg nouns; they go back to plural *les gants* and *les bas* in Fr, but have been reanalysed because Sg *gant* and *bas* are too short to be good MCA noun shapes, and because they end in a low back vowel which is conveniently reinterpreted as the FSg suffix /-a/. In ACA, on the other hand, these forms are treated as /li-ga/ "gloves" and /li-ba/ "stockings" (apparently with no correponding Sg form permitted), since /li-/ is elsewhere established as a Pl prefix with borrowings. Thus concord is Pl rather than FSg.

Instead of /li-/, we get /liz-/ as Pl prefix when the borrowed stem begins in a vowel. Thus /l-aṛbiṭ/ "the referee" (*l'arbitre*), with /liz-aṛbiṭ/ "(the) referees" as one possible Pl form. We have also recorded /lizafir-at/ "business, business matters" (Fr *les affaires*), but since we have no specifically Sg counterpart in the data we cannot be sure that here /liz-/ is functioning as a segmentable Pl prefix.

Unfortunately, our limited data do not have many examples of Pl forms corresponding to FSg borrowings which retain /la-/ or /ḷa-/ as definite prefix. In one example, /ḷa-/ is replaced by /li-/ to form the Pl: /ḷa-pil/ "the (flashlight) battery", Pl /li-pil/ (cf. Fr *la pile, les piles*). However, in another case we get Pl suffix /-at/, with /la-/ shortened to the regular ACA definite prefix /l-/: /la-pisin/ "the swimming pool", Pl /l-pisin-at/. Further fieldwork is needed on this point.

Some other examples of suffixed plurals with /-at/ or an allomorph are /tikiy-at/ "tickets", /ṭakṣiy-at/ "taxis", /kuliy-at/ "parcels", and /bisklat-at/ "bicycles" (/y/ between /i/ and the suffix is epenthetic). Note also the morphophonemic alternation in /žwæ̃/ "rubber belts (in car engine)" (Fr *joint*), Pl /žwan-at/ (for MCA cf. C-827, 828). Another ACA Pl suffix, /-a/, is also recorded with a borrowing: /ṭṛanǰi/ "foreigner" (*étranger*), Pl /ṭṛanǰiy-a/ (cf. C-766).

Ablaut plurals do not seem as common in ACA as in MCA, but a fair number are attested. Some examples: /zufri/ "playboy" (cf. C-809), Pl /zwafra/; /ṛuḍ-a/ "wheel" (Sp *rueda* or similar Romance form), Pl /ṛwəḍ/ (C-624); /srbit-a/ "napkin, towel" (Fr *serviette* or other Romance form), Pl /srabət/ (as in MCA, C-657).

Some further data on ACA borrowings can be gleaned from Appendices B and C, where occasional ACA counterparts to MCA borrowings are listed to indicate distributions, variants, and other information of possible historical or etymological interest. However, we cannot undertake a more complete analysis here.

In order to treat the historical relationships between borrowings in ACA and MCA more thoroughly, we would clearly need much more information about ACA borrowings, particularly in dialects spoken in the westerly part of Algeria, and in the far east of Morocco around Oujda. It should be mentioned, however, that there is a fairly natural social and geographical divide between Oujda (and Algeria) on the one hand, and the main bulk of the Moroccan population (centred in the Fes-Meknes-Rabat-Casablanca belt in the centre and west, with offshoots on the northern coast and in the south around Marrakech, none of these regions being closely associated with Oujda or with Algeria). These natural divisions have been consolidated in recent years by the closing of the border and the sharp reduction in travel between Morocco and Algeria. It seems sociolinguistically reasonable to assume that the great bulk of Fr and Sp borrowings in MCA are of local Moroccan origin, though we would have to make some exceptions for the very earliest batch of Fr borrowings in the first decade or so of the Protectorate (especially in the military area of lexicon). The assumption of independent sociolinguistic complexes seems to be supported by the linguistic data, which show significant structural differences in the adaptation strategies used for nouns in particular (for verbs MCA and ACA use similar conversion routines, but this seems to have been an independent development, especially in view of the fact that MCA has solidified its preference for weak borrowed stem forms in the period following the introduction of the earliest Fr verbal borrowings, as shown in 6.14).

10 Reflections I: Structural determinism in borrowing processes

10.1 The problem

In this and the following chapter, I reflect on two of the main issues which I see facing those of us concerned with the general theory of language mixing. Though I refer here and there to factual points developed in earlier substantive chapters, I am more interested here in locating this study in a wider perspective. It would have been premature and distracting to have injected these reflections in the earlier chapters.

The relationship between structural analysis and borrowing has long been a matter of intense debate. At the turn of the century, a split developed in Europe between a group of anything-goes diffusionists led by Schuchardt and a more conservative establishment in which Meillet played a leading role; the latter group downplayed diffusion as a factor in the evolution of grammatical systems. In the United States, Sapir reacted against diffusionism (associated with ethnological approaches focusing on "trait" distributions) as a major evolutionary factor and thus sided with Meillet. In general, anti-diffusionist theories were associated with the belief that each language, or at least an important core grammar and lexicon, was a tightly integrated system deeply ingrained in its speakers, subject to (usually very slow) historical changes which were themselves heavily constrained by or immanent in the initial system.

At mid-century, Einar Haugen and Uriel Weinreich emerged as specialists in language mixing, each carrying out at least one major field study (Haugen on American Norwegian, Weinreich on Romance and German dialects in Switzerland) and subsequently producing general monographs on the classification and analysis of borrowings and other forms of interference (Weinreich 1963[1953], Haugen 1956). Both had roots in European structuralist linguistics, and although their empirical studies showed considerable quantities of borrowings in intensive contact zones, they argued that the extent and type of borrowing was heavily constrained and channelled by structural factors. Of the two, Haugen was perhaps somewhat more conservative in recognizing the extent of the borrowing.

Some of Haugen's conclusions, also taking Weinreich's findings into account, were these:

> (4) Interlingual identification occurs when speakers equate items in one language with items in another because of their similarities in shape, distribution, or both. (5) When the items involved are phonemes, the identification leads to the phonemes of one language becoming diaphones of phonemes in another; when they are morphemes, the identification makes the morphemes of one language into diamorphs of morphemes in the other. (6) Identifications can be established a priori by linguistic description and enable the linguist to predict certain types of interference, since identification is the necessary but not sufficient condition of interference. (7) A complete language switch is possible at any lexeme boundary and may embrace only one lexeme; it avoids the necessity of interference, though it may be the initiation of later interference... (9) Language distance is a factor in the promotion or hindrance of interlingual identification ... (14) Integration of a diffused item into the new language is a process which is differently accomplished by different speakers, resulting in some vacillation of form...
>
> (Haugen 1956:67-8)

Comment (6) represents what we might call the "axiom of structural determinism"; that is, given a satisfactory prior structural analysis of languages L_2 and L_1, it is possible to predict the adaptation processes which will be applied to L_2 borrowings in L_1 (and of course vice versa). Within this framework, residual uncertainty is due to the fact that we cannot predict which items from L_2 will be borrowed, and to variable degrees of adaptation for a given item (and a given speaker) ranging from unintegrated code-switching (comment 7) to intermediate and fully adapted borrowing (comment 14). These uncertainty factors do not seriously undermine the determinism axiom, which argues only that the adaptation processes applied to borrowings are predetermined; the processes do not have to apply instantaneously to produce fully adapted borrowings. Bilingual agents of transfer may themselves retain some or all L_2 features (pronunciation, morphology) in L_2 items used in an L_1 base, so that monolingual L_1 speakers are the ones who complete the adaptation eventually. In general, half-adapted forms should be seen as unstable and as on the way to eventual full adaptation:

> Loans which are accepted from bilinguals into a monolingual community will pass through various stages of integration until they achieve their commonly accepted form.
>
> (Haugen 1956:55-6)

Therefore Haugen expresses skepticism about analyses of a language (L_1) which distinguish an archaic core grammar (including phonology) from a separate, stabilized "coexistent system" applied to borrowings (from L_2) (Haugen 1956:57).

Moreover, while the theory does not predict precisely which

items from L_2 will enter L_1 as borrowings, it does provide for significant structural constraints on this selection. Thus, for Haugen, bound grammatical morphemes "are seldom if ever borrowed" while isolated elements such as exclamations are most easily borrowed (1956:66-7).

Weinreich's theory of borrowability shares this general viewpoint, but does recognise that borrowing of bound morphemes has occurred under favourable conditions. With some rephrasing and regrouping, Weinreich's factors favouring bound-morpheme borrowing are: (a) affective quality (diminutives); (b) transparent, unitary function of morpheme in L_2; (c) borrowing L_2 morpheme into L_1 will have therapeutic value by formal renewal of a zero or other very short and indistinct L_1 morpheme or by replacing a messy proliferation of allomorphs in L_1 by a simple unitary morpheme (Weinreich 1963[1953]:31-7).

The general picture which emerges from this body of research is essentially consistent with the axiom of structural determinism. The prior structural analysis (chiefly identification of phonemes and morphemes, identification of sequencing/distribution rules for phonemes and morphemes, specification of allophones and allomorphs, and identification of grammatical value of morphemes) of L_1 and L_2 was considered sufficient to permit predictions of which L_2 items might be borrowed and of the adaptation processes (based on the prior structure of L_1) which would be applied to them. Functional defects in L_1 (e.g. use of a zero morpheme for a marked grammatical category) could act as a factor favouring borrowing, but even this is basically a structural matter (perhaps more in tune with Martinet's version of structuralism than Jakobson's). Residual uncertainty factors apply to individual items rather than general classes of items, and to the degree of adaptation of particular borrowings for a given speaker.

10.2 Complications

In the present study, I dispute the position that adaptation processes applying to foreign material in MCA can be satisfactorily accounted for merely by initially presenting structural descriptions of the several systems and then projecting direct L_2-to-L_1 correspondences (cf. Haugen's diaphones and diamorphs, representing interlinguistic correspondences or associations which affect borrowing patterns). Instead, I argue for recognition of (a) a degree of ambiguity or tension in linguistic systems generally such that speakers' internalized grammars may be fuzzy on some points; (b) additional complexities in borrowing due to the fact that different structural principles in L_1 point to different adaptation processes applied to the same L_2 item so that we either get compromise outputs or have some principles outweighing others; (c) development over time of specific psycholinguistic adaptation routines based analogically on earlier borrowings, but perhaps evolving over several decades of contact; (d) "false" borrowing routines and related complexities due to convergence of borrowings from two or more source languages: (e) some "unexplained" residual fluctuation not attributable to any obvious structural factors. We omit from this section matters related to simplification and pidginization covered in the next chapter, and now exemplify the points just made, in order.

(a) Structural ambiguity

Even without reference to interference from other languages, the structuralist and now generativist assumption of rigid, well-integrated internalized "grammars" is dubious in general and is difficult to apply to MCA in particular. The point is not merely that there is some output variation (of the sort analysed by quantitative sociolinguists), but also that there may be some ambiguity in the speaker's mind as to, say, the phonological representation of everyday forms whose output pronunciation is standardized. With respect to MCA, I have a monograph (Heath 1987) on phonetics/phonology making this general point, using data from ablaut (e.g. diminutives) and play-speech perturbations as well as loanword phonology and dialectal variation. I omit a general discussion here, since many of the examples are not related to the topics covered in this study.

Consider, however, the treatment of MCA /r/ and pharyngealized /ṛ/. Structural analysis of this opposition in inherited MCA items shows two conflicting tendencies — one for the opposition to be predictable from neighbouring vowels, the other for the opposition to have underlying phonemic status (and thus to be maintained even in ablaut forms with new vocalic environments). The opposition is not present (structurally) in CA or in the European languages. CA borrowings into MCA follow the first MCA tendency, so that /r/ vs. /ṛ/ in the borrowing is usually determined by neighbouring vowels, and separately borrowed Sg/Pl ablaut doublets or verbal noun/participle doublets frequently have /r/ in one form and /ṛ/ in the other (5.4). In European borrowings, on the other hand, the tendency is to establish either /r/ or /ṛ/ on the basis of the initial borrowed form, then to keep this consonant in internally derived ablaut forms from this borrowing; this tendency goes so far as to create /baṛ/ "bar, tavern", Pl /biṛ-an/ (C-52) and similar Sg/Pl pairs even though the immediate analogical models are of the type /faṛ/ "mouse", Pl /fir-an/ (inherited MCA item) with consonant alternation (6.5). These data only make sense if we conclude that even without reference to borrowings, MCA speakers are subconsciously aware of two conflicting "analyses" of the data, each of which is consistent with a selection of the facts but neither of which accounts for everything. In connection with borrowings, the two conflicting analyses turn into two conflicting adaptation routines (and perhaps more generally into two conflicting developmental tendencies).

(b) Conflicting adaptation principles

Conflicting adaptation processes applied to borrowings from L_2 may apply even when L_1 is internally consistent and harmonious. This is because a satisfactory structural analysis of L_1 may operate at many levels — identification of phonemes, of allowable clusters, canonical-shape restrictions at word level or involving sequences of two or three syllables, etc.

In the case of MCA, problems arise in assimilating European items because we have, on the one hand, segment-to-segment correspondences (Haugen's diaphones), and on the other hand canonical shape and sequencing restrictions on MCA stems. Thus MCA verb roots originally had to be in one of a small number of possible shapes, basically strong verbs with three or four root consonants and no full vowels, along with certain types of hollow or weak verbs with one or rarely two (nonadjacent) vowels filling a consonantal slot (3.4, 3.6). There are also various restrictions on sequencing the root consonants, and phonological implications involving pharyngealization (3.1). MCA nouns also show canonical shape patterns, but they are less rigid and are more liberal in allowing full vowels.

In borrowing Fr and Sp verbs, some fluctuation arises because we can either transpose the Fr/Sp stem into MCA by segmental conversions, resulting in long stem shapes like /CVCCVC-/ with full vowels (not permitted in traditional MCA), or we can squash the Fr/Sp stem into an MCA-type canonical shape, throwing out vowels and perhaps a consonant or two. The first pattern is now preferred, especially by bilinguals, but the earlier stratum of Fr borrowings favours squashing, e.g. /ẓṛṭ/ or /ẓṛṭa/ B-183 "he deserted" (Fr *déserter*), and there are also intermediate forms (6.14-15). Concerning syllable-to-syllable implications involving pharyngealization, see also 6.1-2.

The same conflict between segmental and canonical shape adaptation processes applies to CA borrowings. In the case of verbs, the vowels in the CA form (e.g. perfective /katab-/, imperfective /-ktub-/ "to write") are thrown out of the borrowed form, which acquires the MCA pattern (simple triliteral /CCəC/, for example); however, CA nouns with the same vowels come into MCA with full vowels under most conditions (Chapter 5). Whereas in borrowing European verbs, MCA has gradually shifted from canonical shape to segmental adaptation, with CA verbs the canonical shape adaptations are still dominant.

In general, nominal borrowings are handled by segmental conversions with some readjustments in connection with pharyngealization; this applies both to European and CA loans. As a result, we must recognize very different adaptation strategies for borrowings depending on their word-class affiliations. It is necessary to recognize contextually variable weightings of segmental and canonical adaptation processes, along with occasional compromise forms. Thus even a full structural analysis of L_1 and L_2 does not permit us to predict the detailed treatment of borrowings, since there may be several distinct but interacting levels of structure, each pointing toward a different type of adaptation strategy.

(c) Psycholinguistic adaptation routines

It is important to understand that ongoing borrowing (and code-switching, for that matter) is not regulated directly by abstract structural comparisons between the languages in contact. Not only do bilingual speakers have a knowledge of the languages (say, MCA, CA, and Fr), they are also well aware of standardized conversion routines for going from one to another. These routines are based on the analogy of many borrowings which have come in earlier and become at least partly established in MCA, but which are still recognizably derived from the foreign source. In addition, they observe other speakers using these routines for what are obviously on-the-spot "adaptations" of foreign items (perhaps including comical mixings) rather than stabilized borrowings.

For example, CA affricate /ǰ/ comes into MCA as /ž/, on the analogy of many MCA/CA doublets with /ž/ corresponding to /ǰ/, representing both inherited vocabulary and earlier borrowings. On the other hand, the occasional recent borrowing involving English /ǰ/ shows /dž/ in MCA, as in /džin/ C-179 "(pair of) jeans" (Eng via Fr). In morphology, new verb borrowings from Fr regularly take the weak stem form, with final vowel /a/ or /i/ depending on inflectional category. This is now a standardized borrowing routine, though in the first decades of intensive French penetration in Morocco there was no clearcut preference for weak stems; some older strong-verb borrowings are still present as an archaic stratum, e.g. /ẓṛṭ/ variant of B-183 "to desert" (Fr *déserter*), and some Jewish dialects now spoken outside of Morocco retain strong forms like /ḍiṛãž/ instead of the now more regular /ḍiṛãža/ B-44 "to disturb" (Fr *déranger*), see 6.14.

Other examples of evolving adaptation routines have already been mentioned above (this section) under the headings "structural ambiguity" and "conflicting adaptation principles". Some of the most convincing evidence for the importance of these routines as intervening factors between the structures of L_1 and source languages shows up in connection with "false borrowing routines"(below).

(d) False borrowing routines

In the examples just given, say of CA /ǰ/ being borrowed as MCA /ž/ because of analogy to many preexisting MCA/CA doublets, we have what might be called a "true" borrowing routine.

On the other hand, we have also seen cases in the present study of a "false" borrowing routine, where the analogically basic L_1/L_2 doublets are in reality cases where L_1 originally borrowed items from another language L_3 which may be no longer known to present-day speakers (or to speakers in regions never affected directly by L_3).

One example is of the type MCA /ḅal-a/ C-40 "shovel" and Fr *pelle*, where the original borrowing was from Sp *pala*. On the basis of a number of examples of this type, Fr/MCA bilinguals appear to have identified FSg suffix /-a/ as characteristically added to Fr nominal borrowings, especially if the Fr noun is grammatically feminine, so that /-a/ has been added gratuitously to some more recent Fr borrowings (including some masculines), see 6.25.

We have just mentioned that, over a few decades, a routine developed for incorporating Fr verbal borrowings as MCA weak verbs. This pattern has now been extended to recent Eng verbal borrowings for which mediation via Fr is often unlikely (6.16, see also end of 7.15 for more examples). Since Eng verbs commonly end in consonants (including diphthongs), and since most of the salient Eng verbal suffixes do not involve full vowels (*-ed*, *-s*), it is doubtful whether Eng verbs would have been borrowed as weak forms, e.g. /spika/ "he spoke" B-144 were it not for this "false" routine initially designed for Fr verbs (which do have several important vocalic suffixes).

These examples, among other things, attest to the importance of psycholinguistic routines in general (see above). At the same time, it is worth recalling that routines which may apply interchangeably to Eng, Fr, and Sp borrowings are not extended to CA, nor vice versa. Both because of its status as diglossic superordinate and because of its general structural similarities to MCA, CA provides a reservoir of potential on-the-spot borrowings which can be readily assimilated by simple conversions which are backed up by analogy to many existing MCA/CA doublets, the only real mechanical problems occurring in connection with highly marked verbal "conjugations" (5.8). On the other hand, the primary European languages involved in Morocco (Fr, Sp, Eng) are somewhat difficult to sort out because of the many Fr/Sp cognates and because some Eng borrowings (e.g. in the drug subculture) are either filtered through Fr or at least have Fr counterparts. So it is more reasonable to apply routines based on Fr borrowings to new Eng borrowings than it is to extend these routines to CA.

(e) Unexplained residual fluctuation

For most of the complexities alluded to so far in this section, we can basically understand what has been going on, though we might not have predicted it. On the other hand, it does appear that there is a residual amount of oscillation in forms, or even stabilization of unexpected borrowed forms, which cannot easily be accounted for by invoking L_1 or L_2 structural patterns, conversion routines, or hidden substratum (L_3) influences.

Perhaps the best example of this is the data on segmental conversions involving nasals and liquids in Fr and Sp borrowings into MCA (6.5). Since the MCA set of basic phonemes /m n l r ṛ/ includes several which match Fr and Sp consonants, and since even Fr uvular *r* ("grasséyé") is clearly associated with MCA /r ṛ/, it is surprising to find an appreciable number of variants or even stabilized forms of borrowings showing unexpected switches among these nasals and liquids, e.g. /ṭiṇifizyu/ variant of C-724 "television" (full list in 6.5). Some such switches may reflect co-occurrence patterns of nasals and liquids in MCA roots, but in the C-724 variant and several others there is no such explanation available.

Without reproducing here a large block of data, we may simply remark that in many sections of Chapter 6 in particular, we found two or more alternatives for a segmental conversion, presence of FSg /-a/, or some other matter. There is reason to believe that in many instances a variant or stable form of a Fr or Sp borrowing has been affected by groping attempts at pronunciation by Moroccans with little command of the European language, which not only involve regular adaptation routines but also involve transmission distortion. The position expressed in the earlier literature on mixing that borrowing is a smooth process of gradual adaptation of elements beginning as code-switches in bilingual speech, then being partially adapted to L_1 norms by these bilinguals, before finally being fully adapted by monolingual L_1 speakers, would not lead us to expect the degree of structurally unmotivated deviation from expected outputs which we have seen.

The general conclusion is that borrowing in this type of post-colonial context is quite complex, involving the gradual stabilization of conversion routines used by bilinguals, but also an appreciable amount of variation and unpredictability due to differences in chronological strata, conflicting structural principles, substratum interference, and transmission distortion. This is over and above the variation in degree of adaptation of a given form, which was clearly recognized by Haugen and Weinreich.

11 Reflections II: Pidgins/creoles vs. "ordinary" language mixing

11.1 Identifying parallels

The question of comparability of results from pidgin/creole studies to studies of "ordinary" language contact has been raised by a number of earlier publications, but has hardly been resolved. Unfortunately, most pidgin/creole specialists have their hands full keeping up with studies within this subfield and do not have extensive experience with other forms of language mixing, while specialists in "ordinary" mixing (European contact zones, American immigrant languages or European Gastarbeiter languages, American Indian acculturation studies, etc.) tend not to have much exposure to pidgins and creoles. Nor is it particularly easy to find the information one needs for synthesizing purposes in libraries; for example, there are hardly any decent monographs on mixing involving small neighbouring tribal groups, and the situation is not much better concerning (post-)colonial contact zones (which is, of course, why the present case study was undertaken). The situation is not helped by the widely publicized disagreements among pidgin/creole specialists as to the basic dynamics of these speech varieties, nor by less visible but none the less present diagreements among students of "ordinary" language contact as to the nature of code-switching and borrowing. I will therefore confine my attention here to considering some relatively uncontroversial aspects of pidgin/creole research on the one hand, and the present case study of language contact on the other.

At first sight, the Moroccan data do not suggest promising parallels with pidgins or creoles. Although a "foreigner talk" register used by domestics with European employers has been identified and briefly exemplified here (8.2), this register represents only a limited formal simplification of MCA and in any event has probably played only a modest role in the adoption of Fr items into MCA over several decades and is no longer widespread. Moreover, the Fr and Sp borrowings we have examined show extensive integration in most instances into the MCA morphological system – borrowed nouns have definite prefixes, suffixal or ablaut plurals, ablaut diminutives etc., while borrowed verbs have full inflectional paradigms and often form derivatives such as verbal nouns and participles. A stronger case for a parallel with pidgins and creoles could be made if borrowed nouns and verbs were resistant to L_1 (borrowing language) morphology. Instances of such resistance can indeed be found, as in many instances where L1, instead of directly borrowing inflectable verb stems from L_2, borrows a single L2 form (either an unmarked verb form, or a derivative such as a verbal noun) and inflects it indirectly by juxtaposing a native L_1 verb ("to do", "to be", "to make") which thus functions as a kind of auxiliary – Turkish borrowings from Arabic like *teşekkur etmek* "to thank" (Arabic verbal noun plus Turkish *etmek* "to make"), for example.

While European borrowings into MCA scarcely have an overall pidgin- or creole-like status in the sense of avoiding complex inflectional and derivational structures, we have none the less identified a functional stratum of the borrowings which do have pidgin-like characteristics (6.31). These are items showing varying degrees of phonological integration (and varying degrees of usage frequency), but little or no morphological adaptation even when they belong to functional word-class types which typically do have morphological structure in MCA (and often in the source language as well). For example, there are adjectives like /frišk/ C-233 "fresh", /kaḷm/ C-310 "calm", and /himri/ C-290 "hungry" which are not compatible with FSg /-a/ or pluralizers for some or all dialects. Of these, /himri/ is an example displaying fluctuating word-class status in its MCA form (adjective "hungry" or noun "hunger"), a frequent pattern in pidgins but not typical of MCA and not present in the source form (Sp *hambre*).

In addition to a number of (usually) adjectival or adverbial cases like these, we also mention in 6.31 that some borrowed nouns resist taking definite prefix /l-/ or the relevant allomorph even while taking case prefixes (prepositions) and permitting a plural suffix if semantically reasonable.

The resistance of adjectives and perhaps adverbs to normal L_1 morphology (e.g. gender and plural marking) is apparently widespread. In the case of English-influenced Spanish in the United States, it is sometimes stated that English adjectives are not borrowed (Sobin 1982:168 on Texas), but it would seem that this means that functionally borrowed Eng adjectives simply are not adapted morphologically and so are formally not very distinct from code-switches (Pfaff 1979:305).

It would seem, then, that even in intensive contact zones where productive adaptation routines (including integration of borrowed verbs into inflectional paradigms) are developed, there may be a set of borrowings (mainly adjectival and adverbial, perhaps nouns, and in some languages "verbs" which require a juxtaposed auxiliary) which show some features of pidgins: avoidance of inflection and derivation, partially unstable word-class status (hence variable syntactic usage), and perhaps some fluctuation in pronunciation in early stages.

11.2 Chronological development

It is also advisable to consider whether we have (in the Moroccan data) any parallels to the typical developmental cycle linking pidgins with creoles, perhaps through a complex set of intergrading stages (jargon, pidgin, stabilized pidgin, creole, decreolizing creole continuum).

Indeed, there are some possible analogies. In the present case study, we have been concerned (among other things) with the historical dimension, and have taken advantage of the existence of relevant publications going back to early in this century to document changes in adaptation processes applied to borrowings. We have been able to show, for example, that borrowings from Fr into MCA during the early part of the Protectorate period differed from newer borrowings not only in number but also to some degree in type. For example, the earlier stratum of borrowings permitted few inflectable verb roots from Fr (and those which were brought in showed MCA-like canonical shapes, requiring severe formal squashing in some instances). The early loans also appear to have been pronounced with traditional MCA phonemes.

As time has gone on, adaptation routines have developed permitting the introduction of a much larger number of borrowings. Canonical shape restrictions on stems have been gradually relaxed, so that even Fr verbs like *utiliser* "to use" with radically non-MCA-like stem shape can be instantly provided with MCA inflectional frames (6.14). At the same time, non-MCA phonemes like nasalized vowels and front rounded vowels which formerly would have been converted into MCA phonemes are often retained unchanged in the more recent strata, and show signs of stabilizing in these forms to some extent.

Without trying to reproduce all of our data on these points, we should emphasize strongly that patterns of borrowing (and code-switching) in Morocco have experienced a developmental cycle over time. Just as jargons and early pidgins are typically used by persons not accustomed to them and who therefore must grope and fumble their way through interactions using them, there must have been generations of Moroccans who had to fumble with Fr borrowings in their MCA, not having fixed community-wide forms to be learned and not even having an extensive set of earlier Fr borrowings from which standardized conversion routines could be extrapolated (to a degree, uneducated rural Moroccans even now may be not very far removed from this stage). For later generations, the adaptation routines had already been settled to some extent by their predecessors, and one can speak at least loosely of a more stable "grammar" for borrowings.

This line of thought suggests a connection with the development of unstable jargons and pidgins into stabilized pidgins and then creoles. However, the analogy is far from perfect. In the early days of French influence in Morocco, while native Moroccans may have had to fumble when speaking Fr to the colonists, the Fr items which found their way into MCA (as used among natives) were relatively few in number and (especially for verbs) required extensive formal modification. As time has gone on, while productive conversion routines have been developed for new borrowings, these routines have incorporated an appreciable relaxation of the originally tight phonological and morphological structure of MCA, permitting new sounds and canonical shapes while maintaining the inflectional apparatus. Because of the continued direct influence of Fr during the entire Protectorate and Independence periods, the frequent reborrowing of the same Fr item in successive waves (each new form being closer to the Fr model), and the development of more productive code-switching patterns, the historical developments in Morocco have something of the character of post-creole continua (DeCamp 1971, Bickerton 1975), in which a formerly distinctive creole is gradually being brought back closer to the (usually European) lexifier language.

Clearly, a specific analogy between the Moroccan system and any particular segment of the pidgin/creole developmental cycle is going to be problematic. Nevertheless, a loose comparison would not be amiss, and makes us remember that language dynamics in colonial societies reflect systems of social relations not entirely unlike those found in some pidgin/creole zones, particularly some of the Pacific ones where demographic disruptions were less abrupt and drastic than in the Caribbean. Above all, it is essential to make the basic point that systems for handling borrowed (and code-switched) material do change over time, even though at any given moment a wide range of individual variation exists.

There is another respect in which the Moroccan material converges with pidgin/creole studies, to which we now turn.

11.3 Multiple lexifier languages

When we think of language contact and resultant mixing, we are usually thinking of interactions between two languages, L_1 and L_2. Such one-on-one cases are not only the bread and butter of immigrant, migrant, and acculturating indigenous sociolinguistic studies, but are also typical of the many small and large case studies of borrowing and interference carried out in the European context.

A wider perspective is obtained by studies in "areal linguistics", which present geographical distributions of selected diagnostic features over large areas. The classic case is the Balkans (Sandfeld 1930, Schaller 1975, Petrovici 1957), where daughter languages representing highly divergent Indo-European stocks (Romance, Slavic, Greek, Albanian) have been in contact for centuries. Among other more recent studies dealing with larger blocks of languages, we may mention Masica (1976) for South Asia and Sherzer (1976) for North American Indians.

However, areal linguistics does not necessarily require revisions in the basic one-on-one model. Given a configuration of, say, fifty languages in a geographically bounded territory, the actual dynamics of borrowing and interference might well be broken down into a large number of dyadic, one-on-one contacts. Over a very long period, a degree of typological uniformity and of lexical sharing could emerge even from initially unrelated languages in roughly the same way that gene flow operates in large biological populations. In general, the literature on the Balkans is compatible with one-on-one interference analyses, while the other larger-scale areal studies have eschewed or deferred consideration of the mixing dynamics which have produced the attested distributions.

One useful function of the present volume might be to emphasize that a language L_1 may be subject to influence from several other languages L_2, L_3, L_4, etc., either simultaneously or sequentially. Moreover, L_1 may be subject to quite different influences in different sectors of its territory. These facts do not require adjustments in the one-on-one model if the borrowings and other forms of interference from the several foreign languages are mechanically independent; we will then see L_1 evolving from its primitive state to a new form in which L_2, L_3, and L_4 elements (lexicon, perhaps some typological features) are present.

In possible contrast to this additive model, we can visualize an interactive model, in which the borrowings and other interference from L_2, L_3, and L_4 have been difficult to dissociate from each other. In the present volume, for the most part the influence of the diglossic superordinate CA has been independent of the influence of the European languages. In a few cases ("bank" C-48, "doctor" C-188) there may have been some joint influence of CA and European languages on an MCA borrowing, but in general this has been rare, due largely to the fact that official CA has been controlled by linguistic purists who have avoided extensive adoption of "international" vocabulary of European (including Latin/Greek) origin, with exceptions in scientific language which are of little concern to the average Moroccan.

On the other hand, we have emphasized that the various European languages have interacted in complex ways in Morocco. We have seen that a number of individual borrowings are hybrids, often involving an original borrowing from Sp (or It) and subsequent partial contamination from Fr (6.29), and that in addition to this some conversion routines applied to Fr items are based on analogies to earlier borrowings from Sp which have Fr cognates and have been secondarily associated by MCA/Fr bilinguals with Fr (e.g. gender marking in 6.25).

Similarly, pidgin/creole studies have now indicated that some attested varieties may have involved the gradual replacement of one lexifier language L_1 by a second lexifier language L_2. In particular instances this historical interpretation is a matter of debate, as in the continuing discussion of "monogenesis" theories which claim that a large number of pidgins/creoles all originated in a single Mediterranean form, perhaps based on Portuguese (e.g. Whinnom 1965). However, a careful and well-documented study of New Guinea Pidgin (Mühlhäusler 1979) has concluded that "the number of lexical items which can be derived equally well from German or English is quite large, and it can be assumed that many of them are the result of conflation..." (p.219). A variety of other types of conflations are discussed in the same volume (e.g. two distinct but phonologically similar Eng words, or an Eng word and a fortuitously similar item from native Melanesian languages).

In the case of Ger and Eng interaction in New Guinea Pidgin, the precise etymology may be indeterminate unless the historical documentation (giving time and location of establishment of the NGP item) is unusually clearcut. This is because the examples chiefly involve noun stems (e.g. *garden* and *Garten*) in the lexifier languages, and because the form borrowed will in either case be a morphologically simple stem. In the Moroccan case, the phonological and morphological differences between Fr and Sp (and between Fr and Eng) are sufficient to make it possible, at least in many instances, to distinguish borrowed reflexes from the several source languages and even to identify contaminated (hybrid) variants.

Mühlhäusler expresses the hope "that a theoretical concept of 'mixture of linguistic systems' will eventually form part of a theory of pidgins and pidginisation" (1979:23fn.). Improved sharing of results between pidgin/creole specialists and those working on "ordinary" (but none the less very intensive) language contact would indeed be mutually beneficial. At the same time, we must not underestimate the complexity of language mixing even in a single contact zone, and I suspect that readers who have made it through to the end of this volume will be inclined to agree.

Appendix A: CA borrowings in MCA

This appendix has the modest aim of giving representative examples of clear or probable CA borrowings into MCA. It is not exhaustive and is based on a specific textual corpus with some supplementary elicitation to get examples of particular structural types. Some items are used only occasionally, by educated speakers.

CA borrowings usually come in as complete stems. Plurals are usually borrowed separately rather than internally generated; participles and verbal nouns are likewise usually borrowed directly. Regular MCA inflectional frames are provided, but at the level of stems we basically have one-to-one CA-to-MCA borrowings. For this reason, our entries do not group distinct stems from the same root together; plurals, participles, etc. are listed as separate items.

The appendix has three sections: A-1 has nouns and adjectives including verbal nouns and specialized participles; A-2 has verbs; A-3 is miscellaneous, including particles, prepositions, and fixed expressions. Subsections within each section are based primarily on canonical shape (of the CA prototype) and/or morphological type.

Glosses given are for MCA. It can usually be assumed that the CA prototype has the same or similar meaning. Some MCA glosses may be based on the particular contextual usage of the attestation and may not be generally valid. Since our main concern here is phonological and morphological, such glossing discrepancies may be disregarded.

1 Nouns and adjectives

	CVCVC- (singular)	
A-1-1	/taman/ "price"	CA *θaman-*
A-1-2	/walad/ "boy" (less common than /wld/)	CA *walad-*
A-1-3	/ᶜamal/ "work, labour"	CA *ᶜamal-*
A-1-4	/ᶜadad/ "number (quantity)"	CA *ᶜadad-*
A-1-5	/sabab/ "reason"	CA *sabab-*
A-1-6	/ᶜalam/ "flag"	CA *ᶜalam-*
	(for MCA homonym see A-1-97 below)	
A-1-7	/baṭal/ "hero"	CA *baṭal-*

CVCVC- (plural)

A-1-8 /fiṛaq/ "teams" CA *firaq-*
A-1-9 /xuḍaṛ/ "vegetables" CA *xuḍar-*
A-1-10 /ᶜuṭal/ "vacations" CA *ᶜuṭal-*
A-1-11 /šuᶜab/ "fields (of study)" CA *šuᶜab-*
A-1-12 /duwal/ "countries" CA *duwal-*
A-1-13 /ṣuwaṛ/ "chapters (of Koran)" CA *suwar-*
A-1-14 /nuqaṭ/ "points (of view)" CA *nuqaṭ-*
A-1-15 /mudun/ "cities" CA *mudun-*
A-1-16 /žuẓuṛ/ "islands" CA *ǰuzur-*
A-1-17 /ṭuṛuq/ "ways, methods" CA *ṭuruq-*

CVCVC-a(t-) (feminine singular)

A-1-18 /kalim-a/ "word (alongside /klm-a/) CA *kalim-a*
A-1-19 /daṛaž-a/ or /ḍaṛaž-a/ "step, degree" CA *daraǰ-a*
A-1-20 /ḥaṛak-a/ or /ḥ̣aṛak-a/ "movement" CA *ḥarak-a*
A-1-21 /baṛak-a/ "blessing" CA *barak-a*

CVCVC-a(t-) (plural)

A-1-22 /ṭalab-a/ "students" CA *ṭalab-a*

CaCaC-iyy- (adjective)

A-1-23 /madan-i/ "civil" CA *madan-iyy-*
A-1-24 /nabaw-i/ "of the Prophet" CA *nabaw-iyy-*
A-1-25 /žabal-i/ "of the mountains" CA *ǰabal-iyy-*
A-1-26 /waṭan-i/ "national" CA *waṭan-iyy-*
A-1-27 /malak-i/ "royal" CA *malak-iyy-*
A-1-28 /badaw-i/ "rural, bedouin" CA *badaw-iyy-*

CVCV̄C- (singular)

A-1-29 /ṣiyam/ "fasting" (vbl. noun) CA *ṣiyām-*
A-1-30 /niḍam/ "organization" CA *nið̣ām-*
A-1-31 /munax/ "climate" CA *munāx-*
A-1-32 /mudir/ "director" (participle) CA *mudīr-*
A-1-33 /mufid/ "useful" (participle) CA *mufīd-*
A-1-34 /šita?/ "winter" CA *šitā?-*
(Used in MCA only occasionally, in sense "winter" only; normally both "winter" and "rain" are /šta/.)
A-1-35 /hawa/ "breeze" CA *hawā?-*
A-1-36 /qiṭaṛ/ "train" (cf. C-487) CA *qiṭār-*
A-1-37 /kalam/ "speech, words" CA *kalām-*
(Less common than /klam/.)
A-1-38 /ḥaṛam/ "forbidden (in Islam)" CA *ḥarām-*
(Less common than /ḥṛam/.)
A-1-39 /šamal/ "north" CA *šamāl-*
(Inherited /šmal/ means "left side".)
A-1-40 /žawaž/ "marriage" CA *zawāǰ-*
(Considerably less common than /žwaž/, with both sibilants palatal, and its variants.)
A-1-41 /ᶜaša/ "evening meal" CA *ᶜašā?-*
(Not common; used occasionally to redifferentiate MCA /ᶜša/ "evening meal, evening prayer", which reflects merger of CA *ᶜašā?-* and *ᶜišā?-*.)

A-1-42 /žanub/ "south" CA *ǰanūb-*
A-1-43 /žalid/ "ice" CA *ǰalīd-*
A-1-44 /žami^c/ "entirety, all"(alongside/žmi^c/) CA *ǰamī^c-*
A-1-45 /ṣaḍiq/ "friend" CA *ṣadīq-*
A-1-46 /kabir/ "big" CA *kabīr-*
(Much more commonly /kbir/; similar occasional restoration of *a* with other *CaCīC-* adjectives, especially those associated with literary or religious style.)
A-1-47 /muyul/ "inclination" (vbl. noun) CA *muyūl-*
A-1-48 /ḥuḍuṛ/ "attendance" (vbl. noun) CA *ḥuḍūr-*
(alongside /ḥḍuṛ/)

CVCV̄C- (plural)
A-1-49 /ḥuṛuf/ "letters (of alphabet)" CA *ḥurūf-*
(/ḥṛuf/ also attested but appears to be less common)
A-1-50 /^{c}ulum/ "sciences" CA *^{c}ulūm-*
A-1-51 /wuḥuš/ "wild animals"(/wḥuš/also found) CA *wuḥūš-*
A-1-52 /tuluž/ "snows" CA *θulūǰ-*
A-1-53 /ḍuṛuf/ "conditions" (alongside /ḍṛuf/) CA *ð̣urūf-*
A-1-54 /fuṛu^c/ "branches" CA *furū^c-*
A-1-55 /duṛuṣ/ or /duruṣ/ "studies" CA *durūs-*
A-1-56 /sinin/ "years" CA *sin-īn*
(Infrequent variant of /snin/; CA form contains oblique case plural suffix *-īn-*, but the morpheme boundary after *sin-* is probably opaque because of the unusual root shape and the infrequency of the nominative counterpart.)
A-1-57 /ližan/ "councils" CA *liǰān-*

CVCV̄C-a(t-) (feminine singular)
A-1-58 /madin-a/ "city" CA *madīn-a*
(infrequent variant of /mdin-a/)
A-1-59 /ṭaṛiq-a/ "method" CA *ṭarīq-a*
A-1-60 /waḍif-a/ "position (employment)" CA *wað̣īf-a*
A-1-61 /ṭabi^c-a/ "nature" CA *ṭabī^c-a*
A-1-62 /ḥadiq-a/ "garden" CA *ḥadīq-a*
A-1-63 /qaḍyy-a/ "case, situation" CA *qaḍiyy-a*
(Also /qḍyy-a/; in either case the /yy/ is indistinguishable from /iy/, and CA *iyy* is indistinguishable here from *īy*.)
A-1-64 /ḍaḥyy-a/ "victim" CA *ḍaḥiyy-a*
(For transcriptions see comments for preceding entry; CA *ḍaḥiyy-a* is also the etymon for inherited MCA /ḍḥyy-a/ "sacrificial lamb"; compare A-1-114.)
A-1-65 /sa^{c}ad-a/ "happiness" CA *sa^{c}ād-a*
A-1-66 /šahad-a/ "primary school diploma" CA *šahād-a* (general meaning: "attestation")
A-1-67 /ḥaṛaṛ-a/ "heat" CA *ḥarār-a*
(Competes with /sxun-iy-a/ and other lexical items.)
A-1-68 /ḥaḍaṛ-a/ "civilization" CA *ḥaḍār-a*
A-1-69 /baṣaṭ-a/ or /basaṭ-a/ "simplicity" CA *basāṭ-a*
A-1-70 /taqaf-a/ "culture" CA *θaqāf-a*
A-1-71 /siyas-a/ "politics" CA *siyās-a*
A-1-72 /ḥiṛas-a/ "defence (e.g. in sports)" CA *ḥirās-a* (lit. "guarding, watching")

A-1-73 /filaḥ-a/ "agriculture" CA *filāḥ-a*
A-1-74 /tižaṛ-a/ "commerce" CA *tiǰār-a*
A-1-75 /ḍiṛaṣ-a/ or /diras-a/ "studying" CA *diṛāṣ-a*
A-1-76 /ṣinaᶜ-a/ "trade, industry" CA *ṣināᶜ-a*
A-1-77 /wizaṛ-a/ "(government) ministry" CA *wizār-a*
A-1-78 /siyaḥ-a/ "tourism" CA *siyāḥ-a*
A-1-79 /nihay-a/ "end, conclusion" CA *nihāy-a*
A-1-80 /biday-a/ "beginning" CA *bidāy-a*
A-1-81 /tilaw-a/ "textbook" CA *tilāw-a*
(also used in slang as collective: "girls, chicks") "reading,recital"
A-1-82 /diᶜay-a/ "publicity, propaganda" CA *diᶜāy-a*
A-1-83 /ᶜibad-a/ "worship" CA *ᶜibād-a*
A-1-84 /wilay-a/ "state", in expression CA *wilāy-a*
/l-wilay-at l-muttaḥid-a/ "the United States"
A-1-85 /ziyaṛ-a/ "journey, visit" CA *ziyār-a*
A-1-86 /kitab-a/ "(hand-)writing" CA *kitāb-a*
A-1-87 /qiṛa?-a/ "(level of) study" CA *qirā?-a*
(Compare the much more common /qṛay-a/ "studying".)
A-1-88 /qiyad-a/ "directorship" CA *qiyād-a*
A-1-89 /ṛiyaḍ-a/ "sports" CA *riyāḍ-a*
A-1-90 /ḥukum-a/ "government" CA *ḥukūm-a*
A-1-91 /xuṭub-a/ "(marital) engagement" CA *xuṭūb-a*
(alongside /xṭub-a/)
A-1-92 /buṭul-a/ "championship" CA *buṭūl-a*
(same root as A-1-7)
A-1-93 /suhul-a/ "ease" in /b-suhul-a/ "with ease" CA *suhūl-a*

CVCV̄C-iyy- (adjective)

A-1-94 /ḍaṛuṛ-i/ "necessary" CA *ḍarūr-iyy-*
A-1-95 /taqaf-i/ "cultural" (for base cf.A-1-70) CA *θaqāf-iyy-*
A-1-96 /ṛiyaḍ-i/ "athletic, sporting" (cf.A-1-89) CA *riyāḍ-iyy-*

CV̄CVC- (singular)

A-1-97 /ᶜalam/ "world" (for MCA homonym see A-1-6) CA *ᶜālam-*
A-1-98 /nadi/ "club, association" CA *nādi-*
(structurally *CāCiy-* in CA)
A-1-99 /talit/ "third (ordinal numeral)" CA *θāliθ-*
(Similarly for other *CāCiC-* ordinals in CA, mostly reclassicizations of earlier MCA /CaCC/ forms.)
A-1-100 /ḥaris/ "goalkeeper (in soccer etc.)" CA *ḥāris-*
(formally a participle)
A-1-101 /qa?id/ "leader" CA *qā?id-*
(Also inherited /qayd/; another participle formally.)
A-1-102 /na?ib/ "representative, delegate" CA *nā?ib-*
(another participle)
A-1-103 /katib/ "writer", also used as adjective in /?āl-a kātib-a/ "typewriter" (lit. "writing machine") CA *kātib-* (participle)
A-1-104 /walid/ "(biological) father" CA *wālid* (participle)
A-1-105 /mahid/ "pioneer" (e.g. rank in boy scouts), usually in plural /l-mahid-un/ "the pioneer scouts", with otherwise rare use of CA plural suffix seen in CA *māhid-*, pl.*māhid-ūn-*.
A-1-106 /daxil/ "interior, inside" (noun or adj.) CA *dāxil*
A-1-107 /xariž/ "exterior, outside" CA *xāriǰ*

A-1-108 /ᶜamm/ "general (not specific)" CA *ᶜāmm-*
(from underlying *ᶜāmim-*)

CV̄CVC-a(t-) (feminine singular)

A-1-109 /ᶜaʔil-a/ "family" CA *ᶜāʔil-a*
A-1-110 /žaʔiz-a/ "prize" CA *ǰāʔiz-a*
(occasionally /žayz-a/)
A-1-111 /madd-a/ "material" (noun) CA *mādd-a*
(from underlying *mādid-a*)
A-1-112 /žamiᶜ-a/ "university" CA *ǰāmiᶜ-a*
A-1-113 /naḥy-a/ "environment" CA *nāḥiy-a*
(more common in pl. form *nawaḥi*, see A-1-128)
A-1-114 /ḍaḥy-a/ "vicinity" CA *ḍāḥiy-a*
(more common in pl. *ḍawaḥi*, see comment on preceding entry; contrast with phonological form seen in A-1-64)
A-1-115 /dariž-a/ "vernacular, colloquial (Arabic)" (usually a noun with "Arabic" understood as referent)
CA *(ᶜarab-iy-a) dāriǰ-a*
A-1-116 /walid-a/ "(biological) mother" CA *wālid-a*
(feminine of A-1-104)

CV̄CVC-iyy- (adjective)

A-1-117 /madd-i/ "material" (cf. A-1-111) CA *mādd-iyy-*
A-1-118 /tanaw-i/ "secondary (school, etc.) CA *θānaw-iyy-*
A-1-119 /xariž-i/ "exterior, external" (cf.107) CA *xāriǰ-iyy-*
A-1-120 /ᶜaʔil-i/ "family", as in
/smiy-a ᶜaʔil-iy-a/ "family name" CA *ᶜāʔil-iyy-*

CV̄CV̄C- (singular)

A-1-121 /qanun/ "(the) law, legal system" CA *qānūn-*
A-1-122 /midan/ "(playing) field" CA *mīdān-*
A-1-123 /taṛix/ "history" CA *taʔrīx-* or *tārīx-*

CVCVCV̄C- (singular)

A-1-124 /ṛamaḍan/ "Ramadan (Muslim holy month)" CA *ramaḍān*
(optional reclassicization of /ṛmḍan/)

CVCCV̄CVC- (singular)

A-1-125 /baṛnamaž/ "(broadcast) programme" CA *barnāmaǰ-*
(also pronounced /bṛnamaž/)

CaCāCā (plural)

A-1-126 /qaḍaya/ "cases" (pl. of A-1-63) CA *qaḍāyā*
A-1-127 /ḍaḥaya/ "victims" (pl. of A-1-64) CA *ḍaḥāyā*

CawāCiC- (plural)

A-1-128 /nawaḥi/ "environment, surroundings" CA *nawāḥi-*
(from underlying *nawaḥiy-*) (pl. of A-1-113)
A-1-129 /fawakih/ "fruit (collective)" CA *fawākih-*
A-1-130 /mawadd/ "materials, subjects" CA *mawādd-*
(underlying *mawādid-*) (pl. of A-1-111)
A-1-131 /žawaʔiz/ "prizes" (pl. of A-1-110) CA *ǰawāʔiz-*
A-1-132 /sawaḥil/ "coasts" (also /swaḥl/) CA *sawāḥil-*
A-1-133 /šawariᶜ/ "streets" (occ. /swarᶜ/) CA *šawāriᶜ-*
A-1-134 /ḥawadit/ "(vehicular) accidents" CA *ḥawādiθ-*

CaCāCiC- (plural)

A-1-135 /baṛamiž/ "programmes" (pl. of A-1-125) CA *barāmiǰ-*
A-1-136 /?amakin/ "locations" CA *?amākin-*
A-1-137 /hayakil/ "frameworks, components" CA *hayākil-*
A-1-138 /?ažanib/ "foreigners" CA *?aǰānib-*
A-1-139 /salasil/ "chains (of mountains)" CA *salāsil-*
A-1-140 /ᶜanaṣiṛ/ "elements" CA *ᶜanāṣir-*

CaCāCiC-a(t-) (plural)

A-1-141 /?asatid-a/ "teachers" CA *?asātið-a*

CawāCīC- (plural)

A-1-142 /qawanin/ "laws, canons" (pl. of A-1-121) CA *qawānīn-*

CaCāCīC- (plural)

A-1-143 /talamid/ "pupils" CA *talāmīð-*
(reclassicization of /tlamd/)

maCāCiC- (plural of derived noun)

A-1-144 /maṛasim/ "rituals" CA *marāsim-*
A-1-145 /maᶜamil/ "factories" CA *maᶜāmil-*
A-1-146 /maṛatib/ "steps (taken), positions" CA *marātib-*
A-1-147 /mazariᶜ/ "farms" CA *mazāriᶜ-*
A-1-148 /makatib/ "offices" CA *makātib-*
A-1-149 /mašakil/ "problems" CA *mašākil-*
A-1-150 /masa?il/ "matters, questions" CA *masā?il-*
A-1-151 /madaris/ "schools" CA *madāris-*
(optional reclassicization of /mdars/, var. /mdaṛṣ/)
A-1-152 /mabadi?/ "principles" CA *mabādi?-*
A-1-153 /masažid/ "mosques" CA *masāǰid-*
(Optional reclassicization of /msažd/; there is also an uncommon intermediate form /msažid/ in my data.)
A-1-154 /manaṭiq/ "regions" CA *manāṭiq-*
A-1-155 /ma?atir/ "monuments, ruins" CA *ma?āθir-*
(CA form often means "feats, exploits" but other CA forms of this root mean "monuments".)
A-1-156 /mawani?/ "ports" CA *mawāni-*
(The historically false /?/ in the MCA form attested in my data is probably carried over from the sg. form /mina?/ from CA *mīnā?-*.)
A-1-157 /malaᶜib/ "playing fields" CA *malāᶜib-*

maCāCīC- (plural of derived noun)

A-1-158 /mawaḍiᶜ/ "topics" CA *mawāḍīᶜ-*

CaCā?iC- (plural)

A-1-159 /ḥada?iq/ "gardens" CA *ḥadā?iq-*

CVCCV̄ (singular)

A-1-160 /dikra/ "souvenir, commemoration" CA *ðikrā*
A-1-161 /fuṣḥa/ "classical (Arabic)" CA *fuṣḥā*

CVCCVy-āt- (plural)

A-1-162 /dikray-at/ "commemorations" (pl.of 160) CA *ðikray-āt-*

CVCCV̄C- (singular)

A-1-163 /žumhur/ or /žumhuṛ/ "crowd, audience" CA *ǰumhūr-*
A-1-164 /kuttab/ or /k^{w}ttab/ "school" CA *kuttāb-*
A-1-165 /tyyaṛ/ "(air) current" CA *tayyār-*

CVCCV̄C- (plural)

A-1-166 /b^{w}ldan/ "countries" CA *buldān-*
(reclassicization of /bldan/ "countries, cities")
A-1-167 /^{c}^{w}mmal/ "workers; governors" CA *^{c}ummāl-*

CuCayC-a(t-) (frozen dimunitive)

A-1-168 /buḥayr-a/ "lake" (cf. *baḥr-* "sea") CA *buḥayr-a*

?aCCāC- (plural)

A-1-169 /?a^{c}yad/ or /?^{c}yad/ "holidays,festivals" CA *?a^{c}yād-*
A-1-170 /?atman/ "prices" CA *?aθmān-*
A-1-171 /?anwa^{c}/ "types" CA *?anwā^{c}-*
A-1-172 /?afkaṛ/ "thoughts" CA *?afkār-*
A-1-173 /?aṛa?/ "views, opinions" CA *?ārā?-*
(underlying *?ar?ā?-*)
A-1-174 /?ataṛ/ "ruins, monuments" CA *?āθār-*
(In normal MCA pronunciation this pl. form is indistinguishable from its own sg., which reflects CA *?aθar-*; solutions to this problem include use of suffixal Pl form /?ataṛ-at/, use of synonym seen in A-1-155 especially in pl., or attempt to carry over CA vowel-length opposition into MCA.)
A-1-175 /?aflam/ "films, movies" CA *?aflām-*
(Of course this is ultimately a European loanword, but this pl. form is clearly from CA.)
A-1-176 /?ayyam/, /?yyam/ "days" CA *?ayyām-*
(An infrequent reclassicization; cf. older /yyam/ invariably used in construction with "short form" of numeral: /sb^{c} yyam/ "seven days", etc.)
A-1-177 /?aḥbab/ "loved ones, kin" CA *?aḥbāb-*
(infrequent reclassicization of /ḥbab/)
A-1-178 /?afrad/ "individuals" CA *?afrād-*
A-1-179 /?aṣḥab/ "friends" CA *?aṣḥāb-*
(Occasional reclassicization of /ṣḥab/, which becomes either /ṣ-ṣḥab/ or l-ṣḥab/ with def. prefix.)
A-1-180 /?al^{c}ab/ "games" CA *?al^{c}āb-*
A-1-181 /?abṭal/ "heroes" (pl. of A-1-7) CA *?abṭāl-*
A-1-182 /?ažwaq/ "(musical) bands" CA *?aǰwāq-*
(reclassicization of /žwaq/, def. prefix form /l-žwaq/)
A-1-183 /?asṛaṛ/ or /?asṛaṛ/ "secrets" CA *?asrār-*
(optional reclassicization of /sṛaṛ/, def. l-sṛaṛ/)
A-1-184 /?aqsam/ "divisions, grades" CA *?aqsām-*

CVC-a(t-) (feminine singular)

A-1-185 /san-a/ "year" CA *san-a*
(uncommon in sg., where /^{c}am/ is normal word in MCA; for pl. forms see next entry and A-1-56)

CVC-aw-āt- (irregular plural)

A-1-186 /san-aw-at/ "years" CA *san-aw-āt-* (pl. of preceding entry; for the more common form /snin/ and its reclassicized variants, see A-1-56)

ʔaCCaC- (comparative form of adjective)

A-1-187 /ʔaqll/ or ʔaqall/ "fewer, less", most common in expression /ᶜl l-ʔaqll/ "at least" and variants, CA *ʔaqall-* (with geminate metathesis). (Inherited /qll/ from same etymon used in time expressions, as in /l-xms-a qll qṣm/ "five minutes to five".)

A-1-188 /ʔahmm/ or /ʔahamm/ "more important, the main thing", especially in expression /mn ʔahmm X/ "one of the most important Xs (is...)", CA *ʔahamm-* (with geminate metathesis)

A-1-189 /ʔaḥsn/ or /ʔaḥsan/ "better", especially in expression /ml l-ʔaḥsn/ "it would be better (to...)" and variants, CA *ʔahsan-*. (In more general sense inherited /ḥsn/ "better" is preferred.)

A-1-190 /ʔakbaṛ/ "bigger", not only in standard religious expression *ʔaḷḷāh-u ʔakbar* (CA) but also in intellectual speech in such forms as /ʔakbaṛ ᶜadad mumkin/ "(the) largest possible number", CA *ʔakbar-*. (In ordinary contexts inherited /kbṛ/ "bigger" is used.)

A-1-191 /ʔqṛǝb/ or /ʔqṛb/ "nearer", CA *ʔaqrab-*

A-1-192 /ʔāshăl/ or /ʔshl/ "easier", CA *ʔashal-*

ʔaCCaC-iyy-a(t-) (noun derived from preceding type)

A-1-193 /ʔaktar-iy-a/ "majority, most" CA *ʔakθar-iyy-a*

A-1-194 /ʔaġlab-iy-a/ "majority" CA *ʔaġlab-iyy-a*

A-1-195 /ʔahamm-iy-a/ or /ʔahmm-iy-a/ "importance" (cf. A-1-188) CA *ʔahamm-iyy-a*

CVCC- (singular)

A-1-196 /ᶜǝhd/ "era, period" and /ᶜahd/ "promise, word of honour, both from CA *ᶜahd*

A-1-197 /qṛn/ "century" CA *qarn-* "century, horn" (In sense "horn" MCA shows inherited /gṛn/ with /qṛn/ as a regional dialect variant.)

A-1-198 /fǝᶜl/ "act, fact", chiefly in expressions like /b-l-fǝᶜl "in fact" CA *faᶜl-*

A-1-199 /nǝṣf/ "half" CA *niṣf-* (infrequent reclassicization of inherited /nǝṣṣ/, /nʷṣṣ/)

A-1-200 /ḥǝfḍ/ "memorization (esp. of Koran) CA *ḥifð̣-*

A-1-201 /nʷṭq/ "pronunciation" CA *nuṭq-*

A-1-202 /wǝfd/ "delegation" CA *wafd-*

A-1-203 /sinn/ "age" CA *sinn-*

A-1-204 /silk/ "cycle (division in secondary school levels)" CA *silk-* "thread, corps"

A-1-205 /qism/ or /qǝsm/ "class (in school)" CA *qism-* (general meaning "piece, division") (From same etymon MCA has inherited /qṣm/ "unit of five minutes", common in time expressions.)

A-1-206 /ṭifl/ or /ṭǝfl/ "small boy" CA *ṭifl-* (occasional reclassicization of inherited /ṭfl/)

A-1-207 /ṣifṛ/ or /ṣəfṛ/ "zero" CA *ṣifr-*
(grade on homework, soccer score etc.)
A-1-208 /ṣəbṛ/ "self-control, patience" CA *ṣabr-*
A-1-209 /qadr/ or /qədṛ/ "amount" CA *qadr-*
A-1-210 /baḥṛ/ or /bəḥṛ/ "sea" in name /nadi l-baḥṛ l-mutwṣṣiṭ/ "Club Méditerranée", CA *baḥr-*. (Usual term for "sea, ocean" is inherited /bḥṛ/.)
A-1-211 /fəṣl/ "season" CA *faṣl*
(apparently a reclassicization of /ḟṣl/ "season", which is however used only in part of Morocco)
A-1-212 /šuġl/ "work, occupation" CA *šuġl-*
(infrequent reclassicization of /šġ^{w}l/)
A-1-213 /ḥ^{w}km/ "governing, rule" CA *ḥukm-*
A-1-214 /dəxl/ "intervention, interference" CA *daxl-*

CVCC-a(t-) (feminine singular)

A-1-215 /wžb-a/ "meal" CA *wajb-a*
A-1-216 /bhž-a/ "joy" CA *bahj-a*
A-1-217 /rəḥl-a/ or /riḥl-a/ "journey" CA *riḥl-a*
A-1-218 /žuml-a/ "(linguistic) sentence" CA *juml-a*
A-1-219 /šahw-a/ "lust" CA *šahw-a*
A-1-220 /^{c}uṭl-a/ "vacation" CA *^{c}uṭl-a*
A-1-221 /šw^{c}b-a/ "field (of study)"(pl.seeA-1-11)CA *šu^{c}b-a*
A-1-222 /m^{w}dd-a/ or /mudd-a/ "while (length of time)" CA *mudd-a*
A-1-223 /^{c}uqd-a/ or /^{c}qd-a/ "contract" CA *^{c}uqd-a*
(A rural variant /^{cw}gd-a/ is also recorded; from the form this would appear to be an old inherited form, but in view of semantics this may be just a variant of the intrusive CA borrowings, with *q*→/g/ by analogy to other forms.)
A-1-224 /n^{w}qṭ-a/ "point(of view)"(pl.see A-1-14) CA *nuqṭ-a*

CVCC-iyy-a(t-) (feminine singular)

A-1-225 /wḍ^{c}-iy-a/ "situation" CA *waḍ^{c}-iyy-a*
A-1-226 /kšf-iy-a/ "scouting CA *kašf-iyy-a*
(i.e. being boy/girl scout)"

CayC- or CawC- (singular)

A-1-227 /ṣəyd/ "hunting" CA *ṣayd-*
A-1-228 /dəwr/ "role" CA *dawr-*
A-1-229 /dəwq/ or /dăwq/ "taste" CA *ðawq-*

nouns containing glottal stop /?/ in MCA

A-1-230 /quṛ?an/ "Koran" CA *qur?ān-*
A-1-231 /su?al/ "question, query" CA *su?āl-*
A-1-232 /?uṛžuḥ-a/ "(children's) swing" CA *?urjūḥ-a*
A-1-233 /?iqlim/ or /?qlim/ "region" CA *?iqlīm-*
A-1-234 /?ustad/ "teacher" (pl. see A-1-141) CA *?ustāð-*
A-1-235 /?ăhl/ "family" CA *?ahl-*
(reclassicization found when definite prefix present, /l-?ăhl/; contrast /hl-u/ "his family" etc.)
A-1-236 /?akl/ "food" CA *?akl-*
(rare, the common term in MCA being /makl-a/)
A-1-237 /?insan/ "human being" CA *?insān-*
(In MCA the /?/ sometimes drops when definite prefix /l-/ is present.)

A-1-238 /?əsm/ "name" CA *(?)ism-*
(uncommon reclassicization; usual form is /smiy-a/, etymologically a diminutive)

A-1-239 /?al-a/ "machine, apparatus" CA *?āl-a*

A-1-240 /?axir/ "end", as in /f-?axir s-san-a/ "at the end of the year", CA *?āxir-* "last; end". (In MCA the usual adjective for "last" is /lxxr/ or /tali/, the former ultimately from *?āxir-* via resegmentation and analogy to the shape of /lwwl/ "first".)

A-1-241 /?ax^{w}ṛ/ "other" CA *?āxar-*
(more common is inherited /ax^{w}ṛ/ with /^{w}/ due to analogy of fem. and pl. forms)

A-1-242 /?awwl/ or /?wwl/ "first" CA *?awwal-*
(occasional reclassicization of /lwwl/)

A-1-243 /?aṣl/ "origin" CA *?aṣl-*

A-1-244 /?aḷf/ "thousand" CA *?alf-*
(usual inherited form is /alf/)

A-1-245 /?əx/ "brother" in definite form /l-?əx/ CA *?ax-*
(usual inherited form is /xa-/ or /xu-/ depending on dialect and possessive suffix)

A-1-246 /?ǎb/ or /?ǎbb/ "father" in def.form /l-?ǎb(b)/ CA *?ab-*
(inherited form normally /ḅḅa-/ via restructuring; archaic definite form /l-^{w}ḅḅ/, modelled on forms for "mother", see next entry)

A-1-247 /?^{w}mm/ "mother" in definite form /l-?^{w}mm/ CA *?umm-*
(normal MCA form is /ṃṃ-/ plus possessive suffix, archaic definite form /l-^{w}mm/)

A-1-248 /?^{w}xt/ "sister" in definite form /l-?^{w}xt/ CA *?uxt-*
(usual MCA form is /x^{w}t-/ plus possessive; archaic definite form /l-^{w}xt/)

?aCCiC-a(t-) (plural)

A-1-249 /?ažhiz-a/ "outfits, units" CA *?aǰhiz-a*

A-1-250 /?anšiṭ-a/ "activities" CA *?anšiṭ-a*

?aCCiC-ā?- (plural)

A-1-251 /?aṣdiqa?/ "friends" CA *?aṣdiq-ā?-*

maCCVC- (derived noun of place, etc.)

A-1-252 /maḥall/ "house, place" (pl.see A-1-270) CA *maḥall-*

A-1-253 /masžid/ or /msžid/ "mosque" CA *masǰid-*
(for pl. see A-1-153)

A-1-254 /mṛkəz/ "centre" (e.g. cultural centre) CA *markaz-*

A-1-255 /musim/ or /musm/ "(sports) season" CA *mawsim-*
(MCA also has /musm/, apparently inherited, in sense "saint's festival")

A-1-256 /mwlid/ "holiday, anniversary" CA *mawlid-*

A-1-257 /mtḥəf/ or /mtḥaf/ "museum" CA *matḥaf*

A-1-258 /ml^{c}əb/ or /ml^{c}ab/ "(playing) field" CA *mal^{c}ab-*
(for pl. see A-1-157)

A-1-259 /mədxl/ or /madxal/ "introduction" CA *madxal-*

A-1-260 /mbdə?/ "principle" (pl.: A-1-152) CA *mabda?-*

A-1-261 /mžlis/ or /mažlis/ "council" CA *maǰlis-*

A-1-262 /mktəb/ "desk, office" (cf. A-1-148) CA *maktab-*

A-1-263 /msṛḥ/ or /msṛəḥ/ "theatre" CA *masraḥ-*

maCCVC-iyy-a(t-) (feminine singular)
A-1-264 /msṛaḥ-iy-a/ "play (theatrical production)", particularly in pl. /msṛaḥ-iy-at/ CA *masraḥ-iyy-at-*

maCCVC-iyy- (adjective)
A-1-265 /maṣiṛ-i/ "crucial" CA *maṣīr-iyy-*

maCCVC-a(t-) (feminine singular derived noun)
A-1-266 /mḍṛaṣ-a/ "school" CA *madras-a*
(consonantism in MCA influenced by inherited verb /ḍṛṣ/ from *daras-*, but cf. pl. A-1-151)
A-1-267 /mṛḥal-a/ or /maṛḥal-a/ "stage, level" CA *marḥal-a*
A-1-268 /ms?al-a/ "question, matter"(Pl.A-1-150) CA *mas?al-a*
A-1-269 /mktb-a/ or /maktab-a/ "desk, office" CA *maktab-a*
(cf. A-1-262 and pl. A-1-148)

maCCVC-āt- (plural)
A-1-270 /maḥll-at/ "houses, places"(pl.of A-1-252) CA *maḥall-āt-*

ma-CCūC- (passive participle)
A-1-271 /mwḍu^c/ "subject, topic" CA *ma-wḍū^c-*
(MCA also has /muḍu^c/, probably an older form)
A-1-272 /mžhud/ "effort" CA *ma-ǰhūd-*
A-1-273 /m^{c}zul/ "isolated" CA *ma-^{c}zūl-*
A-1-274 /mwzun/ or /muzun/ "balanced" CA *ma-wzūn-*
A-1-275 /ms?ul/ "responsible" CA *ma-s?ūl-*

mu-CaCCiC- (active participle)
A-1-276 /mu?hhil/ "preparation, potential", attested in pl. /mu?hhil-at/, CA pl. *mu-?ahhil-āt-* "qualifications"
A-1-277 /mu^{c}llim/ "teacher" CA *mu-^{c}allim-*
(The same etymon appears in inherited /m^{c}llm/ or /m^{wc}llm/ "boss".)
A-1-278 /mumttil/ "actor, representative" CA *mu-maθθil-*
(Compare synchronic true participle /m-mttl/ "acting", derived internally from verb /mttl/ "to act", also probably borrowed from CA.)
A-1-279 /mufttiš/ "inspector" CA *mu-fattiš-*
A-1-280 /muqṛṛiṛ/ "(legal) clerk" CA *mu-qarrir-*
A-1-281 /muṛbbi/ "trainer" CA *mu-rabbi*
(underlying *mu-rabbiy-*)

mu-CaCCaC- (passive participle)
A-1-282 /muqṛṛaṛ/ "programme, agenda" CA *mu-qarrar-*
(passive counterpart of A-1-280) (Contrast true synchronic participle /m-qṛṛəṛ/ "decided" from verb /qṛṛəṛ/.)
A-1-283 /muxyyam/ "campground" CA *mu-xayyam-*
A-1-284 /muqallaq/ "annoyed" CA *mu-qallaq-*
(much less common than /m-qlləq/)
A-1-285 /mušddad/ "doubled (letter of alphabet), fortified", CA *mu-šaddad-* (cf. true participle /m-šddəd/ "strengthened")

mu-CāCiC- (active participle)

A-1-286 /muṛaqib/ "supervisor" CA *mu-rāqib-*
A-1-287 /muhažir/ "émigré" CA *mu-hāǰir-*
(cf. /m-hažṛ/ "having emigrated")
A-1-288 /muṛadif/ "synonym" CA *mu-rādif-*
A-1-289 /mušarik/ "participant" CA *mu-šārik-*
(cf. /m-šark/ "participating, associated")

mu-CCiC- (active participle)
(Note: for "weak" forms see also A-1-32,33)

A-1-290 /muxriž/ "(film) producer) CA *mu-xriǰ-*
A-1-291 /muhimm/ "important,(the)main thing" CA *mu-himm-*
(with geminate metathesis)
A-1-292 /muškil/ "problem" CA *mu-škil-*
A-1-293 /muslim/ "Muslim" CA *mu-slim-*
(occasional reclassicization of /mslm/)
A-1-294 /muṛšid/ "(tourist) guide" CA *mu-ršid-*
(MCA also has fem. /muṛšid-a/ "girl scout/guide")
A-1-295 /musinn/ "elderly" CA *mu-sinn-*

mu-CCaC-a(t-) (feminine passive participle)

A-1-296 /mufṛad-a/ "term, expression", mostly in pl. /mufṛad-at/, in CA usually masc. in sg. form *mu-frad-*.
(MCA fem. form may be a back-formation from the pl.)

mu-ta-CaCCiC- (active participle)

A-1-297 /mutwṣṣiṭ/ or /mutwssiṭ/ "Mediterranean" CA *mu-ta-wassiṭ-*
(For /ss/ cf. related word /wəṣṭ/ "middle" with /ṣ/ in MCA; cf. regular synchronic participle /m-t-wṣṣəṭ/ "middle, average"; cf. also A-1-210.)
A-1-298 /m-t-^{c}wwəd/ "accustomed" CA *mu-ta-^{c}awwid-*
(MCA form in this case derived internally from verb /t-^{c}wwəd/, but probably influenced by CA participle.)

mu-ta-CāCiC- (active participle)

A-1-299 /mutawažid/ "available, present" CA *mu-ta-wāǰid-*
(cf. regular synchronic participle /m-t-wažd/)

mu-CtaCiC- (active participle)

A-1-300 /mu^{c}tadil/ "balanced, even, middle" CA *mu-^{c}tadil-*
(cf. true synchronic participle /m^{c}tadl/ "even, standing at attention")
A-1-301 /muttaḥid/ "united" (cf. A-1-84) CA *mu-ttaḥid-*
A-1-302 /m-xtalf/ "different" CA *mu-xtalif-*
(MCA form appears to be formed directly from verb /xtalf/, but influenced by CA participle.)
A-1-303 /m-žtam^{c}/ "combined" CA *mu-ǰtami^{c}-*
(MCA form based on verb /žtam^{c}/ but influenced by CA participle.)
A-1-304 /m-ṛtaf^{c}/ "elevated" CA *mu-rtafi^{c}-*
(MCA form based on verb /ṛtaf^{c}/ but influenced by CA participle.)

mu-CtaCaC- (passive participle)

A-1-305 /mustawa/, pl. /mustaway-at/ "level(s)" CA *mu-stawa-* pl.*mu-staway-āt-*
A-1-306 /muntaḍam/ "organization" CA *mu-ntað̣am-*
A-1-307 /muntaxab/ "selected (e.g. team)" CA *mu-ntaxab-*
(cf. also regular synchronic participle /m-ntaxb/ "choosing, chosen")
A-1-308 /mu?tamaṛ/ "conference" CA *mu-?tamar-*
A-1-309 /muḥtaṛam/ "respected" CA *mu-ḥtaram-*
A-1-310 /muṣṭalaḥ/ "term, expression" CA *mu-ṣṭalaḥ-*
A-1-311 /muḍṭṛṛ/ "forced, required" CA *mu-ḍṭarr-*
(regular participle /m-ḍṭṛṛ/ is more common)
A-1-312 /mu^{c}taṛaf/ "recognized" CA *mu-^{c}taraf-*
(regular participle /m-^{c}taṛf/ "having recognized"

mu-sta-CCiC- (active participle)

A-1-313 /mustaḥil/ "impossible" CA *mu-sta-ḥīl-*
A-1-314 /musthlik/ "consumer" CA *mu-sta-hlik*
(cf. regular participle /m-st^hlək/)
A-1-315 /must^{c}mir/ or /must^{c}miṛ/ "colonist" CA *mu-sta-^{c}mir-*
(Variant with /ṛ/ shows influence of verb /st^^{c}mṛ/ "to colonize" and its regular participle /m-st^^{c}mṛ/.)

mu-sta-CCaC- (passive participle)

A-1-316 /mustqbal/ "future" (noun, adj.) CA *mu-sta-qbal-*

mu-CCaCiCC- (participle)

A-1-317 /m-ṭma?nn/ "reassured" CA *mu-ṭma?inn-*
(Form is directly from verb /ṭma?nn/, but influenced by CA participle.)

ta-CCīC- (verbal noun)

A-1-318 /t-^{c}lim/ "education" CA *ta-^{c}līm-*
A-1-319 /t-?min/ or /ta-?min/ "insurance" CA *ta-?mīn-*
A-1-320 /t-kwin/ "formation, training" CA *ta-kwīn-*
A-1-321 /t-shil/ "facilitation, easing" CA *ta-shīl-*
A-1-322 /t^-drib/ "training" CA *ta-drīb-*
A-1-323 /t-šġil/ "labour" CA *ta-šġīl-*
A-1-324 /t-qṛiṛ/ "report" CA *ta-qrīr-*
A-1-325 /t-wṣil/ "receipt" CA *ta-wṣīl-*
A-1-326 /t-sbiq/ "advance (payment)" CA *ta-sbīq-*
A-1-327 /t-?tir/ "influence" CA *ta-?θīr-*

mu-CāCaC-a(t-) (verbal noun)

A-1-328 /munasab-a/ "occasion" CA *mu-nāsab-a*
A-1-329 /musa^{c}ad-a/ "assistance, help" CA *mu-sā^{c}ad-a*
(optional reclassicization of /m-sa^{c}d-a/)
A-1-330 /muqabal-a/ "(sports) match, encounter" CA *mu-qābal-a*
A-1-331 /musabaq-a/ "competition" CA *mu-sābaq-a*
(MCA also has /m-sabq-a/ and /m-ṣabq-a/)
A-1-332 /musawat/ "equality" CA *mu-sāwā-t-*
(underlying *mu-sāway-at-*).

ta-CaCCuC- (verbal noun)

A-1-333 /tažmmu^c/ or /tažammu^c/ "colony, aggregation" CA *ta-ǰammu^c-*
A-1-334 /tafqqud/ "study, examination" CA *ta-faqqud-*
A-1-335 /tabddul/ or /tabaddul/ "exchange" CA *ta-baddul-*

ta-CāCuC- (verbal noun)

A-1-336 /ta^{c}adul/ "equality, (sports) draw" CA *ta-^{c}ādul-*
A-1-337 /tawažud/ "(co-)existence" CA *ta-wāǰud-*
A-1-338 /tafahum/ "(mutual) understanding" CA *ta-fāhum-*
A-1-339 /tasawi/ "equality" CA *ta-sawi-* (underlying *ta-sāwiy-*)
A-1-340 /taṛaḍi/ "mutual consent" CA *ta-rāḍi-*
A-1-341 /ta?axi/ "brotherhood" CA *ta-?āxi-*

?iCCāC- (verbal noun)

A-1-342 /?islam/ "Islam" CA *?islām-*
A-1-343 /?išhaṛ/ "publicity, advertising" CA *?išhār-*
A-1-344 /?ižra?/ "measure, step" CA *?iǰrā-*
(most common in pl. /?ižra?-at/)

?iCCāC-a(t-) (feminine form of verbal noun)

A-1-345 /?iqam-a/ "sojourn, stay" CA *?iqām-a*
(Contrast MCA /l-iqam-a/ "the mint", with def. /l-/ often unsegmentable.)
A-1-346 /?iġat-a/ "assistance" CA *?iġāθ-a*
A-1-347 /?ida^c-a/ "broadcast" CA *?iðā^c-a*
A-1-348 /?ižaz-a/ "licence, permit" CA *?iǰāz-a*
A-1-349 /?idaṛ-a/ "administration" CA *?idār-a*
A-1-350 /?intaž-a/ "production" CA *?intāǰ-a*

?iCCāC-iyy- (adjective from verbal noun)

A-1-351 /?idar-i/ "administrative" (cf.A-1-349) CA *?idār-iyy-*

?iCCāC-iyy-āt- (plural verbal noun)

A-1-352 /?imkan-iy-at/ or /mkan-iy-at/ "possibilities" CA *?imkān-iyy-āt-*

(?)iCtiCāC- (verbal noun)

A-1-353 /?iqtiṣad/ or /qtiṣad/ "economy" CA *(?)iqtiṣād-*
A-1-354 /mtiḥan/ "exam, test" CA *(?)imtiḥān-*
A-1-355 /ttiṣal/ "relation"
attested in pl. form /ttiṣal-at/ CA *(?)ittiṣāl-*
A-1-356 /?imtiyaz/ "benefit, privilege"
attested in pl. form /?imtiyaz-at/ CA *(?)imtiyāz-*
A-1-357 /ntima?/ "affiliation" CA *(?)intimā?-*
A-1-358 /?xtilaf/ or /xtilaf/ "difference" CA *(?)ixtilāf-*

(?)iCtiCāC-iyy- (adjective from verbal noun)

A-1-359 /btida?-i/ "primary (school)" CA *(?)ibtidā?-iyy-*

(?)isti-CCāC- (verbal noun)

A-1-360 /st^{c}maṛ/ or /sti^{c}maṛ/
"colonization, colonial period" CA *(?)isti-^{c}mār-*
A-1-361 /stqbal/ or /istiqbal/ "reception" CA *(?)isti-qbāl-*
A-1-362 /st^{c}dad/ or /isti^{c}dad/ "preparation" CA *(?)isti-^{c}dād-*

(?)isti-CCāC-a(t-)

A-1-363 /stiraḥ-a/ "recreation" CA *(?)isti-rāḥ-a*

other verbal nouns

A-1-364 /ṭmi?nan/ "reassurance" (cf. A-1-317) CA *(?)iṭmi?nān-*

A-1-365 /taṛžam-a/ or /tṛžam-a/ "translation" CA *tarǰam-a*

2 Verbs

simple triliterals

A-2-1 /s?l/ "he asked" CA *sa?al-a*

A-2-2 /dəll/ "he pointed" CA *dall-a*

A-2-3 /zhəd/ "he was devout" CA *zahad-a*

A-2-4 /qam b-/ "he undertook" CA *qām-a bi-*
(includes preposition /b-/ attached to following noun; as simple verb /qam/ "he got up" occurs in some MCA dialects)

root quadriliterals

A-2-5 /bṛhn/ "he proved" (with prep. /ᶜla/) CA *barhan-a*

A-2-6 /ṣiṭṛ/ "he dominated" CA *sayṭar-a*

CaCCaC- (factitive, "conjugation II")

A-2-7 /?kkəd/ "he insisted (on)" CA *?akkad-a*

A-2-8 /hyyə?/ "he prepared" CA *hayya?-a*

A-2-9 /ᶜbbṛ/ "he expressed" (prep. /ᶜla/) CA *ᶜabbar-a*

A-2-10 /?ttṛ/ "he influenced" CA *?aθθar-a*

A-2-11 /?žžl/ "he delayed" CA *?aǰǰal-a*

A-2-12 /klləf/ "he put in charge" CA *kallaf-a*

A-2-13 /ṭbbəq/ "he practised" CA *ṭabbaq-a*

A-2-14 /fssr/ "he explained" CA *fassar-a*

A-2-15 /ḥddəd/ "he limited" CA *ḥaddad-a*

A-2-16 /mttl/ "he acted, imitated" CA *maθθal-a*

A-2-17 /sžžl/ "he registered, recorded" CA *saǰǰal-a*

A-2-18 /wḥḥəd/ "he unified" CA *waḥḥad-a*

CāCaC- ("conjugation III")

A-2-19 /nada/, imperfect /-nadi/ "he called (for)" CA *nāda*
(underlying *nāday-a*) (preposition /b-/)

A-2-20 /naqḍ/ "he contradicted, violated" CA *nāqaḍ-a*

A-2-21 /qawm/ "he fought, opposed" CA *qāwam-a*

A-2-22 /ḥafḍ/ "he kept, maintained"(prep./ᶜla/) CA *ḥāfað̣-a*

A-2-23 /šark/ "he participated" CA *šārak-a*

A-2-24 /qabl/ "he met (with)" CA *qābal-a*

A-2-25 /qaṛn/ "he compared" CA *qāran-a*

A-2-26 /ḥawl/ "he tried" CA *ḥāwal-a*
(actually a CA-motivated semantic shift of older MCA /ḥawl/ "he was careful" from same etymon)

?aCCaC- (causative, "conjugation IV")

A-2-27 /mkn/ "he/it made possible" CA *?amkan-a*
(in MCA differs only in semantics from simple intransitive /mkn/ "it was possible")

A-2-28 /ᶜln/ "he called (for)" (prep./ᶜla/) CA *?aᶜlan-a*
(preposition /ᶜla/)

ta-CaCCaC- ("conjugation V")

A-2-29 /t-qddm/ "he made progress" CA *ta-qaddam-a*
A-2-30 /t-wffṛ/ "it abounded" CA *ta-waffar-a*
A-2-31 /t-^{c}ttṛ/ "it was damaged, it failed" CA *ta-^{c}aθθar-a*
A-2-32 /t-wffa/, imperfect /-t-wffa/ "he passed away, died" (underlying *ta-waffay-a*) CA *ta-waffā*
A-2-33 /t-^{c}wwəd/ "he was accustomed" CA *ta-^{c}awwad-a*
A-2-34 /d-žwwl/ "he wandered, travelled" CA *ta-ǰawwal-a*
A-2-35 /t-xrrəž/ "he got his diploma, graduated" CA *t-xarraǰ-a*

ta-CāCaC- ("conjugation VI")

A-2-36 /t-rasl/ "they corresponded (wrote letters)", used in pl. only (third pl. forms are /t-rasl-u/ and CA *ta-rāsal-ū* "they corresponded") CA *ta-rāsal-ū*
A-2-37 /t-wafq/ "they came to an agreement" CA *ta-wāfaq-a* (as with preceding entry, actually used only in pl.)
A-2-38 /t-ṣalḥ/ "they patched up their friendship (after quarrel)" (attested in pl. form) CA *ta-ṣālaḥ-a*
A-2-39 /t-xaṣm/ "they quarrelled" (attested in pl.) CA *ta-xāṣam-a*
A-2-40 /d-žawz/ "he overstepped" (can be used in sg.) CA *ta-ǰāwaz-a*

(?)in-CaCaC- (passive, "conjugation VII")

A-2-41 /n-qasm/ "it was divided" CA *(?)in-qasam-a*
A-2-42 /n-fa^{c}l/ "he overdid" CA *(?)in-fa^{c}al-a*

(?)iCtaCaC- ("conjugation VIII")

A-2-43 /ntaha/, imperfect /-ntahi/ "it ended" (from underlying *intahay-a*) CA *(?)intahā*
A-2-44 /^{c}tabṛ/ "he considered" CA *(?)i^{c}tabar-a*
A-2-45 /ḥtafl/ "he celebrated" CA *(?)iḥtafal-a*
A-2-46 /ntahz/ "he took advantage (of opportunity)" CA *(?)intahaz-*
A-2-47 /ḍṭṛṛ/ "he was compelled" (cf. A-1-311) CA passive *(?)uḍṭurr-a*
A-2-48 /htəmm/ "he was interested (in)" CA *(?)ihtamm-a*
A-2-49 /ḥtəžž/ "he protested" CA *(?)iḥtaǰǰ-a*
A-2-50 /ttafq/ "he agreed" (same CA root as A-2-37) CA *(?)ittafaq-a*
A-2-51 /ḥtaž/ "he needed" CA *(?)iḥtāǰ-a* (probably a CA-inspired semantic restitution in this sense; also occurs as old MCA form in sense "ought to" with following verb)
A-2-52 /ḥtaṛm/ "he honoured, showed respect to" CA *(?)iḥtaram-a* (cf. A-1-309)
A-2-53 /btaġa/, imperfect /-btaġi/ "he desired" CA *(?)ibtaġā* (underlying *ibtaġay-a*) (much less common than /bġa/ "he wanted" or, in some dialects, /ḥəbb/ "he wanted")
A-2-54 /xtalf/ "he differed, was different" CA *(?)ixtalaf-a* (for other forms from same CA root see A-1-301, A-1-358)
A-2-55 /žtahd/ "he formulated ideology (in Islam) CA *(?)iǰtahad-a*
A-2-56 /ktasb/ "he possessed" CA *(?)iktasab-a*

A-2-57 /ž tam^c/ "they gathered" (used normally in pl. forms) — CA *(?)iǰtama^c-a*
A-2-58 /ntama/, imperfect /-ntami/ "he belonged (to)" (underlying *intamay-a*) (preposition /l-/) — CA *(?)intamā*
A-2-59 /xtaṛ^c/ "he invented" — CA *(?)ixtara^c-a*

(?)ista-CCaC- ("conjugation X")

A-2-60 /st^{c}ml/ "he utilized" — CA *(?)ista-^{c}mal-a*
A-2-61 /stqbl/ "he received" — CA *(?)ista-qbal-a*
A-2-62 /stafəd/ or /stafad/ "he profited" — CA *(?)ista-fād-a*
A-2-63 /st^{c}ədd/ or /sta^{c}dd/ "he prepared himself)" — CA *(?)ista-^{c}add-a*
A-2-64 /starəḥ/ or /staraḥ/ "he took a rest" — CA *(?)ista-rāḥ-a*
A-2-65 /stažəb/ "he heeded, agreed" — CA *(?)ista-ǰāb-a*
A-2-66 /st^{c}mṛ/ "he colonized" (cf. A-1-315) — CA *(?)ista-^{c}mar-a*
A-2-67 /stḥml/ "he tolerated" — CA *(?)ista-ḥmal-a*
A-2-68 /stnṭəq/ "he interrogated" — CA *(?)ista-nṭaq-a*
A-2-69 /stḥla/, imperfect /-stḥli/ "he enjoyed (e.g. food)" (underlying *ista-ḥlay-a*) — CA *(?)ista-ḥlā*
A-2-70 /staḥqq/ "he deserved" — CA *(?)ista-ḥaqq-a*
A-2-71 /stahl/ "he deserved (reward, result)" — CA *(?)ista-?hal-a*
A-2-72 /st?dn/ "he requested permission" — CA *(?)ista-?ðan-a*
A-2-73 /stanəf/ "he prolonged" — CA *(?)ista-?naf-a*
A-2-74 /staqm/ "he straightened" (attested in corpus in participle /m-staqm/ "standing straight" — CA *(?)ista-qām-a*
A-2-75 /st^tna/, imperfect /-st^tni/ "he excluded" (underlying *ista-θnay-a*) — CA *(?)ista-θnā*
A-2-76 /st^d^{c}a/, imperfect /st^d^{c}i) "he invited, summoned" (underlying *ista-d^{c}ay-a)* — CA *(?)ista-d^{c}ā*
A-2-77 /st^dṛk/ "he reached, arrived at" — CA *(?)ista-drak-a*
A-2-78 /st^dṛž/ "he did (series of things) in succession" — CA *(?)ista-draǰ-a*
A-2-79 /stadll/ "he based (decision) on" (preposition /b-/ with "on" phrase) — CA *(?)ista-dall-a*
A-2-80 /staṭ^c/ "he was able" — CA *(?)ista-ṭā^c-a*
A-2-81 /staṭl/ "he persisted, kept doing" — CA *(?)ista-ṭāl-a*

other conjugations

A-2-82 /ṭma?nn/ "he was reassured" (functions as intransitive counterpart of /ṭm?n/ "he reassured", CA *ṭam?an-a*; cf. also A-1-317) — CA *(?)iṭma?ann-a*

3 Miscellaneous

clause introducers and particles

A-3-1 /li?inna/, /li?anna/, or /li?nna/ "because", CA *li-?anna* (If the MCA form takes a pronominal suffix, representing in most cases the clause subject NP, the suffix is often in CA form: /li?inna-hu/ "because he...", not /li?inna-h/, at least for educated persons. Older forms for "because" are /^{c}la ḥqq-aš/, ^{c}la ḥqet-aš/, etc.)

A-3-2 /bi?inna/, /bi?anna/, or /bi?nna/ "that" (conjunction used in various complement clause types) CA *bi-?anna* (remark on pronominal suffixes for A-3-1 holds here; older forms: /billa/, /b-aš/)

A-3-3 /ḥet/ "because, since", CA *ḥayθu* (recorded many times with /e/ vowel; not attested as /ḥəyt/ or /ḥit/; near synonym of A-3-1)

A-3-4 /bin-ma/ "while" (conjunction), CA *bayna-mā* (Modelled on this CA form, but modified by analogy to /bin/ "between" from CA *bayna*. Less common than /mnin/, /f-aš/, and other MCA forms meaning "when".)

A-3-5 /?aw/ "or", CA *?aw* (less common than older MCA forms like /awlla/ and its variants, or regional form /yaw/)

A-3-6 /kama/ "as, in the same way as", CA *ka-mā* (used with verbs; becoming frequent in certain phrases such as /kama g^wl-t-l-ək/ "as I (already) told you"; another example is A-3-12, below)

A-3-7 /r^wbbama/ "possibly", CA *rubba-mā* (less common than old MCA phrases based on verb /mkn/ "to be possible")

adverbial phrases

A-3-8 /li-mitli-h/ "each, apiece" CA *li-miθl-i-hi*

A-3-9 /mn qabl/ "earlier, previously" CA *min qabl-u*

A-3-10 /b-l-xuṣuṣ/, /b-xuṣuṣ/, or /bi-l-xuṣuṣ/ "especially", based on CA noun *xuṣūṣ-* (perhaps a little less common than the related CA borrowing seen in A-3-45, below)

A-3-11 /b-l-fə^{c}l "in fact, actually" CA *bi-l-fi^{c}l-i* (cf. A-3-51, below)

A-3-12 /kama yažib/ "as it should be" CA *ka-mā ya-ǰib-u*

A-3-13 /la ba?s-a bi-hum/ "they are doing fine" (refers to economic prosperity or sometimes to medical condition) CA *lā ba?s-a bi-hum*

A-3-14 /(?)ila ?axiri-h/ "et cetera, and so forth" CA *(wa) ?ilā ?āxir-i-hi*

A-3-15 /fi-l-?axir/ "at last, finally" CA *fi-l-?axīr-i*

A-3-16 /bi-duni šəkk/ "without doubt" CA *bi-dūn-i šakk-i-n*

A-3-17 /li-?awwl mṛṛ-a/ "for the first time" CA *li-?awwal-i marr-at-i-n* (/mṛṛ-a/ "time" is common in MCA, though absent from some dialects; usual MCA adjective "first" is /lwwl/, inherited from CA *?awwal-* but restructured)

A-3-18 /l-?an/ "now", CA *(?)al-?ān-a* (much less common in MCA than old form /daba/, regional alternative /ḍṛuk/)

A-3-19 /ḥawalay/ "approximately", CA *ḥawālā* or *ḥawālay* (less common than MCA preposed /ši/, as in /ši xms-in/ "around fifty"; cf. A-3-42)

prepositions and simple prenominal elements

A-3-20 /ḥasab/ "according to, depending on" CA *ḥasab-a* (cf. next entry)

A-3-21 /^{c}la ḥasab/ "depending on, according to" CA *^{c}alā ḥasab-i* (cf. preceding entry)

A-3-22 /xilal/ "during" (cf. following entries) CA *xilāl-a*
A-3-23 /f-xilal/ "during" (based on A-3-22) CA *fi xilāl-i*
A-3-24 /mn xilal/ "on the basis of" (based on A-3-22) CA *min xilāl-i*
A-3-25 /ḥəwl/ or /ḥəwla/ "concerning, about" CA *ḥawl-a*
A-3-26 /ḍun/ "without" (cf. next entry) CA *dūn-a*
A-3-27 /bi-dun/ "without" CA *bi-dūn-i* (based on A-3-26; for example with vocalic suffix retained in fixed expression, see A-3-16)
A-3-28 /amma/ "as for" CA *?ammā*
A-3-29 /bəᶜd/ "some of" CA *baᶜd-*
A-3-30 /ḍəḍḍ/ or ḍəḍḍa/ "against, in opposition to" CA *ḍidd-a* (not very common; MCA /ᶜla/ "against, for" can be used in many contexts including this one)
A-3-31 /b-xilaf/ "contrary to" CA *bi-xilāf-i*
A-3-32 /ᶜla ṣaᶜīd/ "on the basis of, at the level of" CA *ᶜalā ṣaᶜīd-i* (also used, with adjective, in non-genitive definite NP construction, as in /ᶜl ṣ-ṣaᶜid l-ᶜali/ "at the high level")
A-3-33 /mn naḥiy-ət/ "with respect to" CA *min nāḥiy-at-i*
A-3-34 /b-n-nsb-a l-/ "with respect to, in comparison with" CA *bi-n-nisb-at-i ?ilā*
A-3-35 /f-ma y-xʷṣṣ/, /fi-ma ya-xʷṣṣ/, and variants "as far as ... is concerned", CA *fī-mā ya-xuṣṣ-u* (takes following NP as direct object of verb /y-xʷṣṣ/ "concerns")
A-3-36 /l-ṭul/ "throughout" CA *li-ṭūl-i*
A-3-37 /b-l-?iḍaf-a l-/ "in addition to" CA *bi-l-?iḍāf-at-i ?ilā*
A-3-38 /b-sabab/ "because of" (with following NP) CA *bi-sabab-i* (for simple noun stem see A-1-5)
A-3-39 /l-?ažl/ or /li-?ažl/ "for the sake of" CA *li-?ajl-i*
A-3-40 /ᶜla qbl/ "for the sake of" attested in corpus in form /ᶜla qbl-ək/ "for your sake" with pronominal suffix, CA *ᶜalā qibal-i* (distinct from /qbl/ "before", a common MCA preposition inherited from CA *qabl-*)
A-3-41 /li-munasab-at/ or /li-munasab-ət/ "on the occasion of" CA *li-mu-nāsab-at-i* (with verbal noun *mu-nāsab-a*, see A-1-328)

denominative adverbs with suffix -an

A-3-42 /tqrib-n/ or /tqṛib-n/ "approximately" CA *ta-qrīb-an* (now fairly common, along with /ši/; cf. A-3-19, a less common form)
A-3-43 /matal-an/ "for example" (very common) CA *maθal-an*
A-3-44 /naḍaṛ-an l-/ "considering, in consideration of, in the light of" CA *naẓar-an ?ilā*
A-3-45 /xuṣuṣ-an/ or /xuxuṣ-n/ "especially" CA *xuṣūṣ-an* (cf. A-3-10)
A-3-46 /niha?-iy-n/ "definitely, conclusively" CA *nihā?-iyy-an*
A-3-47 /xaṣṣ-at-an/ or /xaṣṣ-at-n/ "especially" CA *xāṣṣ-at-an* (from same CA root as A-3-45, but stem-form different)
A-3-48 /ṭbᶜ-an/ or /ṭbᶜ-n/ "naturally" CA *ṭabᶜ-an*

A-3-49 /da?im-an/, /da?im-n/, or /daym-n/ "always" CA *dā?im-an* (now tending to replace the inherited form /dima/, which reflects a variant of *dā?im-an*)

A-3-50 /^{c}ad-at-an/ or /^{c}ad-at-n/ "usually" (common) CA *^{c}ād-at-an*

A-3-51 /f^{c}l-an/ or /f^{c}l-n/ "in fact" CA *fi^{c}l-an* (alternative to form in A-3-11 from same stem)

A-3-52 /ḥaqiq-at-an/ or /ḥaqiq-at-n/ "truly, in fact" CA *ḥaqīq-at-an*

A-3-53 /šay?-an ma/ "to some extent" CA *šay?-an mā*

A-3-54 /naw^c-an ma/ "to some extent, in a fashion" CA *naw^c-an mā*

A-3-55 /ziyad-at-n ^{c}la/ "in addition to" CA *ziyād-at-an ^{c}alā* (synonym of A-3-37)

A-3-56 /?ayḍ-an/ "also", CA *?ayḍ-an* (uncommon except in highly classicized style; usual MCA construction is with preposition /ḥtta/ "even X", i.e., "X too")

A-3-57 /ždd-an/ "very" CA *ǰidd-an* (uncommon; usual expression is /bzzaf/ which also means "much, many")

A-3-58 /katir-n ma/ "frequently" CA *kaθīr-an mā* (cf. MCA /ktir/ "much" inherited from same stem)

A-3-59 /sawa?-n ... ?aw .../ "either ... or ..." (add two NPs or other parallel constituents) CA *sawā?-an ... ?aw ...* (cf. A-3-5)

A-3-60 /šxṣ-iy-an/ or /šxṣ-iy-n/ "personally" CA *šaxṣ-iyy-an*

A-3-61 /sabiq-an/ or /sabiq-n/ "previously" CA *sābiq-an*

A-3-62 /?awwal-an/ or /?awwal-n/ "initially, (at) first" CA *?awwal-an* (cf. A-1-308; the usual MCA adjective for "first" is /lwwl/)

A-3-63 /btida?-an mn/ or /?btida?-n mn/ and variants "starting from", CA *(?)ibtidā?-an min*

A-3-64 /nṭilaq-an mn/ "on the basis of, starting from" CA *(?)inṭilāq-an min*

A-3-65 /šukṛ-an/ "thank you" CA *šukr-an* (the standard expression for this meaning; for the standard reply see next entry)

A-3-66 /la šukṛ-a ^{c}la wažib/ "you're welcome" CA *lā šukr-a ^{c}alā wāǰib-i-n* (lit., "no thanking [is needed] for a duty") (standard response to preceding item)

A-3-67 /tamam-n/ "completely, definitely" CA *tamām-an*

phrases containing demonstrative pronouns

A-3-68 /ka-dalik/ or /ka-dalika/ "in that way, thus, like that" CA *ka-ðālika*

A-3-69 /m^{c}a dalik/ "nevertheless, notwithstanding that" CA *ma^{c}a ðālika* (lit., "with that")

A-3-70 /li-dalik/ or /fa-li-dalik/ "(and) for that reason, consequently", CA *(fa) li-ðālika* (here *fa* is a conjunction roughly meaning "and" or "and so")

A-3-71 /li-hada/ or /fa-li-hada/ "(and) for this reason" CA *(fa) li-hāða* (same structure as preceding entry, but here with proximate demonstrative)

Appendix B: European borrowings in MCA – Verbs

In this appendix we list MCA verbs recorded in F (Fes), Meknes (Mk), and/or Marrakech (Mr) from Muslim informants during the fieldwork period. We also give variants from other locations for these items, but items which occur (in my data) only in these other locations are not presented here. These locations are abbreviated Alg, Casa(j), Tt, etc., as indicated in the list of place abbreviations, (j) meaning Jewish dialect. Items in this appendix are borrowed from European languages.

It should be emphasized again that although we specify locations for each item and variant, these materials do not purport to be highly reliable in dialectological terms. A large master set of items was obtained from recorded texts, lengthy participant observation, and supplementary elicitation from informants in the F/Mk area, mostly young men. The primary F informant had lived in Mk as well as F and was of village origin, but spoke what we might consider a supralocal F/Mk regional educated dialect (and was able to provide rural variants for many items). From this master list, variants from Mr and the other locations were obtained by elicitation with one or two informants.

Each entry contains a formula of the general type: F Mk *Mr *Casa(j). This particular one means that the item is attested from F and Mk informants, but was explicitly rejected (or not understood) by Mr and Casa(j) informants. The formula F Mk by itself means that the item was obtained from F and Mk informants, but no information is available as to whether the item also occurs in other locations. A formula of this type is usually followed by further information in brackets [ ] giving variants from other locations, and also indicating attestations in the existing published literature. The principal publications of relevance here are abbreviated DMA-AE, DMA-EA, EDA, GJA, MAG, NLVM, TAR, TAT, and ZLMA (see list of bibliographical abbreviations). Where the form given in the publication cited matches the form I recorded (leaving aside differences in transcriptional convention), I frequently do not bother to present the transcription here. Where the transcription is divergent, or where the item has several variants and it is of interest to know which variant occurs in the earlier source, the form is presented here, retranscribed according to my conventions (except when presented in quotation marks). Specialist readers whould be warned that this retranscription is sometimes problematic, and they may find it useful to consult the original sources directly. Borrowed items which occur in the earlier sources, but which my informants from F, Mk, and Mr rejected or did not understand, are not presented here but in some cases are discussed in the theoretical chapters of this book.

As noted above, the items in this appendix are verbs of European origin. Some of these have been directly borrowed from verb forms in those languages, chiefly Sp (Spanish) and Fr (French). Others are clearly internal MCA derivatives based on earlier borrowings (mostly nouns) from European languages; for some items either direct borrowing or internal denominative formation is possible.

The citation form given at the beginning of the entry, and the basis for alphabetization, is the 3Sg masculine perfective (which has no inflectional affixes). In the great majority of instances the other inflected forms are easily predictable from this form; for example, unless otherwise specified, final /a/ vowel in the citation form changes to /i/ in all imperfective forms, and in the perfective before consonant-initial subject-marking suffixes, so that from /gaža/ B-63 "he enlisted" we can automatically produce /ta-y-gaži/ "he enlists" and /gaži-t/ "I enlisted". For the handful of triliteral hollow verbs such as /šat/ B-162 "he shot", the imperfective form is also listed. Stems with more than three root phonemes containing medial vowels, such as /faḷṭ/ B-47 "he made a mistake", show no vocalic alternations unless otherwise indicated.

Transcriptions of the MCA borrowings are based on normal MCA phonemic structure to the extent possible. For example, phonetic [e], [o], and (back) [ạ] are interpreted as allophones of the phonemes /i/, /u/, and /a/, respectively, if and only if it is possible to attribute the feature pharyngealization to a neighbouring consonant. In those forms where such a phonetic vowel occurs in environments where no pharyngealized consonant can be posited, the phonemic transcription contains /e/, /o/, or /ạ/. In less well-assimilated stems we also find Fr vowels such as /ɔ/, /ɛ/, /ü/, /ö/, /ạ̃/, /æ̃/, /õ/, and /ɔ̃/. For a fuller discussion of transcriptional conventions see the note on this matter and the discussions of phonological structure in the theoretical chapters.

In general, attempts were made to elicit verbal nouns related to the borrowed verb forms, and these are presented here when obtained. Some are internal MCA derivatives, others are direct from Fr; thus, from /ḍipana/ B-43 "he repaired", we have verbal noun /ḍipạnaž/ directly from Fr dépannage. Since participles are essentially predictable from inflected verb forms they are usually not explicitly given here, but they are given when they are especially common and/or when they have special meanings; there are some verb stems, moreover, which seem to be used in participial forms but are unattested or notably uncommon in regular inflected forms.

Although verbal nouns and participles are presented in this appendix within the entry for the related simple verb, there are still many other nouns and adjectives given in Appendix C which are formally relatable to verbs in the present Appendix B. Usually the entries in the present appendix mention the forms in question but do not present them in detail; they are in Appendix C.

-- /?aḅạ̃ḍuna/ See /bạ̃ḍuna/ B-4.
-- /?anṣṭala/ See /ṣṭala/ B-155.
-- /?aṛạ̃ža/ See /ṛạ̃ža/ B-126.
-- /?aṭaka/ See /ṭaka/ B-176.

B-1 /?nṭək/ Currently uncommon, used only in participle /m-?ntək/ "well-dressed, elegant" (mainly of persons), dimin. /m-?intək/ (same gloss, endearing or jocular); from Fr antique via earlier borrowings now out of use. F Mk *Mr *Casa(j). [See EDA 403 for earlier forms.] Syn: /?aniq/, /zwin/.

B-2 /?uṛganiza/ "he organized", mediopassive /t-?uṛgạniza/ "he got organized", participle /m-?uṛgạnizi/ "(well) organized, in order"; from Fr organiser; educated usage. F *Mr. Syn: /ṛttəb/, /nḍḍm/.

B-3 /?ütiliza/ "he used, utilized", mediopassive /t-?ütiliza/ "it was used"; from Fr utiliser; educated usage, uncommon. F *Mr. Syn: /stᶜml/, /xddm/.

B-4 /bạ̃ḍuna/, educated variant /?aḅạ̃ḍuna/ "he abandoned, left behind; he gave up (fight, etc.)"; from Fr abandonner, not common. *F Mk (two speakers). Syn: /xlla/.

B-5 /baṛa/ "he blocked off"; example /baṛa ᶜli-ya ṭ-ṭriq/ "he blocked my way" (lit., "he blocked the way for me"); Fr barrer. Said to be used in eastern Morocco (Oujda). Cf. noun /baṛaž/ C-56.

B-6 /bgbəṣ/. Used in mediopassive /t-bgbəṣ/ and most common in dimin. (jocular) form /t-bigbəṣ/ "he acted like a big shot (wheeler-dealer, underworld chief, etc.); he acted like a big strong man (flexing muscles, etc.)"; denominative from /bigbuṣ/ C-79 (Eng big boss); used in slang; verbal noun /t-bgbiṣ/. F *Mk *Mr *Alg.

-- /bidṛ/ See /piḍala/.

B-7 /bḷaga/ with preposition /ᶜla/: (1) "he spoke angrily to (subordinate), he chewed (him) out" (F); (2) "he deceived, lied to" (Mk). From Fr blaguer. F Mk *Mr. Syn (sense 1): /ġwwət ᶜla/.

B-8 /blaka/ "he slammed on brakes, screeched to a stop"; origin unclear but canonical shape suggests European borrowing. Mr *F.

B-9 /bḷana/ "he schemed, made plans" (often pejorative); probably denominative from noun /bḷan/ (Fr Sp plan). F Mk *Mr *Alg. Syn: /xṭṭəṭ/. Cf. C-99.

B-10 /blanda/: (1) "he fortified, made strong"; (2) "he acted like a strong man, showed off his robustness". Mediopassive (sense 1) /tt-blanda/ "he fortified himself" (e.g. put on warm clothing in cold weather); participle (sense 1) /m-blandi/ "armoured"; Fr blinder (common in military contexts); earliest MCA borrowing perhaps participle, modelled on Fr blindé; cf. adjective C-100 /blandi/ from same source. F Mk *Mr. [Alg: /m-blandi/ only.]

B-11 /blaṣa/: (1) "he placed, located, put in place" (e.g. automobile); (2) "he replaced" (less common sense). Denominative from /bḷaṣ-a/ (Fr place, etc.) or possibly Fr verb placer. F Mk Mr. [Attested from Alg informants in reflexive phrase /blaṣa ṛuḥ-u/ "he placed himself, took his place".] More common MCA stems are /hət̩t̩/ "to place", /bddl/ "to change, replace". [EDA 375] Cf. C-102.

B-12 /blisa/ "he wounded" (mainly military usage), mediopassive /tt-blisa/ "to get wounded", participle /m-blisi/ "wounded"; Fr blesser (participle blessé). F Mk Mr *Casa(j). [Alg has mediopassive form.] Syn: /žr̥h/ (still common).

B-13 /blufa/ "he bluffed (in poker)"; Fr bluffer [blöfe]. F Mk (rare) Alg *Mr.

B-14 /bl̥uka/ "he blocked (shot)" (soccer, etc.); Fr bloquer (Sp blocar). F Mk *Mr. Syn: /wqqəf/.

B-15 /bntr/ "he painted (wall, house)"; etymology probably complex involving earlier MCA borrowings from Sp pintar with subsequent influence of Fr peindre but also possible denominative formation from noun /bantur-a/ "paint" (cross of Sp pintura, Fr peinture), cf. also /bantur-i/ "painter"; verbal noun /t-bntir/. F Mk *Mr. [Alg has /bntr/ "painter"; for other references see GJAF 17, NLVM 13, DMA-AE; Tt /pintar/ "he painted" with unpharyngealized /r/, 3 Pl /pintr-u/.] Cf. C-49, 50. Syn: /ṣbəġ/ (more common).

-- /bra/ See /-bri/ below.

B-16 /br̥ḁ̃ša/ "he branched off (electric outlet, etc.), plugged in"; example /br̥ãši-t l-priz dyal ḍ-ḍuw/ "I branched off the electric outlet (with extension cord)"; Fr brancher; compare separately borrowed noun /br̥ašm-a/ (unnasalized). F. Cf. C-106.

B-17 /brda/: (1) "it (tire, etc.) became dislocated, came off"; (2) "he lost (possession)"; (3) "he farted" (slang). Participle /m-brdi/ also has sense "deflowered, no longer virgin" in fem. form /m-brdy-a/. From Fr perdre (Sp perder) "to lose", with special participial meaning perhaps a special contextual usage of Fr participle perdue (fem.). F (senses 1, 2) Mk (3) *Mr *Casa(j). [EDA 371 indicates that these MCA forms were formerly more common than they are now; he plausibly suggests an initial connection between Fr participle perdu and MCA /m-brdi/; DMA-AE.] Syn: /xṣr̥/ "to lose", /ḥzəq/ "to fart". For more recent loans from the same Fr (Sp) verb(s) see /pir̥da/, below (B-113).

B-18 /-bri/ (imperfective only; corresponding perfective */bra/ not used) "it is/was shining" (said of sun, etc.); Fr briller; use of imperfective only perhaps due both to inherently durative meaning of verb and to avoidance of form with /a/ vowel which is sharply different from vowel in Fr source form; not in very common use; cf. parallel borrowing /briya/, below. F Mk Mr. Syn: /lmᶜ/.

B-19 /brikula/: (1) "he improvised (contraption), did miscellaneous odd jobs, found a way to make or fix (machine)"; (2) "he did something in a haphazard fashion, threw (machine) together; (3) "he swindled, cheated, or exploited (other person)". May be transitive or intransitive; passive participle /m-brikuli/ "(object) made haphazardly, pieced together"; verbal noun /brikul/, agentive /brikulur/; from Fr bricoler (agentive bricoleur). F Mk Alg *Mr. Syn: /qḍa b-aš-mma kan/ "he got it done in whatever way".

B-20 /briya/ "it shone" (regular imperfective /-briyi/); Fr briller; variant of more common but defective /-bri/ (B-18 above). The form /-bri/ presumably directly reflects Fr (il) brille, while /-briyi/ (whence /briya/ by analogy) appears to be directly related to Fr bisyllabic forms (briller, brillait, brillé). Mk *F.

B-21 /brnəz/ "he varnished (it)"; probably denominative from noun /brniz/, variant of /virni/ (Sp barniz, Fr vernis). F. [DMA-AE] (C-789)

B-22 /bṛõza/ Attested as mediopassive /tt-bṛõza/ "he got a suntan", participle /m-bṛõzi/ "tanned", verbal noun /m-bṛõzy-a/, /t-bṛõzy-a/, or /bṛõẓaž/ (/ẓ/ pharyngealized in last form only); Fr se bronzer. F Mk Mr. [Alg has /bṛõẓa/ without mediopassive prefix in same intransitive sense; note pharyngealization.] Syn: /t-šmməš/ "to get suntanned", /ḥmaṛ/ "to become red (e.g. to get badly sunburned)".

B-23 /bṛẓəṭ/ "he pestered (constantly)"; example /ma-t-bṛẓṭ-ni-š/ "don't keep pestering me!"; participle usually in active sense /m-bṛẓəṭ/ "pestering (someone)"; verbal noun /t-bṛẓiṭ/; agentive /bṛẓaṭ/ or /mu-bṛẓiṭ/ "pest (person)"; denominative from /baṛaẓiṭ/ "pest (person)" with meaning influenced by Fr verb parasiter; agentive /bṛẓaṭ/ presumably derived internally on /CCCaC/ agentive model, but /mu-bṛẓiṭ/ is (curiously) patterned on /mu-CCCiC/ pattern for active participles borrowed from CA (see A-1-276ff.) and is perhaps a pseudo-learned (hypercorrect or jocular) restructuring of /m-bṛẓəṭ/ (participle, see above). F Mk Mr *Casa(j) *Alg. Syn: /šṭn/, /ḍiṛãža/ (B-44 below).

B-24 /bṛžəz/ Occurs in mediopassive /t-bṛžəz/ "he acted like a bourgeois (rich person)", often in jocular dimin. form /t-biṛžəz/; denominative from /buṛžwa/, variant of /buṛžwa/ C-149 "bourgeois" (Fr bourgeois); verbal noun /t-bṛžiz/; F informant who gave this verb form has /r/ not /ṛ/ in /buržwa/ and adj. /buržwaz-i/, but /ṛ/ found elsewhere. F *Mk *Mr *Alg.

B-25 /budr/ Occurs as mediopassive /t-burd/ "he flexed or showed off muscles; he was well built or muscular"; probably denominative but exact origin unclear, said by some informants to be semantically connected with noun /budr-a/"pillar, column" (Fr poutre), but /badr-a/ "muscular man" (uncommon word) is also recorded (origin unclear, probably not European); verbal noun is /t-budir/; formation of verb is /t-CuCC/ (cf. in this appendix /ḅugəṣ/, /fuḅṛ/, /kumək/, /kunəb/, /ṛufəẓ/, /zufr/). F Mk Mr.

B-26 /ḅugəṣ/ Occurs as mediopassive /t-ḅugəṣ/ "he acted like a fop or dandy" (pejorative, said of Europeanized boys or men who wear flashy clothes, etc.); denominative from noun /ḅuguṣ/ (Fr beau gosse) on /t-CuCəC/ pattern; verbal noun /t-bugis/. F *Mk *Mr. [Alg has distinct formation /t-bggəṣ/ from same source.] Syn: /t-?ṇṇəq/ "he acted elegant" (also, in this appendix, /frkəs/, /bṛžəz/, /stika/, /šyyək/, /zufr/).

B-27 /buks/(F) or /buksa/(Mr) "he boxed (someone)" (transitive); example /buks-ni/ "he boxed with me"; reciprocal /t-buks/ (F) in pl., e.g. /t-buks-u/ "they boxed (each other)"; combination of direct borrowing from Fr verb boxer and internal denominative from /buks/ (Fr boxe "boxing"). F Mr. [Alg has /ḅukṣa/.] Syn: /lakm/.

B-28 /buṃḅa/ "he bounced (e.g. ball)", mediopassive /t-buṃḅa/ "it (ball, etc.) bounced"; Fr bomber crossed with rebondir (?). F. For semantically different nouns see /ḅumb-a/, /ḅumbiy-a/ C-135.

B-29 /bwaṭa/ Occurs only as participle /m-bwaṭi/ "canned (in tin can)"; probably directly based on Fr emboîté, cf. also Fr en boîte(s), perhaps influenced by noun /bwaṭ-a/ "tin can" (Fr boîte); cf. /ḅwwəṭ/ below (B-30). F *Mk *Mr. Cf. C-161.

B-30 /ḅwwəṭ/ "he beat (someone) up, he beat the tar out of (someone)". Mediopassive /t-ḅwwəṭ/ has several meanings: (1) "he got beaten up (badly)"; (2) "he got stoned, plastered (on liquor, drugs)". Participle /m-ḅwwəṭ/ has these meanings (F Mk) or means "fat, bloated" (Mr). Probably modelled on Fr emboîter, which can mean "to beat up" (slang), but form is factitive-causative /$C_1C_2C_2C_3$/ and may therefore be formally a denominative from /bwaṭ-a/ "tin can" (Fr boîte, related to emboîter via the latter's main meaning "to can") or possibly to /buṭ/ C-155 "boots". F Mk Mr(participle) *Alg. Syn: /nfəx/ "he inflated" or (slang) "he beat up" (cf. /gufl/ below, this appendix; association "to inflate" with "to beat up" alludes to black eyes and other swollen parts after beating), /ḍ-ḍwwəx/ "he got high (on drugs, liquor)", adjectives /ġliḍ/ and /smin/ "fat". Cf. B-29 above.

-- /ḅyḍṛ/ See /piḍala/.

B-31 /bznəs/ "he used narcotics" (Mr). In F used as mediopassive /t-bznəs/ "he was a drug dealer, he engaged in illegal commerce (drugs, other contraband items)" (tends to imply swindling customers as well). Verbal noun /t-bznis/, agentive /bznas/ C-163 "dealer" and variants (Appendix C). From Eng business via Fr bisness [biznəs]. F Mr *Mk.

B-32 /bẓwəṭ/ "he hazed (new student)" (refers to a traditional treatment of new students at some institutions, said to be notorious at engineering schools), verbal noun /t-bẓwiṭ/; modelled on Fr bizuter "to haze", but in fo may be denominative from noun /bẓwiṭ/ "new student subject to hazing" (variants /bizu/ and unassimilated /bizü/) (Fr bizut). The form /bẓwiṭ/ itself has a complex origin in which the various Fr forms (bizut, verb bizuter, verbal noun bizutage) are crossed with each other. F *Mk *Mr. Cf. C-96, 164.

B-33 /dimirda/ "he acted by himself, he saved his own skin, he looked out for himself"; Fr démerder. F Mk *Mr. [Alg has reflexive construction /dimirda ṛuḥ-u/ "he saved himself, he looked out for himself".]

B-34 /diwana/ "(official) assessed customs tax to (object)"; sense from Fr dédouanier but formally denominative from /diwan-a/ "customs" (see Appendix C for discussion of this item). F.

B-35 /dribla/: (1) "he dribbled (soccer, basketball)"; (2) he cheated (other person)" (slang, transitive); (3) "he beat around the bush, was evasive" (slang, intransitive). Verbal noun: /driblaž/, unpharyngealized. From Fr dribbler (ex Eng), dribblage. F Alg. Syn: /luppa/ B-96.

-- /dubl/ See /ḍubl/.

B-36 /dwwəš/ "he took a shower"; modelled on Fr doucher (perhaps) but form is denominative from /duš/ (Fr douche); verbal noun /tə-dwaš/. F Mk Mr Tt Alg *Casa(j). Cf.C-177.

B-37 /ḍala with preposition /ᶜla/ "he was obsessed with (food, wọrk, etc.), he threw himself (figuratively) into (it)"; now entirely assimilated and not considered foreign by Moroccans but an old loan from Sp imperative dale "give (it) to him!". F Mk *Mr *Alg *Casa(j). [DMA-AE; for the etymology see EDA 351.]

B-38 /ḍạ̃ṣa/ "he danced"; Fr danser; not very common, used occasionally with reference to modern rock 'n' roll rather than traditional Moroccan dancing. F Mk *Mr. Syn: /šṭəḥ/ (usual word for "to dance"), /ṛqəṣ/ (from CA, uncommon).

B-39 /ḍifuṛma/ Used chiefly in participial form /m-ḍifuṛmi/ "deformed, mutilated (person)"; Fr déformer (participle déformé) (Sp deformar). F.

B-40 /ḍiklaṛa/ with preposition /b-/: (1) "he accused (culprit to police), ratted on", example /ḍiklaṛa bi-ya/ "he accused me (of the crime)"; (2) "he declared (article, to customs official)", ex. /ḍiklaṛi-t b-l-wiski/ "I declared the whisky"; (3) "to declare, announce", ex. /ḍiklaṛa bi?nna-hu kan tmma/ "he declared that he had been there". Mostly educated usage in all senses; from Fr déclarer (Sp declarar). F.

B-41 /ḍikuṛa/ "he decorated, embellished (room, etc.)", participle /m-ḍikuṛi/ "decorated"; educated usage; Fr décorer (Sp decorar). F Mk *Mr. Syn: /ẓwwəq/, /zyyn/.

B-42 /ḍimaṛa/: (1) "he moved forward"; (2) "(motor) started up"; verbal noun /ḍimaṛaž/; Fr démarrer (démarrage). F Mk Mr. (Alg dimaṛa.]

B-43 /ḍipana/: (1) "he repaired (e.g. automobile, after malfunction or accident)"; (2) "he bailed out (friend, e.g. with badly needed help or loan)" (figurative); (3) "he was in trouble, in need of help". Senses 1 and 2 (F Mk), sense 3 (Mr). Verbal noun /ḍipaṇaž/. From Fr dépanner (dépannage). F Mk Mr. [Alg has /dipaṇa/.] Syn: /ṣləḥ/ "to repair", /ᶜawn/ "to help".

B-44 /ḍiṛạ̃ža/ "he disturbed, bothered, annoyed (someone)"; Fr déranger. F Mk Mr *Casa(j). [Alg /ḍiṛạ̃ža/ or /diṛạ̃ža/, not so common as in Morocco; attested as /ḍiṛạ̃ž/ in some Jewish Moroccan dialects including Rabat.]

B-45 /ḍṛuga/ Occurs in mediopassive /tt^-ḍṛuga/ "he became drugged, he got high on drugs"; participle /m-ḍṛugi/ "high on drugs, addicted to drugs"; from Fr droguer. F Mk *Mr. Syn: /t-ḥššəš/ "to smoke hashish (or use drugs in general)".

B-46 /ḍubl/(Mk Mr) or /dubl/(F): (1) "he doubled (it), increased two-fold"; (2) "he repeated (action), did it over"; (3) "he passed (another automobile)". Influenced by Fr doubler (Sp doblar) but probably most directly related to noun /ḍubl/ or /dubl/ (Fr double, Sp doble). F Mk Mr *Casa(j). [Tt variant /ḍawbal/ shows characteristic Tt verb shape; Alg has /dubla/.] Syn: /zad/ "to increase", /^{c}awd/ "to repeat" (or adverb "once again"), /tna/ or /tnna/ "to fold, double".

B-47 /faḷṭ/ "he made a mistake, he was wrong"; probably denominative from noun /faḷṭ-a/ "error, fault" (Sp falta). F *Mk *Mr *Alg. [DMA-AE; recorded in Casa(j) in phrase /faḷṭ f-/ with preposition /f-/ in sense "to treat (someone) wrongly, to make a mistake regarding (person)".] Syn: /ġləṭ/, /xṭə?/. Cf. C-198, 250, 252.

B-48 /fanta/ "he dodged (opposing player), he gave a fake" (sports); probably denominative from /fant-a/ "(a) fake, dodge" (Fr feinte) rather than directly from Fr verb feindre. F Mk Mr Alg. Syn: /ṛawəġ/ (from CA, used in broadcasts). Cf. C-201.

B-49 /fiksa/: (1) "he looked directly or piercingly at (person, thing)"; (2) "he assembled (device, from pieces)"; (3) "he set or fixed (e.g. time for appointment or rendezvous)"; (4) "he fixed, repaired". From Fr fixer. F(senses 1 2) Mk(3) Mr(4).

B-50 /fikta/ or /fikṭa/ "he posted (employee or soldier, to a given location, often far away)", mediopassive /t-fikta/ or /t-fikṭa/ "he got posted (to a given city, e.g.)"; Fr affecter. F.

B-51 /flippa/ Occurs in mediopassive /tt-flippa/ "he flipped out, he started acting silly or berserk", participle /m-flippi/ "flipped out, acting strangely" (both forms often used in context of narcotic or alcoholic high); either an internal derivative from adjective /flipp/ "flipped out" (Eng flipped via Fr flip), or possibly direct from Fr verb flipper (participle flippé); slang usage but common in this style. F Mk Mr. Syn: /ḥmaq/ "to become crazy", /ḅwwəṭ/ (B-30, above). (Cf. also B-31, B-45.)

B-52 /fngḷ/ "(man) he copulated with (woman)" (transitive, uncommon and vulgar slang)"; from noun /fangaḷ-a/ "penis" (uncommon vulgar slang), a possible European loan. F. Syn: usual word is /ḥwwa/, numerous slang forms. Cf. C-200.

B-53 /fnṭəẓ/ or /fnṭəz/ Occurs in mediopassive t-fnṭəẓ/, /t-fnṭəz/ "he acted like a big shot, put on airs, acted pompously"; denominative from /fnṭaziy-a/ "pompousness" (Sp fantasia and other Romance forms); verbal noun /t-fnṭiẓ/, /t-fnṭiz/. F Mk Tt *Mr. [DMA-AE]

B-54 /fõṣa/ "he tried very hard, exerted himself, threw himself into activity"; Fr foncer. F. [In Alg "he went very fast, charged ahead", literal or figurative.]

B-55 /frkəs/ Occurs in mediopassive /t-frkəs/ "he acted like a dandy or fop" (smartly dressed, etc.); denominative from noun /friks/, said to be from Fr; slang usage. F *Alg. Syn: several in this appendix (B-24, 26 etc.). Cf. C-232.

B-56 /frma/ or /frm/ Occurs in mediopassive /t-frma/ or less commonly /tt-frm/ "it became worn out or no good"; originally used in military in sense "discharged from army (for injury or illness)"; Fr réformer [see EDA 400]. F *Mr *Casa(j). [Alg /firma/.]

B-57 /fuḅṛ/ Occurs in mediopassive /t-fuḅṛ/ with preposition /ᶜla/ "he gave tip or small gift to (person)", example /t-fuḅṛ-u ᶜli-ha/ "they gave her a tip"; verbal noun /t-fuḅiṛ-a/; denominative /t-CuCC/ type from noun /faḅuṛ/ "tip, gift" C-193 (Sp favor). F Mk Mr Tt *Alg. [Tt variant /t-fawḅaṛ/ has characteristic Tt stem shape; DMA-AE.] Syn: /ᶜṭa/ "to give" (usual word).

B-58 /fuk/ "must". Invariable form used with following finite clause (like Fr il faut que), example /fuk t-mši/ "you must go", /fuk n-mši-w/ "we must go"; occasionally in form /y-fuk/ with same usage; uncommon in Morocco but occurs in Algeria and adjoining parts of Morocco (Oujda area in northeast, southeast area around Zagora where I have recorded it from a Jewish dialect); based on Fr il faut, with /k/ in /fuk/ originally from following Fr conjunction que or from MCA 2Sg object suffix /-k/ (in which case the form was originally /y-fu-k/ "you must", il te faut); now an unsegmentable unit treated either as a particle /fuk/ or, in the case of /y-fuk/, as an imperfective 3Sg masc. form (with dummy, invariable 3Sg subject). *F *Mk. [Used occasionally by my Alg informants but, unlike in Morocco, restricted to 2nd person subject in subordinated clause: /i-fuk t-mši/ "you must go".] Syn: /xəṣṣ/ "must" with similar syntax, e.g. /xṣṣ-ək t-mši/ "you must go", /xəṣṣ-ni n-mši/ "I must go".

B-59 /fuṛa/ Occurs in mediopassive /t-fuṛa/ "it (nail, screw) got worn out", participle /m-fuṛi/ "worn out"; Fr forer (foré). F.

B-60 /fuṛma/ Occurs in mediopassive /t-fuṛma/ "he showed off his strength, showed off his muscles", participle /m-fuṛmi/ "strong, well-built, muscular (person)"; Fr former (formé). F Mr. [GJA 99 has noun /fuṛm-a/ but participle /m-fuṛm/; Alg /t-fuṛma/ means "to be trained, educated" from Fr se former, cf. formation "training".] Syn: see /budr/, /müskla/ (both in this appendix).

B-61 /fuṛṣa/: (1) "he forced open (door)"; (2) "he worked on something hard, he exerted himself", in this sense in expressions like /fuṛṣa ᶜla ṛaṣ-u/ "he pushed/exerted himself" (with preposition /ᶜla/ and reflexive pronoun) and /fuṛṣi-t ᶜla žhd-i/ "I strained, exerted force". From Fr, perhaps based on both forcer and (s')efforcer. F Mk Mr. [Alg in sense 1.]

B-62 /gaṛḍa/: (1) "he guarded, protected, defended" (F Mk Alg); (2) "he supervised, watched over (workers, students)" (F Mr); (3) he guarded (opposing player, in sports)" (British English: "he marked") (Mk). From Fr garder. F Mk Mr Alg. Syn: /ḥḍa/ "to watch over", /ᶜəss/ "to be on guard duty", /dafᶜ/ (from CA) "to guard, mark (in sports)".

B-63 /gažа/ "he enlisted (in army, in travel group, etc.), he signed up"; example /gaži-t mᶜa-hum/ "I signed up with them"; verbal noun /m-gažy-a/; Fr (s')engager "to enlist", old loan brough in from Algeria in early Protectorate period. F Mk Mr Tt. [Alg now has /gaǰa/ with affricate.] Syn: /ltazm/ (from CA, not common). [EDA 384]

B-64 /gida/ "he guided (tourists)"; noun of profession /ta-gyyad-t/; Fr guider (Sp guiar), reinforced by noun /gid/ "guide" C-269 (Fr guide) with noun of profession based on /ta-CCCaC-t/ pattern; cf. also verbs /gwwəd/ and /gyyəd/, below. F Mk *Mr *Alg. Syn: /ṛšəd/ (from CA, not common except in formal contexts).

B-65 /glaṣa/(F Mk) or /gḷasa/(F) "he froze (it), he made (it) very cold, he chilled (drink)"; participle /m-glaṣi/ or /m-gḷasi/, verbal noun /m-glaṣy-a/ or /m-gḷasy-a/; from Fr glacer (participle glacé). F Mk *Mr. [Alg. has participle.] Cf. noun /glaṣ/ and variants "ice cream". Syn: /brrəd/ "to make cold", /žməd/ "to freeze". Cf.C-273.

B-66 /grisa/: (1) "he greased (it)" (Mk); (2) "he attacked, mugged (him)" (F Mk Mr); verbal noun /grisaž/ (unpharyngealized), /m-grisy-a/, or /t-grisy-a/; Fr graisser (sense 1), agresser (sense 2). F Mk Mr.

B-67 /gṛṣn/ Occurs as mediopassive /t-gṛṣn/ "he did servile or domestic labour"; denominative from /gaṛṣun/ "waiter" (Fr garçon); verbal noun /t-gṛṣin/. F Mk(rare) *Mr.

B-68 /gufl/: (1) "he inflated (tyre, balloon)"; (2) "he beat up (in fist-fight)". Mediopassive /t-gufl/ "it became inflated or swollen" or "he got beat up" (with black eye, etc.); from Fr gonfler. F Mk Mr *Casa(j). [Alg now has /gõfla/ in both senses; EDA 400 gives /gnfḷ/ as older Moroccan borrowing.] Syn: /nfəx/ "to inflate"; see also discussion of B-30 above.

B-69 /guma/ "he erased (something written)"; Fr gommer or denominative from /gum-a/ "(rubber) eraser" (Fr gomme and Sp goma). F Mk *Mr. Syn: /mḥa/ "to erase", /ḥyyəd/ "to eliminate, get rid of".

B-70 /gwwəd/ "he guided, led; he drove (vehicle)"; actually not a European loan but inherited from CA root √qwd (in a dialectal stem-formation); now secondarily associated with loanwords /gid/ "guide" (person) and /gida/ B-64 and /gyyəd/ B-71 "to guide (tourists)", so that /gwwəd/ is sometimes used in this touristic context. F Mk Mr Alg. [DMA-AE; MAG 115 gives /gwwad/ "guide", a regular agentive from /gwwəd/.] Syn: /ṣag/.

B-71 /gyyəd/: (1) "he guided (tourists)" (F Mk Mr); (2) "he led (person) astray (into sin, danger, etc.)" (F Mk). Verbal noun /t-gyad/. Denominative from /gid/ "(tourist) guide"; see also verbs /gida/ B-64 and /gwwəd/ B-70 above. Syn: /ṣag/ "to lead, drive", /ṛšəd/ (from CA) "to guide (tourists)", /žṛṛ/ "to pull".

B-72 /hippa/ Occurs in mediopassive /t-hippa/ "he behaved like a hippie"; participle /m-hippi/ "hippie" and fem. /m-hippy-a/; verbal noun /t-hippy-a/ or /m-hippy-a/; denominative from noun /hippi/ (pl. /hippiy-in/) "hippie" (Eng via Fr hippie); noun of profession /ta-hippiy-ət/ "being a hippie, hippiehood" also elicited. F Mk *Mr. Cf. C-291.

B-73 /kaṣa/: (1) "he cut corner (driving)" (F); (2) /kaṣa ḷa-kṛuṭ/ "he had midafternoon snack (sandwich, etc.)" (F Mk); (3) "he suffered" (Mk). Participle (sense 1) /m-kaṣi "(driver or vehicle, e.g. motorcycle) taking sharp corner, angled to take sharp corner" (F). From Fr casser (basic meaning "to break" but occurring in various expressions), for sense 2 Fr casser la croûte "to take midafternoon sandwich". F Mk *Mr *Casa(j). For sense 2 see also /qṣṣa/ B-122 below. [EDA gives /kssṛ/ in sense 2, actually an old MCA stem with secondary meaning due to phonological similarity to the Fr verb; NLVM 120 has /kaşa/ "lift!" (imperative) from Sp caza!, an independent borrowing probably with no historical relationship to those cited in this entry.] Syn: /hrrəs/ (sense 1), /t-^{c}gba/ (sense 3).

B-74 /kḷakṣuna/(F Mk), /kḷakṣuṇa/(Mr), or /kḷakṣa/(Mr) "he honked (automobile horn)"; Fr klaxonner or denominative from noun /kḷakṣuṇ/ "(automobile) horn" (Fr klaxon [klakson]); note that for F Mk the /n/ in verb is not pharyngealized, but /ṇ/ in noun is (hence pl. /kḷakṣuṇ-at/ with final syll. pharyngealized). F Mk Mr. Syn: /ṭyyəṭ/ or /ṭwwəṭ/ (from onomatopoeia /ṭuṭ/ "honk!", cf. Eng. toot but probably a native form). Cf. C-355.

B-75 /klaṣa/: (1) with preposition /^{c}la/ "he chewed (person) out, he rebuked (him) forcefully"; ex. /klaṣi-t ^{c}li-ha/ "I chewed her out" (F); (2) (simple transitive with no preposition) "he put (something unwanted) to side" (Mr). From Fr classer in minor idiomatic uses. F Mr *Mk. [Used in Alg in sense "he classified, arranged" following main Fr sense.] Syn: /ġwwəṭ/ "to shout", /bḷaga/ B-7 "to chew out".

B-76 /klaṭa/ Attested as mediopassive /tt-klaṭa/ "(balloon, tyre, bomb) blew up, exploded" (intransitive); Fr (s') éclater. F. Syn: /t-fṛg^c/.

B-77 /kɔ̃pa/ "he camped out (in tents)"; Fr camper. Obtained from F informant but he said used mainly in east around Oujda. [Alg /ką̃pa/.] Cf. borrowed noun /ką̃ping/ "camping ground" and variants (Fr camping ex Eng).

B-78 /kṛaẓa/ "he smashed, crushed (it)"; Fr écraser. F. [Alg /kṛaẓa/.]

B-79 /k^{w}rrəz/ "he embraced (person), he held in bear hug"; origin unclear, possible connection to Fr caresser. Mr *F.

B-80 /kruva/(F) or /krufa/(Mr) "it (tyre) was punctured, went flat"; mediopassive /tt-kruva/, /tt-krufa/ in same sense; example /(tt-)kruva-t-l-u ṛ-ṛwiḍ-a/ "he had a flat tyre" (lit., "the tyre got flat for him"); participle /m-kruvi/, /m-krufi/ "flat (tyre)" (can be used by itself as noun); Fr crever (crevé) reinforced by noun /kruvi/ "flat tyre" (crevé). F Mr *Mk. [Alg /kriva/, /kröva/ "to be punctured.] Syn: /t-fšša/.

B-81 /kruwa/ "he screwed (nut, into bolt)"; Fr écrouer reinforced by noun /kru/ "nut" (Fr écroux). F.

B-82 /kṛwaẓa/ (/ṛ/ not syllabic) "he crossed (legs, etc.); (they) crossed (e.g. cars at intersection, perpendicularly)"; participle /m-kṛwaẓi/ "crossed; having limbs crossed", example /ana m-kṛwaẓi ržl-i-ya/ "I have my legs crossed"; Fr croiser (croisé). F Mk Mr(rare). [Alg /kṛwaza/ with /z/ instead of /ẓ/.] Syn: /ṛbb^c/.

B-83 /kufṛ/ "he preserved (insect, etc.) in alcohol; he stuffed (bird, game animal) for preservation"; origin ambiguous, associated by some speakers with borrowed noun /kufṛ/ "vault, safe" (Fr coffre, Sp cofre), but perhaps really from /kafuṛ/ "camphor, mothballs" (CA kāfūr-). F Mr. [DMA-AE; Tt has /kawfaṛ/.]

B-84 /kuṃanḍa/ (with preposition /f-/) "he bossed (person) around, he gave lots of orders to"; example /ta-y-kuṃanḍi fi-ya/ "he bosses me around"; Fr commander. F Mk Mr. [Alg /kuṃạ̄ḍa f-/; EDA 391.] Syn: /ḥkm f-/.

B-85 /kuṃanṣa/ (F Mr) or /kuṃaṣa/ (Mk, unnasalized) "he began" (especially, "he began work"); Fr commencer; not common, used mostly in European-type contexts. F Mk Mr. Syn: /bda/ "to begin" (usual word).

B-86 /kumək/ In mediopassive /t-kumək/ "he clownedaround, did a funny routine"; denominative from /kumik/ "comedian" (Fr comique); verbal noun /t-kumik/. F Mk *Mr. Syn: /ḍḥək/, /ḍḥḥək/.

B-87 /kunəb/ In mediopassive /t-kunəb/ "he acted like a country hick"; denominative from pejorative slang noun /kambu/ "country hick" C-311 (Sp campo "field"). F.

B-88 /kuṇṭakṭa/ or /kuṇṭakṭa/ "he contacted (someone, by touch or by communication)"; also used as euphemism for "he copulated with (woman)"; Fr contacter, cf. borrowed noun /kuṇṭak/. F Alg. Syn: /qaṣ/ "to touch", /ḥwwa/ "to copulate with".

B-89 /kuṇṭṛula/ "he supervised (workers, etc.); he controlled"; nouns /kuṇṭṛul/ "control", agentive /kuṇṭṛulör/ "(train, bus) ticket-collector"; Fr contrôler. F Mk Mr. [Alg /kõṭṛula/.] Syn: /ṛaqəb/ (from CA, cultivated).

B-90 /kupa/(Mk), /kuppa/(F), or /kuppya/(F) "he copied" (used in context of cheating on homework); verbal noun /kuppyaž/ ([kuppyæž]), or /t-kupy-a/; Fr copier. F Mk *Mr *Casa(j). [Alg /kopiya ^{c}la-/ "to copy (something)".] Syn: /nql/, /ql^c/. For variant /kuppa/ see also homophonous B-91.

B-91 /kuppa/: (1) "he cut (finger, etc.)"; (2) "he cut off, intercepted (pass, in sports)", example /kuppa ^{c}li-ya l-kuṛ-a/ "he cut off the ball (i.e. the pass) to me"; Fr couper; note that for some speakers this is homophonous with preceding entry B-90. F. [Alg /kupa/ "to cut off", used especially in context of driving automobiles.] Syn: /qṭ^{c}/.

B-92 /kura/ "he ran"; Fr courir; not normally used, attested once from uneducated Mk informant, apparently used for the linguist's benefit instead of usual word /žra/, definitely rejected as MCA form by other informants. Mk.

B-93 /kuvra/ with preposition /^{c}la-/: (1) "he fouled (other player, in sports)"; (2) "he covered up for (friend, e.g. when friend has missed class or work)". From Fr couvrir (sense 2) or denominative from /kufṛ-a/ "foul kick (soccer)" (Fr coup franc). F(sense 2) Mr(sense 1). [Alg "to follow (other soldier in march formation)", related to sense 2.]

B-94 /kwansa/ "he bumped (into), rammed, collided with"; Fr coincer. F Mk Mr. [Alg /kwæ̃sa/.]

B-95 /liva/ "he made (ball, etc.) spin, curve, or swerve"; mediopassive /t-liva/ "it (ball) swerved"; denominative from /livi/ "curving shot"; informant from F claimed these are from Fr verb *liver and noun (participle) *livé, but these forms do not occur in Fr dictionaries and were not recognized by Fr speakers; perhaps we are dealing with Fr lever "to lift" or some other form. F Mk *Mr. Syn: /^{c}wwəž/. Cf. also B-96.

B-96 /luppa/ "it missed or eluded (someone, something), he was evasive or slippery (in speech), he beat around the bush"; ex. /luppa-t-hum/ "it (soccer ball) eluded them, it got away from them"; Fr louper. F Mk Mr. Cf. /dribla/ B-35.

B-97 /maṛka/ "he scored (goal)"; Fr marquer (Sp marcar), perhaps with some support from noun /maṛk-a/ "brand, type" (Fr marque, Sp marca) despite divergent semantics; verbal noun /t-maṛky-a/. F Mk Mr Tt Alg. Syn: /sžžl/ (also "to register"), /dxxl/ "to put in". Cf. C-91.

B-98 /miḷãža/ or /miḷãňza/ "he mixed (things)"; Fr mélanger; fairly uncommon. F. Syn: /xlləṭ/ (the common term), cf. also /rwwn/ B-137. Cf. noun /miḷãžž/ C-501.

B-99 /mirda/ "he annoyed, pestered"; Fr emmerder. F Mk *Mr. [Alg /mrda/.] Syn: /qlləq/ (more common), /šṭn/ (also more common), cf. /bṛẓəṭ/ B-23 and /ḍiṛãža/ B-44.

B-100 /miza/ "he anted (in poker), he put his ante in"; from Fr miser or else directly modelled on Fr noun mise "ante"; cf. noun C-505 /miss-a/. F Mk Mr. Syn: /ṭawl/.

B-101 /mṇṇək/ "he failed to show up (for work, school), he was a no-show"; verbal noun /t-mṇak/; probably an old loan brought in from Algeria, from Fr manquer or It mancare, now showing factitive-causative form in MCA. F Mk Mr *Casa(j). [Alg now has /mãka/, /maṇka/.] Syn: /ġab/ "be absent", /t-ġyyəb/ "be absent".

B-102 /müskla/ or /müskl/ Occurs in mediopassive /t-müskla/ (F Mk) or /t-müskl/(Mr) "he showed off or flexed his muscles"; probably denominative from adjective /müskli/ "muscular, having large muscles" (Fr musclé). F Mk Mr. Cf. C-523.

B-103 /musəq/(F) or /mwssəq/(Mr) "he played or turned on some music for (person, direct object)"; example is imperative /musəq-na/ "play music for us! give us some music!"; possibly modelled on Fr musiquer, but most direct source is noun /musiq-a/ "music", from CA mūsīqā, a fairly old European borrowing. F Mr *Mk. Syn: /smm^c l musiq-a/ "to cause to hear music". For semantically similar verb type see /žwana/ B-187, below, sense 2.

B-104 /myyək/ with preposition /^{c}la/ "he would have nothing to do with (person), he deliberately avoided (person)" (slang); common in insulting imperative /myyək ^{c}li-ya/ "stay away from me!, get lost!"; denominative from /mik-a/ "plastic; money", cf. parallel expression /mik-a ^{c}li-ya/ (same gloss as /myyək ^{c}li-ya/); informants explaining these forms suggest a basis in Fr slang (faire oeil de plastique "to avoid, to give the cold shoulder"); however, Fr speakers did not recognize such expressions and they do not occur in Fr slang dictionaries; actually /mik-a/ "plastic; money" and /myyək/ are probably associated synchronically only by a secondary convergence, since /myyək/ appears to be a reshaping of vulgar Alg /nyyək/, as in /nyyək ^{c}li-ya/ "get fucked!" (i.e. "get the fuck away from me"); MCA normally has /ḥwwa/ in sense "to copulate with" and rarely has /nak/, /-nik/ (but not /nyyək/), so an older expression with */nyyək/ might have been opaque in MCA and subject to restructuring by association to /mik-a/. F Mk Mr. [Alg also has /ṛuḥ t-nyyək/ "go get fucked!" in addition to the expression quoted above.] Syn: /d-žnnəb ṭṛiq-i/ "get lost!, out of my way!".

B-105 /nirva/ In mediopassive /t-nirva/ "he was worried, agitated, anxious"; participle /m-nirvi/ "worried"; associated by bilinguals with Fr nerveux, but Fr énervé may also be involved historically; it is likely that participle /m-nirvi/ was the first borrowed form. F Mk Mr *Casa(j). [Alg has /t-niṛva/, participle /m-nirvi/, also transitive simplex /niṛva/ "to worry, bother (someone)", and Alg informants associate this with énerver, énervé.] Syn: /t-qlləq/.

B-106 /ṇuma/ In mediopassive /t-ṇuma/ "he was appointed (named) (to a post)" or "he was named (personal name)"; participle /m-ṇumi/ "named" (both senses), the participle being the only common form; Fr nommer (nommé). F Mk *Mr. [EDA 401 gives /numa/ and emphasizes the appointment sense.] Syn: /smma/ "to give name".

B-107 /numr/: (1) "he numbered (several items)"; (2) he singled out, picked out (one man in a crowd), he spotted (man in crowd)". Denominative from /nmr-a/ and /nimiru/ "number" (Fr nombre and numéro, Sp número); verbal noun /t-numir/.

F Mk *Mr *Casa(j) *Alg. Syn: /ṛqqm/ "to number", /šaf/ "to see".

B-108 /nuṭa/: (1) "he took notes"; (2) "he assigned grades (to student, direct object)". From Fr noter (sense 2 also influenced by Fr noun note "grade".) F Mk *Mr. [Alg in sense 2.]

B-109 /paṛḷa/ "he spoke"; Fr parler; rare, used by educated bilinguals mainly in jocular sense, used ostentatiously by some half-educated speakers, mainly in context of speaking Fr. F. For a similar ex. see /spika/ (below, this appendix). The usual word is /hḍṛ/ with /t-kllm/ the second most common stem.

B-110 /paṣa/: (1) "he advanced to higher level (in educational system, by passing difficult exam at end of preceding level)"; (2) "he passed (food at table, soccer ball to teammate, etc.)"; (3) "he went past, he passed by"; Fr passer, passage. Verbal noun (sense 1) /paṣaž/; cf. C-544 noun /paṣ-a/ (related to sense 2). F(senses 1 2) Mk(1 2) Mr(2) Tt(3) Alg(2). Syn: /nžəḥ/ "he passed exam", /daz/ (regional variant /gaz/) "he went past".

B-111 /pãṣa/ "he thought"; Fr penser; rare, used in ostentatious speech of semi-educated person in F, also overheard in Mr. Syn: /fkkṛ/ or /xmməm/.

B-112 /piḍala/ (F Alg), /pidala/(Mr), /biḍṛ/(F area but rural), or /ḅyḍṛ/(F area but rural) "he pedalled (bicycle)"; Fr pédaler or denominative from /piḍal/ (variant /biḍaṛ-a/) "pedal (of bicycle)"; rural forms show assimilation to traditional MCA canonical shape (quadriconsonantal verb stem); verbal noun /piḍaḷaž/ (Fr pédalage) or /t-biḍiṛ/. F Mk Mr Alg. No common native synonym. For noun see C-77.

B-113 /piṛda/(F Alg) or /pirda/(Mk): (1) "he wasted (time, money)"; (2) it (tyre, balloon) lost air, was disinflated". Fr perdre (Sp perder), cf. earlier borrowing /brda/ B-17 from same source; not very common. F Mk *Mr *Casa(j). [Alg sense 1; NLVM 18.] Syn: /xṣṛ/ or /xsr/ "to lose", /ḍyy^c/ "to waste".

B-114 /plõža/ "he dived, plunged", mediopassive /tt-plõža/ "he jumped in (literal or metaphorical), he immersed himself"; Fr plonger (se plonger). F Mk Mr Alg.

B-115 /pṛipaṛa/ "he prepared (food, lesson, etc.)", mediopassive /tt-pṛipaṛa/ "he prepared himself, got prepared", participle /m-pṛipaṛi/ "prepared, ready", example /l-makl-a m-pṛipaṛy-a mzyan-a/ "the food is well prepared" (calque on Fr bien préparé); Fr préparer; mainly educated usage. F Mk Alg *Mr. Syn: /wžžəd/.

B-116 /pṛiṣa/ "he pressed (oil from olives, hashish from kif, etc.)"; participle /m-pṛiṣi/ "pressed"; Fr presser or denominative from noun /(ḷa-)pṛiṣ/ "press, pressing machine". F Mr *Mk. [Alg has /m-prisi/ "pressed for time, very busy" from another sense of Fr pressé.] Syn: /^{c}ṣṛ/ "to squeeze, wring out".

B-117 /p̣ṛiẓạ̃ṭa/ "he presented, introduced (one person to another); he displayed, showed off (something)", mediopassive /tt-p̣ṛiẓạ̃ṭa/ "he was introduced or displayed; he showed himself off, put on airs (said mainly of women); he showed up (for appointment)"; Fr (se) présenter (Sp presentar). F Mk Alg *Mk. Syn: /qddm/ "to introduce", /t-?ṇṇəq/ "to put on airs", /ḥḍṛ/ "to be present, show up", /^{c}ṛḍ/ "to display".

B-118 /p̣ṛunõṣa/ "he pronounced"; Fr prononcer; educated usage, not very common. F Mk(rare) Alg *Mr. Syn:/nṭəq/(from CA).

B-119 /puṣṭa/ "he mailed, posted (letter or package)"; Fr poster or denominative from /buṣṭ-a/ "post office, postal system" (Fr poste, Sp posta). F Alg. Syn: /ṣifəṭ/ "to send". Cf. C-151.

B-120 /puẓa/ Mediopassive /t-puẓa/ "he sat with legs crossed"; Fr (se) poser or perhaps reposer. Mr *F. [Alg has /puẓa/ "he posed (for photo); he showed off".]

B-121 /pwanta/ (with /pw/ pharyngealized as [p̣p̣^{w}]) "he punched in (an employee at work indicating time of arrival for shift)"; in participle also has slang sense, /hwwa m-pwanti ^{c}li-ha/ "he is chasing her, he is courting her"; Fr pointer. F. Syn: /ṣyyəḍ/ "to hunt; (man) to court (woman)".

B-122 /qṣṣa/: (1) "he ate, consumed"; (2) "he copulated with (woman)"; (3) in expression /qṣṣa ḷa-kṛuṭ/(Mk) or /qṣṣa l-kaṣkruṭ/(Mr) "he had midafternoon snack (sandwich)". It is possible that in sense 1 this is a native form (sense 2 being a metaphorical extension), but sense 3 is modelled on Fr casser la croûte; cf. also /kaṣa/ B-73, sense 2. F(senses 1 2) Mk(3) Mr(3). Syn: /kla/ "to eat" (metaphorically "to copulate with"), /ḥwwa/ "to copulate with".

B-123 /ṛabuṭa/ "he used lathe on (material, object)"; Fr raboter. Cf. noun /ṛabu/ "lathe" (Fr rabot). F *Mk *Mr.

B-124 /ṛamaṣa/ "he collected (several things), he gathered in (e.g., money and cards after a play in a card game)"; Fr ramasser. F *Mk *Mr *Casa(j). [Alg has /ṛmməṣ/ in similar sense.] Syn: /žm^c/ (very common).

-- /rata/ See /rita/ B-128.

B-125 /ṛaṭa/ "he missed (train, exam, etc.)"; Fr rater. F Mk *Mr. [Alg has /ṛata/.] Syn: /fat-l-i/ (lit. "it passed for me" with different syntax).

B-126 /ṛạ̃ža/ or occasionally educated /?aṛạ̃ža/: (1) "he put (it) in order"; (2) "he arranged (meeting, business, etc.)". Long form /?aṛạ̃ža/ possible only in sense 2 and not common there. Mediopassive /t-ṛạ̃ža/ or rarely /t-?aṛạ̃ža/ with preposition /m^{c}a/ "with" means "to make arrangements with (someone), to fix things up with (someone)"; Fr arranger (and s'arranger avec) for both senses, also Fr ranger "to arrange, put in place" for sense 1. F Mk(/ṛạ̃ža/ but not /?aṛạ̃ža/) *Mr *Casa(j). [Alg has /ṛạ̃ǰa/ and /t-ṛạ̃ǰa m^{c}a/. Syn: /rttəb/ or /sttəf/ (sense 1), /t-fahm/ or /klləf/ (sense 2).

B-127 /rigl/ "he fixed, repaired (something)". Mediopassive /t-rigl/ has the corresponding mediopassive sense, but is also very common in slang in form /t-rigl ^{c}la/ in sense "he teased (someone), he poked fun at (person), he put (person) down with wry humour, he used sarcasm against (person)"; verbal noun in this sense /t-rigil/; participle /m-rigl/ "sarcastic (person), person who teases others" (note active sense); Fr régler (and se régler avec, cf. Sp arreglar) with some senses influenced by Fr rigoler. F Mk Mr. Syn: /sawa/ "to fix". Cf. C-600.

B-128 /rita/(F Mk Alg) or /rata/(Mr) "it (bus, etc.) stopped; he stopped (doing something), ceased (activity)"; example /riti-t ml-l-xdm-a/ "I stopped working, I gave up my job"; Fr arrêter, not very common in either sense. F Mk Mr *Casa(j). [Alg, also participle /m-riti/ "stopped, having stopped".] Syn: /wqəf/ "to stop, come to a halt", /ḥbəs/ "to stop", /qaḍa/ "to finish (activity)". Cf. C-19.

B-129 /ritma/ Occurs only as participle /m-ritmi/ "rhythmic, rhymed"; based directly on Fr rhythmé. F *Mk *Mr. Syn: /m-wzun/. Cf. C-604.

B-130 /ṛiyaža/ "he reacted (to/against something)"; Fr réagir; educated usage. F. No common synonym.

B-131 /ṛiẓiṛva/ "he reserved (seat, ticket)"; Fr réserver. F. No common MCA synonym, but "this seat is reserved (taken)" is expressed by "this seat is full" /had l-bḷaṣ-a had-i ^{c}amṛ-a/.

B-132 /r^{w}ppiṛa/ "he noticed (landmark, to remember route), he took a good look at (landmark, to fix it in his mind)". Mediopassive can mean the same thing as /r^{w}ppiṛa/, or can have the passive meaning "he was spotted (by police, etc.)". From Fr repérer. F *Mk *Mr. Syn: /lqa/ "to find", /tt-^{c}ṛf/ "to be recognized".

B-133 /ṛuḍa/ "he broke in (new car, wild horse, inexperienced employee, naive young wife), he trained (person)"; Fr roder. F Mk Mr. Syn: /drrəb/ "to train" (preposition /^{c}la/ or /f-/)

B-134 /ṛufəẓ/ or /ṛuvəz/ In mediopassive /t-ṛufəẓ/ (F Mk) or /t-ṛuvəz/ (Mr) with preposition /^{c}la/, "he was insolent or disobedient to (person)"; verbal noun /t-ṛufiẓ/; Fr refuser, originally in army in context of refusing orders. F Mk Mr *Casa(j). [Alg /ṛufẓa/ "he refused", mainly rural usage; EDA 405-6.] Syn: /t-ḥnkṛ/.

B-135 /rula/: (1) "he rolled (cigarette, hashish joint); (2) "he let (vehicle) roll, he got (vehicle) under way". Sense 2 is not very common; however, an imperative /ṛul/ "let her roll!" is used to tell bus drivers to start the bus after letting passengers off (this form, if taken as MCA, would be a hollow triliteral presupposing perfective */ṛal/, but the only form which can occur is /ṛul/ and the only use is imperative with no affixes permitted). From Fr rouler (and imperative roule!). F Mk Mr.

B-136 /rutira/ "he took (ojbect) out, he withdrew (object, money from bank, etc.)"; Fr retirer; not common. F Mk *Mr. Syn: /xrrəž/ "to take out". Cf. /tira/ B-168.

-- /ṛuvəz/ See /ṛufəẓ/ B-134.

-- /rʷppiṛa/ See B-132.

B-137 /rwwn/ "he mixed (several things) together; he threw or stirred (things) together haphazardly"; mediopassive /t-rwwn/ used in pl. forms "they got mixed or thrown together" (in Tt this also can mean "he got into trouble (with police, etc.)" and thus may have sg. subject); participle /m-rwwn/ "mixed or thrown together" (Tt also "mixed up, in trouble, behaving in a mixed-up way"); denominative from /rwin-a/ (Sp ruína, Fr ruine) "mixture, disturbance, struggle". F Mk Mr Tt. [Casa(j) with sense "he disturbed, annoyed"; Alg rare in sense "he ruined, wasted", rejected by informants in second interview.] Syn: /xlləṭ/ "to mix".

B-138 /sbira/: (1) "he took advantage of (weak or gullible person), he exploited (person), he got something for nothing from (person, direct object)"(F); (2) (with preposition /ᶜla/) "he was stronger than (person), he overpowered or dominated (person)"(Mr). Origin unclear; one informant suggested derivation from noun /sbiritu/ "liquor, spirits" (Sp espíritu), but this may be a folk etymology; Fr supérer (Sp superar) "to overcome" may also be involved. F Mr *Mk *Casa(j). Syn: /t-ḍllm/.

B-139 /sdr/ "he welded" (literal sense); Fr soudre or, more likely, denominative from noun /sudur/ "welding; welder" (Fr soudure, soudeur) fitting into triconsonantal root type in MCA. Mr *F. For F form see /suda/, below.

B-140 /sinya/(F Alg), /sina/(Mk Mr), or /sna/(F Mk) "he signed (contract, etc.), he put his signature on (something)"; verbal noun /sny-a/ or /sinyatur/; Fr signer (noun signature). The participle (passive sense "signed") may be /m-sinyi/ or /m-sini/ but never */m-sni/; the imperfective corresponding to /sna/ is /-sni/. F Mk Mr Alg. [Casa(j) /sinyaṛ/, 1Sg perfective /sinyaṛ-t/, has form of Sp verb loans and suggests an earlier form for /sinya/, but Sp *siñar or *señar is not standard, cf. the normal verb firmar. Thus /sinyaṛ/ is either based on a substandard dialectal Sp form or is a pseudo-Sp formation based on Fr signer.] Syn: /wqqᶜ/ (but /sinya/ and variants are now dominant). [EDA 407 /snya/.]

B-141 /sira/(F Mk Casa(j)), /sirž/(F), or /sirža/(Mr) "he shined (shoes)"; mediopassive /t-sira/ "he had his shoes shined, got a shine; it (shoe) got shined"; verbal noun /siraž/ [siræž]; agentive noun /sirur/ "shiner, shoeshine boy". /sira/ direct from Fr cirer, /sirž/ and /sirža/ denominative from verbal noun (Fr cirage). F Mk Mr Casa(j). [Alg /sirž/, /sirža/.] Syn: /msəḥ/. [EDA409]

B-142 /skanta/ "he ruined (machine, appliance, etc.), he wore out (machine, etc.)"; mediopassive /tt-skanta/ "he got sick; it (machine) malfunctioned, became no good, got worn out"; Fr esquinter. F. [Alg in sense "he wore me out", etc.]

-- sna/ See /sinya/ B-140.

B-143 /spida/ Occurs in mediopassive /tt-spida/ "he used Speed (name of a narcotic); he used narcotics (of all sorts) excessively"; denominative from /spid/ "Speed" (Eng, perhaps via Fr slang). F Mr *Mk.

B-144 /spika/ "he spoke"; Eng speak; strictly found in affected or jocular style by persons who know some English. F. Cf. comments regarding /paṛla/ B-109 above.

B-145 /srba/(F Mk Mr Tt Casa(j) Alg) or /srva/(Tt): (1) "he (waiter or bartender) served (food or drink, direct object)" (person served normally in dative) (F Mk Mr Tt Casa(j)); (2) "he dealt out (cards, in card game)"(F Mk); (3) "he hurried up"(F Mk Mr Tt Casa(j)). Sense 3 chiefly in imperative /srbi/ "hurry up!", also /srbi-ni/ (same gloss) with meaningless 1Sg object marker. Verbal noun /m-srby-a/ or /t-srby-a/ (one F informant says the first of these means "service", the second "hurrying, haste"); cf. /srbay/ "server, waiter" (agentive derivative) and noun /srbis/ "service; queue, line (of people, waiting for something)". Old, well-integrated loan across North Africa from Fr servir, Sp servir, It servire, but with sense 3 (perhaps a Moroccan innovation) showing semantic contamination with native /zrb/ "he hurried". F Mk Mr Tt Casa(j). [NLVM 58; MAG 75; Alg /srba/ in sense 1, also permitting person served to be direct object; DMA-AE; EDA 407.] Syn: /qddm/(sense 1), /fṛṛəq/ or /wzzᶜ/(sense 2), /zrb/(sense 3).

B-146 /srkl/: (1) "he surrounded, circled around (them)"; (2) "he weaved his way through (crowd, obstacles)". Mediopassive /t-srkl/ "he was surrounded" or (slang) "he was crazy, nuts"; participle /m-srkl/ "surrounded; crazy, nuts"; Fr cercler, encercler or denominative from /siṛkl/ "circle" (Fr cercle). F Mk(participle) *Mr. [Alg has /srkla/ "he surrounded".] Syn: /ḍaṛ b-/, /t-mšša/.

-- /srva/ See /srba/ B-145.

B-147 /stika/ with preposition /ᶜla/. "he polished (it) up, he made (it) pretty, he dressed (person) up nicely"; mediopassive /tt-stika/ "he got dressed up (in fancy clothes), he showed off (with clothes and slick behaviour)"; participle /m-stiki/ "well-dressed, polished, embellished"; origin problematic, possibly connected with /šiki/ (Fr chiqué) and verb /šyyək/ B-167, but presumably also involves some other unknown form. F *Mk *Mr *Alg. Syn: /t-ʔṇṇəq/.

B-148 /suda/ "he welded (objects)"; Fr soudre. F *Mr. [Alg.] For Mr variant /sdr/ see B 139. Cf. also agent noun /sudur/.

B-149 /sugr/: (1) "he matched, paired (e.g. cards with others, in card game)"(F Mr); (2) "he beat (person) up, in fight" (Mk); (3) "he fixed or repaired (it)"(Mk; (4) "he insured (home, etc.), he took out insurance on (home, etc.)"(Tt pronounced /sawgar/with usual Tt form). Mediopassive /t-sugr/ "it was matched, paired", verbal noun of mediopassive /t-sugir-a/ "matching, pairing". From Sp seguros "insurance" (verb asegurar) for sense 4, with sense 3 possibly an offshoot of this; presumably Sp seguir "to follow" for sense 1. F Mk Mr Tt *Alg. [Casa(j) has /sugr/ in sense 4, like Tt; see DMA-AE "to insure, to register"; NLVM 74 gives participle /m-ṣugṛ/ "registered (letter)" from Sp seguro as urban Rabaṭ form.] Syn: /žwwəž/ "to pair" (also "to marry"), /ḍṛb/ "to hit" (cf. other loans like sense 2 here such as /bwwəṭ/ B-30, /gufl/ B-68), /ṣawb/ "to fix", /sura/ "to insure" B-150.

B-150 /ṣura/ "he insured (home, etc.), he took out insurance on (it)"; verbal noun /m-sury-a/, cf. also noun /aṣuranṣ/ "insurance"; Fr assurer. F Mk Mr *Casa(j). [For Tt form, presumably once more widespread butnow completely ousted by /sura/ in much of Morocco, see B-148, above, sense 4 from Sp seguros.] Syn: /?mmn/ (uncommon, from CA). Cf.C-23.

B-151 /ṣabuṭa/ or /ṣbbəṭ/: (1) "he attacked (former friend, etc.) verbally, he turned against (former friend)"; (2) "he kicked" (/ṣbbəṭ/ only). From Fr saboter (first form), or (second form) from noun /ṣbbaṭ/ "pair of shoes" (old MCA form related to Sp zapato, Fr sabot, etc., but where the Romance forms may be from Arabic not vice versa historically); since /ṣbbəṭ/ can also be used in sense 1 we may have convergence due to phonological similarity; verbal noun /ṣabuṭaž/ or /t-ṣbaṭ/ (the latter derived regularly from /ṣbbəṭ/). F Mk *Mr *Casa(j). Syn: /ḥṭṭm/ "to destroy, hurt" (perhaps from CA).

B-152 /ṣaka/ "he swindled (gullible person)"; said to be based on Fr sacquer; slang usage. F.

B-153 /ṣbbn/ "he washed (clothing) with soap" (not used for washing dishes or body); denominative from /ṣabun/ or /ṣabun/ "soap" (possible loanword from Sp jabón, Fr savon, It sabone, but directionality of borrowing unclear in this case); verbal noun /t-ṣban/; feminine agentive noun /ṣbban-a/ "washerwoman". F Mk Mr Tt Casa(j) *Alg. [DMA-AE; TAR 422 refers to an etymological study suggesting that /ṣbbn/ is an old Semitic form while /ṣabun/ is a more recent loan; MAG 83 gives verbal noun as /t-ṣbin/ instead of /t-ṣban/, but this is a common alternation in this verbal noun pattern.] No synonym, but note /ġsl/ "to wash" (body, dishes).

-- /ṣbbəṭ/ See B-151.

B-154 /ṣkurṭa/ "he escorted" (used mainly in military context); participle /m-ṣkurṭi/ "escorted" (passive sense); Fr escorter. F Mk *Mr. Syn: /həzz/ "to take", /nqql/ "to transport", /ḥml/ "to carry".

B-155 /ṣṭala/ or (educated) /?anṣṭala/ (in latter form first syllable has plain [æ]) "he installed (piece of furniture, etc.), he put (large object) in its place"; mediopassive /tt-ṣṭala/, /t-?anṣṭala/ "he settled in (e.g. in new home)"; Fr installer. F Mk Mr. [Alg /ṣṭala/ "he installed" or intransitive "he settled in" without /t-/ prefix.] Syn: /ḥəṭṭ/ "to put down", /staqṛṛ/ (CA) "to settle in".

-- /ṣṭṭa/ See /suta/ B-159.

B-156 /ṣṭuppa/(F Mk) or /ṣṭuppa/(Mk) "he stopped (e.g. his car)"; imperative can be regular /ṣṭuppi/, /ṣṭuppi/ or irregular short form /ṣṭup/; Fr stopper (and stop!) ex Eng; cf. noun /ṣṭup/ "stop" and /luṭuṣṭup/ "hitchhiking" (Fr autostop); uncommon as verb. F Mk Mr. [NLVM 57 gives /stap/, /stop/ (phonemic interpretation not clear).] Syn: /wqəf/ "he stopped".

B-157 /ṣufəž/ Occurs in mediopassive /t-ṣufəž/ "he acted wild, acted like a savage"; participle /m-ṣufəž/ "acting wild, savage"; denominative from /ṣuvaž/ "savage" (Fr sauvage), with participle probably central historically. F. [Alg /t-sufəǰ/ "he became savage".] Cf. /wḥš-i/ "savage, wild".

B-158 /ṣuna/ "he rang (doorbell)"; example /ṣuni-t s-srsar/ "I rang the doorbell"; Fr sonner (Sp sonar). F Mr. [Alg has /ṣuni-t f-l-bab/ "I rang at the door".] Cf. /ṣuniṭ/C-692.

B-159 /ṣuṭa/: (1) "he jumped"; (2) "it (light, electricity) went out". Mediopassive /t-ṣuṭa/ has meanings corresponding to sense 2 and also "he went berzerk, he went crazy" (slang); participle /m-ṣuṭi/ "out (lights, electricity); nuts, berserk"; Fr sauter. Participle has variant /m-ṣṭṭi/ in slang sense "nuts, berserk"; this presupposes a verb */ṣṭṭa/, */t-ṣṭṭa/ which, however, is not used. F Mk Mr. [Alg /ṣuṭa/ "he jumped (on to train)" or "it went out (electricity, lights)" without /t-/.] Syn: /nqqəẓ/ "to jump", /wqᶜ ᶜaṭab/ from CA "there was a (power) failure", /ḥmaq/ "he went crazy". [DMA-AE /ṣuṭi/, /ṣṭṭa/.]

B-160 /šanṭa/: (1) "he sang" (mainly referring to European and American singing, not traditional Moroccan singing); (2) "he blackmailed (person, direct object)". From Fr chanter (cf. chantage "blackmail"). F *Mk *Mr. Syn: /ġnna/ "to sing", /ṛawd/ "to lure, entice" (CA).

B-161 /šaṛža/: (1) "he loaded up (truck, etc.)"; (2) "he (re-) charged (batteries)". From Fr charger, now very common; cf. noun /šṛžm-a/ "load" (Fr chargement). F Mk Mr Tt Casa(j). [Alg /šaṛža/, not */šaṛǰa/; NLVM 122 gives older MCA form based on Sp cargar.] Syn: /ᶜmmṛ/ (both senses).

B-162 /šat/, 1Sg perfective /šət-t/, imperfective /šut/ "he shot" (in context of soccer or similar sport); verbal noun /šut/ "shooting", /šut-a/ "(a) shot"; perhaps influenced by Fr shooter [šute] ex Eng, but probable direct source is Egyptian Arabic (via television broadcasts) where /šat/, /-šut/ is probably direct from Eng shoot. F Mk Mr *Casa(j). [Alg /šuta/ as in /šuta l-baḷu/ "he shot the ball" probably direct from Fr shooter.] Syn: /qdəf/ (Moroccan broadcast style), /ḍrb/ (also "to hit"), /tira/ B-168. [EDA 412; Tt /čaṭ/, /-čuṭ/.]

B-163 /šãža/: (1) "he changed, switched (hotel room)"; (2) "he exchanged (currency)"; (3) "he changed (tyres)"; (4) "he drew (new cards, in card game)". From Fr changer; note that this is used chiefly in "modern" contexts. F Mk Mr. [Alg in sense 3.] Syn: /bddl/, /ġyyṛ/.

B-164 /škḷəṭ/ "he masturbated" (slang); mediopassive /t-škḷəṭ/ (same meaning). Probably metaphorical denominative from /škḷaṭ/ "chocolate" (Fr chocolat, Sp chocolate); a synonymous slang expression /kffət/ "he masturbated" is similarly based on /kft-a/ "ground meat, hamburger meat". F.

B-165 /šuṃa/ "he was unemployed"; Fr chômer. In addition to regular imperfective /šuṃi/ I have heard /-šuṃ/ as in /ta-y-šuṃ/ "he is unemployed", suggesting direct influence of Fr present il chôme in this instance. Syn: negative of /xdm/ "to work".

-- /šuta/, /-šut/. See /šat/ B-162.

B-166 /šwạza/, imperfective /-šwạzi/ (back vowel /a/ but /z/ not pharyngealized) "he chose"; Fr choisir; not common but used sometimes by educated bilinguals. F *Mk *Mr. Syn: /xtaṛ/ (common).

B-167 /šyyək/ In mediopassive /t-šyyək/ "he acted suave, acted chic"; probably denominative from /šiki/ "suave, (ostentatiously) chic" (Fr chiqué), possibly influenced by Fr chic. F Mk Mr *Alg. [EDA 411] Syn: /t-?ṇṇəq/; see also B-24, 26, 53, 55, 117, 147. For /šiki/ see C-707.

B-168 /tira/: (1) "he shot (gun"; (2) "he shot (ball)"; (3) "he pulled (it), he withdrew (it)". Exx.: /tiri-t fi-h/ "I shot at (lit. in) him"; /tiri l-bab muṛa-k/ "pull the door (shut) behind you"; /tiri-t l-fluṣ ml l-ḅank-a/ "I withdrew the money from the bank". From Fr tirer (and retirer), Sp tirar. F Mk Mr. [Alg in sense 2.] Syn: for sense 2 /q̣dəf/, /ḍṛb/, /šat/ B-162; for sense 1 /ḍṛb/; for sense 3 /žṛṛ/ "to pull", /xrrəž/ "to take out".

B-169 /tka/, imperfective /-tki/ "he knocked out (opposing boxer or antagonist in fistfight)"; probably related to /kaw/, /kạw/ "knockout" (Fr K.O.), perhaps via a longer variant reflecting something like Fr coup de K.O. "knockout blow", now having regular triliteral weak stem shape. Mr *F.

-- /trika/ See /trüka/ B-172.

B-170 /trina/ "he trained (athlete, direct object)" or "he (athlete) trained, was in training"; mediopassive /tt-trina/ also used in second sense; Fr entraîner, s'entraîner; verbal noun /anṭṛinm-a/ (initial syllable pron. [æn]) or /ãṭṛim-a/ (Fr entraînement). F Mk Mr(mediopassive). [Alg in sense "he trained, also "he fooled around".] Syn: /drrəb/. Cf. C-16, 26.

B-171 /triša/ "he cheated" (intransitive, used chiefly in context of schools); Fr tricher. F. Syn: /ġəšš/, /trüka/ B-172.

B-172 /trüka/ or /trika/ "he cheated, he used devious gimmicks, e.g. to win card game" (can be intransitive or transitive, with other person in game as direct object); Fr truquer (cf. Fr noun truc); verbal noun /trükaž/. F Mk *Mr. Syn: /ġəšš/, cf. also /triša/ B-171.

B-173 /truna/ "he took his turn (e.g. to buy drinks for group)"; probably denominative from /turni/ "(his) turn" (Fr tournée). Mr *F. Cf. /turna/ B-174.

B-174 /turna/: (1) "he turned (object), he turned (it) over"; (2) "he did (a film, said of actor, director, etc.)". From Fr tourner (for sense 2 cf. tourner un film); verbal noun /turṇaž/ with initial syllable unpharyngealized. F Mk Alg *Mr. Syn: /ḍwwṛ/.

B-175 /tuša/: (1) "he touched"; (2) "he earned, made (a certain amount of money, normally as salary)". From Fr toucher (used in Fr in both senses, cf. combien tu touches? "how much (money) do you make?"). F Mk *Mr. [Also heard in Oujda; uncommon in Alg but occasional in sense 2.] Syn: /qaṣ/ "to touch" (the usual word), /məss/ "to touch", /lmə̇s/ "to touch" (perhaps CA).

B-176 /ṭaka/ or (educated) /?aṭaka/: (1) "he attacked (enemy, etc.)"; (2) "he (soccer player) went after the ball (in scramble)". From Fr attaquer (Sp atacar). F Mk Mr. [Alg has /ṭaka/ or /taḳa/ but it is not common now.] Syn: /hžm/ "to attack".

B-177 /ṭṛafika/(F Mk Mr Alg) or short form /ṭṛafik/(Mr) "he swindled, he was involved in swindling" (generally intransitive); verbal noun /ṭṛafik/ means "swindling" or else "irritating, bumbling behaviour"; Fr trafiquer (noun trafic). F Mk Mr. Short form is uncommon as verb and seems to be morphologically defective, avoiding most suffixes. Syn: /ẓwwṛ/.

B-178 /ṭṛaṣa/: (1) "he drew (line)"; (2) "he occupied (seat) for a long time", ex. /ṭṛaṣa f-l-kursi/ "he was in the seat for a long time". Verbal noun: /ṭṛaṣaž/ or /m-ṭṛaṣy-a/. From Fr tracer (Sp trazar). F(sense 1) Mk (sense 2) Alg(sense 1). Syn: /xṭṭəṭ/ "to draw".

B-179 /ṭṛạ̃ṣpuṛṭa/ "he transported, conveyed (load, etc.)"; Fr transporter; educated usage, not very common, cf. noun /ṭṛạ̃ṣpuṛ/. F Alg. Syn: /ḥml/ "to carry".

B-180 /ṭulạ̃ṭa/, imperfective /-ṭulạ̃ṭa/ (not */-ṭulạ̃ṭi/) "he acted smart (pejorative), showed off his cleverness, was a smart alec"; diminutive verb form /ṭwilạ̃ṭa/; denominative from adjective /ṭulạ̃ṭi/ "smart alec, wise guy" (complex origin involving Fr intelligent, Sp inteligente, and other prototypes); note that imperfective inflection suggests morphological connection with medio-passive type /t-CCCa/. F Mk *Mr *Casa(j). Syn: /ṭ-ṭwwṛ/.

B-181 /tuṛiza/ "he authorized, allowed"; Fr autoriser; educated usage. F. Syn: /sməḥ/ "to permit".

B-182 /vizita/: (1) "he visited (city, relatives)"; (2) "he (doctor) visited (patient)" (this more common than sense 1). From Fr visiter (Sp visitar) reinforced by nouns /vizit/, /vizit-a/ C-797 (Fr visite, Sp visita). F. Syn: /ẓaṛ/ "to visit" (used traditionally only in sense of visiting cemetery or religious site, now used more broadly by influence of CA).

B-183 /ẓṛṭa/(F Mk Alg) or /ẓṛṭ/(Mr) "he deserted (from army), he escaped (from jail)" (normally intransitive); participle /m-ẓṛṭi/ "deserter, escapee"; Fr déserter (Sp desertar), probably an old loan first common in military context. F Mk Mr Alg *Casa(j). [DMA-AE /ẓṛṭa/.] Syn: /hṛb/ "to flee, run away".

B-184 /zufr/ Occurs in mediopassive /t-zufr/, pronounced /d-zufr/ (with /ᶜla/ if indirect object expressed) "he acted like a playboy or swinger (chasing girls, getting drunk), he was a debauchee" or (less pejoratively) "he was a bachelor"; denominative from noun /zufri/ "swinger (back formation from Fr plural les ouvriers "the workers"); participle /m-zufr/ "swinger, debauchee"; verbal noun /d-zufir/. F Mr. Syn: /t-ᶜzra/ "to be a bachelor", /t-ṣlgəṭ/ "to be a swinger, debauchee".

B-185 /žangla/ "he zigzagged, moved crookedly, weaved in and out" (e.g. soccer player dribbling effectively); Fr jongler. F Mk *Mr. [Alg /žõgla/ "he juggled", closer to normal sense of Fr form.]

B-186 /žiṇiṛaliza/ "he (over-)generalized"; Fr généraliser; uncommon but overheard a few times in educated speech. F.

B-187 /žwana/: (1) "he put (letter) in envelope"; (2) "he gave a joint of hashish to (person, direct object)", ex. /žwana-ni/ "he gave me a joint , he fixed me up with a joint". Denominative from /žwa/ "envelope" (Fr joint) and /žwan/ "joint" (same Fr form). F *Mr. Syn: /ġlləf/ (sense 1), /ḥššəš/ or /ḍwwəx/ (sense 2). For semantics of sense 2 cf. parallel B-103. Cf. C-827, 828. Variant form /žwwn/ in sense 2.

B-188 /žwwn/ Same meaning as sense 2 of /žwana/B-187. From /žwan/ C-828.

Appendix C: European borrowings in MCA – Other stems

In this appendix we list MCA words other than verbs which are considered to be borrowings from European languages, mainly Fr and Sp. Most are nouns and adjectives; there are some adverbial elements and a few which are difficult to classify. Verbal nouns and participles related to verbs listed in Appendix B are given along with those verbs in that appendix and are usually not reproduced here, but some nouns and adjectives with some other relationship to verbs in that appendix are listed here as separate entries, with appropriate cross-references.

For transcriptions, abbreviations, etc., see the relevant notes and lists elsewhere in this book. Some general remarks on the organization of the entries given in the introductory note to Appendix B are also valid for this appendix. Some additional remarks for the present appendix follow.

The basic citation form given at the head of each entry is the Sg or MSg (masculine singular). Pl (plural) and Dimin (diminutive) forms are given in the same entries and are not separately listed. The FSg form of adjectives, with suffix /-a/ added to the MSg form, is usually not explicitly given except when its form and/or meaning is unpredictable.

The Pl is often given simply as /-at/, which of course is to be taken as a suffix added to the Sg stem. If the Pl involves ablaut the entire Pl form is transcribed. The Dimin Sg form always involves ablaut and is therefore always fully transcribed. The Dimin Pl is always /-at/ added to the Dimin Sg and is not explicitly presented.

Although technically unnecessary, instead of giving the Pl suffix in its phonemic form /-at/, we usually give it in phonetic form as either [-ạt] with back vowel or [-æt] with front vowel. The choice between the two depends on whether the final consonant of the preceding stem is pharyngealized or uvular, or not. The point of this practice is that often the phonetic form of the Pl suffix is the only reliable evidence for taking the stem-final consonant as pharyngealized or plain. For example, the Sg form for "diploma" (C-172) is phonetic [diplom] for my informants from F, Mk and Mr. However, for F and Mk the Pl is [diplom-æt], with unpharyngealized final syllable, while for Mr it is [diplom-at] with back vowel allophone in the final syllable. We account for this by representing the stem as /dipḷum/ for F and Mk, with pharyngealized /ḷ/ accounting for the realization of the /lum/ syllable as [lom] in the unsuffixed Sg form. For Mr, we take the stem as /dipḷum/ or /dipluṃ/ (we choose the latter for simplicity), since this accounts both for Sg [diplom] and Pl with [-ạt] (the /ṃ/ has automatic effects on preceding as well as following segments). It is technically sufficient to list the stem forms as shown, with Pl /-at/ simply listed in its phonemic form; however, it may be helpful to readers to know explicitly that a particular Pl form was recorded with [-ạt] or [-æt] as surface form of the Pl suffix, this being the evidence on which the phonemic transcription of the stem was made. When Pl /-at/ is shown as part of a fully transcribed form like /dipluṃ-at/ in phonemic transcription, we usually do not bother to mark the surface vowel allophones.

It should be noted that the detailed morphological information (concerning plurals, diminutives, etc.) is often based primarily or solely on data from F or Mk. Even when other locations (Mr Tt Casa(j) Alg, etc.) are listed as part of the distribution of the lexical item, the special grammatical forms mentioned may be valid only for F and Mk.

It should also be noted that some half-assimilated items from Fr fluctuate between code-switched and assimilated forms. The distinction is most obvious in the Pl, where the code-switched form involves Fr les and where the assimilated form involves suffix /-at/ or some MCA ablaut pattern. In many of the entries we indicate "no Pl", which means merely that no assimilated MCA plural form is recorded. If the citation form is a Sg form of an obviously countable noun, it can be assumed that my informants indicated that they preferred a code-switched Fr plural form.

Unless otherwise specified, the definite forms are based on the (indefinite) citation form and the Pl and Dimin forms given, plus the usual MCA definite prefix /l-/, which becomes /C_1-/ when the initial stem consonant /C_1/ is coronal (including /ž/). This applies even to nouns borrowed from Fr or Sp feminine nouns which would take la as the definite article in the source language. However, for some borrowings the definite form in MCA is /la-/ or /ḷa-/, and in this event the definite form is explicitly given. (Use of this definite form does not necessarily mean code-switching, since MCA Pl /-at/ and other MCA morphology may co-occur with the same form.)

For purposes of gender concord, unless otherwise indicated we get FSg agreement if and only if the borrowed form in MCA ends in /-a/, the usual FSg suffix in MCA (which must be segmented by a hyphen). Because of this, commonly the gender of the MCA borrowing does not match the grammatical gender of the form in the source language. (This is not true for Algeria.) Even the generalization of the /la-/ or /ḷa-/ definite allomorph for a given borrowing does not affect this rule, so /(ḷa-)gaṛ/ "(the) train station" (Fr feminine la gare) is grammatically MSg in MCA. On the other hand, some Fr masculines ending in -ment or the like are resegmented in MCA so that they end in /-a/ and are treated as FSg, as in the case of /bṛašm-a/ C-106 "intersection" (Fr branchement). (For

Algerian Arabic, Fr gender is usually retained in borrowings, and since gender is often not predictable from the form of the borrowing itself it must often be explicitly stated.) For further details see the discussion in Chapter 6.

-- /abiḷā̃s/ See /baḷansiy-a/ C-41.
-- /aḅugaḍu/ See /ḅugaḍu/ C-125.
C-1 /aḍris-a/ "address, location"; Pl [-æt]; Fr adresse. F Mk *Mr. [Alg definite /ladris-a/, indefinite either /adris-a/ or /dris-a/, EDA 374-5.] Syn: /ᶜunwan/, /nəᶜt/ (but /adris-a/ is most common).
C-2 /aḍviṛṣiṛ/ "opponent" (in sports); no Pl; Fr adversaire. F. Syn: /xəṣm/.
C-3 /ạkt/, /ạkṭ/, /ḷakt/, or /ḷakṭ/. Occurs in /ạkt d-l-maṛyaž/ "marriage certificate"; no Pl; Fr acte de mariage. F Mk. Syn: /ᶜəqd/.
C-4 /aḷaṛm/ "alarm" (e.g. in alarm clock); no Pl; Fr alarme. F.
C-5 /aḷbum/ "(photo or record) album"; Pl [-æt]; Fr album [albɔm]. F *Mr.
-- /alkul/ See /ankul/ C-10.
C-6 /aḷṃan/ "Germans (people)", Sg /aḷṃan-i/ (masc.), /aḷṃan-iy-a/ (fem.), count Pl /aḷṃan-iy-in/; Fr allemand(s), Sp alemán(es), but possibly mediated by CA ?almān- (from these sources). F Mk.
-- /-am-a/ See /lam-a/ C-436.
C-7 /aṃaṛš/ (adverb) "in motion, under way", used with verb /dar/ "he did/made" as in /dar aṃaṛš ṭ-ṭumubil/ "he got the car moving"; Fr en marche. F Mk Mr(rare). Syn: /qllᶜ/, /nwwəḍ/ (verbs).
C-8 /aṃḅriyaž/ (last syllable pron. [æž]) "(automobile) transmission"; no Pl; Fr embrayage. F Mk Mr.
C-9 /aṇaṇaṣ/ (collective) "pineapple(s)"; Sg /-a/, Pl [-ạt]; Fr ananas ([ananas] or [anana]), Sp ananás. F Mk. [Tt /?aṇaṇaṣ/.]
C-10 /ankul/ (F Mk Mr) or /alkul/ (Casa(j) Alg) "(drinking or industrial) alcohol"; Fr alcool [alkɔl], Sp alcohol [alkól], though the Fr and Sp words are themselves medieval loans from Arabic (cf. CA al-kuḥūl-). F Mk Mr Casa(j) Alg. [Tt /kul/, def. /l-kul/.]
C-11 /antiris/ "interest (on loan)"; no Pl; cross of Sp interés and Fr intérêt. F Mk. [Casa(j) and TAR 303 have older /(l-)intiris/ based on Sp.]
C-12 /antrit/ "(retirement) pension", as in /qbṭ-u l-antrit/ "they are retired (on a pension)"; early loan from Fr (la) retraite, perhaps brought in from Algeria; Pl [-æt]. F Mk Mr. [Alg /(l-)antrit/ is feminine for concord purposes.] Syn: /taqaᶜud/ (uncommon, CA). [EDA 394]
C-13 /anṭiṛ/ ([æ nṭeṛ]) (F), /ā̃ṭiṛ/ (F Mk), /ā̃tiṛ/ (Mr) "antenna, aerial"; Pl [-æt]; Fr antenne. F Mk Mr. [Tt /intiṛṇ-a/ and variant /linṭiṛṇ-a/ involve crossing with /linṭiṛṇ-a/ "flashlight", from Sp linterna "lamp", etc.] Syn: /xiṭ/ (lit. "thread").

C-14 /antịrdi/([aenteṛdi]) Occurs in phrase /ṣã̤ṣ antịrdi/ "no entry (traffic direction)"; Fr sens interdit. F. Syn: /m-mnu^c/ is usual for "prohibited", cf. also /ḍifaṇḍi/ C-183.

C-15 /anṭịṛṇ-a/([æ nṭeṛṇ-a]) "campus (of elementary or secondary school, not university)"; Pl [-ạt]; Fr internat. F.

C-16 /anṭṛinm-a/([æ nṭṛenm-a])(F) or /ã̤ṭṛim-a/(Mk) "training, conditioning"; Fr entraînement; cf. verb /trina/ B-170. Syn: /tˆ-drib/ (verbal noun of /(t-)drrəb/).

C-17 /aṛaf/(F Mk) or /aṛaf̣/(Mr), definite form /l-aṛaf/ or /l-aṛaf/, indefinite either /aṛaf/, /aṛaf̣/ or same as definite. (1) "police car or van"; (2) "police raid or round-up". Pl [-æ t](F Mk), [-ạt](Mr). From Fr (la) rafle. Cf. C-203, 204.

C-18 /aṛbiṭ/ "referee"; Pl [-ạt], alternative Pl /aṛbiṭṛ-at/(F) with extra /ṛ/ not found in Sg; Fr arbitre (Sp árbitro). F Mk Mr. [Tt has /aṛbitṛu/ or shortened /bitṛu/ from Sp; Alg /aṛbiṭ/ has Pl /liz-aṛbiṭ/ from Fr les arbitres.] Syn: /ḥakam/ (from CA, used in broadcasts).

C-19 /aṛi/ "(bus or train) stop"; Pl /-yat/; Fr arrêt. F *Mk *Mr. Syn: /muqəf/, /wuquf/. Cf. related verb /rita/ B-128.

C-20 /arivi/(F) or /ạrivi/(Mk) "finish point (in race, etc.)"; Pl /-yat/; Fr arrivée. F Mk *Mr. Syn: /wuṣul/ "arrival" (CA).

-- /aṛmwaṛ/ See /maryu/ C-481.

C-21 /aspirin/ "aspirin"; no Pl; Fr aspirine (Sp aspirina). F Mr. [EDA 394]

-- /asurti/ See /aṣuṛṭi/ C-24.

-- /ạsyæ̃/, /ạsyan/ See /aṣyæ̃/ C-25.

C-22 /aṣṭa/ Occurs in the slang expression /aṣṭa ḷa muxiṛṛ-a/ "(until) some other time, not now" (discussed under /muxiṛṛ-a/ C-525), and in /aṣṭa luwego/ "see you later, until tomorrow"; from Sp conjunction or preposition hasta [asta] "until" (originally a borrowing from dialectal Arabic, cf. MCA /ḥtta/ "until"), hasta luego "until then, see you later". Both expressions attested in F from educated speakers who do not know Sp, but are used by a small segment of the population.

C-23 /aṣuṛanṣ/ "insurance"; no Pl; definite form /l-aṣuṛanṣ/ may also be used as indefinite; Fr assurances. F. [EDA 368 gives /asurans/; Alg has /l-asirã̤ṣ/, treated as feminine.] Cf. verbs /sura/ B-150 and /sugr/ B-149 (sense 4). Syn: /t-?min/ (from CA).

C-24 /aṣuṛṭi/(F Mk) or /asurti/(Mr) "security policeman"; Pl /-ya/; Fr (la) Sûreté "security (force)", involving resegmentation as /l-aṣuṛṭi/. F Mk Mr. [EDA 395 /lasurti/.]

C-25 /aṣyæ̃/, /ạsyæ̃/, or /ạsyan/([ạsyæ n]) Occurs in variants of the expression /aṣyæ̃ kuṃḅaṭa/ "retired serviceman, military veteran", definite form /l-aṣyæ̃ kuṃḅaṭa/ (with just one /l-/ prefix, but pronounced as two words); forms above used as Sg or Pl in concord depending on meaning; Fr ancien combattant. This is a well-known expression but is linguistically not fully assimilated to MCA.

-- /ạ̃tiṛ/ See /anṭiṛ/ C-13.

-- /ạ̃ṭiṛ/ See /anṭiṛ/ C-13.

-- /ạ̃ṭṛim-a/ See /anṭṛinm-a/ C-16.

C-26 /ạṭṛinyur/ "(athletic) coach"; no Pl; Fr entraîneur (Sp entrenador). F Mk. Syn: /mu-drrib/ (from CA, but now common). Cf. verb /trina/ B-170.

C-27 /aỵuka/ (masculine): (1) "lawyer, attorney"; (2) "avocado". Pl in both senses /aỵuk-at/([aỵok-æt]); Fr avocat. F Mk. Syn: for sense 1 /muḥami/ (CA) or (very common) /ḅugaḍu/ C-125.

C-28 /aỵyaṣyuṇ/(F), /aỵyaṣun/(Mk), or /abyasun/(Mr) "airport, airplane landing strip or runway; aviation, flying airplanes"; no Pl; Fr aviation, Sp aviación. F Mk Mr. Syn: /maṭaṛ/ (now the common word for "airport").

C-29 /ḅaḅa/ "father, dad"; no Pl; used principally among Gallicized urban bourgeoisie; Fr papa, Sp papá. F Mk Casa(j). [DMA-AE; Alg has /baba/ as vocative.] Usual form for "father" is /ḅḅa-/, but /baba/ or /ḅaḅa/ may be native in some MCA dialects. Cf. /ṃaṃa/ C-465. Cf. also C-581.

C-30 /baḅuṛ/: (1) "steamer, ferry"; (2) "port (left side of ship facing toward prow, nautical term)"; (3) samovar (large tea urn or container)". Pl (senses 1 and 3) is [-ạt] or /bwaḅṛ/. Sense 1 from Sp vapor, Fr vapeur; sense 2 from Fr bâbord. F(senses 1 2 3) Mk (1 3) Tt(1 3) Alg(1) *Mr. [DMA-AE has /babbuṛ/; cf. NLVM 3, MAG 55, 57.] Syn: /baxiṛ-a/ or /safin-a/ "ship" (both from CA), /brrad/ "tea container".

C-31 /bạ̃d, definite /ḷa-bạ̃d/ "band, pack (of thieves)"; no Pl (hence hard to tell whether final segment is /d/ or /ḍ/; Fr (la) bande. F. Syn: /ᶜiṣab-a/. Cf. C-32.

C-32 /bạ̃ḍ-a/ "(head)band"; Pl [-ạt]; Fr bande, Sp banda. F.

-- ḅagaḍu/ See /ḅugaḍu/ C-125.

C-33 /bagaž/ (unpharyngealized) "loose possessions" (things usually taken with one on journeys, but not necessarily already in luggage); no Pl; Fr bagages. F Mk Mr. [Alg /bagaǰ/, uncommon.] Cf. also /baliz-a C-42, /ṗakṭaž/ C-539.

C-34 /ḅagiṭ/ "long, thin bread loaves" (collective); individual Sg /-a/, Pl [-ạt]; Fr baguette; still less common than the old Sp loan /kumir/ C-401. F. [eAlg has Sg /ḅagiṭ-a/.]

C-35 /ḅak/ "baccalaureat diploma" (abbreviated form); Pl [-aet]; Fr bac. F Mk Mr Alg. Syn: see C-36.

C-36 /ḅakaḷuṛiy-a/(the common form), /bakaṛuṛiy-a/(rural), or /ḅakaṛuḷiy-a/(rural) "baccalaureat diploma (from lycée)"; Pl [-aet]; Fr baccalauréat. F Mk. Cf. C-35.

C-37 /bakiy-a/: (1) "packet, pack (of cigarettes, tea, etc.)"; (2) "rear end, arse" (slang, mildly vulgar). Pl [-æt] or ablaut /bwaki/, Dimin /bwikiy-a/; Fr paquet, probably replacing older loans from Sp paquete. F Mk Mr. [Casa(j) has /ṗaket/, Pl /ṗaket-iṣ/ with ordinary MCA assibilated /t/, pronounced [tˢ], not pharyng. /ṭ/ despite surrounding vowels, the Pl being from Sp paquetes and the Sg back-formed by analogy to other Sg/Pl loan doublets from Sp with Pl /-iṣ/; Alg /baki/, Pl /-at/ or /bwaka/; Tt /pakiy-a/; EDA 369 and DMA-AE both give /bakit/.] Syn: /qabs-a/ (uncommon) "pack", /ṭiẓ/ "arse".

C-38 /ḅal/(F Mk) or /baḷ/(Mr) (collective) "haystack(s)"; individuative Sg /-a/, Pl [-æt](F Mk) or [-ạt](Mr); Fr balle. F Mk Mr. Do not confuse with next two entries.

C-39 /ḅal/, definite /la-ḅal/ "ball"; Pl [-æt]; Fr balle perhaps reinforced by Fr ballon; not common. F *Casa(j). Note that long definite form /la-/ distinguishes this from preceding entry in definite form (at least for F informants). Syn: /kuṛ-a/ (the usual word).

C-40 /ḅal-a/(F Mk) or /baḷ-a/(Mk Mr) "shovel"; Pl [-æt](F Mk) or [-ạt](Mk Mr); Fr pelle, Sp pala. F Mk Mr. [DMA-AE; NLVM 17 gives Sp form as etymon; TAT 241 gives /pal-a/.] This item may be confused with C-38 and C-39, especially in Pl forms. This is now the common term for "shovel".

C-41 /baḷansiy-a/(F), /ḷabilạ̃ṣ/(Mk), /ạbilạ̃ṣ/(Mr), or /ḷabiḷans/(F but uncommon) "ambulance"; Pl [-æt](F, both forms) or [-ạt](Mk Mr); Fr ambulance. F Mk Mr. [Tt has /bulaṇsy-a/ or aṃbulaṇsy-a/, Sp ambulancia, and this Sp form may also be behind /baḷansiy-a/; Alg has /l-ambilạ̃ṣ̤/, grammatically feminine.] Syn: /syyaṛ-a d-l-?isᶜaf-a/ (complex CA phrase).

C-42 /baliz-a/: (1) "suitcase"; (2) "rear end, arse". Pl [-æt] or /bwalz/, Dimin /bwiliz-a/; Fr valise, possibly with Sp also involved. F Mk Mr. [Casa(j) /valiz-a/; Alg /valiz-a/, Pl /-at/, with rural pronunciation /faliz-a/; DMA-AE.] Syn: /mḥfaḍ-a/, /šanṭ-a/ (but /baliz-a/ now the usual word).

C-43 /balko/ "balcony"; Pl [balko-næt]; Fr balcon, Sp balcón.F.

C-44 /baḷu/ "ball; balloon"; Pl /-yat/, /-wat/, or /-nat/; Fr ballon (Sp balón); most common sense is "balloon", since /kuṛ-a/ is usual word for "ball". F *Casa(j). [This seems to be the common word for "ball" in Alg, which has Pl /baḷu-wat/; Alg does not seem to use /kuṛ-a/ very often.] Cf. also /ḅal/ C-39.

C-45 /ban/, definite /la-ban/. Occurs in expression /kamyu d-la-ban/ "dump-truck" with stem /kamyu/ "truck" C-313; Fr (camion de) la benne. F.

C-46 /banan/ (collective) "banana(s)"; individuative Sg /-a/, Pl [-æt]; Dimin /bwinin-a/ (Sg); Fr banane, Sp dialectal (and Portuguese) banana (but the normal continental Sp word now is plátano). F Mk Mr Tt.

-- /ḅandi/ See /bwandi/ C-160.

C-47 /ḅani/, definite /la-ḅani/ "vanilla (flavour)"; no Pl; Fr (la) vanille. F.

C-48 /ḅank/, /ḅank/, /ḅank-a/, or /bank-a/ "bank (financial)"; Pl [-æt]; Fr banque, Sp banco ("bank") and banca ("banking system" as abstraction); forms with FSg /-a/ suffix common in F/Mk area, but unsuffixed form preferred by Mr informant; CA bank-, Pl bunūk- (also of course a modern borrowing) possibly involved but does not by itself account for MCA forms. F Mk Mr. [Casa(j) /bank-a/; Tt and Alg /ḅaŋk-a/, with Tt Pl /ḅnuk-a/ and Alg Pl [-æt]; EDA 369-70; MAG 51, 69; NLVM 14; DMA-AE; Pl /bnak/ in some of these early sources.] Dimin /ḅniyk-a/(F Mk), /bniyək/ (Mk Tt), /bwiŋk-a/(Mk).

C-49 /bantur-a/ "paint (substance); painted area"; Pl [-æt]; probable cross of Sp pintura, Fr peinture; cf. C-50 and verb in B-15. F Mk *Mr *Casa(j). [GJA 17 /pntuṛ-a/, from Sp.] Syn: /ṣbaġ-a/.

C-50 /bantur-i/, FSg /bantur-iy-a/ "painter"; Pl /-iy·in/(F) or /-iy-a/(Mk), FPl /-iy-at/(F Mk); perhaps modelled on Fr peintre, Sp pintor, but formally from C-49 with /-i/ derivational suffix. F Mk. Syn: /ṣbbaġ/.

C-51 /ḅanyu/ "bathtub"; Pl /-wat/ or -yat/; Sp baño (reinforced by Fr bain). F Mk Mr. [Tt /ḅanyo/; Algrs /ḅanyu/, Pl /-wat/; eAlg prefers /binwaṛ/, grammatically feminine, from Fr baignoire; DMA-AE.]

C-52 /baṛ/ "bar, tavern"; Pl [-ạt] or /biṛ-an/, Dimin /bwiyṛ/; Fr Sp bar. Tt F Mk Mr *Casa(j). [Alg prefers /tbrn-a/, a distinct Romance loan.] Syn: /ḥan-a/ (uncommon, probably from CA).

C-53 /baṛašit/, /baṛašid/, /paṛašit/, /paṛašid/ (these first four from F area), /parašit/(Mk), or /paṛašiḍ/(Mr) "parachute"; Pl [-æt](F Mk) or [-ạt](Mr); Fr parachute. F Mk Mr. Syn: /miḍll-a/ (from CA).

C-54 /baṛaṭu/ "small payment to owner of establishment made in each hand of poker (or similar game)"; no Pl; Sp barato "cheap" (apparently also used in this sense in card game). F. [GJA 8]

C-55 /baṛaẓiṭ/ "parasite, pest" (pejorative word for human pest); no Pl; Fr parasite; cf. /bṛẓaṭ/ C-119 and verb /bṛẓəṭ/ B-23. F *Casa(j).

C-56 /baṛaž/ "checkpoint, barrier for police check"; Pl [-æt]; Fr barrage. F Mk Mr.

C-57 /baṛb-a/ (collective) "beets"; no other Sg or Pl; probably an old loan brought in from Algeria based on It barbabietola or a short form thereof, cf. /biṭṛav/ C-92, a more recent loan from Fr betterave. F Mk Mr Casa(j)(uncommon) *Tt. [EDA 370]

C-58 /baṛku/ "fishing boat"; Pl /-wat/; Sp barco "boat". Mr. [Tt has /baṛko/.] Old loan used mainly in coastal areas. Cf. C-71.

C-59 /baṛṃan/ "bartender"; no Pl; Fr barman [barman] ex Eng; not common. F(rare) Mk *Mr. Syn: /mu-wqqif/ (from CA). Cf. /baṛ/ C-52 and /baṛmiṭ/ C-60.

C-60 /baṛmiṭ/ or /baṛmiṭ-a/ (both forms grammatically feminine for concord) "barmaid, female bartender"; Pl [-at]; Eng, perhaps via Fr. F. Syn: /muwqqif-a/. Cf. C-59.

C-61 /basin-a/ "(washing) basin"; Pl [-æt]; Fr bassine. F. Syn: /bstiliy-a/ C-120.

C-62 /baṣaḍuṛ/ "ambassador"; no Pl; Sp embajador (possibly also Fr ambassadeur); now rare in comparison to /safir/ (from CA) or code-switched Fr ambassadeur. F. [MAG 55 gives /bašaḍuṛ/ as earlier form, suggesting direct origin in Sp, so that /baṣaḍuṛ/ may merely have been slightly remodelled by the influence of the Fr form.]

C-63 /baṣaži̇ṛ/ "passenger(s)" (Sg or Pl, no difference); Fr passager perhaps crossed with earlier loan from Sp pasajero. F *Casa(j). [NLVM 18-19; MAG 63; these sources suggest earlier form /bašažir/ meaning "passenger" or "(very) rich person", later partly remodelled under influence of the Fr form.]

-- /baṣbbuṛ/, /baṣbuṛ/. See /paṣpuṛ/ C-545.

C-64 /baṣkiṭ/ "basketball"; no Pl; Fr and Sp basket ([baskɛt] in Fr) ultimately from Eng. F Mk.

C-65 /baṣṭ-a/ "ice-cream cone"; Pl [-ạt]; exact history unclear but perhaps related to Sp pasta (a type of pastry). F. [Tt /paṣṭ-a/ "ice-cream cone"; GJA 16 /baṣṭ-a/, a Jewish pastry type; DMA-AE "ice-cream".] Cf. /gufrit/ C-282, /glaṣ/ C-273.

C-66 /batri/ or /ḅatri/: (1) (definite /l-batri/) "large battery (especially of automobile)"; (2) (definite /la-batri/ or /ła-ḅatri/) "drums, set of drums". Pl /-yat/. Distinction between /l-/ in sense 1 and /la-/ in sense 2 obtained from F and Mk informants. From Fr batterie (Sp batería). F Mk Mr(sense 1 only). [Alg has /(la-)batri/ "car battery", grammatically feminine; NLVM 3 gives an older form used by sailors from the Sp word.] Syn: /ḥžṛ/ "(small) battery" (also "stone"), /ṭbl/ "drum", /ṭnbuṛ/ "drum" C-763.

C-67 /baṭaṭ-a/(F Mk Mr Casa(j) Alg) or /bṭaṭ-a/(F Tt) (collective) "potato(es)"; no separate Sg, Pl optionally /bwaṭaṭ/; Dimin Sg /bwiṭiṭ-a/; early loan from Sp batata or patata (ultimately of American Indian etymology). F Mk Mr Tt Casa(j) Alg. [DMA-AE gives both forms; TAR 53 has /bṭaṭ-a/; TAT 231 gives /bṭaṭ-a/ with /baṭaṭ-a/ listed as Alg or Tunisian form.] Cf. C-326. Dimin also /bṭiyṭ-a/.

C-68 /baṭim-a/(F Mk Mr) or /vaṭim-a/(Mr) "apartment building"; Pl [-æt]; Fr bâtiment with semantics partially influenced (perhaps) by Fr appartement (cf. /bṛṭm-a/ C-114). F Mk Mr. [Alg also has /baṭim-a/, Pl /-at/, grammatically feminine as in Morocco, despite usual Alg tendency to preserve Fr gender value.] Syn: /ᶜimaṛ-a/ "building" (from CA), /ḍaṛ/ "house", /mubl/ C-517.

-- /baṭṛun/. See /paṭṛõ/ C-547.

C-69 /baṭṛuṇ-a/ "madame (female pimp or bordello proprietress)"; Pl [-ạt]; either direct from Sp patrona (Fr patronne) or an internal MCA form with feminine /-a/ added to /baṭṛun/ (see C-547). F. Syn: /qwwad-a/.

C-70 /baṭṛwi/ (with /ṛ/ usually syllabic) "military patrol"; Pl /-yat/; Fr patrouille. F Mk. [EDA 370-1]

C-71 /baṭu/ "ship, boat"; Pl /-wat/ or /-yat/; Fr bateau. F Mk Mr. Syn: /safin-a/ (from CA), /baṛku/ C-58.

C-72 /baṭwaṛ/ "slaughterhouse, abattoir"; Pl [-at]; Fr abattoir. F. Syn: /mdbəḥ/, /gʷrn-a/.

C-73 /ḅaz/, definite /la-ḅaz/ "military base"; Pl [-æt]; Fr (la) base; not very well assimilated and code-switched Pl les bases rather common among bilinguals. F Mk Mr.

C-74 /baẓaṛ/: (1) "bazaar" (large, all-purpose shopping area); (2) "messy or untidy thing or area". Pl in sense 1 only: [-ạt]. From Fr bazar (itself ultimately a Perso-Arabic borrowing). F Mk. [DMA-AE; EDA 371 rules out direct CA etymology and points out that the bazaar was a colonial innovation.] Cf. /suq/ or /suq/ "(ordinary) marketplace".

-- /bbiluṭ/ See /piluṭ/ C-551.

-- /bbisi/, /bbisin/ See /pisin/ C-556.

-- /bbist/ See /pist/ C-557.

-- /bidal-a/ See /biḍaṛ-a/ C-77.

C-75 /bidu/ "canister, water tank" (portable, usually plastic); Pl /-wat/, /-yat/, Dimin /bwidu/; Fr bidon. F Mk Mr. [EDA 373 gives /bidun/, Pl /byadn/; DMA-AE gives both /bidu/ and /bidun/.] Dimin rarely /bwiydu/ (Mk).

C-76 /bidžiz/ "Bee-Gees" (name of a popular rock 'n' roll group) also used in slang as a pejorative nickname for national guards (auxiliary police), cf. /biṇiṭ/ C-82. The Bee-Gees were very popular in Morocco at the time of fieldwork because of their music in hit films starring John Travolta (cf. C-770).

C-77 /biḍaṛ-a/(F), /piḍal/(F Tt), /piḍaḷ-a/(Mk), or /bidal-a/ (Mr) "(bicycle) pedal"; Pl [-æt](Mr and second F form) or [-ạt](Mk and first F form); Fr pédale, Sp pedal. F Mk Mr.

C-78 /bifi/ "pantry; dresser" (furniture); Pl /-yat/; Fr buffet. F *Mr.

-- /biftik/ See /buftik/ C-124.

C-79 /bigbuṣ/(F) or /bikbuṣ/(Mr) "huge, very muscular man; giant"; Pl [-ạt](F Mr) or /bgabṣ/(F); English big boss, apparently through karate films (heard in Morocco chiefly with Fr dubbing) where this was the name of a character; cf. verb /bgbəṣ/ B-6. F Mr *Mk.

-- /bikini/ See /ppikini/.

C-80 /bikub/ "pick-up truck"; Pl [-æt]; Eng via Fr pick-up [pikǒp]. F. Cf. /kamyu/ C-313, /ban/ C-45.

C-81 /bilanti/, /bilaniti/, or /pinalti/: (1) "penalty shot" (soccer); (2) "(successful) copulation" (slang, fairly vulgar, cf. Eng score in this context). Pl /-yat/. Eng via Fr penalty (pronounced [penalti] or occasionally [penaliti]), Sp penalty [penálti]. F.

C-82 /biṇiṭ/ "national guard, auxiliary forces"; used as Sg or Pl; a popular etymology recorded in F is that this is a corruption of Fr menottes "handcuffs"; pejorative slang. F *Mr. Cf. /bidžiz/ C-76.

-- /biniz/ See /piniz/.

C-83 /binu/ "wine", especially "red wine"; no Pl; slang; from Sp vino. F. Syn: /šṛab/ (the usual word for "wine" in general), cf. /ruž/ C-623.

C-84 /biriy-a/ "beret", also "skullcap" (of Jews or others); Pl [-æt]; Dimin /bwiriy-a/; Fr béret; now applied mainly to berets of military cadets. F Mk Mr. [Casa(j) /biri/; similar form given GJA 15.] Syn: /ṭṛbuš/, /qubba^{c}-a/ (but /biriy-a/ is now common for cadets' berets).

-- /birmi/ See /pirmi/ C-554.

C-85 /birnus/ or (more archaic) /brnus/ "hooded garment worn by men (especially native employees of Moroccan colonial administration)"; Pl /brans/; Fr burnous ([bürnu] or [bürnus]), probably brought in from Alg; the garment (hence the term) no longer in common use. F Mr *Mr. [DMA-AE and EDA 372 give /bṛnuṣ/.]

C-86 /birr-a/(F Mk Mr) or /byiṛ/(Mr) "beer"; Pl [birr-æt], [byiṛ-ạt]; Dimin /bwirr-a/; form /birr-a/ probably from It birra and brought in from Alg, form /byiṛ/ more recent and based on Fr bière. F Mk Mr. [Alg /birr-a/; Casa(j) /ṣiṛbis-a/ is from Sp cerveza and represents an alternative borrowing formerly more widespread and now mainly confined to the Tangier/Tt area; DMA-EA under "beer" gives /biṛṛ-a/ along with /srbis-a/, but the pharyng. /ṛṛ/ instead of /rr/ may be a typo; DMA-AE gives only /srbis-a/.]

-- /biṛṣuṇil/ See /piṛṣuṇil/ C-555.

C-87 /biru/ "office (workplace)"; Pl /-wat/ or /-yat/, Dimin /bwiru/; Fr bureau (Sp buró). F Mk Mr Alg. [EDA 373] Syn: /mktǝb/.

-- /bisklit/ See /biškliṭ/ C-90.

C-88 /birsi/(F Mk) or /pisri/(Mr) "grocery store" (small store, always run by Soussi Berbers, selling canned and packaged foods and similar products along with eggs and milk, but usually not meat or produce); Pl /-yat/; Fr épicerie. F Mk Mr *Tt. [EDA 374]

C-89 /bisṭuli/ or /pisṭuli/ "pistol"; Pl /-yat/; Fr pistolet. I have also recorded /bastuli/ as a slang form of this. F Mk *Mr. Syn: /kabus/ C-306.

C-90 /biškliṭ/(F Mk), /biškliṭ-a/(Mk), /bisklịṭ/(Mk), /bisklịṭ-a/(Mk), /bisklit/(F Mr), or /bŭsklịṭ/(rural around F) "bicycle"; Pl [-ạt] after /ṭ/, [-æt] after /t/; Fr bicyclette, Sp bicicleta. F Mk Mr. [Casa(j) /bisklịṭ-a/; Alg /bisklat/, grammatically feminine, Pl [-æt], though rural Alg dialects often use /ṛuḍ-a/ cf. C-624; Tt has /bšklịṭ-a/; DMA-AE gives /bisklit/, /bišklịṭ/, while DMA-EA has /bšklịṭ-a/ or /bišklịṭ-a/; EDA 374 gives several variants with /bisklit/ most widespread but with /bšklịṭ/ and similar forms common in F.]

C-91 /bit: (1) "room (in house or other building)"; (2) "goal, score" (in soccer etc.). In both senses, Pl /byut/, Dimin /bwiyǝt/. In sense 1 an old MCA form (cf. CA bayt-), but sense 2 from Fr but [büt]. Syn: /hadaf/ or /ʔiṣab-a/ "goal" (both from CA, less common than /bit/ in vernacular), cf. verb /maṛka/ B-97. F Mk Mr Alg.

C-92 /biṭṛav/ (collective) "beets" (British "beetroot"); individuative Sg /-a/, Pl [-æt]; Fr betterave. F. [Alg /biṭṛav/ may be grammatically masculine or feminine, the Fr prototype being feminine.] Syn: /baṛb-a/ C-57.

C-93 /biṭṛul/ or /piṭṛul/ "oil, petroleum"; no Pl; Fr pétrole (Sp petróleo). CA has bitrūl- (also a European borrowing) and the form /biṭṛul/ may be influenced by it, but /piṭṛul/ is more common in vernacular MCA. F Mk *Mr. Syn: /zit/ "oil" (including olive oil).

C-94 /biyi/ "ticket"; Pl /-yat/; Fr billet; not very common, the usual word being native /wṛq-a/, cf. also /tikiy-a/ and variants C-722. F Mk *Mr.

C-95 /bizagr-a/(F Mk Casa(j) Tt), /bizạgr-a/(Mr), or /bizạgaṛ-a/(Mr) "hinge or jamb (of door)"; Pl [-æt](F Mk) or [-ạt](Mr); Sp bisagra. [DMA-AE /bizạgṛ-a/; NLVM 9.]

-- /biznis/ See /bznas/ C-163.

C-96 /bizu/(F) or /bizü/(Mk) "new student subjected to hazing, hazing initiate"; Pl /bẓawṭ/(F) (also the Pl of /bẓwiṭ/ C-164); Fr bizut. F Mk *Alg. Related to /bẓwiṭ/ C-164 and verb /bẓwəṭ/ B-32.

-- /bižam-a/ See /pižam-a/ C-558.

C-97 /b^{w}kk/ "handsome, pretty" (slang); Pl /b^{w}kak/, Dimin /b^{w}kiyək/; F informant says this feels like a loan (perhaps Sp), but etymology unclear. F *Mk *Mr. Syn: usual words are /zwin/ (in Mr /zin/) and /mzyan/, with many slang equivalents.

C-98 /blak-a/(F Mk Mr) or /bḷak-a/(F Mr) "sign (on road); badge"; Pl [-æt](F Mk Mr) or /blayk/, /bḷayk/; Dimin /bliky-a/, rural variant /blayk-a/; Fr plaque, Sp placa. F Mk Mr. [Casa(j) has /pḷak-a/, Pl [-æt]; Alg /bḷak-a/; EDA 374-5.]

-- /bḷakaṛ/ See /pḷakaṛ/ C-559.

C-99 /bḷan/(F Mk Alg) or /blaṇ/(Mr): (1) "plan, scheme, intention" (sometimes but not always pejorative); (2) "outline, map". Pl [-æt](F Mk Alg) or [-ạt](Mr), Dimin /bliyn/; from Fr plan, Sp plan. Idiom: /bddl l-bḷan/ "he changed his mind" (lit. "he changed his plan"). Alg has expression /^{c}ml l-bḷan/ "he made a plan", but MCA has a verb /bḷana/ B-9. [DMA-AE] Syn: /t-xṭiṭ/ (CA, uncommon).

C-100 /blandi/ "very strong, solid (person, object); armoured"; adjective with invariable form for numbers/genders; Fr blindé. F Mk *Mr. Cf. verb /blanda/ B-10. Syn: /m-ġlləf/.

C-101 /bḷasuz/, /bḷasöz/, /pḷasuz/, or /pḷasöz/ "female usher (in cinema)"; Pl [-æt]; Fr placeuse. F Mk *Mr. No synonym.

C-102 /bḷaṣ-a/ "place" (all senses, very common); Pl [-ạt] or /bḷayṣ/, Dimin /bḷiyṣ-a/; Fr place, perhaps at one time crossed with Sp plaza (usual meaning: "square, plaza, large intersection"). Also used in expressions like /f-bḷaṣ-t-i/ "in my place" (literal or figurative, as in Eng), presumably a calque on Fr au lieu de, Fr en ma place, Sp en lugar de. F Mk Mr Casa(j). [Tt /plaṣ-a/ "specialty marketplace" from Sp plaza is perhaps not directly related; Alg /blaṣ-a/ or /plaṣ-a/, Pl /playṣ/; TAT 242; EDA 375; DMA-AE.] This form is well on its way to displacing /muḍ^{c}/ "place" in the F/Mk area (I am unsure about Mr), but /muḍ^{c}/ or variant /muṭ^{c}/ is still common in the north (Tt, Tangier); /maḥall/ A-1-252 (from CA) is not very common and usually means "home" (cf. Eng. my place); for "in place (instead) of" the other forms are /f-maḥll-/ and /f-^{c}əwḍ/. All of these "instead of" expressions take an ending /-ma/ when preceding a verb, as in /f-bḷaṣ-t-ma t-mši/ "instead of you going". Cf. verb /bḷaṣa/ B-11.

-- /bḷay-a/ See /pḷay-a/ C-560.

-- /bḷaž/ See /pḷaž/ C-561.

C-103 /bḷḷuṭ/: (1) "acorns" (collective), individuative Sg /-a/, Pl [-ạt](F Casa(j)); (2) "a card game played with Spanish card deck", no Pl (F). In sense 1 probably an old loan from Sp bellota or similar form; sense 2 now equated with Fr belote, but mechanically perhaps just a semantic extension of the older loan. F Casa(j). [DMA-AE;NLVM 454-5.] Similar games: C-616, C-710, /tuti/.

C-104 /bluz-a/(F Mk Mr) or /blus-a/(Tt Casa(j)) "blouse" (woman's garment); Pl [-æt] or /blayz/, Dimin /bliyz-a/ (and presemably variants with /s/); Sp blusa, Fr blouse. F Mk Mr Casa(j). [DMA-AE gives /bluz-a/; DMA-EA under "blouse" has /bḷuẓ-a/, perhaps a typo; GJA 13 has Jewish /blus-a/ from Sp vs. Muslim /bluz-a/ from Fr referring to two distinct garments, the former one worn by boys.] Syn: /qššab-a/, a roughly similar native Moroccan garment.

C-105 /blyun/ "an old coin worth fifty centimes"; Pl /blayn/; fairly old loan, probably ultimately Fr billon via Sp vellón; word remembered but not applied to current fifty-centime coin. F *Mr. [MAG 51; NLVM 12; TAT 237 with further refs.]

-- /bnu/ See /pnu/ C-562.

C-106 /bṛašm-a/ (no vowel nasalization) "intersection, crossing" (now mainly for street intersections); Pl [-æt]; Fr branchement; cf. verb /bṛã̄ša/ B-16, a more recent loan from Fr brancher keeping nasalized vowel. F Mk *Mr. [EDA 377 gives meaning "electrical extension".] Syn: /mlqa ṭ-ṭṛq-an/ "meeting of roads".

C-107 /brgad-i/ "brigadier (rank in military or police)"; Pl /brgad-iy-a/; Fr brigadier; cf. C-108. F Mk Mr. [EDA 372 has bṛgad-i/.]

C-108 /brigad/, definite /la-brigad/(F Mk) or /l-brigad/(Mk) "brigade" (unit of military or police); Pl [-æt]; Fr brigade. Compare C-107 above. F Mk Mr. Syn: /takan-a/.

-- /brik-a/ See /briki C-109.

C-109 /briki/(F) or /brik-a/(Mr): (1) "flashlight", British "torch" (F); (2) "cigarette lighter" (F Mr). Pl /-yat/ (F) or [-æt](Mr); from Fr briquet. F Mr. [EDA 377] Syn: /ḍuw/ (also "light"), /fnaṛ/ C-225, /pil/ C-549.

-- /briz/ See /priz/ C-569.

C-110 /brmil/ "barrel"; Pl /braml/; Sp bermil. F Tt. [DMA-AE; NLVM 8 has /brmil/ with Sp barril as suggested prototype.]

C-111 /bṛmsyun/ (/ṛ/ is syllabic) "military leave, permission"; no Pl; Fr permission (Sp permisión). F. Cf. /pirmi/C-554.

-- /brniz See /virni/ C-785.

-- /brnus/ See /birnus/ C-85.

-- /brövi/, /bröve/ See /bruvi/ C-117.

C-112 /brrak-a/: (1) "shack in shantytown or bidonville (ramshackle slums on fringe of city)", as Pl often used as designation for such a shantytown; (2) "shop, store" (uncommon meaning). Pl [-æt] or /brark/; from Fr baraque, Sp barraca (the loan was perhaps originally used to designate military barracks). F and Mk have sense 1, Mr sense 2. F Mk Mr. [DMA-AE "barracks", "hovel", or "cabin"; Tt /bṛṛak-a/.] Syn: /nwal-a/ or /nwwal-a/ (sense 1), /ḥanut/ (regular term in sense 2).

-- /bṛtiy-a/ See /paṛtiy-a/ C-542.

-- /bṛtm-a/ See /bṛṭm-a/ C-114.

C-113 /bṛṭal/: (1) "small bird" (general term); (2) "sparrow" (called moineau in Fr). Pl /bṛaṭl/, used in some dialects as the only general collective term for "birds" (though referring mainly to smaller species). Old, precolonial loan from Sp pardal. In sense 1 attested in several rural and Jewish dialects, now used in F area only in sense 2. F *Casa(j) Taf(j). [GJA 9; DMA-AE.] For "sparrow" a synonym /žəwš/ is common in rural areas around F, /bṛṭal/ being urban; for "bird" the usual word in F/Mk area is now /ṭiṛ/, Pl /ṭyuṛ/, while Casa(j) has /fṛx/, Pl /fṛax/.

-- /bṛṭiy-a/ See /paṛṭiy-a/ C-542.

C-114 /bṛṭm-a/(F Mk) or /bṛtm-a/ (said to occur in Mr area) "apartment, flat"; Pl [-æt]; Fr appartement; note apparent semantic convergence with /baṭim-a/ C-68 (from Fr bâtiment). F Mk *Casa(j). [Alg /baṛtm-a/, Pl [baṛtm-æt].] Syn: /ḍaṛ/ "house, home".

C-115 /bṛuḍkạn/(F), /bṛuḍkan/(pronounced [bṛoḍkæn])(Mr), or /bṛuḍk-a/ (Mr) "(type of) military boots"; Pl [-æt]; Fr brodequin. F Mr.

C-116 /ḅṛuṣ/, definite /la-ḅṛuṣ/ "brush"; Pl [-ạt]; Fr brosse. F.

C-117 /bruvi/(Mk), /brövi/(Mr), or /bröve/(F) "degree or diploma on graduation from first cycle of secondary school"; no Pl; Fr brevet. F Mk Mr. Syn: /šahad-a/ (from CA).

C-118 /bṛwiṭ-a/ "wheelbarrow"; Pl [-ạt] or /bṛawṭ/; Dimin /bṛiwiṭ-a/ or rural /bṛəywiṭ-a/; Fr brouette. F Mk Mr. [DMA-AE] 3 syllables.

C-119 /bṛẓaṭ/ "parasite, pest" (pejorative reference to person); Pl /-a/ (parallel to regular Pl of /CCCaC/ agentive type /xddam/ "worker", Pl /xddam-a/); probably an internal MCA derivative from denominative verb /bṛẓəṭ/ B-23, which is based on borrowed noun /baṛaẓiṭ/ C-55 (Fr parasite). F.

C-120 /bstiliy-a/ "(washing) basin"; Pl [-æt]; probably a loanword but details uncertain. F. [TAR 46 suggests Sp origin and gives Pl alternate /bsatl/; ZLMA 27 with etym.] Syn: /basin-a/ C-61.

C-121 /bṣṣiṭ-a: (1) "peseta" (unit of Spanish currency); (2) "Moroccan ten-centime coin" (this sense in north around Tt and Tangier); (3) "small Moroccan coin worth (about) one centime" (this sense formerly used in F, now obsolete). Pl [-ạt] or /bṣaṣṭ/; Sp peseta (Fr pessète). F Mk Tt *Mr. [MAG 49; TAT 231; Tt /pṣṣiṭ-a/.]

C-122 /bṣṭil-a/(F Mk) or /bṣṭiḷ-a/(Mr) "pastilla (famous Moroccan dish made with meat baked in pastry shell)"; Pl [-æt] (F Mk) or [-ạt](Mr), also /bṣaṭl/; Sp pastilla, Fr pastilla. F Mk Mr. [Tt has /paṣṭiḷḷ-a/; DMA-AE; TAR 52.]

-- /bṭaṭ-a/ See /baṭaṭ-a/ C-67.

-- /bu̇bbiy-a/, /bubbuy-a/ See /puppiy-a/ C-577.

C-123 /budr-a/ "pillar, column"; Pl [-æt]; Fr poutre; cf. verb /budr/ B-25. There is also a form /badr-a/ "muscular man" which may be related.

C-124 /buftik/ "steak"; no Pl; Fr bifteck (or perhaps variant boeufteck), Sp biftec ex Eng; not common. F. [Alg /biftik/, more common than /buftik/.]

C-125 /ḅugaḍu/(Mk) or /ḅagaḍu/(F) "lawyer, attorney"; Pl /-wat/ or /-yat/; Sp abogado; still more common than /aṿuka/ C-27 from Fr avocat. F Mk *Mr. [Casa(j) /l-aḅugaḍu/, Pl /l-aḅugaḍu-ş/ with definite prefix; Algrs /bugaţu/possibly from It vs eAlg /aṿuka/; GJA 2 gives Jewish /aḅugaḍu/, Pl /aḅugaḍut/ with Hebraized Pl, vs. Muslim /aḅugȧdu/, /bṛgaḍu/, etc., suggesting these forms brought in from Algeria; DMA-AE /bugadu/ perhaps a typo; DMA-EA sub "lawyer" /ḅugaḍu/.] Now about equally common as /muḥami/ "lawyer" from CA, but the latter is gaining.

C-126 /ḅuguṣ/ "dandy, dashing young man" (often pejorative); Pl [-ạt], no feminine form; Fr beau gosse; cf. verb /ḅugəṣ/ B-26. F Mk(occasional) *Mr. [Alg /buguş/, also feminine /buguş-a/.]

C-127 /bukan/ Occurs in Pl form /bukan-at/ "comics, comic books"; Fr (les) bouquins. F Mk Mr. Cf. C-498.

C-128 /buks/ "boxing (sport)"; no Pl; Fr boxe; cf. verb /buks(a)/ B-27. F Mr. Syn: /mu-lakam-a/ (CA). Cf. C-129.

C-129 /buksur/ "boxer"; Pl [-æt]; Fr boxeur. F Mk (occasional) Mr. Syn: /mu-lakim/ (CA). Cf. C-128 and verb B-27.

C-130 /ḅul-a/(F) or /buḷ-a/(Mk Mr) "light bulb"; Pl [-æt](F) or [-ạt] (Mk Mr), also /bwali/(Mk); Dimin /bwiḷ-a/(Mk); perhaps Sp bola (though bombilla is now the usual Sp word for "light bulb") reinforced by Fr ampoule. F Mk Mr Casa(j). [DMA-AE /buḷ-a/; EDA 375 /bul-a/.] Syn: /žaž-a/ (lit. "glass"). Cf. C-798.

C-131 /bulasarrut/ "highway patrol (police)"; no difference between Sg and Pl; Fr police de route. F *Mk. Syn: /bulis/ C-132.

C-132 /bulis/ (collective) "police"; Sg /bulis-i/, FSg /bulis-iy-a/; Fr police (Sg perhaps influenced by Fr policier). F Mk Mr. [Casa(j) /p̣ulis/; Alg /l-bulis/ or more recent /ḷa-pulis/ shown in definite forms, Sg /l-pulis-i/; DMA-AE /bulis/ Sg /bulis-i/, Pl /bwals/; MAG 60 /ḅulis-a/ and NLVM 19 /p̣uliş-a/ designate inspectors of merchandise on ships, the form presumably from Sp policía with possible Fr influence overlain; EDA 377 has /bulis/ "police", Sg /bulis-i/, Pl variants including /bwals/.] Syn: /šʷṛṭ-a/ C-716, cf. /bulasarrut/ C-131, /aṣuṛṭi/ C-24, /žaḍaṛmi/ C-810, /biṇiṭ/ C-82, /bidžiz/C-76.

C-133 /buḷun/ "bolt"; Pl [-æt], Dimin /bwiḷin/; Fr boulon, Sp bulón. F Mk *Mr. [DMA-AE]

C-134 /ḅumb-a/ "pump" (especially gasoline/petrol pump); Pl [-æt], uncommon Dimin /ḅwimb-a/; Fr pompe, Sp bomba; cf. verb /buṃḅa/ B-28 and /ḅumbiy-a/ C-135. F Mr. [Tt distinguishes /ḅumḅ-a/ "bomb" from /p̣ump̣-a/ "pump"; TAT 237 gives /bumb-a/ "bomb" with Alg equivalents, plus several verb forms; DMA-AE /bumḅ-a/ "pump" or "bomb".]

C-135 /ḅumbiy-a/ (collective)(F Mk) with no other forms; alternatively Sg /pumbi/, Pl / pwambiy-a/ (Mr); "firemen" (sometimes also "firetruck"); Fr pompier(s). The Fr noun is most often used in the Pl and it is likely that MCA first borrowed the Pl form as /ḅumbiy-a/ or the like, with forms like Mr /pumbi/ a back-formation involving identifying /-a/ as Pl suffix; Mr /pwambiy-a/ seems to be reshaped to match /CCaCC-iy-a/ agentive Pl pattern. F Mk Mr. [DMA-AE /ḅumbi/ Sg, /ḅumbiy-a/ Pl; Alg /ḷi-pɔ̃pyi/ always Pl; Tt has /ḅumbiy-a/, Pl /-at/ in sense "light bulb" from Sp bombilla, cf. C-130.]

C-136 /bun/ "coupon"; Pl [-æt] or /bwan/, Dimin /bwiyn/; Fr bon; idiom /ᶜam l-bun/ "the year of the coupon" (Alg /wəqt l-bun/ "time of the coupon") refers to a period of wartime rationing through government coupons, now used figuratively for any period of short supplies. F Mk Mr Alg. [EDA 378 has /bun/; DMA-AE has /ḅun/, Pl /ḅwan/.] Syn: /t-wṣil/ (also "receipt").

C-137 /bunani/ "Happy New Year" or "New Year's Day"; no Pl; Fr bonne année. Mk Mr *F.

C-138 /buni/ "swimming cap; bonnet"; Pl /-yat/; Fr bonnet. F Alg.

C-139 /bunt-a/: (1) "cigarette butt", in this sense usually in Dimin form /bwint-a/; (2) "shot with toe (not instep, in soccer)", in ordinary form. Pl [bunt-æt] or /bwant/, Dimin Pl /bwint-at/; from Sp punta, with Dimin form perhaps influenced directly by Fr pointe (but Fr for "cigarette butt" usually mégot, see C-495). F Mk Mr. [Alg has /bunt-a/, not in Dimin form, "cigarette butt", also /bunt/ in /žbəd bunt/ "he took a puff"; Tt /punt-a/ "tip, point" is from Sp; DMA-AE gives /bunt-a/ and Dimin /bwint-a/ in sense 1.] Syn: /ṃigu/ C-495, /nful-a/.

C-140 /buny-a/ "fist; punch (with fist)"; Pl [-æt]; Sp puño, puña reinforced by Fr poign, poignée. F Mk Mr. [Casa(j) /puny-a/; Tt distinguishes /punyu/ "fist" from /puny-a/ "punch", showing both Sp forms; Alg /buny-a/ "fist"; DMA-AE.] Syn: /lkm-a/ (rare).

-- /bunž/, /bunž-a/ See /pụnž/C-576.

C-141 /buṛbu: (1) "baby powder" (F); (2) "a dish made from vegetables" (Mr). No Pl. F Mr. From Sp polvo "powder", at least in sense 1. [Casa(j) /puḷḅu/; DMA-AE /buṛbu/ "powder".]

C-142 /burdil: (1) "bordello" (word now uncommon, applied in colonial period to military bordellos); (2) "unpleasantly noisy or disorderly place; unpleasant commotion". In sense 1, Pl [-æt], Dimin /bwirdil/; Fr bordel. [EDA 378-9.] F.

C-143 /burmid-a/ "knee-length shorts, Bermudas"; Pl [-aet] (two or more pairs); Fr bermuda from the geographical name. F *Mr. Cf. C-717.

C-144 /buṛṛu/(F), /burru/(Mk), or /bwaṛṛu/(F Mk) "leek (vegetable)"; no Pl; Fr poireau. F Mk *Mr. [Casa(j) /puṛṛu/; Alg /puṛu/, masculine; EDA 376 also gives variant /buṛu/.]

C-145 /burs/(F) or /buṛṣ/(Mr) "scholarship stipend (for student)"; Pl [-æt](F) or [-ạt](Mr), Dimin /bwirs-a/(F) with FSg /-a/; Fr bourse; forms with /ṛṣ/ perhaps indicate crossing with Sp bolsa (but Sp usually has beca in the sense given). F Mr. [Alg /(ḷa-)burs/, grammatically feminine.] Syn: /mnḥ-a/ (the usual term). Cf. /buṛṣ-a/ C-146.

C-146 /buṛṣ-a/ "stock exchange, trading market"; Pl [-æt]; Fr bourse, Sp bolsa (possibly a crossing of these two). Mk *F *Mr.

C-147 /buṛṭfuy/ "wallet"; Pl [-æt]; Fr portefeuille. Less common than native /bẓṭam/. F.

C-148 /buṛṭṃuni/ "change-purse" (used to carry coins); Pl /-yat/; Fr porte-monnaie. F. [EDA 372 /bṛṭmuni/.] Less common than native /bẓṭam/. Cf. C-147.

C-149 /buržwa/(F Mk) or /buṛžwa/(F Mr) "upper middle-class, well-off, bourgeois"; invariable form used for Sg/Pl and for either gender; first form from Fr bourgeois, second form with /ṛ/ as discussed above, p.77; cf. verb /bṛžəz/ B-24 and /buržwaz-i/ C-150. F Mk Mr. In F at least, second form seems archaic. [Casa(j) has /snyuṛ/, Pl /-iṣ/ in this sense from Sp señor, señores.] Syn: /tažr/ "rich man; merchant".

C-150 /buržwaz-i/(F Mk) or /buṛžwaz-i/(Mr Tt) "bourgeois" (adjective), FSg /-iy-a/, Pl /-iy-in/; Fr bourgeois [buržwa], FSg bourgeoise [buržwaz], perhaps influenced also by Fr bourgeoisie (which closely resembles the MSg form), with Sp burgués, It borghese dubiously involved; cf. also C-149. F Mk Mr. [Alg /buržwaz-i/.]

C-151 /buṣṭ-a/ "post office (place)" or "postal service"; Pl [-ạt], Dimin /bwiṣṭ-a/; Fr poste, perhaps initially crossed with dialectal Sp posta (though correo(s) is the usual Sp word) or It posta (in Algeria); cf. verb /puṣṭa/ B-119. F Mk Mr. [Casa(j) and Alg /puṣṭ-a/; DMA-AE; MAG 68; EDA 377 suggests direct Fr borrowing with /-a/ added by analogy to (mostly Sp) loans already in MCA.] Syn: /barid/ (CA, much less common).

C-152 /bušun/ "cork, stopper"; Pl [-æt]; Dimin /bwišin/; Fr bouchon. F Mk Mr. Syn: /ǧṭṭay-a/. Cf. C-153.

C-153 /bušun-a/ "bottle-cap"; Pl [-æt]; Fr bouchon with added feminine /-a/. F. (Not always distinguished from /bušun/ C-152.)

C-154 /butik/(Mr) or /butik-a/(F) "shop, boutique" (flattering word); Pl [-æt], Dimin /bwitik-a/(F); Fr boutique, Sp botica. F Mr. [GJA 96 /butik-a/; MAG 69 /buṭik-a/; DMA-AE /butik-a/.] Syn: /ḥanut/ (usual term for "shop").

C-155 /buṭ/: (1) "pair of boots"; (2) "basin (especially women's basin in washroom)"; (3) abdominal bulge (especially of women)". Pl /bwəṭ/(F), /bwaṭ/(F Mk, distinct from /bwat/ "pow!"), or /buṭ-at/(Mr); Dimin

/bwiyəṭ/; Fr botte(s). F Mk Mr. [DMA-AE] Contrast C-156.

C-156 /buṭ-a/ "large gas bottle"; Pl [-ạt], Dimin /bwiyṭ-a/; perhaps a cross of Fr butane "butane gas" and Sp bota "pair of boots" (the latter supplying the form, the former the meaning). F Mk Mr. [Casa(j) has /buṭaṣ/ "boots", Sp plural botas; DMA-AE.] Syn: /qṛ^c-a/ "(any) bottle". Cf. C-155.

C-157 /buṭuṇ/: (1) "button"; (2) "irrigation channel". Pl [-ạt], Dimin /bwiṭiṇ/; Fr bouton, Sp botón. F Mr *Mk *Tt. Cf. C-158. Syn: /ṣḍaf-a/ "button"; /sagy-a/ (regular word) "irrigation channel".

C-158 /buṭun-a/(F) or /buṭuṇ-a/(Mr) "button"; Pl [-æt](F) or [-ạt] (Mr), Dimin / bwiṭin-a/(F); Fr bouton, Sp botón with added feminine /-a/. Note that F informant distinguishes Pl forms [boṭoṇ-at] C-157 from [boṭon-æt] C-158. For Mr informant, /buṭuṇ-a/ C-158 functions as individuative Sg of /buṭuṇ/ C-157 so the two entries should be combined for this speaker. F Mr *Casa(j). [Alg /buṭun/ means "knob", not referring to button on clothing.] Syn: /ṣḍaf-a/ or /ṣḍf-a/.

C-159 /bwan/ (invariable form used as predicate) "broke, without money, destitute" (slang); ex. /ana bwan/ "I am broke", /huwa gals bwan/ "he is broke" (lit. "he is sitting broke"); Fr en panne. F *Mk *Mr. Pronounced [bwaen] without pharyngealizing /bw/. Syn: /mskin/ "poor, indigent", most common slang form /ḥazəq/ (lit. "farting"). Cf. /ðp̤p̤an/ C-537. Cf. /bwan/, Pl of /bun/ C-136.

C-160 /bwandi/([b̤b̤andi])(F Mk) or /b̤andi/(Mr) "bandit"; Pl /bwandiy-a/ (F Mk) or /b̤andiy-at/(Mr); Fr bandit (Sp bandido). F Mk Mr. [EDA 379-80; DMA-AE has /b̤b̤andi/, /b̤wandi/.] Syn: /šffaṛ/ is most common word for "thief", but /bwandi/ fairly common to refer to gangs of bandits, e.g. in films. Also pronounced [bwaendi].

-- /bwaṛṛu/ See /buṛṛu/ C-144.

C-161 /bwaṭ/ (collective) "tin cans"; individuative Sg /-a/, Pl [-ạt]; Dimin Sg /bwiyṭ-a/; Fr boîte. F *Mr. Syn: /ḥukk/ (less common). Cf. verb /bwwəṭ/ B-30 and /bwaṭa/ B-29.

-- /bwint-a/ See /bunt-a/ C-139.

-- /b^{w}kk/ Alphabetized as though /bkk/, see C-97.

C-162 /byas-a/: (1) "(spare) part" (of car, etc.)(F Mr Mk); (2) "patch (on clothing)"(F); (3) "hole, opening" (F, uncommon sense). Pl [-æt]; Fr pièce. F Mk Mr. [Alg /pyas-a/ "spare part".] Syn: /ṭṛf/ "piece", /ṛq^c-a/ "patch", /tqb-a/ "hole".

C-163 /bznas/(F Mr), /biznis/(Mk), or /bznəs/(F): (1) "drug dealer; racketeer"; (2) businessman" (less common sense). No Pl; from Fr business [biznɛs] ex Eng; cf. verb /bznəs/ B-3]. The usual word for "businessman" is MCA /tažr/ "merchant" (also "rich man") or a code-switched form like Fr négociant or homme d'affaires.

C-164 /bẓwiṭ/ "new student subjected to hazing"; Pl /bẓawṭ/; related to noun /bizu/ C-96 (Fr bizut) and verb /bẓwəṭ/ B-32 (cf. Fr bizuter, bizutage), but the precise mechanical development and chronological order of these MCA forms is problematic (it is possible that /bẓwiṭ/ is an internal derivative from the verb /bẓwəṭ/, which has verbal noun /t-bẓwiṭ/). F *Alg.

-- /daksi/ See /ṭaksi/ C-754.

C-165 /dambir-a/ or /danbir-a/ "large cart or similar device used by construction workers; dump-truck"; Pl [-æt]; Fr dumper locally pronounced [dæ̃ber] from English (usual Eng form dump-truck). F. Cf. /kamiyu/ C-313, /bikub/ C-80, /ban/ C-45.

-- /dibblum/ See /dipḷum/ C-172.

-- /dibbu/ See ḍipu/ C-184.

C-166 /difili/: (1) 'parade' (usual sense, F Mk Mr); (2) "rapid succession of copulations by same pair" (slang, rather vulgar), or more generally "rapid succession of identical events"(F). Pl /-yat/, Dimin /dwifili/; Fr défilé (Sp desfile). F Mk Mr. [Tt /disfili/ from Sp.] Syn: /(?)isti^{c}ṛaḍ/ and variants (from CA, less common than /difili/ but gaining).

C-167 /dihuġ-a/ "whore" (infrequent slang word); Pl [-ạt]; German die Hure with definite article. F. Usual word is /qḥb-a/, several slang expressions.

C-168 /dikti/ or /dikte/ ([dikt^{s}e]) "dicté, dictation exercise (in school)"; no Pl; Fr dicté, not a well-assimilated loan. F Mk. Syn: /?imla?/ (CA).

C-169 /dilwi/ "tell him!" (frozen expression, no inflected forms); Fr dis-lui! F.

C-170 /dinamu/ "generator (of automobile etc.)"; Pl /-wat/ or /-yat/; Fr dynamo. F Mk Mr.

C-171 /dipaṛ/(F Mr) or /ḍipaṛ/(Mk) "starting point, departure (of train, bus)"; Pl [-ạt]; Fr départ. F Mk Mr.

C-172 /dipḷum/(F Mk), /dipluṃ/(Mr), or /dibblum/(F, uneducated) "degree (from school), diploma"; Pl [-æt](F Mk) or [-ạt] (Mr); Fr diplôme (Sp diploma). F Mk Mr. [Tt /dipluṃ-a/ from Sp.] Syn: /šahad-a/, /bruvi/ C-117, /ḅak/ C-35 (these are specific types).

C-173 /disk/ or (rural) /diks/ "record, disc" (music); Pl [-æt] (F) or /dyask/(F Mk Mr), Dimin /dwisk/. F Mk Mr. Syn: /t-bṣil/ (rare). Fr disc.

C-174 /diwan-a "customs bureau"; no Pl; perhaps a cross of Sp aduana and (recently restored) CA dīwān- (the Sp form is historically from the CA form); cf. verb /diwana/ B-34. F Mk. [DMA-AE; NLVM 44.]

C-175 /dörti/ "dirty" (student slang); Eng dirty. F. Syn: /m-wṣṣəx/.

-- /dubl/ See /ḍubl/ C-187.

C-176 /dublsumil/ "walking, steps" (name of a foul called in basketball for taking too many steps without dribbling); no Pl; Fr double semelle. F.

-- /duktuṛ/ and variants: See /ḍuktuṛ/ C-188.

C-177 /duš/ "shower" (for taking a shower); Pl [-æt] or /dwaš/, Dimin /dwiyəš/; Fr douche; cf. verb /dwwəš/ B-36. F Mk Mr. [Alg /duš/, definite /la-duš/; DMA-EA under "shower"; Tt /dučč-a/ from Sp ducha.]

C-178 /dyaṃanḍ/ "diamonds" (collective, jewellery); individuative Sg /-a/, Pl [-ạt]; idiom /bənt dyaṃanṭ/ with /ṭ/ "diamond girl" (i.e. a very beautiful girl); idiom /ṭl^{c}-at-l-i d-dyaṃanḍ-a/ "I got high, smashed" (on liquor, etc.; slang), literally "the diamond rose up for me"; Fr diamant crossed with Sp diamante. Tt F. [Casa(j) Sg /dyamạ̃ṭ-a/; ZLMA 25 gives Tangiers /dyamant/ vs. Rabat /ḍyamant/, and suggests that Catalan diamant in addition to Sp diamante may have been involved.]

-- /džikit-a/ See /žạkiṭ-a/ C-811.

C-179 /džin/ "(pair of) jeans (pants)"; Pl [-æt], Dimin /džiyn/; Eng jeans via Fr jean [ǰin]. F Mr Mk. Rarely /džim/ (rural F area) .

-- /džuḅ/ See /žuḅ/ C-821.

C-180 /ḍam-a/ "checkers, draughts" (chess-like games); Pl [-æt] (only in sense "sets of checkers"); Fr (les) dames, Sp (las) damas. F Mk Mr. [DMA-AE; apparently widespread across North African Arabic dialects; TAT 364 gives this form and also Pl variant /ḍyum/ and verb /ḍam/, imperfective /-ḍim/.]

C-181 /ḍạ̃tifris/ "toothpaste"; no Pl; Fr dentifrice. F Mk *Mr. Syn: /m-^{c}zun d-s-snan/.

C-182 /ḍbḷun/ "old gold coin, doubloon"; Pl [-æt]; Sp doblón. F. [ZLMA 44.]

C-183 /ḍifanḍi/ (adjective) "prohibited"; Fr défendu. F. [EDA 380.] Syn: /m-mnu^{c}/ (most common form), /ḥṛam/ (prohibited by religion, sacriligious), rarely /anṭiṛdi/ C-14.

-- /ḍipaṛ/ See dipaṛ/ C-171.

C-184 /ḍipu/(F Mk), /ḍippu/(F), or /dibbu/(F) "depot, warehouse"; Pl /-wat/ or /-yat/, Dimin /ḍwipu/; Fr dépôt. F Mk Syn: /ḥri/.

C-185 /ḍiṭay/. Occurs in phrase with preposition /b-ḍ-ḍiṭay/ "retail" (adverb, as in "it is sold/bought retail"), used with verb /šra/ "he bought" or /ba^{c}/ "he sold"; Fr en détail. For opposite "wholesale" see /gṛu/ C-279.F.

C-186 /ḍṛappu/ "flag"; Pl /-wat/ or /-yat/; Fr drapeau. F *Mr. Syn: /^{c}alam/, /ṛay-a/. (Borrowings from Sp bandera are attested in the east and north of the country but are not used by my F/Mk informants.)

C-187 /ḍubl/(Mk), /dubl/(F Mr) "double, twice as much" (formally a noun but often translated as an adverb), ex. /xlls-ni ḍ-ḍubl/ "he paid me double"; no Pl; Fr double, with Mk form probably involving Sp doble as well. F Mk Mr. [Tt /ḍubḷi/ is direct from Sp doble, and this also occurs in some rural or Jewish dialects.]

C-188 /ḍukṭuṛ/(F), /dukṭuṛ/(Mk), /ḍukṭuṛ/(Mr), or /duktur/ (rural around F) "doctor, physician"; Pl [-ạt] except [-æt] in last form (rural around F), Pl also /dakatir-a/ or /ḍakạṭiṛ-a/ (with /t/ not /ṭ/); Fr docteur, Sp doctor.

F Mk Mr *Casa(j). [DMA-EA under "doctor" has /doktuṛ/, Pl /dakatiṛa/; not in DMA-AE.] Syn: /ṭbib/ (about equally common). Probably via CA duktūr-.

C-189 /ḍulaṛ/ "dollar" or (slang) "money" (in general); Pl [ạt]; Eng dollar probably via Fr and Sp. F Mk *Mr. [DMA-EA.]

C-190 /ḍuṛu/ "coin worth five centimes"; Pl /-wat/ or /-yat/; Sp duro (still used in Spain for five-peseta coin); in MCA this is an archaic word no longer in active use except in some rural areas and in the east around Oujda. F Mk Mr *Casa(j). [Algrs.] Syn: /ryal/ is very common around F/Mk in the sense "five centimes" (as a unit of currency, hence "twenty riyals" to mean "one dirham"), cf. C 626.

C-191 /ḍuṣ/ "two (in cards)"; no Pl; Sp dos. F Mk Alg. [Tt with Pl /ḍiṣ-an/.]

C-192 /fabrik-a/ "factory"; Pl [-æt], Dimin /fwibrik-a/; Fr fabrique, Sp fábrica. F Mk Mr. [DMA-AE; Tt /f̣abrik-a/; Alg /f̣abrik-a/ or /fabrik-a/.] Syn: /m-ᶜml/ (about equally common) and (not very common) /wzin/ C-801.

C-193 /faḅuṛ/(F Mk Mr) or /faỵuṛ/(F) "small gift; tip; free (adverb)"; Pl [-ạt]; old, well-established loan from Sp favor reinforced by Fr faveur (form /faỵuṛ/ probably reshaped under Fr influence); cf. verb /fuḅṛ/ B-57. F Mk Mr Tt. [NLVM 50; DMA-AE /fabuṛ/.] Syn: /hdiy-a/ and /kaḍu/ C-308, both "gift".

C-194 /fagu/ "car (of train)"; Pl /-wat/, /-yat/, or /-nat/; Fr wagon, Sp vagón. F Mk Mr Alg. [Tt /vagun/ from Sp; Casa(j) /ỵago/ from Fr; DMA-AE; EDA 380-1.] Syn: /ᶜaṛab-a/ (CA, not common).

C-195 /f̣akā̤ṣ/ or /f̣akaṇṣ/ "Moroccan working in France"; this form used as Sg or Pl without change; Fr vacances "vacation" (because these people are normally seen in Morocco while on vacation). F (common). Syn: /mu-hažir/ (CA) "emigré".

C-196 /f̣aktö̤r/, /faktur/, or /f̣aktur/ "mailman, man who delivers mail"; Pl [-æt]; Fr facteur. F.

C-197 /faktur-a/ "invoice, bill (to be paid), check (in restaurant)"; Pl [-æt]; Fr facture, Sp factura. F Mk Mr. [Tt /f̣aktur-a/; DMA-AE has variant form /fituṛ-a/, Pl /fyatṛ/, not recognized by my informants.] Syn: /ḥsab/ "account".

-- /fal̤gaṭ-a/ See /fṛgaṭ-a/ C-231.

C-198 /fal̤ṭ-a/ "fault, error"; Pl [-ạt], Dimin /fwil̤ṭ-a/; Sp falta reinforced by Fr faute; can occur in calqued expressions like /l-fal̤ṭ-a dyal-ək/ "it is your fault"; cf. verb /fal̤ṭ/ B-47. Tt F Mk Mr Casa(j). [In Tt has same meanings plus "foul (in sports)"; ZLMA 25; DMA-AE.] Cf. C-250, 252.

C-199 /family-a/(Tt and many Jewish dialects) or /famil-a/(F Mk Mr Casa(j)) "family"; Pl [-æt]; Sp familia, Fr famille; occurs in forms with pronominal suffix like /famil-t-i/ "my family" (F Mk). F Mk Mr Tt Casa(j). [Alg /famil-a/ or /f̣amily-a/.] Syn: /ᶜaʔil-a/ (CA, less common than the Fr/Sp borrowing).

C-200 /f̣angaḷ a/ "penis" (vulgar slang, uncommon); Pl [-ạt]; exact etymology unclear but appears to be of Romance origin on the basis of canonical shape; cf. verb /f̣ngḷ/ B-52. F. Syn: the most common word is /zəbb/.

C-201 /fant/ or /fant-a/ "(a) dodge, (b) fake (in soccer, etc.)"; Pl [-æt]; Fr feinte; cf. verb /fanta/. F Mk Mr. Syn: /mu-ṛawaġ-a/ (CA, used in broadcast style). Cf. B-48.

C-202 /faṛ/ "bright headlights (of car)"; Pl [-ạt]; Fr phare. F Alg. In Sg this is homophonous with native /faṛ/ "mouse" (but the latter has Pl /fir-an/).

C-203 /faṛgo/ "police van (equipped to carry prisoners)"; no Pl (Pl supplied by C-204); possibly Fr fourgon (borrowed meaning, however, based on Fr fourgonette, see C-204), other possibility might be Wells Fargo (bank with stage coaches in western films). F.

C-204 /faṛguṇiṭ/(F) or /faṛgunit/(Mr) "police van (equipped to carry prisoners)"; Fr fourgonette "van (main part of truck, excluding cab)"; cf. C-203. F. Cf. C-17.

C-205 /farin-a/ "type of wheat"; no Pl; Fr farine (Sp harina, perhaps It farina). F Mk Mr Alg. [TAR 598; DMA-AE.] Syn: /qəmḥ/, /ẓṛ^c/ (more general words for "wheat").

C-206 /faṣ/ Occurs in expression /pil w-faṣ/ "heads or tails"; Fr pile ou face?. Cf. /pil/ C-549.

C-207 /faṣm-a/(F Mk) or /faṣm̩-a/(Mr) "bandage"; Pl [-æt](F Mk) or [-ạt](Mr); Fr pansement. F Mk Mr. [EDA 381; DMA-AE.] Syn: /ḥzam/.

-- /fayuṛ/ See /faḅuṛ/ C-193.

C-208 /f̣ayạž/(F Mk) or /ṿayạž/(Mr) "(a) haul (i.e. a trip in truck with a load)"; Pl [-æt](F Mk); Fr voyage. F Mk Mr. [Alg has /l-ṿayaǰ/, phonetic [l-vayaej] "the voyage" with conventional Fr meaning; for a somewhat similar earlier borrowing from Sp viaje "trip, voyage" see NLVM 6.] Syn: see /kuṛṣ-a/ C-423.

C-209 /figur-a/: (1) "face" (uncommon sense); (2) "guy" in expressions in slang like /škun dak l-figur-a/ "who is that guy?" (somewhat pejorative). Pl [-æt] (but rarely used in Pl); Sp figura, Fr figure. F (both senses) Mk (sense 1) Mr (sense 1). Syn: usual word for "face" is /wžəh/; other slang words for sense 2 are /fiṇumin/ C-216 and /maṛk-a/ C-476.

C-210 /fil/ "commission, percentage (of transaction)" (slang); no Pl; perhaps Fr fil "thread"; probably unconnected with native fil "elephant". F. Syn: /ž^{c}b-a/.

C-211 /fil-a/, /fill-a/, /vill-a/(usual F Mk form), or /vil-a/ (F Mr) "villa, elegant house"; Pl [-æt], Dimin /vwill-a/, etc.; Fr villa (Sp villa), applied mainly to homes built by Europeans or in the same style. F Mk Mr. [Alg and Tt /vill-a/.]

C-212 /fili/ "net (in tennis or soccer)"; Pl /-yat/; Fr filet. F. Syn: /šbk-a/.

C-213 /filil/ "safety pin"; Pl /flayl/; probably Sp alfilel (which is itself an old borrowing from CA al-xilāl-). F. [DMA-AE; ZLMA 54; these two sources give Pl /fyaləl/, ZLMA giving Sp form as etymon.] Syn: /fnt-a/.

-- /fill-a/ See /fil-a/ C-211.

C-214 /film/ (/m/ optionally syllabic) "film, motion picture"; Pl [-æt] or /?aflam/, Dimin /fwilm/; Fr and Sp film; this loan is also well established in CA and the MCA form has been reinforced by CA; of the two Pl forms /?aflam/ is from CA, /film-at/ an internal MCA form. F Mk Mr. [DMA-EA under "movie".]

C-215 /filṭaž/ (1st syll. unpharyngealized) "grooves in screw" no Pl; Fr filetage. F Mk.

C-216 /fiṇumin/ "guy" (pejorative), used like /figur-a/ C-209 (sense 2); no Pl; Fr phénomène. F *Mr.

C-217 /firm-a/ "(modern) farm"; Pl [-aet] or /fwarm/, Dimin /fwirm-a/; Fr ferme. F Mk Mr. [MDA-AE; EDA 382.] F Mk Mr. Syn: /ḍay^c-a/ (but /firm-a/ is common).

C-218 /firuž/(F), /furuž/(F), or /föruž/(Mk) "stoplight, red light, traffic signal"; Pl [-æt]; Fr feu rouge. F Mk.

C-219 /fist-a/ "(man's) coat" (as in coat-and-tie); Pl [-æt], Dimin /fwist-a/; Fr veste (and perhaps veston). F Mk Mr.

C-220 /fišṭ-a/(F Mk), /fižṭ-a/(F Mk, mostly rural), or /ṿižṭ-a/ (Mr) "celebration, (non-religious) holiday characterized by festive activities"; Pl [-ạt], Dimin /fwižṭ-a/ or /fwišṭ-a/; early loan from It festa, Sp fiesta, Fr fête probably brought in from Algeria. F Mk Mr. [Alg /fišṭ-a/; Casa(j) /fiẓṭ-a/ with regular depalatalization; Tt /fyiṣṭ-a/ based on Sp fiesta; DMA-AE /fišṭ-a/; ZLMA 23-4 /fišṭ-a/ or fiṣṭ-a/.] Syn: /^{c}id/ "religious holiday", /ḥfl-a/ "party".

C-221 /fitɛs/(F) or /vitɛs/(F Mk Mr) "gears (of vehicle)"; no Pl; Fr vitesse "speed"; common but formally not well assimilated. F Mk Mr.

-- /fižṭ-a/ See /fiṣṭ-a/ C-220.

C-222 /fḷaš/: (1) "flash attachment (of camera)"; (2) flash, (an) excerpt (overheard fragment of conversation, brief interview segment shown in broadcast, etc.)". Pl [-æt] (F Mk) or [-ạt] (Mr), imin /fḷiyəš/; Fr and Sp flash ex Eng. F (both senses) Mk (sense 1) Mr (sense 1).

C-223 /flik/ "policeman, cop" (slang); no Pl; Fr flic "cop"; not very common. F. Syn: see /bulis/ C-132 and refs.

C-224 /flipp/ "crazy, flipped (out)" (slang); invariable form for all numbers/genders; Fr flip and flippé ex Eng; cf. verb /flippa/ B-51. F. Syn: /ḥməq/ "crazy", many slang synonyms.

C-225 /fṇaṛ/ or /fnaṛ/ "flashlight"; Pl [-ạt] or /fṇayṛ/; Dimin /fṇiyṛ/ (F Mk) or /fniyṛ/ (F Tt); Mediterranean word, perhaps ult. Gk phanarion. Tt F Mk. [DMA-AE; NLVM 105 "ship's searchlight' from Sp fanal.] Syn: /briki/ C-109.

C-226 /fnṭaziy a/ or /fnṭaẓiy-a/ "showing off" (noun), ex. /fi-h l-fnṭaziy-a/ "he is a show-off" (in-him [is] showing-off)"; early loan, It fantasia, Sp fantasía via Algeria; not used for Moroccan equestrian performance (Fr fantasia); related verb /fnṭəẓ/ B-53. Mk F Tt Casa(j) Alg *Mr. [DMA-AE; TAT 418; see G. Cifoletti, La parola fantasia nelle linque del mediterraneo, pp.139-45, "Incontri linguistici", vol.5, Licosa and Firenze, Italy, 1979.]

C-227 /fɔlɔ̃ṭi/ "willingly, gladly" (adv.); ex. /n-nqqẓ-u fɔlɔ̃ṭi/ "I will gladly jump it"; Fr volontiers influenced by volonté. F.

C-228 /fran/, rarely /fṛan/ (rural F area) "brake(s)", Pl [-æt], Dimin /friyn/; Fr frein (Sp freno), related verb /frana/ (F Mk Mr) "he braked". F Mk Mr Tt Casa(j). Syn: /ḥṣṣaṛ/ (uncommon).

C-229 /fṛanṣaw-i/ "French (adj.), Frenchman"; FSg /fṛanṣaw-iy-a/ "French language, Frenchwoman"; Pl /fṛanṣaw-iy-in/ "French people"; has Gentilic /-i/ added to /fṛanṣa/ (var. /faṛanṣa/) "France", probably via CA. F Mk. [DMA-AE.] The form /fṛanṣiṣ/, C-230 below, is older in MCA.

C-230 /fṛanṣiṣ/ "French"; invariable form for all genders/numbers; from Sp francés. Common in the north (Tt) and in rural and Jewish dialects, now being replaced by C-229 in the F/Mk area but formerly widespread there. Tt. [NLVM 14; GJA 97; DMA-AE.] Casa(j) dialect prefers /nṣṛan-i/ "Christian" as designation for French; in other locations this is a general term for Europeans (mostly tourists and teachers).

C-231 /fṛgaṭ-a/(F Mk) or /faḷgaṭ-a/(F) "large rowboat"; Sp fragata, Fr frégate. F Mk *Mr. [DMA-AE with gloss "warship"; NLVM 101; TAR 4 /fṛgaṭ-a/; Tt /fṛgaṭ-a/ now rare.]

C-232 /friks/ "chic, modish, flashy (person); form invariable for all genders/numbers; said by F informant to be from a colloquial Fr expression with same pronunciation, but this has not been confirmed yet by Fr speakers; cf. verb /frkəs/ B-55. F Mr.

C-233 /frisk/(F Mk), /frišk/(F Mk), or /frisku/(Mk) "fresh (said of fruit, etc.)"; form invariable for all genders/numbers; Sp fresco (reinforced by Fr frais, feminine fraîche). F Mk *Mr. [Casa(j) /frisk/ permits Pl /-in/, FSg /-a/ unlike other dialects; Alg /frišk/, form invariable, also can mean "cool drink" as noun; NLVM 100; TAT 412; DMA-AE.] Syn: /ṭṛi/.

C-234 /frit/ "French fried potatoes" ("chips" in British English); no Pl; from Fr les frites. F Mk Mr. Syn: /baṭaṭ-a m-qliy-a/ "fried potatoes" (less common).

C-235 /friy-a/(F Mr) or /friwi/(F) "no good, worthless (thing)" (slang); Pl /friy-at/; origin unclear, possibly Sp fría "cold (FSg)" or the like; a recent slang word now current among some student groups as general insulting or pejorative word (for food, ugly person, etc.); forms antonym pair with /nugᶜ-a/ "great, terrific thing" (apparently not a European loan). F Mr *Mk. Syn: /xayb/ "bad, foul", /qbiḥ/ "ugly".

C-236 /friz/ or /fṛiz/ "strawberry, strawberries" (collective); some speakers permit individuative Sg /-a/, Pl [-æt]; Fr fraise, Sp fresa. F Mk *Mr. [EDA 388.]

C-237 /frizi/ "frizzy (haircut)"; no Pl; Fr frisé. F Mk. [DMA-AE; EDA 383.]

C-238 /frižidir/ "refrigerator"; Pl [-æt]; trade label Frigidaire; fairly common but competes with synonym /tllaž-a/. F Mk *Mr. [Alg /frižidir/ with masculine concord.]

C-239 /frmasyan/(F) or /fṛṃasyan/(Mk Mr), last syllable [yæn] "pharmacist" (by extension "pharmacy", as in "I am going to the pharmacist"); Pl [-æt], but code-switched Pl les pharmaciens common among bilinguals; Fr pharmacien. F Mk Mr. [DMA-AE with /ṛm/; EDA 381; GJA 96.] Syn: /ṣaydal-i/ (from CA, not common).

C-240 /fṛṃaž/(F Mk Mr) or /fṛuṃaž/(F Mk, mostly rural) "cheese"; no Pl, Dimin /fṛiṃiž/; Fr fromage (possibly earlier It formaggio). F Mk Mr. [Casa(j) /fṛumaẓ/; Alg /frmaǰ/, unpharyngealized; DMA-EA under "cheese".] Syn: /žḅn/ (applied mainly to native cheeses while European types are called /fṛṃaž/).

C-241 /frmli/ (syllabic /r/) "male nurse"; FSg /frmliy-a/ "(female) nurse"; Pl /frmliy-at/ (either gender) or /framliy-a/ (male); Fr infirmier, FSg infirmière (Sp enfermero, -a), possibly influenced by Fr infirmerie. F Mk Mr Alg. [Casa(j) /frmiṛ-a/ "nurse" from Sp enfermera; EDA 381-2; DMA-AE.] Syn: /mu-mṛṛiḍ/ (CA).

C-242 /fṛəŋk/(F Mk), /fṛaŋk/(F Mk Tt), or /fṛank/(Mk) "franc, centime" (French or Moroccan, the latter 1/100 of a dirham); Pl [-æt] elicitable but Sg form normal with numeral; Dimin /fṛinək/ or /fṛink/ with alveolar /n/ consistently; Fr franc. F Mk Mr Tt. [Casa(j) /fṛank/; EDA 383; DMA-AE.]

C-243 /fṛšiṭ-a/(F Mk Mr), /f^wṛšiṭ-a/(F), or /f^wršiṭ-a/(F) "fork"; Pl [-aṭ] or /fṛašəṭ/; Fr fourchette. F Mk Mr. [Alg /fṛšiṭ-a/; DMA-AE.] Syn: /šuk-a/ (uncommon in this sense); some Jewish dialects still have /gaṛf̣u/, Pl /gaṛf̣u-ṣ/ or /gwaṛf̣/, from Judeo-Spanish garfo(s).

C-244 /frut-a/ "fruit"; Pl [-æt]; Sp fruta. Casa(j) (also Tt and some additional rural and Jewish dialects). Syn: /fakih-a/, Pl /fawakih/ from CA, now the dominant forms in the F/Mk area.

C-245 /fsyan/(F Mk), /ufisyi/(F Mk), or /ofisyi/(Mr) "(military) officer" Pl /fsyan-at/(F) along with code switched les officiers (F Mk), or /fsyan/(Mr — note that this matches the Sg form in F/Mk); /fsyan/ brought in from Algeria, It uffiziale or Sp oficial, the other two from Fr officier; Mr plural /fsyan/ probably identical to Sg /fsyan/ historically but reinterpreted as Pl on the model of /CCC-an/ plurals like /xrf-an/ "lambs", /ždy-an/ "goat kids". F Mk Mr *Casa(j). [DMA-AE; EDA 382.]

C-246 /fuḷaṛ/(Mr), /fuḷaṛ-a/(F Mk), or /fuṇaṛ-a/(F Mk) "kerchief, handkerchief, shawl"; Pl [-aṭ]; Fr foulard. F Mk Mr *Casa(j). [Alg /fulaṛ-a/.] Syn: /drr-a/, /sbniy-a/ C-634.

C-247 /fundu/ "depths of sea" (slang); no Pl; Sp fondo "base, bottom". F. [GJA 99 in different context.]

C-248 /fuṛfi/ "forfeit (of game, in sports)"; no Pl; Fr forfait. F.

-- /furuž/ See /firuž/ C-218.

C-249 /fusi/ "ditch"; Pl /-yat/; Fr fossé. F Mk Mr.

C-250 /fut/, definite /la-fut/(F Mk, nonpharyng.) or /ḷa-fut/ (Mr) "fault"; generally less common than /faḷṭ-a/ C-198 but used in similar expressions like /la fut dyal-ək/ "it is your fault"; Fr faute. F Mk Mr *Casa(j). [Alg /(ḷa-)fuṭ/ with /ṭ/; Tt has /(la-)fut/.] Syn: /ġlṭ-a/. In practice may easily be confused with /fuṭ/ C-252 below.

C-251 /futöy/ (F Mk) or /futi/(Mr) "armchair, easy chair"; Pl /futöy-at/ (F Mk) or /futiy-at /(Mr); Fr fauteuil. F Mk Mr. Syn: /tkkay-a/.

C-252 /fuṭ/, definite /la-fuṭ/ "foul (in sports)"; no Pl; Fr faute. F. Cf. /fut/ C-250 and /faḷṭ-a/ C-198, above, also /kufṛ-a/ C-392, below.

C-253 /fuṭu/ "photograph"; Pl /-yat/ or /-wat/; Fr photo [fɔto], Sp foto; not very common, the usual word being /t-ṣwiṛ-a/ "picture". F Mk Mr.

C-254 /fuṭukoppi/ "photocopy"; Pl /-yat/; Fr photocopie; exx. /dar l-fuṭukoppi/ "he made the photocopy", also slang expression /n-mši-w b-l-futukoppi/ "let's live in sin, let's shack up together (illegally), let's live together without being married". F Mk (minus slang expression).

C-255 /galuri/ "gallery (low cost seating area in stadium); crowd of spectators (e.g. after automobile accident)"; Fr galerie (Sp galería). F *Mr.

C-256 /gamil-a/ "cooking pot; food cooked in cooking pot"; Pl [-æt] or /gwaml/, Dimin /gwimil-a/; Fr gamelle. F Mr. [EDA 384; DMA-AE.] Syn: /ṭnžṛ-a/.

C-257 /gan-a/ "character (of person), propensities" or (in Tt) "appetite, desire"; no Pl; early loan from Sp gana "desire, whim"; ex. /k^{w}ll waḥəd w-gan-t-u/ "everyone has his own character (or tastes)", lit. "everyone and his character"; ex. from Tt /^{c}nd-i l-gan-a d-l-makl-a/ "I feel like (having) some food" (Sp tengo ganas de comer). F Mk Mr. [Casa(j) has same sense as Tt; not recognized by Alg informants; DMA-AE; NLVM 98; TAR 686-7 also indicates earlier form /ġan-a/ with fricative /ġ/.] Syn: /xaṭṛ/ (from CA).

C-258 /ganšu/ or /gantšu/ "pitchfork"; Pl /-wat/ or /-yat/; from Sp gancho (It gancio, Old Fr ganche), which is also the source for /ġanžu/ C-288, below. F and vicinity. *Casa(j). [NLVM 97-8 gives /ġanžu/ as "harpoon" or "pitchfork", while I have /ganšu/ or /gantšu/ for "pitchfork" and a very different sense for /ġanžu/ C-288; the form with /g/ presumably reflects restoration of /g/ under continuing Sp influence.]

C-259 /gaṛ/, definite /ḷa-gaṛ/ "(railroad) station"; Pl [-ạt]; Fr (la) gare; the ordinary word for this sense. F Mk Mr Casa(j). Generally used in definite form; some speakers do not accept simple form. [Algrs /ḷa-gaṛ/, feminine grammatically, vs. eAlg /ḷaŋgaṛ/, masculine; the latter perhaps a cross of la gare (sense) with le hangar (form); EDA 393.] Syn: /maḥṭṭ-a/ "station" (CA, also "bus station"), cf. /ṣṭasyu/ C-688.

C-260 /gaṛanṭi/(F), /gaṛãṭi/(Mk), or /gaṛãti/(Mr) "guarantee, warranty (from shop, manufacturer, etc.)"; Pl /-yat/; Fr garantie (Sp garantía). F Mk Mr. [DMA-AE has /gaṛantiy-a/ from Sp.] Syn: /ḍman-a/ (variant /ḍaman-a/).

C-261 /gaṛaž/ "garage (especially in sense of auto repair shop)"; Pl [-æt]; Fr garage (Sp garaje). F Mk Mr. [DMA-AE; Alg has /garaž/ or /gaṛaǰ/.] Syn: /mu-stwda^{c}/ (CA).

C-262 /gaṛdyan/([gaṛdyæn]) "goalie, goalkeeper (soccer, etc.)"; Pl [-æt]; Fr gardien. F. Syn: /ḥaris/ (CA).

-- /gaṛfu/ See /fṛšiṭ-a/ C-243.

C-263 /gaṛṛu/ "cigarette" (the usual word); Pl /gwaṛṛu/, also /-wat/ or /-yat/; Sp cigarro or similar Romance form. F Mk Mr. [Also Tt, which has Pl /gaṛṛu-ṣ/ from Sp cigarros; Alg /gaṛṛu/, grammatically masculine; DMA-AE; MAG 15; TAT 440-1 with plural /gṛaṛu/ or /gaṛṛi-wat/.] Syn: /d^{W}xxan/, /sižaṛ-a/ (both from CA, though the second is a European borrowing originally). Note that Sp cigarro really means "cigar" (also Sp puro), while Sp cigarillo (diminutive) means "cigarette".

C-264 /gaṛṣun/: (1) waiter (in restaurant or café)"; (2) "(man's) underpants". Pl [-æt] or /gṛaṣn/ in both senses, in sense 1 also FSg /gaṛṣun-a/ "waitress", Pl [-æt]; Fr garçon (sense 1), Sp calzón (and diminutive calzoncillo, sense 2). Both senses in F, sense 1 also Mk Mr Casa(j). [DMA-AE; EDA 384-5; Alg /qṛṣun/ connected with Fr caleçon; Tt has /kaṛsusiyu/ "underpants" from calzoncillo.] Syn: /slipp/ C-653 "underpants" (more common than /gaṛṣun/ at least in F/Mk area), /srbay/ C-656 "waiter" (not very common, /gaṛṣun/ being the usual word in this sense). Cf. also C-265.

C-265 /gaṛṣuniy-a/ "studio apartment, bachelor's apartment"; Pl [-æt]; Fr garçonnière. F *Mr. Syn: /ḍ-ḍaṛ d-l-^{c}zar-a/ "the house of the bachelors". Cf. /bṛṭm-a/ C-114.

C-266 /gaṭu/(F) or /gaṭṭu/(Mk Mr) "cake" (collective); individuative Sg /-wa/(F) or /-ya/(F Mk Mr) "piece of cake"; Pl /-wat/ or /-yat/, Dimin Sg /gwiṭṭu-ya/(Mr); Fr gâteau. F Mk Mr *Casa(j). Syn: /ḥlw-a/.

C-267 /gaz/ "(lamp) oil"; no Pl; Fr gaz; idiom /ṭl^{c}-l-i l-gaz/ "I am fed up, irritated" (lit., "the gas has risen for me, has come up to my head"), for similar idiom cf. C-178 (also /ṭl^{c}-l-i d-dəmm/ "I am fed up" with /dəmm/ "blood"). F Mr. [DMA-AE; EDA 385; TAR 287; Alg in sense "cooking gas".] More common than /ġaz/, which is based on the CA variant.

C-268 /gaẓu/ "lawn, turf"; no Pl, Dimin /gwiẓu/; Fr gazon. F.

C-269 /gid/ "tourist guide (person, not guidebook)"; Pl /gyad/ (for analogical pattern cf. /bir/ "well (of water)", Pl /byar/), Dimin /gwiyəd/; Fr guide (Sp guía). F Mk Mr Alg. [DMA-AE.] Syn: /mu-ṛšid/ (from CA, see A-1-294), also /gyyad/ C-287 and verbs /gida/ B-64, /gwwəd/ B-70, and /gyyəd/ B-71.

C-270 /gidun/ "handlebar (of bicycle, etc.)"; Pl [-æt], Dimin /gwidin/; Fr guidon. F Mk Mr. [DMA-AE.] Syn: /dwwas/.

C-271 /girr-a/(F Mk Tt) or /giṛṛ-a/(Casa(j) and some other Jewish dialects) "war"; Pl [-æt], Dimin /gwirr-a/; old, well-established loan from Sp guerra, reinforced by Fr guerre. Syn: /ḥṛb/ (from CA apparently, now gaining).

C-272 /gitaṛ/(F Mk Mr), /gitaṛ-a/(F Mk), or /giṭaṛ-a/(Casa(j)), definite usually the normal form /l-/ but Mk informant also permits /ḷa-/, "guitar"; Pl [-ạt]; Fr guitare, Sp guitarra. F Mk Mr. Syn: /qiṭaṛ-a/ (based on the CA form).

-- /gəwri/ See C-286.

C-273 /glaṣ/, definite /l-/ or /ḷa-/ "ice cream"; Pl [-ạt]; Fr (la) glace. F Mk *Mr. [Alg /(ḷa-)glaṣ/, feminine.] Syn: /tlž/ (also "snow"), cf. /puḷu/ C-575, /baṣṭ-a/ C-65, and /gufrit/ C-282. Cf. also verb /glaṣa/ B-65.

-- /gṛafaṭ/, /gṛafaṭ-a/ See /kṛavaṭ-a/ C-367.

C-274 /gṛafiṭ/ "gravel"; no Pl; perhaps Fr gravier with form influenced by Fr graphite "graphite". F.

C-275 /gṛam/(F Mk) or /g^{w}ṛam/(Mr) "gram"; Pl [-æt] (F Mk Mr), but normally in Sg form with numeral: /tlat-a gṛam/ or /tlat-a d-l-gṛam/ "three grams"; Fr Sp gram. F Mk Mr. [DMA-AE.] Syn: /ġṛam/ (from CA).

C-276 /gṛayd-i/ "graded, ranked" (adjective); Pl /gṛayd-iy-a/, FSg also /gṛayd-iy-a/; Fr gradé, assimilated to derivational type seen in native /skayr-i/, Pl /skayr-iy-a/ "drunkard(s)" from root √skr. F.

C-277 /grisun/ "bus driver's assistant" (man who signals to driver to let passengers off from the back door and sometimes sells tickets); Pl [-æt]; Fr graisseur. F Mk Mr. [EDA 386 and Tt /gṛiṣuṛ/.]

C-278 /griyaž/ (unpharyngealized) "(wire) fence"; Pl [-æt]; Fr grillage. F Mk Mr. Syn: /slk/ "wire".

C-279 /gṛu/. Occurs in prepositional phrase (used as adverb) /b-l-gṛu/ "in bulk, wholesale" (used with verb /šra/ "he sold" or /ba^{c}/ "he bought"); Fr en gros. For antonym see /ḍiṭay/ C-185. F Syn: /žml-a/, /g^{w}rž-a/.

C-280 /grupp/ "group (especially, organized tourist group, or musical ensemble)"; Pl [-æt]; Fr groupe (Sp grupo); note that this is used in European-type contexts. F Mk Mr. (Tt /grupu/ is from Sp.] Syn: /fṛq-a/ (also "team").

-- /g^{w}ṭaṛ/ See /kṭaṛ/ C-385.

C-281 /gudṛun/(Mk Mr) or /guḍṛun/(F) "blacktop, bitumin, asphalt (highway material)"; no Pl; Fr goudron. F Mk Mr. Syn: /zəft/, also /qṭṛan/ (from CA; this is the original source of the Fr form).

C-282 /gufrit/ or /gufṛiṭ/ "ice-cream cone"; no Pl; Fr goufrette usually refers to a wafer-like cream-filled biscuit/cookie, rather than ice-cream cones. F. Syn: see /glaṣ/ C-273 and refs there.

C-283 /guḷ/: (1) "goalie, goalkeeper (soccer, etc.)"; (2) "goal, score". Pl /gwal/ (for analogical pattern cf. /buš/ "marble", Pl /bwaš/; for other Sg/Pl pairs involving loanwords see /bun/ C-136, /buṭ/ C-155); Sp goal (occasional Fr gol,though but is the usual Fr word); less common than /bit/ C-91 except in northern Morocco formerly under Sp control. F. [Tt /guṇ/, Pl /guṇ-iṣ/ from Sp goles; Alg "goalie" /(l-)gul/, Pl /ḷi-guḷ/ from Fr les gols.] For "goalie" see also C-262, A-1-100.

C-284 /guḷf/(Mk Mr) or /gɔlf/(F) "golf"; no Pl; Fr golf [gɔlf], Sp golf. F Mk Mr. [EDA 385.] Syn: /kuṛ-at l-^{c}aṣa/ (from CA, uncommon).

C-285 /gum-a/:(1) "(rubber) eraser"(F Mk Mr Tt); (2) "type of hashish"(F). Pl [-æt], Dimin /gwim-a/ or /gwiym-a/; Sp goma, Fr gomme; cf. verb /guma/ B-69. F Mk Mr Tt. [DMA-AE.] Syn: /mimsaḥ-a/ (CA).

C-286 /gwri/ "stranger; foreigner, European tourist"; Pl /gwr/ (with syllabic /r/), FSg /gwriy-a/, Pl /gwriy-at/; etymological history unclear but probably related to Turkish gâwur; either a fairly old form from Algeria (where Turkish influence was substantial) or spread by dialectal Fr (now rare) giaour. Has recently become very common in Morocco among hotel staff, illegal guides, etc., replacing /nṣṛan-i/ (which these Moroccans suspect is now "picked up" by Europeans who overhear the hotel staff or illegal guides talking about them). F Mk *Casa(j). [Alg, both Sg and Pl forms as given above.] Syn: /nṣṛan-i/ (also "Christian"), cf. /ṭṛanži/ C-766. (I thank Haim Blanc, p.c., for suggesting the Turkish connection.)

C-287 /gyyad/ "tourist guide (person)"; Pl /-a/, FSg /-a/, FPl /-at/; internal derivative on /CCCaC/ professional-agent pattern from verb /gyyəd/ B-71; less common than /gid/ C-269.

C-288 /ġanžu/ "hick, country bumpkin"; Dimin /ġwinžu/(F); FSg /-ya/, Pl /ġwanž/ or /ġwanža/; from Sp gancho (It gancio, Old Fr ganche) in sense "pitchfork" (which is still the meaning of more recent borrowing /ganšu/ C-258), with subsequent semantic shift; for similar shift see /kambu/ C-311. F(and region) *Casa(j). [For older forms in sense "pitchfork" or "harpoon" see NLVM 97-8, TAT 406.]

C-289 /ġiwan/: (1) "great, wonderful" (invariable in form); (2) "a type of native song style". F *Casa(j). [NLVM 98 suggests that this was formerly an MCA Pl form of /ġan-a/, see /gan-a/ C-257, from Sp gana "desire, whim".]

C-290 /himri/ "hungry" or "hunger"; no Pl; Sp hambre; used with unstable syntax in recent slang expressions like /ana himri/ "I (am) hungry" (in this usage, adjectival but invariable in form) or /ana fi-ya l-himri/ "I am hungry" (lit., "in me is hunger", parallel to /ana fi-ya ž-žu^{c}/, same gloss and structure), Mr variant /ža-ni l-himri/ "I am hungry" (lit., "hunger has come to me", parallel to the Mr type /ža-ni ž-žu^{c}/, same gloss and structure). F Mr *Mk. Syn: /žu^{c}/ (the normal word for "hunger"). Now often thought to be from Eng hungry.

C-291 /hippi/ "hippie"; Pl /-yin/(F Mr), /hwappa/(F), or /hpappa/(Mr), FSg /hippiy-a/, Pl /-at/, MSg Dimin /hwippi/; Eng hippie, probably via Fr; used as pejorative slang, applied almost exclusively to foreign hippies; cf. verb /hippa/. Used by hotel staff, guides, etc., referring to one characteristic type of tourist. F Mk Mr. Syn: /bu š^{c}kak-a/, /m-š^{c}kək/ (words literally indicating unkempt hair).

C-292 /hiġipuġ/ "airport" (Mr); no Pl; Fr aéroport with unusual loan phonology (notably /ġ/ for Fr uvular r, normally becoming /r/ or /ṛ/ in loans), probably a poorly assimilated uneducated form; usual term for "airport" is /maṭaṛ/ (from CA). Mr *F *Mk. Cf. also /ayyaṣyuṇ/ C-28.

-- /ikip/ See /kibb/ C-351.

-- /ikul/ See /skwil-a/ C-654.

C-293 /ilyan/ (interjection) "it's a goal!" (British English broadcast style: "it's there!"); Fr il y est (used in Fr soccer broadcasts). F. [Alg has /ilyi/ in this sense.] Cf. C-294.

C-294 /ilyi/ "wing (position in soccer team)"; no Pl; Fr ailier. F. [For Alg /ilyi/ see C-293.] Syn: /žanih/ (from CA).

C-295 /ingliz/, /iŋgliz/, /?ingliz/, /ngliz/ "English (people, collective)"; MSg and adjectival form /-i/, FSg /-iy-a/ "Englishwoman; English language"; Sp inglés with later influence of Fr anglais (FSg anglaise) and CA ?inglīz-. F Mk Tt. [MAG 14, 57, 68; DMA-EA under "English" has /ngliz-i/, but for language also /ngliz-a/.] Human Pl also /ngalza/ (Mk).

-- /intiṛṇ-a/ See /anṭiṛ/ C-13.

C-296 /iṣạ̃ṣ/(F Mr) or /iṣanṣ/(Mk), for some speakers requiring definite /l-/ prefix, "gasoline"; Fr (l')essence. F Mk Mr. [Alg /lisạ̃s/; DMA-EA under "gas" /liṣanṣ/; EDA 395.] Although not used in standard CA, Moroccan petrol (gas) stations sometimes use this word in written form (with pharyngealized ṣ, and with n written). Cf. /gaz/ C-267, /biṭṛul/ C-93.

C-297 /iššir/ "little boy", usually with definite /l-/; no Pl, FSg /-a/; F informant claims this is from Fr (le) cher "the dear one", but this may be a folk etymology. F Mk. [DMA-AE; Alg /iššir/ has Pl /išašra/.] Syn: /wəld/, /drri/.

C-298 /itṛu/(Mk Mr Casa(j)) or /yṭṛu/(F) "litre"; Pl /-wat/, /-yat/, /itaṛa/, or /iṭaṛa/, but with numeral normally found in Sg form, as in /tlat-a yṭṛu/ or /tlat-a d-l-iṭṛu/ "three litres"; Sp litro with l reinterpreted as definite prefix and segmented out. F Mk Mr Casa(j). [Algrs /ritl-a/, eAlg /itṛ-a/ perhaps with slightly different history; DMA-AE /iṭṛu/ and /liṭṛu/; DMA-EA under "liter" /litru/, not pharyngealized, perhaps a typo; EDA 395-6 /litr/(Fr litre) or /liṭṛu/(Sp litro); Tt /litru/ or /liṭṛu/.]

C-299 /iṭaž/(F Mk Mr) or /ṭaž/(F Mk) "floor, storey (of building)"; Pl [-æt](F Mk) or [-ạt](Mr); Fr étage. F Mk Mr. Syn: /ṭabaq/ or /ṭabaq-a/(CA). Cf. C-300 below.

C-300 /iṭažiṛ/ "shelf"; Pl [-ạt]; Fr étagère. F. Cf. C-299.

-- /iṭṛ-a/ See /ṭṛiṭ-a/ C-773.

-- /iṭṛu/ See /itṛu/ C-298 above.

C-301 /kab/, definite /la-kab/ ([læ-kæb]) "cellar (of house)"; Pl [-æt]; Fr (la) cave. F.

C-302 /kaḅal/ "knight (card worth eleven in Spanish card deck)"; Pl [-æt](Mk) or /kwaḅl/; Sp caballo "horse" (or related Portuguese or Catalan form). F Mk Mr. Cf. /ṣuṭ-a/ C-693.

C-303 /kabin/, definite /la-kabin/ "cab (of truck)"; Pl [-æt]; Fr (la) cabine. F. Cf. C-304, 332.

C-304 /kabin-a/ "(modern) bathroom"; Pl [-æt]; Fr cabinet (de toilette). F Mk Mr. [EDA 387.] Syn:/visi/ C-791 or /bit l-ma/.

C-305 /kabṛan/([kæbṛan]) "corporal (in army); leader of group or pack"; Pl [-æt], Dimin /kwibṛin/; Fr and Sp caporal, probably an old loan brought in from Algeria. F Mk *Mr. [EDA 387; DMA-AE.] Occurs also in compound /kabṛan šaf/ "chief corporal" (with /šaf/ C-697 from Fr chef).

C-306 /kabus/ "pistol (especially children's toy pistol)"; Pl /kwabs/; perhaps a Romance loan but history unclear; perhaps Sp cabos "corporals" or Fr caboche; cf. CA kābūs- "nightmare; phantom" with semantics making connection to the MCA form difficult. F Mk Casa(j) Alg *Mr. [DMA-AE.] Syn: /frd-i/, cf. /bisṭuli/ C-89.

-- /kade/ See /kaḍi/ C-307.

C-307 /kaḍi/(F Mk) or /kade/([kæde])(F) "cadet (player in cadet soccer league, in late teens)"; no Pl; Fr cadet. F Mk. Cf. C-814.

C-308 /kaḍu/ "gift, present"; Pl /-wat/ or /-yat/, Dimin /kwidu/; Fr cadeau. F Mk Mr. Syn: /hdiy-a/ (about equally common). Cf. C-193.

C-309 /kafatir-a/ "coffee-brewer" (machine in café); Pl [-æt]; Sp cafetera reinforced by Fr cafetière. F *Mr. [DMA-AE; TAT 233.]

C-310 /kaḷm/ "placid, calm" (person or thing); used as adjective, form invariable; Fr calme. F.

C-311 /kambu/ "hick, country bumpkin" (currently a common slang term in F/Mk area); Pl /kwanb/ or /kwanəb/ (suggesting that /m/ in /kambu/ is interpreted as underlying /n/ assimilating to /b/); probably ultimately Sp campo "field, country (not city)". F *Casa(j). Syn: /ᶜṛub-i/, /ġanžu/ C-288. Cf. verb /kunəb/ B-87.

C-312 /kaṃiṛ-a/ "camera"; Pl [-ạt], Dimin /kwiṃiṛ-a/; Fr caméra. F Mk Mr. Syn: /mu-ṣwwiṛ-a/ (from CA but fairly common.

C-313 /kamiyu/(F), /kamyu/(Mk Mr and area around F), /kamiyun/ (F), /kamyun/(Mk), or /kamayun/(attributed to far north and Rif) "truck"; Pl /-wat/ or /-yat/ after /u/, [-æt] after /n/; Sp camión, Fr camion. F Mk Mr. [Casa(j) /kaṃyun/; Alg /kamyu/, Pl /-wat/; DMA-AE /kamiyu/; EDA 388 has several variants; Tt /kamyun/.] Syn: /šahin-a/(rare). Cf. /ban/ C-45, /bikub/ C-80.

C-314 /kanappi/ "armchair"; Pl /-yat/; Fr canapé. F. Syn: /ḟutöy/ C-251.

C-315 /kaṇaṛ/ "canary"; Pl [-at]; Sp canario, Fr canari, or similar form, possibly influenced by Fr canard "duck" for form. F Mr. [DMA-AE.]

C-316 /kantin-a/ "tavern; canteen (restaurant)"; Pl [-æt]; Sp cantina, Fr cantine. F Mk Mr Tt. [DMA-AE.]

C-317 /kanz-a/: (1) "fortnight, period of two weeks"; (2)"a card game based on getting fifteen points". Pl [-æt]; Fr quinzaine "group of fifteen; fortnight" or perhaps direct from Fr quinze "fifteen". F.

C-318 /kạ̃piŋg/(F), /kạ̃piŋk/(F), /kɔ̃piŋg/(Mk), or /kõpin/(Mr) "camping ground (official area reserved for camping out)"; Fr camping [kãpiŋg] "camping ground" ex Eng. F Mk Mr. Syn: /mu-xyyam/ (CA) is now becoming equally common.

C-319 /kapitan/ "captain (especially of sporting team)"; Pl [-æt]; Fr capitaine, Sp capitán. F Mr. This is a more recent form than /qbṭan/ C-581 (used in military context).

C-320 /kaṛ/ "intercity bus"; Pl /kiṛ-an/, Dimin /kwiyṛ/, with Pl form based on pattern seen in /faṛ/ "mouse", Pl /fir-an/ (section 6.5) but note /ṛ/ retained in Pl; Fr car. F Mk Mr Tt Casa(j). [DMA-AE; Alg /kaṛ/; EDA 388.] Sg/Pl forms obtained from all these sources except Casa(j) (Sg only from this dialect), all showing constant /ṛ/. Syn: for "local bus" see /ṭubis/ C-778. I have also heard /kaṛ/ used in cheap rotisseries to mean "quarter (of a chicken)" (Fr quart) but this seems to be a code-switched form and I have not (yet) heard it with affixes or in an MCA plural form.

C-321 /kaṛabin/ or /kaṛabil/ "small rifle, carbine"; Pl [-æt]; Fr carabine. F *Mr. Syn: /m^wkḥl-a/.

C-322 /kaṛakṭiṛ/(F) or /kaṛaktir/(Mr) "character (of a person)"; no Pl; Fr caractère, Sp carácter. F Mr. Syn: cf. /gan-a/ C-257.

C-323 /kaṛḅun/ "carbon; coal"; no Pl; Sp carbón, Fr carbone (cf. Fr charbon "coal"), perhaps via CA karbūn- "coal". F Mk. [DMA-AE.]

C-324 /kaṛni/(F Mk Mr) or /kaṛṇi/(F) "identity card" (or any similar card); Pl /-yat/, Dimin /kwiṛni/ or /kwiṛṇi/; Fr carnet (cf. Fr carte d'identité). F Mk Mr. [Alg /kaṛni/ "card" (not specifically identity card, which is called /kaṛḍạ̃titi/ in Alg.)]

-- /kaṛṛuṣ-a/ See /kṛṛuṣ-a/ C-374.

-- /kaṛtun/ See /kaṛṭun/ C-331.

C-325 /kaṛtuš/(F Mk Mr) or /qaṛtuš/(F): (1) "shells, bullets" (collective) (F Mk); (2) "small box" (Mr). Individuative Sg /-a/ in sense 1, Pl [-æt] in both senses; Fr cartouche (Sp cartucho); a fairly recent loan still less common than the older form /qṛṭaṣ/. F Mk Mr. [Casa(j) /kaṛtus/ with regular depalatalization; Alg /kaṛtuš/; DMA-AE has only /qṛṭaṣ/.]

C-326 /kaṛtuvn/ or /kaṛṭuvn/ "potato(es)" (Sg or collective); no Pl; German Kartoffeln (Pl); a recently popularized slang word. F *Mk *Mr *Casa(j). Usual word is /baṭaṭ-a/ C-67.

C-327 /kaṛtyi/ "quarter, neighbourhood (in city)"; Pl /-yat/; Fr quartier. F. Syn: /ḥum-a/ (much more common).

C-328 /kaṛṭ/, definite /ḷa-kaṛṭ/ "(credit or identity) card"; Pl [-ạt]; Fr (la) carte. F Mr. Syn: /kaṛni/ C-324, and /kaṛṭ-a/ C-329.

C-329 /kaṛṭ-a/: (1) "(playing) card"(F Mk Mr Alg); (2) "card game"(F Mk Mr); (3) "credit card"(F, least common sense). Pl [-ạt]; Dimin /kwiṛṭ-a/; Sp carta (but Sp naipe is usual in the sense "playing card"), Fr carte. F Mk Mr Alg. [DMA-AE; GJA 115; NLVM 122; TAT 448.] Syn: see C-328.

C-330 /kaṛṭbuṣṭ-a/(F), /kaṛṭpuṣṭal/(F Mk), or /kaṛṭpuṣṭal/(Mr) "postcard"; Pl [-æt] from second form, [-ạt] from first/third; Fr carte postale, with first form perhaps influenced by /buṣṭ-a/ C-151 "post office". F Mk Mr.

C-331 /kaṛṭun/(F Mr) or /kaṛtun/(Mr) "cardboard" (collective); individuative Sg /-a/ "piece of cardboard", Pl [-æt], Dimin Sg /kwiṛṭin-a/; Fr carton, Sp cartón. F Mr.

-- /kaṛṭuvn/ See /kaṛtuvn/ C-326.

C-332 /kaṛusri/ "van (of truck)"; Pl /-yat/; Fr carrosserie. F. Cf. /kabin/ C-303, /kamiyu/ C-313.

-- /kaṛwel-a/, /kaṛwil-a/. See /kṛwel-a/ C-381.

-- /kaskṛuṭ/ See /kaṣkṛuṭ/ C-335.

C-333 /kạ̃ṣiṛ/ or /kə̃ṣiṛ/ "cancer"; no Pl; Fr cancer. F. Competes with /saṛaṭan/ from CA, but common among bilinguals.

C-334 /kaṣiṭ-a/ "cassette (tape)" or "cassette tape recorder"; Pl [-ạt]; Dimin /kwiṣiṭ-a/; Fr cassette. F Mk Mr.

C-335 /kaṣkṛuṭ/(F) or /kaskṛuṭ/([kæskṛoṭ])(Mk Mr) "sandwich; midafternoon snack"; Pl [-ạt], Dimin /kwiṣkṛuṭ/(F); Fr casse-croûte. F Mk Mr. [EDA 388 /kaṣkṛuṭ/; Alg /kaṣkrut/, Pl [-æt].] For related forms see /kṛuṭ/ C-376, verbs /kaṣa/ B-73, /qṣṣa/ B-122.

C-336 /kaṣṛun-a/(F Mk) or /kaṣṛuṇ-a/(Mr) "cooking pot"; Pl [-æt](F Mk) or [-ạt](Mr); Fr casserole. F Mk Mr. Cf. /gamil-a/C-256.

C-337 /kạš/ (adverb) "in cash, by cash"; example /xlləṣ kạš/ "he paid cash"). F *Mr. Cf. /nikl/ C-532.

C-338 /kạši/ "seal, stamp"; Pl /-yat/; Fr cachet. F. Syn: /ṭampụ/ C-756.

C-339 /kạškạš/(Mk Mr) or /kaškaš/([kæškæš])(F) "children's hide-and-seek game"; no Pl; Fr cache-cache; does not permit definite prefix /l-/. F Mk Mr. Syn: /ġʷmmayḍ-a/(F), /ġmmayḍu/(Mr).

C-340 /kaškul/ "scarf"; Pl [-æt]; Fr cache-col. F Alg. Cf. /kašni/ C-341.

C-341 /kašni/ "scarf worn over nose"; Pl /-yat/; Fr cache-nez. F Alg. Cf. C-340.

C-342 /kạw/(F Mk) or /kaw/ ([kæw]) (rural, F/Mk region) "knockout (in boxing)"; examples /ṭaḥ kạw/ "he was knocked out" (lit. "he fell K.O."), /žab l-kạw/ "he got knocked out (boxing)" or figuratively "he got plastered (very drunk)", lit. "he brought the K.O."; Fr K.O. [kao] ex Eng. Cf. /kutknut/ C-429.

C-343 /kawatšu/ "rubber"; Pl /-yat/ or /-wat/; Fr caoutchouc, Sp caucho. F Mk Mr. [Casa(j) /kawtšu/; Alg /kawiču/; EDA 389 /kawatšu/ or /kawtšu/; GJA 113 /kawtšu/ as Muslim form; DMA-AE /kawatšu/; DMA-EA under "rubber" has "kawetšu"; Tt /kawaču/.]

C-344 /kawkaw/([kæwkæw])(F Mk Tt) or /kạwkạw/(Mr, Casa(j), also said to be used in east around Oujda) "peanuts"; perhaps a cross of Fr cacahouète (also spelled cacahuète), Sp cacahuete, and CA kākāw-. F Mk Mr Tt Casa(j). [Alg /kawkaw/([kæwkæw]); DMA-AE.]

-- /kawtšu/ See /kawatšu/ C-343.

C-345 /kayaṣ/: (1) "gravel, small stones"; (2) "bulldozer"(F only). From Fr caillasse. F Mk Mr. [DMA-AE /kayaṣ/ "gravel", also individuative Sg /-a/ "rock, stone"; EDA 389.]

C-346 /kaẓa/: (1) "Casablanca" (largest city in Morocco); (2) "Casa" (a brand of cigarettes). No Pl; Dimin /kwiẓa/ in either sense; Fr Casa (conventional abbreviation of Casablanca, ultimately from Sp casa blanca "white house"). Normal MCA for the city is the calque /ḍ-ḍaṛ l-biḍ-a/ "the white house" (also used in CA).

C-347 /kazyu/(F), /okazyu/(F), or /okaẓyu/(Mk) "second-hand" (adverb); ex. /šri-t ṭ-ṭuṃubil kazyu/ "I bought the car second-hand"; form invariable with no definite prefix permitted; Fr d'occasion. F Mk *Mr. [Alg /ukazyu/ and Tt /okaẓyuṇ/, same syntax.] Syn: /x^wrd-a/ (mainly of clothing), /qdim/ "old".

C-348 /k^wbb-a/: (1) "ball of yarn"; (2) "wine". Pl [-æt] in sense 1. Original MCA in sense 1, but sense 2 may involve semantic reshaping by influence of Sp copa "(brandy) glass", with original MCA verb /k^wbb/ "he poured" a linking factor. The second sense attested in F along with the first (which is the only sense thus far recorded from Mk). Cf. /kubb-a/ C-387. For "wine" usual word is /šṛab/, cf. also C-83, C-622, C-623.

C-349 /k^wbbaniy-a/(F Mk) or /kubbaniy-a/(around F, rural) "business enterprise, company; (pejoratively) pack of children, pack of thieves"; Pl [-æt]; Sp compañía, Fr compagnie. F Mk Mr. [DMA-AE with /k^wbb.../.] Syn: /šarik-a/ "business enterprise".

C-350 /kbbuṭ/ "shirt" (especially knitted); Pl /kbabṭ/; It cappotto or Sp capote. F Alg. [DMA-AE; TAT 446; ZLMA 23.] Syn: /trikku/ C-739.

C-351 /kibb/ "team (sports)"; Pl [-æt]; Fr équipe. F *Mr. [Alg /l-ikip/.] Somewhat less common than /fṛq-a/,/faṛiq/.

C-352 /kulu/ "kilo"; Pl /-wat/ or /-yat/, but Sg form usual with numeral, as in /ᶜšṛ-a kilu/ "ten kilos"; Fr Sp kilo. F Mk Mr Tt. [DMA-AE; EDA 389.]

C-353 /kiluṃiṭ/(F Mk Casa(j)), /kiluṃiṭṛ/(Tt), /kuḷumiṭ/(F Mr), or /kulumiṭ/(rural near F) "kilometre"; Pl [-ạt] but Sg normal with numeral (as with /kilu/ C-352 and other borrowed measure terms); Fr kilomètre (Sp kilómetro), perhaps influenced by CA kilumitr- and/or by /mitr/ C-506. F Mk Mr Tt Casa(j). [Alg /kilumitr/ probably via CA; DMA-EA /kilumitr/ under"kilometer"; EDA 390 lists several variants.]

C-354 /kipkul/ "unruffled, cool under pressure"; used as adverb or predicate adjective, form invariable, also as interjection with imperative force; Eng keep cool, perhaps via Fr slang. F *Mr. Syn: /brrəd d-dəmm/ "cool (your) blood" (possible calque).

C-355 /kḷakṣuṇ/ "automobile horn"; Pl [-ạt]; Fr klaxon [klakson], Sp claxon; verb /kḷakṣuna/ B-74 has unpharyngealized /n/. F Mk Mr.

C-356 /kḷaṣ/ or /kḷaṣ-a/ "class (in school)"; Pl [-ạt] or /kḷayṣ/, Dimin /kḷiyṣ-a/; Fr classe (Sp clase). F Mk Mr. [Alg /kḷaṣ-a/.] Less common than /qism/ from CA; cf. semantically unrelated verb /klaṣa/ B-75.

C-357 /kḷaṭ-a/(F Mk Tt) or /k^{W}ḷaṭ-a/(F Mk) "rifle"; Pl [-ạt] or /kḷayṭ/ (probably also */k^{W}ḷayṭ/, not in data); Dimin /k^{W}ḷaṭ-a/ with /k^W/ even for F/Mk speakers using /k/ in non-Dimin Sg; source unclear, possibly related to Fr éclater "explode", cf. verb /klaṭa/ B 76. Syn: /m^{W}kḥl-a/, /kaṛabin/ C-321. F Mk Casa(j) Tt *Mr *Alg. [DMA-AE.]

C-358 /kliṛ/ "clear, certain"; normally invariable form, but FSg /kliṛ-a/ heard once in /ma-kayn ḥtta ši ḥaž-a kliṛ-a/ "nothing is clear" in hot retort to other speaker who had just said that a matter was /kliṛ/. F. Fr clair. Syn: /bayn/.

C-359 /kliru/ or /kriru/ "in a single draught" (with "to drink"); ex. /šṛb-ha kliru/ "he drank (beer) in one gulp, chugged it"; Fr clairon "small military bugle" (held to mouth like beer bottle). F Mk *Mr. Syn: /f-ḍṛb-a wḥd-a/ "in one blow".

C-360 /kliyan/(F Mk Mr) or /klyan/(F, pronounced as one syllable) "client, customer"; Pl [-æt] or identical to Sg; Fr client (Sp cliente). F Mk Mr. [Tt /klyinti/, Pl /-s/.] Syn: /zabun/(CA).

C-361 /klüb/(F), /klöb/(F Mk), or /klupp/(Mr) "(sporting, recreational) club"; Pl [-æt]; Fr club (usually [klöb], sometimes spelling pronunciation [klüb]), Sp club [klub]. F Mk Mr. [Tt /klub/ from Sp.] Syn: /nadi/ (CA).

-- /klyan/ See /kliyan/ C-360 above.

C-362 /k^{W}ṇiniṛ/(Mk), /k^{W}niniṛ/(F), /kuṇiniṛ/(Mr), /kuṛuniḷ/(F), or /kuṇuniḷ/(F) "colonel"; Pl [-ạt]; Fr colonel, Sp coronel; /kuṇuniḷ/ seems to be becoming common in cities. F Mk Mr *Casa(j). [DMA-AE /kniniṛ/; EDA 390 /kninṛ/ or /kninir/.]

-- /kõba/, /kõb-a/ See /kumb-a/ C-399.

C-363 /kõfuṛ/ "de luxe", normally in phrase /d-l-kõfuṛ/ "de luxe" as modifying adjectival phrase; Fr de confort. F *Mk *Mr. Syn: /luks/ C-454.

C-364 /koki/ or /kokiy/: (1) "shell; shellfish"; (2) "plastic groin protector worn by soccer goalie". No Pl; Fr coquille. F Mk. Syn: /qšr-a/.

C-365 /kokuṭ/ "stewpan"; Pl [-ạt], Dimin /kwekiṭ/; Fr cocotte. F Mk Mr. Cf. C-366.

C-366 /kokuṭminut/ "(cooking) pots and pans"; no Pl; Fr Cocotte-Minute (brand name). F Mk. Cf. C-365.

-- /kõpin/, /kõpiŋ/ See /kạpiŋ/ C-318.

-- /kõpp-a/ See /kuṃp-a C-404.

-- /kõṭṛ-a/, /kõṭṛaḍ-a/ See /kuṇṭṛ-a/ C-410.

C-367 /kṛavaṭ-a/(Mk Casa(j)), /kṛafaṭ/(Mk), /gṛafaṭ-a/(F), or /gṛafaṭ/(Mr) "necktie"; Pl [-ạt], Dimin /gṛifiṭ-a/ and variants; Fr cravate crossed (in some forms) with Sp corbata. F Mk Mr Casa(j). [Algrs /gṛbaṭ-a/, eAlg /kṛavaṭ-a/; DMA-EA under "necktie" /gṛabaṭ-a/; EDA 385

/gṛafaṭ(-a)/; MAG 85 has Pl /kuṛbaṭ-as/ from Sp corbatas; Tt /kṛbaṭ-a/, Pl /-at/.]

C-368 /krballu/ "sieve"; Pl /-wat/, /-yat/; old loan, Sp cribello or similar form (perhaps via Berber), possibly influenced by MCA /$ġ^{w}$rbal/ "sieve". F Mk *Casa(j). [DMA-AE; TAR 710; TAT 447.]

C-369 /kridi/(Mr) or /kṛidi/(F), generally in prepositional phrase /b-l-kridi/ "on credit, not for cash"; Fr à crédit. F Mr. Syn: /slləf/ "to lend".

C-370 /krik/(F Mk) or /k^{w}rik/(Mr): (1) "jack (to raise car while changing tyre)"; (2) (slang) "short person, dwarf". Pl [-æt]; from Fr cric "jack". F Mk Mr. [DMA-AE under "jack".]

C-371 /kṛim/, definite /ḷa-kṛim/ "cream"; Fr (la) crème. F. [Alg /(la-)krim/ "cream" or "ice cream", grammatically feminine.] Cf. C-372.

C-372 /kṛimkạkạwiṭ/ "peanut cream (cosmetic for lips)"; no Pl; Fr crème cacahouète; pronounced more or less as in Fr, definite /l-kṛimkạkạwiṭ/. F. Cf. C-371.

-- /kriru/ See /kliru/ C-359.

C-373 /kriyu/ "pencil"; Pl /-wat/ or /-yat/; Fr crayon. F Mk Alg *Mr. Syn: /qalam ṛ-ṛaṣaṣ/(CA).

-- /k^{w}ṛniṭ-a/ See /kuṛniṭ-a/ C-421.

C-374 /kṛṛuṣ-a/ "cart"; Pl [-ạt] or /kṛaṛṣ/, Dimin /kṛiṛiṣ-a/; early loan from Fr carrosse, Sp carroza, perhaps It carrozza. F Mk Mr Casa(j). [Tt /kaṛṛuṣ-a/ from Sp; Alg /kṛṛuṣ-a/ "car, automobile"; DMA-AE; MAG 72 with Sp etymology; TAR 712 with Sp etymology, also mentioning a second sense "twelve dozen" from Sp gruesa.] Cf. /kṛwel-a/ C-381.

C-375 /kru/: (1) "nut" (as in "nuts and bolts")(F); (2) "small hole bored before screw is inserted"(Mr). No Pl; Fr écroux. F Mr. Cf. verb /kruwa/ B-81.

C-376 /kṛuṭ/, definite /ḷa-kṛuṭ/ "(midafternoon) snack; sandwich"; no Pl; Fr (la) croûte, cf. variant borrowing /kaṣkṛuṭ/ C-335 (from casse-croûte) and verbs /kaṣa/ B-73 and /qṣṣa/ B-122. F Mk. [EDA 388.]

C-377 /kruvi/ "flat tyre"; Pl /-yat/; Fr crevé; cf. verb /kruva/ B-80. F *Mr.

C-378 /kṛw-a/(/ṛ/ syllabic for Mk informant, optionally for F Mr): (1) "cross, mark in shape of cross (including Christian symbol)" (F Mk); (2) "belt(s) (rubber strips in motor)"(F Mk Mr). Pl [-ạt]; Fr croix "cross", Fr courroie "belt". F Mk Mr. Syn: /ṣlḅan/ "cross"; /ṣmṭ-a/ "belt (including that worn on body)".

C-379 /kṛwaṣ-a/(/ṛ/ syllabic for Mk informant, not for F Mr) "croissant", also "petit pain au chocolat" (pastry similar to croissant but with chocolate bits); Pl [-ạt], Dimin /kṛiwiṣ-a/; Fr croissant. For "petit pain au chocolat" this can optionally be extended as /kṛwaṣ-a b-š-šklạṭ/ (lit., "chocolate croissant"). F Mk Mr.

C-380 /kṛwaẓm-a/(/ṛ/ not syllabic) "intersection of streets)"; Pl [-æt]; Fr croisement. F Mk *Mr. Syn: /mu-ltaqa/(CA), cf. /ṛɔ̃p̣p̣-a/ C-607.

C-381 /kṛwel-a/(F Mr with syllabic /ṛ/) or /kaṛwel-a/(Mk Mr): (1) "chariot"; (2) "horse drawn cart"; (3) "jalopy" (pejorative term for automobile). Pl [-æt], Dimin /kṛiwel-a/; Fr carriole, Sp carriola, perhaps It carriuola. Possibly analysable as /kṛwil-a/ but it is unclear why the /i/ is pronounced [e] in this case. F Mk Mr Casa(j). [DMA-AE] Syn: see /kṛṛuṣ-a/ C-374, /kutši/ C-430.

C-382 /ksidạ̃/(Mk Tt), /ksid-ã/(Mk Tt), /ksid-a/(Mk Tt), /kṣiḍ-a/(F Tt), or /ḷakṣiḍ-a/(F) "automobile accident"; Pl [-æt] (Mk Tt) or [-ạt](F), also /kṣayḍ/(F); Dimin /kṣiyḍ-a/(F); Fr accident. F Mk Mr Tt. Forms shown with /-ã/ or /-a/ suffix are feminine, but /ksidạ̃/ is masculine. [Alg /ạksid-a/, feminine.] Less common than /ḥadit-a/ from CA.

C-383 /ksiratur/ "automobile accelerator (pedal on floor)"; Pl [-æt]; Fr accélérateur. F Mr [DMA-AE under "accelerator" has /ksiliṛaṭuṛ/.]

C-384 /kššin-a/(F) or /k^{w}ššin-a/(Mk Mr and F area) "cooking area, kitchen (especially as part of a larger room used for storage); (pejorative) dirty or messy kitchen area"; Pl [-æt], /kšašn/(F), or /k^{w}šašn/(Mk Mr), Dimin /kšišin-a/ or /k^{w}šišin-a/; Sp cocina (It cucina). F Mk Mr *Casa(j). [DMA-AE /kššin-a/; MAG 72; TAT 446 /kəčin-a/.] Cf. /kuzin-a/ C-431. Syn: /m-ṭbəx/.

C-385 /kṭaṛ/(F), /k^{w}ṭaṛ/(Mk), /g^{w}ṭaṛ/(F), or /hikṭaṛ/(Mr) "hectare"; Pl [-ạt], Dimin /g^{w}ṭiyṛ/ and variants; Fr hectare (Sp hectárea). F Mk Mr *Casa(j). [Tt /kṭaṛ/, Alg /kṭaṛ/; DMA-AE /kṭaṛ/.]

C-386 /ku/. Occurs in a few expressions like /ku-d-ktəf/ "blow or nudge with shoulder" and /ku d-z^{w}kk/ "blow or nudge with rear end" (somewhat vulgar); no Pl; Fr coup as in coup d'épaule and similar phrases ending in body-part noun, with fortuitous similarity between Fr de and MCA /d-/ (genitive) facilitating the transfers. F *Mk. Syn: /ḍṛb/ or ḍṛb-a/ (more common).

C-387 /kubb-a/ "(large) bowl (for soup, etc.)"; Pl [-æt]; perhaps Sp copa (Fr coupe), with with possible interaction with existing forms like /q^{w}bb/ "bucket", /q^{w}bb-a/ "dome", verb /k^{w}bb/ "he poured", and also with /k^{w}bb-a/ C-348 and /kupp/ C-414. The main F informant distinguishes C-387 from C-348 and C-414. F.

-- /kubbaniy-a/ See /k^{w}bbaniy-a/ C-349.

C-388 /kud/: (1) "road signs, traffic directions"; (2) "dimmed headlights (of car)". Pl [-æt]; Fr code. F.

C-389 /kuf-a/ "(military) convoy"; Pl [-æt]; Fr convoi, Sp convoy. F Mk. [EDA 392 states that this stem could not then take definite /l-/, but it can now.] Syn: /ᶜṛṛam/.

C-390 /kufitir/ "marmalade"; Pl [-æt] (meaning "kinds of marmalade"); Fr confiture (Sp confitura). F Mk Mr.

C-391 /kufṛ/: (1) "vault, safe"; (2) "truck (of car)"; (3) "glove compartment (of car)". Pl [-ạt]; Fr coffre, Sp cofre; cf. /kufṛfuṛ/ C-393, and possibly verb /kufṛ/ B-83. F. [MAG 49 gives older forms from Sp cofre.]

C-392 /kufṛ-a/: (1) "foul; free kick after a foul" (soccer); (2) "worthless, bad, or ugly thing" (slang). Pl [-ạt]; Fr coup franc "free kick". F Mk Mr. [EDA 392 /kufr-a/.] Cf. verb /kuvra/ B-93. Syn: /xaṭa?/ "error".

C-393 /kuf̣ṛfuṛ/ "strongbox, vault (e.g. in bank)"; Pl [-ạt]; Fr coffre fort. F.

C-394 /kuḷ-a/(F Mk Casa(j)) or /kul-a/(Mr): (1) "glue, paste" (agreement is feminine); (2) "drunkard, alcoholic" (agreement depends on actual sex of person). Pl [-ạt](F Mk Casa(j)) or [-æt](Mr), Dimin /kwiḷ-a/(F); Fr colle, Sp cola "paste, glue" with sense 2 perhaps suggested by /ankul/ C-10 "alcohol". In F at least, in sense 2 the Dimin is regularly used so the simple form is normal only in sense 1. F Mk Mr Casa(j)(sense 1 only). [Alg /(ḷa-) kuḷ/ "glue", grammatically feminine, possibly to be analysed as /kol/ since the related verb in Alg is /kola/ "he glued" with second syllable unpharyngealized.] Syn: /lṣaq/ "glue, paste", /skayr-i/ "drunkard".

C-395 /kuliy-a/ "(postal) parcel"; Pl [-æt], Dimin /kwiliy-a/; Fr colis. F Mk Mr. [Casa(j) has /koli/ "parcel"; Tt has /kuliy-a/ "parcel" or "cigarette butt", the latter from Sp colilla; Alg /kuli/, Pl /-yat/ "parcel"; DMA-AE /kuliy-a/ "parcel"; EDA 390 gives /kolibuṣṭ/, /kolibuṣṭu/, /koly-a/, /kolliy-a/ as Sg variants, all pluralized as /koly-at/, with Fr colis postaux "postal parcels" involved in some Sg forms; NLVM 125 also has /kolibuṣṭ/.] Syn: /ḥawal-a/ (less common).

-- /kuliyi/ See /kuryi/ C-425.

C-396 /kuliž/ "first section (cycle) of secondary school"; Pl [-æt]; Fr collège. F. Cf. /lisi/ C-448.

-- /kuḷumiṭ/ See /kiluṃiṭ/ C-353.

C-397 /kuḷuṣ/: (1) "big, muscular man"; (2) "bouncer (man who throws drunks or fighters out of bar)". Pl [-ạt]; Fr colosse "giant".

C-398 /kuṃanḍaṛ/ or /kʷṃanḍaṛ/(rural variant) "(army) major"; Pl [-ạt]; Fr commandant, Sp comandante; cf. verb /kuṃanḍa/. F Mk Mr Tt. [EDA 391.] Cf. B-84.

C-399 /kuṃḅ-a/, /kumb-a/, /kõb-a/ (these three feminine) or /kuṃḅa/ (masculine) "(big) fight, brawl, combat"; ex. /dar waḥəd l-kuṃḅ-a/ "he got into (lit. did) a fight"; Fr combat (Sp combate). F Mk Mr. Syn: /ṣiṛa^c/.

C-400 /kumik/ "comedian, funny person"; no FSg or Pl forms; Fr comique (Sp cómico), cf. verb /kumək/ B-86. F Mk *Mr. Syn: /mu-ḍḥḥik/.

C-401 /kumir/ (collective) "long thin bread loaves" (called baguette in Fr); individuative Sg (-a), Pl [-æt]; early, well-established loan from Sp comer "to eat" (infinitive), F Mk Mr. [Casa(j) /kuṃiṛ-a/; Tt /kummir/; DMA-AE /kumir/; GJA 117 /kuṃiṛ/; EDA 351 /kuṃiṛ/.] Syn: /ḅagiṭ/ C-34 (but /kumir/ is more common).

C-402 /kumisariy-a/ "police station, police headquarters"; Pl [-at]; Fr commissariat, Sp comisaría. F Mk Mr. [EDA 391.] Syn: /mṛkəz š-šuṛṭ-a/ (CA, "police centre").

C-403 /kumisir/ "police chief"; Pl [-æt], Dimin /kwimisir/; Fr commissaire (Sp comisario). F Mk Mr. [EDA 391; DMA-AE.] Syn: /m-ndub/.

C-404 /kuṃp̣-a/(tt), /kõpp-a/(F) "compass (direction-finding instrument)"; Fr compas (Sp compás). F Tt. Unrelated to verb /kɔ̃p̣a/ B-77 (Fr camper).

C-405 /kuṃp̣aṛtimą̃/(F, masculine), /kumpaṛtim-a/(F, feminine), or /kuṃp̣aṛtim-a/(Mk, feminine) "compartment (in train)"; Pl [-æt](Mk), though F speaker uses code-switched Fr plural; Fr compartiment. F Mk *Mr. Syn: /bit/ "room".

C-406 /kun-a/ "cradle"; Pl [-aet]; old loan from Sp cuna, perhaps going out of use in some areas. F Casa(j) Tt *Mk *Mr. [DMA-EA under "cradle"; EDA 351; GJA 118; TAR 736.]

C-407 /kuṇkur/ or /kõkur/ "contest, competition"; Pl [-æt]; Fr concours. F Mr.

C-408 /kuṇṣiṛv/ "canned goods"; ex. /huwa ^{c}ayš b-l-kuṇṣiṛv/ "he is living on canned goods"; no Pl; Fr conserve(s). F Mk. Cf. /bwaṭ/ C-161.

C-409 /kuṇṭak/(F Mr) or /kuṇṭakt/(Mk) "ignition (in car)"; Pl [-æt]; Fr contact. F Mk Mr. Cf. verb /kuṇṭakṭa/ B-88.

C-410 /kuṇṭṛ-a/(F Mk Mr), /kõṭṛ-a/(Mk), /kuṇṭṛaḍ-a/(F Mk Casa(j)), /kuṇṭṛad-a/(F), or /kõṭṛaḍ-a/(Mk) "contract"; Pl [-ạt] after /ṛ/ or /ḍ/, [-æt] after /d/; Dimin /kwiṇṭṛ-a/(F); Fr contrat (bisyllabic forms), perhaps Fr crossed with Sp contrato and similar Romance forms in trisyllabic MCA forms. F informant suggests semantic distinction with bisyllabic forms meaning "contractual relationship" while trisyllabic forms refer to "contract" as an actual written document, but this is a fine distinction not always made in real speech. F Mk Mr Casa(j). [DMA-AE /kuṇṭṛaḍ-a/; Tt /kuṇṭṛatu/, Pl /-ṣ/ from Sp contrato, contratos; TAR 419, 733 gives /kuṇṭṛaḍ-a/ with list of other dialect forms and earlier references it should be noted that some formal interaction may have occurred between this set and borrowings from Sp contra, Fr contre "against, opposed to", cf. Alg /xrəǰ kõṭṛa ^{c}li-ya/ "he is (lit., has come out) against me", with Sp contra reinforced by Alg Arabic preposition /^{c}la/ "against".] Syn: /ltizam/ (CA, uncommon).

C-411 /kuṇṭṛaḅanḍ/(F), /kuṇṭṛaṿan/(Mr), /kuṇṭṛbą̃ḍ/(F), /kuṇṭṛḅanḍ/(Mr), /ṭṛaḅanḍu/(F, pronounced [ṭṛabæ ndu]), or /ṭṛaḅanḍu/(Mr) "contraband, smuggled goods, smuggling"; no Pl; these forms variously from Fr contrebande, Sp contrabando. F Mr. [Casa(j) /kuṇṭṛaḅanḍu/ from Sp; MAG 54 and NLVM 126 give forms based on the Sp form.]

-- /kuṇṭṛad-a/, /kuṇṭṛaḍ-a/ See /kuṇṭṛ-a/ C-410.

C-412 /kuṇṭṛul/ "control, supervision"; no Pl; Fr contrôle; cf. verb /kuṇṭṛula/ B-89. Cf. also C-413.

C-413 /kuṇṭṛulur/(Mk) or /kuṇṭṛulör/(F) "supervisor; ticket-collector (on train)"; Pl [-æt]; Fr contrôleur. F Mk.

-- /kuṇuniḷ/ See /k^{w}ṇiniṛ/ C-362.

C-414 /kupp/ or /kup/, definite /ḷa-kup(p)/: (1) "cup, trophy"; (2) "haircut style". Pl [-æt]; Fr coupe. Form with /pp/ more common than that with single /p/. F. [Tt /kupp̣-a/ "cup, trophy" from Sp copa.] Cf. similar borrowings /k^Wbb-a/ C-348 and /kubb-a/ C-387.

C-415 /kuṛ-a/ (1) "ball (in soccer, etc.)"; (2) "soccer (name of the sport)"; (3) "electric current". Pl [-ạt] in sense 1 only. Senses 1 and 2 are native MCA forms, but sense 3 is from Fr courant (Sp corriente). F Mk Mr. [DMA-AE /kuṛ-a/ in sense 1 only; Alg /kuṛ-a/ in all three senses but grammatically masculine in sense 3, following Fr gender, vs. feminine in senses 1 and 2; in MCA, by contrast, the form is feminine in all senses.]

C-416 /kuṛḅ-a/(F Mr), /kuṛb-a/(F Mk), or /kurb-a/(Mk) "crate, box (e.g. of oranges)"; Pl [-ạt](F Mr) or [-æt](F Mk Mr), Dimin /kwiṛḅ-a/(F); Fr corbeille. F Mk Mr. [eAlg /kurbay-a/; DMA-AE /kuṛḅ-a/ "open basket".] Syn: /ṣnḍuq/.

C-417 /kuṛḍuni/(F Mr) or /kuṛḍunyi/(F) "shoemaker, cobbler"; Pl /-yat/; Fr cordonnier. F Mr. Syn: /ṭṛṛaf/, /xrraz/, cf. also /ṣbbaṭ/ C-681 "pair of shoes" and derivative /ṣbabṭ-i/ C-679.

C-418 /kuṛfi/ "hard labour"; no Pl; Fr corvée. F Mk. Syn: /tamar-a/ "hardship".

C-419 /kuri/ "stable (for horses)"; Pl /-yat/ or /kwara/, Dimin /kwiri/; Fr écurie. F Mk Mr. [DMA-AE.] Syn: /mṛbəḍ/.

C-420 /kuṛniṛ/ "corner kick (in soccer)"; Pl [-ạt]; Eng corner via Fr corner [kɔrnɛr], Sp córner [kórner]. F.

C-421 /kuṛniṭ-a/(F Mk) or /k^Wṛniṭ-a/(F Mk Mr) "bugle, horn"; Pl [-ạt], Dimin /kṛiniṭ-a/; Sp corneta, Fr cornet. F Mk Mr. [DMA-AE with /k^W/.]

C-422 /kurs/, definite /la-kurs/ ([læ-kurs]) "race"; Pl [-æt]; Fr (la) course. F. [EDA 391 /kuṛṣ/.] Cf. next entry.

C-423 /kuṛṣ-a/ "(payment for) transporting a load of passengers (in intercity taxi carrying a fixed number of passengers, usually four to six)"; ex. /šḥal l-kuṛṣ-a/ "how much is (the price for) a load (to a given destination)?". F Mk Casa(j) Tt. [EDA 391 has /kuṛṣ/ in sense "race", Fr course, cf. C-422.] This form /kuṛṣ-a/ is now equated with Fr course by Moroccans, requiring r→/ṛ/ after [u] and adding FSg suffix /-a/. Alternative: perhaps this is really an older form involving either obsolete Sp nautical term corsa "(a) cruise", or (if brought in from Alg) It corsa "(a) run, (a) running" (or some similar Romance form). Cf. C-208.

-- /kuṛuniḷ/ See /k^Wṇiniṛ/ C-362.

C-424 /kurur-a/ "racing bicycle"; Pl [-æt], Dimin /kwirir-a/; presumably from Fr coureur "runner, racer" with feminine /-a/ added by analogy to /biškliṭ-a/ "bicycle" C-90. F. Cf. verb /kura/ B-92.

C-425 /kuryi/(F) or /kuliyi/(Mr) "mail, letters"; no Pl; Fr courier, with second form perhaps crossed with /kuliy-a/ C-395. F Mk. Syn: /bṛa-wat/ "letters".

C-426 /kusan/ "seat (in vehicle)"; Pl [-æt]; Fr coussin "cushion". F Mk Mr. Syn: /kursi/ "chair" (CA).

C-427 /kuṣṭ-a/ "(police) deposition or affidavit"; Pl [-ạt]; now equated with Fr constatation, but possibly involving phonological crossing with Sp costa "coast". F. [For earlier borrowings based on Sp costa see ZLMA 25-6.]

C-428 /kušiṭ/(F) or /kušɛt/(Mk) "sleeping berth, couchette (on train)"; no Pl; Fr couchette. F Mk.

C-429 /kutknut/ "knockout (in boxing)"; no Pl; unusual form obtained from middle-aged Mk man who boxed as a youth; perhaps based on Fr coup de K.O. or a regional Fr pronunciation of Eng knockout. For the currently usual form see /kạw/ C-342.

C-430 /kutši/ "two-horse carriage"; Pl /-yat/; Dimin /kwitši/; old loan from Sp coche (cf. Fr coche). F Mk Mr Casa(j). [Tt /kuči/ "hand cart"; DMA-AE /kutši/ or /kudši/ "surrey", Pl /kwatša/ or /kwadša/.] Cf. /kṛṛuṣ-a/ C-374, /kṛwel-a/ C-381.

C-431 /kuzin-a/ "kitchen" (especially when this is a separate room and not just a corner of a large storage room); Pl [-æt], Dimin /kwizin-a/; Fr cuisine, Sp cocina (note that the Fr form might be identified with the MCA dimin, with back-formation to produce /kuzin-a/, but the Sp form may well be involved as well). F Mk Mr Casa(j) Alg. [Tt /kozin-a/, /kuzin-a/; NLVM 124 bases this form on Sp; TAT 446; DMA-AE.] Cf. the distinct borrowing /kššin-a/ C-384 from the same set of Romance forms (perhaps including It cucina). Cf. C-432.

C-432 /kuzin-i/(F) or /kwizinyi/(Mr) "cook, chef"; Pl /-yat/, Dimin /kwizin-i/(F), simple FSg /kuzin-iy-a/(F); Fr cuisinier or derivative from C-431 with suffix /-i/. F Mr. Syn: /ṭbbax/.

C-433 /kwạfur/ or /kwạfőr/ "barber"; Pl [-æt]; Fr coiffeur. F. Syn: /ḥžžam/, /ḥffaf/ (both more common than /kwạfur/).

C-434 /kwan/([kwæn]) "corner"; Pl [-æt], Dimin /kwiyn/; Fr coin; heard several times, but seems less common than /ṛk^{w}n-a/ or /qnt/. F *Mr.

C-435 /kwaṭṛu/ "four (card in Spanish playing cards)"; Pl /-wat/ or /-yat/, Dimin /kwiṭṛ/(Mr); Sp cuatro "four". Mk Mr Alg.

-- /kwiḷ-a/ Diminutive of /kuḷ-a/ C-394.

-- /kwizinyi/ See /kuzin-i/ C-432.

C-436 /lam-a/([læm-æ]) "hand-ball" (foul, in soccer); used normally as interjection, so morphemic analysis problematic; some speakers permit a Pl form /lam-at/([læm-æt]); Fr la main. F Mk.

C-437 /ḷamb-a/(Mk) or /ḷamḅ-a/(F Mr): (1) "lamp"; (2) "light bulb". Pl [-æt](Mk) or [-ạt](F Mr), Dimin /ḷwimb-a/, /ḷwimḅ-a/; Fr lampe, Sp lampa "lamp", with Fr (l')ampoule possibly indirectly involved in sense 2. F Mk Mr. [DMA-AE /laṃḅ-a/ "lamp; bulb", really identical to /ḷamḅ-a/; Alg /ḷamp̣-a/ or /ḷamḅ-a/ "lamp; bulb"; EDA 393 /lamb-a/ "lamp; bulb"; MAG 81 /lamb-a/ "lamp".] Syn: /miṣbaḥ/ or /fanus/ (CA, both senses).

C-438 /lanḍṛuvir/ "Landrover (or similar four-wheel-drive vehicle)"; Pl [-æt]; Eng brand name Landrover via Fr. F.

C-439 /lastik/ "rubber band"; Pl [-æt]; Fr élastique. Definite form usually just /lastik/, not */l-lastik/. F. [Alg /lastik/, grammatically masculine; DMA-EA under "elastic"; GJA 121.]

-- /l-asurti/, /l-aṣuṛṭi/ See /aṣuṛṭi/ C-24.

C-440 /laṣ/, definite /laṣ/ or /l-laṣ/ "ace (playing card)"; Pl /liṣ-an/ (on pattern of /faṛ/ "mouse", Pl /fir-an/, etc., suggesting that the /l/ in /laṣ/ is a root consonant and not the definite prefix /l-/); Sp (el) as (Fr l'as). F Mk Alg Tt.

C-441 /ḷažnyuṛ/ "engineer"; Pl [-ạt]; Fr l'ingénieur (with article). Definite form /ḷažnyuṛ/ or /ḷ-ḷažnyuṛ/. F Mk *Casa(j). A fairly early loan now being displaced by /mu-hndis/ (Casa(j) /mu-hndiz/) from CA.

C-442 /liḅ-a/, definite /l-liḅ-a/ "stocking (of athlete, or woman's nylons)"; Pl [-ạt]; Fr Pl les bas treated as Sg. F Mk Mr. [Alg /li-ba/ has plural concord and is thus analysable as containing Pl /li-/, which occurs in several Alg loans from Fr.] Syn: /tqašr/ "socks", also /miḍyaṣ/ (Casa(j) and the Tt area) from Sp medias.

C-443 /lig-a/, definite /l-lig-a/: (1) "glove"; (2) "ball (of wool or cotton)". Pl [-aet], Dimin /lwig-a/; Fr les gants reanlaysed as Sg. F Mk Mr *Casa(j). [DMA-AE; EDA 395; Alg /li-ga/ has same origin but is grammatically plural.] Syn: for sense 2 /k^{w}bb-a/ is more common; for "gloves" this is the common term in much of Morocco, but Casa(j) has /waṇṭiṣ/ from Sp guantes.

C-444 /limun/ (collective): (1) "lemon"(F Mk); (2) "orange (fruit)" (Rabat and Casablanca region). Individuative Sg /-a/, Pl [-æt], Dimin Sg /lwimin-a/. F Mk *Mr. These forms are related to Fr limon, Sp limón, and CA līmūn- or laymūn-, but it is difficult to determine whether the MCA form is straight from older Arabic or is (re-)borrowed from a Romance language. The two different senses constitute a well-known semantic isogloss which many well-travelled Moroccans are aware of (cf. DMA-AE, which also restricts sense 2 to the Rabat area); in F and Mk the usual word for "orange" is /ltšin-a/ C-452, and cf. /lṛənž/ C-451.

C-445 /limuṇaḍ/ "soft drink; lemonade"; Pl [-ạt]; Fr limonade (Sp limonada). F Alg *Mr. Cf. the more common /muṇaḍ-a/ C-520 (with variants including /limuṇaḍ-a/).

C-446 /lin/, definite /ḷa-lin/ "line" (used mainly in sports, e.g. for foul-throw line in basketball); Fr (la) ligne (Sp la línea). F.

C-447 /liṛ-a/ or /niṛ-a/: (1) "type of flute" (either pronunciation); (2) "lira" (Italian currency; first pronunciation only). Pl [-ạt]; probably an old Romance or Latin loan in sense 1 (It lira or the like), ultimately Greek; for sense 2 a more modern borrowing from It lira perhaps via Fr or Sp. F Mr. [DMA-AE, both senses.]

C-448 /lisi/ "secondary school, especially the second cycle"; Pl /-yat/, Dimin /lwisi/; Fr lycée. F Mk Mr. Syn: /t-tanaw-iy-a/ "secondary (school)", cf. /kuliž/ C-396, /primiṛ/ C-567, /skwil-a/C-654.

-- /liṭṛ-a See /ṭṛiṭ-a C-773.

C-449 /livi/ "hooking, curving shot (in soccer)"; Pl /-yat/; from a Fr form, possibly levé (see discussion of related verb /liva/ B-95). F. Syn: /m-ᶜwwž-a/ "twisted".

C-450 /livr/ "book"; Pl [-æt]; Fr livre; uncommon, used occasionally in school contexts. F. Usual word is /ktab/.

C-451 /lṛənž/(F), /lṛnəž/(Mk, syllabic /ṛ/), or /ṛənž/(F) "sour orange"; individuative Sg /lṛnž-a/, /ṛnž-a/, both with syllabic /ṛ/; Pl [-æt]; related to the set Fr (l')orange, Sp naranja, CA naranǰ-, but the historical relationships are complex and unclear. F Mk *Mr. Cf. /limun/ C-444, /ltšin/ C-452.

C-452 /ltšin/ or /lččin/ (same pronunciation, different analysis), also rural variant /lššin/ "oranges (collective)", individuative Sg /-a/; Dimin /lčičin-a/, /ltitin-a/, etc. (often hard to elicit in F/Mk area), rural /lšišin-a/; old borrowing, Sp la China "China (country)". F Mk. [DMA-AE; TAT 455-6.] Fruit usually called /limun/ C-444 in Rabat and Casablanca, sometimes Mk; cf. also C-451 for different variety of fruit.

C-453 /ḷukaḷ/ "premises (of shop, etc.), locale"; Pl [-æt](F Mk); Dimin /ḷwikiḷ/(F Mk) or /ḷwikil/(Mk), Dimin Pl [-ạt](F Mk) or [-æt] (Mk); Fr local (Sp local). F Mk *Mr. Syn: /maqṛṛ/.

C-454 /luks/ "de luxe, elegant; (person) doing well, happy"; adverb, by itself or in phrase /d-l-luks/; ex. /ši ḥaž-a (d-l-)luks/ "something luxurious"; Fr de luxe. F Mk. [EDA 396.] Syn: /kõfuṛ/ C-363.

C-455 /luṭuṣṭup/(F) or /ṭuṣṭup/(Mr) "hitchhiking"; definite /luṭuṣṭup/(F) or /ṭ-ṭuṣṭup/(Mr); verb expressed by /dar luṭuṣṭup/ "he did hitchhiking"; Fr (l')autostop. F Mk Mr.

C-456 /luwego/: Occurs in phrase /aṣṭa luwego/ "until tomorrow", discussed under entry for /aṣṭa/ C-22; Sp luego "then, later".

C-457 /madam/(F Mk Mr, unpharyngealized), /maḍam/(F): (1) "wife" (with possessive); (2) "woman" (esp. French); (3) "effeminate man (insult)". Pl [-æt]; Fr Madame; elegant word (senses 1, 2). F Mk Mr(rare) *Casa(j). [Algerian dialects can use /maḍam-a/ "dame, lady", either admiringly or sarcastically, occasionally "wife" with possessive; EDA 396.] Usual term for "woman" or "wife" is /mṛa/.

C-458 /madri/ (collective) "beams, timbers"; individuative Sg /madriy-a/, Pl /-at/; Fr madrier; many speakers permit the Sg and Pl but not collective forms in MCA, and it is clear that /madriy-a/ is the form related to madrier, with collective /madri/ produced by some speakers by back-formation. F Mk Mr. [DMA-AE /madriy-a/; Alg /madriy-a/.

-- /maḍam/ See /madam C-457.

C-459 /maḷiṭ-a/ "suitcase"; Pl [-ạt]; Sp maleta. F. [NLVM 137; MAG 49, 116.] Nowadays in F this is much less common than /baliz-a/ C-42 (Fr valise), but is perhaps still common in the Spanish colonial area down to Casablanca.

C-460 /magan-a/ "clock, watch"; Pl [-æt] or /mwagn/, Dimin /mwigin-a/; perhaps of Romance origin (Sp máquina "machine" or the like), but D. Cohen (p.c.) points out that there are many formal variants in North African dialects whose origin(s) is(are) problematic. F Mk Mr Tt *Casa(j). [ZLMA 4 fn. ex Greek; DMA-AE; MAG 46, 95; my Alg informants use /sa^{c}-a/ "hour" in this sense.] Derivative /mwagn-i/ C-528, below. Cf. /makin-a/ C-463, /mašin-a/ C-487. This is the common word for this sense.

C-461 /magaz-a/ "large store, department store"; Pl [-æt] or /mwagz/, Dimin /mwigiz-a/; Fr magasin (itself formerly a borrowing from CA maxāzīn-). F *Mr. [EDA 397; Alg informants accept only in Pl /magaz-at/.] Syn: /xazin/. Small shops are /ḥanut/, cf. also /maṛši/ C-478, /butik/ C-154.

C-462 /makanik/(F) or /mikanik/(Mk) "mechanics (as a profession or study, not the plural of "mechanic")"; no Pl; Fr mécanique. F Mk. Cf. /mikanisyan/ C-497.

C-463 /makin-a/ "machine, device"; Pl [-æt] or /mwakn/, Dimin /mwikin-a/; Sp máquina (Fr machine). F Mk Mr Tt. Syn: /?al-a/ (CA, but about as common as /makin-a/).

C-464 /makiyaž/([mækiyæž]) or /ṃakiyạž/(Mk Mr) "cosmetics, make-up"; no Pl; Fr maquillage. F Mk Mr. Syn: /t-zyin/ "beautification".

-- /maksyan/ See /mikanisyan/ C-497.

C-465 /ṃaṃa/ "mother, Mom"; no Pl; Fr maman, Sp mamá; characteristic of the speech of westernized bourgeois persons. F Mk Casa(j) *Mr.

C-466 /manḍ-a/ "paycheck, money order"; Pl [-ạt] or /mwanḍ/ (compare Pl /mwaṇəḍ/ or /mwanḍ/ from /muṇaḍ-a/ C-520 "soft drink"), Dimin /mwinḍ-a/ (compare /mwiṇiḍ-a/ from C-520); Fr mandat. F Mk Mr. [DMA-AE /manḍ-a/ "salary"; EDA 397-8.]

C-467 /manifir/ "crank (e.g. for starting old-fashioned car)"; Pl [-æt]; Fr manivelle. F *Mk. [NLVM 137 has /manibiṛ-a/, suggesting dialectal Sp or Fr origin.]

C-468 /maṇiṛ-a/: (1) "way, manner (of doing something)"; (2) "trick, ruse, clever technique"; example /^{c}l-aš ta-d-dir m^{c}a-ya l-maṇiṛ-at/ "why are you using ploys with me?"; Sp manera reinforced by Fr manière. F Mk Tt(rare) Casa(j) *Mr. [DMA-AE /maniṛ-a/] Syn: /ṭaṛiq-a/.

C-469 /mantik-a/ "pure alcohol"; no Pl; etymology unclear but looks like Romance canonical shape (Sp manteca "lard" would fit phonologically but is divergent semantically). Recognized in F but said to be used in the east around Taza. Cf. /sangriy-a/ C-627.

C-470 /manṭ-a/ "blanket (especially types with synthetic fabric)"; Pl [-ạt]; early loan from Sp manta. F Casa(j). [GJA 130; Alg has /manṭu/ from Sp manto or similar Romance form.] Syn: /ġṭa/.

C-471 /maṛi/ "tide"; no Pl; Fr marée. F Mk *Mr *Casa(j). Syn: /mariy-a/ C-474, also /mədd/ "high tide", /žazṛ/ "low tide" (Mr informant gave /mun/ "tide" if correctly understood).

C-472 /marikan/ "American, the United States; American (adjective, or person)"; form invariable for genders/numbers, though a variant adjectival form /marikan-i/ occurs with FSg /-iy-a/, Pl /-iy-in/; Eng American. F Mk. [MAG 68; DMA-EA under "America" has /blad l-mirikan/.]

C-473 /mariwan/(F) or /mariwan-a/(Mr) "marijuana"; no Pl; Fr marihuana, Sp marihuana; not normally used to refer to Moroccan kif.

C-474 /mariy-a/ "tide"; no Pl; Sp marea; recognised in F/Mk but used in Rabat/Casablanca area. F Mk *Casa(j). [DMA-AE /mariy-a/; DMA-EA under "tide" has /mariy-a/ and /maṛiy-a/; NLVM 95, 131; Tt /mary-a/.] Competes with /maṛi/ C-471 from Fr.

-- /mariyu/ See /maryu/ C-482.

C-475 /maṛk/ or /ḍuytšmaṛk/ "Mark (German currency unit), Deutschmark"; no Pl (Sg form normally used with numeral); German Mark, Deutschmark perhaps via Fr and Sp. F Mk.

C-476 /maṛk-a/: (1) "brand, trade-mark"(F Mk Mr Casa(j) Alg); (2) "kind, type"(F Mk Mr); (3) "guy, fellow"(F only, calqued on Fr type, used like /figur-a/C-209, sense 2). Pl [-æt]; Sp marca, Fr marque. F Mk Mr Casa(j) Alg. [DMA-AE.] For sense 2, /nu^c/ "kind" is the regular form (in F/Mk at least). Dimin /mwiṛk-a/ (F Mk).

C-477 /maṛšaṛyan/([maṛšaṛyæn])(Mr) or /maṛšaṛyar/([maṛšaṛyaer]) (F Mk) "reverse gear"; no Pl; Fr marche arrière. F Mk Mr.

C-478 /maṛši/(F Mk Mr) or less commonly /maṛše/(Mk) "marketplace" (mainly the big produce and meat market in the European section of each large city); Pl /-yat/, Dimin /mwiṛši/; Fr marché (Sp mercado). F Mk Mr. Smaller or more traditional markets are called /ṣuq/ or /suq/.

C-479 /maṛšiṇwaṛ/ "black market"; no Pl; Fr marché noir. F Mk Mr. [EDA 398 indicates that definite /l-/ could not be added, but my informants permit it.] Cf. C-478.

C-480 /maṛṭu/ "hammer"; Pl /-yat/ or /-wat/; Fr marteau. F Mr. Some speakers normally use this term, others prefer /mṭṛq-a/ or its Dimin /mṭiṛq-a/.

C-481 /maṛyaž/ "marriage". Occurs in an expression presented in C-3; in other contexts /zwaž/ means "(state of) marriage" and /^crs/ or /^cṛṣ/ means "wedding, marriage ceremony". Fr mariage.

C-482 /maryu/(F Mk Mr), /mariyu/(F), or /aṛmwaṛ/(Mk) "wardrobe, dresser (piece of furniture)"; Pl /-wat/ or /-yat/, also /maryu-nat/(F), Dimin /mwiryu/ or /mwiriyu/; Sp armario, with /aṛmwaṛ/ from Fr armoire. F Mk Mr. [Tt /maryu/, Pl /-s/ or /maryo/, Pl /-ṣ/; DMA-AE /mariyu/; TAT 462 /mariyu/, Pl /-s/; Casa(j) has distinct form /gwaṛḍaṛup-a/ from Sp guardaropa.] Syn: /dulab/, cf. /bifi/ C-78.

C-483 /maṣ/ "commission, percentage (of transaction)" (slang); no Pl; perhaps Fr masse "mass" or Sp más "more". F. Syn: /ž^cb-a/, cf. /fil/ C-210.

-- /mastik/ See /maṣtik/ C-486.

C-484 /maṣṣ-a/: (1) "sledgehammer"; (2) "mass, huge amount" (of money, etc.). Pl [-ạt], Dimin /mwiṣṣ-a/; Fr masse, Sp masa (It massa). Sense 1 in F, sense 2 in Mr. Syn: see /maṛṭu/ C-480.

C-485 /maṣṣu/ "mason, bricklayer"; Pl /-wat/ or /-yat/, also /-nạt/; Fr maçon. F Mk *Mr. [DMA-AE has /maṣṣu/ "pile (of coins, jewels, gold); nugget (gold)", presumably from a different source.] Syn: /bnnay/ "builder, construction worker".

C-486 /maṣtik/(F Mr) or /mastik/([mæstik])(Mk) "putty (soft substance which children play with)"; no Pl; Fr mastic. F Mk Mr.

C-487 /mašin-a/ "train"; Pl [-æt] or /mwašn/, Dimin /mwišin-a/; Fr machine "machine"; the common word. F Mk Mr Alg *Casa(j). [DMA-AE; EDA 398-9.] Syn: /qiṭaṛ/ (CA), /tran/ and variants C-736 (common in north).

C-488 /ṃašwaṛ/, definite /l-ṃašwaṛ/(F) or /la-ṃašwaṛ/(Mk) "jaw"; no Pl (code-switched les mâchoires used); Fr (la) mâchoire. F Mk *Mr. Body-part terms are rarely borrowed; this one is favoured by a lexical gap in MCA. Syn: /fəkk/ (CA).

C-489 /maṭš/ "match (in sports)"; Pl [-æt]; Fr and Sp match (ex Eng). F. Syn: /mu-qabal-a/ (CA).

C-490 /maṭiṛyal/([maṭeṛyæl])(F Mk Mr) or /mataryal/([mætæryæl]) (said to be used by older persons in F area) "materials (tools, paper suppleis, etc.)" (collective); no Pl; Fr matériel, Sp material. F Mk Mr. Syn: /?atat/.

C-491 /maṭiš-a/, definite also /maṭiš-a/ without /l-/ prefix; "tomatoes" (collective) or "tomato" (Sg); Pl [-æt]; obviously related to Sp tomates (of New World origin), but probably really a semantic shift based on /maṭiš-a/ "swing" (children's playground device). F Mk. [DMA-AE has both senses; TAR 502 indicates "swing" is old MCA meaning with "tomatoes" a sense imported from Alg; Tt and Alg have /ṭumaṭiš/ "tomatoes" with Alg permitting definite /ṭ-ṭumaṭiš/, the Alg form being grammatically feminine; eAlg also has /ṭmaṭm/ "tomatoes", masculine; some Jewish MCA dialects have /ṭumaṭiṣ/ "tomatoes"; TAT 468 has /maṭiš-a/ "swing".]

C-492 /ṃayṣṭṛu/ "boss" (e.g. of theatre troupe); no Pl; Sp maestro. F. [Formerly common in sense "teacher" in some areas, still the usual word in this sense in some Jewish dialects like Casa(j), which also has Pl /-ṣ/ from Sp maestros; GJA 123; NLVM 135 has variant with /š/.] In the F/Mk area nowadays the usual term for "teacher" is /?ustad/(CA).

C-493 /ṃayu/ "bathing suit, swimming suit"; Pl /-yat/ or /-wat/; Fr maillot. F Mk *Mr. [DMA-EA under "bathing suit" has /mayyu/.]

C-494 /midi/ "mid-length skirt, midi"; Pl /-yat/; Fr midi. F.

C-495 /ṃigu/(F) or /ṃigo/(Mk) "cigarette butt"; Pl /-yat/ or /-wat/; Fr mégot. F Mk *Mr. [Alg /migu/, Pl /-wat/.] Syn: /bunt-a/ C-139 (especially Dimin /bwint-a/).

C-496 /mik-a/: (1) "plastic (including tablecloths etc.)"; (2) "money" (slang but very common). No Pl; Fr and Sp mica "mica" or perhaps a commercial name like Formica. Also used in expression /mik-a ᶜli-ya/ "scram!; get lost!; get away from me!" (slang). For discussion of this last expression see verb /myyək/ B-104. F Mk Casa(j)(sense 1) Tt(sense 2). Syn: /flus/ "money"; for slang words for this sense see /ḍuḷaṛ/ C-189, /nikl/ C-532, /tawzn/ C-721, /trimis-a/ C-740.

-- /mikanik/ See /makanik/ C-462.

C-497 /mikanisyan/(F Mk Mr) or /maksyan/(Mk) "mechanic (person)"; Pl [-æt]; Fr mécanicien (Sp mecánico). F Mk Mr. Cf. /makanik/ C-462.

C-498 /mikiy-at/(F Mk) or /mxxiy-at/(Mr): (1) "cartoons" (television); (2) "comic book(s)". Form is already Pl, hence no Sg/Pl difference; apparently Eng Mickey (Mouse) via F. Cf. /bukan/ C-127.

C-499 /mikṛu/(F Mr), /mikṛufuṇ/(F), /mikṛufun/(Mk), /mikṛafuṇ/ (rural), or /makṛafuṇ/(rural) "microphone"; Pl /-wat/ or /-yat/ after /u/, [-æt] after /n/, [-ạt] after /ṇ/; Fr microphone, micro, Sp micrófono. F Mk Mr. Syn: /midyaᶜ/ (CA).

C-500 /mikṛub/ "microbe, germ"; Pl [-æt]; Fr microbe, or perhaps CA mikrūb-/mīkrūb- (from Eng or Fr). F Mk. [DMA-AE; EDA 400.]

-- /mikṛufuṇ/ and variants. See /mikṛu/ C-499.

C-501 /miḷạ̃ž/ "mixture"; no Pl; Fr mélange; not very common. F. Syn: /t-xlaṭ/. Cf. verb /miḷạ̃ža/ B-98.

C-502 /militir/(F), /miliṭiṛ/(F), or /minitir/(F Mk Mr) "soldier, serviceman (in armed forces)"; Fr militaire (Sp militar). F Mk Mr *Casa(j). Syn: /ᶜṣkṛ-i/.

C-503 /min-a/: (1) "mine (explosive); bomb"; (2) "wharf, pier" (this sense Mr only). Pl [-æt]; Fr mine, Sp mina. F Mk Mr. [DMA-AE "mine".] Syn: /qnbul-a/"bomb".

C-504 /minim: (1) "midgit (player in midgit soccer league, about 10-14 years)"; (2) "young (child)"; ex. /had-a baqi minim/ "he is still a young boy". No Pl; Fr minime. F Mk *Mr. Cf. C-814, 819.

-- /minitir/ See /militir/ C-502.

C-505 /miss-a/ "cards and money on table (in card game)"; ex. /ṛamaṣa l-miss-a/ "he raked in the cards and money (after winning poker hand)"; Pl [-æt]; Sp mesa "table", perhaps influenced by Fr mise "ante" (cf. verb /miza/ B-100). F Mr *Casa(j). [Occurs in Alg in this sense in context of Spanish-type card game /ṛunḍ-a/ C-614; Tt has /miss-a/ "large table".] Syn: /qaᶜ-a/.

C-506 /mitr/(F Mk) or /mitru/(F Mr) "meter (measure of distance)"; Pl /mitru-wat/ or /mitru-yat/ (not */mitr-at/) (F Mk Mr) but Sg form usual with numerals; Fr mètre, Sp metro. F Mk Mr. [Tt has /miṭṛu/; Casa(j) /miṭṛu/, Pl /-ṣ/; EDA 401 /mitr/ or /mitṛu/, the latter older but losing ground; DMA-AE /mitṛ/, /mitru/; MAG 99 /miṭṛ/.]

C-507   /miṭ-a/, definite /l-miṭ-a/ or /la-miṭ-a/ "halftime (in soccer game, etc.)"; Pl [-aṭ]; Fr mi-temps. F.
C-508   /mizaṇṇi/ "suspension from job without pay"; no Pl; Fr mise à pied. F *Mk *Mr.
C-509   /mlyaṛ/(F Mk Mr) or /mnyaṛ/(F) "billion, thousand million"; Pl [-aṭ] or /mlayṛ/, /mnayṛ/; Fr milliard. F Mk Mr. [EDA 399 /mlyaṛ/, DMA-AE /ml̥yaṛ/, DMA-EA under "billion" /mlyaṛ/; Tt /mlyaṛ/.]
C-510   /mlyun/ "million"; Pl [-aet] or /mlayn/, Dimin /mliyn/, Dimin Pl /mliyn-at/ "a few million"; Fr million, Sp millón. F Mk Mr Tt. Modern CA malyūn may be involved at least as a reinforcement. [DMA-AE; EDA 399.] Cf.C-509.
C-511   /mm-u/ "his mother" (old MCA form), now also used as interjection "wow!" (admiration); probably modelled on American Eng slang (what a) mother!, perhaps via Fr slang calque. F.
C-512   /mndil/ "handkerchief"; Pl /mnadl/; old loan from Sp mandil or a similar early Romance form. F. [DMA-AE; NLVM 142.]
--   /mnyaṛ/ See /mlyaṛ/ C-509.
C-513   /mɔš/ or /m̥uš/ "ugly, revolting (e.g. woman)" (infrequent, slang); form invariable for genders/numbers; Fr moche. F *Mk *Mr. Syn: /qbiḥ/ "ugly" (FSg /qbiḥ-a/).
C-514   /mṛmiṭ-a/ "(cooking) pot"; Pl [-aṭ]; Fr marmite, Sp marmita. F. Syn: /ṭnžṛ-a/.
C-515   /mṛṛuk/(F Mk) or /maṛṛuk/(some Jewish MCA dialects, Tt): (1) "Morocco"; (2)"Moroccans" (collective). In sense 2 Sg /mṛṛuk-i/, Pl /mṛaṛk/(F) or /mṛaṛk-a/(Mk), FSg /mṛṛuk-iy-a/, FPl /mṛṛuk-iy-at/. From Fr Maroc (Sp Marruecos) "Morocco" with derivational suffix /-i/, though Fr marocain (Sp marroquí) may also be directly associated with /mṛṛuk-i/. F Mk. [Alg /mṛṛuk/, Pl /mṛaṛk-a/; EDA 399 /mṛṛuk/, Pl /mṛaṛk-a/.] These are the regular terms in certain archaic (mostly Jewish) MCA dialects, but in most dialects these forms are pejorative (like yankee, limey, etc.), the ordinary (and non-pejorative) terms nowadays being /mġrib/ "Morocco", /mġrib-i/ (MSg), and /mġarb-a/ (Pl); EDA already makes this point. Pl /mṛaṛk-a/ has the same pattern as /mġarb-a/.
C-516   /msyu/ "Frenchman, (French) man"; no Pl; Fr monsieur. F Mk. [EDA 402; Alg only as address form.] Common in simplified "foreigner talk" MCA used by maids, otherwise uncommon, mostly ironic, except when used in names like /msyu X/ "Mister X".
C-517   /mubl/ "apartment building"; Pl [-aet]; Fr immeuble. F *Mk. Not common in F/Mk, which uses /baṭim-a/ C-68, but said to be in common use around Casablanca. Syn: /ᶜimaṛ-a/ "building".
--   /mu-bṛziṭ/ See discussion of verb /bṛzəṭ/ B-23.
C-518   /muḍ-a/ "fashions, mode"; ex. /1-muḍ-a dyal had l-ᶜam/ "this year's fashions" (clothing etc.); Pl [-aṭ]; Fr mode, Sp moda. F Mk Mr. [EDA 401-2; DMA-AE.]

C-519 /m̩ukiṭ/ "rug"; Pl [-ạt]; Fr moquette. F. Not applied to the usual Moroccan carpets (/ẓṛbiy-a/).

C-520 /muṇaḍ-a/(F Mk Mr) or /muṇiḍ-a/(rural around F) "soft drink" (any carbonated beverage); Pl [-ạt], also /mwaṇəḍ/ or /mwaṇḍ/ (the latter homophonous with Pl /mwaṇḍ/ from /maṇḍ-a/ C-466 "paycheck"); Dimin /mwiṇiḍ-a/; Sp limonada, Fr limonade, with /muṇiḍ-a/ possibly due to phonological mixing with Sp moneda "coin"; see also less common but more recent /limuṇaḍ/ C-445 from Fr. F Mk Mr. [DMA-AE /munaḍ-a/; Casa(j) /limuṇaḍ-a/ from Sp; MAG "limonāda" perhaps is /limuṇaḍ-a/ with some diacritics supplied; GJA 122 gives Jewish form /limuṇaḍ-a/ vs. Muslim /muṇaḍ-a/ in F.] Syn: /m-šṛub-a/ (not very common).

C-521 /munik-a/ "doll (toy)"; Pl [-æt] or /mwank/, Dimin /mwinik-a/; Mr informant uses Dimin as the regular form; some speakers think this is the Fr personal name Monique, but it is most probably Sp muñeca "doll" (possibly reinforced somewhat by Fr mannequin). Tt F Mk Mr. [Casa(j) /m̩unik-a/; DMA-AE.] Syn: /puppiya-/ C-577, occasionally /dumiy-a/ (CA dumayy-a).

C-522 /muṛṣu/ "piece (of food, etc.)"; Pl /-yat/ or /-wat/; Fr morceau. F (but rare in this area; said to be common in east around Oujda and in west around Casablanca). [Also Alg.] Syn: /ṭṛiyəf/.

C-523 /müskli/(F) or /müskli/(Mk) "muscular, heavily muscled (person)"; form invariable; Fr musclé, not well assimilated. F Mk *Mr. Syn: /ṣḥiḥ/ "strong", cf. verbs /müskla/ B-102, /budr/ B-25, and noun /kuḷuṣ/ C-397.

-- /m̩uš/ See /mɔš/ C-513.

C-524 /mutur/(F Mk), /m̩utur/(Mr F Mk), /m̩utuṛ/(near Mk), /muṭuṛ/ (Casa(j) and generally from Casablanca to Tt in north) "motorcycle"; Pl [-æt](F Mk Mr) or [-ạt](Casa(j) Tt), also /mwatr/(F); Dimin /m̩witir/, /mwitir/, /mwitr/, or /mwiṭiṛ/; mix of Sp motor and Fr moteur but sense influenced by Fr motocyclette (short form moto), Sp motocicleta "motorcycle". F Mk Mr Tt Casa(j). [Alg /mutur/; DMA-AE /muṭuṛ/; EDA 402 /muṭuṛ/ and /motoṛ/ with "motor" as alternative meaning.] No common synonym.

C-525 /muṭaṛ/ "motorcycle policeman, motorcycle gendarme"; no Pl; Fr motard. F Alg.

C-526 /muxiṛṛ-a/. Occurs in jocular slang expression /aṣṭa ḷa muxiṛṛ-a/ "(until) some other time, not now", and in slang /mša ạ ḷa muxiṛṛ-a/ "he's had it, he's done for, his goose is cooked, he's all through". The first of these is an ingenious crossing of Sp hasta la "until the" (as in hasta la próxima "until the next time" and hasta la vista "until the sight", both used in Sp as informal "goodbye, see you later" expressions), Sp mujer "woman" (phonetically identical to MCA */muxiṛ/), and MCA /mṛṛ-a x^{w}ṛ-a/ "another time"; note that /muxiṛṛ-a/ is a kind of hybrid formally of */muxiṛ/ and /mṛṛ-a x^{w}ṛ-a/, which share the consonants /m x ṛ/ and have a rounded vowel /u/ or labialization feature /^{w}/. The second expression, /mša ạ ḷa muxiṛṛ-a/ has MCA /mša/ "he went" plus Sp a la "to the (FSg)" and the same /muxiṛṛ-a/, but the semantic evolution here is considerable. These bizarre slang expressions were obviously concocted by someone who knew Sp, but were recorded in F among persons who had no such exposure. F *Mk *Mr. For another bizarre case of this sort see /xwadri/ C-804.

C-527 /mwaḍṛi/ "mother" (humorous slang); no Pl; humorous deformation of Sp madre with onset influenced by MCA /ṃṃ-i/ "my mother", where /ṃṃ-/ is phonetically labialized. F (but said to be more common in Casablanca). Similar cases: /pwaḍṛi/ C-581, /xwadri/ C-804.

C-528 /mwagn-i/ (with pharyngealized pronunciation) "watch seller; watch repairman"; Pl /-iy-a/; derivative from /magan-a/ C-460. F. [DMA-AE; MAG 95 "watchmaker".]

-- /mxxiy-at/ See /mikiy-at/ C-498.

C-529 /ṇay/ "no!" (interjection), an occasional slang form now "in" among slang-speaking F youth; F informant considers this to be dialectal Eng nay, but it is probably from colloquial German Nee. F. The usual negative interjection is /la/.

-- /ngliz/ See /ingliz/ C-295.

C-530 /nibru/ "cigarette wrapping paper" (used to roll cigarettes or hashish joints); Pl /-wat/ or /-yat/, Dimin /nwibru/; Sp libro; old, well-established loan. F Mk Mr *Casa(j). [DMA-AE; MAG 91 "libro"; Tt /libru/, /libṛu/.] Syn: /wṛq-a d-l-gaṛṛu/ (paraphrase, not in common use).

C-531 /nigru/: (1) "black (person)"; (2) "black (coffee)" (opposed to green coffee, another major type of coffee). In sense 2 form invariable, hence /qhw-a nigru/ "black coffee" with FSg noun /qhw-a/ not requiring FSg agreement; in sense 1 we have FSg /nigru-ya/(F) or /nigrut-a/ (Mk) but no Pl elicitable; from Sp negro reinforced by Fr nègre, with Mk FSg form perhaps related to Sp negrita. Tt F Mk *Mr. Usual word for "black" is /kḥl/, and this word is often used even in the special contexts where /nigru/ is possible. "Green coffee" is /qhw-a xḍṛ-a/ with native MCA lexical items.

C-532 /nikl/: (1) "money" (slang); (2) "(in) cash" (adverb), used like /kạš/ C-337; (3) "nickel" (metal). Sense 1 F Mr, sense 2 F only, sense 3 F Mr, also Tt. From Sp níquel, Fr nickel. F Mr. [Tt /nikiḷ/; EDA 403 /nikl/.] Syn: for "money" see /mik-a/ C-496.

C-533 /nimiru/ "number", used chiefly in common expression /nimiru waḥəd/ "number one, the best, superb"; Pl /-wat/ /-yat/, or /nwamr/; Dimin /nwimiru/; Sp número, Fr numéro. F Mk Mr *Casa(j). [DMA-AE; EDA 403; Tt /numiṛu/, Pl /nwamr/ with the Pl perhaps from paradigm of /nmr-a/ C-534; Alg /numṛu/, Pl /-wat/, now losing ground.] Syn: /nmr-a/ C-534, /ᶜadad/ "number, quantity", /ṛəqm/ "number, numeral" (now gaining, from CA).

C-534 /nmr-a/ "numeral, number"; Pl [-æt] or /nmari/; Dimin /nmir-a/(usual), /nwimr-a/; Fr nombre or perhaps another loan from Sp número, Fr numéro; more common than /nimiru/ C-533 except before a numeral. F Mk Mr *Alg. [Casa(j) /nmṛ-a/; DMA-AE /nmr-a/.] Cf. related verb /numr/ B-107 (DMA-AE has verb /nmmr/, not recognized by my F/Mk informants).

-- /nṭiliža/ See /ṭulạ̃ṭi/ C-779.

-- /nutir/, /nuṭiṛ/ See /uṭil/ C-784.

C-535 /nuṭ-a/ "(musical) note"; Pl [-ạt]; Sp nota, Fr note. F.

-- /nuṭiṛ/ See /uṭil/ C-784.

C-536 /ṇuwiḷ/ or /nuwiḷ/ "Christmas"; no Pl; Fr Noël, Sp Noel; occurs also as /bababanwiḷ/([bæbænweḷ])(Mk) or /ḅaḅaṇuwiḷ/ (F), Fr papa Noël, now used by old-timers. F Mk.

-- /ofisyi/ See /fsyan/ C-245.

-- /okazyu/, /okaẓyu/ See /kazyu/ C-347.

C-537 /õp̣p̣an/ Found as adverb in expression /ṭaḥ õp̣p̣an/ "he had his car break down (and couldn't repair it)" with /ṭaḥ/ "he fell"; Fr en panne. F. Cf. also /bwan/ C-159.

C-538 /p̣ak/ "Easter"; no Pl; Fr Pâcques (Sp Pascua). F Mk.

C-539 /p̣akṭaž/ "baggage, luggage" (collective); no Pl; Fr paquetage. Cf. /bagaž/ C-33.

C-540 /paṇṭaḷu/ "pair of pants"; Pl /-wat/, /-yat/, /-nat/; Fr pantalon, Sp pantalón; less common than /srwal/. F. [ZLMA 30 /paṇṭaḷun/ from Sp.]

C-541 /p̣anyi/ "basket (in basketball, applies to netting only, not to rim)"; Pl /-yat/; Fr panier. F Cf /siṛṣu/ C-651.

-- /paṛašit/, /paṛašid/ See /baṛašit/ C-53.

C-542 /paṛtiy-a/(F Mr), /bṛtiy-a/(F), or /bṛṭiy-a/(Mk): (1) "part, piece (of something)"; (2) "(good/bad) performance (in job, etc.)"; ex. /dr-ti paṛtiy-a zin-a/ "you did a fine job"(Mr); Pl /-at/, Dimin /bṛiṭiy-a/, etc.; Fr partie, Sp parte. Sense 1 F Mk, sense 2 Mr, occurs in Casa(j) but sense(s) unclear. [Alg has /paṛti/ "sports match" from another sense of Fr partie, and is grammatically feminine; Tt informant rejects all forms.]

C-543 /paṣ/: (1) "passport"; (2) "brief encounter with prostitute (single copulation)". Pl [-ạt]; Fr passe. F Mk. Cf. /paṣpuṛ/ C-545.

C-544 /paṣ-a/ "(a) pass (in soccer, etc.)"; Pl [-ạt]; Fr passe with FSg /-a/ added to indicate individual event, or perhaps based on verb /paṣa/ B-110. F. Cf. /paṣ/ C-543.

-- /paṣaž/ Verbal noun of /paṣa/ B-110.

C-545 /paṣpuṛ/(F Mk Mr Casa(j)), /baṣbuṛ/(F area, rural), or /baṣbbuṛ/(F area, rural) "passport"; Pl [-ạt]; Fr passeport (Sp pasaporte). F Mk Mr Casa(j). [Tt has /paṣapuṛṭi/ from Sp and /paṣpuṛṭ/, which may be a Fr/Sp cross; Alg /paṣpuṛ/, Pl /ḷi-paṣpuṛ/.] Cf. also short form /paṣ/ C-543. Syn: /žawaz/ (CA, official style).

C-546 /paṣtiy-a/ or /p̣astiy-a/: (1) "microphone attached to electric guitar/ (2) "pill, tablet". Pl /-at/; Fr pastille, Sp pastilla. Sense 1 F, sense 2 Tt. Two transcriptions almost impossible to distinguish but informants disagree as to whether they feel the sibilant is /s/ or /ṣ/.

C-547 /paṭṛõ/(F Mk) or /baṭṛun/(F Mr) "boss, owner"; Pl /baṭṛun-at/ ([baṭṛon-æt]) from second variant, usually code-switched les patrons for first variant; Fr patron, Sp patrón. F Mk Mr. Cf. /baṭṛuṇ-a/ C-69. Syn: /m-ᶜllm/.

C-548 /p̣ay-a/ "paella (Spanish rice dish)"; no Pl; Sp paella. Called /p̣ahiy-a/ in Tt where it is commonly served; called /p̣ay-a/ in F/Mk area by persons who have heard about it but may never have actually eaten it. F Mk Tt.

-- /piḍal/, /piḍaḷ-a/ See /biḍaṛ-a/ C-77.

C-549 /pil/: (1) "flashlight, torch"(cf./pil-a/ C-550); (2) (adverb at end of time expression) "on the dot, sharp"; ex. /l-xms-a pil/ "five (o'clock) sharp"; (3) part of expression /pil w-faṣ/ "heads or tails". For sense 1 Pl [-æt]. Fr pile "battery; on the dot; tails", cf. Fr il est cinq heures pile "it's five o'clock sharp". F Mk Mr. [Casa(j) "battery"] Syn: /ḥžṛ/ (collective), Sg /ḥžṛ-a/ is regular MCA for "battery" (as well as "stone"), so sense 1 of /pil/ is usually limited to "flashlight", where it competes with /briki/ C-109 (most common) and /fnaṛ/ C-225. [Alg /(ḷa-)pil/ "battery", feminine, Pl /li-pil/, also /pil/ in sense 2.]

C-550 /pil-a/: (1) "flashlight, torch" (variant of /pil/ C-549) (Mk); (2) (slang, pejorative) "drunkard, wino". Grammatically FSg in sense 1, but in sense 2 may be MSG or FSg depending on actual sex (this point is often unimportant since in sense 2 the form is commonly a simple predicate). Sp pila and Fr pile "battery"; development of sense 2 problematic but may be related to such expressions as Fr recevoir une pile "to take a beating, to get clobbered" (the connection between being beaten up and being high on drugs or alcohol is rampant in MCA slang, cf. B-30). F (sense 2) Mk (both senses) Casa(j)(sense unclear) Tt (sense 2). Syn: /skr-an/ "drunk", /skayr-i/ "drunkard", many slang forms.

C-551 /piluṭ/(F Mk), /piḷuṭ/(Mr), or /bbiluṭ/(F area, rural) "pilot"; Pl [-ạt]; Fr pilote (Sp piloto). F Mk Mr. Syn: /ṛa?id/.

-- /pinalti/, /pinaliti/ See /bilanti/ C-81.

C-552 /piniz/ or /biniz/ "thumbtacks" (collective); individuative Sg /-a/, Pl [-æt]; Fr punaise. F.

C-553 /pipp-a/ "pipe (for smoking)"; Pl [-æt]; Fr pipe, Sp pipa. Tt F Mk Alg *Mr. Syn: /sbsi/.

C-554 /pirmi/(F Mk), /piṛmi/(Mr), or /birmi/(F area, rural) "driver's license; permit"; Pl /-yat/; Fr permis (Sp permiso). F Mk Mr. [Alg and Casa(j) /piṛmi/.] Syn: /ṛʷxṣ-a/ (uncommon).

C-555 /piṛṣuṇil/(F Mk) or /biṛṣuṇil/(F) "staff, personnel"; no Pl; Fr personnel. F Mk. Syn: /xddam-a/ "workers".

C-556 /pisin/(F Mk Mr), /bbisin/(rural around F), or /bbisi/ (rural around F), definite normally /la-pisin/([læ-pisin]) rarely /l-pisin/, "swimming pool"; Pl [-æt]; Fr (la) piscine (Sp piscina). F Mk Mr. [Casa(j) and Tt /(ḷa-) pisin/; Alg /(la-)pisin/, grammatically feminine, Pl

/(l-)pisin-at/ with definite /l-/ in Pl form.]
Syn: /msbəḥ/ (uncommon).

C-557 /pist/(F Mk) or /bbist/(rural around F), definite prefix /la-/ or /l-/, "highway, road (especially if unpaved)"; Pl [-æt], Dimin /pwist-a/; Fr (la) piste. F Mk *Mr. Syn: /ṭṛiq/ "road". Cf. /gudṛun/ C-281.

-- /piṭṛul/ See /biṭṛul C-93.

C-558 /pižam-a/(F Mk Mr) or /bižam-a/(F) "pair of pyjamas"; Pl [-æt]; Fr pyjama (Sp pijama). F Mk Mr.

C-559 /pḷakaṛ/ or /bḷakaṛ/ "dresser (furniture) built into wall"; Pl [-ạt]; Fr placard. F.

-- /pḷasuz/, /pḷasöz/ See /bḷasuz/ C-101.

-- /pḷaṣ-a/ See /bḷaṣ-a/ C-102.

C-560 /pḷay-a/ or /bḷay-a/"beach"; Pl [-æt]; Sp playa. Used principally in north around Tt and Tangiers, recognized by some F/Mk people (who regularly use /pḷaž/ C-561. *Casa(j). [DMA-AE /bḷay-a/; NLVM 13 with /p/ or /b/.]

C-561 /pḷaž/, rarely /bḷaž/, definite regularly /ḷa-pḷaž/, "beach"; Pl [-æt]; Fr (la) plage. Common in F and Mk, occasional in Mr. *Casa(j). Syn: /pḷay-a/ C-560 in north; formerly /bḥṛ/ "sea" was commonly used; cf. also /šaṭi?/ "shore, beach" (CA).

C-562 /pḷizir/ "pleasure". Appears to function as a kind of adverb, as in /dar fi-ha pḷizir/ "he did whatever she wanted" (lit. "he-did in-her pleasure"); Fr plaisir (Sp placer). F.

C-563 /pnu/, less often /bnu/ "tyre (of car)"; Pl /-wat/ or /-yat/; Dimin not used but F speaker produced /pniyu/ under badgering; Fr pneu. F Mk Mr *Casa(j). [Alg /pnö/, Pl /li-pnö/; DMA-AE /bnu/; EDA 375 /bnu/.] Syn: /ᶜažal-a/ (CA, uncommon), /ṛwiḍ-a/ C-624.

C-564 /ppiki/ "spike (to nail down tent)"; Pl /-yat/; Fr piquet. F.

C-565 /ppikini/ or /bikini/ "bikini (two-piece woman's swimsuit)"; Pl /-yat/; Fr (and international) bikini. F Mr. Initial /pp/ in this and preceding item unpharyngealized.

C-566 /pṛi/ "ready"; form invariable for numbers/genders; Fr prêt. F Mk. Not common; usual word is /wažd/.

C-567 /primiṛ/ "primary school"; no Pl; Fr primaire. F *Mr. Not well assimilated; competes with /btida?-iy-a/ (CA, FSg form).

C-568 /pṛiṣ/, definite /ḷa-pṛiṣ/ "press (machine for pressing out olive oil or for pressing hashish)"; Pl [-ạt]; Fr (la) presse. F. Cf. verb /pṛiṣa/ B-116.

C-569 /priz/(F Mk Mr) or /briz/(F), definite usually /l-/ but sometimes /la-/([læ-]), "electric plug; electric outlet"; Pl [-æt] or /prayz/, /brayz/; Fr (la) prise. F Mk Mr.

C-570 /pṛuṭiž/ "shin guard (in soccer)"; Pl [-æt]; Fr protège (perhaps really from a compound like protège-jambe). F *Mr. Syn: /rkkab/.

C-571 /pti/ "small", used chiefly with following personal name as in /pti ḥamid/ "little Hamid"; no Pl or FSg form; Fr petit (as in le petit Jean, etc.). F Mk. Usual word for "small" is /ṣġiṛ/. Cf. C-572.

C-572 /ptiwa/ "short person" (slang, like Eng shrimp or shorty); no Pl; grammatically MSg or FSg depending on sex of referent; perhaps a Dimin of /pti/ C-571. F *Mr *Casa(j). Syn: /qṣiṛ/ "short".

C-573 /püblik/ "audience, fans (in sports match)"; no Pl; Fr publique. F.

C-574 /p̣ukiṛ/ "poker"; no Pl; Fr poker (ex Eng). F Mk. Cf. /ṛami/ C-592.

-- /p̣ulis/ See /bulis/ C-132.

C-575 /puḷu/ "ice cream on a stick"; Pl /-wat/; Sp polo. Mr *F Tt. Syn: /glaṣ/ C-273, /baṣṭ-a/ C-65, /gufrit/ C-282.

-- /p̣umbi/ See /ḅumbiy-a/ C-135.

-- /puny-a/, /punyu/ See /buny-a/ C-140.

C-576 /p̣unž/(F Mk Mr), /bunž/(F), or /pɔ̃ž/(F Mk) "sponge(s) [material]"; individuative Sg /-a/, Pl [-æt], Dimin Sg /p̣winž-a/, /bwinž-a/; Fr éponge, Sp esponja. F Mk Mr. [Tt /ṣpux-a/, /ṣpuṇx-a/ and Casa(j) /ṣpuṇǯ-a/ from Sp; Alg /ḷipɔ̃ž/ or /(l-)pɔ̃ž/.] Syn: /žffaf-a/.

C-577 /puppiy-a/(F Mk), /bubbiy-a/(F Mk, but less common), or /bubbuy-a/ (rural) "doll (toy)"; Pl [-æt]; Fr poupée. F Mk *Mr *Casa(j) *Tt. Seems equally common with /munik-a/ C-521, more common than /dumiy-a/ (CA).

C-578 /puṛ/ "port, harbour"; Pl [-ạt]; Fr port. F.

-- /puṛu/, /puṛṛu/ See /buṛṛu/ C-144.

C-579 /puṣṭir/ "poster; poster-like picture taken from magazine 'Poster'"; Pl [-ạt]; Fr poster ex Eng and magazine name.F.

C-580 /puṭu/ "pole, bar (of wood or metal)"; Pl /-yat/ or /-wat/; Fr poteau. F.

C-581 /pwaḍṛi/(phonetic [p̣p̣^{w}aḍṛe]) /pwadri/ "father" (humorous slang); no Pl; concoction based on combining Sp padre with MCA /ḅḅa/, phonetic [ḅḅ^{w}a] "father", similar to /mwaḍṛi/ C-527 and /xwadri/ C-804. F. Syn: /ḅḅa/.

C-582 /qamiž-a/(F Mk Mr), /qamižž-a/(F), or /qmžž-a/(F) "shirt"; Pl [-æt] or /qwamž(ž)/; Dimin /qwiṃiž(ž)-a/, /qwimiž(ž)-a/, /q^{w}miyž-a/; Sp camisa, maybe CA qamīs- (masculine). F Mk Mr. [Casa(j) /?mẓẓ-a/, reflecting older *qmžž-a; Alg /qməǯǯ-a/; GJA 105 /?mizz-a/ or /?amizz-a/, Pl /?mayz/ as Jewish forms meaning "shirt" vs. Muslim /qmžž-a/, Pl /qmayž/ "sweater"; DMA-AE /qamižž-a/ or /qmžž-a/, Pl /qwamž/; DMA-EA under "shirt" /qamžž-a/; MAG 77, 85 /kamis-a/ or /qamiṣ-a/; Tt /qmiǯǯ-a/.] Cf. /qmiṣ/ C-585.

-- /qaṛtuš/ See /kaṛtuš/ C-325.

C-583 /qbṭan/(F Mk) or /qbṭaṇ/(Mr) "captain (in military)"; Pl [-æt](F Mk) or [-ạt](Mr); Fr capitaine (Sp capitán) along with CA qubṭān-. F Mk Mr. [DMA-AE, with Pl also /qbaṭn/; EDA 404.] Cf. also /kapitan/ C-319.

C-584 /qimṛun/: (1) "shrimp"; (2) "squid". Used as Sg or as collective; Pl also [-æt]; Sp camarrón "shrimp". F (sense 2) Mr(sense 1) *Mk *Casa(j). [DMA-AE /qmṛun/ collective, with Sg /-a/ "shrimp"; NLVM 24, 113 "shrimp".] These foods are not common in the interior.

C-585 /qmiṣ/(F Mk) or /qamiṣ/(Mr): (1) "sweater"; (2) "blouse"; (3) "upper body garments"(collective). Pl /qmayṣ/, Dimin /qmiyəṣ/; Sp camisa or similar Romance form perhaps via CA qamīṣ-. F Mk *Casa(j). [DMA-AE /qmiṣ/; GJA 105.] Cf. also /qamiž-a/ C-582. Not very common; for sense 2 the usual word is /bluz-a/ C-104.

-- /qmžž-a/ See /qamiž-a/ C-582.

-- /qṛṣun/ See /gaṛṣun/ C-264.

C-586 /qṛṭaṣ/ "bullets, shells"(collective); individuative Sg /-a/; Pl [-ạt]; Fr cartouche or cognate. F Mk *Casa(j). [Tt /qaṛṭaṣ/; DMA-AE /q^{w}ṛṭaṣ/, verb /qṛṭəṣ/ "to shoot"; TAT 424.] Cf. /kaṛtuš/ C-325.

C-587 /ṛabu/ "lathe or plane" (tool); no Pl; Fr rabot; cf. verb ṛabuṭa/ B-123. F Mk *Mr.

C-588 /ṛãdivu/ or /ṛadifu/ "appointment (to meet someone), rendezvous"; Pl /-wat/ or /-yat/; Fr rendez-vous. F.

C-589 /ṛadyu/(Mk), /ṛaḍyu/(F), or /ṛaḍyun/(F area, uncommon) "radio, x-ray"; Pl /-wat/ or /-yat/ after /u/, [-æt] after /n/; Dimin /ṛwidyu/, /ṛwiḍyu/, /ṛwiḍyun/; Fr and Sp radio. F Mk Mr. [Alg /ṛadyu/, masculine or feminine, definite /ṛ-ṛadyu/, Pl /-wat/; DMA-AE /ṛadyu/; Tt /ṛadyo/, Pl /-ṣ/; EDA 405.]

C-590 /ṛaḍaṛ/ "radar"; no Pl; Fr and Sp radar (ex Eng). F.

-- /ṛaḍyu/, /ṛaḍyun/ See /ṛadyu/ C-589.

C-591 /ṛakiṭ/, definite /ṛ-ṛakiṭ/ or /la-ṛakiṭ/, also FSg /ṛakiṭ-a/, definite /ṛ-ṛakiṭ-a/: (1) "scoring area (near basket, in basketball)"; (2) "tennis racket". No Pl; Fr (la) raquette, Sp raqueta. F.

C-592 /ṛami/ "rommy, rummy (card game)"; no Pl; Fr (gin) rommy, Sp rummy ex Eng. F.

C-593 /ṛan-a/ "open space between rows of grapevines in vineyard"; Pl [-æt], Dimin /ṛwin-a/ (contrast /rwin-a/ C-625); F informant claims this is a Fr loan but exact source unclear (Fr has (la) rêne "rein", (l')arène "the arena", (la) reine "queen", and (le) rang "row"). F *Mr. Syn: /faṛiq/.

C-594 /ṛapuṛ/ "report" (especially, official report of student's bad behaviour in school); Pl [-ạt]; Fr rapport. F.

C-595 /ṛaṭu/ "rake (tool)"; Pl /-wat/ or /-yat/; Fr râteau. F Mk *Mr. Syn: /xbbaš-a/.

-- /ṛay/ See /ṛiy/ C-605.

-- /ṛaẓwaṛ/ See /ṛiẓwaṛ/ C-606.

C-596 /ṛḍum-a/ "bottles of wine" (Pl only); Sp redoma, old loanword originally Sg, reinterpreted as Pl by analogy to such patterns as /^{c}ḍm/ "bone", Pl /^{c}ḍum-a/. F *Casa(j). [DMA-AE and Tt Sg /ṛḍum-a/ with /ṛḍaym/ Pl; same forms given ZLMA 44.] Usual word for "bottle" is /qṛ^c-a/.

C-597 /ridu/ "curtain"; Pl /-wat/ or /-yat/; Fr rideau. F.

C-598 /rigi/ "reggae (Jamaican music style)"; no Pl; Eng reggae via Fr; for some speakers, associated with /rigli/ C-600. F.

C-599 /rigl-a/ "ruler (measuring instrument)"; Pl [-æt]; Fr règle, Sp regla. F Mk *Mr. Syn: /msṭṛ-a/, /misṭaṛ-a/(F), or /^{c}baṛ/(Mr).

C-600 /rigli/ "teasing, (person) who teases or is sarcastic"; no Pl; Fr réglé (or rigolé?); cf. discussion of verb /rigl/ B-127 (and participle /m-rigl/); now secondarily associated by some with /rigi/ C-598 because of clever, inscrutable lyrics of reggae music. F.

C-601 /risil/ "eyelash brush"; Pl [-æt]; based on a French trademark locally pronounced [resil]. F.

C-602 /ṛiṣṭuṛ-a/(F Mk Mr), /ṛiṣṭuḷ-a/ (uneducated person in Mk), or /liṣṭuṛ-a/(rural near F) "restaurant"; Pl [-ạt]; Fr restaurant (Sp restaurante). F Mk Mr *Casa(j). [EDA 405 says that /ṛiṣṭuṛ-a/ cannot take definite prefix, but now it can; EDA indicates that this form, from Fr, is ousting /fund-a/ from Sp.] Syn: /mṭ^{c}m/ (CA, not common).

C-603 /rišu/ "stove"; Pl /-wat/ or /-yat/, Dimin /rwišu/; Fr réchaud. F Mk *Mr. Syn: /sxxan-a/ (less common).

C-604 /ritm/ "rhythm"; no Pl; Fr rythme (Sp ritmo). F Mk. Cf. verb /ritma/ B-129 (occurring only as participle /m-ritmi/). Syn: /mizan/.

C-605 /ṛiy/(F Mk Mr) or /ṛay/(Tt) "king (card in Spanish card deck)"; Pl /ryay/(F w. plain /r/); Sp rey. F Mk Mr Tt *Casa(j). [Alg /ṛiy/; Tt /ṛay/ has Pl /ṛyuy/.] There may have been some interference between this item and an item given by DMA-AE as "ṛeyy" with Pl "ṛyay" "irrigation; opinion" (presumably /ṛiy/, /ṛyay/ in my transcription). Syn: normal term for "king" is /malik/ (from CA).

C-606 /ṛiẓwaṛ/(F Mk), /ẓiẓwaṛ/(F Mk Mr and rural near F), or /iẓwar/ (Mr) "razor"; Pl [-ạt]; Fr rasoir. F Mk Mr *Casa(j). [Alg /ṛaẓwaṛ/, grammatically masculine.] Syn: /mus d-l-ḥsan-a/ "shaving knife".

C-607 /rmiz/: (1) "rebate, discount (off regular price)"; ex. /^{c}ṭa-ni r-rmiz/ "he gave me a/the discount"; (2) "final payment, tip"; (3) occurs in slang expression /ḥši-t-l-u r-rmiz/, lit. "I stuck (or jabbed) him with the discount", i.e. "I played a trick on him". No Pl; Fr remise. F Tt. [DMA-AE "trump" in bridge game.]

C-608 /ṛṃuk/ "trailer attachment to automobile (like U-Haul)"; Pl [-æt]; Sp remolque, Fr remorque. F. [NLVM 51, DMA-AE in sense "tugboat"; Tt /ṛimuṛke/ "big truck".] Cf. /šaryu/ C-703, /simaṛmuk/ C-642.

C-609 /ṛɔ̃pp-a/ (feminine) or /ṛɔ̃pwæ/ (gender fluctuating) "intersection, roundabout"; Pl /ṛɔ̃pp-at/ or /ṛɔ̃pwa-nat/ [rɔ̃pwæ-næt]; Fr rond point. First form more widespread and older. F. Cf. also /kṛwaẓm-a/ C-380.

-- /rökan/ See /rukan/ C-614.

C-610 /rösövör/ "ticket-seller (in booth at bus or train station)"; no Pl; Fr receveur. F Mk.

C-611 /ṛubḅ-a/ "robe, gown"; Pl [-ạt], Dimin /ṛwibḅ-a/; has sense of Fr robe but perhaps originally from Sp ropa "clothing". F *Casa(j). [Alg /rubb-a/ or /rupp-a/ "robe".]

C-612 /ṛubyu/ "blond and fair-skinned (person)"; FSg like MSg or else /-ya/; Pl /-wat/ or /-yat/; MSg Dimin /ṛwibyu/; old loan, Sp rubio "blond (MSg)". F Mk *Mr. [DMA-AE; NLVM

45 as name of a fish sp.; Tt MSg /ṛobyo/, MPl /-ṣ/, FSg /ṛuby-a/ from Sp rubia, also pronounced /rubyu/, etc.] Syn: /ẓᶜṛ/ "blond".

-- /ṛuḍ-a/ See /ṛwiḍ-a/ C-624.

C-613 /ṛuk/ "rock (music)"; no Pl; Eng rock via Fr. Cf. /rigi/ C-598, /ṛuknṛul/ C-615. F Mk *Mr.

C-614 /rukan/(Mr) or /rökan/(F Mk) "shark" (known in interior mainly through films like Jaws); Pl [-æt]; Fr requin; in most areas a recent, poorly assimilated term.

C-615 /ṛuknṛul/ "rock 'n' roll (music)"; no Pl; Eng via Fr. F Mk *Mr. Short form /ṛuk/ C-613.

C-616 /ṛunḍ-a/ "a popular card game played with Spanish cards"; no Pl; Sp ronda. F Mk Tt. [GJA 53.] Other card games: /bḷḷuṭ/ C-103, etc.

C-617 /ṛupp-a/ "meal"; Pl [-æt]; Fr repas; not common, but used (for example) among hotel staff in doing accounts for tourists who have taken meals at the hotel restaurant. F *Casa(j). Syn: /wžb-a/ (CA, not too common). Distinct from /ṛuḅḅ-a/ C-611.

C-618 /ṛuppu/ "rest, time off from work" (noun or adverb); exx. /ana l-yum ṛuppu/ "I am off work today", /ši siman-a d-ṛuppu/ "about a week off"; no Pl; Fr repos. F Mk Mr. Syn: /ṛaḥ-a/.

C-619 /ṛuṣul/(F), /ṛusul/(Mk Mr), or /ṛuṣuṛ/(Mk Tt) "metal spring"; Pl [ṛoṣol-æt], [ṛosul-æt], or [ṛoṣoṛ-at]; Fr ressort (Sp resorte). F Mk Mr.

C-620 /ṛutin/ "routine", standardized or repetitive pattern of activity"; Pl /ṛutin-iy-at/ "routines"; Fr routine; there is also a more or less code-switched pronunciation with /r/ for /ṛ/. F.

C-621 /ṛuṭaṛ/ "late (for work)" (adverb); ex. /ža ṛuṭaṛ/ "he came late for work, he showed up late"; Fr en retard. F. Usual word for "late" is /m-ᶜṭṭl/. There appears to be a secondary association with /ṭṛuṭaṛ/ C-776.

C-622 /ṛuẓi/ "rosé wine" (especially one particular brand); no Pl; Fr rosé. F Mk.

C-623 /ruž/ "red wine"; no Pl; Fr (vin) rouge. F Mk. Cf. /binu/ C-83, /šṛab/ "wine" (most general term).

C-624 /ṛwiḍ-a/: (1) "wheel (of vehicle)"; (2) "rear end, arse" (occasional, slang but not very vulgar). Pl [-ạt]; early loan from Sp rueda; without prefix /ṛ/ optionally syllabic in Mk, nonsyllabic in F Mr, in all locations syllabic in def. /ṛ-ṛwiḍ-a/. F Mk Mr Casa(j). [Tt and DMA-AE with Pl /ṛwayḍ/; NLVM 52; Alg /ṛuḍ-a/ "wheel" (also "bicycle" in rural areas), Pl /ṛwəḍ/, rural Pl forms /ṛwənḍ/ and /ṛwanəḍ/, is either from a different Romance source or else involves analysis of /ṛwiḍ-a/ as Dimin form with /ṛuḍ-a/ derived by back-formation; in Morocco /ṛuḍ-a/ is a distinct word meaning "cemetery".]

C-625 /rwin-a/ "mix, mixture; mess, disturbance; noisy place; commotion, struggle"; Pl [-æt]; Sp ruína, Fr ruine; /r/ usually nonsyllabic except with definite /r-/. F Mk Tt *Casa(j). [Alg has senses "ruin" and "type of cake", also idiom /y-ᶜṭi-k r-rwin-a/ "may He (God) give you ruin!".] Related to verb /rwwn/ B-137. Distinct from /ṛwin-a/, Dimin form of /ṛan-a/ C-593.

C-626 /ryal/ "riyal" (unit of currency); Pl [-æt], Dimin /rwiyl/ (F Mk); Sp real. F Mk Mr Tt. [DMA-AE.] The /r/ is non-syllabic. In the F/Mk/Mr area (central and south Morocco) one riyal is worth five centimes (one-twentieth of a dirham) and is commonly used in counting values at any level (/ᶜšr-in ryal/ "twenty riyals" is one dirham, /myat ryal/ "one hundred riyals" is five dirhams, etc.); in the north around Tt a riyal is fifty centimes, and this is a common source of miscommunication with travellers. Cf. /ḍuṛu/ C-190, /fṛəŋk/ C-242.

C-627 /sangriy-a/ "sangria (alcoholic fruit punch)"; no Pl; Sp sangría (possibly via Fr). F.

C-628 /santur/ "military belt"; Pl [-æt]; Fr ceinture, possibly crossed with Sp cintura. F. Usual word for "belt" in general is /ṣmṭ-a/.

C-629 /sarut/ "key"; Pl /swart/. F Mk. [DMA-AE and many other refs.] NLVM 58 gives Berber tasarut as source, but same author elsewhere suggests Sp cerrado "closed, shut" as source. Syn: /mftaḥ/.

C-630 /saṛžan/([saṛžæn])(F Mk Mr) or /šaṛžan/([šaṛžæn])(F Mk, older form) "sergeant"; Pl [-æt]; Fr sergent (Sp sargento). F Mk Mr. [EDA 411 has /š/ form and suggests early introduction from Alg; my Alg informants now have /ṣaṛžan/ ([ṣaṛžaen]).]

C-631 /sạtimiṭ/, /sạtimiṭṛ/, /ṣạtim/, /ṣạtimiṭ/, or /ṣạ̄ṭimiṭ/ "centimetre"; Pl [-ạt]; Fr centimètre (Sp centímetro); these forms unstable and interchangeable, first two common among modern educated persons. F Mk Mr *Casa(j). Third variant not usually confused with Fr centime since MCA uses /fṛəŋk/ C-242 for the latter sense.

C-632 /sbiktur/ "inspector"; Pl [-æt]; Fr inspecteur, Sp inspector. F. [Taf(j) has fuller form [ænṣp̣ektoṛ], perhaps a Fr/Sp cross.] Syn: /mu-fttiš/ (CA, but common nowadays).

C-633 /sbiritu/: (1) "liquor, booze" (slang); (2) "person resembling human figure on wine bottle label" (slang). No Pl; Sp espíritu "spirit". F *Mk *Mr *Casa(j) *Tt. [TAT 328 /spiritu/ "match (for lighting fire); DMA-AE /sbiritu/ "alcohol (never for beverage)" appears to restrict the sense to medicinal and cooking alcohol, but my informants apply it to alcoholic beverages.] Not very common; /šṛab/ "wine" is the common term, cf. /wiski/ C-800, /ankul/ C-10.

C-634 /sbniy-a/ "shawl"; Pl /-yat/ or /sbani/; Sp sabanilla (old loan). Tt F. [DMA-AE; GJA 58-9; MAG 79; TAT 327-8.] Syn: /šan/ C-700.

C-635 /sbrdil-a/(F Mr) or /sbrdin-a/(Casa(j) and apparently generally in north and east Morocco) "pair of sneakers (basketball shoes)"; Pl [-æt], Dimin /sbirdil-a/; Sp esparteña, Fr espadrilles. F Mr Casa(j). [DMA-AE

/sbrdil-a/; GJA 57 /sbrdin-a/ or /sprdin-a/; Algrs /sprdin/ collective, individuative Sg /-a/; other Alg /spadri/ from Fr, grammatically masculine.] Syn: /ḥdiy-at ṛ-ṛiyaḍ-a/ (CA "sports shoes").

C-636 /si/ "yes!" (contradicting addressee); Fr si! (or mais si!). Now fairly common among educated bilinguals, filling a gap in MCA. F.

C-637 /sigaṛ/(F Mk Mr) or /ṣigaṛ/(less common, rural) "cigar"; Fr cigare. F Mk Mr. [DMA-EA under "cigar" /sigaṛ/.] Syn: /sižaṛ-a/ "cigar, cigarette", cf. /gaṛṛu/ C-263.

-- /silim-a/ See /sinim-a/ C-634.

C-638 /silul/(preferred F) or /silun/(preferred Mk) "cell (in jail, etc.)"; Pl [-æt], Dimin /swilil/; Fr cellule, possibly influenced by Sp célula (but this Sp word used mainly in botanical and other scientific senses, vs. Sp celda for jail cell). F Mk *Tt [DMA-AE /silun/.] Syn: /bniq-a/.

C-639 /sim-a/ "cement", no Pl; Fr ciment. F Mk Mr. [Alg has /sima/, grammatically masculine.]

C-640 /siman-a/(F), /ṣiman-a/(Mk Tt), /ṣiṃan-a/(Tt Casablanca), or /ṣimaṇ-a/(Mr) "week"; Pl [-ạt] in Mr, elsewhere [-æt], Dimin /swimin-a/(F); Sp semana with later influence of Fr semaine (especially in F/Mk forms). F Mk Mr Tt *Casa(j). [Alg /sman-a/; DMA-AE /siman-a/ or /ṣiman-a/.] Now the common term in many of these cities; formerly /žmᶜ-a/ "Friday" was used in counting; /?usbuᶜ/ from CA is gaining but still uncommon.

C-641 /simaṛmi/ "plaster"; no Pl; said to be from Fr, perhaps ciment armé. F Mk Mr. Cf. /sim-a/ C-639 and /simaṛmuk/ C-642.

C-642 /simaṛmuk/ "large truck"; Pl [-æt], said to be from Fr, perhaps ciment-remorque. F. Cf. /sim-a/ C-639, /simaṛmi/ C-641, and /ṛṃuk/ C-608.

C-643 /sinim-a/(F Mk Tt) or rural variants /silim-a/, /sulim-a/ "cinema, movie theatre"; Pl [-æt], Dimin /swinim-a/; Fr cinéma (Sp cine, less often cinema). F Mk Tt. [Alg /sinim-a/ or /silim-a/; DMA-AE /sinim-a/; EDA 408 /siniṃ-a/.] The common term.

C-644 /sint-a/ "(recording) tape; (photographic) film"; Pl [-æt], Dimin /swint-a/; Sp cinta. F Mk Tt. [DMA-AE.]

C-645 /sinyal/ "blinker (signal on front and back of car indicating turns)"; Sp señal, Fr signal. F.

-- /sinyatur/ See verb /sinya/ B-140.

C-646 /sinyuṛ/: (1) "senior (player in senior soccer league)"; (2) "señor" (referring to Spaniard, or jocular). No Pl; Fr sénior (presumably from Eng) in sense 1, Sp señor in sense 2. For other soccer levels see /minim/ C-504, /žiṇyuṛ/ C-814, /kaḍi/ C-307. F.

C-647 /siran/, definite /la-siran/ "siren" (of ambulance, or loud siren indicating fasting period in Ramadan); Pl [-æt]; Fr (la) sirène, Sp sirena. F *Mk *Mr. The more common word is /zwwag-a/(F Mk) or /zwwaq-a/(Mr).

-- /siraž/ See verb /sira/ B-141.

C-648 /siri/, definite /la-siri/: (1) "series (e.g. numbered series of bank notes)"; (2) "money" (slang). No Pl; Fr (la) série. Not very common; usual slang for "money" is /mik-a/ C-496.

C-649 /sirkilasyu/ "automobile traffic; (any) congestion or hubbub"; no Pl; Fr circulation, Sp circulación. F. Syn: /ḥarak-at s-sayr/ "everybody moving around".

C-650 /siṛkl/ or /ṣiṛkl/ "circle"; Pl [-æt]; Fr cercle (Sp círculo); cf. verb /srkl/ B-146. F. Seems less common than /ḍa?ir-a/ or /ḍwwaṛ-a/.

C-651 /siṛṣu/ "hoop, rim (of basketball net)"; Pl /-wat/, /-yat/; Fr cerceau. F.

C-652 /sirur/ "shoe-shine boy (or man)"; Pl [-æt]; Fr cireur; cf. verb /sira/ B-141. F Mk.

-- /skaṃb-a/ See /škamb-a/ C-710.

-- /skaṛṭiṛ/ See /ṣṭaṛṭiṛ/ C-687.

C-653 /skuṭš/ "Scotch tape" (or any tape of this type); individuative Sg /-a/ "piece of Scotch tape", Pl [-æt]; trade mark Scotch (Eng via Fr). F Mk.

C-654 /skwil-a/ "primary school"; Pl [-æt] or /skawl/, Dimin /skiwil-a/; Sp escuela, reinforced by Fr école. F Mk *Mr. [Casa(j) /skwiḷ-a/; Tt /ṣukwel-a/, Pl [-æt]; Alg has /(l-)ikul/ in this sense from Fr (l')école, but eAlg has /škul-a/ which is either directly from another Romance form or from Sp via back-formation with earlier */škwil-a/ or the like interpreted as a Dimin; DMA-AE /skwil-a/; GJA 63.]

C-655 /slipp/ "underpants, undershorts"; Pl [-æt] or /slayp/; Fr slip. F Mk Mr Tt. [Alg /slip/, Pl /slip-at/.]

C-656 /srbay/ "waiter, servant"; Pl /-a/ (usual Pl of agentive type /CCCaC/); agentive from verb /srba/ B-145. F. [DMA-AE; EDA 408; NLVM 58.] Now less common than formerly, since /gaṛṣun/ C-264 is now frequent.

-- /srbis/ Discussed with verb /srba/ B-145.

C-657 /srbit-a/: (1) "towel"; (2) "high-priced black market". Pl [-æt] or /srabt/; Fr serviette, Sp servilleta. Sense 1 F Mk Alg, sense 2 Mr. [MAG 85 and 112 has /srbis-a/, possibly a typo, and /srbyiṭ-a/ from Sp.] For "towel" the usual word is /fuṭ-a/.

C-658 /srdin/ "sardines" (collective); individuative Sg /-a/, Pl [-æt]; widespread Mediterranean cognate set involving Sp sardina, etc. F. [NLVM 59.]

C-659 /srtifik-a/(F Mk Mr), /srtafik-a/(F Mk), or /srfakit-a/ (rural) "certificate"; Pl [-æt]; Fr certificat. F Mk Mr. Syn: /šahad-a/.

C-660 /stilu/ or (rarely) /ṣṭilu/ "ballpoint pen"; Pl /-wat/ or /-yat/; Fr stilo. F Mk Mr Tt Alg. [EDA 409.] Syn: /qalam/ (CA, uncommon).

C-661 /stitu/ "small"; Pl /stitw-in/, FSg /stitw-a/, MSg Dimin /stiwt/ ("very short person"); early loan, probably based on Sp chiquito (Dimin of Sp chico) "small". This word is one of the two most notorious indicators of the northern dialect (Tt Tangiers), the other being /^{c}ayl/ "boy, child"; in most of Morocco /ṣġiṛ/ is the basic form for "small" (it also occurs in the north as an alternative to /stitu/); the Dimin /stiwt/ is occasionally used in the F/Mk area. [TAT 328.] *Casa(j).

-- /sṭaž/ See /ṣṭaž/ C-689.

C-662 /sudur/: (1) "welding"; (2) "welder". Pl [-æt] mainly in sense 2; Fr soudure "welding" and soudeur "welder"; cf. verbs /sdr/ B-139, /suda/ B-148.

C-663 /sutyan/ "bra, brassiere" (woman's garment); Pl [-æt]; Fr soutien. F Alg.

C-664 /swirti/ "game of luck"; Pl /-yat/; Sp suerte "luck". F Mk Mr Casa(j). [Tt /swiṛṭi/, perhaps really /ṣwiṛṭi/; DMA-AE.] Syn: /ẓhṛ/ "luck".

C-665 /syas/(F) or /syast/(Mk Mr), definite /ḷa-syas/, /ḷa-syast/ "siesta, midday rest or nap"; ex. /dar ḷa-syas/ "he took ('did') a siesta", /n-dir-u ši syas/ "shall we take a nap?"; no Pl; Fr sieste, Sp siesta. F Mk Mr. [Tt /syiṣṭ-a/.] Syn: /qilul-a/.

C-666 /ṣabun/(F Mk Casa(j)), /ṣaḅun/(F Tt Casa(j)), /ṣabuṇ/(Mr), or /ṣab^{w}n/(F) "soap"; FSg /ṣabun-a/ and variants may be used in place of /ṣabun/ or may have the meaning of individuative Sg "bar of soap"; Pl [-ạt] in Mr, elsewhere [-æt], also /ṣwabn/; Dimin FSg /ṣwibin-a/(F); Fr savon, Sp jabón (old word with complex history). F Mk Mr Tt Casa(j). [Alg /ṣabun/, with informants reporting /ṣavun/ as variant used by Kabylls; DMA-AE /ṣabun/; MAG 66, 78 /ṣabun/ or /ṣaḅun/; TAR 422 /sabun/ with further refs.] No synonym. Related forms: B-153, C-680.

C-667 /ṣạ̃driyi/(F), /ṣạ̃driye/(Mk), /ṣandriyi/(F), or /sạ̃ḍṛiyi/ (Mr) "ashtray"; Pl /-yat/, also haplologic /ṣạ̃dri-yat/, etc.; Fr cendrier. F Mk Mr. [eAlg /ṣạ̃driyi/.] More common than /ṭffay-a/.

-- /ṣạ̃ḍwitš/ and variants: see /ṣanḍwitš/.

C-668 /ṣạ̃fṛwa/ (/ṛ/ not syllabic) "fearless, cool under pressure"; form invariable for numbers/genders; Fr sang-froid. F *Mk. Syn: see /kipkul/ C-354.

C-669 /ṣak/ "(large) sack, bag"; Pl /ṣik-an/ pronounced [ṣek-æn](F) or [ṣek-ạn](Mr Tt); Dimin /ṣwiyək/; Fr sac Sp saco). F Mr Tt. [EDA 413 with Pl /ṣak-at/; Alg masculine /ṣak/, Pl /li-ṣak/.] Syn: /qṛab/, /xnš-a/.

C-670 /ṣak-a/ "tobacco shop"; Pl [-æt](F Mk) or [-ạt](Mr); probably Sp saca "export (of merchandise)". F Mk Mr Tt. [DMA-AE.]

C-671 /ṣakaḍu/ "knapsack"; Pl /-wat/ or /-yat/, Dimin /ṣwikiḍu/; Fr sac à dos. F Mk. Syn: /žarib/ (uncommon).

C-672 /ṣal-a/(F Mk Casa(j))or /ṣaḷ-a/(Mr) "living room"; Pl [-æt](F Mk Casa(j)) or [-ạt](Mr); Dimin /ṣwil-a/(F area); Sp sala, Fr salle. F Mk Mr Casa(j). [Tt /ṣaḷ-a/, Pl /ṣiḷ-an/; MAG 79; DMA-AE /ṣaḷ-a/, Pl [-ạt] or /ṣyəḷ/; Alg /ṣal-a/, Pl [-æt].] Syn: cf. /ṣaḷu/ C-675.

C-673 /ṣaliṛ/ "salary, wages"; no Pl; Fr salaire (Sp salario). F. Syn: the usual word is /xlaṣ/, cf. also /manḍ-a/ C-466.

C-674 /ṣalũ/ Occurs in expression /^{c}ṭa-h ṣ-ṣalũ/ "he gave him a salute, he saluted him"; no Pl; Fr salut. F.

C-675 /ṣaḷu/(F Mr), /ṣaḷun/(F Mk Casa(j)), or /ṣaluṇ/(Mr Tt) "(large) guest room, salon"; Pl /-wat/ or /-yat/ after /u/, [-æt] after /n/ (F Mk Casa(j)), or [-ạt] after /ṇ/ (Mr Tt); Dimin /ṣwiḷu/, /ṣwiḷun/, or /ṣwiḷin/; Fr salon, Sp salón. F Mk Mr Casa(j). [Alg /ṣalu/, Pl /-wat/.] Syn: /bit ḍ-ḍyaf/ "guest room".

-- /ṣandriyi/, etc. See /ṣạ̃driyi/ C-667.

C-676 /ṣanḍal-a/(F Mk) or /ṣanḍaḷ-a/(Mr Tt) "sandal (strapless type)"; Pl [-æt](F Mk) or [-ạt](Mr Tt), also /ṣnaḍl/(Mk) or /ṣwanḍl/(Mr), Dimin /ṣniḍil-a/(rural near F); Fr sandale (Sp sandalia). F Mk Mr Tt. [EDA 406 /sndal/; Tt also /ṣanḍaliy-a/ from Sp.] Syn: /mššay-a/ "slippers", /n^{c}al-a/ "sandals" (but /ṣanḍal-a/ very common).

C-677 /ṣanḍwitš/, /ṣandwitš/(Mk), /ṣạ̃ḍwitš/(F), or /ṣạ̃ḍwiš/(rural near F) "sandwich"; no Pl; Eng sandwich via Fr and Sp. F Mk. [DMA-AE under "sandwich" has /sandwiš/.] Cf. /kaṣkṛuṭ/ C-335.

C-678 /ṣạ̃ṭṛ/ "centre" (esp. of basketball court, or in sense of cultural centre); no Pl; Fr centre. F Mk.

C-679 /ṣbabṭ-i/ "shoemaker, shoe-seller"; Pl /ṣbabṭ-iy-a/; derived from /ṣbbaṭ/ C-681 or verbal counterpart (B-151). F. [DMA-AE.]

C-680 /ṣbban-a/(F Mk) or /ṣbbaṇ-a/(Mr) "washerwoman, cleaning woman, maid"; Pl [-æt](F Mk) or [-ạt](Mr), Dimin /ṣbibin-a/(F); noun of profession /ta-ṣbban-t/ "cleaning (as occupation)"; internal derivative from /ṣabun/ C-666 "soap", probably mediated by verb /ṣbbn/ B-153. F Mk Mr. [DMA-AE; MAG 81, 83.]

C-681 /ṣbbaṭ/(F Mk Mr) or /ṣ^{w}bbaṭ/(rural) "pair of shoes" or (single) shoe"; Pl /ṣbabṭ/, Dimin /ṣbibiṭ/ or rural /ṣbəybiṭ/; derivatives include /ṣbabṭ-i/ C-679 "shoemaker" and /ṣbbaṭ-in/ (Pl only) "shoe sellers (collective), shoe market" (presupposing Sg */ṣbbaṭ/ "shoe seller", which however is not used since it would be homophonous with /ṣbbaṭ/ "pair of shoes"); part of an old and difficult cognate set including Sp zapato, Fr sabot, with exact origin and direction of borrowing uncertain. F Mk Mr *Casa(j). [Tt /ṣubbaṭ/; DMA-AE /ṣbbaṭ/; TAT 352-3.] Traditional Moroccan foootwear usually called /blġ-a/, or for women /riḥiy-a/.

C-682 /ṣbiṭaṛ/ "hospital"; Pl [-ạt]; probably brought in from Algeria, where it was based on It spedale crossed with or reinforced by Fr hôpital, Sp hospital. F Mk. [Tt and Casa(j) /ṣpiṭaṛ/; DMA-AE; Alg /ṣbiṭaṛ/; EDA 413 with discussion of Algerian connection.] This is the usual term.

C-683 /ṣblyun/ or /ṣpnyul/ "Spaniards (collective)"; adjective /ṣblyun-i/ or /ṣpnyul-i/ "Spanish", also MSg "Spaniard"; Sp español, Fr espagnol. F Mk. [DMA-AE /ṣbnyul/; NLVM 14, 68; Casa(j) /ṣpaṇyuḷ-i/; Tt /ṣpanyuḷ/ or /ṣpanyul/.] Maybe forms like Casa(j) /ṣpaṇyuḷ-i/ are partly due to resegmentation of Sp Pl españoles as españole-s.

-- /ṣiman-a/ and variants. See /siman-a/ C-640.

-- /ṣišwaṛ/ See /šišwaṛ/ C-709.

C-684 /ṣlguṭ/ "rascal, good-for-nothing, rogue" (pejoratively or playfully insulting); Pl /ṣlagəṭ/, Dimin /ṣligiṭ/; I have been told by two informants that this is a borrowing from Fr sale gosse "dirty lad", but this may be a folk etymology and the form seems rather old. F Mk. [DMA-AE.] Cf. /ḅuguṣ/ C-126, /zufri/ C-809.

-- /ṣpanyuḷ/ See /ṣblyun/ C-683.

-- /ṣpiṭaṛ/ See /ṣbiṭaṛ/ C-682.

-- /ṣpnyul/ See /ṣblyun/ C-683.

C-685 /ṣpuṛtif/ or /spuṛtif/ "athletic, sporty" (adjective); no Pl or distinct FSg; Fr sportif. F.

C-686 /ṣṭad/(F Mk), /ṣṭaṭ/(F), or /ẓṭaṭ/(F) "sports stadium"; Pl [-æt] after first variant, [-ạt] after the others; Dimin /ṣṭiyəd/(F); Fr stade (Sp estadio). F Mk *Mr. Syn: /ml^{c}əb/, but /ṣṭad/ common.

C-687 /ṣṭaṛṭiṛ/(F), /sṭaṛṭiṛ/(Mk), or /skaṛṭiṛ/(Mr): (1) "choke (of automobile)"; (2) "(person) who is just coasting" (said of athlete or employee who is not working very hard but just going through the motions); ex. /m-kmml ġi b-ṣ-ṣṭaṛṭiṛ/ "he is finishing (the game) by coasting"; Pl [-ạt]; Fr starter (ex Eng). F Mk Mr. Cf. /kuṇṭak/ C-409.

C-688 /ṣṭasyu/(F), /ṣṭasyun/(F), or /ṣṭaṣyuṇ/(Mr), definite prefix /ṣ-/(F) or /la-/(Mr), "bus station"; Pl /-wat/ or /-yat/ after /u/, [-æt] after /n/, [-ạt] after /ṇ/; Fr station, Sp estación. F Mr. Syn: /maḥṭṭ-a/. Commonly, however, the local bus station is referred to by its company name, hence often C.T.M., pronounced /ṣiṭyiṃ/ or the like.

-- /ṣṭaṭ/ See /ṣṭad/ C-686.

C-689 /ṣṭaž/(Mk) or /sṭaž/(F Mr Tt) "practical training period (regular part of some university programmes)"; Pl [-æt] (F Mk) or [-ạt](Mr), Dimin /ṣṭiyəž/; Fr stage. F Mk Mr Tt. Syn: /t^-drib/.

C-690 /ṣubb-a/: (1) "soup" (excluding the thick Moroccan soup /ḥrir-a/); (2) "in a heap, unsorted, unboxed" (adverb); ex. /šaṛži-t baṭaṭ-a ṣubb-a/ "I loaded potatoes in a heap, loose" (this sense F Mk only); Sp sopa, Fr soupe. F Mk Mr Tt. [Casa(j) /ṣup-a/ "soup"; DMA-AE "soup"; MAG 112; ZLMA 24fn; Alg "soup" especially in army context.] Syn: /š^{w}ṛb-a/ "soup".

C-691 /ṣulḍi/ "an old coin, formerly worth about two centimes" (now remembered but no longer in use); Pl /ṣwalḍ/, /ṣwalḍ-a/, or /ṣulḍiy-at/; probably originally It soldi (Pl of soldo). F Casa(j) *Mr. [DMA-AE /ṣuḷḍi/, /ṣuṛḍi/; Alg /suṛdi/, with Pl /swaṛəd/ also in sense "money".]

C-692 /ṣuniṭ/, definite /la-ṣuniṭ/ "doorbell"; Pl [-ạt]; Fr sonnette; cf. verb /ṣuna/ B-158.

-- /ṣušwaṛ/ See /šišwaṛ/ C-709.

C-693 /ṣuṭ-a/ "card worth ten in Spanish card deck"; Pl [-ạt]; Sp sota. F Mk Mr. Cf. /kaḅal/ C-302.

C-694 /ṣuvaž/ "wild, savage"; form invariable for numbers/genders; Fr sauvage (Sp salvaje). F. Cf. verb /ṣufəž/ B-157. Usual term for "wild (animal)" is /wḥš-i/.

C-695 /šạbṛ/, definite /ḷa-šạbṛ/, or else /šạbṛ-a/, definite /š-šạbṛ-a/ "room (in hotel)"; Pl [-ạt]; Fr (la) chambre; fairly common among hotel staff. F Mr. [Alg /šạbṛ-a/.] Syn: /bit/ "room".

C-696 /šạbṛiṛ/: (1) "air chamber (of tyre)"; (2) "room (in hotel)" (an occasional variant of C-695, mainly pejorative). Pl [-ạt]; Fr chambre à air "air chamber". F Mr. [EDA 410.] Form possibly influenced by /šmrir/ "hat".

C-697 /šaf/(F Mk Casa(j)) or /šaff/(Mk Mr) "chief, head (of gang, etc.)"; Pl /šaf-at/(F), /šif-an/(F), /šaff-at/(Mk Mr), the form /šif-an/ being modelled on the type /kaf/ "cavern", Pl /kif-an/; Dimin /šwiyəf/(F); Fr chef (Sp jefe). F Mk Mr Casa(j). [EDA 409-10 with /šif-an/ Pl; Alg /šaf/, Pl /li-šaf/; Tt /šaf/, Pl /šif-an/.] Cf. /paṭṛõ/ C-547. Syn: /m-ᶜllm/ (more common).

-- /šak/ See /šik/ C-706.

C-698 /šakuš/ "bag, sack"; Pl [-æt](Mr) or /šwakš/(F Mk), Dimin /šwikiš/; Fr sacoche, early and well-established loan. F Mk Mr. [EDA 413.] Possible contamination with CA šākūš- "hammer".

-- /šal/ See /šan/ C-700.

-- /šaḷaḍ-a/ See /šḷaḍ-a/ C-712.

C-699 /šalimu/ "blowtorch"; Pl /-yat/ or /-wat/; Fr chalumeau. F Mk *Mr. Syn: /kwway-a/.

C-700 /šan/(F Mk Mr) or /šal/(F Mk): (1) "shawl, scarf"; (2) (good) reputation" (/šan/ is the only variant in this sense). Pl [-æt] (F Mk Mr); sense 1 from Fr châle, Sp chal, Turkish şan, CA šāl-; sense 2 old, from CA ša?n-, with possible confusion between this old MCA form and the Fr/Sp forms for "shawl" responsible for the /šan/ variant in the latter sense. F Mk Mr *Casa(j). [Alg /šal/, masculine, "shawl"; DMA-AE gives Pl /šil-an/ "shawls", but my informants except Tt reject this.] Syn: /sbniy-a/ C-634.

-- /šạp̣p̣an/ See /šạpwaṇ/ C-702.

C-701 /šap̣p̣u/ "bravo!, superb job!" (exclamation of admiration for a heroic feat or the like); Fr chapeau "hat", presumably from Fr expression similar to Eng "hats off!". F. [Alg /šappu/ "hat".]

C-702 /šạpwaṇ/(F), /šạpwæ̃/(Mk), /šạp̣p̣an/([šạp̣p̣ʷan])(Mr), /šaṃbwan/([šaṃbwæn])(F), or /šaḅḅan/([šaḅḅan] or [šaḅḅʷan])(rural and uneducated) "tube or bottle of shampoo"; no Pl; Fr shampooing [šạpwæ̃] ex Eng (Sp champú). F Mk Mr. [Tt /čaṃpwan/[čạṃpwæn].]

C-703 /šaryu/ "trailer attachment to automobile (U-haul type); Pl /-yat/ or /-wat/; Fr chariot. F. Syn: /ṛṃuk/ C-608. [eAlg has /šaṛiṭ-a/, presumably Fr charrette.]

-- /šaṛžan/ See /saṛžan/ C-630.

C-704 /šifluṛ/(F Mk), /šifṛuṇ/(Mr), or /šufluṛ/(F Casa(j)) "cauliflower" (collective); individuative Sg /-a/, Pl [-ạt]; Fr chou-fleur, Sp coliflor. F Mk Mr. [DMA-AE /šifluṛ/; Alg /šifluṛ/; EDA 412.]

C-705 /šifuṛ/(F Mk Mr), /šifuṛ/(F), or /šufiṛ/(rural near F) "driver, chauffeur"; Pl [-ạt], also /šyafṛ/; Dimin /šwifṛ/ or /šwifiṛ/ (pharyngealized /f/)(F); Fr chauffeur, Sp chófer. F Mk Mr *Casa(j). [Tt /čawfir/ or /cawfiṛ/ from Sp; NLVM 70 /šufuṛ/; EDA 412; DMA-AE /šifuṛ/.]

C-706 /šik/(Mr) or /šak/(F Mk) "cheque (from bank)"; Pl /šak-at/ (F), /šik-at/(Mk Mr); Fr chèque (Sp cheque). F Mk Mr. [Tt /ček/, /čik/; DMA-EA under "check" /šik/, Pl /-at/.] Modern CA ṣakk- is only indirectly related.

C-707 /šiki/ "chic, stylish, fancy"; ex. /ksw-a d-š-šiki/ "a chic dress"; form invariable; syntactically a noun but translation often requires adjective; Fr chiqué (cf. Fr chic); cf. verb /šyyək/ B-167. F Mr. [DMA-AE; EDA 411.]

-- /šikul-a/ See /šklaṭ/ C-711.

C-708 /šinw-i/ "Chinese" (adjective, or MSG); FSg /-iy-a/, collective Pl /šinwa/ (this also means "China" and can be treated as FSg /šinw-a/ in this sense); Fr chinois with /-i(y-)/ Gentilic suffix, influenced by CA ṣīn-iyy- "Chinese". F Mk. [Alg /šinwa/ or /šinwan/ as collective for Chinese people, adjective form /šinwaz-i/, FSg /šinwaz-iy-a/ based on Fr FSg form chinoise; DMA-AE under "Chinese" has /ṣin-i/ from the CA form.]

C-709 /šišwaṛ/, /šušwaṛ/, /ṣišwaṛ/, or /ṣušwaṛ/ "hair-dryer" (machine); Pl [-ạt]; Fr séchoir. F.

C-710 /škamb-a/(F), /škaṃb-a/(Tt), or /skaṃb-a/(Mr) "a card game using Spanish cards"; no Pl; presumably a Romance loan but exact source unclear (possibly a form of Sp escampar or It scampare with various meanings including "to escape from danger"). F Mr Tt.

C-711 /šklaṭ/(F), /škʷlaṭ/(Mk Mr), or /šikul-a /(Oujda area) "chocolate" (collective); individuative Sg /-a/ "piece or bar of chocolate", Pl [-ạt](F Mk Mr), [-æt](Oujda), or /škalṭ/(F); Dimin /škilṭ/ or /škiliṭ/(F); /šklaṭ/ and /škʷlaṭ/ probably based on Sp chocolate, Oujda form probably on Fr chocolat; cf. verb /škləṭ/ B-164 with skewed meaning "to masturbate". F Mk Mr Oujda. [Casa(j) /šklaṭ/ shows regular depalatalization and pharyngealization of the sibilant; Alg has /šikul-a/ in most areas, but Algrs has /čoklaṭ/, masculine, perhaps a Fr/Sp/It crossing or possibly a new form from Eng; DMA-AE has /šklaṭ/; Tt /čoklaṭ/.]

C-712 /šlaḍ-a/(F Mk Mr), or /šalaḍ-a/(F) "salad"; Pl [-ạt] or /šlayḍ/; Dimin /šliyḍ-a/; Fr salade, Sp ensalada. F Mk Mr. [Tt /šlaḍ-a/; Casa(j) /ṣalaḍ-a/ with regular treatment of sibilant; Algrs /šlaḍ-a/ but eAlg /ṣlaṭ-a/ presumably from It insalata; DMA-AE /šlaḍ-a/.] Now often applied to the "Moroccan salad" consisting of finely sliced tomatoes and onions. Verb /šlləḍ/ (DMA-AE) now rejected.

C-713 /šlux/ or /ašlux/ "homosexual" (pejorative slang, not common); form invariable for genders/plural; F informant says this is from a German word, but German informants contacted do not know it and perhaps it is actually related to /šlx-a/ "chip, splinter", in slang "chick (girl)". F. Perhaps secondarily associatied with German schwul.

C-714 /šly-a/ "chair"; Pl [-æt] or /šli/; Sp silla; old loan still found in archaic dialects (including several Jewish ones), now vestigial in dominant dialects where /kursi/ from CA is gaining. Mk F [Several Jewish dialects; DMA-AE; MAG 4; Tt /šuly-a/.]
C-715 /šmandifir/ "railroad"; no Pl; Fr chemin de fer. F Alg. [DMA-AE under "railroad"; EDA 412.] Cf. /mašin-a/ C-487 and /tran/ C-736.
C-716 /šʷṛṭ-a/ or /šuṛṭ-a/ "police"; no Pl; probably really from CA šurṭ-a but now closely connected to Fr Sûreté (Nationale). F Mk. [DMA-AE under "police" /šʷṛṭ-a/; EDA 378.] Cf. /aṣurṭi/ C-24. Syn: /bulis/ C-132.
-- /šufiṛ/ See /šifuṛ/ C-705.
-- /šufluṛ/ See /šifluṛ/ C-704.
-- /šut/, /šut-a/ Discussed with verb /šat/ B-162.
C-717 /šuṛṭ/ "pair of shorts"; Pl [-ạt]; Dimin /šwiṛṭ/; Fr short (ex Eng). F Mr Alg. Syn: /burmid-a/ C-143. Distinct from C-716.
-- /šuṛṭ-a/ See /šʷṛṭ-a/ C-716.
-- /šušwaṛ/ See /šišwaṛ/ C-709.
C-718 /šwiŋgɔm/(F Mk), /šwiŋgum/(F Mk), /šwingum/(F), or /šwingu/(F) "chewing gum"; no Pl; Eng via Fr chewing-gum [šwiŋgɔm]. F Mk. [Alg /šwiŋgɔm/, e Alg also /šiŋgum/.]
C-719 /taff-a/ "stack of wheat grains"; Pl [-æt]; Dimin /twiff-a/; F informant claims this is from Fr, and a connection with Fr touffe "bunch, clump" is conceivable but uncertain. F *Mr *Mk. Syn: /ᶜṛṛam/, /ᶜṛm-a/.
-- /taksi/ See /ṭaksi/ C-754.
-- /tambr/, /tanbr/ See /tnbr/ C-734.
C-720 /taqniy-at/ or /tiqniy-at/ (Pl only) "technique, skill (e.g. of athlete)"; apparently from Fr technique(s), Sp técnica (and Eng technique(s) if via modern CA), but in form looks like a factitive-causative verbal noun from CA of type ta-CCiyy-āt- (Pl, from weak root); this seems also to be associated (secondarily) with CA verb ?atqan-, root √tqn "he mastered (it), he became proficient at (it)". F Mk.
C-721 /tawzn/ "money" (slang); no Pl; Eng thousand or German Tausend. F. Uncommon, cf. /mik-a/ C-496, the common slang term.
C-722 /tikiy-a/(F Mk), /tikit-a/(Mr), /tiki/, or /tikit/: (1) "paper label (on mail parcel, etc.)"; (2) "ticket" (this sense uncommon). Pl [-æt]; Fr étiquette "label" and Fr ticket [tike] "ticket". F Mk Mr. [Tt /tikiṭ/ and Casa(j) /tikit-a/ mean "label", the latter perhaps from Sp etiqueta; Casa(j) distinguishes this from /tiki/ or /tikit/ "ticket"; Alg has /tiki/, Pl /-yat/ "ticket".]
C-723 /tilifun/(F Mk), /tilifon/(Mr), /tiniful/(rural around F), or /ṭiṛifun/(rural around F) "telephone"; Pl [-æt] (F Mk Mr), hence Mr [tilifon-æt]; Fr téléphone (Sp teléfono). F Mk Mr. [Casa(j) /ṭiḷifuṇ/, also given as a variant by EDA 416, and also found in Tt; Alg /tilifun/, masculine; CMA-AE /tilifun/.]

-- /tiligr̥am/ See /ṭiḷigr̥am/ C-760.

C-724 /tilivizyun/(Mk), /tilivizyu/(Mk), /tilifizyun/(F Mr), /ṭiḷivizyõ/(F), /ṭiḷivizyun/(F), /ṭiṇifizyu/(rural near F), /ṭiṇifizyul/(rural near F), short form /ṭiḷi/(F); Pl [-æt] after /n/, /-wat/ after /u/, /-yat/ after /i/; Dimin /twilifizyu/, etc.; Fr télévision, Sp televisión (Sp also has televisor "television apparatus, television set" but this is apparently not borrowed), short form Fr télé, Sp tele. F Mk Mr. [Alg /tilivizyõ/, feminine.] More common than /tlfaz-a/ from CA.

C-725 /timid/ "timid, afraid" (occasional as pejorative epithet for a cowardly or indecisive person); form invariable; Fr timide (Sp tímido). F. Syn: /ḥššum-i/ "shy, ashamed".

-- /tiniful/ See /tilifun/ C-723.

C-726 /tinis/ or /ṭinis/ "tennis"; no Pl in this sense; FSg /tinis-a/ "tennis ball" has Pl [-æt], Dimin /twinis-a/; Fr tennis [tɛnis], Sp tenis, now reinforced by CA tanīs-. F(both forms) Mr(with /t/). [EDA 414.]

-- /tiqniy-at/ See /taqniy-at/ C-720.

C-727 /tir/ "shot (in sports or from gun)"; Pl [-æt]; Fr tir (Sp tiro). F Mk Mr. Syn: /ḍṛb-a/, /qədf/. Cf. verb /tira/ B-168.

C-728 /tiran/(F) or /ṭiran/([ṭeræn])(F) "playing field; empty lot"; Pl [-æt]; Fr terrain (Sp terreno). F. Cf. /tirr-a/ C-731.

C-729 /tirbušun/ "corkscrew"; Pl [-æt]; Fr tire-bouchon. F.

C-730 /tiṛminis/(F) or /tiṛminüs/(Mk) or /ṭiṛminüs/(F) "last stop (on bus route, etc.)"; Pl [-æt]; Fr terminus. F Mk *Mr. Syn: /t-tali/ "the last (one)", about equally common. Cf. /nihay-a/ "end".

C-731 /tirr-a/: (1) "open square or plaza"; (2) "vacant lot used as playing ground". Pl [-æt]; perhaps a cross of Fr terrain with Fr terre, Sp tierra "land". F Mk Mr *Casa(j) *Tt. Idiom /m-qwwd-a ᶜli-h t-tirr-a/ "he is in bad physical condition (eats poorly, doesn't take care of himself)" (F); also /xʷrəž l-t-tirr-a/ "get lost!, go to hell!" (Mr, same structure as Mr /xʷrəž l-l-xla/, same general sense). Syn: /saḥ-a/ "square, plaza" (the common term); cf. /tiran/ C-728.

C-732 /tirwaṛ/ "drawer (of desk, bureau, etc.)"; Pl [-ạt]; Fr tiroir. F *Mr. Syn: /mžṛṛ/, cf. also /iṭažiṛ/ C-300.

C-733 /tiyu/ "hose"; Pl /-yat/ or /-wat/, Dimin /twiyu/; Fr tuyau. F Alg.

C-734 /tnbr/(F Mk), /tanbr/(Mr Taf(j)), or /tambr/(Mr Casa(j)) "postage stamp"; Pl /tnabr/(F Mk) or /tanbr-at/(Mr); Dimin /tnibr/(F Mk) or /tnibir/(F); Fr timbre. F Mk Mr. [Alg /tambr/, Pl /li-tambr/; EDA 413-4 /tnbr/; DMA-AE /tnbr/.] Syn: /ṭ-ṭabᶜ l-barid-i/ (from CA, in official language).

C-735 /traktur/ "tractor"; Pl [-æt]; Fr tracteur, Sp tractor. F and vicinity. [EDA 415 /tṛaktör/; Alg /traktor/, Pl [-æt].]

C-736 /tran/(F Mk Mr) or /trən/(Tt and the north, with what is often a syllabic /n/) "train"; Pl /tran-at/(F Mk) or /trun-a/(Tt), Dimin /triyn/(F); Sp tren, with /tran/ variant perhaps based more on Fr train. F Mk Mr Tt *Casa (j). This appears to be the normal word in Tt, but is far less common than /mašin-a/ in the F/Mk area at least. Cf. also /šmandifir/ C-715.

C-737 /tribin/(F Mr) or /tribun/(F) "tribune (upper section of seats in stadium), upper deck"; Pl [-æt]; Fr tribune. F Mr. Cf. /galuri/ C-255.

C-738 /tribuṛ/ "starboard (right hand side, facing ahead on ship)"; no Pl; Fr tribord. F. Opposite: /baḅuṛ/ (sense 2) C-30.

C-739 /trikku/ "knitted shirt or undershirt"; Pl /-wat/ or /-yat/; Fr tricot. F Taf(j) (and other Jewish dialects). [Alg /triku/.] Syn: /kbbuṭ/ C-350.

C-740 /trimis-a/: (1) "three-month period, quarter (of year)"; (2) "money" (slang). Pl [-æt] in sense 1 only; Fr trimestre. F. Origin of sense 2 unclear; usual slang for "money" is /mik-a/ C-496.

C-741 /tris/(Tt) or /ṭṛiṣ/(F Mk Alg): (1) "card worth three (in Spanish card deck)"; (2) "a card game based on winning three points". No Pl; Sp tres "three". F Mk Alg Tt. [NLVM 84 /ṭṛiṣ/.]

C-742 /trisinti/ "electricity"; no Pl; Fr électricité. F Mk Mr Casa(j) Taf(j). [DMA-AE; EDA 415 /trisinte/; Alg /trisiti/.] More common than /khṛab-a/ (from CA), but /ḍuw/ (variant /ḍaw/) "light" is often used also to mean "electricity"; cf. also /kuṛ-a/ C-415, sense 3, and C-743.

C-743 /trisyan/ "electrician"; Pl [-æt]; Fr électricien. F Mk Mr. Cf. C-742 above.

-- /trən/ See /tran/ C-736.

C-744 /turist/ or /turis/ "tourist"; no Pl; Dimin /twirist/; Fr touriste, Sp turista, Eng tourist. F *Mr. Not very common; European visitors are usually referred to simply as /nṣṛan-i/ "Christian" (so that /masiḥ-i/ is used to mean "Christian" referring specifically to religious affiliation), cf. slang form /gəwr-i/ C-286. Other words for "traveller" are /sa?iḥ/, /m-ṣafṛ/.

C-745 /turni/ "(someone's) turn"; ex. /t-turni dyal-ək/ "it is your turn"; no Pl; Fr tournée. F Mk Mr. [NLVM 85 gives older regional forms based on Sp turno.] Syn: /nub-a/, /dəwṛ/.

C-746 /turnvis/(F), /turnfis/(F), /ṭuṛṇuvis/(Mk), or /tuṛṇifis/ (Mr) "screwdriver"; Pl [-æt]; Fr tournevis. F Mk Mr.

C-747 /turnwa/ (MSg) "tournament"; no Pl; Fr tournoi. F.

C-748 /tuš/, definite /la-tuš/ "out of bounds area" (in soccer); Fr (la) touche. F.

C-749 /ṭab-a/ or /ṭaḅ-a/ "loose tobacco (for rolling cigarettes)"; no Pl; Dimin /ṭwib-a/ elicitable but not used since it is common as the Dimin of /ṭub-a/ "sugar cube"; Fr tabac (Sp tabaco). F Mk *Mr. [DMA-AE /ṭab-a/; MAG 15; EDA 415.] Syn: /d^{w}xxan/.

C-750 /ṭabḷ-a/(Mr), /ṭabl-a/(F Mk[rare] Tt), or /ṭbl-a/(F Mk, common) "table"; Pl [-ạt](Mr), [-æt](F Mk), /ṭwabl/(F), /ṭbali/(Mk); Dimin /ṭwibl-a/(F Mk), /ṭbil-a/(F Mk), or /ṭbəyl-a/(F Mk); archaic Sp tabla and later Fr table, reinforced by CA ṭāwil-a (from It tavola or the like) and CA ṭabl-a. F Mk Mr *Casa(j) Tt. [DMA-AE /ṭbl-a/ and /ṭabl-a/; Alg /ṭabl-a/, Pl /ṭwabl/; TAT 367; NLVM 83; TAR 469, 470 and refs there.] Syn: /mid-a/ "low table".

C-751 /ṭabliy-a/ "apron"; Pl /-at/; Dimin /ṭwibliy-a/; Fr tablier. F Mk Mr. [DMA-AE.]

C-752 /ṭablu/(F Mk) or /ṭabḷu/(Mr) "blackboard"; Pl /-wat/ or /-yat/, also /-nat/; Dimin /ṭwiblu/ or /ṭwibḷu/; Fr tableau (noir). F Mk Mr. [DMA-AE /ṭablu/.] Syn: /sbbuṛ-a/.

C-753 /ṭaks/(F Mk) or /ṭakṣ/(Mr) "tax"; Pl [-æt](F) or [-ạt](Mr), but Mk speaker rejects Pl forms; Fr taxe. F Mk Mr. Syn: /wažib/ (also "duty, obligation").

C-754 /ṭaksi/(F Mk Casa(j)), /daksi/(Mr) "taxi"; Pl /-yat/; Dimin /ṭwiksi/; Fr and Sp taxi. F Mk Mr Casa(j). [Tt /taksi/, unpharyngealized; Alg /ṭaksi/ or /ṭakṣi/, Pl /-yat/; DMA-EA under "taxi" has /ṭaksi/.] No synonym. The unusual Mr form is a well-known regional indicator.

C-755 /ṭaṃṭaṃ/ "drum, tom-tom"; Pl [-ạt]; Fr tam-tam [tamtam]. Mr. More common words for drums are /ṭnbuṛ/ C-763, /batri/ C-66 (sense 2).

C-756 /ṭamp̣u/(F Mk) or /ṭampu/(F) "stamp, official seal" (not postage stamp); Pl /-nat/; Fr tampon. F Mk *Mr. Syn: /ṭab^{c}/, also /kạši/ C-338.

-- /ṭaṃubil/ See /ṭuṃubil/C-780.

C-757 /ṭaṛif/ "price; price-list"; Pl [-æt]; Fr tarif, Sp tarifa. F. [DMA-AE /ṭarif-a/ from Sp.] The word is fairly well known since cafés display price-lists labelled "tarif des consommations".

C-758 /ṭaṛṛu/ "metal pail or similar implement"; Pl /-wat/ or /-yat/; Sp tarro. F Tt. [DMA-AE; TAR 494.]

C-759 /ṭas-a/(F Mk) or /ṭaṣ-a/(Mr Tt, sometimes F Mk): (1) "cup, bowl"; (2) "can (of soft drink)"; (3) "liquor, alcohol, booze" (in slang idioms); ex. /ḍṛb ṭ-ṭas-a/ "he became alcoholic; he got drunk" (lit. "he hit the cup"). Pl [-æt](F Mk), [-ạt](Mr Tt, sometimes F Mk), also /ṭis-an/ ([ṭes-æn])(F Mk); from CA ṭās-a but apparently strongly influenced secondarily by Fr tasse, Sp taza (It tazza). F Mk Mr Tt. [Alg /ṭas-a/, Pl [-æt] or /ṭis-an/; DMA-AE /ṭaṣ-a/ in sense 1; GJA 78; MAG 79; TAT 373-4.] There is also a stem /ṭaṣ/ "washing basin" (DMA-AE; GJA 78; MAG 79; TAT 373-4), CA ṭās-, which does not seem to be influenced by the Romance forms.

-- /ṭaybus/ See /ṭubis/ C-778.

-- /ṭaž/ See /iṭaž/ C-299.

-- /ṭbl-a/ See /ṭabl-a/ C-750.

C-760 /ṭiḷigṛam/(F Mk), /tiligṛam/(Mr), /ṭiṛagṛam/(archaic), or /ṭiṛigṛam/(archaic) "telegram"; Pl [-æt](F Mk) or [-ạt] (Mr); Fr télégramme (Sp telegrama). F Mk Mr. [Tt /ṭiḷigṛaṃ/, Pl [-ạt]; MAG 69; DMA-AE /ṭiligṛam/; DMA-EA under "telegram" /tiligṛam/; EDA 414 gives /tilġṛaf/, and Mr variant /ṭiṛaġṛaf/, as either "telegram" or "telegraph", but these forms with /ġ/ instead of /g/ seem to have given way.] Syn: /bṛq-iy-a/.

-- /ṭiṇifizyu/, /ṭiḷivizyõ/, etc. See /tilivizyun/ C-724.

-- /ṭiran/ See /tiran/ C-728.

C-761 /ṭiṛaṣ/, definite /la-ṭiṛaṣ/ "rooftop terrace"; Pl [-ạt]; Fr (la) terrace. F.

-- /ṭiṛifụn/ See /tilifun/ C-723.

-- /ṭiṛminüs/ See tiṛminis/ C-730.

C-762 /ṭiṛmus/(F) or /ṭiṛṃus/(F Mk) "thermos bottle"; Pl [-æt]; Dimin /ṭwiṛmus/ or /ṭwiṛṃus/; Fr thermos [tɛrmos], Sp termos, ex Eng trademark. F Mk *Mr.

C-763 /ṭnbuṛ/ "drum"; Pl /ṭnabṛ/; Dimin /ṭnibṛ/; apparently from Fr tambour, Sp tambor or similar Romance forms; CA now has ṭunbūr- referring to a mandolin-like stringed instrument, but the MCA form seems borrowed from Fr and/or Sp directly. F Mk *Mr. [DMA-AE; EDA 416 with etymology; TAR 494.] Syn: /ṭbl/, /batri/ C-66, /ṭaṃṭaṃ/ C-755 (various types).

C-764 /təŋg/ (really with syllabic /ŋ/): (1) "tank, armoured carrier"; (2) "very strongly built man" (figurative, cf. Eng "he is built like a tank"). Pl /ṭnug-a/(F Mk Tt), [-ạt](Mr), Dimin /ṭniyəg/(F Mk); Fr tank [tạ̃k] (Sp tanque) ex Eng. F Mk Mr Tt. [DMA-AE.] Syn: /mdfᶜ/.

-- /ṭṛabandu/ and variants. See /kuṇṭṛaḅanḍ/ C-411.

C-765 /ṭṛạ̃kil/(F) or /ṭṛaŋkil/(Mk) "alone, unbothered", occurring commonly only with verb /xlla/ "to let", as in /xlli-ni ṭṛạ̃kil/ "leave me alone!" (calqued on Fr laissez-moi tranquille); form invariable for numbers/genders; Fr tranquille (Sp tranquilo). F Mk *Mr. [Tt /ṭṛaŋkil/ or /ṭṛaŋkilo/, the latter from Sp; Alg /ṭṛaŋkil/ in same expressions.] Syn: /qil-ni/ (surface variant [qin-ni]) "get away!; leave me alone!".

C-766 /ṭṛanži/ "foreigner(s)"; invariable for numbers/genders; Fr étranger (Sp extranjero). F. [Alg also has Pl /-ya/.] This form was elicited but not noticed elsewhere; the ordinary ways to refer to European visitors are with /nṣṛani/ "Christian" and the slang /gwri/ C-286; apparently /ṭṛanži/ was once more common than it is now.

C-767 /ṭṛạ̃ṣmisyu/ "communications (as branch of military service), signal corps"; no Pl; Fr transmission(s). F Mk. Syn: /l-lasilk-i/ "the wireless (service)" (with definite /l-/).

C-768 /ṭṛạ̃spuṛ/ "transport, transportation"; no Pl; Fr transport. F. Cf. verb /ṭṛạ̃ṣpuṛṭa/ B-179.

C-769 /ṭṛạ̃ši/(F) or /ṭṛạ̃še/(Mk) "trench, bunker (military context)"; Pl /-yat/(F); Fr tranchée. F Mk. Syn: /ḥfṛ-a/ or /ḥfr-a/ "pit".

C-770 /ṭṛaṿulṭa/ (masculine) "a style of haircut" (named after film star John Travolta); no Pl; Eng proper name via Fr. F.

C-771 /ṭṛibiṇaṛ/ "tribunal, court"; no Pl; Fr tribunal. F. [EDA 418 /ṭṛiḅuṇaṛ/, Pl [-ạt].] Formerly common referring to colonial courts, but /mḥkam-a/ (from CA) is now usual for present-day courts.

C-772 /ṭṛinbu/(Mk) or /ṭṛimbu/(F) "top (spinning toy)"; Pl /-wat/, /-yat/, or /-nat/; Sp trompo. F Mk. [DMA-AE /ṭṛinbu/; Casa(j) /ṭṛumba-a/ and Tt /ṭṛumṗ-a/ appear to reflect Sp variant trompa or the Catalan form trompa; GJA 79 gives Jewish /ṭṛinbu/ vs. Muslim /tṛinbu/ with unassibilated but unpharyngealized /t/, which must be a very fine surface distinction, mentioning /ṭṛumb-a/ as occurring elsewhere in Morocco; TAT 371 gives /ṭṛumb-a/, Pl /ṭṛambi/ from Catalan, but mentions /ṭṛimbu/ elsewhere in Morocco, adding that these forms do not occur in Alg.] No regular synonym except that /ṭṛumbiya/ C-774 sometimes acquires this meaning (sense 2).

-- /ṭṛiṣ/ See /tris/ C-741.

C-773 /ṭṛiṭ-a/ or /liṭṛ-a/ "monthly payment"; Pl /ṭṛiṭ-at/ or /liṭaṛi/; crossing of Sp letra with Fr traitement (the first variant being a partial Fr-based remodelling of the second variant, which is direct from Sp). F. [DMA-AE /iṭṛ-a/ or /liṭṛ-a/; Casa(j) /iṭṛ-a/; Tt /liṭṛ-a/; F /liṭṛ-a/ seems to take the /l/ as definite prefix /l-/ at least in not allowing doubled */l-liṭṛ-a/; ZLMA 24.]

-- /ṭṛiṭwaṛ/ See /ṭṛuṭwaṛ C-777.

C-774 /ṭṛumbiy-a/(F Mk Mr) or /ṭṛəmbiy-a/(F, archaic): (1) "local bus"; (2) "top (spinning toy)". Sense 1 in F Mk Casa(j), sense 2 Mr. Pl /-at/; Sp tranvía "trolley", with sense 2 probably based on interference from C-772. [Tt /ṭṛambiy-a/ "bus".] In the F/Mk area, /ṭubis/ C-778 is usual for "local bus" and /ṭṛinbu/ C-772 for "top", so C-774 is uncommon. For "long-distance (inter-city) bus" the word is /kaṛ/ C-320.

C-775 /ṭṛumḅun/ "paper clip"; Pl [-æt]; Fr trombone. F.

C-776 /ṭṛuṭaṛ/ "late for work" (adverb), ex. /ža ṭṛuṭaṛ/ "he arrived late for work"; Fr trop tard "too late" (influenced by /ṛuṭaṛ/ C-621, Fr en retard). F. Syn: /m-ᶜṭṭl/ "late" (adjective).

C-777 /ṭṛuṭwaṛ/ or /ṭṛiṭwaṛ/ "sidewalk"; Pl [-ạt]; Fr trottoir. F Mk Mr.

-- /ṭuḅḅ-a/ See /ṭuṗṗ-a/ C-782.

C-778 /ṭubis/(F Mk Mr) or /ṭaybus/(said to occur in Casablanca) "local bus" (not intercity bus); Pl [-æt](F Mk) or [-ạt] (Mr), Dimin /ṭwibis/; Fr autobus, Sp autobús. F Mk Mr. [Casa(j) /ṭubüs/ from Fr; DMA-EA under "bus" /ṭubis/; Alg /ṭubis/, less common in Alg than /bis/, Pl /li-bis/ from Fr abbreviated form bus; EDA 416-7 /ṭubis/, Pl /-at/ or /ṭwabs/, or /luṭubis/.] This is the common word for "local bus" in much of Morocco, but in the north around Tt /ṭṛumbiy-a/ C-774 is usual; for "intercity bus" the form is /kaṛ/ C-320.

C-779 /ṭulə̃ṭi/ or /nṭiliža/ "clever, tricky, smart; wise guy, smart aleck"; Pl and FSg coincide as /ṭulə̃ṭiy-a/ from first variant, FPl /ṭulə̃ṭiy-at/; MSg Dimin /ṭwiliṇṭi/ with /ṇ/ instead of nasalized vowel. Second variant from Fr intelligent, first form originally */ṭiṇiṇṭi/ from Sp teniente "lieutenant" with later influences from Fr.

intelligent (with which it is now associated), Sp inteligente, Fr talent and talentueux, Sp talento and talante, perhaps influenced also by related verb /ṭulạ̄ṭa/ B-180. F Mr. [Tt /ṭulanṭi/ or /ṭunanṭi/, obsolescent.] Syn: /m-ṭwwṛ/.

-- /ṭumaṭiš/ and variants. See /maṭiš-a/ C-491.

C-780 /ṭumubil/(F Mk), /ṭunubil/(F and some rural areas), /ṭamubil/(Mr), /ṭanubil-a/(Mk) and others, also FSg counterparts like /ṭumubil-a/, "car, automobile"; Pl [-æt]; Dimin /ṭwimibil/, etc.; Fr automobile, Sp automóvil. F Mk Mr. [Casa(j) /ṭumubil/; DMA-AE /ṭumubil/; EDA 417 /ṭumubil/, masculine or feminine; Alg /ṭunubil/ with feminine concord, but /uṭu/ from Fr auto preferred in Oran; Tt /ṭumubịḷ/ or /ṭunubịṛ/.] Syn: /syyaṛ-a/(CA).

C-781 /ṭun/: (1) "tuna"; (2) "metric ton". Pl /ṭwan/ only in sense 2; from Fr thon, Sp atún (sense 1), Fr tonne (sense 2). Widespread in both senses: F Mr. [DMA-AE; NLVM 23, 87 /ṭ^{w}nn/ in both senses.]

-- /ṭunubil/ See /ṭumubil/ C-780.

C-782 /ṭupp-a/(Mr and some Jewish dialects), /ṭubḅ-a/(F Mk) "rat"; Pl [-ạt]; older Sp dialectal *topa or the like, related to modern Sp topo "mole". F Mk Mr Casa(j). [Tt /ṭawp-a/; DMA-AE /ṭ^{w}bb-a/; ZLMA 24fn has /ṭupp-a/ for Rabat, along with list of other forms and etymology.]

-- /ṭusṭup/ See /luṭusṭup/ C-455.

-- /ṭẓẓin-a/, /t^{w}ẓẓin-a/. See /ẓin-a/ C-806.

-- /ufisyi/ See /fsyan/ C-245.

-- /ukazyu/ See /kazyu/ C-347.

C-783 /uṛžu/ "off sides" (in soccer, formally a noun); no Pl; Fr hors (de) jeu. F.

C-784 /uṭil/(F Mk Mr Casa(j)), /uṭịḷ/(Mr), /nutir/(rural), or /nuṭiṛ/(Rural) "hotel"; Pl [-æt](F Mk), [-ạt](Mr), also /uṭayl/(F Mk), Dimin /uṭiyl/ or /nwitir/; Fr hôtel, Sp hotel. F Mk Mr Casa(j). [Tt /?uṭiḷ/ with glottal stop, Pl [-ạt]; Alg /(l-)util/, /(l-)uṭil/, or /(n-)nutil/; TAR 611 /l-util/; EDA 396; DMA-AE under "hotel" and crops up in DMA-AE in an ex. under /nnit/.] This is the common term since /fndəq/ (cf. funduq- "hotel" in CA) has a different meaning in MCA.

-- /uzin/ See /wzin/ C-801.

-- /vaṭim-a/ See /baṭim-a/ C-68.

C-785 /vidridu/ "preliminary bout, warmup (e.g. minor boxing bout preceding the main event)"; Pl /-wat/ or /-yat/; Fr levée de rideau "lifting of the curtain", cf. /ridu/ C-597. F.

C-786 /vikiŋ/ "savage person, reckless person" (pejorative); form invariable for numbers/genders; Fr viking [vikiŋ] "Viking". F.

C-787 /viktim/: (1) "elderly man with a much younger, attractive wife (who may be having affairs with other men)"; (2) "rich man who has other persons (especially women) living off his wealth". No Pl; Fr victime (Sp víctima). F. Not ordinarily used in general sense of "victim".

-- /vill-a/, /vil-a/ See /fil-a/ C-211.

C-788 /viṛaž/(F Mk), /viṛaž/(F), less often /fiṛaž/(F area) "turn (in road)"; Pl [-æt]; Fr virage. F Mk *Mr.

C-789 /virni/(F Mk) or /brniz/(F, uncommon) "varnish"; no Pl; Fr vernis and Sp barniz, respectively. F Mk. [DMA-AE /brniz/, apparently more common formerly.] Syn: /ḍuṛ-a/, /luy-a/.

C-790 /vis/ "screw"; Pl [-æt]; Fr vis [vis]. F Mk Mr. Syn: /lulb/, /dulb/.

C-791 /visi/: (1) "toilet, bathroom"; (2) "material inside soccer ball". Pl /-yat/; Fr W.C. [vese] in sense 1, Fr vessie "bladder" (including "bladder of soccer ball") in sense 2. F. For variant of sense 1 see C-792.

C-792 /viṣi/ "toilet, bathroom"; Pl /-yat/; Fr W.C. [vese] (abbreviation from Eng water closet). F. See also C-791.

-- /vitɛs/ See /fitɛs/ C-221.

C-793 /vitrin-a/ "shop window, display window"; Pl [-æt]; Dimin /vwitrin-a/; Fr vitrine, Sp vitrina. F Mk.

C-794 /viṭu/ "veto"; ex. /ḥəqq l-viṭu/ "the right of veto" (e.g. in United Nations); no Pl; Fr veto [veto], Sp veto. F Mk.

C-795 /viyuz/ "parking lights (of automobile)"; Pl [-æt]; Fr veilleuse. F.

C-796 /viz-a/ "visa"; Pl [-æt]; Dimin /vwiz-a/; Fr and Sp visa (MCA pronunciation that of Fr not Sp). F Mk.

C-797 /vizit/(F) or /vizit-a(F): (1) "social visit, social call"; "house call, visit (by doctor)". Usually /vizit/ in sense 1, /vizit-a/ in sense 2; Fr visite. F. [Tt /bisit-a/ in sense 2, from Sp visita; GJA 10 /bizit-a/, Jewish only, perhaps a Fr/Sp cross.] Cf. related verb /vizita/ B-182.

C-798 /ṿul-a/(F) or /buḷ-a/(Mr) "steering wheel (of car)"; Pl [-æt]; Fr volant (Sp volante). F Mr. Distinct from /ḅul-a/ and variants C-130.

C-799 /ṿuli "volleyball"; no Pl; Fr volley [vɔlɛ] ex Eng. F.

C-800 /wiski/ "whiskey"; Pl /-yat/; Dimin not in use but informant said /wwiski/ would be the form; Fr whisky, Sp wiski ex Eng. F Mk. [EDA 418.]

C-801 /wzin/ with /w/ syllabic but unstressed, "factory"; Pl [-æt]; Fr usine. F Mk. Syn: /fabrik-a/ C-192, /m-ᶜml/.

C-802 /xiṇṭi/ "people" (slang, occasional); no Pl distinct from this form; Sp gente (apparently a recent loan). F Tt [rare]. Syn: /nas/.

C-803 /xuruṭu/ "fellow" (slang, occasional); no distinct Pl; sounds like Sp but etymon not yet identified. F Tt. Syn: /maṛk-a/ C-476, /figur-a/ C-209, /finumin/ C-216.

C-804 /xwadri/ "brother" (humorous slang); no Pl; FSg /-ya/ "sister"; playful nonce formation modelled on /pwaḍṛi/ C-581, /mwaḍṛi/ C-527, which are themselves humorous concoctions combining Sp padre, madre with MCA /ḅḅa/ "father" and /ṃṃ-/ "mother"; the present form is based on the /...aḍṛi/ sequence, plain form /...adri/, with the /xw/ initial segment taken from MCA /xu-/ "brother". F. Plain /pwadri/, /mwadri/ are also recorded.

-- /yṭṛu/ See /itṛu/ C-298.

C-805 /ẓaḷamiṭ/ "match (for striking light)"; form invariable for number; Fr Pl form les allumettes with article-noun boundary resegmented. F Mk *Mr *Casa(j). [EDA 418 also gives individuative Sg /-a/; Algrs /zalamit/, eAlg /ẓaḷamiṭ/.] Syn: /wqid/ (more common term).

C-806 /ẓin-a/(Mk Casa(j)), /ẓiṇ-a/(F Mr), /ṭ^ẓẓin-a/(Mk), /t^{w}ẓẓin-a/(F Tt), /ṭẓẓin-a/(Tt) "dozen" (especially one dozen eggs); Pl [-æt] after /n/, [-ạt] after /ṇ/; Sp docena, Fr douzaine. F Mk Mr Tt Casa(j). [DMA-AE /ẓin-a/, Pl /-at/ or /ẓyən/.] It dozzina perhaps original source.

C-807 /ziru/(F) or /ẓiṛu/(F Mk Mr) "zero" (especially as grade in school), also a general pejorative "worthless (thing or person)"; Pl /-wat/ or /-yat/, Dimin /zwiru/ or /ẓwiṛu/; Fr zéro (Sp cero). F Mk Mr. Syn: /ṣifṛ/ (from CA) is more common in the simple numeral sense (e.g. in sports scores).

-- /ẓiẓwaṛ/ See /ṛiẓwaṛ/ C-606.

C-808 /zəng/(F Mk), /zənk/(F), also pharyngealized /ẓəng/ or /ẓənk/ "zinc (metal); tin (material in tin cans)"; no Pl; Fr zinc [zæ̃g]. F Mk *Mr. The /n/ does not become velar although it is not separated from the following velar consonant. F Mk. [DMA-AE /ẓəng/; EDA 419 /zəng/, also /zng-a/ individuative Sg; Tt /ẓaṇg/.]

C-809 /zufri/: (1) "playboy, swinger, debauched man"; (2) bachelor" (not necessarily pejorative in this sense). Pl /-yat/ or /zwafr/, no FSg form in normal use; Fr les ouvriers "the workers" with resegmentation, giving Pl /zufriy-a/, with Sg derived by back-formation; cf. verb /zufr/ B-184. F Mk Mr Casa(j). [DMA-AE; Alg /zufri/, Pl /zwafr-a/; EDA 419 with the etymology.] For the Pl pattern cf. /tufri/ "barn", etc., Pl /twafr/.

C-810 /žaḍaṛmi/ "gendarme"; Pl /-ya/, Dimin /žwiḍiṛmi/; Fr gendarme probably with /-i/ suffix as in /ᶜṣkṛ-i/ "soldier", /bulis-i/ "policeman" (see C-132). F Mk Mr. [Casa(j) /ẓaḍaṛmi/ with regular sibilant shift; DMA-AE; Alg MSg /ǰaḍaṛmi/, collective /-ya/.] Syn: /rižal d-daṛak/ (Pl, not common, from CA). [EDA 386.]

C-811 /žạkiṭ-a/(F Mk), /žạkiṭ/(F Mk), /žkiṭ-a/(Tt), /džikit-a/ (Mr and perhaps the Casablanca pronunciation) "light coat, jacket"; Pl [-ạt] (F Mk) or [-æt] (Mr), also /žwạkt/(F Mk); Dimin /žwekiṭ-a/; Fr jaquette, Sp chaqueta. F Mk Mr Tt. [Casa(j) /žakiṭ-a/ [žækeṭ-a].]

C-812 /žaṇṭ-a/ "wheel axle (wheel without tyre)"; Pl [-ạt] or /žwaṇṭ/; Fr jante, Sp junto or a form of Sp verb juntar; also idiom /ṛa-h ᶜl ž-žwaṇṭ/ "he is down and out, he is broke" (lit. "he is (driving) on wheel axles without tyres"). F Tt. [For additional forms and Sp etymology see NLVM 27.]

C-813 /žili/ "vest (garment), waistcoat"; Pl /-yat/; Dimin /žwili/; Fr gilet. F Mk.

-- /žiṇiṛal/ See /žṇṇiniṛ/ C-817.

C-814 /žiṇyuṛ/(F), /žinyuṛ/(Mk), or /žnyuṛ/(F) "junior" (especially player in junior soccer league); Pl [-ạt]; Fr junior. F Mk. Other soccer leagues: /sinyuṛ/ C-646, /kaḍi/ C-307, /minim/ C-504.

C-815 /žip/ or /žipp/ "jeep"; Pl /žipp-at/; Fr jeep [ǰip] ex Eng. F. [In Alg /žip/ "skirt" belongs with C-823 below.]

C-816 /žmafu/([žmæfu]) "I don't care, I don't give a damn" (frozen expression); Fr je m'en fous.

C-817 /žṇṇiniṛ/, /žṇinaṛ/, or /žiṇiṛal/(now the common form) "general (in military)"; Pl [-ạt] after /ṛ/, [-æt] after /l/; Fr général (Sp general). F Mk Mr. [DMA-EA under "general" /žiniṛal/; EDA 386 also adds /žḷḷiṇaṛ/.]

C-818 /žnwiyir/ with syllabic /n/ "knee guard (in soccer)"; Pl [-æt]; Fr genouillère. F.

-- /žnyuṛ/ See /žinyuṛ/ C-814.

C-819 /žön/ "young" (adjective); form invariable for numbers/genders; Fr jeune; not well assimilated, but fairly common in speech of bilinguals to fill a partial lexical gap, since in MCA the only common word in this sense is /ṣġiṛ/ "small", so that borrowing this Fr word creates a lexical opposition between "young" and "small". F Mk. Cf. C-504.

C-820 /žṛd-a/(F Mk) or /žṛḍ-a/(F Mk Mr) "garden (any kind, any size)"; Pl [-æt](F Mk) or [-ạt](F Mk Mr), also /žṛadi/ (apparently never */žṛaḍi/ even for speakers who pronounce the Sg /žṛḍ-a/); Fr jardin (Sp jardín). F Mk Mr. [Casa(j) /ẓaṛdan/, pronounced [ẓạṛdæn], with regular sibilant treatment; DMA-AE /žṛd-a/.] Syn: /ḥadiq-a/ (now becoming fairly common).

C-821 /žuḅ/ or /džuḅ/ "job, position, employment"; Pl [-ạt]; Dimin /žweyəḅ/; Eng job via Fr job [ǰɔb]. F *Mk *Mr. F speaker knows the term but rarely uses it; he says it is common in Rabat and Casablanca. The usual word is /xdm-a/.

C-822 /žumil/ "pair of binoculars, field glasses"; Pl [-æt]; Fr jumelles (Sp gemelos), literal meaning "twins". F.

C-823 /župp-a/ "skirt"; Pl [-æt]; Dimin /žwipp-a/; Fr jupe. F. Mk *Mr *Casa(j). [Alg /žip/, definite /ž-žip/, grammatically feminine, also overtly FSg form /žipp-a/.] Syn: /ṣay-a/, /žlṭiṭ-a/ (less common terms).

C-824 /žuṛṇal/(F Mk, common), /žuṛnal/([žoṛnæl])(Mr), /žuṛnan/ ([žoṛnæn]) (rural), /žurnal/(rural) "newspaper"; Pl [-æt], Dimin /žwiṛṇil/(F); Fr journal. (Sp jornal is not normally used in this sense, but usually means "day work, day wages".) F Mk Mr. [Casa(j) uses a distinct loan /gaẓiṭ-a/.] Syn: /mažll-a/ or /žarid-a/ (both from CA, not very common).

C-825 /žuṛṇi/(F Mk) or /žuṛni/(F Mr) "wages, day wages, day work"; Pl /-yat/; Dimin /žwiṛṇi/, /žwiṛni/; Fr journée. F Mk Mr. Syn: /xlaṣ/ "salary". Cf. comments on C-824.

C-826 /žuwur/ "player (on team)"; Pl [-æt]; Fr joueur. F. Not very common, since /la^{c}ib/ and /la^{c}ib-i/ are fairly common (from CA).

C-827 /žwa/ (may be either MSg or FSg in concord) "envelope (for letter); sheath, scabbard"; Pl /-yat/ or /-wat/; Dimin not in normal use but F informant produced /žwiw/ and /žwiyu/; Fr joint. F Mr Mk. DMA-AE; Alg has /žwæ̃/, Pl /žwan-at/ "belts (in car engine)".] The same Fr word is the source for C-828. Syn: Casa(j) has /ṣubṛi/ from Sp sobre.

C-828 /žwan/ "hashish joint"; Pl [-æt]; Dimin /žwiyn/; Fr joint from Eng joint. F Mr. Same Fr word (in different sense) is involved with C-827, above. Cf. verb /žwana/ B-187.

Bibliography

Abbasi, Abdelaziz (1977) A sociolinguistic analysis of multilingualism in Morocco, PhD dissertation, University of Texas at Austin (University Microfilms no. 77-22908)

Amastae, Jon and L. Elías-Olivares, eds (1982) "Spanish in the United States", Cambridge University Press

Bickerton, Derek (1975) "Dynamics of a Creole System", Cambridge University Press

Blanc, Haim (1970) Dual and pseudo-dual in Arabic dialects, "Language", vol.46, pp.42-57

Brunot, Louis (1920) "Notes lexicologiques sur le vocabulaire maritime de Rabat et de Salé", Paris (Abbreviation: NLVM)

Brunot, Louis (1949) Emprunts dialectaux arabes à la langue française depuis 1912, "Hespéris", vol.36, pp.347-430 (Abbreviation: EDA)

Brunot, Louis (1952) "Textes arabes de Rabat", vol.2 "Glossaire", Publications de l'Institut des Hautes Etudes Marocaines, vol.49, Paris, Paul Geuthner (Abbreviation: TAR)

Brunot, Louis and Elie Malka (1939) "Textes judéo-arabes de Fès", Publications de l'Institut des Hautes Etudes Marocaines, vol.33, Rabat

Brunot, Louis and Elie Malka (1940) "Glossaire judéo-arabe de Fès", Publications de l'Institut des Hautes Etudes Marocaines, vol.37, Rabat (Abbreviation: GJA)

DeCamp, David (1971) Toward a generative analysis of a post-creole speech continuum, in Hymes (1971) pp.349-70

Ferguson, Charles A. (1959) Diglossia, "Word", vol.15, pp.325-40

Ferguson, Charles A. (1971) Absence of copula and the notion of simplicity: a study of normal speech, baby talk, foreigner talk, and pidgins, in Hymes (1971) pp.141-50

Fischer, August (1917) "Zur Lautlehre des Marokkanisch-Arabischen", Leipzig (Abbreviation: ZLMA)

Fishman, Joshua (1971) The sociology of language: an interdisciplinary social science approach to language in society, in Fishman (ed.) "Advances in the Sociology of Language", vol.1 (Contributions to the Sociology of Language, vol.1), The Hague, pp.217-404

Forkel, Fritz (1980) Die sprachliche Situation im heutigen Marokko, PhD dissertation, Hamburg University
Gravel, Louis-André (1979) A sociolinguistic investigation of multilingualism in Morocco, PhD dissertation, Teachers College, Columbia University (University Microfilms no.79-13197)
Harrell, Richard S. (1962) "A Short Reference Grammar of Moroccan Arabic", Institute of Languages and Linguistics, Georgetown Univ.
Harrell, Richard S. (1966) "A Dictionary of Moroccan Arabic: Arabic-English", Institute of Languages and Linguistics, Georgetown University (Abbreviation: DMA-AE)
Haugen, Einar (1956) "Bilingualism in the Americas: A Bibliography and Research Guide", Publications of the American Dialect Society, vol.26, University of Alabama Press
Heath, Jeffrey (1978) "Linguistic Diffusion in Arnhem Land", Australian Institute of Aboriginal Studies, Canberra and Humanities Press, Atlantic Highlands, N.J.
Heath, Jeffrey (1981) A case of intensive lexical diffusion: Arnhem Land, Australia, "Language", vol.57, pp.335-67
Heath, Jeffrey (1983) On structural determinism in borrowing: Moroccan Arabic, in Peter H. Nelde (ed.), "Theorie, Methoden und Modelle der Kontaktlinguistik", Bonn, pp.49-58
Heath, Jeffrey (1978) "Ablaut and Ambiguity: Phonology of a Moroccan Arabic Dialect", SUNY Press, Albany
Heath, Jeffrey and Moshe Bar-Asher (1982) A Judeo-Arabic dialect of Tafilalt (southeastern Morocco), "Zeitschrift für arabische Linguistik", vol.9, pp.32-78
Hymes, Dell, ed. (1971) "Pidginization and Creolization of Languages", Cambridge University Press
Kampffmeyer, Georg (1912) "Marokkanisch-Arabische Gespräche im Dialekt von Casablanca", Berlin (Abbreviation: MAG)
Lanly, André (1962) "Le français d'Afrique du Nord", Paris
Marçais, William (1911) "Textes arabes de Tanger, Paris (Abbreviation: TAT)
Masica, Colin (1976) "Defining a Linguistic Area: South Asia" Chicago University Press
Mercier, Henry (1951) "Dictionnaire Arabe-Français" (vol.4 of Méthode Moderne d'Arabe Parlé Marocain), Rabat
Mühlhäusler, Peter (1979) "Growth and Structure of the Lexicon of New Guinea Pidgin" (Pacific Linguistics vol.C-52), Dept. of Linguistics, Research School of Pacific Studies, Australian National University, Canberra
Petrovici, Emil (1957) "Kann das Phonemsystem einer Sprache durch fremden Einfluss umgestaltet werden? Zum slavischen Einfluss auf das rumänische Lautsystem" (Janua Linguarum vol.3), The Hague
Pfaff, Carol (1979) Constraints on language mixing: Intrasentential code-switching and borrowing in Spanish/English, "Language", vol.55, pp.291-318 (also reprinted in Amastae (1982) pp.264-97)
Sandfeld, Kristen (1930) "Linguistique balkanique: Problèmes et résultats" (Publications de la Société de Linguistique de Paris, vol.31), Paris (reprinted 1968)
Schaller, Helmut Wilhelm (1975) "Die Balkansprachen: Eine Einführung in die Balkanphilologie", Heidelberg

Sherzer, Joel (1976) "An Areal-Typological Study of American Indian Languages North of Mexico" (North-Holland Linguistic Series vol.20), Amsterdam and New York

Sobin, Nicholas (1982) Texas Spanish and lexical borrowing, in Amastae (1982) pp.166-81

Sobleman, Harvey and Richard S. Harrell (1963) "A Dictionary of Moroccan Arabic: English-Moroccan", Institute of Languages and Linguistics, Georgetown University

Stevens, Paul (1974) French and Arabic bilingualism in North Africa with special reference to Tunisia: a study of attitudes and language use patterns, PhD dissertation, Georgetown University (University Microfilms no.75-7868)

Talmoudi, Fathi (1986) A Morphosemantic Study of Romance Verbs in the Arabic Dialects of Tunis, Susa and Sfax, Part 1, Derived Themes II, III, V, VI and X, Orientalia Gothoburgensia, 9, Göteborg

Weinreich, Uriel (1963)[1953] "Languages in Contact: Findings and Problems", The Hague (first edition 1953, Publications of the Linguistic Circle of New York)

Whinnom, Keith (1965) The origin of the European-based pidgins and creoles, "Orbis", vol.14, pp.509-27

Glossary of technical terms

adjective	نعت
adverb	ظرف
affricate	شديد رخو
base language	لغة أساسية
borrowing	مستعار
case suffixes	لواحق إعرابية
code-switching	التحويل اللغوي
compound	مركبة
definite prefix	أداة التعريف
denominative verb	فعل مشتقّ من اسم
diasystem	نظام ثنائي
diglossia	الثنائية اللغوية
diminutive	تصغير
dual	مثنّى
feminine suffix	لاحق تأنيث
fricatives	أصوات إحتكاكية
gemination	تشديد
genitive	إضافة
glottal stop	همزة
hollow (stem)	أَجْوَف
hybrid (contamination, crossing)	مُزْدَوِج الأصل
imperative	أمر

imperfective	مضارع
infinitive	مصدر
labial	شفوي
labialization	تشفية
lengthening	تطويل
liquid	مائع
metathesis	قلب
nasalization	غُنّة
negation	نفي
noun inflection	إمالة اسمية
palatoalveolar	لثوي حنكي
participles	اسم الفاعل واسم المفعول
passive (mediopassive)	مبني للمجهول
perfective	ماض
pharyngealization	تفخيم
plural	جمع
prepositions	حروف الجرّ
pronoun	ضمير
quadriliteral	رباعي
reborrowing	إعادة الاستعارة
reclassicization	كلمة متأثّره بالفصحى
register	مستوى كلامي
resegmentation	إعادة التقسيم
strong (stem)	صحيح
syllabification	تقطيع
triliteral (stem)	ثلاثي
vowel	حركة
weak (stem)	معتلّ

مقدمة المؤلف

إنّ العربية المغربية الدارجة مهمّة في بحث تمازج اللغات لانها تأثّرت تأثّراً قويّا بكل من الفرنسية والاسبانية منذ بداية العصر الاستعماري ، ولانها لازالت تتأثر باللغة العربية الفصحى ، وفي هذا الكتاب نصف تكيّف الكلمات المستعارة من هذه المصادر في اللغة الدارجة .

يجب على الباحث في المستعارات من اللغات الأوربية أن يفرق بين عدّة طبقات تاريخية ، فقد طوّر المغاربة روتينات لاستعارة الأسماء والأفعال من الفرنسية ، لكنّ المستعارات القديمة لها أشكال أخرى ، وتتعلق بعض الروتينات بتشابهات نحوية بين العربية المغربية والفرنسية - التشابه بين أداة التعريف الفرنسية «le ,'l وال - «l-» المغربي ، أو التشابه بين الأفعال الفرنسية مثل «il chantait» (il X-ait) والأفعال المغربية مثل «y-gnni» (y-X-i) ، وكذلك نرى أنّه ليس هنالك فرق واضح بين استعارة الكلمات من جانب والتحويل اللغوي من جانب آخر .

وأغرب المستعارات هي الكلمات المغربية التي لها أصلان أجنبيان ، مثل المستعارات القديمة من الاسبانية التي تأثرت حديثا بالفرنسية ، أو المستعارات الفرنسية التي تأثرت بروتينات قديمة إسبانية ، أو المستعارت الجديدة من الانجليزية التي تأثرت بروتينات قديمة إسبانية ، أو المستعارت الجديدة من الانجليزية التي تأثّرت بروتينات فرنسية الخ ، كما نجد عدّة مستعارت هزلية تمزج اللغات قصدًا .

إن بعض المستعارت لا تتكيف مع العربية فتكوّن مجموعة جديدة من المفردات التي لاتتغير في شكلها لكنّ الأغلبية من المستعارت تتكيف مع قواعد العربية وهكذا قد أنشأت مشتقات جديدة مثل الجمع والتصغير والاسم الفعلي واسم الفاعل ، ونرى كيف تخضع هذه المشتقّات لقواعد الاشتقاق وللقواعد الفونولوجية كذلك .

أما المستعارات من العربية الفصحى فإنها تخضع لقواعد راسخة ، ولا تُنْشَأ مشتقّاتٌ من هذه المستعـارات باستعمال قواعد اللهجة المغربية ، بل تستعار استعارة مباشرة من اللغة الفصحى إلاّ الأفعال فهي تُصرَّف حسب قواعد اللغة الدارجة .

ونعتمد في بحثنا على ما جمعناه من معلومات عن لهجة مدينتي فاس ومكناس في المغرب ، كما يتحدث بها الشباب والطلبة ، ونصف أيضا في فصل آخر بعض مميزات لهجة مدينة تطوان في شمال المغـرب ولهجـة الجـزائر ، كما نصف كلام الاذاعات الرياضية وكلام الخادمات في الفنادق عندما يتحدثن مع المسافرين الاوربيين بعربية مسهلّة ، وفي نهاية الكتاب نعرض معجماً قصيراً من حوالي ١٠٠٠ من المستعارت الاجنبية مع أشكالها المختلفة ومشتقّاتها ومعانيها وأصولها .

جفري هيث

وكتاب البروفيسور «هيث» كما يقرر هو نفسه هو دراسة لمنطقة حدث بها اتصال بين لغتها الأصلية ولغة المستعمر الجديدة ، وقد تمكن من التمييز - على مختلف مستويات التداخل التي تحدث بين لغتين - بين «حديث الأجانب» أى الطريقة التي يتحدث بها العمال المغاربة إلى مستخدميهم - وبين المواقف اللغوية الاكثر انتشاراً والتي استخدمت فيها العربية المغربية - أو بالأحرى - معظم أنماط العربية التي كان يتكلمها أهل الشمال الافريقي بالغرب من ليبيا حيث كان سكان هذه المنطقة أثناء احتلال بلادهم على اتصال وثيق باللغة الفرنسية وكذلك بالاسبانية ولكن إلى درجة أقل ، واستمر هذا الاتصال حتى بعد جلاء المستعمر عن هذه البلاد . وقد أدى هذا إلى ظهور عدد هائل من المفردات الاجنبية في اللغة اليومية (الدارجة) ، ليس في باب الأسماء وحده ولكن في باب الأفعال أيضاً وهذا شائع حتى بين طبقات الناس الذين لايوجد لديهم أي نوع من الاتصال مع الاوربيين .

ويتحدث الكاتب عن نظام نحوى (أجرومى) للاقتباس يشتمل على «أساليب محادثة مثمرة (توالدية)» - وكذلك على «تبسيط» (تسهيل) التراكيب الصوتية والصرفية المقيِّدة الموجودة في العامية المغربية مما يسمح بإيجاد أصوات جديدة وأشكال معترف بها مع الاحتفاظ في الوقت نفسه بأساليب الاشتقاق الخاصة باللهجة نفسها .

وتتبع الدراسة طريقة تكرار استعارة نفس المفردات الموجودة في الفرنسية بطريقة تتابعية ويكون كل شكل جديد أكثر قربا للنموذج الفرنسي . وتتبع الدراسة أيضا أسلوب تطوير أنماط التحول المبني على استخدام الرموز بطريقة أكثر فاعلية . ويميز الكاتب هذا بأنه شبه استمرار لما بعد «الكريول» Post-Creole Continua والتي يتم بها الارجاع التدريجي «للكريول» الذي كان مميزاً من قبل ليكون أكثر قرباً من اللغة الاصلية التي اشتقت منها .

ويشير عنوان الكتاب إلى التمييز المبنى على استخدام الرموز والذي يشتمل على استخدام واضح لأشكال من لغة مختلفة - سواء كانت لغة أجنبية أو صورة مختلفة لنفس اللغة - وهي في هذه الحالة اللغة العربية الفصحى . وفي الغالب يمكن أن يعتبر هذا الاستخدام تكوينا مصغراً لعناصر أجنبية موجودة في داخل تكوينات أكبر للغة الأصلية . وعلى نفس المنوال فإن هذا النوع من الترصيع اللغوي بواسطة مادة لغوية أجنبية من الممكن أن يحدث عشوائيا أو على نطاق شخصى محض . ومن ناحية أخرى فإن الاقتباس يشمل على درجة عالية من التكيف الشكلي للغة وهو أكثر رسوخاً في المجتمع اللغوي - ولايعالج المؤلف التغيير الرمزى على أنه إحدى الوسائل لاقتباس الكلمات فقط ولكنه أيضاً يمثل مرحلة يمكن عدم الالتزام بها وذلك لوجود وسائل المحادثة التوالدية (المنتجة) انظر المقدمة - ويشير المؤلف إلى أنه في هذا السياق لايتأثر كل من الاقتباس والتغيير الرمزى بالأمية اللغوية على الاطلاق والتي هي ذات أهمية خاصة فيما يتعلق باللغة الأساسية التي لها (أو كان لها في الأصل) انماط محددة جداً ومعترف بها ولها صلة بالأقسام الصرفية ، وهذه الأنماط بدورها تؤدى إلى تداخل بين العوامل الصرفية والتكيفات الصوتية الجديدة .

ويعتبر كتاب هيث Heath دراسة ميدانية مفصلة ومنظمة لاتصال لغوى حدث في فترة مابعد الاستعمار ويغطى الاستعارات اللغوية (استعارة الألفاظ) من كل من الفرنسية ، والأسبانية والانجليزية والعربية الفصحى - ولا أعرف دراسة أخرى كُتبت بالانجليزية وتغطى هذا الموضوع تغطية شاملة . والبروفيسور «هيث» استاذ للغويات في جامعة ميشجان وقد نشر دراسة عن التداخل اللغوي في العالم العربي وفي استراليا .

بروس انغام
محرر

تقديم

منذ أن نشر لأول مرة كتاب Weinreich المميز «الاتصالات بين اللغات» في عام ١٩٥٣ ، ظهر اهتمام ملحوظ في مجال التداخل والترابط بين اللغات بعضها البعض وكذلك في الميادين التي يمكن ان يحدث فيهـا هذا التداخل . وقد بنيت هذه الدراسة التقليدية على النظرية أن اللغات أنظمة متناسقة ومتساوية فإنه ينشأ من اندماج وتداخل إحداها بالأخرى نظاماً متناسقاً جديداً . وقد انتقل محور الاهتمام حديثاً إلى الاتصال الذي يتم بين لغات ليست على مستوى واحد ، بمعنى أن متحدثي هذه اللغات غير متساويين من ناحية الطبقة الاجتماعية التي ينتمون إليها . ويتمثل هذا في كتابات De Camp ١٩٧١ و Bickerton ١٩٧٥ . ويبدو هذا واضحاً إذا أخذنا في الاعتبار بصفة خاصة فترة الاتصال بين الثقافات الغربية والمناطق الأخرى من العالم .

ويؤدي هذا في حالات كثيرة إلى وجود حالة من عدم التساوى اللغوى ، أى أنه نتيجة للاتصال الذي يحدث بين لغتين تكون إحداهما عادة لغة «المُسْتَعْمِر» واللغة الأخرى هي لغة «المُسْتَعْمَر» - تظهر لغة ثالثة ليست على قدم المساواة مع أى من اللغتين حيث أنها تكون لاتزال في طور النمو . وهذا مايسمى باللغة الـ Pidgin وهي كلمة مشتقة من الكلمة البرتغالية التي تعني «صغير» Piqueno . وهذا النوع من اللغات يمثل تلك التي يتحدث بها علية القوم مع الرعايا حول موضوعات قليلة ومحدودة جداً لعكس الصلة الضعيفة الموجودة بينهما .

وتتكون اللغة الجديدة عادة من كلمات تنتمي إلى اللغة الاولى ، أما قواعد النمو وتركيب الجمل فتقتبس من اللغة الثانية . ومن وجهة نظر أخرى فإن اللغة الجديدة لاتحتوي على أية أحكام خاصة بقواعد نحو أو تراكيب جمل ، وغالبا لايوجد بها قواعد خاصة بالصرف بالمعنى الدقيق للكلمة ، وتعتمد كثيراً على لصق المفردات احداها مع الآخر لتكوين مفاهيم أجرومية (نحوية) معقدة .

ولايعتبر علم الاجتماع اللغوى الـ Pidgin لغة أصلية لأية مجموعة من البشر ، ولكنها نتاج لتداخل واندماج حدث بين شعبين على نطاق محصور . وقد وجدت مثل هذه الأنماط من الـ Pidgins في غرب أفريقيا ، وجزر الكاريب ، وجنوب شرق آسيا منذ بداية عصر الاستعمار . وعندما يتخذ السكان مثل هذا النوع من اللغة «الهجين» أو «المولدة» كلغة أصلية خاصة بهم أي يتناقلونها من جيل إلى جيل فإنه يصبح أداة للتعبير مستقلة لها سمات اللغة التامة المكتملة النمو ، يظهر فيها الاتساق بين التراكيب وتشمل على عمليات التساوى والتغير القياسي . وفي هذه المرحلة يطلق عليها «الكريولية» Creole وليس من المستبعد أن الانجليزية الحديثة قد نشأت نتيجة وضع شبيه بهذا حيث تم التداخل بين لغتى النورمانديين الذين كان يمثلون الطبقة الحاكمة والذين كانوا يستخدمون اللغة الفرنسية وبين الساكسونيين الذين كانوا يتحدثون الجرمانية في الجزء الأول من الألف سنة الأخيرة ، وقد تكون اللغة الفارسية الحديثة قد ظهرت على نفس المنوال من خلال الاتصال بين السكان الفرس والحكام العرب .

بسم الله الرحمن الرحيم

الكتاب التاسع

الاختلاط اللغوى
في اللهجة العربية المغربية

تأليف
البروفيسور جفري هيث
جامعة ميشجان

مؤسسة كيغان بول العالمية
لندن -هنلى - بوستن
١٤٠٩ هـ/ ١٩٨٩م

مكتبة اللسانيات العربية
سلسلة كتب عالمية في الدراسات اللغوية العربية

هيئة التحرير
د. محمد حسن باكَلّا
جامعة الملك سعود - الرياض
المملكة العربية السعودية
د. بروس انغام
جامعة لندن
د. كلايف هولز
جامعة كمبردج

هيئة التحرير الاستشارية

البروفيسور يوسف الخليفة أبو بكر (جامعة الخرطوم) ، البروفيسور آرنه امبروس (جامعة فيينا - النمسا) ، البروفيسور بروس انغام (جامعة لندن) ، البروفيسور السعيد محمد بدوي (الجامعة الأمريكية في القاهرة) ، البروفيسور بوغوسلاف زغوريسكي (جامعة وارسو) ، البروفيسور أحمد محمد الضبيب (جامعة الرياض) ، البروفيسور محمد حسن عبد العزيز (جامعة نيروبي - كينيا) ، البروفيسور بيتر فؤاد عَبود (جامعة تكساس الولايات المتحدة الأمريكية) ، البروفيسور صالح جواد الطعمة (جامعة انديانا - الولايات المتحدة الأمريكية) ، البروفيسور مارتن فورستنر (جامعة جوهانس غونتبرغ - المانيا الغربية) ، البروفيسور تشارلس فيرستيغ (الجامعة الكاثوليكية في نيجميغن - هولندا) ، البروفيسور مايكل كارتر (جامعة سيدني - استراليا) ، البروفيسور رجا توفيق نصر (الكلية الجامعية في بيروت) ، البروفيسور أوتو ياسترو (جامعة ارلانغن - نورنبرغ في المانيا الغربية) .

الاختلاط اللغوى
في اللهجة العربية المغربية

مكتبة اللسانيات العربية

الحمد لله وحده . والصلاة والسلام على من لا نبي بعده . أما بعد : فإن هنالك أسباباً عدة دعت إلى إنشاء هذه السلسلة من الكتب في حقل اللسانيات والصوتيات العربية .

أولاً : إن هذا الحقل يمر بتطور سريع في إطار الدراسات اللغوية المعاصرة . كما أن كثيراً من الجامعات العربية والغربية قد بدأت تدخل علم اللسانيات وعلم الصوتيات وبعض العلوم اللغوية الحديثة ضمن مواد التدريس بها . بالإضافة الى الإهتمام المتزايد في الدوائر اللغوية العالمية بهذا الميدان .

ثانياً : ومع ازدياد الاهتمام بالدراسات اللسانية والصوتية العربية بدأت تصل هذه الدراسات إلى مرحلة متقدمة في النضوج ليست مستفيدة من معطيات علم اللسانيات العام والعلوم الأخرى النسبية فحسب . بل وأيضاً من معطيات الدراسات اللغوية العربية القديمة .

ثالثاً : بدأت تظهر في حقل اللسانيات العربية فروع ونظريات مختلفة تشمل الصوتيات والفونولوجيا والنحو والدلالة ، وعلم اللغة النفسي ، وعلم اللغة الاجتماعي ، وعلم اللهجات العربية ، وصناعة المعاجم . ودراسة المفردات . وتدريس العربية أو تعلمها كلغة أولى أو ثانية أو أجنبية ، وعلم الاتصال ، وعلم الإشارات اللغوي . ودراسة المصطلحات . والترجمة . والترجمة الآلية ، وعلم اللغة الإحصائي ، وعلم اللغة الرياضي ، وتاريخ العلوم الغوية العربية . وما إلى ذلك .

يضاف إلى هذا كله أن الاقبال على اللغة العربية دراسة وتدريساً وبحثاً يزداد يوماً بعد يوم على الصعيدين المحلي والدولي . ولما لم يكن هناك منبر يرتفع منه نداء لغة الضاد وتعلو منه أصوات الباحثين والمتخصصين فيها لذا وجدت مكتبة «اللسانيات العربية» لتسد هذا الفراغ الكبير والفجوة العميقة وتدفع بالبحث اللغوي العربي قدماً إلى الأمام خدمة للغة القرآن الكريم والتراث العربي الأصيل ، وسيراً بالبحث اللساني العربي للحاق بركب اللسانيات العامة المتقدم . وإثراءً للدراسات اللغوية واللسانية العربية .

وتحرص هذه السلسلة العالميّة على تقديم الجديد من البحث اللغوي وإعطاء الفرصة للبحاثين من العرب وغيرهم للمشاركة في بناء صرح اللسانيات العربية حتى تستعيد الدراسات اللغوية مجدها الماضي العريق .

ولأن هذه السلسلة تعد الأولى من نوعها في الدراسات اللسانية العربية المتخصصة . فإننا نهيب بكل باحث متخصص في مجال اللسانيات العربية بمختلف فروعها النظرية منها والتطبيقية أن يشارك بجهوده وأفكاره وأبحاثه وألا ينجل بتقديم أجود ما لديه من عطاء في سبيل دعم أهداف هذه السلسلة وتطوير مجالاتها الواسعة . والباب مفتوح أمام جميع الأقلام العربية والشرقية والغربية التي تخدم هذه الأهداف الخيّرة .

ونسأل الله العلي القدير أن يحقق لهذه السلسلة ما تصبو اليه من نجاح وتقدم . قال سبحانه وتعالى :

«وقل اعملوا فسيرى الله عملكم» . صدق الله العظيم . والله الموفق لما فيه الخير والصواب لصالح أمتنا العربية الإسلامية المجيدة ولغتها العريقة الأصيلة . إنه سميع مجيب .

For Product Safety Concerns and Information please contact our EU
representative GPSR@taylorandfrancis.com
Taylor & Francis Verlag GmbH, Kaufingerstraße 24, 80331 München, Germany

www.ingramcontent.com/pod-product-compliance
Lightning Source LLC
Chambersburg PA
CBHW052142300426
44115CB00011B/1484
9781138869950